THE CONSTITUTIONALIZATION OF EUROPEAN BUDGETARY CONSTRAINTS

The recently enacted Treaty on the Stability, Coordination and Governance of the Economic and Monetary Union (generally referred to as the 'Fiscal Compact') has introduced a 'golden rule', which is a detailed obligation that government budgets be balanced. Moreover, it required the 25 members of the EU that signed the Treaty in March 2012 to incorporate this 'golden rule' within their national constitutions. This requirement represents a major and unprecedented development, raising formidable challenges to the nature and legitimacy of national constitutions as well as to the future of the European integration project. This book analyses the new constitutional architecture of the European Economic and Monetary Union (EMU), examines in a comparative perspective the constitutionalization of budgetary rules in the legal systems of the Member States, and discusses the implications of these constitutional changes for the future of democracy and integration in the EU. By combining insights from law and economics, comparative analysis and legal theory, the book offers a comprehensive survey of the constitutional incorporation of new fiscal and budgetary rules across Europe and a systematic normative discussion of the legitimacy issues at play. It thus contributes to a better understanding of the euro crisis, of the future of the EU, and the reforms needed towards a deeper and more genuine EMU.

Volume 47 in the series Modern Studies in European Law

Modern Studies in European Law

Recent titles in this series:

Empowerment and Disempowerment of the European Citizen
Edited by Michael Dougan, Niamh Nic Shuibhne and Eleanor Spaventa

Legal Reasoning and the European Court of Justice
Gunnar Beck

Lawyering Europe: European Law as a Transnational Social Field
Edited by Antoine Vauchez and Bruno de Witte

Services and the EU Citizen
Edited by Frank S Benyon

The Accession of the European Union to the European Convention on Human Rights
Paul Gragl

Normative Patterns and Legal Developments in the Social Dimension of the EU
Edited by Ann Numhauser-Henning and Mia Rönnmar

The European Neighbourhood Policy and the Democratic Values of the EU: A Legal Analysis
Nariné Ghazaryan

EU Security and Justice Law: After Lisbon and Stockholm
Edited by Diego Acosta Arcarazo and Cian C Murphy

EU Environmental Law, Governance and Decision-Making
Maria Lee

Shaping the Single European Market in the Field of Foreign Direct Investment
Philip Strik

Nationalism and Private Law in Europe
Guido Comparato

EU Asylum Procedures and the Right to an Effective Remedy
Marcelle Reneman

For the complete list of titles in this series, see 'Modern Studies in European Law' link at www.hartpub.co.uk/books/series.asp

The Constitutionalization of European Budgetary Constraints

Edited by
Maurice Adams
Federico Fabbrini
and
Pierre Larouche

·HART·
PUBLISHING

OXFORD AND PORTLAND, OREGON
2016

Published in the United Kingdom by Hart Publishing Ltd
16C Worcester Place, Oxford, OX1 2JW
Telephone: +44 (0)1865 517530
Fax: +44 (0)1865 510710
E-mail: mail@hartpub.co.uk
Website: http://www.hartpub.co.uk

Published in North America (US and Canada) by
Hart Publishing
c/o International Specialized Book Services
920 NE 58th Avenue, Suite 300
Portland, OR 97213-3786
USA
Tel: +1 503 287 3093 or toll-free: (1) 800 944 6190
Fax: +1 503 280 8832
E-mail: orders@isbs.com
Website: http://www.isbs.com

First published in hardback 2014
Paperback edition, 2016

Hart Publishing is an imprint of Bloomsbury Publishing plc.

British Library Cataloguing in Publication Data

Data Available

ISBN: HB: 978-1-84946-580-9
PB: 978-1-50990-705-2

Typeset by Forewords Ltd, Oxon
Printed and bound in Great Britain by
Lightning Source UK Ltd

Foreword

Fiscal Capacity and Constitutional Reform in the EMU

MIGUEL POIARES MADURO

I AM PLEASED to write the foreword to this volume, collecting the proceedings of a Conference held at Tilburg Law School, in the Netherlands on 30–31 May 2013 and organized by Federico Fabbrini, Maurice Adams and Pierre Larouche. This book explores the challenges of effectiveness and legitimacy produced by the constitutionalization of European budgetary rules and is highly recommended to anyone interested in European constitutional law, comparative fiscal federalism and the implications of the euro crisis.

The origins of the financial and economic crisis of the euro system are state- and market-based democratic failures that the original regime of euro governance did not adequately address. It is only by fully understanding the democratic character of the crisis that we can appropriately understand the extent of the democratic challenges faced by Europe and the role of the European Union in this context.

Two narratives of the current crisis exist. Whichever we may adopt, at the very core of the explanation lies the recognition of a democratic failure.

The first is the dominant narrative. It puts most of the blame for the crisis on some Member States and their irresponsible fiscal policies and lack of economic competitiveness. Capital flight from those Member States is a simple consequence of those irresponsible fiscal policies and underlying economic problems. But, in the meanwhile, the interdependence generated by the euro resulted in the financial problems of those states becoming a problem for all. This can be presented as a democratic problem since the interests of the latter Member States are not taken into account in the democratic process of the former Member States. But it is also a democratic problem internal to the former, since it reflects the extent to which domestic politics is more responsive to the political cycles than to the interests of future generations.

The second narrative does not see markets punishing the mismanagement of Member States but, instead, as the main causes of the crisis. The crisis is a product of unfettered capital flows. After the creation of the euro an excessive influx of capital occurred from northern banks to several EU Member States, particularly in the south. Those banks benefited from the euro to inject liquidity into other Member States in search of increased profits. This artificially lowered interest rates in their economies, creating a credit bubble. When the financial crisis took place in the United States and expanded to European financial institutions it was only a matter of time before markets lost confidence and suddenly cut off access to credit in those countries. This narrative can (and ought) also to be presented in democratic terms. This is a form of transnational democratic externalities imposed on states. Or, in other words, capital movements can be presented as having a profound impact inside a state without being subject to its democratic control.

The failure to internalize the democratic consequences of interdependence also explains what many perceive as the erosion of solidarity within the EU. In fact, the reverse is rather the case. Rather than being the product of the absence of a European cultural or social identity, lack of European solidarity is the result of that very lack of internalization of the consequences of interdependence: this time, of the benefits it generates.

Whatever our view on capital controls it is impossible to conceive of a European internal market subject to national capital controls. A fortiori, it is an impossibility within a monetary union. In fact, a stronger normative justification for the euro might be the opportunity it offers to Europe to address the democratic challenges posed by capital flows.

As to the first narrative and the possible answer to the democratic failure explicit therein, whatever our view on the benefits and costs of constitutionalizing fiscal discipline, two things are clear in the current EU context: this discipline is a necessity to re-establish market trust, and also to re-establish trust between Member States; but this discipline is also insufficient to address the current crisis, for both economic and democratic reasons.

It starts by ignoring that the fiscal situation of a state is closely dependent on its underlying economic situation. Several states that are now in a profound fiscal crisis were until recently fully compliant with the Maastricht criteria. The reasons for their fiscal crisis have to be found in deeper economic problems that rapidly turned into a fiscal crisis.

Let me illustrate this last point with an example. Real divergence instead of convergence occurred inside the euro area. Portugal, for example, between 2000 and 2007 posted a 0.6 per cent GDP per capita annual growth rate, which compares to 3.3 per cent the previous decade. In the euro area as whole growth during the period between 2000 and 2007 was more than twice as high as in Portugal. We interrupted a process of catching-up of half a century. We may call the first decade of the present century as a lost decade. The crisis was the moment at which the vulnerabilities of our economies were shown in full.

We need to take seriously the economic part of Economic and Monetary Union. A Fiscal Union requires fiscal discipline and co-ordination of economic policies between states. But it also requires fiscal capacity, albeit limited to the correction of the asymmetries emerging in a monetary union.

A regime relying exclusively on fiscal discipline to be enforced by the EU would undermine the already limited political and social legitimacy of the Union: either national political processes would preserve autonomy and the effectiveness of the rules would be put into question or the disciplining of national political processes by a non-political space would put democracy itself into question.

In light of the dominant discourse on the crisis it may seem to many that our choice is between a Union anchored almost exclusively on discipline and that, sooner or later, will enter into a destructive conflict with national democracies, and a Union prisoner of permanent negotiation between those national democracies, in an intergovernmental setting that is increasingly incapable of providing effective and legitimate governance. But that is not so. There is an alternative.

Any answer to the current crisis and the form of EU governance adopted to that effect will have to fulfil certain conditions to be both effective and legitimate. What follows is a list of those conditions.

1. *We need political authority.* Any successful model of EU governance will have to make clear that political authority stands behind the euro and the EU. It is the absence of this political authority that undermines the effectiveness and credibility of EU governance of the euro.
2. *We need accountability.* The current crisis is a prime example of the need for accountability. Who exactly was responsible for the crisis? Markets or Member States? And who in the EU was responsible for the failure of the Maastricht instruments of surveillance and co-ordination of national fiscal policies? Who should citizens hold accountable for the results of the adjustment programmes 'imposed' on some Member States: their national governments or the EU? And if the EU, does that mean the Commission, the ECB, the Council, or some Member States within the Council? The diffuse character of EU political authority makes accountability virtually impossible and favours its manipulation by political actors: national political actors may use the nature of intergovernmental bargaining to transfer political costs to the EU. But, increasingly, the EU institutions might use the fact that its policy choices will have to be enforced by national governments to evade accountability too.
3. *We need to re-establish mutual trust between states and between citizens.* This has been severely affected by the crisis. Some Member States and their citizens believe they are paying for the mistakes and even cheating of others. These others believe that that it is the former that have not shown sufficient solidarity and are, instead, imposing a form of collective punishment on the latter. We need both the rules and solidarity to be traced back by all citizens to collective goods shared by all. In other words, they must be linked to the broader purposes of European integration and the fair distribution of its costs and benefits.
4. *We need to render both the benefits and the democratic consequences of interdependence visible to citizens.* This will never be achieved by information

campaigns, no matter how well designed. The real source of communication by a political authority with its citizens is through the policies that it enacts and how they impact and are perceived by citizens. The benefits and costs of the European Union are only properly internalized by citizens if they are inherent in the character of EU policies, including its revenues. EU policies must be simultaneously capable of informing citizens about the benefits of European integration and the reasons for their contribution to it.

5. *We need to legitimate financial solidarity by relating it to the wealth generated by European integration and not the wealth of some states.* The idea that the EU is an instrument to transfer the wealth of some states to other states is a poisonous tree that undermines any form of solidarity within the Union. We must detach financial solidarity and financial transfers between states. Financial solidarity must be a product of the wealth that the process of European integration itself generates and be guided by the goal of a fair distribution of the benefits of integration among all European citizens and all economic players.
6. *We need political integration to support increased transfer of powers to the Union and its financial solidarity.* The starting point for this political integration must be a European political space. Any form of political integration based only on national political spaces will, as described above, both lack sufficiently clear political authority and be incapable of internalizing the democratic consequences of interdependence. The suggestions to be put forward are aimed at promoting that political integration even in the absence of the treaty reform involved.

The following suggestions are based on three pillars: an increased EU or euro budget supported by real EU revenue sources; new EU policies and a different kind of policies; and more effective political authority supported by a European political space.

I favour an increase of the EU or euro budget so that it should provide the Union with the firepower necessary to play two fundamental roles in the context of a Monetary Union. First, introducing policies capable of addressing the asymmetries affecting the good functioning of the monetary union. Second, using the EU or euro budget to address financial emergencies such as the one that the Union is currently living through.

Solidarity through transfers between states is not only limited but also undermines the social and democratic legitimacy of the Union. The citizens of Member States which at a particular moment in time would be net contributors would tend to construe it as an unjustified transfer of their funds to cover risks assumed by other Member States. Use of the EU or euro budget would prevent that direct link from being established. It would also signal to citizens in all Member States that their financial solidarity will be limited to their obligations towards the EU or euro budget and is the price to be paid for the general benefits and costs of being part of the EU.

The legitimacy of this form of financial solidarity would also be made stronger by changing the character and origin of EU revenues. The argument I want to put forward next is that what would make an increased EU budget possible, new own resources, could actually also serve to legitimate the Union. Again, I must articulate clearly and carefully what is another counterintuitive argument.

A polity, including the political authority exercised therein and the necessary solidarity between its members, must be made meaningful and intelligible to its citizens not only by how it represents itself but also by what it does. One fundamental aspect is certainly how revenues are collected and taxes organized. These are not simply a source of revenue. They are also a way for the reasons for solidarity to be made clear to the members of the polity. How revenues are collected in a polity, and taxation allocated, also informs citizens of the reasons for that polity and what it means to be a member of it. EU or euro revenues should not simply be determined on a pragmatic basis of how much is required to fund the Union budget and what is the easiest way to obtain it. Instead, the sources of EU or euro revenues should be determined by what makes the Union more legitimate to its citizens by making visible the reasons for the Union's existence and linking its revenues to the benefits and costs that different social groups obtain from European integration.

If conceived in this way, the new EU or euro own resources would not only provide the EU with the funds necessary to support the proposed budget increase but would also contribute to a clearer justification of the project of European integration. Furthermore, only in this way will we be able to legitimate solidarity within the Union on any meaningful and lasting basis. It is essential that the Union is seen as redistributing Union wealth and not merely the wealth of some Member States. It is equally important for this solidarity to be related to the different degree to which different social groups benefit from European integration and, particularly, the internal market.

In this light, the choice of EU resources should focus on the following areas: economic activity enabled by the internal market; economic activity that, while taking place in a Member State, has important externalities in other Member States; or economic activity that Member States can no longer individually regulate and tax on their own. In all these domains, the Union would be justified in obtaining revenues from the activity in question either because that activity would not exist without the Union or because the intervention of the Union is the only way to limit the negative effects of that activity in some or all states. In addition, the way those EU resources (in particular taxes) should be designed must take into account who benefits most from European integration.

These principles should shape any possible proposals for new own resources. It is the link with democracy and a theory of justice that sheds a new light over the choice of some and not other resources and makes them both politically more viable and better capable of reinforcing EU legitimacy.

Union policies also need to be rethought in light of what justifies European integration. The European Union can increase its democratic legitimacy by more closely aligning its policy priorities to the problems that, given the ineffectiveness of Member State solutions, it should address.

But the problem with EU policies concerns more than having the right policies. The structure and character of EU policies also needs to be rethought. Politics remains intergovernmental at the decisive level of EU policy-making. Policy decisions continue, in spite of the enhanced role of the European Parliament, to be a product of intergovernmental bargaining. More importantly, they continue to be often framed in intergovernmental terms. National governments aggregate the preferences of their citizens and EU policies strike a balance between those aggregated preferences.

Since, however, EU rules often affect individuals directly they can, in fact, be constructed as discriminating on the basis of nationality. This affects citizens' understanding of what determines the redistributive effects of EU policies and the idea of justice that guides them.

It is unrealistic (and also wrong) to eliminate intergovernmental bargaining from EU policy-making. But one should require EU decisions, whatever the bargaining underlying them, to be designed along EU citizenship and not nationality lines and conform to universality criteria. This would require in the future a higher percentage of Union expenditure to be allocated to policies structured around citizen benefits and rights instead of simply funds allocated along national quotas.

One hears endlessly about the European democracy deficit, real and imagined. But, as I tried to underline, Europe's real democratic deficit is to be found in its excessive reliance on national politics that have not internalized the consequences of European and global interdependence.

The democratic problem of the Union is also one of effectiveness. A democracy that cannot effectively govern is no democracy. There is no self-government without government. Europe needs a strengthened political authority if it is to become a legitimate and accountable democratic authority.

All this is only made more urgent by the powers being transferred to the Union. A fiscal Union does require a political Union. This problem is particularly acute with respect to the Commission's position. On the one hand, the Commission has lost part of its powers of political leadership to the Council. But, on the other hand, it has acquired significantly more powers with respect to the Member States under the Fiscal Compact and other fiscal crisis related legislation such as the six-pack. To be effective and legitimate, the Commission must be able to rely on the kind of legitimacy that comes with a direct link to the outcome of European elections.

Elections to the European Parliament should be 'transformed' into an electoral competition for the government of Europe. The most important step in this direction would be for the different European political groups to present competing candidates for the role of President of the Commission before the next election to the European Parliament. The Treaties attribute to the European Council the power to propose the President of the European Commission but its subjection to approval by the European Parliament, and the electoral focus on the choice of a President, will ensure that the 'winner' of the elections would be the selected President.

The cohesion of the Commission would also be reinforced by the fact that the President elected would have much stronger bargaining power vis-à-vis the Member States in selection of the other members of the Commission. One may even consider whether the Commission should not fully reflect the political majority in the European Parliament following the elections.

I am well aware of the risks this approach involves. The politicization of the Commission is bound to affect its perceived neutrality and the authority it derives from being conceived as a semitechnocratic body. But the reality is that the latter authority is already under attack. The expansion of EU and Commission powers into the core of social and economic policy issues is bound to immerse the Commission in politics. The only question is the nature of this politics. As what is happening in some Member States is already making clear, the Commission will not succeed in preserving an appearance of technocratic neutrality in the face of deeply contested political issues. It will simply come across as a limit on democracy and politics. It will no longer be perceived as bringing reason into the passions of national politics but as passion without politics. In order for the Commission effectively and legitimately to exercise the role required by the new EU governance it will have to embed itself in a political space where the legitimacy of the reason that it will impose on Member States will gain the authority of political deliberation.

A first consequence of transformation of EP elections into an electoral competition for the government of Europe would be promotion of transnational politics. Once each European political group selects a candidate for President of the Commission they must also come up with a political platform or government programme. Clearly, these political platforms, in order to be agreed within that political group and to be successful in all Member States, would have to focus on genuinely European issues: issues where citizens are not divided along national lines but across them. The simple need to come up with these European political platforms is bound to generate European politics.

The Commission and its President would not simply gain stronger legitimacy. They would gain political capital. EU political authority would also be reinforced. The link established between the election and a specific political platform would provide the Commission and Parliament with a strong political claim in pursuit of the proposals contained in that platform.

The effects of the change of paradigm that I propose with respect to EU politics would be profound. In a democratic Europe citizens can disagree about the right policies to respond to the current economic and financial crisis. If they are not presented with alternative EU policies then the only alternative that remains for them is to be for or against Europe. Disagreement on the right European response must take place and be arbitrated in a European political space. The extent to which European citizens from different Member States increasingly feel engaged in national elections in other Member States, particularly those understood as playing a key role in EU policies, is revealing. This signals the extent to which European citizens perceive the EU as shaping their lives.

But it also highlights the risk that they will see those lives being determined by national politics in which they have no voice. The only viable alternative is to offer such politics at European level.

Contents

List of Contributors

Maurice Adams is Professor of Jurisprudence and 'vfund' Professor of Democratic Governance and the Rule of Law at Tilburg Law School.

Marek Antoš is Assistant Professor of Constitutional Law at Charles University, Prague.

Kenneth Armstrong is Professor of European Law and the Director of the Centre for European Legal Studies, University of Cambridge.

Samo Bardutzky is a Research Associate at the University of Kent, UK.

Stefania Baroncelli is Professor of Public Law at the University of Bolzano/Bozen.

Francesco Costamagna is Assistant Professor of EU Law at the University of Turin.

Paul Craig is Professor of English Law, St John's College Oxford.

Giacomo Delledonne is a PhD candidate at Sant'Anna School of Advanced Studies, Pisa.

Alexandre de Streel is Professor of EU Law at the Universities of Namur and Louvain and Advisor to the Belgian Deputy Prime Minister.

Michal Diamant is a PhD candidate at Leiden University.

Angelos Dimopoulos is Lecturer in EU Law at Queen Mary University London.

Federico Fabbrini is Assistant Professor of European & Comparative Constitutional Law at Tilburg Law School.

Elaine Fahey is a Senior Postdoctoral Researcher at the Amsterdam Centre for European Law and Governance (ACELG), University of Amsterdam, the Netherlands.

Pierre Larouche is Professor of Competition Law at Tilburg Law School.

Peter Lindseth is Olimpiad S Ioffe Professor of International and Comparative Law, and Director of International Programs, University of Connecticut School of Law (USA).

Miguel Maduro is Minister in the Cabinet of the Prime Minister and for Regional Development in Portugal, formerly Professor of Law at the EUI and Advocate General, European Court of Justice.

Roderic O'Gorman is Lecturer at Dublin City University.

Lina Papadopoulou is Assistant Professor of Constitutional Law at the Aristotle University of Thessaloniki.

Ingolf Pernice is Professor Dr jur, Dr h c chair of public, international and European law at the Humboldt-Universität zu Berlin, Direktor of the Walter Hallstein Institute for European constitutional law .

Sonia Piedrafita is a Research Fellow at the Centre for European Policy Studies in Brussels.

Marijn van der Sluis is a PhD candidate at the EUI.

Michiel van Emmerik is Associate Professor of Constitutional and Administrative Law at Leiden University and Deputy Judge at the Amsterdam District Court.

Pieter-Augustijn Van Malleghem is a Research Fellow (Research Foundation Flanders), PhD candidate at KU Leuven and SJD candidate at Harvard Law School.

1

Introduction
The Constitutionalization of European Budgetary Constraints: Effectiveness and Legitimacy in Comparative Perspective

MAURICE ADAMS, FEDERICO FABBRINI and
PIERRE LAROUCHE

I

THE TREATY ON the Stability, Coordination and Governance of the Economic and Monetary Union, generally referred to as the Fiscal Compact, has introduced a 'golden rule', which is a detailed obligation that government budgets be balanced. Moreover, the Fiscal Compact requires the 25 members of the European Union (EU) that signed the Treaty in March 2012, to incorporate this 'golden rule' within their national constitutions.[1] This requirement represents a major and unprecedented development, which raises formidable challenges on the nature and legitimacy of national constitutions as well as on the future of the European integration project. The purpose of this book is to analyse the new constitutional architecture of the European Economic and Monetary Union (EMU), to examine in a comparative perspective the constitutionalization of budgetary rules in the legal systems of the member states, and to discuss the implications of these constitutional changes on the future of democracy and integration in the EU. Three threads run throughout the volume. First, the book explores the effectiveness of the new fiscal rules introduced at the supranational level and domesticated in the constitutional systems of the member states, addressing the question whether they are able to ensure sustainable budgetary policies in the EMU. Secondly, it evaluates the legitimacy of the constitutionalization of budgetary constraints, addressing a number of questions about the nature of public authority at the EU and national level, constitutional checks and balances, and the mechanisms to ensure accountability of decisions

[1] See further F Fabbrini, 'The Fiscal Compact, the "Golden Rule" and the Paradox of European Federalism' (2013) 36 *Boston College International & Comparative Law Review* 1.

in the field of EMU. Thirdly, the book enlarges our perspective on the challenges of effectiveness and legitimacy of fiscal governance in the EMU by embracing a comparative viewpoint, open to the insights that can be learned from the experience of other fiscal unions.

II

A first theme of this book concerns the effectiveness of the new EMU rules, meaning their capacity legally to shape and constrain action by policymakers in fiscal affairs at the national level. The original design of the EMU broke new ground by attempting to combine centralized monetary policy with a loose co-ordination of economic and fiscal policy.[2] In federal states such as the United States (US), Canada or Australia, monetary union is accompanied by strong central fiscal powers and economic policy steering, offset with solidarity mechanisms. Instead, beyond policy co-ordination and the weak obligation to respect specific deficit and debt rules enshrined in the Stability and Growth Pact (SGP),[3] the EMU relied heavily on the pressure of international markets in order to incentivize underperforming member states.[4] In the original design of the EMU, fear of unsustainable bond spreads should have lead national governments to reform their policies to converge with the better-performing member states, and so ensure the stability of the euro. The no-bailout clause now at Article 125 of the Treaty on the Functioning of the European Union (TFEU) epitomized this design.[5] To some extent, the original setup of the EMU placed too much faith in markets or, more precisely put, in the benevolence of markets and the readiness of market actors to accept the no-bailout clause at face value. Certainly, the influx of capital into the weaker eurozone members throughout the 2000s shows that many market actors believed that no eurozone member would be allowed to fail. Many speculators bet—successfully as it turned out—that the no-bailout clause would not ultimately stand.

Since the outburst of the euro crisis, EU institutions and member states have attempted to reform the architecture of EMU and improve its effectiveness. However, the policy response adopted during the last four years has suffered

[2] See already D MacDougall, 'The Role of Public Finance in European Integration', report commissioned by the Commission of the European Communities (1977) (discussing prospects for economic and monetary integration in Europe in comparative perspective).

[3] On the weaknesses of the SGP, see eg Case C-27/04, *Commission v Council of the EU* [2004] ECR I-6649 (conferring wide discretion on the Council whether to impose sanctions under the SGP or to hold in abeyance the excessive deficit procedure against two member states recommended by the Commission).

[4] See J Rodden, *Hamilton's Paradox: The Promise and Perils of Fiscal Federalism* (Cambridge, Cambridge University Press, 2005) (discussing the enforcement of fiscal rules in economic and monetary unions and distinguishing between a decentralized, market-based enforcement of fiscal rules, and a centralized, rule-based enforcement).

[5] See M Ruffert, 'The European Debt Crisis and European Union Law' (2011) 48 *Common Market Law Review* 1777.

from ambivalence, torn between a need to rely on market discipline (including sanctions for failure, in order to avoid moral hazard) for lack of stronger fiscal and economic policy tools, and knowledge that the consequences of such discipline might tear the eurozone apart. The Fiscal Compact and the Treaty on the European Stability Mechanism (ESM) vividly illustrate this ambivalence. On the one hand, the Fiscal Compact—together with the 'six-pack' and 'two-pack' legislative packages—marks a strengthening of the economic policy co-ordination approach, whilst avoiding the transfer of fiscal capacity to the EU level.[6] Both the substantive standards and the co-ordination procedure have been strengthened, with the European Semester.[7] At the same time, the sanction mechanisms now provided—fines and compulsory deposits—appear ill-suited to the situation of member states that would find themselves unable to bring their deficit and debt under control. On the other hand, the ESM Treaty—despite all efforts by the European Court of Justice (ECJ) in *Pringle*[8] to show the opposite—does create a solidarity mechanism, which may aim to safeguard the eurozone but does so by shoring up eurozone members in difficulty.[9] Of course, support under the ESM Treaty is linked with compliance with fiscal and economic policy co-ordination measures (conditionality), but here as well the question arises whether the sanctions for non-compliance (discontinuance of support) are really appropriate in such a situation.

Considering the above, the Fiscal Compact and ESM Treaty might be no more than a step in the evolution of economic and fiscal policy in Europe.[10] In the end, the level of policy co-ordination required for the euro to be successful cannot be achieved only through the threat of fines or compulsory deposits; rather, every eurozone member should comply out of a political commitment to shared objectives. That political commitment was undermined during the euro crisis: policy reform became a way for beneficiaries to atone to what was often perceived as a diktat from the contributors. Austerity and fiscal orthodoxy took center stage, at the expense of the longer-term objectives. When seen in a broader context, all member states share an interest in improving the competitiveness of EU economies as a way to retain economic significance in the world. The next step, beyond the Fiscal Compact and ESM Treaty, is to restore that shared political commitment; as things now stand, this could involve either more centralized policymaking, or even an EU-level fiscal and economic policy competence that matches that of its monetary policy.

[6] See also M Maduro, 'A New Governance for the European Union and the Euro: Democracy and Justice', report commissioned by the European Parliament Constitutional Affairs Committee, PE 462.484 (2012).

[7] On the European Semester see K Armstrong, 'The New Governance of EU Fiscal Discipline' (2013) 38 *European Law Rewiew* 601.

[8] Case C-370/12 *Pringle v Government of Ireland*, judgment of 27 November 2012, nyr.

[9] See H Hofmeister, 'To Bail Out or Not to Bail Out? Legal Aspects of the Greek Crisis' (2011) 13 *Cambridge Yearbook of European Legal Studies* 113.

[10] See President of the European Council, 'Towards a Genuine EMU', report issued 25 June 2012, SN 25/12 and Commission Communication, 'A Blueprint for a Deep and Genuine EMU: Launching a European Debate', 28 November 2012, COM(2012) 777 final.

One of the lessons from the crisis is indeed that, for all the attention dedicated to EU institutions and governance in the 2000s, politically as well as academically, those institutions were apparently not up to the challenge of the first serious post-Lisbon test. Through its constant and seemingly haphazard involvement, the European Council might have inflated the sense of crisis as much as it signalled a high-level political resolve to address that crisis.[11] For lack of any other credible institution, the European Central Bank (ECB) was drawn out of its mandate and its isolation from politics, which could prove harmful in the longer run.[12] In the end, one could even argue that the lack of a trustworthy and trusted institutional framework, by which member states could commit to shared economic and fiscal policy goals, drove member states to push forward austerity measures as a precondition for financial support. In so doing, member states pre-empted the—avowedly more Keynesian—option of first increasing public spending to overcome the crisis, and only thereafter bringing public finances on a sustainable path.

III

Beyond the question of efficiency, but closely connected to it, lies a second central theme of this book: the legitimacy of the constitutionalization of European budgetary constraints. Of course, as a multifaceted term, legitimacy is notoriously difficult to utilize. It can, inter alia, be explored from a legal, political, sociological or moral point of view.[13] Moreover, as the French political theorist Pierre Rosanvallon recently said, legitimacy, like trust, is an invisible institution. Nonetheless, it might signal a firm foundation for the relation between the government and those who are governed.[14] Rosanvallon adds that if legitimacy, in its most generic sense, means the absence of coercion, then *democratic* legitimacy must mean something more than that, ie a fabric of relationships between government and society. And this fabric works to the benefit of the European project if, in this case, the 'European citizens' believe in such project. In other words, if they have confidence in it, regardless of whether they agree with each of the decisions and actions taken by the European Council, the Commission, the Council of Ministers, the European Parliament, or their national government.

The debate about legitimacy in the EU has often centred on the distinction

[11] On the institutional role of the European Council in the management of the euro crisis, see F Eggermont, *The Changing Role of the European Council in the Institutional Framework of the European Union* (Antwerpen, Intersentia, 2012).

[12] See also S Collignon, 'The Various Roles of the ECB in the New EMU Architecture', report commissioned by the European Parliament Economic Affairs Committee, PE 507.482 (2013).

[13] See RH Fallon Jr, 'Legitimacy and the Constitution' (2005) 118 *Harvard Law Review* 1787 and N Huls, 'From Legitimacy to Leadership' in N Huls, M Adams and J Bomhoff (eds), *The Legitimacy of Highest Courts' Rulings: Judicial Deliberations and Beyond* (The Hague, TMC Asser Press, 2009) 13–18.

[14] P Rosanvallon, *Democratic Legitimacy. Impartiality, Reflexivity, Proximity* (Princeton, Princeton University Press, 2011) 8–9.

between output legitimacy—namely the capacity of the EU to justify itself to the citizens through the attainment of public policy objectives—and input legitimacy—namely the subjection of the EU to the dynamics of democratic representation presupposing mechanisms or procedures that link political decisions with citizens' preferences. Traditionally, in the EU the main source of legitimacy was output, referring (generically) to the willingness of citizens to support the decisions made by the European institutions or their national governments concerning the EU for the benefits they produce to them.[15] It should be clear that this definition of legitimacy has clear, though not exclusive, sociological overtones.[16] In this sense legitimacy and effectiveness are closely connected: because not only do the political actors and institutions have to be worthy of confidence, they also need the ability to actually live up to the aforementioned confidence. 'The efficacy of public action depends on legitimacy, and the sense of legitimacy affects the way in which citizens judge the quality of their country's democracy', Rosanvallon states.[17] Nevertheless, the euro crisis has severely challenged the ability of the EU to attain public policy objectives, undermining one of the main sources of justification of the European integration project. For this reason, calls are increasingly made to strengthen the input side of EU legitimacy, through an enhanced framework of democracy and accountability at the level at which decisions are taken.[18]

In any case, no democracy can survive a prolonged weakening of any of these input or output elements, which are mutually reinforcing. The European project depends first and foremost on its continuing acceptability to the real human beings whose lives it affects.[19] This observation leaves open many pressing questions, among them empirical ones with which this volume does not deal (eg how minimal does the level of acceptance have to be for a political entity such as the EU to be able to command authority and acceptance to its population over time?). Certainly, the EU has to deal with a very particular set of problems; and there exists no objective set of rules for matching a people and its specific situation with a set of institutions, or no inherently stable or objectively superior constitutional system.[20] That makes it all the more telling that almost all of the contributors to this volume identify significant challenges regarding the legitimacy of the EU as a result of the constitutionalization of budgetary constraints—challenges which were already looming large even before the 'golden rule' was introduced.

[15] See also JHH Weiler, 'The Political and Legal Culture of European Integration: An Exploratory Essay', (2011) 9 *International Journal of Constitutional Law* 678 (discussing output and input legitimacy, together with political messianism, as a source of justification for the EU integration project).

[16] The two may be positively correlated, with output legitimacy resulting from input legitimacy. See M Adams et al, 'Introduction: Judging Europe's Judges' in M Adams et al (eds), *Judging Europe's Judges. The Legitimacy of the Case Law of the European Court of Justice* (Oxford, Hart Publishing, 2013) 4–5 (with further references).

[17] Rosanvallon (n 14) 9.

[18] See I Pernice et al, *A Democratic Solution to the Crisis: Reform Steps Towards a Democratically Based Economic and Financial Constitution for Europe* (Baden-Baden, Nomos, 2012).

[19] See R Kay, 'Constituent Authority' (2011) 59 *American Journal of Comparative Law* 756.

[20] DS Lutz, *Principles of Constitutional Design* (Cambridge, Cambridge University Press, 2006) ix.

If the euro crisis and the constitutionalization of budgetary rules bring the need for input legitimacy centre-stage, the question arises of how to meet this challenge. Most of the contributors to this book address the issue from the perspective of representative democracy, articulating alternative visions whether this should be grounded in the democratic processes of member states, or rather enhanced at the European level. A perspective that is less developed in the contributions of this book, but has increasingly attracted attention in the scholarly debate, is that of participatory democracy. In his recent history of democracy, John Keane signals the emergence of a new type of democracy that complements representative democracy, and which he calls 'monitory democracy'. This type of democracy is a species of participatory democracy, as it looks at the involvement of citizens with public affairs.

> What is distinctive about this new type of democracy is the way all fields of social and political life come to be scrutinized, not just by the standard machinery of representative democracy but by a whole host of non-party, extra-parliamentary and often unelected bodies, operating within, underneath and beyond the boundaries of the territorial states. … These watchdog and guide-dog and barking-dog inventions are changing both the political geography and the political dynamics of many democracies, which no longer bear much resemblance to textbook models of representative democracy, which supposed that citizens' needs are best championed through electoral parliamentary representatives chosen by political parties.[21]

More research is needed to see to what extent this also is a viable democratic option in the next phase of the development of the European legal and political space. It might well be in line with the Treaty on the European Union (TEU), which in Article 10 now states that 'the functioning of the Union shall be founded on representative democracy', based on direct and indirect public participation; a model that at the same time is extended in Article 11 TEU, where elements of participatory democracy are strongly stressed.

IV

To address these central questions, the book embraces a comparative perspective. The third distinctive *Leitmotiv* of this book, in fact, is the systematic use of the comparative method to enquire as to the effectiveness and legitimacy of the constitutionalization of European budgetary constraints. As a substantive literature has emphasized, the comparative approach presents manifold advantages.[22] At its core, the comparative method constitutes a privileged instrument

[21] J Keane, *The Life and Death of Democracy* (London, Simon and Schuster, 2009) 695.

[22] For a useful overview, see G Dannemann, 'Comparative Law: Study of Similarities or Differences?' in M Reimann and R Zimmermann (eds), *The Oxford Handbook of Comparative Law* (Oxford, Oxford University Press, 2006) 383 and M Tushnet, 'Some Reflections on Method in Comparative Constitutional Law' in S Choundhry (ed), *The Migration of Constitutional Ideas* (Cambridge, Cambridge University Press, 2006) 67.

to understand legal phenomena, explain juridical process, and underline similarities and differences between legal regimes. In the absence of a laboratory to test their theses, moreover, lawyers can resort to the comparative method to identify the expected outcomes of various choices of constitutional design and hypothesize inferences between the existence of specific rules and the effects that they have on the social fabric.[23] Last but not least, comparative law might also offer a benchmark to evaluate from a normative perspective the arrangements introduced in a legal system,[24] as well as a rich source of inspiration to advance proposals for legal reform.[25]

In this book, the comparative method is exploited in two forms. On the one hand, the book engages in a widespread examination of how balanced budget rules are incorporated in the constitutional systems of the EU member states. In this way, the book surveys treaty ratifications, court decisions and constitutional revisions in a plurality of member states, including Belgium, Estonia, France, Germany, Greece, Hungary, Ireland, Italy, the Netherlands, Poland, Portugal, Slovakia and Spain. This allows an in-depth appreciation of the challenges that the introduction of budgetary constraints at the supranational level triggers for the EU member states. As a number of chapters make clear, the capacity of the EU member states to adapt their domestic regimes to the requirement of the Fiscal Compact depends on pre-existing constitutional features, such as the existence of judicial review of legislation, the flexibility with which a constitution can be amended and the status of international law within the domestic hierarchy of norms. All in all, therefore, a comparative perspective provides a complete picture of the variations among the member states and raises some cautionary tales on the viability of exporting one constitutional solution (such as the balanced budget rule of the German Basic Law, and later of the Fiscal Compact)[26] in member states with different constitutional arrangements.[27]

On the other hand, the book resorts to comparative law to put the case of the EU in a global context. While the constitutionalization of budgetary rules in the member states and in the EU is a recent phenomenon, other constitutional regimes have been dealing with these issues for longer time. In particular, as a number of contributions emphasize, the case of the US can provide some key insights to appraise the effects of the introduction of fiscal rules and to discuss

[23] See M Cappelletti et al, 'General Introduction', in M Cappelletti et al (eds), *Integration Through Law: Europe and the American Federal Experience*, vol 1, book 1 (Berlin, de Gruyter, 1986) 3, 5.

[24] See R Schütze, *From Dual to Cooperative Federalism. The Changing Structure of European Law* (Oxford, Oxford University Press, 2009), 59.

[25] For a view of how the comparative legal method needs to be enhanced with greater regard for policy matters in order to deliver useful normative results, see P Larouche, 'Legal Emulation between Regulatory Competition and Comparative Law' in P Larouche and P Cserne (eds), *National Legal Systems and Globalization: New Role, Continuing Relevance* (The Hague, TMC Asser Press, 2012) 247.

[26] See Editorial, 'The Fiscal Compact and the European Constitutions: "Europe Speaking German"' (2012) 8 *European Constitutional Law Review* 1.

[27] On the challenges of exporting constitutional solutions from one system to another, see V Perju, 'Constitutional Transplants, Borrowing and Migration', in M Rosenfeld and A Sajó (eds), *The Oxford Handbook of Comparative Constitutional Law* (Oxford, Oxford University Press, 2012) 1304.

the legitimacy questions that they raise.[28] Beginning in the 1840s, the states of the US started enshrining balanced budget rules in their constitutions, and, although the federal government never required the states to adopt such rules, by now almost all US states are endowed with a form of debt or deficit break. The experience of the constitutionalization of budgetary constraints in the US certainly presents many historical and political differences with the dynamics currently at play in the EU. However, it can serve as a mirror to appreciate how the Fiscal Compact affects the vertical balance of powers in the EU.[29] And it offers several warnings about the effective capacity of fiscal rules to constrain the action of the political branches in the budgetary domain. By enlarging our perspectives, therefore, a comparison with the US constitutional system sheds light on the challenges that the constitutionalization of budgetary rules poses in the EU and encourages a debate about the possible way forward toward a deeper and more genuine EMU.

V

The book is opened by the speech that Miguel Poiares Maduro delivered at Tilburg Law School on 31 May 2013. In his contribution Maduro overviews the two main narratives on the euro crisis—one based on the irresponsible fiscal policies of several member states, the other premised on the failure of the markets and uncontrolled capital flows—and maintains that at its heart the crisis represents a failure to internalize the democratic consequences of interdependence in the EMU. To address this situation, Maduro advances a proposal to take more seriously the economic part of EMU. To this end, he pleads in favour of an increased EU or eurozone budget, supported by real revenue sources, new EU policies and a more effective political authority supported by a European political space. As Maduro emphasizes, fiscal discipline and the constitutionalization of budgetary constraints is necessary, but it is not sufficient. Further steps are therefore needed to re-establish mutual trust between states and citizens, to render visible the benefits of economic interdependence and to link the solidarity of the EU to the wealth that it generates. As such, in a broad brush, Maduro's contribution touches upon all the themes that are addressed in the three parts of this book.

The first part of the book sets the context, introducing the new constitutional architecture of EMU and outlining the major innovations brought about by the Fiscal Compact from the perspective of EU law and economics. In his

[28] See R Henning and M Kessler, 'Fiscal Federalism: US History for Architects of Europe's Fiscal Union', (2012) *Bruegel Essay and Lecture Series* 6 and J Rodden, 'Market Discipline and US Federalism', in P Conti-Brown and D Skeel (eds), *When States Go Broke: The Origins, Context and Solutions for the American States in Fiscal Crisis* (Cambridge, Cambridge University Press, 2012) 123.

[29] On the role of comparative law as a mirror to understand better our own legal system, see also V Jackson, 'Narrative of Federalism: Of Continuities and Comparative Constitutional Experience' (2001) 51 *Duke Law Journal* 223, 258.

contribution Paul Craig aptly uses the metaphor of the triptych to structure his account of the substantive dimension of the constitutional architecture arising from the measures taken in the wake of the euro crisis. On one side, one finds various measures aimed at providing assistance to those member states that suffered severe economic problems. The ESM Treaty created a permanent institution to take over from the European Financial Stability Facility and the prior European Financial Stabilisation Mechanism. These mechanisms were complemented with actions from the ECB, including Outright Monetary Transactions (OMTs). On the other side, oversight and supervision were strengthened, both as regards financial institutions (Banking Union)[30] and national fiscal and economic policies ('six-pack', 'two-pack'), leading to the Fiscal Compact. The two sides are already linked now, and will be so even more if the proposals set out in the Report by the President of the European Council are implemented. At the same time—as Craig points out– from a formal perspective, a divide runs through all three panels of the triptych, between EU and non-EU measures. Some measures, such as the OMTs, find themselves in an improbable grey zone between EU and non-EU measures. Craig then discusses three major constitutional implications of these measures. First of all, the decision in *Pringle* may overextend the scope of the precedents referred to therein, resulting in a situation where EU institutions face little procedural or substantive constraints to stepping outside of the EU framework. Secondly, these measures mark a paradigm shift from legislation to contract, which may seem to enhance flexibility but may mask a loss of legitimacy and accountability. Thirdly, the measures increase the complexity and opacity of the legal and regulatory framework. Craig finally provides an assessment of the economic and political implications of these measures. On the economic side, he underlines the difficulty in finding the balance between assistance and moral hazard considerations. In political terms, he remarks how the euro crisis has severely shaken the faith and trust of citizens in the EU. Despite perceptions that the crisis strengthened the powers of a few member states, in the end the Commission might be the main political beneficiary of the measures. Beyond that, the measures taken to respond to the crisis will have lasting effects on EU unity and national politics.

Angelos Dimopoulos focuses on the difficult questions raised by the use of extra-EU avenues in dealing with the euro crisis. Both the ESM Treaty and the Fiscal Compact are international treaties concluded between EU member states outside of the EU framework, yet both are intimately linked with the EU. They borrow the EU institutions and they relate to the EU measures taken in the wake of the euro crisis, such as the 'six-pack' and 'two-pack' legislative packages. In the case of the ESM Treaty, *Pringle* makes painfully clear that the relationship with the EU is difficult to square within the framework of EU law. Neither the

[30] The pieces of the new EU Banking Union are slowly coming together with the creation of the Single Supervisory Mechanism—see Council Regulation (EU) No 1024/2013 of 15 October 2013—and now with a first agreement on the Single Resolution Mechanism—see Council of the EU, press release of 18 December 2013, Doc No 17983/13.

ESM nor the Fiscal Compact may affect the existence or exercise of EU competences, and to the extent that they help in achieving the goals of the EU, they are welcomed by EU law. On that latter point, one may however question whether the two treaties truly improve EU governance or rather undermine it, especially as regards legitimacy and accountability. The EU institutional balance is also affected, with new decision-making and law-making rules and procedures tilting the balance between member states, sidelining the European Parliament, and stripping the Commission of some of its traditional powers (initiative, enforcement before the ECJ). Dimopoulos considers that both treaties could legally have been elaborated under the EU framework, which might have been a more sustainable solution in the long run.

Kenneth Armstrong relates the measures addressing the euro crisis to the academic discussion on EU governance. These measures cannot be seen simply as a turn to rules-based governance. Even that claim must be qualified in the light of variations in the rules-based aspects of the response to the euro crisis. The 'six-pack' and 'two-pack' legislative packages did not follow traditional law-making models, and they feature a large amount of policy co-ordination. The two extra-EU treaties, the ESM Treaty and Fiscal Compact, evidence the limits of EU legislative capabilities in the light of its political and economic ambitions. Behind the rules, one also sees the emergence of 'infranational' governance, with the Commission and Council taking the central role in the European Semester where member state fiscal and economic policies are reviewed and co-ordinated. According to Armstrong, the response to the euro crisis also borrows from other forms of governance, namely governance by co-ordination (the European Semester), by markets and by contract (conditionality under the ESM Treaty). These governance forms coexist in a hybrid governance structure. Questions of governance also are at the core of Alexandre de Streel's contribution. De Streel considers the effectiveness of the 'six-pack', the 'two-pack' and the Fiscal Compact. These reforms addressed a number of weaknesses in the original design of the eurozone, such as the arbitrariness of the deficit and debt targets, the poor quality of budgetary data, the lack of 'ownership' on the part of the member states, the inadequacy of sanctions and of the decision-making leading to sanctions. Yet, according to De Streel additional reforms are likely to be needed, to resolve pressing issues of legitimacy and incentives (moral hazard).

Closing off the first part of this book, the contributions by Marijn van der Sluis and Stefania Baroncelli discuss the role of the ECB. Van der Sluis revisits the comparison between the ECB and the German Bundesbank, trying to go beyond legal analysis to look at the political and economic context. Whilst independent, the Bundesbank built up political capital and credibility over the first decades of its existence, which it did not refrain from using—with great care and prudence—to keep German economic policy on the 'right' path. In contrast, the ECB was conceived as an independent institution, operating at a distance from politics, and with a narrow mandate (price stability as the prime objective). The ECB had in any event no partner on the political scene at European level. The euro crisis changed the position of the ECB by bringing it closer to the political actors. Contrary to van der Sluis, Baroncelli sees a more direct lineage between the Bundesbank and the ECB, both being independent central banks in the monetarist-neoclassical mold, as opposed to accountable banks along a more Keynesian perspective. Yet, in its case law, the ECJ explicitly limited the ambit of that independence only to the conduct of monetary policy (eg allowing the ECB to be subject to the controls of OLAF, the Europan Anti-Fraud Office). In addressing the euro crisis, member states chose to work outside the EU, with the string of measures culminating in the ESM Treaty. Nevertheless, it could be argued that the actions of the ECB, eg through OMTs, were more influential in taming restless world markets. Yet, through these actions, the ECB moved closer to a political role and expanded upon its narrow mandate. These actions have now been challenged before the German Constitutional Court. Furthermore, the ECB's mandate is being further enlarged with the Banking Union, which entrusts banking supervision to the ECB.

The second part of the book focuses on the constitutionalization of European budgetary constraints in comparative perspective. It begins with a contribution by Pieter-Augustijn Van Malleghem, who draws a broad picture of balanced budget rules in the EU in comparison with the US. Van Malleghem examines the historical emergence of a various types of budgetary constraints in the constitution of the US states and contrasts this with introduction of a 'golden rule' in the constitutions of the EU member states as a result of the top-down obligation of the Fiscal Compact. By drawing cautionary tales from the centennial experience of the US states with balanced budget constraints, Van Malleghem warns about the effectiveness of these constitutional rules in preventing excessive government deficits and debts. He underlines how courts have traditionally shied away from vigorously enforcing compliance with these rules. Moreover, developing insights from the literature on fiscal federalism, he explains that in the US the existence of balanced budget rules at the state level is counterbalanced (at least since the New Deal) by a strong role of the federal government in managing countercyclical economic policies. As he emphasizes, the absence (as of now) of a comparable role for the EU budget, casts some shadows on the introduction of 'golden rules' at the state level, because it forces the member states to run procyclical policies without any possibility to rely on supranational support in times of economic recession. In the worst-case scenario, this would lead to the break-up of the Eurozone—a threatening prospect that only the establishment of a genuine fiscal capacity for the EU would prevent.

Part 2 includes contributions by Giacomo Delledonne and Marek Antoš, which offer a broad comparative assessment of the constitutionalization of balanced-budget rules in the EU member states. Giacomo Delledonne focuses on four countries of Western Europe—France, Germany, Italy and Spain—and traces the export of the German model of the constitutional 'golden rule', via the Fiscal Compact, into the basic (or organic) laws of the larger member states of the eurozone. Marek Antoš, instead, considers the constitutionalization of budgetary constraints in four countries of Central and Eastern Europe—Germany, Hungary, Poland and Slovakia—and contrasts the effects of constitutional debt and deficit brakes in two EU member states that are part of the eurozone and two that are not. According to Delledonne, the constitutionalization of 'golden rules' in the EU member states signals a movement of fiscal issues from the political to the legal constitution, ie a shift from a process-based management of budgetary issues in the political domain to a legal entrenchment of substantive fiscal rules. As he argues, however, the effects of this shift are uncertain due to the existence of derogations in the 'golden rules' and the limited experience of courts in this field. Approaching the theme through the prism of the theory of precommitment, Antoš explains that balanced-budget rules can be assessed on the basis of three criteria: effectiveness, democratic legitimacy and flexibility with regard to the business cycle. As he argues, reconciling these three criteria represents a daunting task. But he regards the German solution as the most suitable, and welcomes its use as a model EU-wide.

Part 2 then features the contributions of Lina Papadopoulou, Michal Diamant and Michiel van Emmerik, and Roderic O'Gorman which focus specifically on the constitutionalization of budgetary constraints in three EU member states: Greece, the Netherlands and Ireland. Each of these member states presents several peculiarities which make it particularly apt for an ad hoc examination. Greece is where arguably all started: the unsustainability of Greek public deficit, and the need to provide European aid to rescue the country, prompted a call for tighter budgetary rules at the EU level—a recipe that was later imposed also on other states, such as Spain or Ireland, where the problems actually lay in banks, rather than governments. As Papadopoulou explains, Greece has not yet constitutionalized a 'golden rule', but the obligation to steer budgets toward a sustainable path has become the *summa lex* of the country, due to its subjection to the economic adjustment programme established in the Memorandum of Understanding between Greece and its foreign lenders. The Netherlands has not constitutionalized a balanced-budget rule—mainly because, as Diamant and van Emmerik explain, changing the Dutch constitution is almost impossible. Entrenching a 'golden rule', furthermore, raises special challenges in a state such as the Netherlands in which judicial review of legislation does not take place. As Diamant and van Emmerik make clear, however, the openness of the Dutch legal system vis-à-vis international law provides a convenient means to ensure the incorporation of the Fiscal Compact and the obligation by the Dutch legislature to comply with its terms. The case of Ireland, which is at the centre of O'Gorman's chapter, is remarkable as this is the only EU member state where the ratification of the Fiscal Compact was subject to a public referendum. Yet, the approval of the Treaty was largely driven by the necessity of continued EU financial support, and was not followed up by a constitutionalization of the 'golden rule' in the national basic law.

The third part of the book, finally, addresses a number of questions about legitimacy and accountability, discussing the role of courts, legislatures and social partners in the new constitutional architecture of EMU and advancing a number of proposals on how to improve the EU institutional regime towards the creation of a deeper and more genuine EMU. Part 3 begins with the contribution by Ingolf Pernice, who in a most ambitious vein argues for a new 'social contract' at the EU level, including all citizens of the member states, determined to organize their common European future most effectively and democratically. This is indeed an undertaking of great constitutional importance and impact, not just a matter of treaty revision. It is also—according to Pernice—an urgent undertaking, because of the fragility of the present situation, and it should involve all the citizens of the EU. The political process towards the negotiation of a new social contract has to be initiated before the electoral campaigns for the European elections are launched, and the Blueprint of the Commission is meant to start the debate. Many questions and challenges remain. For instance, Pernice asks whether a new Union should be adopted by parallel referenda in all the member states, or better by a European Referendum? Also, many provisions would have to be simplified in order to make them understandable for the people, before they can reasonably vote on a new treaty. This could be the 'new European social contract', which could give the Union a legitimacy that some believe the existing EU treaties' 'simple' ratification procedure, which rests in the hands of the national parliaments according to their respective constitutional procedures, cannot provide.

In her chapter, Sonia Piedrafita focuses more on procedural legitimacy, ie the democratic principles of traditional national representation and checks-and-balances, and especially the role that national parliaments have played in the adoption process of the new EU budgetary constraints. For a long time, national parliaments have been considered one of the main sources of the EU's democratic legitimacy. There thus seems ample reason to deal with this topic. More specifically, Piedrafita looks into how Ireland and Spain ratified the Fiscal Compact, and incorporated the 'golden rule' in their respective legal orders. She examines the parliamentary debates as well as the position of the political parties along the process. Both member states—she claims—constitute crucial cases to analyse the degree of contestation of these decisions at national level. In Spain, despite strong opposition from the main opposition parties when the implementing law was debated, parliamentary scrutiny of the Fiscal Compact, as well as the ratification itself, was not very well developed. More generally, and notwithstanding the so-called Lisbon Treaty provisions on the enhanced role of national parliaments in decision-making concerning EU affairs, parliamentary scrutiny in this regard is rather weakly developed in Spain. This is also due to the strong position of the executive in the political system. In Ireland, however, the ratification of the Fiscal Compact (through referendum) and the enactment of its implementing law (by ordinary procedure) were subject to more thorough parliamentary scrutiny. This raises as a result fewer concerns in terms of procedural legitimacy.

Samo Bardutzky and Elaine Fahey consider the adjudication of the ESM Treaty as a rich case study of the character of law in contemporary EU integration and the state of postnationalism. According to the two authors, the ESM constitutes an example of suboptimal adjudication in the EU courts (both national and supranational). Their argument is rooted in both the character of eurozone law and a rather flawed procedural matrix for judicial review, in the form of the preliminary reference mechanism. They argue that, in retrospect, courts possibly offered a unique forum for participation and contestation. They examine the preliminary reference mechanism as the tool that could have facilitated a more participatory and orchestrated judicial response. According to Bardutzky and Fahey, the ESM 'saga' indicates that if the member states continue to avail themselves of creative instruments of esoteric postnational character curbing or purporting to curb judicial review or national plebiscites on their character, this will require a rethink of the architecture of the EU judiciary, at supranational and national level, as much as the instruments themselves. Francesco Costamagna's contribution assesses instead the impact of the measures taken to strengthen the relationship between economic and social objectives in the context of the European integration process. He claims that the need to balance economic and social dimensions of the integration process represents indeed an essential prerequisite for the legitimacy of the EU as such. Costamagna observes that, whereas previously economic objectives were clearly prioritized, there are signs of a reorientation of the strategy adopted at supranational level: the recommendations adopted in the 2013 cycle of the European Semester pay greater attention to social objectives. Nevertheless, the adopted measures are too limited and too occasional. There is the need to ensure that, at a minimum, the action fully contributes to the pursuit of fundamental social objectives that lay at the core of national welfare states and that are now enshrined in the list of EU aims. According to Costamagna, this step, connected with input legitimacy, is necessary to preserve the output legitimacy of the integration process and, ultimately, its very raison d'être.

The two final contributions of the book debate alternative perspectives on the future of the EMU. Peter Lindseth begins his contribution with his challenging 'administrative' interpretation of European governance. European integration—Lindseth claims—is best understood as an extension of modern administrative governance, as it developed over the course of the twentieth century. What administrative bodies, however, lack despite their autonomous *power*, is autonomous democratic and constitutional *legitimacy* to exercise that power without some oversight by strongly legitimated bodies residing elsewhere. This means that, in the case of European integration, supranational institutions lack democratic and constitutional legitimacy of their own, despite the fact that they have been partly constructed to mimic strongly legitimated legislative, executive, and judicial bodies on the national level. As a result, supranational institutions ultimately depend for democratic and constitutional legitimacy on the legislative, executive, and judicial bodies of the member states. He argues that democratic and constitutional legitimacy are inextricably connected in the modern era, and that the EU is not 'constitutional' in itself, but rather technocratic and juristocratic.

According to Lindseth, for instance, the European Parliament is not experienced by the citizens of Europe as an embodiment or expression of the capacity of a new European 'demos' to rule itself. The evolution of European public law and supranational authority is for Lindseth much more than a matter of institutional engineering, often revolving around expanded powers for the European Parliament. As for the crisis in the Eurozone, Lindseth argues that a plausible, democracy-based normative theory is needed to share responsibility for the legacy costs of a poorly designed monetary union. Such theory can be persuasive because it can be recast in terms of fault, causation, responsibility and proportionality that are deeply familiar to the legal mind of national high court judges who might be asked to rule on the constitutionality of such burden-sharing. The challenge—Lindseth claims—is to avoid idealist appeals to intra-European solidarity and instead ground the normative principle of burden-sharing in the idea of democratic and constitutional responsibility of each participating state in the EMU.

Whereas Lindseth is reserved about employing a primarily constitutionalist terminology to describe integration, Federico Fabbrini is doing precisely that. In his contribution Fabbrini focuses on the possibilities and the challenges towards a new phase of economic integration in the EMU, based on fiscal capacity besides fiscal constraints. Fabbrini deals with three 'constitutional' challenges for a fiscal capacity to succeed. These he terms the challenges of asymmetry, unanimity and representation. They all raise critical hurdles to the establishment of a fiscal capacity which is to avoid falling prey of endless negotiations on interstate money transfers, insurmountable deadlock in decisions about the adoption of EU own resources and lack of representation by those individuals who would be directly subject to new EU taxation. Although these challenges are significant, Fabbrini nonetheless does not believe them to be insurmountable, and proposes three remedies: (a) the introduction of EU own resources can break the vicious equation between financial solidarity and interstate transfers; (b) the resort to enhanced co-operation can address the challenge of unanimity and sidestep the deadlock that virtually automatically arises in the field of tax policy whenever proposals are made for new EU taxes; (c) the possibility of the '*passerelle* clauses' can address the challenge of representation and ensure that the only institution directly representing the European citizens—the European Parliament—has a say on decisions which involve EU taxation. Endowing the EMU with a fiscal capacity is, according to Fabbrini, a desirable development to solve the euro crisis and strengthen democracy in the EU. As such, Fabbrini's conclusions link back to the opening contribution by Maduro, who pleaded in favour of an EU budget, based on authentic EU resources and grounded in a new democratic decision-making framework as the least impossible among the impossible options for saving the eurozone from its current quagmires.

Whether the reader will share optimism on the possibility to establish a deeper and more genuine EMU or not, we hope that the Tilburg conference and the present collection of contributions will be considered as one more step in the new debate and stimulate further discussions on the future of Europe.

Part 1

The New Constitutional Architecture of European Economic and Monetary Union

2

Economic Governance and the Euro Crisis: Constitutional Architecture and Constitutional Implications

PAUL CRAIG

I. INTRODUCTION

THE FINANCIAL CRISIS, and resulting crisis with the euro, has had profound effects on the EU, and its Member States, even those that do not form part of the eurozone. It has generated a welter of measures to combat the 'problem' and this flurry of initiatives has not yet come to an end, nor is it likely to do so in the short term. This chapter considers the emerging constitutional architecture resulting from these measures, from both a substantive and a formal dimension. This is followed by an examination of the constitutional implications of the measures adopted thus far. The discussion considers these implications from a legal, economic and political perspective, and it will be seen that there are significant constitutional challenges in all three areas.

II. CONSTITUTIONAL ARCHITECTURE

There will doubtless be continued debate as to the ascription of responsibility for the financial crisis. The reality of the crisis was not, however, to be denied, and it generated a whole raft of legal responses.[1] This section considers the constitutional architecture resulting from the measures enacted to combat the crisis. The discussion begins with the substantive dimension, and it will be seen that the measures can be divided into those designed to provide assistance to eurozone Member States, and those where the primary objective was to strengthen over-

[1] J-V Louis, 'Guest Editorial: The No-Bailout Clause and Rescue Packages' (2010) 47 *Common Market Law Review* 971; M Ruffert, 'The European Debt Crisis and European Union Law' (2011) 48 *Common Market Law Review* 1777; R D'Sa, 'The Legal and Constitutional Nature of the New International Treaties on Economic and Monetary Union from the Perspective of EU Law' [2012] *European Current Law* xi; E Chiti and P Teixeira, 'The Constitutional Implications of the European Responses to the Financial and Public Debt Crises' (2013) 50 *Common Market Law Review* 683.

sight of national budgetary policy. This is followed by an examination of the formal dimension to the constitutional architecture, which connotes the distinction between the measures that took legal effect as norms of EU law, and those measures that took effect as non-EU legal measures. It will be seen that the formal dimension cuts across the substantive.

A. The Substantive Dimension: Assistance and Oversight

The plethora of measures enacted to address the financial crisis represents in reality a secular triptych, in which the two wing panels consist of measures designed respectively to assist and oversee ailing Member States, while the middle panel is comprised of current and future initiatives that reveal the interconnection between the two wings.

(i) Assistance

The EU put in place a range of measures to give assistance to Member States that were in severe economic problems as a result of the euro crisis. The most important common element is conditionality, connoting the basic precept that funds are given on strict conditions concerning reforms that must be put in place by the recipient state.

The assistance was initially provided through the European Financial Stabilisation Mechanism (EFSM), which was financed from the EU budget and from bonds. It was used to give financial assistance to Ireland and Portugal. The EFSM was enacted as a Council Regulation pursuant to Article 122(2) TFEU.[2] The sums available for disbursement under the EFSM were, however, limited to only €60 billion.

The principal vehicle for provision of assistance then shifted to the European Financial Stability Facility (EFSF), a company established by the eurozone countries on 9 May 2010.[3] It was incorporated in Luxembourg under Luxembourgish law. Its objective was to preserve the financial stability of Europe's monetary union by providing temporary financial assistance to eurozone Member States if needed. Its overall capacity was €780 billion. This was backed by guarantees given by the then 17 eurozone Member States, divided in accordance with their share in the paid-up capital of the European Central Bank (ECB). The EFSF Board of Directors is composed of high-level representatives of the 17 eurozone Member States. The Commission and the ECB have observers. The EFSF Board of Directors is headed by the Chairman of the EU's Economic and Financial Committee.

The 'baton' for provision of assistance has, however, now passed to the

[2] Council Regulation (EU) No 407/2010 of 11 May 2010 establishing a European financial stabilisation mechanism [2010] OJ L118/1.

[3] www.efsf.europa.eu/about/index.htm .

European Stability Mechanism (ESM),[4] which entered into force on 8 October 2012, although the EFSF continued to finance ongoing programmes for Greece, Portugal and Ireland.[5] The Euro Group summit agreed on the principle of the ESM in July 2011, but it took time for the details to be ironed out. The ESM was finally agreed on 2 March 2012, and entered into force on 8 October 2012. Article 136 TFEU was amended through recourse to the simplified revision procedure, the result being a new paragraph 3, which stated that 'the Member States whose currency is the euro may establish a stability mechanism to be activated if indispensable to safeguard the stability of the euro-area as a whole'.[6] However this amendment was not in force when the ESM was established and could not therefore form the legal basis for the ESM. The ESM thus took effect as an intergovernmental organization based on an international treaty between the eurozone Member States, and is located in Luxembourg. It shares facilities with the EFSF. The ESM has a total subscribed capital of €700 billion, €80 billion of which is in the form of paid-in capital provided by the eurozone Member States in five instalments of €16 billion.

This brief overview of measures to assist Member States in financial difficulty would be incomplete without mention of the ECB. The no-bail-out clause in Article 125 TFEU, and the prohibition on credit facilities to national governments in Article 123 TFEU, precluded the grant of direct financial assistance to such states. Notwithstanding these provisions, the ECB, acting pursuant to Article 127(2) TFEU, which provides inter alia that the ECB shall define and implement the monetary policy of the EU, made a formal decision establishing a securities markets programme, which sanctioned ECB intervention in the eurozone private and public debt markets;[7] but the scheme was only intended to be temporary, and was terminated in September 2012. It was, however, replaced by Outright Monetary Transactions (OMTs), which concern transactions in secondary sovereign bond markets 'that aim at safeguarding an appropriate monetary policy transmission and the singleness of the monetary policy'.[8]

(ii) Oversight

The grant of assistance to Member States in serious financial difficulty is but one half of the overall strategy to cope with the euro crisis. The other half is increased supervision over national financial institutions. This has assumed various forms. Thus the regulatory apparatus for banking, securities, insurance and occupational pensions has been thoroughly overhauled,[9] and new measures

[4] www.esm.europa.eu/ .

[5] Arts 39–40 ESM.

[6] European Council Decision 2011/199 of 25 March 2011 amending Art 136 TFEU with regard to a stability mechanism for Member States whose currency is the euro [2011] OJ L91/1.

[7] Decision 2010/281/of the European Central Bank of 14 May 2010 establishing a securities markets programme [2010] OJ L124/8.

[8] www.ecb.int/press/pr/date/2012/html/pr120906_1.en.html .

[9] Regulation (EU) No 1093/2010 of the European Parliament and of the Council of 24 November

such as the Single Supervisory Mechanism and the Single Resolution Mechanism will increase EU oversight over national banking facilities. There have also been major changes designed to increase oversight over national economic policy, because of the proximate connection between economic and monetary union. The driving force behind these changes was to tighten EU control over national economic policy in order to prevent any recurrence of the sovereign debt and banking crises that precipitated the crisis with the euro.

The legislative framework for economic union was amended through the 'six-pack' of measures in 2011,[10] which were enacted pursuant to Articles 121, 126 and 136 TFEU.[11] The measures were designed to render economic union more effective by tightening the two parts of the schema, surveillance and excessive deficit, the details of which were contained in the Stability and Growth Pact.[12] Further measures, the two-pack, were enacted on 21 May 2013.[13] Space precludes detailed elaboration of these complex provisions. Suffice it to say for the present that they included changes to enhance budgetary oversight by focusing on its timing, the format of national budgetary determinations and the need for these to be independently verified. Further changes to the surveillance mechanism are substantive and require Member States to make significant progress towards medium-term budgetary objectives for their budgetary

2010 establishing a European Supervisory Authority (European Banking Authority) [2010] OJ L331/12; Regulation (EU) No 1095/2010 of the European Parliament and of the Council of 24 November 2010 establishing a European Supervisory Authority (European Securities and Markets Authority) [2010] OJ L331/84; Regulation (EU) No 1094/2010 of the European Parliament and of the Council of 24 November 2010 establishing a European Supervisory Authority (European Insurance and Occupational Pensions Authority) [2010] OJ L331/4.

[10] http://ec.europa.eu/economy_finance/economic_governance/index_en.htm .

[11] Regulation (EU) No 1175/2011 of the European Parliament and of the Council of 16 November 2011 amending Regulation (EC) No 1466/97 on the strengthening of the surveillance of budgetary positions and the surveillance and coordination of economic policies [2011] OJ L306/12; Council Regulation (EU) No 1177/2011 of 8 November 2011 amending Regulation (EC) No 1467/97 on speeding up and clarifying the implementation of the excessive deficit procedure [2011] OJ L306/33; Regulation (EU) No 1173/2011 of the European Parliament and of the Council of 16 November 2011 on the effective enforcement of budgetary surveillance in the euro area [2011] OJ L306/1; Council Directive 2011/85/EU of 8 November 2011 on requirements for budgetary frameworks of the Member States [2011] OJ L306/41; Regulation (EU) No 1176/2011 of the European Parliament and of the Council of 16 November 2011 on the prevention and correction of macroeconomic imbalances [2011] OJ L306/25; Regulation (EU) No 1174/2011 of the European Parliament and of the Council of 16 November 2011 on enforcement measures to correct macroeconomic imbalances in the euro area [2011] OJ L306/8; Results of in-depth reviews under Regulation (EU) No 1176/2011 on the prevention and correction of macroeconomic imbalances, COM(2013) 199 final.

[12] Council Regulation (EC) 1466/97 of 7 July 1997 on the strengthening of the surveillance of budgetary positions and the surveillance and coordination of economic policies [1997] OJ L209/1; Council Regulation (EC) 1467/97 of 7 July 1997 on speeding up and clarifying the implementation of the excessive deficit procedure [1997] OJ L209/6.

[13] Regulation (EU) 472/2013 of the European Parliament and of the Council of 21 May 2013 on the strengthening of economic and budgetary surveillance of Member States experiencing or threatened with serious difficulties with respect to their financial stability in the euro area [2013] OJ L140/1; Regulation (EU) 473/2013 of the European Parliament and of the Council of 21 May 2013 on common provisions for monitoring and assessing draft budgetary plans and ensuring the correction of excessive deficit of the Member States in the euro area [2013] OJ L140/11.

balances. The EU also strengthened the excessive deficit procedure, the other limb of economic union.

The rules on oversight over national economic policy analysis have also been affected by the Treaty on Stability, Coordination and Governance (TSCG),[14] also known as the Fiscal Compact, which was signed by 25 contracting states in March 2012.[15] Article 3(1) TSCG contains the 'balanced budget' rule[16] and is the heart of the new Treaty. The budgets of the contracting parties must be balanced or in surplus.[17] This is deemed to be respected if the annual structural balance of the general government is at its country-specific medium-term objective, as defined in the revised Stability and Growth Pact, with a lower limit of a structural deficit of 0.5 per cent of gross domestic product at market prices.[18] The contracting parties must ensure rapid convergence towards their respective medium-term objectives. The time-frame for such convergence is proposed by the Commission taking into consideration country-specific sustainability risks. While the obligation to balance the national budget is the core of the TSCG, it is nonetheless arguable that almost everything therein might have been done under the existing Lisbon Treaty provisions, including those on enhanced co-operation.[19] It is also important to recognize that the provisions concerning assistance and those concerning oversight are 'joined at the hip', in the sense that grant of assistance under the ESM is conditional from 1 March 2013 on ratification by the applicant state of the Fiscal Compact.

(iii) Assistance and Oversight: The Next Steps

The efforts made to address the euro crisis through the admixture of assistance and supervision considered above do not, however, exhaust EU initiatives in this area. The next steps can be gleaned from the report produced by the President of the European Council in close collaboration with the presidents of the Commission, ECB and Eurogroup, hereinafter referred to as the Four Presidents' Report.[20] It lays the groundwork for further policies to secure, as the title suggests, genuine economic and monetary union. It was produced at the behest of the European Council,[21] and was endorsed by it in December

[14] P Craig, 'The Stability, Coordination and Governance Treaty: Principle, Politics and Pragmatism' (2012) 37 *European Law Review* 231; S Peers, 'The Stability Treaty: Permanent Austerity or Gesture Politics?' (2012) 8 *European Constitutional Law Review* 404.

[15] Treaty on Stability, Coordination and Governance in the Economic and Monetary Union, 1–2 March 2012, available at www.european-council.europa.eu/eurozone-governance/treaty-on-stability?lang=en .

[16] The rules in Art 3 TSCG are without prejudice to obligations under EU law.

[17] Art 3(1)(a) TSCG.

[18] Art 3(1)(b) TSCG, as qualified by Art 3(1)(d) TSCG.

[19] Craig (n 14); Peers (n 14).

[20] H Van Rompuy in close collaboration with J M Barroso, J-C Juncker and M Draghi, 'Towards a Genuine Economic and Monetary Union', 5 December 2012, www.consilium.europa.eu/uedocs/cms_data/docs/pressdata/en/ec/134069.pdf. See also 'A Blueprint for a Deep and Genuine EMU, Launching a European Debate' COM(2012) 777 final.

[21] www.consilium.europa.eu/uedocs/cms_data/docs/pressdata/en/ec/133004.pdf.

2012.[22] The report is framed in terms of an integrated financial framework, an integrated budgetary framework and an integrated economic policy framework. These proposals can nonetheless be explicated within the frame of assistance and supervision.

Thus some proposals are principally aimed at provision of assistance of a kind that will render it less likely that Member States will need to seek help from the ESM. There are in essence two elements to this proposed schema. The first limb of the proposed reform seeks to address national economic vulnerability through 'limited, temporary, flexible and targeted financial incentives'[23] made operational through contractual arrangements between Member States and the EU, which would be mandatory for eurozone Member States and voluntary for other Member States. The second limb of the proposed reform is to endow the EU with fiscal capacity, the Four Presidents' Report noting that all other currency unions have this.[24] The objective is to facilitate adjustment to economic shocks.[25]

There is, however, also an oversight/supervisory aspect to the proposals, which finds its expression principally in the proposals for an integrated financial framework. Their importance and content are captured in the following extract:

> The current European arrangements for safeguarding financial stability remain based on national responsibilities. This is inconsistent with the highly integrated nature of the EMU and has certainly exacerbated the harmful interplay between the fragilities of sovereigns and the vulnerabilities of the banking sector. The set-up of the Single Supervisory Mechanism (SSM) will be a guarantor of strict and impartial supervisory oversight, thus contributing to breaking the link between sovereigns and banks and diminishing the probability of future systemic banking crisis.[26]

The core idea is for the SSM to be run by the ECB, which will have direct oversight of banks, the objective being 'to enforce prudential rules in a strict and impartial manner and perform effective oversight of cross border banking markets'.[27] Ensuring that banking supervision across the eurozone abides by high common standards is regarded as an essential precondition for introduction of any further support mechanisms, such as use of ESM funds for direct bank recapitalization.[28] The importance of this aspect of the overall plan is attested to by the speed with which the European Council agreed to the idea of the SSM, which has now been formally enacted.

[22] European Council, 13–14 December 2012.

[23] 'Towards a Genuine Economic and Monetary Union' (n 20) 7.

[24] Ibid 7.

[25] Ibid 7.

[26] Ibid 4.

[27] COM(2012) 511 final, 2; Council Regulation (EU) No 1024/2013 of 15 October 2013 conferring specific tasks on the European Central Bank concerning policies relating to the prudential supervision of credit institutions [2013] OJ L287/63.

[28] ESM Direct Bank Recapitalization Instrument, Main Features of the Operational Instrument and Way Forward, 20 June 2013, http://ec.europa.eu/economy_finance/focuson/crisis/index_en.htm.

B. The Formal Dimension: EU Measures and Non-EU Measures

The discussion of constitutional architecture thus far has focused on the substance of the measures, with the divide falling between provisions concerning assistance and those dealing with oversight. There is, however, a further important dimension to this constitutional architecture, which concerns the form through which the relevant measures have taken effect.

Viewed from this perspective the principal fault-line is between measures that have taken effect as EU measures stricto sensu, and those that have not. This fault-line cuts across the assistance/supervision divide. Thus some measures to provide assistance, such as the EFSM, were enacted as formal EU law pursuant to the Lisbon Treaty, and so too were many measures to increase EU oversight over national economic policy, including the six-pack and two-pack.

The ESM and Fiscal Compact have, by way of contrast, taken effect as treaties between Member States, in which EU institutions have participated, but in relation to which the EU is not itself a party. The rationale for this modus operandi differed in the two instances. In relation to the ESM, the rationale was that the Treaty amendment authorising Member States to proceed in this manner was not yet in force, coupled with the fact that the EU itself was not empowered to establish such a stability mechanism. In relation to the Fiscal Compact, the rationale for proceeding outside the formal EU Treaty was more political than legal. Germany and France sought amendment to the primary Lisbon Treaty to strengthen EU oversight over Member State economic policy. This was prevented by a UK veto. It is arguable that almost everything in the TSCG could have been enacted as EU legislation pursuant to the Lisbon Treaty. Germany and France had, however, committed themselves to changing the primary Lisbon Treaty, and did not wish to back down in the light of the UK veto and accept change in the form of EU legislation. This explains the insistence on finding some other method of enshrining the desired precepts in 'primary law', even if this had to be a treaty distinct from the Lisbon Treaty.

The legitimacy of EU institutional involvement in the ESM was tested in *Pringle*.[29] The Court of Justice of the European Union (CJEU) reiterated the holding from its previous case law[30] that Member States 'are entitled, in areas which do not fall under the exclusive competence of the Union, to entrust tasks to the institutions, outside the framework of the Union, such as the task of coordinating a collective action undertaken by the Member States or managing financial assistance'.[31] It then added the caveat that this was subject to the proviso that 'those tasks do not alter the essential character of the powers conferred on

[29] Case C-370/12 *Pringle v Government of Ireland, Ireland and the Attorney General*, judgment of 27 November 2012, nyr.

[30] Cases C-181 and 248/91 *European Parliament v Council and Commission* [1993] ECR I-3685, [20]; Case C-316/91 *European Parliament v Council* [1993] ECR I-653, [41].

[31] *Pringle* (n 29) [158].

those institutions by the EU and FEU Treaties',[32] drawing this principle from case law concerning international agreements made by the EU.[33] The CJEU concluded that the duties allocated to the Commission and ECB in the ESM Treaty met these criteria. We shall return to this issue when considering the constitutional implications of these developments.

It should not, however, be assumed that the divide between formal EU measures and those that take effect outside the formal contours of the Lisbon Treaty is clear cut. The messiness of reality undermines such 'neatness'. There are some measures, such as the ECB's Outright Monetary Transactions, that exist in a netherworld, in the sense that their precise foundation in the Lisbon Treaty is unclear and contestable. There are other measures, such as the Memorandum of Understanding (MoU) made between Member States in receipt of financial assistance and the ESM, which straddle both worlds, in the sense that they are made pursuant to the ESM and hence are outside the formal contours of EU law, while at the same time being formally linked to criteria under the Lisbon Treaty. Thus Article 13(3) ESM stipulates that the MoU must set out the conditions attached to the grant of assistance, and that these must be 'fully consistent with the measures of economic policy coordination provided for in the TFEU, in particular with any act of European Union law, including any opinion, warning, recommendation or decision addressed to the ESM Member concerned'.

III. CONSTITUTIONAL IMPLICATIONS: THE LEGAL DIMENSION

The measures enacted to combat the financial crisis have constitutional implications, three of which are discussed in this section. They prompt inquiry as to: the manner and legitimacy of legal change within the EU; the doctrinal legal form through which this change is effectuated; and resultant issues of transparency and complexity for the overall body of law in this area.

A. Legal Principle, Legal Change and Legitimacy

The limits of law are always going to be tested in times of emergency, and that is true in the modern day for economic as well as physical threats. Indeed the very language of the law is itself expressive, as reflected in the rhetoric of

[32] Ibid [158].

[33] Opinion 1/92 *Draft agreement between the Community, on the one hand, and the countries of the European Free Trade Association, on the other, relating to the creation of the European Economic Area* [1992] ECR I-2821, [32], [41]; Opinion 1/00 *Proposed agreement between the European Community and non-Member States on the establishment of a European Common Aviation Area* [2002] ECR I-3493, [20]; Opinion 1/09 *Draft agreement—Creation of a unified patent litigation system—European and Community Patents Court—Compatibility of the draft agreement with the Treaties* [2011] ECR I-1137, [75].

recent legislation, in which phrases speaking to the need to avoid 'contagion', and the necessity to avoid 'negative spill over' from national budgetary policy, frequently appear. We should be mindful of this 'Schmittian' dimension, but it should nonetheless not preclude reasoned analysis of the legal difficulties attendant on measures enacted to meet the crisis.

This is exemplified by the CJEU's jurisprudence concerning the ability of EU institutions to participate in treaties outside the framework of EU law, such as the ESM and the Fiscal Compact. There is an endemic difficulty in crafting legal rules so as to ensure that they are neither over- nor under-inclusive. There may also be an 'imperfect match' between the legal principle and its sphere of application. Thus a potentially broad legal principle may initially be applied to very limited facts, with the consequence that it is given little attention and is not deemed to be of 'real' constitutional significance. The same legal principle is then applied to a factual situation that is considerably broader, with the consequence that its constitutional significance assumes centre stage. There is a related endemic difficulty in crafting legal rules, which concerns the very idea of reasoning by analogy. The courts must necessarily decide what constitutes an appropriate analogy from an earlier decision, which can be used as the foundation for a later case. In some instances this is straightforward; in others it is not. These twin difficulties of legal reasoning provide the backdrop to the legal story in this area.

It has been argued that the decision in *Pringle*, so far as it concerns the ability of an EU institution to participate in agreements made outside the legal framework of the EU, is satisfactory.[34] I do not share this view, and it is clear moreover that the Commission is wary of intergovernmental initiatives outside the formal confines of the Lisbon Treaty, stating they should only be used on an exceptional and transitional basis, pending a Treaty change.[35] Space precludes detailed analysis of the issues, which can be found elsewhere.[36] Suffice it to say the following in the present context, which is that there are constitutional concerns of a foundational, procedural and substantive nature flowing from the CJEU's decision.

In foundational terms, the ruling begs the question as to the derivation of the principle affirmed in the case and the values that underpin it. In procedural terms, the ruling leaves a legal black hole, according a broad substantive discretionary power to EU institutions with no legal procedural safeguards. Thus there are no formal procedural constraints relating to: reasoned justification for the institutional decision to participate in such an agreement; the form in which the institutional decision is to be taken; consultation with other institutions; or securing the agreement of other institutions. There are additional procedural

[34] S Peers, 'Towards a New Form of EU Law? The Use of EU Institutions outside the EU Legal Framework' (2013) 9 *European Constitutional Law Review* 37.

[35] Commission Blueprint (n 20) 13.

[36] P Craig, '*Pringle* and Use of EU Institutions outside the EU Legal Framework: Foundations, Procedure and Substance' (2013) 9 *European Constitutional Law Review* 263.

concerns raised by the decision, such as the relationship between the ruling in *Pringle* and the rules on enhanced co-operation, which have been imperfectly understood in the discourse thus far. There are moreover unresolved issues as to when, if ever, a dissenting state can prevent EU institutions from participating in agreements of this nature.

In substantive terms, the twin conditions imposed by the judgment, namely that the agreement in which the EU institution participates must be compatible with the Lisbon Treaty and that the powers accorded to it must not undermine the essential character of that institution's powers under the Lisbon Treaty, impose in reality little by way of legal constraint. The conditions are moreover implicitly predicated on a false equation or elision between compatibility and substantive choice: there are very many choices that may be made in any substantive area within the EU's sphere of competence, all of which may be compatible with EU law, none of which alter the essential nature of the powers conferred on the institutions by the constituent treaties, and none of which would find the requisite majority support for enactment. We should think long and hard before according a very broad discretionary power to an EU institution to choose to privilege one such option by participating in an agreement made with states outside the EU. The substantive concerns raised by such participation are exacerbated by the fact that there are very real problems in securing accountability, ex ante and ex post, and in ensuring the applicability of important substantive protections such as the Charter of Rights.

B. Legal Principle, Legislation and Contract

The developments in this area reveal an interesting shift from legislation to contract. To be sure, contractual language and metaphor were already present in this area, as exemplified by the relationship between Member States and the EU pursuant to the broad economic policy guidelines.[37] It is also clear that contracts will subsist against the backdrop of Treaty provisions and EU legislation. Notwithstanding this, contract assumes enhanced prominence as the policy delivery tool of choice within the blueprint for a 'genuine economic and monetary union'.[38]

This is especially prominent in the Four Presidents' Report and in the subsequent endorsement by the European Council. These contracts constitute the mechanism for delivery of the integrated economic policy framework, whereby the EU in tandem with the Member States will review structural features of the national economy in order to reduce economic vulnerabilities and increase competitiveness and growth. This will provide the basis for 'a tailor-made and detailed agreement on some specific reforms'.[39] The European Council encouraged further investigation as to the 'feasibility and modalities of mutually agreed

[37] Art 121 TFEU.
[38] See also K Armstrong in this volume.
[39] 'Towards a Genuine Economic and Monetary Union' (n 20) 12.

contracts for competitiveness and growth', and as to the 'solidarity mechanisms that can enhance the efforts made by the Member States that enter into such contractual arrangements for competitiveness and growth'.[40]

The competence of the EU to engage in these contractual arrangements is not self-evident. The general Treaty provisions on economic policy empower the passage of formal legal acts,[41] and this is true also of the broad competence in relation to eurozone Member States enacting formal measures.[42] Competence to use the contractual route could be grounded in general empowering legislation made pursuant to Articles 121, 126, 136 TFEU. The Commission's thinking is developing on this issue. It envisages that the contractual arrangements will be put in place pursuant to what it terms a 'Convergence and Competitiveness Instrument', which is seen as being integrally linked to the six-pack measures concerned with prevention and correction of macroeconomic imbalances.[43]

It is nonetheless interesting to reflect on the rationale for and consequences of this regulatory choice. The rationale for the shift from legislation to contract is in part because of the very flexibility that inheres in the contract paradigm. It was Maine who famously coined the phrase 'from status to contract'[44] to capture the idea that in modern societies individuals could operate as autonomous agents expressing their choice through agreement, rather than being bound by obligations derived from status over which they had little control. Agreement is, however, a double-edged sword in this respect. It functions as a tool whereby contracting parties can express their autonomy, but also operates as a flexible mechanism for imposition of obligations, which can be tailored to a particular case. This is achieved with the added legitimacy that comes from the fact that the overall package was 'agreed' by both parties, rather than being imposed through legislation, although how much freedom of choice exists in the making and terms of the contract may well be questioned. The choice of contract as a regulatory tool is also explicable in part because it does not require approval in the manner of legislative, delegated or implementing acts. The deal, whatsoever it might be, can be struck between Commission and individual Member States without the need for the formal imprimatur of other EU decision-making institutions. It should, however, be acknowledged that imperatives of legitimacy and accountability as discussed in the Four Presidents' Report mean that there will be some involvement of national parliaments and the European Parliament in order to enhance the 'joint ownership' of the agreement, and it is moreover clear that the Commission conceives of such contracts as but part of the evolving regulatory landscape for economic governance.[45] The 'fit' between such agreements and the existing plethora of regulatory instruments is not, however, self-evident.

[40] European Council (n 22) [12].

[41] Arts 121, 126 TFEU.

[42] Art 136(1), (2) TFEU.

[43] Commission Blueprint (n 20) Annex 1, 43–44.

[44] H Maine, *Ancient Law: Its Connection with the Early History of Society and its Relation to Modern Ideas* (London, J Murray, 1861).

[45] Commission Blueprint (n 20) Annex 1, 42–44.

The consequences of this shift to contract remain to be seen. It will at the very least increase the complexity of the overall regulatory landscape. It will moreover not be easy to ensure the desired legitimacy and accountability. This will be difficult in purely formal terms, as judged by the practical difficulties of involving national parliaments and the European Parliament before the deal has become de facto 'done'. It will also be difficult to achieve the desired legitimacy and accountability in substantive terms, as judged by the extent to which the contract really is a mutual bargain, rather than unilateral imposition of prescribed economic change by the Commission acting in paternalist management consultant mode.

C. Legal Principle, Transparency and Complexity

The range of measures enacted pursuant to the financial crisis will exacerbate problems of transparency and complexity that already beset this area, even for those skilled at navigating this complex terrain. There were prior to the recent reforms three layers of legal rules pertinent to control over national economic policy: the provisions of the Lisbon Treaty, EU legislation, and broad economic policy guidelines. These rules were complex and created difficulties in terms of transparency, because they were spread across primary Treaty provisions, complex EU legislation and high-level soft law.

The ESM and TSCG add a fourth layer to the existing schema through treaties operating outside of the Lisbon Treaty. This exacerbates difficulties of complexity and transparency, more especially because there is in relation to the TSCG very significant overlap between obligations incumbent on states through the six-pack and two-pack of EU legislation, and those in the TSCG. It may indeed be difficult for states to know in advance whether they should be structuring their documentation in terms of the six-pack plus two-pack, or in terms of the TSCG.

The further reforms posited in the Four Presidents' Report, as endorsed by the European Council, add a fifth layer, through the prominence accorded to contracts as the legal medium via which new obligations concerning economic policy should be realized. The broader implications of this move are considered in the next section.

IV. CONSTITUTIONAL IMPLICATIONS: THE ECONOMIC DIMENSION

The measures enacted to meet the euro crisis have been concerned with assistance and supervision. The general economic consequences of these measures will be considered from these perspectives in turn.

A. Assistance: Funding and Moral Hazard

From the perspective of assistance, the central economic issues are funding, who pays for the assistance, and moral hazard, the concern that the recipient state will take excessive risks and free ride on the greater fiscal rectitude practised by others.

The numbers involved with financial assistance/bail-outs are significant indeed—normally of the order of magnitude of the tens of billions, conceivably even more. The money has to come from somewhere, and thus far this has been from the Member States, with Germany bearing the principal burden. This is likely to continue for the foreseeable future, given that financing of the ESM is predicated on state contributions. The economic impact of contributions from smaller countries should nonetheless be kept firmly in mind. Thus, for example, Finland's contribution to the ESM is €12.5 billion, which is one-quarter of that country's annual government budget.[46] This regime is only viable because the ESM is structured on a divide between paid-up and callable shares, with the former amounting to €1.4 billion for Finland, a still not insignificant amount relative to its overall budget.

Eurostat has indicated that such contributions will not increase the government debt of the shareholder countries. They will rather be treated analogously to similar international financial organizations such as the International Monetary Fund (IMF).[47] Therefore, unlike the loans provided by the EFSF, the loans provided by the ESM will not be re-routed through the accounts of other eurozone countries and will therefore not increase their government debt. An alternative conclusion would in any event have risked adding economic insult to injury. If shareholder contributions did increase government debt of donor countries, then they might thereby have crossed the forbidden line of the TSCG, the Fiscal Compact, and been subject to the sanctions imposed by that regime. To show financial solidarity with other Member States and then to be held liable for breach of the Fiscal Compact would have been ironic indeed.

While this accounting regime is therefore defensible it cannot conceal the obvious reality, which is that the contributions are real money, and that sums expended for one purpose will not be available for alternative uses. This is of course recognized by all, although normally in somewhat muted tones. Thus the Four Presidents' Report noted that support to financial institutions had been substantial and that it had 'unduly weighed on public finances and reduced the ability to use fiscal policy to stave off the effects of the recession'.[48] This is a fortiori the case for assistance given to states pursuant to the ESM and its predecessors.

[46] K Tuori, 'The European Financial Crisis—Constitutional Aspects and Implications', EUI Working Papers, Law 2012/28, 40.

[47] Loans from the ESM to a Eurozone country are recorded in the same way as a loan from the IMF to a Member State, ie as a direct loan from an international organization to the country in question.

[48] 'Towards a Genuine Economic and Monetary Union' (n 20) 5.

The very fact that the contributions are real money also explains the concern about moral hazard and the consequential emphasis placed on conditionality throughout the reforms enacted thus far. The overall assistance regime is delicately poised between the desire to intervene fast, prevent contagion and shore up the system, with the equally firm desire to ensure that the recipient state does not free ride on the greater fiscal rectitude practised by others. This explains the emphasis placed on structural reform and conditionality, these being intended as the twin guarantors of fiscal probity, the one operating ex ante to try to prevent a state from getting into trouble in the first place, the other being applied ex post if it does get into trouble as the price of the bail-out. The delicate balance between these impulses is forcefully exemplified by proposals in the Four Presidents' Report, which attempt to prevent the likelihood of contagion through the insurance-based shock absorption system, funded by Member State contributions, while at the same time avoiding the risk of moral hazard of states claiming on the insurance system as a result of their fiscal irresponsibility.[49] The delicate balance is revealed once again by the insistence that fiscal risk-sharing should not be seen as unidirectional or permanent transfers between countries.[50]

There are real challenges to maintaining this delicate balance going forward. They are if anything greater than hitherto, which is evident from a close reading of the Four Presidents' Report, laying the blueprint for a 'genuine economic and monetary union'. The challenge in terms of financial solidarity is still present: how long will the Member States be willing to support their fellow travellers in the eurozone? The report seeks to provide reassurance in this respect, but the reassurance is itself predicated on the recognition that this is not a short-term problem, but rather one that owes its origin to substantial divergence in economic structures and performance between the Member States. This explains the emphasis placed on structural adjustment of national economies to improve them, making them more competitive and robust and hence able to withstand shocks. The mandatory contractual arrangements for those in the eurozone are to be the medium through which this problem is addressed. Willingness to recognize the scale of the problem is in many ways laudable. It also serves to place in perspective the challenge that lies ahead.

The discussion thus far has focused on the issues of funding and moral hazard that are central to the assistance regime. This is not, however, the only way in which assistance could be organized. Maduro has challenged the status quo and argued that financial solidarity in the EU should be detached from transfers between states and related rather to the wealth generated by the process of European economic integration.[51] It is integral to his view that the EU budget should be increased from 1 per cent to at least 3 per cent of EU gross domestic

[49] Ibid 8.

[50] Ibid 10.

[51] M Maduro, 'A New Governance for the European Union and the Euro: Democracy and Justice', European Parliament, Directorate-General for Internal Policies, Policy Department C: Citizens' Rights and Constitutional Affairs, PE 462.484 (2012).

product (GDP). The extra revenue would be derived from new EU taxes, such as a financial transaction tax and an EU corporation tax. Maduro argues that these taxes are justified because the economic activity was made possible by the internal market, or because the economic activity, while taking place within a state, has externalities for other Member States, or because it is an economic activity that states can no longer tax on their own.[52]

The idea is that such revenues would then provide the EU with the requisite economic firepower to address economic problems and prevent future crises, while removing the need for Member States to insure each other in the manner that underpins the ESM. The enhanced EU budget would be used for a stability fund that would provide collateral to state-issued debt when necessary, albeit subject to an adjustment programme, and would also be used for EU policies that would address asymmetries in the EU's economic and monetary union.[53] Maduro contends that this is preferable to the ESM-type regime because it would have greater funds at its disposal, the adjustment programme would come fully within the scope of EU policies thereby increasing accountability, and since funding would come from the EU budget, citizens would no longer think of themselves as bailing-out ailing states since there would be no direct link to such state support. This is an interesting proposal. Space precludes detailed analysis, but the following brief comments on funding and moral hazard can be made.

In terms of funding, the proposal is premised on an increase in the EU budget from 1 per cent to at least 3 per cent of EU GDP. It is extremely unlikely that this will occur, given the political difficulties of securing far more modest increases in the EU budget in 2012–13, and in previous budgetary negotiations. A proposal that would effectively triple the EU budget would seem doomed at the outset, whatever its merits might be. If this hurdle were to be overcome, that would still leave open a plethora of issues concerning the proposed taxation. Maduro's criteria for new tax revenue entail normative and practical assumptions. It would, for example, be difficult to determine whether an economic activity was made possible by the internal market and it is clearly not the case that all financial transactions occur because of the internal market. There are similar difficulties with application of the precept that a tax is warranted because the activity, even though it takes place within a state, has externalities for other states. It is not clear who or how such matters would be determined. It would moreover also be difficult to ensure that such revenues would be ring-fenced within the EU budget to be used for the ends that Maduro specifies. There would always be the temptation to use such revenues for other purposes, more especially because they constitute such a sizable increase over the budgetary status quo.

[52] Ibid 21.
[53] Ibid 19–21.

In terms of moral hazard, Maduro's proposal might have some impact on public sentiment or perception, but it would not affect the substance of the issue. The public might be more accepting of financial solidarity where the link with their money is less direct, given that assistance would come from enhanced EU revenue rather than from direct state disbursement. Even if this were so it would not alter the moral hazard dimension to the provision of assistance. This would still have to be secured through an admixture of conditionality/adjustment programmes, and measures designed to address imbalances in economic performance as between the Member States.

B. Supervision: Oversight and Direction

The whole is greater than the sum of its parts. This aphorism is particularly apposite in relation to the supervisory measures enacted to deal with the financial and euro crisis. The aggregate constraints thereby placed on Member States' economic freedom are far-reaching and will increase further when the proposals from the Four Presidents' Report are realized. The very complexity and legal heterogeneity of the proposals makes it difficult to perceive the overall impact. There are in effect four kinds of supervisory oversight in the current regime, each of which places detailed regulatory duties on Member States, especially those in the eurozone and those that have signed the Fiscal Compact, or on national financial institutions.

First, there are ex ante supervisory constraints designed to enhance EU budgetary oversight by focusing on the timing and format of national budgetary determinations, and the need for independent verification. These are ex ante in the sense that they are consciously designed so as to ensure that EU budgetary principles are embodied in national budgets prior to their approval by national parliaments. Draft national budgets must be detailed. The Commission is assigned the role of 'assessor', decides whether national budgets meet the requisite criteria and can request an amended budget.

Secondly, there is the detailed regime of procedural and substantive obligations that flow from the Treaty provisions on economic union. The twin pillars of the Stability and Growth Pact dealing with multilateral surveillance and excessive deficit have been strengthened through the six-pack and two-pack. Thus, for example, changes made in relation to multilateral surveillance impose enhanced obligations on Member States to make significant progress towards medium-term budgetary objectives for their budgetary balances, which is backed up by a sanction regime. It is reinforced through the Excessive Imbalance Procedure, which provides minimum requirements for national budgetary frameworks, including numerical fiscal rules to promote compliance with the Treaty reference values for deficit and debt. The reforms have also ratcheted-up the controls applicable to the excessive deficit procedure, which can be triggered by government debt or government deficit. The TSCG, the Fiscal Compact, adds a further layer to this set of obligations and is built on the duty to balance budgets.

Thirdly, there is a novel regulatory architecture for banks and financial institutions. Its core elements are the new regulatory agencies established to replace the previous Lamfalussy regime, the weaknesses of which were felt to have contributed to the EU's poor regulatory performance in the banking crisis. This has been augmented by the SSM run by the ECB, which will have direct oversight of banks, and enforce prudential rules to ensure that EU banking abides by high common standards. The SSM will itself be complemented by the Single Resolution Mechanism, through which supervisory responsibility will be exercised and conditions set in relation to individual banks that get into financial difficulty.

The fourth component consists of measures that will impact significantly on broader economic policy in Member States, the object being to reduce national economic vulnerability through temporary, targeted financial incentives. These are in one sense a form of assistance from the EU, but they also come with 'supervisory bite' in the sense that the contractual arrangements through which they are made operational are mandatory for eurozone Member States, and carry the indirect sanction that Member States will not be eligible to participate in the insurance-based shock absorption function unless they comply with contractual arrangements aimed at instilling sound economic precepts. This aspect of 'genuine EMU' is akin to mandatory management consultancy directed at national economic policy broadly conceived, which will be 'good' for the recipient even if it does not quite like it at the time.

There is, as Fabbrini has pointed out,[54] a paradox in the EU regime. The EMU system was structured with the intention of preserving national fiscal sovereignty, which was thought to entail rejection of a more 'US-style federalist' model for governance of the eurozone. However, as he points out, the reality is that the constraints on fiscal choice are greater in the EU and will become ever more so as the measures designed for a 'genuine economic and monetary union' come on line.

It is moreover worth noting that the rules have been devised or ratcheted-up on the logic that only such tighter constraints can produce a genuine economic and monetary union, although whether this is so is for economists to debate. The corollary is that the schema imposes far-reaching duties on EU institutions, especially the Commission, to deliver this overall policy. The complexity of the tests that the Commission has to apply to determine whether Member States and financial institutions are fulfilling their numerous duties is daunting, and ever more so given the political sensitivity of such exercises. Getting the legislation on to the statute book may with hindsight turn out to be the easier part of this venture. Making it work may prove a lot more difficult.

[54] F Fabbrini, 'The Fiscal Compact, the "Golden Rule" and the Paradox of European Federalism' (2013) 36 *Boston College International & Comparative Law Review* 1.

V. CONSTITUTIONAL IMPLICATIONS: THE POLITICAL DIMENSION

A. Impact on the EU's Defining Political Credo

The consequences for the EU of the financial crisis and the measures taken to meet it are, as we have seen, many and varied. It is nonetheless easy when considering complex economic and constitutional implications to miss what may be the most important and long-lasting impact on the 'EU brand', when viewed from the perspective of the ordinary citizen.

The EU was founded on the promise of peace and prosperity. This was the original Monnet vision, to be realized through technocratic-led expertise. The EU has largely delivered on this vision, although the technocracy-driven leadership that Monnet envisioned has been qualified. There has not been armed conflict within the EU countries, and Member States have benefited from the economic gains of the single market. There have been economic ups and downs during this period, but this was to be expected, more especially given that the EU is affected by trading conditions in other parts of the world. These bumps along the economic road were in general accepted with equanimity by the citizenry of the EU.

The financial crisis that led to the euro crisis has cast a very long shadow over this credo at the heart of the EU. Politicians and academics might engage in complex arguments about the relative degree of responsibility for the current malaise. This, however, matters little, if at all, from the perspective of ordinary citizens, especially those living in countries affected most dramatically by the euro crisis and consequent economic measures imposed under the name of conditionality. For these people it is the EU and the euro that has failed, and this is so irrespective of political and academic discourse as to the 'real' causes of the crisis. The trust in the EU to deliver prosperity as well as peace has been severely shaken, and it will be a long time before the trust can be restored. It is this which may be the single most damaging fallout from the current crisis.

B. Impact on EU Inter-institutional Power

The euro crisis has also impacted on the EU inter-institutional division of political power. It would be tempting to conclude that it has had a predictably Schmittian effect, with power being concentrated to an ever-greater extent in the EU executive, the rationale being that only it can respond with sufficient speed to the profound problems generated by the euro crisis. This conclusion should, however, be resisted, or at the least tempered, since the reality has been more complex. The European Parliament has not been excluded from the process, nor has the EU executive always demonstrated the will and speed to deal with the crisis. Thus the six-pack of measures to bolster the Stability and Growth Pact was enacted by the ordinary legislative procedure in the post-Lisbon world, with input from the European Parliament as well as the Council. This is true also for the two-pack.

There is nonetheless some evidence to sustain the Schmittian perspective. In terms of process, the lead on measures to address the euro crisis has been taken by the European Council, and by Germany and France acting partly within the European Council and partly through bilateral discussion. This is evident in the negotiations for the ESM, TSCG and the Four Presidents' Report. It could, however, be argued that the European Council did not always serve to alleviate the crisis, even though it clearly intended to do so. Thus the very fact that European Council meetings were conducted under intense media scrutiny, often from the perspective of differing countries' respective national interests, combined with the imperative to 'solve' the crisis, was not the ideal way to secure a measured and effective response.

In terms of substance, however, it may well prove to be the Commission within the EU executive whose power is most enhanced. This is readily apparent if one stands back from the principal measures to deal with the crisis. It is the Commission that has a central role in relation to the six-pack, two-pack, ESM and TSCG, and its role will be even greater in relation to the measures enacted pursuant to the Four Presidents' Report. The provisions concerning reverse qualified majority voting in the six-pack and the TSCG are a forceful symbolic and substantive exemplification of this power, but there are numerous other articles in both sets of measures, as well as the ESM, which accord the Commission prominence.

The ratchet-effect of increased EU economic oversight with the Commission in the driving seat, however, carries dangers for the Commission itself. Increased power brings increased responsibility. The hard-pressed Commission will have to deliver on a whole series of fronts, which will bring it face to face with domestic political imperatives. This is more especially so in relation to the new measures foreshadowed in the Four Presidents' Report, given that these are mandatory for all eurozone Member States irrespective of whether or not they are in economic difficulty. It is one thing to write down obligations, whether in EU treaty provisions, legislation, other international treaties or contracts. It is quite another to enforce them.

C. Impact on EU Unity

There was much talk at the time of the UK veto in December 2011 that it would lead to a radical division within the EU, with the UK and the Czech Republic on the fringes and excluded de facto if not de jure from important policy discussion. There has more generally been talk about a two-speed EU and how the response to the euro crisis might lead to this as a result of the tougher controls imposed on the eurozone Member States. It is important for the sake of clarity to disaggregate two senses of the phrase 'two-speed' EU.

The phrase is often used in a loose sense in the literature and in press coverage to capture the idea that closer co-operation on economic union, whether achieved within the confines of the Lisbon Treaty or without, will exert a gravitational force and produce what is in effect a two-speed EU—one speed for those subject to that regime, and another for those that are not. This flows from the very subject matter of economic union, dealing as it does with national budgetary policy, combined with the degree of centralized oversight required to make economic union work. There is force in this argument. Whether and how far it becomes a reality depends on a range of factors, including the extent to which differential rules are imposed on the eurozone Member States, the reality being that some rules apply only to eurozone Member States, whereas others such as the TSCG apply to all 25 Member States. The two-speed vision is moreover predicated, explicitly or implicitly, on the assumption that the inner core will share a common vision, which is opposed to or different from that of the other Member States. This does not represent current reality, at least when one gets down to detail, and this is unlikely to change in the future. A further factor is the extent to which the inner core complies with the extra demands placed on them. It should not be forgotten that it was France and Germany that violated the Stability and Growth Pact in 2003–04, which ended up in legal action before the EU courts.

The phrase 'two-speed EU' has, however, also been used in a tighter, more defined sense by Piris. The central idea is that a two-speed Europe would be taken forward through an additional Treaty, which would specify the nature of the obligations of the participating states, while continuing to respect the existing EU treaties. The separate Treaty would have separate institutions performing functions analogous to those of the Commission, EP, Council and ECJ. It is integral to this vision of a two-speed EU that '*all* participating states should be fully committed to participate in *all* areas of cooperation, no areas being optional'.[55] Piris contends that there is a broad range of areas in which such co-operation could be undertaken by the avant-garde group pursuant to the additional Treaty: the economic component of EMU; security and defence policy; aspects of justice and home affairs; social policy; taxation; environmental protection; public health; culture and education; and certain procedural aspects of foreign policy implementation. It is the fact that the same states form the avant-garde across all such areas that distinguishes Piris' conception of a two-speed EU from the current reality of a multi-speed EU. There are, however, very considerable difficulties with this conception of a two-speed EU. Thus there is, for example, no reason to believe that the inner core would share beliefs across these different subject matter areas, and there are formidable difficulties associated with creation of a parallel set of institutions for the avant-garde states.[56]

[55] J-C Piris, *The Future of Europe, Towards a Two-Speed EU?* (Cambridge, Cambridge University Press, 2012) 122 (original emphasis). Piris also considers the possibility of a two-speed EU without an additional Treaty, but the idea that all avant garde states must participate across all areas is still central to his vision.

[56] P Craig, 'Two-Speed, Multi-Speed and Europe's Future: A Review of Jean-Claude Piris on the Future of Europe' (2012) 37 *European Law Review* 800

D. Impact on National Politics

The crisis has had very significant implications for the precepts on which the democratic regimes of Member States operate. This flows in part from the degree of economic oversight to which eurozone Member State budgets are subject, as seen above. The focus here is on the more direct political impact of the crisis.

This is manifest most significantly in the regime change at national level precipitated by the need to satisfy the EU and the markets that domestic economic reform will occur. The ousting of Berlusconi and his replacement by Monti in Italy was the most visible manifestation of this phenomenon. It led predictably to criticism that national political leadership was being determined by the EU, which also set the tight parameters within which this technocratic leadership would operate. The reality was rather more nuanced, since many Italians were keen to see Berlusconi go and welcomed the more professional perspective that Monti brought to the job. The Italian experience demonstrates moreover the 'limits', however ill-defined they might be, to this kind of intervention in the normal political process, and to the tensions that this can then produce. Thus Monti's decision to stand down in 2013 after the draft national budget was approved was based in part on the need for the country to get back to 'ordinary politics', but the very announcement precipitated a rise in the interest rate on Italian bonds, as the markets expressed their fears about a return to the bad old days of Italian national economic policy.

The impact on national politics is manifest more generally in the constraints placed on political choices available to national regimes subject to the economic crisis. It is axiomatic that those choices are always constrained by international obligations and economic exigency. There are nonetheless very real differences in degree. Conditionality is on its face a relatively innocuous word, but the consequences for countries such as Greece, Ireland and Spain in terms of dictating the detailed direction of national politics is on a scale rarely if ever seen before in peacetime. This is not to say that the conditions imposed were unwarranted, although there is of course a vibrant debate as to the optimal economic response to the crisis. It is simply to say that whatever position one takes on that debate, the reality is that the national political agenda is set and monitored from outside.

It should also be recognized that if the measures adumbrated in the Four Presidents' Report become a reality, then increased constraints on national political choice will bite on all eurozone Member States, irrespective of whether they are in economic difficulty, and will also have some effect on non-eurozone Member States. Whether this can be sustained remains to be seen. It depends in part at least on whether the EU, and in particular the Commission, has the political authority to carry through such measures. The economic logic is towards ever tighter controls on national budgetary and economic policy. This may or may not be inexorable in economic terms, but it does not mean that it will prove to be politically acceptable to the Member States, nor does it mean that it will be capable of being delivered by the Commission.

The authors of the Four Presidents' Report were mindful of these concerns, which explain discussion of the need to secure democratic legitimacy and accountability for the proposed reforms.[57] The sentiments were echoed by the European Council when endorsing the Report.[58] There was much talk about the need to involve national parliaments and the European Parliament, and to ensure that there was 'national ownership' of the forthcoming changes. These are laudable sentiments, but it remains to be seen whether the reality is joint ownership achieved through discourse leading to consensus, or unilateral imposition of far-reaching constraints that are at best grudgingly accepted by Member States, at worst met with passive resistance or recalcitrance.

VIII. CONCLUSION

The economic and financial crisis has had profound effects on the EU, including its constitutional architecture. Nor is the problem likely to go away in the short term. It has generated a complex array of political responses, some of which have been designed to provide assistance to ailing states, others of which have increased oversight of national economic policy. The measures have assumed varying legal forms, ranging from the enactment of ordinary EU legislation, albeit in an accelerated manner as warranted by the nature of the crisis, to intergovernmental agreements made outside the formal confines of the constituent treaties. The constitutional implications of these developments continue to unfold, with profound consequences for the legal, economic and political dimensions of the EU, and indeed for the balance between the 'economic' and the 'social', a theme that has run through the development of the EEC from its very inception. The EU may weather this particular storm, but the nature of the polity that emerges thereafter remains to be seen.

[57] 'Towards a Genuine Economic and Monetary Union' (n 20) 13–14.
[58] European Council (n 22) [14].

3

The Use of International Law as a Tool for Enhancing Governance in the Eurozone and its Impact on EU Institutional Integrity

ANGELOS DIMOPOULOS*

I. INTRODUCTION

IN ORDER TO strengthen economic co-operation in the EU and prevent the rise and spread of debt crises in the future, EU leaders have over the past three years adopted a number of measures that aim to deal in a permanent and definitive manner with the new threats the crisis has created. In their effort to establish appropriate and sufficient mechanisms to deal with the crisis, EU leaders have relied extensively on international law tools, fostering the creation of new, 'extra-EU' intergovernmental institutions that lie outside the framework provided for currently in the Treaty on the Functioning of the European Union (TFEU).

The use of 'extra-EU' tools has been a key element of the approach taken to tackle the crisis since its emergence.[1] The establishment of the Greek facility in May 2010, which comprised an international loan agreement between Greece, the eurozone countries and the International Monetary Fund (IMF),[2] set up a new institutional pattern within the eurozone, which was further embraced and solidified, as proven by subsequent practice. The European Financial Stability

* The author would like to thank Professor Jean-Victor Louis and Pierre Larouche and the participants of the conference 'The Constitutionalization of European Budgetary Constraints', Tilburg, 30–31 May 2013.

[1] For an overview of the timeline of the crisis and in particular its early stages see JV Louis, 'Guest Editorial: The No-Bailout Clause and Rescue Packages' (2010) 47 *Common Market Law Review* 971; Editorial comments, 'The Greek Sovereign Debt Tragedy: Approaching the Final Act?' (2011) 48 *Common Market Law Review* 1769; L Tsoukalis, 'The Shattering of Illusions—And What Next?' (2011) 49 *Journal of Common Market Studies* 19; Editorial comments, 'Some Thoughts Concerning the Draft Treaty on a Reinforced Economic Union', (2012) 49 *Common Market Law Review* 1.

[2] See Louis (n 1) 974.

Facility (EFSF)[3] and initially and currently the European Stability Mechanism (ESM),[4] which assumed the tasks held by the EFSF and the European Financial Stabilisation Mechanism (EFSM),[5] were established as permanent structures securing the provision of emergency loans to eurozone Member States in difficulty. Despite their strong linkages to the EU treaties, the EFSF and now the ESM constitute institutions based on international law.

In addition to the ESM, the international law toolbox has been used to strengthen economic co-operation among the eurozone Member States. Complementing the ESM and ensuring that it is used only in cases of emergency, EU leaders have adopted a number of measures aimed at enhancing and improving economic governance. Next to the amendment of the Stability and Growth Pact and the introduction of the so-called 'six-pack'[6] and the 'two-pack' legislation,[7] EU leaders have deemed it necessary to create an additional, 'extra-EU' layer of economic governance. Almost two years after the outbreak of the crisis, in February 2012, 25 out of 27 EU Member States[8] concluded the Treaty on Stability, Coordination and Governance in the Economic and Monetary Union (TSCG, also known as Fiscal Compact),[9] and took up international law obligations regarding the co-ordination of their national fiscal policies.

The changes that the ESM and the Fiscal Compact have created in the legal and institutional framework surrounding the European single currency have been highly controversial, as evidenced by the number of legal challenges to these measures in front of national courts[10] and the Court of Justice of the European Union (CJEU).[11] As the ESM and the Fiscal Compact introduce inter-

[3] EFSF Framework Agreement, available at www.efsf.europa.eu/attachments/20111019_efsf_framework_agreement_en.pdf .

[4] Treaty Establishing the European Stability Mechanism, available at: www.europeancouncil.europa.eu/media/582311/05-tesm2.en12.pdf

[5] Council Regulation (EU) No 407/2010 establishing a European financial stabilisation mechanism [2010] OJ L118/1.

[6] Regulation 1175/2011 amending Regulation 1466/97 on the strengthening of the surveillance of budgetary positions and the surveillance and coordination of economic policies [2011] OJ L306/12; Regulation 1177/2011 amending Regulation 1467/97 on speeding up and clarifying the implementation of the excessive deficit procedure [2011] OJ L306/33; Regulation 1173/2011 on the effective enforcement of budgetary surveillance in the euro area [2011] OJ L306/1; Directive 2011/85 on requirements for budgetary frameworks of the Member States [2011] OJ L306/41; Regulation 1176/2011 on the prevention and correction of macroeconomic imbalances [2011] OJ L306/25; Regulation 1174/2011 on enforcement measures to correct macroeconomic imbalances in the euro area [2011] OJ L306/8.

[7] Regulation (EU) No 473/2013 on common provisions for monitoring and assessing draft budgetary plans and ensuring the correction of excessive deficit of the Member States in the euro area; Regulation (EU) No 472/2013 on the strengthening of economic and budgetary surveillance of Member States in the euro area experiencing or threatened with serious difficulties with respect to their financial stability.

[8] The Czech Republic and the UK have opted out of the Fiscal Compact.

[9] Treaty on Stability, Coordination and Governance in the Economic and Monetary Union (1–2 March 2012), available at www.european-council.europa.eu/eurozone-governance/treaty-on-stability?lang=en.

[10] The legality of the ESM Treaty has been tested by the supreme courts of Estonia, Germany, France and Ireland. See also Chapter 20 in this volume.

[11] Case C-370/12 *Pringle* [2012] ECR-I 0000.

national law obligations in an area covered largely by EU law, it is at least questionable as to how these international agreements fit within the existing EU legal framework, and if they are in conformity with EU law. However, in addition to questions of compatibility,[12] which go beyond the scope of this chapter, the introduction of the ESM and the Fiscal Compact cast doubt on the credibility of the EU governance model. Without questioning the contribution of the substantive rules of the ESM and Fiscal Compact Treaties to the effectiveness and efficiency of economic governance in the eurozone, which falls outside the scope of this chapter, it is contestable whether their adoption as international law instruments adds to the efficiency of EU governance or whether it creates new threats and concerns. This is particularly so, since EU law and these extra-EU treaties create two separate institutional frameworks, which, however, do not operate in distinctly different areas of law.

In that respect, this chapter aims to identify and assess the benefits and risks raised by international law as a tool for strengthening economic co-operation in the eurozone. To this end, it examines the governance structure established under the TESM and the TSCG, in order to identify, first, whether and how it is different from economic governance within the EU legal framework, and secondly, how it affects the latter. It is argued that although the ESM and Fiscal Compact create a governance structure that supplements the EU legal order, their intergovernmental nature exacerbates the governance problems that the ESM and TSCG aim to resolve, while in the long term they may threaten the very foundations of the process of European integration. This is particularly so,since there was no legal necessity to conclude them outside the EU legal framework.

Within this chapter, part II highlights very briefly the key institutional characteristics of the ESM and Fiscal Compact treaties. Part III continues with an analysis of the added value of the ESM and Fiscal Compact Treaties, considering how the different governance models regarding co-ordination of economic policies, rule-making and enforcement differ from EMU law and how they affect it. Complementing the assessment of the significance of the ESM and Fiscal Compact as extra-EU treaties, part IV discusses whether it was legally necessary to resort to international law and part V concludes.

II. THE 'EXTRA-EU' NATURE OF THE ESM AND THE FISCAL COMPACT

The ESM and the Fiscal Compact were established as complementary intergovernmental institutions, aiming to foster fiscal responsibility and solidarity within the EMU. The establishment of a new, 'extra-EU' institutional framework in the

[12] For analysis of the *Pringle* case and the questions of compatibility with EU law that arise, see B de Witte and T Beukers, 'Editorial Comments: Case C-370/12, *Thomas Pringle v Government of Ireland, Ireland, The Attorney General*, Judgment of the Court of Justice' (2013) 50 *Common Market Law Review* 637; Editorial (2013) 50 *Common Market Law Review* 805.

eurozone was deemed necessary as the European political leadership intended to introduce changes expediently to the EU Treaties, which were allegedly not achievable without the amendment of these treaties.[13]

A. The European Stability Mechanism

The ESM exists as an international financial institution set up by eurozone Member States, which aims to 'provide stability support under strict conditionality, appropriate to the financial assistance instrument chosen, to the benefit of ESM Members which are experiencing, or are threatened by, severe financing problems, if indispensable to safeguard the financial stability of the euro area as a whole and of its Member States'.[14] In that respect, the ESM has the capacity to provide ESM members with loans, but assistance may also take the form of a precautionary credit line, specific assistance for the recapitalization of banks, and the acquisition of bonds in the primary or secondary markets.[15]

Despite the permanent nature of the ESM as a key institution of the eurozone, it is established as an intergovernmental institution that functions parallel to the eurozone institutional framework. Unlike the EFSF, which is a private-law institution set up under Luxembourg law, the ESM is an international organization with a distinct legal personality.[16] The establishment of the ESM as an international organization is not only relevant for determining its privileges and immunities, but also for its governance structure. More specifically, decision-making powers are awarded to new intergovernmental bodies, the Board of Governors and the Board of Directors, while decision-making is dependent on the capital contributions of the eurozone Member States, thus distinguishing itself from the governance rules that exist under the EU Treaties.[17]

Nevertheless, the ESM Treaty established strong linkages with the EU institutional framework. Indeed, the European Commission is entrusted with the task of carrying out, implementing and monitoring the decisions adopted by the ESM Boards.[18] Moreover, the European Central Bank (ECB) is also given the key roles of assessing the need for emergency financial assistance, negotiating the terms and monitoring compliance with the conditionality attached to financial assistance. Moreover, the ESM Treaty assigns a specific role to the CJEU

[13] A Weber, 'Die Reform der Wirtschafts-und Währungsunion in der Finanzkrise' (2011) *Europäisches Zeitschrift für Wirtschaftsrecht* 935, 937–38.

[14] Art 3 TESM.

[15] Arts 14, 15, 17 and 18 TESM. For a detailed analysis of the ESM provisions, see C Ohler, 'The European Stability Mechanism: The Long Road to Financial Stability in the Euro Area' (2011) 54 *German Yearbook of International Law* 47.

[16] Art 32 TESM.

[17] Compare Art 4 TESM with Arts 121 and 136 TFEU, which provide different rules regarding simple and qualified majority voting and offer a specific role to the European Parliament. See also D Adamski, 'National Power Games and Structural Failures in the European Macroeconomic Governance' (2012) 49 *Common Market Law Review* 1319, 1333-4.

[18] See in particular Art 13 TESM.

as regards the settlement of disputes arising out of its application. It allows an ESM Member to challenge before the CJEU the decisions adopted by the Board of Governors, which decides on first instance on any dispute arising between an ESM member and the ESM, or between ESM members.[19]

In addition to its close link to the EU institutional framework, the ESM is also closely linked to substantive rules of EU economic governance. The CJEU clearly recognized that the ESM falls within the area of economic policy.[20] Although the ESM Treaty does not encroach on EU competences to co-ordinate Member States' economic policies, and in particular EU competences under Articles 122(2) or 126 TFEU,[21] the Court explicitly acknowledged that financial assistance offered by the ESM functions parallel to the system established by the EU Treaties. Conditionality attached to financial assistance substantively overlaps with measures that may be requested from a Member State under EU law.[22] Financial assistance is subject to strict conditionality, which can take the form of a macroeconomic adjustment programme, covering in essence the same measures that can be adopted under Article 126 TFEU and the new Stability and Growth Pact. As the Court ruled, this substantive overlap is not necessarily incompatible with EU law, as the exercise of EU competences is not impeded, while the ESM Treaty guarantees that any stability support has to be fully consistent with the measures of economic policy co-ordination provided for in the TFEU.[23] Nevertheless, ESM conditionality may replicate, or even go beyond, measures agreed under macroeconomic programmes adopted in accordance with the SGP, as long as they do not materially conflict.

The close substantive links between the ESM and the TFEU are further evidenced by the amendment to Article 136(3) TFEU, which aimed to anchor the ESM within the eurozone institutional framework. Even if the Court found that the introduction of Article 136(3) TFEU may not have been necessary to render the ESM compatible with EU,[24] since Member States retain competences to conclude it, the legal value of this provision remains important, as it highlights the substantive overlaps between the different legal instruments, and may serve as an interpretative tool ensuring consistency between them.[25]

[19] Art 37 TESM.

[20] *Pringle*, para 60.

[21] *Pringle*, paras 108–09, 118–20.

[22] *Pringle*, para 111.

[23] Art 13(3) and (4) TESM.

[24] *Pringle*, paras 184–85. *Cf* the decision of the German Constitutional Court, which saw Art 136(3) as an authorization to eurozone Member States to establish the ESM (Bundesverfassungsgericht (n 10) paras 233–36).

[25] A de Gregorio Merino, 'Legal Developments in the Economic and Monetary Union during the Debt Crisis: The Mechanisms of Financial Assistance' (2012) 49 *Common Market Law Review* 1613, 1629.

B. The Fiscal Compact

Turning to the Fiscal Compact, it is important to underline that it does not establish a new institution, but rather defines a set of new, additional obligations for EU Member States. Unlike the ESM, the Fiscal Compact does not create an international organization. Its norms impose international law obligations on the participating EU Member States, which aim to enhance the degree and nature of co-ordination of national economic policies. More specifically, Article 3 contains the most important rule, which requires the participating Member States introduce balanced budgets in their national (preferably constitutional) legal order, and provides elaborate rules as to when Member States satisfy this requirement.[26] Moreover, the Fiscal Compact reiterates one of the key obligations that Member States bear under the EU Treaties and secondary EU legislation, namely to reduce public debt that is in excess of the limits defined in the Fiscal Compact,[27] while it creates an international law obligation for EU Member States to support Commission proposals or recommendations regarding the application of the TFEU rules on excessive deficits.[28]

The function of the Fiscal Compact to build on top of the existing level of co-operation provided in the EU treaties is also reflected in the role assigned to EU institutions. Similar to the ESM, the Commission is entrusted with the task of assessing and monitoring the compliance of the participating Member States with the provisions of the Fiscal Compact, while Member States can initiate proceedings before the CJEU if they consider that another Member State has failed to fulfil its obligations.[29] Moreover, the Fiscal Compact formalizes current practices regarding political governance in the eurozone. Article 12 specifies the tasks of a newly institutionalized political organ, the Euro Summit, which presents a specialized form of the European Council for the eurozone, as well as its President, who is in charge of co-ordinating and preparing Euro Summits.[30]

As the Fiscal Compact aims to strengthen the degree of economic co-operation provided in EU law, it contains numerous provisions concerning the relation between the two different sets of rules. Unlike the ESM, which establishes an emergency mechanism that is not available under the EU legal framework, the Fiscal Compact contains rules regarding the co-ordination of national economic policies, an area that is the subject matter of TFEU provisions and secondary EU legislation. Indeed, Article 126 TFEU contains detailed rules concerning public debt and deficit, while the Commission underwent a major reform of the

[26] For an analysis of the exact obligations imposed under Art 3 TSCG, see C Antpöhler, 'Emergenz der europäischen Wirtschaftsregierung Das Six-pack als Zeichen supranationaler Leistungsfähigkeit' (2012) *Zeitschrift für ausländisches öffentliches Recht und Völkerrecht* 354, 383–86; P Craig 'The Stability, Coordination and Governance Treaty: Principle, Politics and Pragmatism' [2012] *European Law Review* 231, 233–34.

[27] Art 4 TSCG. See also Antpöhler (n 26) 386.

[28] Art 7 TSCG.

[29] Art 8 TSCG.

[30] Antpöhler (n 26) 387–89.

secondary EU law framework in November 2011 and May 2013.[31] In order to avoid potential conflicts with the EU regulatory framework, the Fiscal Compact provides that it should be applied consistently with the EU treaties and only insofar as it is compatible with them.[32]

The strong linkages between the Fiscal Compact and the EU legal framework are further reflected in the preamble of the Fiscal Compact, which indicates the aspirations of its drafters regarding its future status. The Preamble of the Fiscal Compact states that 'the objective … is to incorporate the provisions of this Treaty as soon as possible into the Treaties on which the European Union is founded'. Moreover, the participating Member States declare their readiness to take further action to promote economic co-operation within the EU legal framework, by using the legal tools of enhanced co-operation and involving the EU institutions in any future policy change.[33] Hence, EU political leaders indicate their eagerness to transplant the international law obligations imposed upon the participating Member States to EU law and undertake any future measures within the EU legal framework, or at least, with respect to it and in close co-operation with EU institutions.

To sum up, both the ESM and the Fiscal Compact acknowledge the existence of the relevant EU legal framework and assert that they aim to contribute to its strengthening. They rely heavily on EU law, but they lie outside the EU legal framework, whilst borrowing certain elements of this framework, in particular the EU institutions.

III. A CHANGING INSTITUTIONAL FRAMEWORK: THE ADDED VALUE OF THE ESM AND THE FISCAL COMPACT

The implications arising from the conclusion of the ESM and Fiscal Compact as extra-EU treaties become clear when the role assigned to EU institutions and Member States within their governance scheme is examined. In that respect, a comparison of the different governance models presents a primary indicator of the added value that the ESM and the Fiscal Compact have as extra-EU treaties. Moreover, given the substantive linkages between these treaties and EU law, their added value is also determined by the influence they can exert on EU law.

A. Compatibility with EU Law as a Constraint

Starting from the influence that the ESM and Fiscal Compact Treaties may have on EU law, it is important to understand firstly whether this is legally possible and, if so, to what extent. Despite the widespread impression that EU

[31] For an analysis of the six-pack legislation, see Adamski (n 17) 1336–56.
[32] Art 2 TSCG.
[33] Arts 10 and 11 TSCG.

law is not very favourable towards international agreements concluded between EU Member States, EU law actually allows for the conclusion of agreements between Member States in fields not covered by EU law, encouraging their conclusion under certain circumstances.[34] However, the CJEU has drawn limits to the freedom enjoyed by Member States to conclude agreements between them, requiring that they be compatible with EU law. Therefore, the extent to which the ESM and Fiscal Compact Treaties may influence EU law depends on their compatibility with it. Without entering into a detailed analysis of compatibility questions, which has been largely conducted by the CJEU in *Pringle*, suffice it to underline that neither the ESM nor the Fiscal Compact may affect the existence or exercise of EU competences. Hence, these international agreements cannot amend or deviate from the substantive rules on economic governance that are adopted under EU law.

On the contrary, the use of EU institutions and the existence of linkages to EU law between Member States are actually welcomed by the EU legal order. The CJEU has expressly confirmed the ability of Member States to use EU institutions in order to achieve their collective goals via international co-operation.[35] As the CJEU recently reiterated in *Pringle*, Member States are entitled, in areas that do not fall under the exclusive competence of the EU, to entrust tasks to EU institutions acting outside the framework of the EU. However, this is possible only as long as 'the tasks conferred on [EU institutions] do not alter the essential character of the powers conferred on those institutions by the EU and FEU Treaties'.[36]

On the one hand, the rationale behind this principle is obvious. If Member States opt for co-operation outside the EU legal framework, the best way to ensure compatibility of the international agreement with EU law is to set compliance with EU law as an essential condition for the application of the agreement and have EU institutions involved in the application of the extra-EU agreement.[37] At the same time, this principle is not uncontroversial. As Paul Craig indicates in his chapter, the opportunity to use EU institutions outside the EU legal framework raises constitutional law concerns regarding its normative foundations, and the degree of discretion given to the institutions to decide when, how and in which extra-EU treaties they can participate.[38] Therefore, as there are plenty of options regarding the involvement of EU institutions in extra-EU treaties between Member States that are compatible with EU law, the specific

[34] Until the entry into force of the Lisbon Treaty, Art 293 TEC was the most important expression of the encouragement given to Member States to conclude agreements between them on specific matters. See B de Witte, 'Old-Fashioned Flexibility: International Agreements between Member States of the European Union' in B de Witte, D Hanf and E Vos (eds), *The Many Faces of Differentiation in EU Law* (Antwerp and Oxford, Intersentia, 2001) 32–33.

[35] Case C-181 and 248/91 *European Parliament v Council and Commission* [1993] ECR I-368; Case C-316/91 *European Parliament v Council* [1993] ECR I-653.

[36] *Pringle*, para 162.

[37] S Peers, 'Towards a New Form of EU Law? The Use of EU Institutions outside the EU Legal Framework' (2013) 9 *European Constitutional Law Review* 37.

[38] See Chapter 2 in this volume.

choice made under the ESM and Fiscal Compact Treaties can indirectly influence the way the EU institutional framework functions.

B. Co-ordination of Economic Policies and Executive Powers

The added value of the governance model adopted under the ESM and Fiscal Compact should first be examined with regard to the policy-making mechanisms that they establish, and in particular the role they assign to co-ordination of economic policies. As the EMU has been a primary example of co-ordination-based governance, where new forms of governance such as the Open Method of Co-ordination (OMC) have been widely used,[39] it is only natural to start from governance tools concerning the co-ordination of economic policies. Nevertheless, when one compares the governance model adopted under the ESM and Fiscal Compact Treaties to the EMU, it is difficult to identify any advantages that these Treaties offer. On the contrary they lack the institutional guarantees provided under EU law, which raises concerns about accountability and legitimacy under the adopted governance model.

Since the crisis erupted in 2010 a new, more complex governance system has emerged within the EMU, which is characterized both by the creation of more hard rules and a tightening of co-ordination.[40] Of course, as Kenneth Armstrong highlights in his chapter, it is difficult to oversimplify the situation by stating that the EMU is moving towards more rules-based governance, as co-ordination and legislative powers are inextricably intertwined in the new institutional balance framework set by the six-pack and two-pack legislation.[41] Without entering into a normative discussion about what is the most appropriate institutional design for ensuring efficiency, legitimacy and a high degree of accountability of EMU governance, suffice it to highlight that the EMU is currently undergoing a change of its governance model, which, for the time being, incorporates elements of both legislative and co-ordinative approaches.[42]

Within this framework, the ESM and the Fiscal Compact add little by means of introducing or experimenting with new methods of governance. Both treaties seem to replicate the policy-making choices that have been already adopted within the EU legal framework. Especially as regards co-ordination of economic policies, the Commission and the ECB hold significant executive and monitoring

[39] See indicatively D Hodson and I Maher, 'The Open Method as a New Mode of Governance: The Case of Soft Economic Policy Co-ordination' (2001) 39 *Journal of Common Market Studies* 71; I Maher, 'Economic Governance: Hybridity, Accountability and Control' (2007) 1 *Colombia Journal of European Law* 679.

[40] D Chalmers, 'The European Redistributive State and a European Law of Struggle' (2012) 18 *European Law Journal* 667, 676–82; A Scott, 'Does Economic Union Require a Fiscal Union?' in N Nic Shuibhne and L Gormley (eds) *From Single Market to Economic Union* (Oxford, Oxford University Press, 2012) 33, at 40–42, 45–50.

[41] See Chapter 4 in this volume.

[42] Ibid.

powers, issuing recommendations that present the basis for subsequent action of the decision-making bodies. For example, when one compares the tasks assigned to the Commission under Article 13 TESM and Article 8 TSCG, it is difficult to identify any differences from the executive functions assigned to these institutions within the EMU.

On the contrary, the executive and monitoring powers that the Commission and the ECB hold under the ESM and Fiscal Compact Treaties lack the institutional guarantees attached to their functions under EU law. First and foremost, a question of accountability arises. In contrast with EMU law, where the executive is politically accountable to the European Parliament for its actions,[43] the omission of any reference to the European Parliament under the ESM and the Fiscal Compact highlights the lack of political accountability of the actors involved in the application of these treaties. In addition, the Commission and the ECB have a great degree of discretion to develop new standards and procedures when they exercise their powers to monitor and assess Member States' conduct under the ESM and the Fiscal Compact. The CJEU has clarified numerous times that EU law rules and principles bind the conduct of EU organs and Member States when they act within the framework of EU law.[44] Nevertheless, the Court remains silent on the question of whether basic principles of EU law, including the Charter of Fundamental Rights, bind EU institutions when they act outside the framework of the EU Treaties.[45]

But even if the Commission and the ECB were bound in their extra-EU functions by EU principles, as the Commission tends to consider,[46] it is doubtful whether their action can be challenged in front of the CJEU. On the one hand, the CJEU lacks jurisdiction to control the way EU institutions discharge their extra-EU functions, when they do not affect EU law. As the same time, as argued below,[47] it is contestable whether the CJEU, when exercising its jurisdiction under the ESM or the Fiscal Compact, can utilize EU law as a benchmark for assessing the legality of measures taken under these treaties. As a result, the legal accountability of the EU institutions acting under the ESM and Fiscal Compact is severely limited, given the lack of accountability standards and jurisdictional limitations.[48]

Last but not least, EU institutions enjoy a wide margin of discretion under the ESM and TSCG Treaties. They may exercise their duties in a way that complies

[43] On the notion of political accountability and its function within EU law, see indicatively W van Gerven, *The European Union: A Polity of States and People* (Oxford, Hart Publishing, 2005) ch 2; E Fischer, 'The European Union in the Age of Accountability' (2004) 24 *Oxford Journal of Legal Studies* 495.

[44] On legality review as a means of accountability in the EU, see C Harlow, *Accountability in the European Union* (Oxford, Oxford University Press, 2002) 147–59. For a recent example, see Case C-617/10 *Aklagaren v Ackerberg* [2013] ECR I-000, paras 19–23 regarding the scope of application of the Charter of Fundamental Rights.

[45] *Pringle*, paras 178–79.

[46] European Commission, 2012 Report on the Application of the EU Charter of Fundamental Rights, COM(2013) 271 final.

[47] See Section III.E below.

[48] Craig (n 26) 242.

with fundamental rights or transparency obligations under EU law, but still may deviate significantly from the standards and the procedures adopted within the EU legal framework. The development of new standards and approaches to monitoring and co-ordination under the ESM and Fiscal Compact raises concerns regarding the way EU institutions perform their tasks within the EU legal system. First of all, in light of the degree of overlap between the ESM and the Fiscal Compact on the one hand and the EU treaties on the other, the danger arises that EU institutions could be tempted to free themselves from their EU law obligations simply by claiming they are acting under an extra-EU framework. Although such action would be incompatible with EU law, it would create legal uncertainty and could exacerbate political tensions, which would in the end affect negatively the effectiveness of these economic governance tools. Moreover, the creation of distinct sets of procedures could result in unwanted spillovers. Considering that it is the same Directorates in the Commission and the ECB that carry out the similar tasks assigned to them under EU law and under these extra-EU treaties, the danger of dilution of the different standards and procedures is more than just theoretical.

More importantly, the adoption of different standards and approaches to monitoring and co-ordination could result in the long-term in the replacement of EU standards. The possibility of reintegration of these extra-EU treaties in the EU legal framework, which is more probable for the Fiscal Compact,[49] has been viewed as a brake on the fragmentation of EU law and a signal that resorting to extra-EU solutions is only temporary and thus cannot affect European governance in the long term. Nevertheless, it is unclear how these extra-EU treaties will be integrated in the EU legal system. It is arguable that, if and when the ESM and Fiscal Compact are integrated to EU law, any deviations from the EU legal order that are important for the political sensitivities of the Member States at that time could be 'grandfathered', and thus kept as permanent derogations from the EU institutional framework.

C. Co-ordination of Economic Policies and Decision Making

Similar to the executive powers held by the Commission and the ECB, decision-making under the ESM and Fiscal Compact Treaties relies on existing forms of EMU governance, but departs significantly from the constitutional and institutional guarantees embedded within the EU legal framework. Following the general trends of the EMU, the ESM and the Fiscal Compact are also characterized by tightening of co-ordination. As was already mentioned,[50] decisions are taken by the Member States that are parties to each Treaty, following a recommendation by the Commission and/or the ECB. In that respect, neither of these

[49] Art 16 TSCG.
[50] See Section II above.

Treaties is revolutionary in terms of the institutional actors or the procedures used with regard to decision making.

However, both Treaties lack significant institutional guarantees that ensure democratic legitimacy within the EMU. A simple comparison between the ESM and the Fiscal Compact on the one hand and the EMU rules on the other exemplifies their great differences regarding the participation of Member States in decision making. At the same time, though, it is rather disturbing that both extra-EU treaties borrow terminology from EU law, albeit giving it a different content. The best example is the definition of qualified majority voting (QMV) under the ESM Treaty, where the percentages mentioned and the weight attached to the vote of each Member State are radically different from the rules established within the Union legal order. According to Article 4(5) TESM, '[t]he adoption of a decision by qualified majority requires 80% of the votes cast', while according to Article 4(7), '[t]he voting rights of each ESM Member … shall be equal to the number of shares allocated to it in the authorised capital stock of the ESM'.

These provisions are in sharp contrast with the EU law definition of QMV and the reality of how decision making works in the Council. In essence, by using the threshold of 80 per cent, which does not exist within EU law, Article 4 TESM offers a veto right only to two EU Member States that happen to control more than 20 per cent of the votes.[51] By singling out and offering exceptional powers to only certain Member States, the TESM departs significantly from the tradition and history of decision making within the EU. So far, mutual respect and sovereign equality dictated decision making to be taken either by majority, without any Member State holding veto powers, or in more sensitive policy fields by unanimity, where all Member States hold veto powers.[52] Of course, even within Union law the establishment of different voting requirements, assigning special weight to the votes of different Member State in different areas of EU law, is plausible. However, the ESM Treaty is markedly different from similar policy areas and the institutions established thereunder, such as monetary policy and the ECB. Although Member States do not participate equally in the capital of the ECB, all members of the Governing Board have equal voting rights, in the sense that veto powers are not granted only to two Member States.[53]

The rules determining the participation of Member States in decision making under the ESM and Fiscal Compact also affect directly the way EU institutions are supposed to perform their tasks within the EU legal order. The best example

[51] Under Annex I TESM only Germany and France (marginally) hold more than 20% of the ESM's capital.

[52] On the history of the development of rules concerning decision-making in the Council, see O Costa, R Dehousse and A Trakalova, 'Co-decision and "Early Agreements": An Improvement or a Subversion of the Legislative Procedure?' Notre Europe paper (2011), available at www.eng.notre-europe.eu/011-2606-Co-decision-and-early-agreements-an-improvement-or-a-subversion-of-the-legislative-procedure.html.

[53] On decision-making within the ECB, see F Amtenbrink, 'Economic, Monetary and Social Policy' in AM McDonnell et al (eds), *The Law of the European Union and the European Communities*, 4th edn (Aalphen aan de Rijn, Kluwer, 2008) 881, at 951–55.

of such influence is Article 7 TSCG, which imposes an obligation on Member States to support the Commission under the excessive deficit procedure, when the latter considers that a Member State is in breach of the deficit criterion.[54] It is only when a majority of Member States disagrees with the Commission's recommendations that Member States do not have such an obligation. In that respect, Article 7 TSCG establishes in essence a reverse qualified majority rule within the Council when the latter decides under Article 126 TFEU.[55]

As a result, Article 7 TSCG intervenes indirectly in the function of the Council and changes the balance of power that has been deemed appropriate for decision making on similar subject matters within the EMU. By imposing international law obligations on Member States on how to exercise their voting rights within the EU legal framework, Article 7 carefully sidesteps the procedures established within the EMU, though without creating an outright conflict.[56] Moreover, the longer-term implications arising from the introduction of Article 13 TESM and Article 7 TSCG become obvious when the potential of reintegration of these extra-EU treaties in the EU legal framework is considered. It is unclear how these rules will be integrated in EU law and if the deviations from the EU legal order will be kept as permanent derogations from the EU institutional framework or even expand to other EU policy areas.

In these respects, the ESM and the Fiscal Compact Treaties seem to indicate a clear shift in the institutional balance between Member States and between Member States and EU institutions. Decision making under both Treaties favours bigger and stronger Member States, and deprives smaller and weaker Member States of effective participation in the adoption of crucial decisions. At the same time, the extra-EU treaties offer significant power to the Commission and the ECB in decision making, as a majority of Member States is now required so as not to adopt their recommendations. These deviations from the principles underpinning the EU legal framework become even more problematic when one considers the criticism regarding the lack of accountability and legitimacy of EU action in the field of economic governance.[57]

But what is more worrisome is that the introduction of such rules is occurring outside the EU legal framework. Similar trends regarding the rebalancing of powers between Member States have also been voiced within the EMU, for example, with the introduction of reverse qualified majority voting under the six-pack[58] and the proposal for a restriction of a Member State's voting rights

[54] Art 7 TSCG provides 'the Contracting Parties whose currency is the euro commit to supporting the proposals or recommendations submitted by the European Commission where it considers that a Member State of the European Union whose currency is the euro is in breach of the deficit criterion in the framework of an excessive deficit procedure'.

[55] Adamski (n 17) 1348.

[56] Reverse qualified majority voting is also introduced under secondary EU law, such as in Arts 5(2) and 6(2) of Regulation 1466/97, as amended by Regulation 1177/2011 (n 6 above). However, decision-making rules under the excessive deficit procedure provided for in Art 126 TFEU have not changed.

[57] See indicatively Chalmers (n 40) 687–91.

[58] See n 56 above.

when it violates EU law.[59] Nevertheless, these suggestions have been the subject of European debate, where different institutional actors, as well as the affected Member States have the opportunity to express their opinion and participate in the drafting of new rules. All of this is missing from the ESM and the Fiscal Compact.

D. Rule-Making

The governance approaches to rule-making under the ESM and Fiscal Compact have also significant differences from the EU legal framework. As already discussed,[60] both treaties establish additional standards and set very detailed technical rules regarding the co-ordination of economic policies and the conditions attached to the grant of financial assistance. However, the ESM and Fiscal Compact introduce a new institutional balance that differs significantly from EU law.

Being international agreements that are negotiated and concluded by sovereign states, these extra-EU treaties have not involved EU institutional actors in the way the latter would have been involved within the EU legal framework, departing from the 'Community method'. First of all, under the ESM and Fiscal Compact Treaties, the Commission does not enjoy the same prerogatives as within the EU legal order, where its role is to 'promote the general interest of the Union and take appropriate initiatives to that end'.[61] The Commission is deprived of its basic power to initiate legislative action and present proposals to the Council and the European Parliament for consideration. For example the Commission has formally no say in the formation of by-laws and subsidiary bodies of the ESM, which are exclusively created by the Member States.[62]

More importantly, the European Parliament is excluded from rule-making under the ESM and Fiscal Compact Treaties. The complete lack of its involvement in the original drafting and negotiating of these Treaties and their subsequent implementation are in stark contrast with the proven interest the European Parliament has in EMU affairs. Following the introduction of the Ordinary Legislative Procedure after the Lisbon Treaty and the use of 'trialogues' in the EU legislative process,[63] the European Parliament had been very actively involved with the reform of the SGP and the adoption of the six-pack and the two-pack.[64]

[59] See eg the Report of the Task Force to the European Council on 'Strengthening Economic Governance in the EU', Brussels, 21 October 2010.

[60] See above Section II.

[61] Art 17(1) TEU.

[62] Art 5(7) TESM.

[63] O Costa 'The European Parliament and the Community Method' in R. Dehousse (ed), *The 'Community Method': Obstinate or Obsolete?* (London, Palgrave, 2011) ch 4.

[64] F Amtenbrink and CPS van Duin, 'The European Central Bank Before the European Parliament: Theory and Practice After Ten Years of Monetary Dialogue' (2009) 34 *European Law Review* 561.

On the contrary, both the ESM and the Fiscal Compact Treaties deliberately avoid any reference to the European Parliament.

Of course, one may argue that EU institutions would be excluded from rule-making anyway, at least as far as the rules are concerned. Irrespective of the fact that both Treaties, or significant parts thereof, could have been adopted under secondary EU law,[65] it is uncontestable that EU institutions would have participated more actively in the adoption of primary EU rules introducing similar rules. In fact, EU institutions were involved in the amendment of Article 136(3) TFEU, where they had the opportunity to raise their concerns about the legality and the substance of what proved later to be a purely declaratory provision.[66] Their involvement there provides an indication of how EU institutions could have influenced the debates around the ESM and the Fiscal Compact, and accordingly the degree of accountability and democratic legitimacy of these two Treaties, were they to be adopted as primary EU law.

But even with regard to secondary rule-making, the exclusion of EU institutions does not seem to be founded on any legal necessity, but rather on political choices. The CJEU accepted that EU institutions can be used under extra-EU treaties as long as they do not affect their function under EU law.[67] However, although the rules permitting the use of EU institutions in extra-EU treaties apply to the European Parliament as well,[68] Member States decided to omit the Parliament from the institutional balance established under the ESM and the Fiscal Compact. Besides, there is no rule limiting the use of EU institutions under extra-EU treaties to executive functions only and not to legislative ones.

E. Enforcement and dispute settlement

A proper assessment of the added value of the ESM and the Fiscal Compact Treaties as extra-EU agreements requires also a consideration of their dispute settlement and enforcement provisions. As already discussed, both Treaties assign the resolution of any disputes arising under their provisions to the CJEU.[69] By granting jurisdiction to the CJEU in extra-EU situations, which is allowed according to Article 273 TFEU, Member States aim to give real teeth to the substantive obligations provided under the ESM and Fiscal Compact Treaties. This is particularly relevant for the Fiscal Compact, which tightens the rules

[65] See below Section IV.

[66] Commission Opinion on the draft European Council Decision amending Article 136 of the Treaty on the Functioning of the European Union with regard to a stability mechanism for Member States whose currency is the euro, Brussels, 15.2.2011, COM(2011) 70 final; European Parliament resolution of 23 March 2011 on the draft European Council decision amending Article 136 of the Treaty on the Functioning of the European Union with regard to a stability mechanism for Member States whose currency is the euro (00033/2010–C7-0014/2011–2010/0821(NLE)).

[67] Above nn 35 and 36.

[68] Tsoukalis (n 1).

[69] See above nn 19 and 29.

on fiscal discipline and requires Member States to initiate cases against other Member States that fail to fulfil their obligations.[70] In that respect, the CJEU's jurisdiction over disputes arising from the application of extra-EU Treaties enables Member States to bypass the obstacles that co-ordination-based governance creates in the enforcement of the corresponding EU law obligations.[71]

As a result, the potential for increased involvement of the CJEU in economic governance appears to present a significant contribution of the ESM and the Fiscal Compact towards greater judicial involvement in economic policy when compared to EMU governance.[72] Nevertheless, a closer look at the legal framework concerning access to the CJEU indicates that this may not be the case. Offering more access to judicial proceedings does not necessarily mean that extra-EU mechanisms can achieve the objective of more or better enforcement and compliance.

More specifically, both the ESM and Fiscal Compact establish a new set of actors that are responsible for ensuring compliance with the law. Unlike EU law, the Commission is stripped of its role in enforcement. The Fiscal Compact reserves the right to proceed before the CJEU to Member States only,[73] while under the ESM Treaty that right is given to the Member States as well as the ESM authority,[74] which represents the Member States.[75] Of course, considering that the CJEU's jurisdiction under Article 273 TFEU concerns disputes between Member States, it is only natural that the Commission be excluded from initiating proceedings. At the same time, it could be argued that the exclusion of the Commission from infringement proceedings is merely a formality, at least under the Fiscal Compact, where Member States are required to initiate proceedings based on the Commission's reports.[76] Besides, the Commission may indirectly trigger the enforcement of the ESM and Fiscal Compact by initiating complaints against Member States under EU law regarding the application of overlapping substantive rules.[77] Even if the Commission indirectly triggers enforcement, however, the reality remains that it is the Member States that are primarily charged with enforcement. It is paradoxical that although the Commission has a significant role in rule-making and decision-making, for example under Article 7 TSCG, it is stripped of its very significant enforcement tools.

The exclusion of the Commission from the enforcement of the ESM and Fiscal Compact may not only limit the effectiveness of judicial involvement in economic governance, but also affect the relations between Member States. Over

[70] See above nn 27 and 28.

[71] Adamski (n 17) 1356–58.

[72] Editorial (n 1) 8.

[73] Art 8 TSCG.

[74] Art 37 TESM.

[75] As the Court ruled in *Pringle* (para 175), 'since the membership of the ESM consists solely of Member States, a dispute to which the ESM is party may be considered to be a dispute between Member States'.

[76] Craig (n 26) 246–47.

[77] *Pringle*, para 174.

the past 60 years, the Commission has been the 'watchdog' of EU law, having primary responsibility for the application and enforcement of EU law rules.[78] Its success has relied, among other things, on its supranational nature which has contributed to the depoliticization of disputes: there are less than a handful of cases before the CJEU brought by one Member State against another under Article 259 TFEU.[79] At the same time, by relying solely on Member States for the enforcement of the ESM and the Fiscal Compact, it is doubtful whether Member States would be willing to bring a case against another Member State to the Court, especially given the political cost that such action may entail.

Moreover, judicial enforcement under the ESM and the Fiscal Compact lacks the procedural guarantees found within EU law. Without entering into a detailed analysis of the different procedures under which the CJEU can assess the legality of Member States' measures and the procedural rules applied in such proceedings, suffice it here to highlight only the key differences that appear in comparison to the infringement proceedings under Articles 258–60 TFEU. Unlike the EU legal order, the ESM and Fiscal Compact lack the administrative stages provided in Article 258 TFEU, which have proven very successful at ensuring Member States comply with EU law and at avoiding Court proceedings.[80] Moreover, contrary to EU law, which sets out in Article 260 TFEU specific rules regarding Member State compliance with CJEU judgments,[81] the enforcement of any judgment rendered under the ESM and Fiscal Compact Treaties relies upon typical international law remedies. Given the unsuitability of international law remedies to sanction the conduct of EU Member States effectively, the very objective of better enforcement could be frustrated.

Last but not least, the very involvement of the CJEU in the enforcement of the ESM and Fiscal Compact Treaties raises concerns regarding the functioning of the CJEU as the supreme court of the EU. Assessing the compatibility of the ESM Treaty with Article 273 TFEU, the CJEU found that 'a dispute linked to the interpretation or application of the ESM Treaty is also likely to concern the interpretation or application of provisions of European Union law'.[82] Nevertheless, by accepting the close substantive linkages between EU law and the ESM, the Court indirectly acknowledges that most of the disputes adjudicated under the ESM

[78] On the role of the Commission under infringement proceedings, see L Prete and B Smulders, 'The Coming of Age of Infringement Proceedings' (2010) 47 *Common Market Law Review* 9, 56–60; Commission Communication, 'A Europe of Results—Applying Community Law', COM(2007) 502.

[79] Case 141/78 *France v UK* [1979] ECR 2923; Case C-388/95 *Belgium v Spain* [2000] ECR I-3121; Case C-145/04 *Spain v UK* [2006] ECR I-7917.

[80] For example, in 2011 the Commission opened 1,201 dossiers, 700 out of which were closed because the Member State offered a satisfactory response, 203 were closed after the Commission sent the formal letter of notice and a further 167 cases were solved after reasoned opinions were sent to the Member States. European Commission, 29th Annual Report on monitoring the application of EU law, 30 November 2012, available at http://ec.europa.eu/eu_law/docs/docs_infringements/annual_report_29/sg_annual_report_monitoring_eu_law_121130.pdf.

[81] On the different guarantees ensuring Member States' compliance with EU law under Art 260 TFEU, see Prete and Smulders (n 78) 47–56; I Kilbey, 'The Interpretation of Article 260 TFEU (ex 228 TEC)' (2010) 35 *European Law Review* 370.

[82] *Pringle*, para 174.

and the Fiscal Compact, which has even closer substantive links with EU law, have a direct bearing on EU law rights and the obligations of Member States.

In that respect, it may be tempting for the Court to use its extra-EU jurisdiction to interpret relevant provisions of EU law that would otherwise have not been submitted to it and vice versa. Given that the degree of involvement of the CJEU in EMU governance has been very limited so far due to political unwillingness and institutional hurdles, the initiation of disputes under the ESM and Fiscal Compact Treaties may prove an excellent opportunity for the Court to be involved in the interpretation of EMU rules. At the same time, the involvement of the Court in disputes concerning the application of EMU rules may result in it deciding on matters related to the compatibility of a Member State's measure with the ESM and Fiscal Compact, without however having followed the procedures established thereunder. As a result, the potential misapplication of the Court's jurisdiction coupled with the lack of institutional guarantees regarding the actors and the procedures of enforcement generates additional concerns for the legitimacy of the ESM and the Fiscal Compact.

IV. THE COMPETENCES OF THE UNION AND THE NEED FOR EXTRA-EU SOLUTIONS

Considering the threats that the conclusion of the ESM and the Fiscal Compact Treaties raise for EU institutional integrity, the question whether they could fit within the existing EU legal framework ultimately begs further clarification. Even if one accepts that they contribute towards enhancing and improving economic governance in the EU, one may still wonder whether the ESM and the Fiscal Compact could have been included under the existing EU Treaty framework, thus avoiding the complications that their extra-EU nature raises.

A. The European Stability Mechanism

Considering firstly the ESM Treaty, the possibility of including it within the EU legal framework depends on whether the EU has the competence to establish an emergency stability mechanism for eurozone Member States. As the CJEU found in *Pringle*, a mechanism of the magnitude of the ESM cannot be based on a specific provision of the EU Treaties. The only relevant provision that would allow the establishment of such mechanism is Article 122(2) TFEU, which foresees the possibility of the EU granting financial assistance to a Member State in difficulties or seriously threatened with severe difficulties caused by exceptional occurrences beyond its control. However, the CJEU found that this provision would not constitute an appropriate legal basis for the establishment of a stability mechanism of the type of the ESM, which aims to 'safeguard the stability of the euro area as a whole'.[83] Although the financial crisis may constitute 'exceptional circumstances' that can trigger the application of Article 122(2) TFEU, and this provision is a sufficient legal basis for measures aiming to preserve the financial stability of the Union,[84] the Court considered, albeit not very convincingly, that a permanent mechanism, such as the ESM, cannot be set up under Article 122(2) TFEU, which concerns only exceptional circumstances.[85]

Nevertheless, the Court left open the possibility of using Article 352 TFEU as a legal basis for establishing a permanent stability mechanism. The Court opined that the mere availability of Article 352 TFEU did not impose an obligation on the EU to act.[86] In that respect, Article 352 TFEU could have been used for setting up a stability mechanism similar to the ESM, as long as safeguarding the stability of the eurozone is considered to be an EU objective and setting a stability mechanism is 'necessary' to attain this objective.[87] As the Court found in *Pringle*, maintaining the financial stability of the eurozone is an objective of the EU Treaties,[88] while the establishment of a stability mechanism is a necessary step to attaining this goal.[89] Consequently, Article 352 TFEU could have been used for the introduction of a stability mechanism similar to the ESM in the EU legal order.

Even if a stability mechanism had been set up within the EU legal framework, it is argued that such a mechanism could not have attained the magnitude of funds that the ESM can provide to eurozone Member States in distress. Considering the EU financial reserves that can serve as collateral for the loans that an EU-financed stability mechanism would provide, it would be impossible for the EU to raise sufficient money in the capital markets to finance a permanent stability mechanism of the same magnitude as the ESM.[90] These inherent limitations of the EU budget were already evident with the establishment of the EFSM, which was set up only as a complement to the EFSF.[91]

Nevertheless, it would have been legally possible to set up a stability mechanism of the magnitude of the ESM within the EU Treaty system without affecting the general budget of the EU. Indeed, in other areas of EU law there exist special-purpose funds, the funding and management of which is driven by the specific economic interests of only certain Member States. A good example is

[83] *Pringle*, para 65.

[84] See eg recitals 2–5 of the EFSM Regulation (n 5).

[85] On the debate regarding the scope of Article 122(2) TFEU before *Pringle*, see indicatively B Ryvkin, 'Saving the Euro: Tensions with European Treaty Law in the European Union's Efforts to Protect the Common Currency' (2012) 45 *Cornell International Law Journal* 227, 237–40.

[86] *Pringle*, para 67.

[87] On the conditions attached to the use of Art 352 TFEU see A *Arnull*, 'Left to its Own Devices? Opinion 2/94 and the Protection of Fundamental Rights in the European Union', in A Dashwood and C. Hillion (eds) *The General Law of EC External Relations* (London, Sweet & Maxwell, 2000) ch 5.

[88] *Pringle*, para 135.

[89] European Council Decision 2011/199 amending Article 136 of the Treaty on the Functioning of the European Union with regard to a stability mechanism for Member States whose currency is the euro, Recital 4.

[90] Adamski (n 17) 1329–31.

[91] The EFSM was worth 'only' €60 billion.

the European Development Fund (EDF), which has been traditionally used by certain Member States that have closer economic interests to the development of African, Caribbean and Pacific countries.[92] The EDF 'is currently the only EU policy instrument that is financed through a specific key that is different from the EU budget key, and which reflects the comparative interests of individual Member States'.[93]

In any case, it is also arguable that Article 136(3) TFEU could have been used to establish the ESM as a eurozone institution, embedded within primary EU law. Such introduction of a permanent stability mechanism for the eurozone could have occurred under the simplified procedure provided in Article 48(6) TEU, as the establishment of the ESM would not result in increasing EU competences. Considering that the stability of the eurozone is an objective of the EU Treaties and a stability mechanism is a necessary step to achieve this objective, the introduction of a euro-specific stability mechanism would not result in any broadening of EU powers. Hence, it seems that it is rather the political unwillingness of Member States to transfer capital to the EU rather than the lack of Union competence that precludes the incorporation of the ESM under the EU legal framework.[94]

B. The Fiscal Compact

Turning to the Fiscal Compact, the question of EU competence and the necessity for concluding it as an international Treaty is easier to answer. As already mentioned, the Fiscal Compact concerns the strengthening of economic co-operation between EU Member States, a field where the EU is clearly vested with powers under its Treaties. In fact, when one takes a closer look to the specific provisions of the Fiscal Compact, it becomes apparent that these rules do not result in any *additional* level of economic co-operation between EU Member States, but rather amend and tighten the methods of economic co-operation already provided by the EU Treaties and secondary EU legislation.[95]

More specifically, under the substantive provisions of the Fiscal Compact Member States are obliged to have balanced budgets (Article 3), to comply with their EU law obligation regarding the reduction of their deficits (Articles 4 and 5), and to support the Commission's view within the relevant procedures under EU law, when the latter considers that a Member State is in breach of the deficit

[92] European Council, Council Regulation (EC) No 215/2008 of 18 February 2008 on the Financial Regulation applicable to the 10th European Development Fund, 18 February 2008.

[93] U Kilnes et al, 'More or Less? A Financial Analysis of the Proposed 11th European Development Fund', Briefing Note no 29, European Centre for Development Policy Management, March 2012, 3–4.

[94] See also European Parliament Legislative Resolution on the draft European Council decision amending Article 136 of the Treaty on the Functioning of the European Union with regard to a stability mechanism for Member States whose currency is the euro (00033/2010–C7-0014/2011–2010/0821(NLE), recital 9.

[95] To this point see also Craig (n 26) 232–33.

criterion (Article 7). However, the budgetary position of Member States, especially in cases of excessive debt or deficit, is already the subject matter of the EU Treaties and the new Stability and Growth Pact, which establishes elaborate procedures concerning decision-making and the voting patterns of individual Member States.[96] In that respect, the introduction of the Fiscal Compact cannot be rationally justified by the need for new rules for which the EU lacks competence.

Of particular merit is the argument that the Fiscal Compact requires Member States introduce these rules in their national constitutions; hence, such rule could not be introduced into the EU legal order without an amendment of the Treaties. However, this argument is superfluous, if not dangerous, for the unity and primacy of the EU legal order. Although this argument may hold merit from a political and democratic legitimacy point of view, if the principle of primacy of EU law is to be taken seriously, then the Member States cannot seriously contend that a sovereign power that has been already transferred to the EU cannot be exercised if it requires an amendment of the national constitution! It would not be the first time that Member States would have to amend their constitution to comply with secondary EU law, although such constitutional amendment has never been as explicit as under the TSCG.

Similar concerns arise with regard to the governance provisions of the Fiscal Compact. The establishment of the Euro Summit as a specialized form of the European Council for the eurozone does not necessarily require an amendment of the Treaties, and it certainly does not fall outside the scope of EU competence. However, following the practice of the European Council until it was formally introduced by the Treaty of Lisbon,[97] Eurozone Heads of Government could have kept meeting as usual, until such rules were formally embedded in the EU institutional structure during the next Treaty reform, whenever it takes place.

Without entering into the debate concerning the reasons why Member States choose not to trust and make use of the EU legal framework, it is crucial to point out the additional procedural hurdles that the introduction of secondary EU law and even an amendment of the EU Treaties require in comparison to the conclusion of an international Treaty. Article 48 TEU, as well as Articles 121–26 TFEU grant a specific role to the European Parliament. But more importantly, *all* Member States have to participate in the decision-making process. In that respect, the introduction of extra-EU mechanisms enables a 'coalition of the willing' to overcome any hurdles the process of Treaty revision may stumble over. However, a Member State's refusal cannot justify not using secondary EU law. In fact, the mechanism of enhanced co-operation is a legal tool that provides a platform for overcoming potential vetoes by unwilling Member States and establishing differentiated rules within the EU legal order. Nevertheless, given

[96] Adamski (17) 1357–58.

[97] On the role and nature of the European Council in the post-Lisbon era, see R Schutze, *European Constitutional Law* (Cambridge, Cambridge University Press, 2012) 100–06.

the substantive and procedural complexities that enhanced co-operation entails,[98] Member States preferred not even to attempt the adoption of the Fiscal Compact under enhanced co-operation. Finally, the conclusion of the Fiscal Compact as international law guarantees its application in the participating Member States in the event of EU law no longer being applicable. Considering the widespread rumours regarding an impending exit of Greece from the eurozone at the time of its adoption,[99] the establishment of fiscal discipline rules in international law, which requires them to be introduced in national constitutions, was considered important to guarantee that any Member States that withdraws from the eurozone or the EU will still be bound and hence be liable to pay off its loans to the lender Member States.

V. CONCLUDING REMARKS

The institutional response to the inefficiencies of the eurozone has been largely found outside EU law. The conclusion of the ESM and the Fiscal Compact Treaties as international agreements indicates continuing mistrust of the EU legal order and a lack of faith on the part of—at least some—Member States in its structures, rules and mechanisms. The fact that both Treaties could have been introduced via secondary EU law or via an amendment of primary EU law based on Article 48(6) TEU renders clear that resort to international law was not legally necessary and has been dictated mainly by political reasons. Within this context, any positive contribution the ESM and Fiscal Compact Treaties may have to the efficiency of economic governance is mitigated by their institutional deficiencies.

First of all, the ESM and Fiscal Compact Treaties affect EU institutional integrity and change the balance of power struck within the EU legal order. Article 7 TSCG presents an excellent example of how extra-EU Treaties may influence indirectly the way EU institutions perform their functions within EU law. Moreover, the overlapping jurisdiction that the CJEU has over extra-EU Treaties and EMU law may result in misapplication of its jurisdiction, avoiding the institutional and procedural guarantees embedded within the different legal frameworks. But more importantly, the danger exists that any deviations of the ESM and Fiscal Compact from the EU institutional framework may in the end become a permanent element of the EU legal order, especially if these Treaties are, as planned, 'integrated' in the future in the EU legal framework.

More importantly, the ample use of EU institutions and procedures in the

[98] On the conditions attached to triggering the procedures under Art 20 TEU and Arts 326–34 TFEU, see Editorial Comments, 'Enhanced Cooperation: A Union à taille réduite or à porte tournante?' (2011) 48 *Common Market Law Review* 317.

[99] On the topic of withdrawal from the EMU, see H Hoffmeister, 'Goodbye Euro: Legal Aspects of Withdrawal from the Eurozone' (2011) 18 *Columbia Journal of European Law* 111; P Kindler, 'Währungsumstellung, Vertragskontinuität und Vertragsgestaltung' [2012] *Neue Juristische Wochenschrift* 1617.

ESM and Fiscal Compact indicates that these extra-EU agreements aim primarily to create a distinct level for governance in the eurozone, which is not hindered by the substantive and procedural 'obstacles' that the Union legal order imposes. Of course, it could be argued that the extensive use of supranational institutions mitigates the problems that the conclusion of the TSCG and ESM as international Treaties entails. However, it is exactly the broad involvement of EU institutions in this extra-EU legal framework that raises additional concerns. The involvement of the Commission under the ESM and Fiscal Compact Treaties is based on a cherry-picking approach that undermines their legitimacy and ultimately their efficiency. Both extra-EU Treaties enable the Commission to perform its executive functions without being bound by EU law principles and accountability mechanisms, while at the same time strip the Commission of its legislative and enforcement functions, which have been a key element for the success of EU governance so far. Moreover, by excluding the European Parliament from their governance scheme, the ESM and Fiscal Compact Treaties create a gap in the accountability and democratic legitimacy regarding the creation and application of their rules. Finally, the involvement of the CJEU in dispute settlement may not be sufficient to increase compliance, given the lack of the institutional and procedural framework attached to its function within the EU legal order.

The use of international law ultimately reveals the political preference of Member States towards intergovernmentalism. Member States obtain direct control over the different phases of creating, applying and enforcing the rules of the ESM and Fiscal Compact Treaties, without however being bound by the constitutional and political constraints that characterize the relations between Member States within the EU. However, with greater power comes greater responsibility. And given that the ESM and Fiscal Compact Treaties rely extensively on the EU legal order and its institutions, it is questionable whether the involvement of national parliaments and national courts can mitigate the threats to legitimacy, democracy and accountability that the extra-EU nature of these economic governance instruments raises.[100] But more importantly, by reverting to intergovernmentalism, Member States cast doubts on the welfare effects of European integration and question the value of the principles of sovereign equality and solidarity that underpinned the EU process so far. In that respect, the EU 'must decide between executive federalism and transnational democracy'.[101]

[100] On the role of national parliaments and courts towards enhancing accountability and legitimacy of EU economic governance see Chapters 15, 16 and 19 in this volume.

[101] J Habermas, 'The Crisis of the European Union in the Light of a Constitutionalization of International Law' (2012) 23 *European Journal of International Law* 335, 342.

4

Differentiated Economic Governance and the Reshaping of Dominium Law

KENNETH A ARMSTRONG

I. INTRODUCTION

ANALYSES OF THE dynamics of European integration are prone to influence by the demands both of the moment and of the discipline.[1] Episodes of European 'crisis' are especially apt to drive scholarly reflection on whether such developments demand revisions to, or the adoption of new, concepts and theories. In this chapter, a governance perspective is adopted to explore the European response to the economic crisis.[2] In other work, it has been suggested that European governance is increasingly differentiated, producing a range of connections and disconnections between law and governance.[3] This contribution takes that argument forward in two senses. Firstly, the specific context of the economic crisis is used as a focal point for the dramatization of the claim that EU governance is differentiated in nature. The range of governance modes and actors deployed in response to the crisis is highlighted. It is argued that it is not enough to analyse the response to the crisis in terms of a turn to hierarchy and forms of rules-based governance. There is differentiation within rules-based governance; deviations from rules-based governance; and 'hybrid' frameworks that combine different modes of governance.

Secondly, the analysis draws particular attention to the way in which differentiation in forms of governance also drives pluralization in the types and forms of legal instruments which have been used to exert fiscal discipline and to enshrine commitments associated with the receipt of financial stabilization support. Drawing on the research methodologies associated with the literature on 'Europeanization', it is suggested that variation in the forms of legal instru-

[1] B Rosamond, 'European Integration and the Social Science Of EU studies: The Disciplinary Politics of a Subfield' (2007) 83 *International Affairs* 231

[2] See generally M Jachtenfuchs, 'The Governance Approach to European Integration' (2001) 39 *Journal of Common Market Studies* 245; B Kohler-Koch and B Rittberger, 'Review Article: The "Governance Turn" in EU Studies' (2006) 44 *Journal of Common Market Studies* 27.

[3] KA Armstrong, 'The Character of EU Law and Governance: From "Community Method" to New Modes of Governance' (2011) 63 *Current Legal Problems* 179.

ments used to create duties and obligations can be expected to produce different effects within the national legal orders.[4] Moreover, the national legal orders are important variables in conditioning the reception of different legal instruments. The object of this 'Europeanization' is identified in terms of Daintith's concept of '*dominium*-law'.[5] For Daintith, 'wealth' is a key power resource available to government, with the law relating to this resource forming a distinct field of legal analysis—*dominium*-law. The capacity for different European legal instruments to reshape this *dominium*-law is highlighted and the constitutional implications of this reshaping of the legal context through a variety of forms of legal instruments is noted.

II. DIFFERENTIATED ECONOMIC GOVERNANCE

The literature on European 'governance' has sought to analyse the complexity of, and variety within, EU policymaking as a means of giving empirical depth and breadth to an understanding of the phenomenon of European integration.[6] That scholarship has highlighted differentiation in the modes, institutions and instruments through which the 'Europeanization' of economic and social life in the EU has been pursued. Governance scholarship has sometimes tended to retreat into its own grand narratives, particularly as regards the dominance or decline of hierarchy as a mode of governance, and whether governance is an activity of public or private actors. While for some scholars, hierarchy and governance by public actors remains the dominant expression of EU governance,[7] for others, changes in European governance are a manifestation of a wider turn away from hierarchy and its associated institutional forms of public democratic will-formation.[8] Not surprisingly, these competing characterizations of EU governance have made it difficult to draw a legal evaluation of the significance of changes in EU governance.[9]

The EU's response to the economic crisis has given added poignancy to these debates. For some, to strengthen the EU's economic governance is necessarily to make a decisive shift in the direction of governance by hierarchy as a response to the perceived failures of decentralized policy co-ordination and intergovernmen-

[4] See especially, S Bulmer and S Padgett, 'Policy Transfer in the European Union: An Institutionalist Perspective' (2005) 35 *British Journal of Political Science* 103; CM Radaelli, 'Europeanization, Policy Learning, and New Modes of Governance' (2008) 10 *Journal of Comparative Policy Analysis: Research and Practice* 239. See generally, P Graziano and MP Vink (eds), *Europeanization: New Research Agendas* (Basingstoke, Palgrave Macmillan, 2007).

[5] T Daintith, 'Legal Analysis of Economic Policy' (1982) 9 *Journal of Law and Society* 191

[6] See generally H Wallace, MA Pollack and AR Young (eds), *Policy-making in the European Union*, 6th edn (Oxford, Oxford University Press, 2010).

[7] See eg T Börzel, 'European Governance: Negotiation and Competition in the Shadow of Hierarchy' (2010) 48 *Journal of Common Market Studies* 191.

[8] CF Sabel and J Zeitlin, 'Learning from Difference: The New Architecture of Experimentalist Governance in the EU' (2008) 14 *European Law Journal* 271.

[9] For a critique of these opposing characterisations of EU governance, see Armstrong (n 3).

talism. The packages of legislative measures adopted by the EU since 2010 are, at least superficially, a visible symbol of this apparent turn to rules-based governance. The attempt to 'constitutionalize' budgetary discipline through demands for a domestically embedded balanced-budget rule can also be viewed as a heightened resort to rules-based governance and hierarchy.

Yet, a closer examination of changes in EU economic governance suggests the emergence of a more complex and differentiated pattern of governance. Indeed, whatever may have been achieved as a result of the turn to patterns of rules-based governance cannot simply be understood as a turn away from, or decline in the use of, other modes of governance.[10] The story of the economic crisis is rather a story of the attempt to expand and strengthen European governance capacity through the deployment of a range of governance modes and institutions rather than a zero-sum game in which rules-based governance occupies an increasing share of a predefined governance pool.

To organize the analysis, the chapter takes rules-based governance as a starting point, with the analysis developed along three axes. The first move is to highlight variation within rules-based governance. It is evident that one characteristic of rules-based governance is the heightened legislative response to the crisis. However, EU numerical fiscal rules are relatively framework in nature. That is to say, the adoption of EU legislation is the beginning rather than the end of a process of normative development as framework norms are elaborated in their concrete application. Moreover, the turn to legislation has not prevented alternative approaches to rulemaking, most clearly in the turn to treaty-revision and international treaties in the form of the Treaty on Stability, Coordination and Governance in the Economic and Monetary Union (TSCG, the 'Fiscal Compact') and the ESM Treaty. Moreover, the package of stabilization support for European countries has been accompanied by a range of forms of executive rulemaking and governance. The second point of departure is to highlight alternative modes and institutions of economic governance. Attention is drawn to governance by co-ordination, governance by markets and governance by contract. The final refinement is to suggest that variation within, and differentiation between, governance responses can also be accompanied by a yoking of different modes and instruments in 'hybrid' governance architectures.[11] The embedding of rules-based governance within the framework of economic policy co-ordination is explored.

Differentiation in the modes of EU governance also gives rise to variety in the roles played by a range of actors, particularly EU institutional actors. The

[10] In recognizing this differentiation in governance, for some authors, this signals not the return of the Community/Union method but rather a more decisive swing towards new forms of intergovernmentalism: E Chiti and PG Teixeira, 'The Constitutional Implications of the European Response to the Financial and Public Debt Crisis' (2013) 50 *Common Market Law Review* 683.

[11] See generally, DM Trubek and L Trubek, 'New Governance and Legal Regulation: Complementarity, Rivalry and Transformation' (2007) 13 *Columbia Journal of European Law* 539. For a more particular discussion of hybridity in EU fiscal governance, see KA Armstrong, 'The New Governance of EU Fiscal Discipline' (2013) 38 *European Law Review* 501.

capacity for institutional actors to take on certain governance tasks is also a function of the changing constitutional landscape of the EU, with the changes made by the Lisbon Treaty providing an important backdrop to the economic crisis and the response to the crisis. However, while the Lisbon Treaty forms a backdrop to the role played by institutional actors, that is not to say that such roles are necessarily directly constituted or anticipated by the Lisbon framework. Indeed, one of the issues raised by the EU's response to the economic response is its potential departure from the constitutional framework elaborated by the Lisbon Treaty.[12]

A. Rules-Based Governance

To the extent that the EU's response to the economic crisis takes the form of the imposition of rules-based duties and obligations on states, variation is exhibited in a number of ways. In anticipation of the later discussion, it may be useful to distinguish between three contexts in which rules-based governance might be advanced: the legislative sphere; the domain of EU and international treaties; and 'executive governance'.

(i) Legislating the Response

There can be no doubt that a key aspect of the post-Lisbon and post-crisis reforms to economic governance can be found in the use of the EU legislative process to put in place key elements of the governance architecture. First there was the 'six-pack' of five regulations and one directive. The regulations amended the 'preventative' and 'corrective' limbs of the Stability and Growth Pact (SGP);[13] created new opportunities to sanction Member States for breaches of the SGP fiscal rules;[14] and established a new 'macroeconomic imbalance procedure' (MIB) to alert Member States to certain risks in the operations of their economies.[15] The sole directive sets out minimum requirements for the conduct of domestic budgetary frameworks.[16] A supplementary 'two-pack' of regulations was added applicable only to those Member States that use the euro as their currency. These regulations extend the surveillance mechanisms for states experiencing finan-

[12] See Chiti and Teixeira (n 10). See also Chapter 3 in this volume.

[13] Regulation 1175/2011 amending Regulation 1466/97 on the strengthening of the surveillance of budgetary positions and the surveillance and coordination of economic policies [2011] OJ L306/12; Regulation 1177/2011 amending Regulation 1467/97 on speeding up and clarifying the implementation of the excessive deficit procedure [2011] OJ L306/33.

[14] Regulation 1173/2011 on effective enforcement of budget surveillance in the euro area [2011] OJ L306/1.

[15] Regulation 1176/2011 on the prevention and correction of macroeconomic imbalances [2011] OJ L306/25; Regulation 1174/2011 on enforcement measures to correct excessive macroeconomic imbalances in the euro area [2011] OJ L306/8.

[16] Directive 2011/85/EU on requirements for budgetary frameworks of the Member States [2011] OJ L306/41.

cial difficulties[17] and establish new procedures for the surveillance of national budgets.[18]

Leaving aside for a moment the content of these deals, these packages of measures illustrate some features of contemporary EU legislative governance. Firstly, the measures were adopted under the ordinary legislative process which was extended into the economic sphere by the Lisbon Treaty. Secondly, and consistent with pre-Lisbon developments, the measures were all adopted as 'early' first-reading measures, relying heavily on informal trilogue negotiations between the EU's legislative institutions.[19] Thirdly, with the exception of the one directive setting out minimum requirements for domestic fiscal frameworks, all the other measures took the form of regulations which are directly applicable and do not require domestic legal implementation. Fourthly, the adoption of packages of legislative measures probably gave some momentum to the legislative process and minimized risk of blockages either in the EU decision-making arena or from national parliamentary scrutiny. Fifthly, the Lisbon Treaty introduces in Article 136 TFEU an authorization for the adoption of legislative measures specific to eurozone countries. While the SGP necessarily differentiates between those states inside and outside the eurozone, when taken with other governance responses that involve only eurozone states (the ESM Treaty), or the eurozone states plus those EU states also willing to take additional measures (the TSCG), the 'two-pack' illustrates more starkly differentiation within EU legislative governance between eurozone and non-eurozone states.

Given the intensity of the legislative activity, and particularly its output in the form of directly applicable regulations, it is understandable that the response to the economic crisis might be understood as signalling a resort or return to rules-based hierarchical governance. However, while fiscal rules may restrict the capacity of states to breach debt and deficit levels, or to incur macroeconomic imbalances, there is nothing self-executing about such rules. As will be highlighted more fully below, EU-level numerical fiscal rules are the starting point rather than the end point of economic governance. Other processes are involved in determining when such rules are breached; when deviation from fiscal discipline is permitted; and in escalating the enforcement regime associated with the reinforcement of fiscal discipline.

It is, however, important not to conflate rules-based governance with the use of the legislative process. What is equally striking about the legislative response is the manner in which it institutionalizes and diffuses policy co-ordination as a governance technique. Thus multilateral surveillance is extended through

[17] Regulation 472/2013 on the strengthening of economic and budgetary surveillance of Member States experiencing or threatened with serious difficulties with respect to their financial stability in the euro area [2013] OJ L140/1.

[18] Regulation 473/2013 on common provisions for monitoring and assessing draft budgetary plans and ensuring correction of excessive deficits of the Member States in the euro area [2013] OJ L140/11.

[19] For an analysis of early agreements and trilogues, see A Rasmussen and C Reh, 'The Consequences of Concluding Codecision Early: Trilogues and Intra-institutional Bargaining Success' (2013) 20 *Journal of European Public Policy* 1006.

the macroeconomic imbalance procedure created under the 'six-pack', while the 'European semester' as an overarching framework for economic and fiscal policy co-ordination is formalized within the amended SGP. This is a point to which the discussion will return later.

(ii) Treaty-Making

Legislative governance as a means of instilling fiscal discipline was found wanting when it came to the idea of introducing enforceable balanced-budget rules. In the end, after a failed attempt to revise the EU Treaties, the balanced budget rule was incorporated as part of the 'Fiscal Compact' under the TSCG. At first glance it might have appeared possible for a balanced-budget rule to be adopted via the legislative process, with the decision to seek a revision to the Treaties driven by the desire to send a stronger political signal to the markets that EU leaders really were serious about fiscal discipline. But insofar as the balanced-budget rule was to be incorporated directly in national law, preferably of a constitutional nature, then the use of EU legislation would encounter two obvious hurdles. The first is that incorporation of a balanced-budget rule in a regulation would not itself entrench the rule in national law directly. While directly applicable rules are, of course, valid and enforceable in domestic law, their legal authority derives from EU law directly and not from the national legal order let alone the national constitutional order (the ironic consequence of the seminal *Van Gend en Loos* judgment). Meanwhile, the use of a directive to instil a uniform rule in national law would at the very least run counter to the very discretion which directives are supposed to afford the Member States' legal orders. The second objection runs deeper and it is the idea that it would be constitutionally inappropriate—and arguably run counter to Article 4(2) TEU—for EU legislation to seek to make domestic legal changes of a constitutionally significant nature.[20] Adopting an international agreement, subject to domestic ratification, paradoxically became a less contestable route through which to seek to enforce a balanced budget rule than might be the case with rulemaking through EU legislative governance.

For rather different reasons, eurozone states also looked beyond the competences and capacities of the EU legislative process when designing a new mechanism to provide financial support to troubled Member States. As the financial and economic crisis developed, the Council adopted a regulation with a legal basis of Article 122(2) TFEU to create a European Financial Stabilisation Mechanism (EFSM) as a means of providing loans and credit lines guaranteed against the EU budget to a maximum of €60 billion.[21] The EFSM drew on the model of financial assistance already available to support Member States' balance

[20] Art 4(2) TEU provides *inter alia*, that: 'The Union shall respect the equality of Member States before the Treaties as well as their national identities, inherent in their fundamental structures, political and constitutional, inclusive of regional and local self-government.'

[21] Council Regulation 407/2010 establishing a European financial stabilisation mechanism [2010] OJ L118/1.

of payments,[22] and together these mechanisms provided a legal basis for the initial response to the problems that were encountered in Ireland, Portugal and Greece. Yet it became readily apparent that these mechanisms lacked the financial muscle that would be required to deal with the scale of the problems. Moreover, given that the EU budget—to which all EU Member States contribute—stood as guarantor for the loans, there was also the issue of the indirect liability of non-eurozone states for problems that were principally confined to eurozone states. Accordingly, eurozone states established a temporary European Financial Stability Facility (EFSF) as a 'special-purpose vehicle', incorporated under Luxembourg law. However, given the inadequacy of the EU response via the EFSM, and given concerns that the EFSF might encounter constitutional challenges before the German Constitutional Court, eurozone states agreed to adopt an international treaty creating the European Stability Mechanism (ESM). While the legality of the ESM was itself subject to challenge in the Irish courts, the CJEU in the preliminary reference in *Pringle* dismissed allegations of an incompatibility between the international agreement and the duties of EU institutions and Member States under EU law.[23]

Although it is apparent that the resort to extra-EU solutions to the economic crisis can give rise to concerns about the compatibility of these responses with the obligations of Member States and responsibilities of EU institutions under EU law, it is also equally clear that the post-Lisbon Treaty legal framework simply did not permit or equip the EU to use its legislative powers to produce more extensive financial support frameworks. Moreover, the increasing watchfulness of national constitutional courts over how and when the EU does use its legislative powers—itself a response to past exercises of legislative governance—also contributes to a constraining constitutional environment that is likely to drive EU states to turn back to the possibilities and potentials of international law as a means of developing European integration beyond the boundaries of the EU order itself. While we have traditionally identified a potential disjuncture between the EU's ambitious social aspirations and its limited social legislative competence,[24] the financial crisis may also have exposed a gap between the EU's broader political and economic ambitions—as embodied in the EMU project—and its legislative capacities in the economic sphere.

[22] Council Regulation 332/2002 establishing a facility providing medium-term financial assistance for Member States' balance of payments [2002] OJ L53/1.

[23] Case C-370/12 *Thomas Pringle v Governement of Ireland, Ireland and The Attorney General* [2012] ECR I, nyr. For extensive analysis, see B de Witte and T Beukers, 'The Court of Justice Approves the Creation of the European Stability Mechanism outside the EU legal order: *Pringle*' (2013) 50 *Common Market Law Review* 805.

[24] MP Maduro, 'Europe's Social Self: "The Sickness Unto Death"' in J Shaw (ed), *Social Law and Policy in an Evolving European Union* (Oxford, Hart Publishing, 2000).

(iii) Executive Governance

The term 'executive governance' is not without its ambiguities, not least because of the distribution of executive responsibilities within and across the structures of EU institutions and national administrations.[25] Indeed, the post-Lisbon and post-crisis constitutional and political environment is one in which executive governance not only has new impetus, it also has new institutional forms.

The most obvious post-Lisbon, post-crisis development is the role played by the office of the President of the European Council. As a creature of the Lisbon Treaty, one of the first tasks for its inaugural office-holder, Herman Van Rompuy, was to manage the unfolding financial and economic crisis. In so doing, a certain level of rivalry with the policy-initiating role of the European Commission—the historic 'executive' supranational authority—appeared evident as the European Council President established his own task force to develop policy responses. It is easy to overstate the extent of the rivalry and the point is rather to highlight the development of working relationships between the President of the European Council and the President of the European Commission. Indeed, that high-level working relationship has been extended to the Presidents of the European Central Bank and European Parliament as evidenced by the so-called 'Four Presidents' paper 'Towards a Genuine Economic and Monetary Union' authored by the President of the European Council 'in close collaboration' with the other three presidents.[26] In this way, we can see the emergence of an 'elite-institutional' form of executive governance with the office of the President of the European Council choreographing responses to the crisis, including the shape of the packages of legislative responses.

Nonetheless, the European Council is first and foremost a forum for 'chief executive' governance in the sense of bringing together the heads of state and government of the Member States. Meetings of the heads of state and government became more frequent as the sovereign debt crisis deepened. In 2011, five formal scheduled meetings of the European Council took place, supplemented by an 'extraordinary' and by an 'informal' meeting of the European Council. In addition, two meetings of the European Council convened as the heads of state and government of the eurozone states were held. The advent of 'Euro Summits' with an elected President—also Herman Van Rompuy—was neither envisaged nor provided for in the Lisbon Treaty, but again highlights a degree of institutional differentiation at the level of the European Council that mirrors the emergence of the Eurogroup as an informal meeting of the Council of Ministers, later formalised by the Lisbon Treaty.[27]

The significance of the European Council as an institutional actor is also

[25] See generally, D Curtin, *Executive Power of the European Union: Law, Practices, and the Living Constitution* (Oxford, Oxford University Press, 2009).

[26] www.consilium.europa.eu/uedocs/cms_data/docs/pressdata/en/ec/134069.pdf.

[27] U Puetter, *The Eurogroup: How a Secretive Circle of Finance Ministers Share European Economic Governance* (Manchester, Manchester University Press, 2006).

underscored by its capacity to amend the treaties under the simplified revision procedure introduced by the Lisbon Treaty (Article 48(6) TEU). This power was used for the first time in the attempt to amend Article 136 TFEU to make provision for a permanent financial stabilization mechanism: the ESM. Although the European Council Decision to amend the treaties was adopted,[28] the full ratification of the treaty amendment was not completed until April 2013 when finally the Czech President signed the instrument of ratification. Meanwhile, the ESM had itself been operational since summer 2012, highlighting that in fact an amendment to the EU treaties had hardly been necessary given that the authority for the ESM derived from an international treaty and not the EU treaties. Nonetheless, the role played by the European Council in seeking to amend Article 136 TFEU was significant insofar as the CJEU recognized the right of the European Council to intervene in the legal proceedings brought by Thomas Pringle to challenge the legality of the ESM.[29] Although the Lisbon Treaty does not recognise the European Council as an institution capable of initiating proceedings under Article 263 TFEU to review the legality of the acts of the institutions, it does now recognize that acts of the European Council which produce legal effects are themselves capable of being challenged. Acknowledgement of the European Council's capacity to intervene in legal proceedings in which it has an interest is a further recognition of the increasing significance of the role it plays in EU executive governance, legally as well as politically.

Nonetheless, while it is right to acknowledge the increasing influence of the European Council over EU economic governance, when thinking more specifically about rules-based fiscal governance it is the role played by the Council of Ministers and the European Commission in a form of 'infranational' executive governance that is perhaps more noteworthy.[30] Even at this 'infranational' level we can differentiate between different manifestations of executive governance. One example is the role played by the Commission and Council in elaborating and enforcing the rules-based framework for fiscal discipline. In the context of the European semester (discussed below), it is the Commission and Council that formulate the country-specific recommendations which Member States are required to follow. Moreover, in the enforcement of fiscal discipline it is the Council, acting on the proposals of the European Commission, that takes the decisive steps in adopting formal recommendations and decisions addressed to states. Revisions made under the TSCG and the 'six-pack' attempt to restrict the

[28] European Council Decision 2011/199 amending Article 136 of the Treaty on the Functioning of the European Union with regard to a stability mechanism for Member States whose currency is the euro [2011] OJ L91/1.

[29] Above n 23.

[30] The term 'infranational' is borrowed from JHH Weiler, UR Haltern and FC Mayer, 'European Democracy and its Critique' (1995) 18 *West European Politics* 4. In that essay, infranationalism is associated with executive 'regulatory policy' governance. Certainly, for some, contemporary developments in fiscal governance may represent an attempt to extend the model of the 'regulatory state' into the fiscal sphere: W Schelkle, 'The Contentious Creation of the Regulatory state in Fiscal Surveillance' (2009) 32 *West European Politics* 829.

capacity of the Council to deviate from recommendations and proposals made by the European Commission. Firstly, Article 7 TSCG instructs eurozone states to support the Commission's proposals in respect of a eurozone state that falls under the excessive deficit procedure. Secondly, in formalizing the European semester in legislative form, amended Regulation 1466/97 also makes clear that the Council is, 'as a rule', expected to make full use of the legal powers to adopt decisions and recommendations under the treaties and under the SGP, based on Commission recommendations.[31] Thirdly, the 'six-pack' introduces the idea of 'reverse' majorities in which determinations of deviations from fiscal discipline and decisions to adopt sanctions are deemed to be adopted by the Council on the basis of Commission proposals or recommendations, unless by a majority (simple or qualified) the Council votes not to adopt the measure. Together, these changes are clearly intended to strengthen the 'supranational' dimension of infranational executive governance at the expense of the collective 'intergovernmental' will of the Council.

One of the aims of the Lisbon Treaty was to delineate more clearly the spheres of legislative and executive power, with the latter primarily being a function of the European Commission. With regard to 'delegated' acts (Article 290 TFEU), the thrust of the reform was to dispense with the complex system of comitology in favour of more direct delegation of powers to the European Commission, subject to oversight by the European Parliament and Council. As regards 'implementing' measures (Article 291 TFEU), a revised form of comitology would be retained with a new legal framework.[32] Yet, insofar as implementing acts have been adopted to provide specific financial assistance to EU Member States, the model of executive governance deviates from the thrust of these reforms in several ways. Thus, in considering the stabilization programmes for Ireland and Portugal supported under the EFSM, Council Implementing Decisions were adopted.[33] The point to note here is that it is formally the Council rather than the European Commission which is granted the power to adopt implementing measures. However, the Member State seeking financial assistance must present a draft adjustment programme to the European Commission and the Economic and Finance Committee. The Commission, in consultation with the European Central Bank, will determine the conditionality to be attached, with the Commission concluding a Memorandum of Understanding (MoU) with the Member State which is communicated to the European Parliament and Council.

[31] Art 2(a)(3) Regulation 14466/97 as amended. Under the revised 'corrective' arm of the SGP it is also made clear that 'as a rule' the Council is expected to follow the recommendations or proposals of the Commission 'or explain its position publicly': Art 2(a) Regulation 1467/07 as amended. Both above n 13.

[32] R Schütze, "Delegated' Legislation in the (New) European Union: A Constitutional Analysis' (2011) 74 *Modern Law Review* 661; S Peers and M Costa, 'Accountability for Delegated and Implementing Acts after the Treaty of Lisbon' (2012) 18 *European Law Journal* 427.

[33] Council Implementing Decision 2011/77/EU on granting Union financial assistance to Ireland (as amended) [2011] OJ L30/34; Council Implementing Decision 2011/344/EU on granting Union financial assistance to Portugal (as amended) [2011] OJ L159/88.

Although the EFSM was modelled on the balance-of-payments support mechanism for non-eurozone states,[34] and notwithstanding that the latter mechanism also gives the Council the authority to authorize support, the decision-making procedure also departs from that model inasmuch as the Commission and European Central Bank appear to play a more decisive role in shaping the adjustment programme and conditions attached to it under the EFSM mechanism. Financial support to Greece, Spain and Cyprus—including support via the intergovernmental EFSF and ESM—has been undertaken within a rather different legal framework. Instead of being based on secondary legislation, Council Decisions authorizing support have been based directly on the TFEU, in particular Articles 126 (dealing with excessive deficits) and 136 (the rules applicable solely to eurozone states).[35] All of which serves to highlight that the 'infranational' executive governance of the crisis manifests itself in different contexts and has been fashioned out of diverse legal resources. Different patterns of institutional interplay are the result. At the level of the implementation and enforcement of fiscal discipline, we see the attempt to tilt the balance of power in favour of the European Commission. Yet the implementation of the financial support mechanisms, at least formally, gives a more authoritative role to the Council.

B. Beyond Rules-Based Governance

The second claim advanced here is that economic governance manifests itself by means other than rules-based hierarchical forms of governance. The governance literature tends to offer a range of taxonomies by which to draw attention to non-hierarchical forms of governance.[36] For present purposes these are taken to include governance by 'co-ordination', by 'markets' and by 'contract'.

(i) Governance by Co-ordination

A common narrative that has emerged in the governance response to the crisis has been the alleged failures of the mechanisms and processes of policy co-ordination in the economic and fiscal spheres.[37] The argument tends to be presented as though the design of EMU post-Maastricht represented a kind of 'original sin' by which monetary policy was centralized yet economic and fiscal responsibilities remained decentralized, subject only to the 'soft' discipline of mechanisms of reporting, monitoring and peer review. It is the apparent failures of

[34] See above n 22.

[35] Council Decision 2010/320/EU addressed to Greece (as amended) [2010] OJ L145/6. Similarly, see the Council Decision addressed to Spain: Council Decision 2012/443/EU [2012] OJ L202/17; Council Decision addressed to Cyprus: Council Decision 2013/236/EU [2013] OJ L141/32.

[36] See eg C Scott, 'The Governance of the European Union: The Potential for Multi-Level Control' (2002) 8 *European Law Journal* 59.

[37] See eg European Commission, 'A Blueprint for a Genuine Economic and Monetary Union' COM(2012) 777.

policy co-ordination to exert fiscal discipline that exposes the inadequacy of 'soft' intergovernmentalism and which, therefore, ought to drive the turn to 'hard' rules-based responses.

Yet whatever the diagnostic accuracy or otherwise of such assertions, it is abundantly clear that the governance response to the crisis cannot be understood as a mere zero-sum game in which whatever may be gained by a heightened legislative response necessarily results in a decline in resort to modes, institutions and instruments associated with governance by co-ordination. Rather, as intimated above, economic and fiscal policy co-ordination has been diffused and intensified through the post-crisis framework of the 'European semester'.

The governance architecture of the European semester has its origins in the structures and processes associated with the Lisbon strategy. Under the Lisbon strategy, the legally distinct economic and employment co-ordination processes were integrated within a framework of common guidelines and a common reporting structure, with Member States producing National Reform Programmes (NRPs) subject to EU evaluation. This type of 'multilateral surveillance' was also applied to fiscal co-ordination under the SGP with Member States producing 'stability' or 'convergence' reports that are analysed by the Commission and the Council. With the adoption of the 'six-pack' and 'two-pack', policy co-ordination is extended first in the development of the macroeconomic imbalance procedure to monitor apparently destabilizing elements of national economies, and secondly in monitoring the budgetary processes of eurozone states. The aim of the European semester is to synchronize and co-ordinate these distinct processes.

In the first half of the semester, the reports required under individual co-ordination processes are produced in light of the Commission's Annual Growth Survey; the conclusions adopted by the Council of Ministers; and the conclusions adopted by the spring European Council. In the second half of the semester the national reports are discussed with the European Commission and ultimately the Council adopts Country-Specific Recommendations (CSRs) for each of the Member States. In this way, the European semester can be seen to represents a 'meta-OMC': [38] an architecture for the 'co-ordination of co-ordination'.[39]

(ii) Governance by Markets

The discussion has concentrated on differentiation in the modes and institutions for the exercise of public governance. Yet fiscal discipline can be exerted via market behaviour. Indeed, part of the inspiration behind the EU's 'no-bailout' clause and the absence of mutualized eurobonds is the idea that moral hazard

[38] The term 'meta-OMC' was originally coined by Tholoniat to describe the integration of the economic and employment policy co-ordination processes, but it is perhaps a more apt nomenclature for the European Semester: L Tholoniat, 'The Career of the Open Method of Coordination: Lessons from a "Soft" EU instrument' (2010) 33 *West European Politics* 93.

[39] KA Armstrong, 'The Lisbon Agenda and Europe 2020: From the Governance of Coordination to the Coordination of Governance' in P Copeland and D Papadimitriou (eds), *The EU's Lisbon Strategy: Evaluating Success, Understanding Failure* (Basingstoke, Palgrave Macmillan, 2012).

should be avoided, and fiscal responsibility supported by the discipline exerted via the bond markets. The strength of that discipline relies upon the capacity of those markets to interpret underlying fiscal conditions and respond accordingly. It is also conditional on the no-bailout provision being taken seriously, otherwise markets will assume that specific risks can and will be absorbed by other eurozone states. It seems apparent it was only as the crisis got underway and, according to some authors,[40] only after the collapse of the investment bank Lehmann Brothers, that bond yields began to reflect growing concerns as to the sovereign debt positions of certain Member States. Unfortunately, this discipline then turned the financial and economic crisis into a sovereign debt crisis.

There is, therefore, a certain ambiguity in the role assigned to markets in enforcing fiscal discipline. On the one hand, the design of EMU assumes that debts and risks are not shared but discrete. Indeed, the legality of European financial stabilization is dependent upon the idea that each state remains responsible and liable for its own debts. In this way, market forces may exert a certain discipline. Yet there is also a sense in which market failure might be viewed as part of the problem both in terms of a failure to anticipate the crisis and as a causal factor in the crisis itself. At the same time, the need for European states to provide substantial financial assistance undermines the discipline that underpinned the no-bailout clause and individual fiscal responsibility.

(iii) Governance by Contract

In his contribution to this volume, Paul Craig identifies a shift in governance from 'legislation to contract'. The nature and form of these 'contracts' varies. On the one hand, it is commonplace to characterize even treaties and legislation as 'contracts' whose incomplete nature often demands the delegation of interpretative power to institutions such as courts. On the other hand, the characterization of certain instruments as contractual in nature is often intended to connote something of less general application and governed not by public law rules of treaty or legislation-making but instead by private law rules of contract and consent. The difficulty in the EU context is that whereas there are at least certain rules governing the making of treaties and legislation; the constitution of policy co-ordination; and certain aspects of executive governance, leaving aside the specific domain of public procurement law as an instance of governance by public contract, the legal framework for the use of contracts in economic governance is less apparent. Indeed, there may even be simple problems of whether to characterize certain instruments as contractual at all.

If we take the example of the recently introduced 'macroeconomic imbalance procedure',[41] states that are subject to the procedure are obligated to adopt a 'corrective action plan'. The plan sets out timetabled policy plans to bring about

[40] J von Hagen, L Schuknecht and G Wolswijk, 'Government Bond Risk Premiums in the EU Revisited: The Impact of the Financial Crisis' (2011) 27 *European Journal of Political Economy* 36.

[41] Above n 15.

an end to the excessive imbalance. On the basis of a Commission recommendation, the Council will 'endorse' the plan if satisfied or require the submission of an amended plan if not satisfied. Another example is the 'economic partnership plan' which must be adopted by a eurozone state that is subject to the excessive deficit procedure.[42] In many ways, these 'plans' are more like unilateral undertakings than bilateral contracts. Yet the plans must obtain the agreement of the Council and their adoption and implementation seeks to avoid the escalation of sanctions for breaches of fiscal or budgetary discipline. In this way, the plans have more of the character of a quasi-contract than a legal instrument of general application.

Perhaps the more visible side of governance by contract is the conditionality that applies to receipt of financial stability assistance. Here the contractual form is more obvious. Thus, the MoU to provide financial support to Greece is expressed as an agreement, 'Between the European Commission, acting on behalf of the Euro Area Member States' and 'The Hellenic Republic', complete with opening contractual recitals explaining the context of the agreement, and signatures by, on the one hand, the Greek Deputy Prime Minister and Governor of the Bank of Greece, and on the other hand, by the European Commissioner responsible for Economic and Monetary Affairs. However, these and the other similar MoUs which have been signed are not merely means of seeking to avoid escalating sanctions for breaches of discipline, but are the necessary precondition for the release of loans and lines of credit, without which the recipient states would default on their existing debts and become insolvent.

C. 'Hybrid' Forms of Governance

Recognition of differentiation in forms of governance can produce different interpretations. One approach is to seek to determine fundamental shifts between different modes of governance. In this way, if the crisis was characterized as a failure of governance by co-ordination for which rules-based governance was the solution, then that characterization has turned itself into a critique of the response to the crisis in which differentiation away from an ideal of the Community/Union method is viewed as a weakness in the resulting governance architecture.[43] There is good reason to take seriously the implications of shifts and movements between modes and forms of governance and between different types of legal instrument. However, too often the analysis overstates the extent to which governance moves from one form to another, while too little attention is paid to the manner in which governance reforms are intended to combine to

[42] Art 9, Regulation 473/2013 (n 18). Where the excessive deficit procedure is opened with regards to a state that has already submitted a corrective action plan under the excessive macroeconomic imbalance procedure, the corrective action plan is amended to include the requirements of the economic partnership plan.

[43] See eg Chiti and Teixeira (n 10).

enhance governance capacity. Therefore, the approach taken here is to explore how different approaches to economic governance combine in 'hybrid' governance architecture. A minimal interpretation of hybridity suggests the coexistence of, and complementarity between, governance techniques. A more elaborated interpretation highlights forms of mutual interaction between different governance approaches.[44]

The first example of interaction is as between rules-based and co-ordination-based forms of governance. This is particularly evident when one considers the relationship between Directive 2011/85/EU adopted under the 'six-pack' and the outputs of economic policy co-ordination. The aim of the directive was to set out certain minimum requirements for domestic fiscal frameworks including the adoption of domestic numerical fiscal rules, medium-term budgetary planning and national fiscal institutions. But in many ways this directive built upon the pre-crisis experience of fiscal policy co-ordination and the role played by peer review in that process. In this way, the intention was to expand upon the directive through the continuing operation of peer review and in light of its output in the form of policy advice. In turn, that policy advice has fed into the country-specific recommendations under the European semester, compliance with which is sought through the repeated cycles of reporting and multilateral surveillance. In this way, policy co-ordination can serve to reinforce and amplify the normative steering potential of the directive.

There is another type of interaction between policy co-ordination and rules-based governance that concerns the institutions and processes for determining and enforcing compliance with EU fiscal rules. If, as has been suggested, EU fiscal rules are far from self-executing norms and more in the nature of benchmark or framework norms, then it becomes apparent that the processes and structures for fiscal policy co-ordination play a central role in determining and enforcing compliance with these norms. Thus, while it may be that domestically embedded rules such as the balanced-budget rule may result in more traditional forms of court-based compliance—something that remains to be seen—compliance with EU numerical fiscal rules remains firmly within the political process of evaluation by the European Commission and the Council. Indeed what remains striking is the absence of the sort of power to bring Article 258 TFEU infringement proceedings for breaches of EU fiscal discipline. In this way, it seems clear that whatever has been achieved by way of a tightening of fiscal discipline through the legislative reforms of the 'six-pack', rules-based governance is firmly embedded within the structures and processes for fiscal policy co-ordination.

If the analysis of public governance highlighted the manner in which rules-based governance often finds itself embedded in co-ordination-based forms of governance, then it may also be the case that market-based fiscal governance is not wholly unrelated to rules-based governance. Indeed, the argument can be made that fiscal rules such as the balanced-budget rule contained in the

[44] Trubek and Trubek (n 11).

TSCG do not rely primarily on judicial enforcement in national systems but ought instead to be viewed as a basis for sending a signal to private as well as public actors. It is clear from the post-crisis governance architecture that national independent fiscal councils are assigned a role in monitoring compliance with numerical fiscal rules. Yet it may also be that the diffusion of these rules is also intended to provide greater transparency to the markets and offer 'focal points' or benchmarks to facilitate the pricing of domestic bonds.[45] However, whatever may be the potential of increasing the transparency of the conduct of domestic fiscal policy, it is the market judgements based on this and other data that ultimately are of importance. In the context of a system where tight domestic fiscal rules may act procyclically and where a small EU budget has no capacity to offset such effects, markets will have to judge the extent to which compliance with fiscal rules is actually a good or a bad thing for a Member State. To put it another way, markets will have to judge whether compliance with rules-based fiscal discipline is actually in a Member State's best economic interests.

A final example of interaction between different governance responses is the relationship between the country-specific recommendations that are the product of co-ordination under the European semester and the conditionality which is associated by governance by contract. For those states in receipt of financial stabilization support, the conditionality that is contained in the MoUs and accompanying Council decisions substitutes for compliance with the CSRs.

III. RESHAPING DOMINIUM-LAW

When it comes to evaluating the legal significance of differentiation in EU economic governance, much contemporary legal analysis has taken a perspective that focuses upon its impact on EU law and the unity of the legal order.[46] While an inescapably important focal point, this does not exhaust the sphere of legal and constitutional enquiry. As the essays in this volume testify, there is at least an important domestic legal context to incorporate into the constitutional conversation. After all, the post-Maastricht structure of EMU is one in which economic and fiscal policy competence was retained by Member States. In this way, Member States have conducted their economic and fiscal policies within their own legal and constitutional frameworks and traditions. The legal conditions under which a state deploys its resources of wealth is considered by Daintith to form a specific area of public law enquiry: '*dominium*-law'. Therefore, an important question is: how has the EU's governance response impacted upon, and reshaped, *dominium*-law?

One starting point is to treat *dominium*-law as state-law and to consider the

[45] RD Kelemen and TK Teo, 'Law and the Eurozone Crisis: Law, Focal Points, and Fiscal Discipline', European Union Studies Association, Baltimore, 9–11 May 2013.

[46] See M Ruffert, 'The European Debt Crisis and European Union Law' (2011) 48 *Common Market Law Review* 1777; Chiti and Teixeira (n 10).

influence of Europe on that law. This would then combine a public law analysis with the analytical framework suggested by research on 'Europeanization'. If we consider this for a moment, it becomes clearer that there are two different potential research methodologies at play: a 'top-down' and a 'bottom-up' approach.[47] Adopting a 'top-down' research design suggests that the *dominium*-law of EU Member States is the dependent variable with differentiation in EU governance and associated differentiation in the sorts of European legal measures adopted as the independent variable. The alternative (or additional) approach is to take a 'bottom-up' research methodology which considers how the domestic constitutional system mediates the capacity of any and each form of European intervention to reach into and reshape the legal framework for economic policy.

Viewed from these different perspectives we can begin to contextualize research on the constitutionalization of European budgetary constraints. The top-down approach asks how variation in the forms and types of legal instruments might impact upon the domestic constitutional and legal orders. These legal instruments include:

- international treaties between European states: eg the TSCG and ESM Treaty;
- international agreements between European states and international organisations, eg the agreement between eurozone states and the EFSF;
- the treaties constituting and regulating the European Union: TEU, TFEU, Charter of Fundamental Rights;
- secondary EU legislative acts: regulations and directives;
- EU executive acts: decisions, delegated and implementing acts;
- policy advice and recommendations;
- MoUs, economic partnership agreements, corrective action plans.

A top-down research strategy would suggest that effects of these different legal instruments on the *dominium*-law of Member States would vary depending upon the choice of instrument.

A bottom-up perspective is also interested in the implications of variation in the choice of instrument but more in terms of how the domestic constitutional and legal order might mediate the reception of different types of legal instrument. Of course, the domestic constitutional orders have themselves been Europeanized to some extent as regards their capacity to receive different EU legal instruments. Yet there is still significant space for the domestic constitutional order to assert itself and to condition the capacity of, or conditions under which, external norms penetrate into and have application within domestic legal orders.

Both of these research methodologies offer considerable potential in their capacity to shed light on the implications for *dominium*-law of the changing European governance and legal landscape. Nonetheless, it is also worth calling to mind the essential point behind Daintith's legal analysis of economic policy.

[47] For a more expanded discussion of 'bottom-up' vs 'top-down' research methodologies, see T Exadaktylos and CM Radaelli, 'Research Design in European Studies: The Case of Europeanization' (2009) 47 *Journal of Common Market Studies* 507.

Albeit that his focus was upon the conduct of economic policy in the UK, his concern was to try and make sense of claims that the use of different types of intervention and instrument raised constitutional issues. In the manner described above, these constitutional issues are confined to working through the interaction between, on the one hand, 'taken-for-granted' variety in the forms of European legal instruments, and on the other hand, domestic constitutional and legal orders. Yet this issue of the choice and form of instruments adopted in pursuit of EU governance is itself a European constitutional issue. In this way, the sphere of *dominium*-law cannot be contained within state-law. In other words, the constitutional dimension of *dominium*-law is reconfigured to beg questions as to the choice and form of European legal instruments deployed to discipline and influence the conduct of economic and fiscal policy within nation states.

Take, for example, debates about whether measures to strengthen fiscal discipline do or do not require treaty change. Is this simply a political question on what is most expedient to national and European political leaders, or is it a question that has constitutional significance? If it does have constitutional significance, what particular aspects are significant? We might draw attention to the national constitutional processes associated with treaty ratification. On the one hand, such processes may be viewed as desirable features which give added constitutional buy-in to the treaty change. On the other hand, they may be viewed as impediments and constraints on the capacity to bring about legal change. We might draw attention to the constitutional environment of the EU itself. Consider the circumstances which lead to the adoption of the Fiscal Compact Treaty and a whole raft of constitutional issues present themselves. Why not simply amend the SGP to include a balanced-budget rule? As suggested earlier, there are potential constitutional objections to the use of regulations to embed such a rule in domestic constitutions. A revision to the TFEU has to overcome the constitutional hurdle of the need for unanimity. Taking the norm outside of EU law raises the issue of the compatibility of international norms with the obligations and duties on Member States within the EU legal order. The examples just given are perhaps the most obvious examples of the way in which the choice of instrument raises constitutional issues. Yet it is also clear that such issues are equally raised by the executive acts, the instruments that set out the conditionality of financial assistance, and the other contracts and agreements under which states incur obligations and duties in the conduct of their economic policies.

Without developing this argument further, the essential point that is being made is that differentiation in EU governance creates variation in the forms and instruments of legal intervention. In turn, the choice of legal instrument through which to create duties and obligations gives rise to a range of important constitutional questions. Significantly those questions include the impact of European law on the domestic constitutional orders and as the essays in this volume show, there is much to research and uncover along this dimension. Yet European integration also reframes the constitutional context and reshapes *dominium*-law in a deeper, structural way giving rise to a different set of constitutional questions that relate to the relationship between, on the one hand, the choice of an instrument, and on the other hand, the processes associated with norm production and adoption; the limits of EU competence; the reviewability of different instruments before courts; and the reach of substantive EU constitutional norms and values.

IV. CONCLUSION

The introduction suggested that episodes of crisis often lead to scholarly reflection on the applicability and durability of theories and concepts. Certainly, the economic crisis and the response to the crisis dramatizes the debate within EU governance scholarship about the character and nature of EU governance. It has been argued that the response to the crisis confirms wider trends in EU governance towards both differentiation but also hybridity as different modes and instruments combine in new governance frameworks. This differentiation in governance has also resulted in increased variety in the forms and types of instrument through which duties and obligations have been assumed by states in the conduct of their economic and fiscal policies. Understanding the legal implications of this increase in variety is, perhaps, not so readily absorbed within contemporary European legal discourse. It has been suggested here that Daintith's concept of *dominium*-law—albeit one developed in a rather different context—may open a conceptual window through which to begin to tease out the constitutional dimension of fiscal and budgetary discipline.

5

EU Fiscal Governance and the Effectiveness of its Reform

ALEXANDRE DE STREEL*

A COMMON CURRENCY area leads to multiple externalities, or spillover effects, among its participating countries. One of these externalities relates to national fiscal policy. This is especially the case when financial markets are, on the one hand, imperfect and do not charge different risk premiums between countries according to their risk profiles, and, on the other hand, are integrated and financial institutions hold significant debts of foreign countries. In such circumstances, there is a risk that a country runs a large fiscal deficit by free-riding on the credit rating of the others.[1] To deal with this externality risk, the architects of EMU decided to constrain national fiscal policies with rules backed by sanctions.[2] Thus the TFEU imposed numerical limits on government deficit and debt (Protocol No 12 on the excessive deficit procedure), established an annual surveillance of national fiscal policies (Article 121 TFEU) and a sanction procedure when the fiscal limits were breached (Article 126 TFEU). Moreover, the TFEU also provided that a national deficit could not be monetized (Articles 123–24 TFEU) and that the EU or the Member States could not be liable for or assume the commitments of another Member

* The author wishes to thank Pierre Larouche and Federico Fabbrini for their very useful comments as well as the participants of the Conference on the Constitutionalization of European Budgetary Constraints, Tilburg, May 2013 for helpful discussions.

[1] For a discussion of this externality, P de Grauwe, *Economics of Monetary Union*, 9th edn (Oxford, Oxford University Press, 2012) 218–26. He shows that, empirically, it is not clear whether fiscal discipline is lower in monetary unions.

[2] The Maastricht negotiations were based on the Report on Economic and Monetary Union in the European Community, prepared by the Committee chaired by J Delors and presented in April 1989. On the background to the negotiations, see K Dyson and K Featherstone, *The Road to Maastricht: Negotiating Economic and Monetary Union* (Oxford, Oxford University Press, 1999). On the model of governance decided, see J Pipkörn, 'Legal Arrangements in the Treaty of Maastricht for the Effectiveness of the Economic and Monetary Union' (1994) 31 *Common Market Law Review* 263; MJ Herdegen, 'Price Stability and Budgetary Restraints in the Economic and Monetary Union: The Law as Guardian of Economic Wisdom' (1998) 35 *Common Market Law Review* 9–32; JV Louis, 'A Legal and Institutional Approach for Building a Monetary Union' (1998) 35 *Common Market Law Review* 33–76; HJ Hahn, 'The Stability Pact for European Monetary Union: Compliance with Deficit Limit as a Constant Legal Duty' (1998) 35 *Common Market Law Review* 77–100.

State (no-bailout clause: Article 125 TFEU). Thus the governance model chosen was based on the maintenance of fiscal decentralization constrained by financial markets and rules and without financial solidarity. Other models were possible, such as more centralized fiscal policy, but they were not politically feasible at the time.

The past decade has showed that the model chosen did not work well. There are several reasons for this, including fiscal rules that were poorly designed and not well implemented. When added to the other banking and macroeconomic difficulties created by the 2008 global financial crisis, this led to some Member States experiencing high levels of financial instability since 2010. In turn, this led to more financial solidarity than envisaged by the architects of EMU[3] and cast doubt on the credibility of the no-bailout clause.[4] To remedy such weaknesses, EU fiscal governance has been substantially reformed in three main waves. The first wave was the adoption in November 2011 of the 'six-pack', a set of five regulations and one directive. These make the fiscal rules stricter and improve the sanction procedure, notably by increasing their automaticity.[5] The second wave was the adoption in March 2012 of the Treaty on Stability, Coordination and Governance in the the Economic and Monetary Union (TSCG, the 'Fiscal Compact'), an international treaty concluded by 25 EU Member States outside the EU legal framework but relying very much on EU institutions.[6] This Treaty provides for the constitutionalization of the EU fiscal rules and the creation of

[3] In 2010, the European Financial Stability Facility (EFSF) with a lending capacity of €440 billion and the European Financial Stabilisation Mechanism (EFSM) with a lending capacity of €60 billion were established. They were replaced in 2012 by the European Stability Mechanism (ESM) with a lending capacity of €500 billion. On those instruments, see A de Gregorio Merino, 'Legal Developments in the Economic and Monetary Union During the Debt Crisis: The Mechanism of Financial assistance' (2012) 49 *Common Market Law Review* 1613–46; JV Louis, 'Guest Editorial: The No-Bailout Clause and Rescue Package' (2010) 47 *Common Market Law Review* 971–86.

[4] Note that the CJEU validated the ESM Treaty with regard to the non-bailout clause by adopting a teleological interpretation of the clause: 'Given the objective pursued by Article 125 TFEU, it must be held that that provision prohibits the Union and the Member States from granting financial assistance as a result of which the incentive of the recipient Member State to conduct a sound budgetary policy is diminished. … However, Article 125 TFEU does not prohibit the granting of financial assistance by one or more Member States to a Member State which remains responsible for its commitments to its creditors provided that the conditions attached to such assistance are such as to prompt that Member State to implement a sound budgetary policy': Case C-370/12 *Pringle v Ireland* [2012], judgment of 27 November 2012, nyr, [136]–[137].

[5] The six-pack was published in [2011] OJ L306. Most of its provisions entered into force on 13 December 2011. The six-pack was negotiated on the basis on the Final Report of 21 October 2010 by the Task Force on Economic Governance which was endorsed by the European Council of 28–29 October 2010. Note that the Stability and Growth Pact regulations had already been amended in 2005 to make the fiscal rules smarter: see F Amtenbrink and J de Haan, 'Economic Governance in the European Union: Fiscal Discipline Versus Flexibility' (2003) 40 *Common Market Law Review* 1075–106; JV Louis, 'The Review of the Stability and Growth Pact' (2006) 43 *Common Market Law Review* 85–106.

[6] P Craig, 'The Stability, Coordination and Governance Treaty: Principle, Politics and Pragmatism' (2012) 37 *European Law Review* 231; S Peers, 'The Stability Treaty: Permanent Austerity or Gesture Politics' (2012) *European Constitutional Law Review* 404.

a national correction mechanism next to the EU sanction procedure.[7] The third wave was the adoption in May 2013 of the 'two-pack', a set of two EU regulations that apply only to Member States whose currency is the euro. These regulations improve the national institutional framework and reinforce the Commission and Council oversight over national fiscal policies. [8]

This paper analyses these three waves of reform. The first section is descriptive and gives a brief overview of the new fiscal governance as modified by the six-pack, the TSCG and the two-pack. The second section is critical and analyses the weaknesses of the original fiscal governance and the effectiveness of the recent reforms. The third section briefly concludes.

I. OVERVIEW OF EU FISCAL GOVERNANCE

EU fiscal governance is based on several legal instruments which are closely related: (i) a number of primary EU law provisions; (ii) two EU regulations composing the Stability and Growth Pact[9] and two EU regulations reinforcing and complementing the Stability and Growth Pact for the Member States whose currency is the euro;[10] (iii) one EU directive and one EU regulation requiring minimal quality for the national institutional framework;[11] and (iv) the TSCG. This section analyses the three main components of EU fiscal governance: first, the rules constraining national fiscal policies; second, the institutions at the EU and national levels in charge of the implementation of the rules; and third, the enforcement mechanisms at the EU and national levels.

[7] The TSCG entered into force on 1 January 2012. It was negotiated on the basis of the Statement by the eurozone heads of state or government of 9 December 2011.

[8] The two-pack was published in [2013] OJ L140. Most of its provisions entered into force on 30 May 2013.

[9] Regulation 1466/97 of the Council of 7 July 1997 on the strengthening of the surveillance of budgetary positions and the surveillance and coordination of economic policies [1997] OJ L209/1 as amended by Regulation 1055/2005 and Regulation 1175/2011; Regulation 1467/97 of the Council of 7 July 1997 on speeding up and clarifying the implementation of the excessive deficit procedure [1997] OJ L209/6, amended by Regulation 1056/2005 and Regulation 1177/2011. For an overview of the revised Stability and Growth Pact, see European Commission, 'Building a Strengthened Fiscal Framework in the European Union: A Guide to the Stability and Growth Pact' (2013) *European Economy: Occasional Paper 150*; European Commission, 'Vade Mecum on the Stability and Growth Pact' (2013) *European Economy: Occasional Paper 151.*

[10] Regulation 1173/2011 of the European Parliament and of the Council of 16 November 2011 on the effective enforcement of budgetary surveillance in the euro area [2011] OJ L306/1; Regulation 473/2013 of the European Parliament and of the Council of 21 May 2013 on common provisions for monitoring and assessing draft budgetary plans and ensuring the correction of excessive deficit of the Member States in the euro area [2013] OJ L140/11.

[11] Directive 2011/85 of the Council of 8 November 2011 on requirements for budgetary frameworks of the Member States [2011] OJ L306/41; Regulation 479/2009 of the Council of 25 May 2009 on the application of the Protocol on the excessive deficit procedure annexed to the Treaty establishing the European Community [2009] OJ L145/1, amended by Regulation 679/2010.

A. Fiscal Rules

EU law and the TSCG provide limiting rules related to actual and structural government deficit and to government debt as well as to the correction path when those limits are violated.

(i) Actual and Structural Government Deficit Rules

Each Member State must maintain its actual government deficit below 3 per cent of GDP, unless either the ratio has declined substantially and continuously and reached a level that comes close to 3 per cent, or, alternatively, the excess over 3 per cent is only exceptional and temporary and the ratio remains close to 3 per cent.[12] Moreover, each Member State must comply with a country-specific Medium Term Objective (MTO). This is a target for the structural deficit (ie the actual deficit corrected for the effects of the economic cycle as well as the one-off and temporary fiscal measures) in the medium term (ie three years). The target is determined for each Member State according to its government debt. The Stability and Growth Pact requires that the MTO must be above a floor of −1 per cent of GDP[13] and the TSCG goes further by requiring that the MTO is above −0.5 per cent of GDP (unless the ratio of government debt is below 60 per cent of GDP and the risks in terms of long-term sustainability of public finances are low).[14] This MTO rule ensures the sustainability of public finance while allowing room for budgetary manoeuvre, in particular for automatic stabilizers or public investment.

Until a Member State reaches its MTO, it must follow an adjustment path towards the MTO by reducing its structural deficit by at least 0.5 per cent of the GDP per year (or more if the Member State has a government debt above 60 per cent of the GDP or presents pronounced risks of overall debt sustainability).[15] There is an escape clause in the case of an unusual event outside the control of the Member State which has a major impact on the financial position of the general government or in periods of severe economic downturn for the eurozone or the EU as a whole. In such exceptional circumstances, the Member State may be allowed temporarily to depart from the adjustment path, provided that this does not endanger fiscal sustainability in the medium term.[16]

[12] Art 126(2) TFEU and Art 1 Protocol no 12 on the excessive deficit procedure.

[13] Art 2(a)(2) Regulation 1466/97 amended. The methodology to calculate the MTO is explained in the Specifications of the Council of 3 September 2012 on the implementation of the Stability and Growth Pact and Guidelines on the format and content of Stability and Convergence Programmes. See also European Commission (n 10).

[14] Art 3(1b) and (1d) TSCG.

[15] Art 5(1) Regulation 1466/97 amended.

[16] Art 5(1) *in fine* Regulation 1467/97 amended and Art 3(1c) and (3b) TSCG.

(ii) Government Debt Rule

Each Member State must maintain its government debt below 60 per cent of GDP, unless the ratio is sufficiently diminishing and approaching 60 per cent at a satisfactory pace.[17] If a Member State has a government debt above 60 per cent of GDP, it must reduce it at a satisfactory pace, which implies a reduction of the differential between the actual debt level and the 60 per cent of the GDP threshold at an average rate of 1/20th per year.[18] Finally, the Member States of the Eurozone must report to the Commission and the Eurogroup, ex ante and in a timely manner, on their national debt issuance plans in order to better co-ordinate the planning of such issuance.[19]

(iii) Transposition of EU Fiscal Rules into National Law

EU law provides that each Member State must enshrine in national law numerical fiscal rules which effectively promote compliance with EU government deficit and debt rules and their annual budget legislation must reflect such rules.[20] The TSCG goes further and requires that Contracting Parties transpose into national law the MTO rule and its adjustment path through provisions of binding force and permanent character, preferably constitutional, or otherwise guaranteed to be fully respected and adhered to throughout the national budgetary processes.[21]

B. Institutional Framework

The second component of the fiscal governance relates to the institutional framework. EU law and the TSCG provides for minimal quality characteristics of the national institutions and for efficient EU co-ordination and oversight.

(i) National Institutional Framework

To facilitate the control of the fiscal rules by national and EU institutions, EU law provides for minimal quality rules for the budgetary framework defined as 'the set of arrangements, procedures, rules and institutions that underlie the conduct of budgetary policies of general government'.[22]

[17] Art 126(2) TFEU and Art 1 Protocol no 12 on the excessive deficit procedure.
[18] Art 2(1a) Regulation 1467/97 amended and Art 4 TSCG.
[19] Art 8 Regulation 473/2013 and Art 6 TSCG; Section III of the Specifications of the Council of 9 July 2013 on the implementation of the two-pack and Guidelines on the format and content of draft budgetary plans, economic partnership programmes and debt issuance reports.
[20] Arts 5–7 Directive 2011/85. Such provisions do not apply to the UK.
[21] Art 3(2) TSCG.
[22] Art 2 Directive 2011/85.

Minimal Institutional Requirements Applicable to All Member States

All Member States must have in place public accounting systems comprehensively and consistently covering all subsectors of general government, based on the European System of Accounts (ESA) 95 standard and subject to internal control and independent audits.[23] Eurostat, the statistics department of the Commission, controls the quality of the national data by running dialogue and methodological visits in the Member States.[24] Member States must also adopt realistic macroeconomic and budgetary forecasts with sensitivity analysis, and must explain any significant divergences from Commission forecasts.[25] In addition, Member States must establish a credible, effective medium-term budgetary framework providing for the adoption of a fiscal planning horizon of at least three years.[26] Finally, Member States must establish appropriate mechanisms of co-ordination across subsectors of general government and promote fiscal accountability of those subsectors.[27]

Additional Institutional Requirements for Member States whose Currency is the Euro

Each Member State of the eurozone must apply a Common Budgetary Timeline with three main deadlines: (i) preferably by 15 April but no later than 30 April, adoption of a national medium-term fiscal plan; (ii) no later than 15 October, adoption of a draft budget for the forthcoming year; (iii) not later than 31 December, adoption of the budget.[28] Each Member State of the eurozone must also establish a national independent fiscal council (IFC) with three main tasks: producing or endorsing macroeconomic forecasts and possibly budgetary forecasts; monitoring compliance with national numerical fiscal rules; and monitoring the implementation of the national automatic correction mechanism in the case of violation of the fiscal rules.[29] These national fiscal councils must be structurally independent or endowed with a high degree of functional autonomy vis-à-vis the national budgetary authorities. That requires: a statutory regime grounded in national law; nomination procedures based on experience and competence; adequacy of resources; and appropriate access to information and freedom to communicate this publicly in a timely manner.[30] In other contexts,

[23] Art 3 Directive 2011/85.
[24] Arts 11–11b Regulation 479/2009 amended.
[25] Art 4 Directive 2011/85.
[26] Art 9 Directive 2011/85.
[27] Article 13 Directive 2011/85.
[28] Art 4 Regulation 473/2013.
[29] Art 5 Regulation 473/2013
[30] Art 2(1a) Regulation 473/2013. Some argue that IFCs should be independent from the government, but not necessarily from the parliaments: C Fasone and E Griglio, 'Can Fiscal Councils Enhance the Role of National Parliaments in the European Union? A Comparative analysis' in B de Witte, A Héritier and A Trechsel (eds), *The Euro Crisis and the State of the European Democracy* (Florence, European University Institute, 2013) 264.

the CJEU has shown strong support for independence by interpreting strictly this requirement and considering it not to be contrary to democratic legitimacy.[31]

(ii) EU Institutional Framework

EU institutional bodies, in particular those active in the eurozone, have been substantially reinforced by the reform of fiscal governance leading to an increased institutional differentiation between the EU and EMU.[32] Regarding bodies composed of national executives, the different levels of Member State representation has been improved. At the top, a Euro Summit, composed of the heads of state or government of those Member States whose currency is the euro and chaired by an elected president, has been created by the TSCG.[33] At the ministerial level, the Eurogroup had already been reinforced by the Lisbon Treaty[34] and it is now envisaged that it will be chaired by a full-time president.[35] At the preparatory level, the Eurogroup Working Group (EWG), which is composed of the representatives of the eurozone countries at the Economic and Financial Committee, is now chaired by a full-time Brussels-based president.[36]

Regarding parliamentary bodies, the six-pack and the two-pack establish an economic dialogue between, on the one hand, the relevant committees in the European Parliament and, on the other hand, representatives of the EU institutions involved in fiscal governance (Commission, Ecofin Council, Eurogroup, European Council) or representatives of the Member States affected by fiscal governance measures.[37] Moreover, a conference of representatives of the relevant committees of the European Parliament and representatives of the relevant committees of national parliaments has been set up by the TSCG.[38]

C. Enforcement Mechanisms

The third component of fiscal governance is the enforcement mechanisms at the EU and the national levels.

[31] See Case C-518/07 *Commission v Germany* [2010] ECR I-1885, in particular paras 30 and 46 interpreting the independence requirement for a national data protection authority provided by Art 28(1) Directive 95/46/EC of the European Parliament and of the Council of 24 October 1995 on the protection of individuals with regard to the processing of personal data and on the free movement of such data [1995] OJ L281/31.

[32] For an analysis of the integration and the differentiation caused by the EMU, see F Snyder, 'EMU—Integration and Differentiation: Metaphor for European Union', in P Craig and G de Búrca (eds), *The Evolution of EU Law*, 2nd edn (Oxford, Oxford University Press, 2011) 687.

[33] Art 12 TSCG.

[34] See Art 137 TFUE and Protocol no 14 on the Eurogroup.

[35] Point 5 of Annex I to the Euro Summit Statement of 26 October 2011: Ten measures to improve the governance of the euro area.

[36] Ibid, points 7 and 8.

[37] Article 2(a), (b) Regulation 1466/97 amended; Art 2a Regulation 1467/97 amended; Art 3 Regulation 1173/2011; Art 15 Regulation 473/2013.

[38] Art 13 TSCG.

(i) EU Enforcement Tools

Annual Multilateral Surveillance Procedure for Fiscal Imbalances

EU law provides for an annual multilateral surveillance procedure, which is integrated into the European semester.[39] This is the preventive phase of the Stability and Growth Pact foreseen by the amended Regulation 1466/97 and complemented, for the eurozone, by Regulation 473/2013.

In April, each Member State submits to the Commission its stability programme (if its currency is the euro) or its convergence programme (if its currency is not the euro).[40] In May, the Commission analyses these programmes and, on that basis, proposes country-specific recommendations for each Member State. In July, the Council adopts the recommendations (Article 121(2) TFEU) by a qualified majority and following the 'comply or explain' principle, under which the Council is expected to, as a rule, follow the proposals of the Commission or explain its position publicly.[41]

If a Member State does not comply with its country-specific recommendations, the Commission may address a warning to this Member State (Article 121(4) TFEU). The Commission may also propose a revision of the country-specific recommendations. The Council adopts the revised recommendations (Article 121(4) TFEU) by a qualified majority and following the 'comply or explain' principle. Moreover, if the Member State concerned is part of the eurozone, the Commission proposes the imposition of an interest-bearing deposit of 0.2 per cent of GDP. Such sanction is deemed to be adopted by the Council unless it decides by a qualified majority to reject it within ten days (reverse qualified majority).[42] Thus, these recommendations do not have direct binding effect as their violation cannot lead to an infringement case before the CJEU. However, they have indirect binding effect as their violation may lead to an investigation by the Commission and the imposition of sanctions by the Council. As in other EU fields (such as electronic communications), the recommendations have important legal effect through ad hoc sanction procedures. In other words, economic governance recommendations have less binding effects than those of the hard law but more binding effects than those of the (standard) soft law.

In addition, Member States of the eurozone are also subject to obligations during the second semester of the year. No later than the 15 October, they must submit to the Commission and the Eurogroup a draft budgetary plan for the forthcoming year.[43] If the Commission identifies serious non-compliance with

[39] The European semester is foreseen by Art 2(a) Regulation 1466/97 amended.

[40] Art 4 Regulation 1466/97 amended and Code of conduct of 3 September 2012 on the Specifications on the implementation of the Stability and Growth Pact and Guidelines on the format and content of stability and convergence programmes.

[41] Arts 2(a), (b)(2) and 6(2) Regulation 1466/97 amended.

[42] Art 4 Regulation 1173/2011.

[43] Art 6 Regulation 473/2013; Section II of the Specifications of the Council of 9 July 2013 on the

EU fiscal rules, it requests within two weeks the submission of a revised draft budgetary plan.[44] Otherwise, the Commission adopts in November an opinion on those draft budgetary plans.

Corrective Procedure: The Excessive Deficit Procedure

If a Member State violates EU fiscal rules, the Council may place this state under an excessive deficit procedure (EDP) which gives the Commission and the Council significant powers to force Member States to comply with their fiscal obligations.[45] The EDP follows a specific timetable that is not necessarily aligned with the EU semester. The EDP is described in Article 126 TFEU, clarified by the amended regulation 1467/97 (the corrective phase of the Stability and Growth Pact) and complemented, for the eurozone, by Regulation 473/2013.

The EDP starts with a proposal from the Commission to place the Member State under EDP and adopt budgetary recommendations with two main elements: a correction date by which the actual government deficit must be below 3 per cent of GDP, and an annual reduction path for the structural deficit.[46] The Council adopts the decision on the existence of an excessive deficit and the budgetary recommendation by qualified majority and under the 'comply or explain' rule (Article 126(6) and (7) TFEU).[47] However, when the EDP is opened against a Member State whose currency is the euro and on the basis of the deficit rule, the TSCG requires that Member States support the Commission proposal unless a qualified majority of them oppose.[48] In practice, that means the Council decides by reverse qualified majority.

If the Member State concerned is part of the eurozone, it presents to the Commission and to the Council an economic partnership programme describing the policy measures and structural reforms that are needed to ensure an effectively durable correction of the excessive deficit.[49] It is also subject to far-reaching reporting requirements to the Commission.[50] Moreover, if the Member State has previously been condemned during the preventive phase of the Stability and Growth Pact or violates significantly EU fiscal rules, the Commission proposes

implementation of the Two-pack and Guidelines on the format and content of draft budgetary plans, economic partnership programmes and debt issuance reports; Communication from the Commission of 27 June 2013, Harmonized framework for draft budgetary plans and debts issuance reports within the euro area COM(2013) 490.

44 Art 7 Regulation 473/2013.

45 Also European Commission (2013b) and (2013c).

46 Art 3(2) Regulation 1467/97 amended.

47 Art 2a(1) Regulation 1467/97 amended. When an EDP is proposed against a Member State whose currency is the euro, only the other Member States whose currency in the euro can vote: Arti 139(4b) TFEU.

48 Art 7 TSCG.

49 Art 9 Regulation 473/2013 and Art 5 TSCG; Section IV of the Specifications of 1 July 2013 on the implementation of the Two-pack and Guidelines on the format and content of draft budgetary plans, economic partnership programmes and debt issuance reports.

50 Art 10 Regulation 473/2013.

the imposition of an non-interest-bearing deposit amounting to 0.2 per cent of its GDP. This sanction is deemed to be adopted by the Council unless it decides by a qualified majority to reject the Commission's recommendation within ten days.[51]

If the Member State does not comply with the Council budgetary recommendation to end the excessive deficit, the Commission needs to establish that no effective action has been taken. The Council decides on the failure to take effective action following the 'comply or explain' rule and acting by reverse qualified majority if the Member State concerned is part of the eurozone and by qualified majority otherwise (Article 126(8) TFEU).[52] Moreover, if the failing state is part of the Eurozone, the Commission proposes the imposition of a fine of 0.2 per cent of its GDP, which is deemed to be adopted by the Council unless it decides by a qualified majority to reject the Commission's recommendation within 10 days.[53] The Commission also proposes to give notice to the Member State concerned to take, within a specified time limit, necessary measures for deficit reduction in order to remedy the situation. The Council decides by reverse qualified majority and following the 'comply or explain' rule (Article 126(9) TFEU).[54] If a eurozone Member State persists in failing to apply the budgetary recommendations, it may be sanctioned by the Council with a fine of up to 0.5 per cent of its GDP and other sanctions such as a revision of the loan policy by the European Investment Bank (Article 126(11) TFEU). Alternatively, if the failing state is not part of the eurozone but benefits from the cohesion fund, the Council may decide to suspend any commitments from the fund until the state concerned complies with its fiscal obligations.

(ii) National Enforcement Tools

As a complement to the EPD, EU law also requires the establishment of a national correction mechanism to increase the effectiveness of the fiscal rules. Directive 2011/85 provides that the national fiscal rules adopted by Member States must entail effective and timely monitoring of compliance with the rules, based on reliable and independent analysis carried out by independent bodies as well as the consequences of non-compliance.[55] However, such obligations are vague because the legal basis of the directive on the budgetary framework (Article 126(14) TFEU) does not allow the imposition of precise and extensive obligations.

[51] Art 5 Regulation 1173/2011.

[52] Art 126(8) TFEU provides for qualified majority rule, but the application of Art 7 TSCG leads to a reverse qualified majority.

[53] Art 6 Regulation 1173/2011.

[54] Art 126(9) TFEU provides for qualified majority rule, but the application of Art 7 TSCG leads to a reverse qualified majority. This step of the EDP does not apply to Member States whose currency is not the euro: Art 139(2b) TFEU.

[55] Art 6 Directive 2011/85.

The TSCG goes further by providing that the Contracting Parties must adopt a national correction mechanism which is triggered automatically in case of significant deviation from the MTO or the adjustment path towards it.[56] The mechanism must be based on seven common principles adopted by the Commission.[57] Those principles provide that the correction mechanism is activated in case of significant deviation from the MTO adjustment path[58] and can only be suspended when the conditions for an escape defined in EU law are met,[59] and that the correction must be proportionate to the deviation and must be monitored by an independent fiscal council. Like the MTO rule, such a correction mechanism must be included in provisions of binding force and permanent character, preferably constitutional, or otherwise guaranteed to be fully respected and adhered to throughout the national budgetary processes.[60] To ensure that the Contracting Parties transpose the MTO rule and the automatic correction mechanism into their national laws, such transposition is monitored by the Commission and subject to the adjudication of the CJEU.[61]

II. EFFECTIVENESS OF EU FISCAL GOVERNANCE AND ITS RECENT REFORMS

Compliance with the EU fiscal rules has varied over time. During an initial period, when the Member States were not yet part of the eurozone, the rules were relatively well respected because of the perceived political and economic benefits of being part of the eurozone. Once Member States had been admitted to the eurozone, however, compliance with the rules weakened substantially because there was no perceived risk of being excluded from the monetary zone and the financial markets no longer discriminated according to the differing risk profiles of the individual Member States.[62] This contributed to increasing economic divergence within the eurozone.[63]

[56] Art 3(1e) TSCG.

[57] Communication from the Commission of 20 June 2012, Common principles on national fiscal correction mechanisms COM(2012) 342.

[58] Art 6(3) Regulation 1466/97 amended stating that the deviation is significant when it is at least 0.5% of GDP in a single year or at least 0.25 % of GDP on average per year in two consecutive years.

[59] Art 5(1) Regulation 1466/97 amended: an unusual event outside the control of the Member State concerned which has a major impact on the financial position of the general government or periods of severe economic downturn for the euro area or the Union as a whole.

[60] Art 3(2) TSCG.

[61] Art 8 TSCG.

[62] For an evolution of the spreads of ten-year government bond vis-à-vis Germany between 1991 and 2011, see de Grauwe (n 1) 219.

[63] For an analysis of the divergences in the competitive positions in the Eurozone, see among others de Grauwe (n 1) 129.

A. The Weaknesses of Fiscal Governance and its Reform

Such poor compliance was also due to several weaknesses in the design of the EU fiscal governance established by the TSCG and the Stability and Growth Pact regulations. The following paragraphs review such weaknesses and the improvements made by the recent reforms of economic governance (six-pack, TSCG and two-pack).

(i) Economic Relevance of the Fiscal Rules

The 3 per cent actual deficit limit and the 60 per cent debt ceiling had no strong economic justification, and have even been claimed to be stupid by former Commission President Romani Prodi. Indeed what is relevant is the sustainability of the public finances as captured by the MTO rule and its adjustment path. Therefore, the shift of focus from the actual deficit rule to the MTO rule, initiated by the first reform of the Stability and Growth Pact regulations in 2005 and reinforced by the six-pack and the TSCG, is welcome. However, those smarter rules are more difficult to apply because the calculation of the structural deficit is complex and methodologies are subject to debate among economists. Moreover, they are less transparent and less easy to explain to the general public, hence the case for painful socioeconomic reforms to meet those rules is more difficult to make. An additional improvement to the rules would be to differentiate between public expenditures for productive investment and expenditures which do not generate return in the future.[64]

(ii) Quality Budgetary Data and Macroeconomic Forecasts

The fiscal rules cannot be applied properly, as shown in the case of Greece, if the national and EU institutions cannot rely on complete, reliable, timely and consistent statistical data as well as on independent macroeconomic forecasts. The recent reforms improve the quality of the data by conferring additional investigative powers on Eurostat[65] and providing for sanction if it is found that statistics have been manipulated.[66] These reforms also improve the quality of the forecasts by requiring, for the eurozone Member States, that forecasts are produced or endorsed by an independent national fiscal council.[67]

[64] In that regard, see European Commission, 'The Quality of Public Expenditures in the EU' (2012) *European Economy: Occasional Paper 125*.

[65] Arts 11–11b of the Regulation 479/2009 amended.

[66] Art 8 Regulation 1173/2011.

[67] Arts 2(1)(b) and 4(4) Regulation 473/2013. The usefulness of the Independent Fiscal Councils has been shown in X Debrun, D Hauner and M Kumar, 'Independent Fiscal Agencies' (2009) 23 *Journal of Economic Surveys* 44.

(iii) National Ownership

Initially, the EU fiscal rules were poorly owned by the national institutions. In most Member States, they were not transposed into national law, and no national institution was specifically in charge of their implementation. However, national ownership of EU fiscal rules is one of the key requirements for the success of EMU because fiscal policies remain decentralized and the Commission alone does not have sufficient knowledge, expertise, political capital and legitimacy to ensure that all Member States comply with EU fiscal rules. Thus, one of the main objectives of the recent reforms was to increase the ownership of fiscal rules. First, the six-pack (Directive 2011/85) provides minimal requirements for the national fiscal framework, in particular by imposing national fiscal rules incorporating some of the EU rules. Then, the TSGC requires the transposition of the MTO rule and national correction mechanism into national law preferably at the constitutional level. Finally, the two-pack (Regulation 473/2013) requires the establishment of an independent fiscal council with an extensive monitoring role. It is now up to the Commission, as the guardian of EU law (and of some TSCG provisions), to ensure that Member States implement and apply correctly Directive 2011/85, Regulation 473/2013 and the TSCG. If this is achieved, the Commission could then partner with independent national institutions to promote fiscal responsibility.

An additional improvement could be the establishment of an European network made of the national fiscal councils and the Commission in order to strengthen independent fiscal council, to exchange best practices, and ultimately to contribute to the diffusion of fiscal discipline within each Member State. Such a network of national authorities has been used successfully in the network industries such as electronic communications with the Body of the European Regulators for Electronic Communications (BEREC)[68] or energy with the Agency for the Cooperation of Energy Regulators (ACER).[69] Those networks of authorities contributed to the acceptance of a new liberalization policy paradigm promoted by the EU institutions, and often opposed by the majority of the Member States, and led to an appropriate implementation of the paradigm. To be sure, there are important differences between economic governance and the regulation of network industries as the former carries more political importance than the latter and the role of the independent fiscal council is merely advisory while the role of national regulatory authority is regulatory, but it remains that the usefulness of the network of authorities in energy or electronic communications offers important lessons for the role and the organization of the independent fiscal councils.

[68] Regulation 1211/2009 of the European Parliament and of the Council of 25 November 2009 establishing the Body of European Regulators for Electronic Communications (BEREC) and the Office [2009] OJ L337/1.

[69] Regulation 713/2009 of the European Parliament and of the Council of 13 July 2009 establishing an Agency for the Cooperation of Energy Regulators [2009] OJ L211/1.

(iv) Typology of the Sanctions

Initially, the sanctions foreseen by the Treaty were of three main types:

- Reputational: a sanction of this kind increases transparency which, in turn, leads to political as well as financial incentives (through an increase of a Member State's borrowing costs) to comply with the rules. Unfortunately, such sanctions do not work very well as financial markets are imperfect and tend to underreact (before the euro crisis) or overreact (after the euro crisis) to financial information.
- Suspending or terminating the allocation of EU funds. In particular, the European Investment Bank may reconsider its lending policy,[70] and cohesion funds may be suspended.[71] Such sanction can be effective and has been applied successfully against Hungary in 2012.[72]
- Imposition of fines. The credibility and the effectiveness of fines is a complex matter. If the Member State is able to pay the fine without undermining its financial stability, the sanction is credible; hence the threat of a fine provides an incentive to comply with the fiscal rules. This has been shown by Belgium which improved its fiscal adjustment plan in June 2013 due to the threat of being fined by the Council.[73] Conversely, if the Member State is unable to pay the fine or if the imposition of the fine jeopardizes its financial stability, the sanction is not credible. In other words, a fine is only effective if it is imposed or threatened to be imposed early in the surveillance procedure when the Member State does not face a liquidity or solvency crisis.

The recent reforms improve the design of the sanctions. First, the possibility of suspending or terminating transfer of EU funds will be extended to all types of structural funds. Second, the financial sanctions are more graduated (going from interest-bearing deposit to non-interest-bearing deposit to fine) and can be imposed earlier in the excessive deficit procedure and even during the preventive phase of the Stability and Growth Pact. Some, notably Germany, have proposed another type of sanction, namely the suspension of the voting right in the Council. However, this new type of sanction requires a Treaty change.

[70] Art 126(11) TFEU.

[71] Art 4 Regulation 1084/2006 of the Council of 11 July 2006 establishing a Cohesion Fund [2006] OJ L210/79, as amended.

[72] Implementing Decision 2012/156 of the Council of 13 March 2012 suspending commitments from the Cohesion Fund for Hungary with effect from 1 January 2013 [2012] OJ L78/19; and Implementing Decision 2012/323 of the Council of 22 June 2012 lifting the suspension of commitments from the Cohesion Fund for Hungary [2012] OJ L165/46.

[73] See Press Speaking Points of 29 May 2013 by Vice-President Rehn, SPEECH/13/481; Decision 2013/370 of the Council of 21 June 2013 giving notice to Belgium to take measures for the deficit reduction judged necessary in order to remedy the situation of excessive deficit [2013] OJ L190/87.

(v) Decision-Making Process for Sanctions

Initially, EU sanctions were proposed by the Commission and decided upon by the Council under qualified majority voting. Inevitably, this led to intense political bargaining between, on the one hand, the Member State susceptible to sanction, and, on the other, the Commission and the other Member States. This was the case during the Ecofin meeting of November 2003 when France and Germany managed to convince a blocking minority of Member States to oppose the Commission proposals for Council decisions to step up the excessive deficit.[74] Moreover, the adjudicating power of the CJEU, with its independence and objectivity, was very limited by the Treaty.[75]

The recent reforms have improved the decision-making process of the sanctions adopted at EU and national levels. Regarding EU sanctions, a distinction should be made between the decision-making process within the Commission (to propose the sanction) and that within the Council (to impose the sanction). Within the Commission, an extensive habilitation has been granted to the Commissioner for Economic and Monetary Affairs and the Euro in order to increase the independence of the decision-making process.[76] Within the Council, most of the sanctions imposed against a Member State whose currency is the euro are decided by reverse qualified majority in order to reduce the possibility of bargaining between Member States. Based on an empirical analysis of other procedures where the reverse qualified majority is applied, Van Aken and Artige show that the change in voting rule has increased substantially the probability of adoption, hence the automaticity in the sanctions proposed by the Commission.[77] In turn, this reinforces the role of the Commission in proposing the sanctions. Regarding national sanctions, Directive 2011/85, but more importantly the TSCG and Regulation 473/2013, provide that they should be automatic[78] and monitored by the independent fiscal council.[79]

However, some problems remain. Regarding the decision-making process within the Commission, there is a tension between the need to reduce the political influence of Member States on Commissioners and the requirement to ensure collegiality among Commissioners. The extensive habilitation of the Euro Commissioner may tilt the balance too much in the first direction. Moreover, the criteria used by the Commission to assess the overall situation of a Member State and decide to propose a sanction are not sufficiently transparent and may

[74] The meeting is summarized in the press release of the Council meeting of 25 November 2003. The Commission requested the annulment of such deliberation at the CJEU, but partly lost its case: Case C-27/04 *Commission v Council* [2004] ECR I-6649. This case triggered the 2005 reform of the Stability and Growth Pact regulations.

[75] Arti 126(10) TFEU.

[76] See Commission press release of 27 October 2011, IP/11/1284.

[77] W Van Aken and L Artige, 'Reverse Majority Voting in Comparative Perspective: Implications for Fiscal Governance in the EU' in B de Witte, A Héritier and A Trechsel (eds), *The Euro Crisis and the State of the European Democracy* (Florence, European University Institute, 2013) 129.

[78] Art 3(2) TSCG.

[79] Art 5(2) Regulation 473/2013.

Table 1. Weaknesses of the original EU fiscal governance and improvements

Weakness	Original system	Improvements by the reforms	Possible additional improvements
Economic relevance of fiscal rules	Actual deficit: same limit for all Member States	Introduction of the Medium Term Objective (MTO): defined in structural terms, on a medium-term basis, and specific to each Member State to ensure the sustainability of its public finances	Distinction between productive and non-productive public investment
Quality of data and forecasts		• Additional investigation powers for Eurostat • Establishment of independent fiscal councils (IFCs)	
National ownership		• Minimum quality for the national budgetary framework • Transposition of the MTO rule into national law • Establishment of an automatic correction mechanism when fiscal rules are violated • Establishment of IFC	Establishment of a network with Commission and IFCs
EU sanction types	• Reputational • Suspension or termination of EU funds • Fines	Financial sanctions are more graduated and imposed earlier	Introduction of an additional sanction consisting in the suspension of voting right
Decision-making process for EU sanctions	• Commission • Council (QMV)	• Habilitation Commissioner for Euro • Council (RQMV)	• Better guarantee for collegiality within the Commission • More transparency for the economic criteria used by the Commission to decide to propose sanctions against the Member States • Possible more adjudicating role for the Court of Justice
Decision-making process for national sanctions	Effective deficit: same for all	National correction mechanism should be based on seven common principles proposed by the Commission	Principles may be reinforced

raise suspicion of discrimination between Member States (eg according to their size). This is all the more important given the enhanced role of the Commission resulting from the reverse qualified majority and the 'comply or explain' rules applicable in the Council. Regarding the national sanction, it is not clear how the automatic requirement will be applied in practice. In particular, it remains to be seen how and by which institution the activation or the suspension of the correction will be decided and what role will be played by the independent fiscal councils.

B. Towards more Radical Reforms

In order to ensure the sustainability of the EMU, additional reforms will probably be needed, first to complement to current governance model, and then to change the model of governance.[80]

(i) Improving Legitimacy of the Current Model of Governance

The first additional reform is to focus on legitimacy as much as on effectiveness. There is indeed a risk that the recent reforms will backfire because of their legitimacy gaps,[81] leading to a rejection by citizens of the new fiscal governance. The perception of legitimacy gaps may be exaggerated or even fuelled by national politicians willing to shift the blame of painful structural reforms on EU institutions, but in politics perception is as important as reality. The first legitimacy issue is that the fiscal rules are constraining the budgetary power of national parliaments. Such constraint exists since the adoption of the Stability and Growth Pact has become more important and visible with the recent reforms. The second legitimacy issue is the increasingly important role of the European Commission (due to the reversed qualified majority voting and the 'comply or explain' rules applicable in the Council)[82] without a parallel increase in parliamentary oversight.

The Four Presidents Report adopts a simple guiding principle that democratic control and accountability should occur at the level at which the decisions are taken.[83] However, legitimacy must be addressed more forcefully. First, the justi-

[80] See also the Communication from the Commission of 28 November 2012, 'A Blueprint for a Deep and Genuine Economic and Monetary Union' COM(2012) 777.

[81] For a description of the legitimacy gaps, see among others, R Baratta, 'Legal Issues for the "Fiscal Compact": Searching for a Mature Democratic Governance of the Euro' in B de Witte, A Héritier and A Trechsel (eds), *The Euro Crisis and the State of the European Democracy* (Florence, European University Institute, 2013) 31; and F Scharpf, 'Monetary Union, Fiscal Crisis and the Preemption of Democracy', Max Planck Institute for Study of Societies Discussion Paper 11/11 (2011).

[82] The legitimacy issue resulting for the introduction of the reverse qualified majority is also analysed by Van Aken and Artige (n 75).

[83] Report of 5 December 2012 by Van Rompuy, Barroso, Draghi and Juncker, 'Towards a Genuine Economic and Monetary Union', 13.

fication of the constitutionalization of fiscal rules and the constraint on parliaments' fiscal power must be better explained, in particular that EU constraint replaces the previous monetary constraint (risk of devaluation) existing before the common currency and aims to protect future generations by limiting the short-term bias of policymakers.

Second, dialogues between institutions should be enhanced to raise awareness of the effects of the budgetary decision between Member States, thereby facilitating the internalization of fiscal cross-country externalities. Dialogues may take different directions. They may be vertical between EU and national executives as well as between EU and national parliaments (as provided for in the interparliamentary conference set up by the TSCG). Dialogues may be diagonal between the European Parliament and national executives (as foreseen in the economic dialogue set up by the six-pack and the two-pack) as well as between EU executive and national parliaments. They may also be horizontal between national parliaments, in parallel with the well-established horizontal dialogue between national executives within the Council.

Third, the oversight of parliamentary bodies over their executives should be strengthened.[84] At the EU level, the European Parliament should be able to supervise Commission actions in economic governance. At the national level, the parliaments may, thanks to the objective analysis of the newly established fiscal councils, be able to better exercise their budgetary scrutiny and oversight.[85]

(ii) Towards a (Not So Radically) New Governance Model

The second additional reform is to complement the current governance model (decentralization and rules backed by sanctions) with other models. One option is to back the rules by a mix of sanctions (sticks) and incentives (carrots). This is the logic of the Competitiveness and Convergence Instrument mentioned in the Four Presidents Report,[86] and recently proposed by the Commission.[87] Member States that undertake structural reforms to improve their public finances in the long run, while incurring short-term costs, could receive financial incentives from the EU or the eurozone.

[84] Also in this sense, not surprisingly the European Parliament (Resolution of the European Parliament 2012/2151 of 20 November 2012 with recommendations to the Commission on the report of the Presidents of the European Council, the European Commission, the European Central Bank and the Eurogroup, 'Towards a Genuine Economic and Monetary Union', point 9); Baratta (n 81).

[85] Fasone and Griglio (n 30).

[86] Ibid 7. Also Resolution of the European Parliament 2012/2151 of 20 November 2012 with recommendations to the Commission on the report of the Presidents of the European Council, the European Commission, the European Central Bank and the Eurogroup 'Towards a Genuine Economic and Monetary Union', point 12.

[87] Communication from the Commission of 20 March 2013, The introduction of a Convergence and Competitiveness Instrument COM(2013) 165.

(iii) Towards a (Radically) New Governance Model

A more radical option would be to centralize some fiscal policies at the EMU (or EU) level as is the case in nearly all currency unions. There are different possibilities for centralizing fiscal policies. One of them is to establish a budget at EMU (or EU) level with insurance characteristics and stabilization functions in case of asymmetric shocks between the Member States.[88] Such a budget and insurance scheme may be provided for financial institutions with the establishment of a common resolution and deposit guarantee mechanism.[89] Another budget and insurance scheme may be foreseen for the labour market with the establishment of a common employment benefit scheme.[90] Another possibility would be the common issuance of eurobonds, to be guaranteed by all the participating Member States. In that regard, several possibilities have been proposed.[91] One of them is the blue bond:[92] Member States can participate in a joint eurobond up to 60 per cent of their GDP (blue bond), while debt above 60 per cent would be issued as a national bond (red bond), with a seniority of the blue bonds over the red bonds.

If those more radical proposals can be justified economically provided they are designed carefully to alleviate moral hazard between the Member States, they can only be acceptable politically with a strong sense of common purpose and an intense feeling of belonging to the same Community, what de Grauwe calls the 'deep variable'.[93] As observed by Habermas:

> If one wants to preserve the Monetary Union, it is no longer enough, given the structural imbalances between the national economies, to provide loans to over-indebted states so that each should improve its competitiveness by its own efforts. What is required is solidarity instead, a cooperative effort from a shared political perspective to promote growth and competitiveness in the euro zone as a whole. Such an effort would require Germany and several other countries to accept short and medium-term negative redistribution effects in its own longer-term self-interest, a classic example of solidarity.[94]

[88] Report of 5 December 2012 by Van Rompuy, Barroso, Draghi and Juncker, 'Towards a Genuine Economic and Monetary Union', 7; de Grauwe (n 1) 128; H Enderlein et al, *Completing the Euro: A Roadmap towards Fiscal Union in Europe* (Notre Europe, 2012) 30.

[89] See the proposals discussed for the banking union.

[90] This fund could be financed by the Member States or their national security systems and activated when one Member State faces an asymmetric macroeconomic shock leading to an increase in its short-term unemployment rate: S Dullien and F Fichtner, 'A Common Unemployment Insurance System for the Euro Area' [2013] *DIW Economic Bulletin* 9.

[91] Green Paper of the Commission of 23 November 2011 on the feasibility of introducing Stability Bonds COM(2011) 818.

[92] P De Grauwe and W Moesen, 'Gains for All: A Proposal for a Common Eurobonds' [2009] *Intereconomics*; J Delpla and J von Weizsäcker, 'The Blue Bond Proposal', Bruegel Policy Brief(2010).

[93] De Grauwe (n 1) 132.

[94] J Habermas, 'Democracy, Solidarity and the European Crisis', lecture delivered at the University of Leuven on 26 April 2013.

III. CONCLUSIONS

In 1992 EU fiscal governance was based on fiscal decentralization constrained by rules (limits of 3 per cent government deficit and 60 per cent government debt), compliance with which was monitored annually and violations of which were sanctioned (via the EDP). Financial solidarity was minimal. The euro crisis and the high level of financial instability of some Member States have shown the severe flaws of such a governance model: the fiscal rules were sometimes inappropriate and often poorly implemented. Inevitably, then, the crisis led to more financial solidarity than expected.

To remedy those flaws, EU fiscal governance has been substantially reformed by the six-pack in 2011, the TSCG in 2012 and the two-pack in 2013. Such reforms, which were probably the only politically feasible options, have improved the three components of governance: on rules, they make the fiscal objectives and limits smarter; on institutions, they improve the quality of data and forecasts needed to apply properly the rules, and ensure a better national ownership; on enforcement, they improve the design and the decision-making process of the sanctions at EU level and create an national correction mechanism. All of this can still be fine-tuned: the fiscal rules could better differentiate between productive and less productive public investment, a network of the Commission and the newly established national fiscal councils could be set up, and the decision-making process and the criteria used by the Commission in proposing the sanctions could be made more transparent.

However, more fundamental reforms are needed to ensure the sustainability of EMU. The legitimacy of the new EU surveillance and sanctions tools should be improved in several ways: explaining better the rationale for the constitutionalization of the fiscal rules, enhancing dialogue between EU and national bodies (economic dialogue, etc.) as well as among national institutions (parliament, independent fiscal councils, etc), increasing the EU parliamentary oversight where the Commission power has been enhanced. Other models of governance may also be developed. The sticks of fiscal governance (sanctions) should be complemented with carrots (financial incentives). More centralization of fiscal policy could be by with the creation of a eurozone budget to absorb asymmetric macroeconomic shocks or the issuance of common eurobonds. Those reforms may be difficult to agree today, but the risk is that the fatigue of the citizens towards the European Union, of which the economic governance is one of the most visible parts, and the rise of nationalism within the Member States, will make any reform even more difficult tomorrow.

6

Maastricht Revisited: Economic Constitutionalism, the ECB and the Bundesbank

MARIJN VAN DER SLUIS

I. INTRODUCTION

THE NEW CONSTITUTIONALIZATION of budgetary constraints represents an evolution of economic constitutionalism: the belief that it is appropriate, necessary or even sufficient to endow constitutions with economic objectives. In a way, all constitutional topics are economic, if we understand economics in a wide sense. This explains why economic constitutional law also encompasses all fields of constitutional law. Nevertheless, the focus of economic constitutionalism and economic constitutional law lies on topics that deal more directly with the economy. European integration has brought forth several such subjects, competition law and the four freedoms being the most prominent examples. The Maastricht Treaty brought a new dimension to European economic constitutional law: Economic and Monetary Union (EMU). This new dimension was not only innovative in its substance—monetary integration and limited economic and fiscal co-ordination—it was also an exercise in constitutional and institutional engineering. The European Central Bank (ECB) was created to conduct European monetary policy, independent from EU institutions and Member State governments. Securing said independence was a main feature of the Maastricht Treaty. Understanding EMU is impossible without taking into account the economic goals that it tried to achieve. The excessive deficit procedure, the no-bailout clauses and the independence of the ECB are not normative objectives by themselves, but parts of a mechanism designed to deliver economic gains: price stability and economic growth. EMU is therefore a prime example of economic constitutionalism.

The constitutionalization of budgetary restraints is not a new phenomenon, but the euro-crisis measures do give it new attributes. Avoiding excessive deficits was—of course—already an obligation under the Maastricht Treaty. The new obligations of the six-pack and the Fiscal Compact are the expanded and more elaborate versions of this earlier commitment. They show the new direction of economic constitutionalism, with a strong emphasis on national constitutional law and national commitments to further European goals. They also show a renewed belief in the capabilities of law in shaping the political and economic future of Europe. To describe the pitfalls and possibilities of this new approach, it would be very interesting to describe and analyse the developments of the fiscal restraints from the Maastricht Treaty to the present. This chapter, however, takes a different approach and focuses on the belief in constitutional law to accomplish economic objectives. It revisits the Maastricht Treaty to look once again at the position of the ECB in the EU's constitutional construct and starts with a comparison of the ECB and the Bundesbank. This comparison shows that it is the constitutionalization of EMU that is vital in explaining the unique position of the ECB. This, in turn, will show how European constitutional law has incorporated the economic objectives under EMU and what can be expected from the new developments in economic constitutionalism. Accordingly, this chapter concentrates on the Treaty of Maastricht: not because I believe subsequent developments of the euro crisis are irrelevant, to the contrary, but because it was such an important step in the evolution of economic constitutionalism. The current reliance on constitutional law to satisfy the demands of European integration cannot be understood without taking into account the particular shape of the constitutional construct, erected in Maastricht. Explaining the euro crisis and the subsequent measures through reference to the substance of the rules is not sufficient: it is the nature of these rules that tells the better part of the story.

The similarities between the Bundesbank and the ECB have been the subject of many academic texts. Mostly, these comparisons focus on the economic context or on the substance of the rules governing the ECB and the Bundesbank.[1] However, and this has received far less attention, the creation of the ECB also provides us with a legal experiment on the nature and role of EU constitutional law.[2] If the rules are, in substance, quite similar for the ECB and the Bundesbank, but different in their legal status, the following question arises: how does the nature of the rules affect their functioning? What did it mean for EMU, and for the ECB, to become part of EU constitutional law? A legal comparison between the Bundesbank and the ECB seems rather troublesome, however, because the Bundesbank was the product of fifty years of German history.[3] No institution can properly be described merely by reference to its legal framework: an institution's culture, traditions and history must always be considered. This seems

[1] F Amtenbrink, *The Democratic Accountability of Central Banks: A Comparative Study of the European Central Bank* (Portland, Hart Publishing, 1999); L Gormley and J de Haan, 'The Democratic Deficit of the European Central Bank' (1996) 21 *European Law Review* 95; J de Haan (ed), *The History of the Bundesbank: Lessons for the European Central Bank* (London, Routledge, 2000).

[2] This paper takes as a given the description of the EU treaties as the Union's 'constitutional charter'. Also see M Everson, 'The Constitutional Law of the Euro? Disciplining European Governance' in PR Beaumont and N Walker (eds), *Legal Framework of the Single European Currency* (Oxford, Hart Publishing, 1999).

[3] The comparison naturally excludes for the Bundesbank the period after 1999.

to be especially true for the Bundesbank. Having said that, the legal framework created the environment in which traditions grew, and therefore can partially explain them.[4] In other words: law matters greatly when it comes to the development of institutions.[5]

II. THE BUNDESBANK

After experiencing several periods of extreme monetary instability, German society after World War II longed for a stable currency and was fearful of possible inflation. It is thus somewhat surprising that the German Constitution (Grundgesetz, GG) does not explicitly secure the independence of the central bank to pursue price stability, but only requires that there is a Federal central bank that possesses certain competences.[6] This requirement is fulfilled by the Bundesbank Act (Bundesbankgesetz) of 1957, which created the Bundesbank and regulated its independence and mandate. With some minor limitations, the GG itself leaves much discretion to the legislature[7] to attribute or withhold competences, to organize the appointment procedure, to determine the institutional structure and to regulate the relations with the federal government.[8] The question whether independence is implicitly guaranteed by the GG has never been directly put before the Federal Constitutional Court (Bundesverfassungsger-

[4] The economics of the story of the independence of the Bundesbank are discussed in J Leaman, *The Bundesbank Myth: Towards a Critique of Central Bank Independence* (New York, Palgrave Macmillan, 2001).

[5] This presumption is criticised in H Berger, 'The Bundesbank's Path to Independence: Evidence from the 1950s' [1996] *Münchener Wirtschaftswissenschaftliche Beiträge* 1–2, 9–11. Berger states that a legal analysis of the independence is a misleading indicator. Interestingly, she infers this, partly, from the fact that the Bundesbank Law could be changed at any moment (ibid 24), in contrast to the earlier legal instruments that created the predecessor of the Bundesbank, the Bank Deutsche Länder. The criticism by Berger has been refined in further work: H Berger and J de Haan, 'A State Within the State? An Event Study on the Bundesbank (1948–1973)' (1999) 46 *Scottish Journal of Political Economy* 17, 18. A counterargument is provided in P Moser, 'Checks and Balances, and the Supply of Central Bank Independence' (1999) 43 *European Economic Review*, 1569. He argues that the legal instruments of independence matter, especially the way the legal instruments can be changed. In a system of checks and balances and hence with multiple veto-players, independence is usually more strongly entrenched.

[6] Comments by C Joerges in F Snyder (ed) *Constitutional Dimensions of European Economic Integration* (Dordrecht, Kluwer Law International, 1996) 23. Art 88 GG now reads (translated): 'Article 88 The Federation shall establish a note-issuing and currency bank as the Federal Bank. Within the framework of the European Union, its responsibilities and powers may be transferred to the European Central Bank, which is independent and committed to the overriding goal of assuring price stability.' The second sentence was added in 1992.

[7] The legislature as an institution must not be confused here with the institution of the Bundestag. Whereas the Bundesbank was not *accountable* to the Bundestag, as a result of its special status as part of the executive, it is not independent from the German legislature. See K Stern, 'The Note-Issuing Bank within the State Structure' in Deutsche Bundesbank (ed), *Fifty Years of the Deutsche Mark: Central Bank and the Currency in Germany since 1948* (Oxford, Oxford University Press, 1999) 111.

[8] See B Schmidt-Bleibtreu and F Klein, *Kommentar zum Grundgesetz*, 10th edn (München, Luchterhand, 2004) Art 88. Also see K Stern, *Das Staatsrecht der Bundesrepublik Deutschland. Bd 2 Staatsorgane, Staatsfunktionen, Finanz- und Haushaltsverfassung, Notstandverfassung*, M Sachs ed (München, Beck, 1994) 4640507.

icht, BverfG). That has not stopped the BverfG from providing ambiguous clues about its opinion on the independence of the Bundesbank.[9] In contrast, the Federal Administrative Court (Bundesverwaltungsgericht) has explicitly stated that there is no constitutional guarantee of the Bundesbank's independence.[10] Legal opinion is equally divided.[11]

The main governing bodies of the Bundesbank were the Central Bank Council (Zentralbankrat, CBC) and the Directorate (Direktorium). The latter was a body of eight members maximum (including the president), centrally nominated and appointed, and responsible for executing the decisions of the CBC, and was responsible for taking the important decisions on monetary policy. The members of the CBC include the members of the Directorate and the presidents of the Landeszentralbanken. The latter were nominated decentrally, by the *Länder*, and appointed by the federal president.[12] There is thus a strong federal element in the setup of the Bundesbank.

Article 3 of the Bundesbank Act describes the main responsibility of the Bundesbank: 'safeguarding the currency'.[13] Its competences were then found in other parts of the law and included, amongst others: issuing banknotes, conducting monetary policy, setting minimum reserve policy and acting as the bank of the federal government.[14] Furthermore, the Bundesbank was obliged to provide advice to the federal government and support its general economic policies, insofar as its own objectives allowed. The mandate of the Bundesbank, safeguarding the currency, was both internally (price stability) and externally (stable exchange rates) oriented, but decisions on external monetary policy were mainly the prerogative of the federal government. As a result, the room for manoeuvre of the Bundesbank was sharply reduced when Germany participated in an exchange rate regime, such as the European Monetary System.

Article 12 of the Bundesbank Act expressly stated that the Bundesbank was independent from instructions of the federal government in the execution of its competences. The latter did have the right to participate in meetings of the CBC and to postpone its decisions by two weeks. Although that option has officially never been invoked, decisions have sometimes been postponed after consultations.[15] Independence from parliament is a result from the Bundesbank's special status in the executive branch. The Bundestag, therefore, could not give direct

[9] BverfGE 14, 125 and BverfGE 62, 169.

[10] BverwGE 41, 354.

[11] See Stern (n 7) 144–47 and Amtenbrink (n 1) 159–64.

[12] The nominating process has remained largely apolitical, with some exceptions. See S Lohmann, 'Federalism and Central Bank Autonomy: The Politics of German Monetary Policy 1957–1992', California Institute of Technology Social Science Working Paper 994 (1996). Also see C-L Holtfrerich, 'Relations between Monetary Authorities and Governmental Institutions: The Case of Germany from the 19th Century to the Present' in G Toniolo (ed), *Central Banks' Independence in Historical Perspective* (Berlin, Walter de Gruyter, 1988) 143; R Sturm, 'The Role of the Bundesbank in German Politics' (1989) 12 *West European Politics* 1.

[13] Translation from Amtenbrink (n 1) 195.

[14] Sections 14–16 of the Bundesbank Act. Stern (n 7) 126 and Amtenbrink (n 1) 96–97.

[15] D Marsh, *The Bundesbank: The Bank that Rules Europe* (London, Heinemann, 1992) 74 and 174.

instructions or hold the members of the CBC or Directorate directly accountable. Judicial control of the Bundesbank was marginal. Bundesbank decisions were subject to administrative law and could thus be challenged in court. In practice, the judiciary was little involved in controlling the monetary policy of the Bundesbank.[16]

Naturally, this brief description of the legal context of the Bundesbank does not fully capture the position of the Bundesbank on the German political scene. To get a glimpse of the political role of the Bundesbank in German (and European) politics, it is interesting to look at the controversy that exists about the role of the Bundesbank in German reunification and European monetary integration. One side, represented by Marsh, argues that the failure of the Bundesbank to set the terms of monetary union in German reunification and the failure to stop EMU revealed the weakness of the Bundesbank.[17] After years of rising power, its success in maintaining the strength of the Deutschmark had become its weakness. First, it was the East Germans who wanted their share of the success of the Deutschmark, then it was the rest of Europe. The Bundesbank failed to protect the Deutschmark. This line of argument is countered by Heipertz, who argues that to ascribe the Bundesbank with the political power to influence these greater political movements of history, and then to say that it failed in doing so, misrepresents the character of the competences and interests of the Bundesbank. During the negotiations, 'the Bundesbank was as strong as one could possibly have expected from a central bank'.[18]

The debate reveals how far the expectations about the powers of Bundesbank have strayed from its legal foundations. The central argument by Heipertz is that it never was the function of a central bank to interfere with these inherently political developments. Marsh correctly points out how, in previous times, the Bundesbank had managed to use its mandate and competences to influence political decisions and that it failed to do so this time. These arguments also point towards another interesting feature of the Bundesbank. Whereas Heipertz based his arguments on the official statements that indicate that the Bundesbank never wanted to stop EMU and actually got what it wanted in Germany's reunification, Marsh interviewed many of the direct participants to paint a different picture.[19] Given that there is a kernel of truth in both arguments, it is revealing in that it lays bare the tactics of the Bundesbank in negotiations with the government. When it came to topics outside the remit of Bundesbank competences,

[16] Stern (n 7) 135–37.

[17] Marsh (n 15) chs 8–9.

[18] MKG Heipertz, 'How Strong Was the Bundesbank? A Case Study in the Policy-Making of German and European Monetary Union', Centre for European Policy Studies Working Document 172/2001 (2001) 20.

[19] See also P Bernholz, 'The Bundesbank and the Process of European Monetary Integration' in Deutsche Bundesbank (ed), *Fifty Years of the Deutsche Mark* (n 7) 774–76. He argues on the one hand that the Bundesbank realised the political reality of the unavoidable progress towards monetary union, and on the other hand that the Bundesbank saw most of its demands for monetary union met in the Maastricht Treaty.

the Bundesbank framed its (official) arguments so as to appeal to the German public, using its authority as 'guardian of the currency'.

Both observations are exemplars of the position of the Bundesbank within the German political system. The Bundesbank has used its monetary policy competence to exert political influence on other policy fields, most notably external monetary policy, fiscal policy[20] and wage formation,[21] and the Bundesbank actively tries to retain public support as a shield against political attacks. The interactions between Frankfurt and Bonn have been most colourfully described by Marsh, who attributes the fall of at least three chancellors to the actions of the Bundesbank. He quotes Bundesbank President Blessing after Chancellor Erhard resigned because of a conflict with the Bundesbank over expansionary fiscal policies: 'We had to use brute force to put things in order.'[22] Marsh notes how Blessing had warned against fiscal profligacy several times and had threatened—and made good on those threats—to raise interest rates. In the recession that followed, Erhard had to resign.[23] In subsequent periods of disagreement, politicians had seen how a conflict with the Bundesbank could hurt their political future and were less inclined to pick a fight. Nevertheless, when, in 1969, the Bundesbank communicated to the federal government its desire for a revaluation of the Deutschmark in the Bretton Woods system, the federal government refused. Chancellor Kiesinger opposed a revaluation, but stood little chance against the continuous actions of the Bundesbank to undermine his position. The Bundesbank knowingly exacerbated the disequilibria that made a revaluation necessary. Kiesinger continued to resist, which eventually led to the fall of his coalition. The new coalition quickly took the formal decision to revaluate the Deutschmark.[24]

Despite its political clout, the Bundesbank might not have been as politically independent as many thought. There is some evidence that in times of conflict, the monetary policy of the Bundesbank has been influenced by the government.[25] One reason why the Bundesbank might have incorporated the demands or wishes of the German government is to avoid conflict with the federal govern-

[20] For a general overview, see W Kitterer, 'Public Finance and the Central Bank' in Deutsche Bundesbank (ed), *Fifty Years of the Deutsche Mark* (n 7). Compare Leaman (n 4) chs 4–6.

[21] See eg D Soskice, 'Wage Determination: The Changing Role of Institutions in Advanced Industrialized Countries' (1990) 6 *Oxford Review of Economic Policy* 36; E Kennedy, *The Bundesbank: Germany's Central Bank in the International Monetary System* (London, Royal Institute of International Affairs, 1991) 47. Also see H Tietmeyer, 'The Bundesbank: Committed to Stability' in SF Frowen and R Pringle (eds), *Inside the Bundesbank* (London, Macmillan, 1998) 5.

[22] Marsh (n 15) 170 and 187. The three Chancellors were Erhard, Kiesinger and Schmidt.

[23] Also see Berger and De Haan (n 5) 34; Holtfrerich (n 12) 146.

[24] See Leaman (n 4) 146–47; Marsh (n 15) 188; Holtfrerich (n 12) 147. See for the influence of the Bundesbank on the negotiations on the EMS, see Kennedy (n 21) 80–81; Bernholz (n 19) 756–57.

[25] See Lohmann (n 12) 28; H Berger, *Does the Bundesbank Give Way in Conflicts with the West German Government?* (Linz, Johannes Kepler Universität Linz, 1997) 23–24; De Haan (n 1); H Berger and F Schneider, 'The Bundesbank's Reaction to Policy Conflicts' in J De Haan (ed), *The History of the Bundesbank: Lessons for the European Central Bank* (London, Routledge, 2000). But see P Maier, J-E Sturm and J de Haan, 'Political Pressure on the Bundesbank: an Empirical Investigation Using the Havrilesky Approach' (2002) 24 *Journal of Macroeconomics* 103.

ment over the best co-ordination of fiscal and monetary policy. Monetary policy is most effective when it is credible and in conformance with fiscal and economic policy, and so the Bundesbank walks a fine line between appearing independent and accommodating pressure from the government. As Marsh notes, both the Bundesbank and the government have an interest in avoiding conflict; differences of opinion are voiced behind closed doors.[26] Whether or not to give in to governmental demands might therefore not always have been a question of the best monetary policy, but a result of strategic reasoning to accomplish the goals of monetary *and* economic policy. To constitutional lawyers such interactions are not unfamiliar, because they resemble a system of checks and balances.[27] Although both actors are formally independent of each other and have different foundations of legitimation, they require each other's support to effectively accomplish the tasks they have been given. Another reason why the Bundesbank might have jeopardized its aura of independence and incorporated government demands is because it knows that its independence is only protected by ordinary law.[28] Bundesbank President Schlesinger once said: 'Our independence is dependent on our ability not to overstep our limits.'[29] If the Bundesbank were to go against the public's (or the political elite's) preferences too often, a political incentive would arise to strip the Bundesbank of its independence. The limits are thus as much defined by the legal division of competences, as by the Bundesbank's ability to persuade the public of the right course of monetary or economic policy and on the legal division of competences.

The Bundesbank's relation with the German public was an intricate one. Whereas the Bundesbank externally needed to portray itself as independent of public opinion in order to be a credible negotiator with the government and in the wage-setting process, there is plenty of evidence that public opinion was an important factor in decision-making and communication.[30] The Bundesbank was all too aware that its independence was, in the long term, dependent on broad support from both politicians and the public. As Berger and De Haan have shown, even the initial enshrinement of independence, first in 1951 for

[26] Marsh (n 15) 169 and 174. Also see Holtfrerich (n 12) 145.

[27] B Dutzler, *The European System of Central Banks: an Autonomous Actor? The Quest for an Institutional Balance in EMU* (New York, Springer, 2003) 133. Also see A Verdun, 'The Institutional Design of EMU: A Democratic Deficit?' (1998) 18 *Journal of Public Policy* 107, 116–18.

[28] On the possibility of revoking independence, see Holtfrerich (n 12) 106; Berger and Schneider (n 25) 60; Lohmann (n 12) 5; P Maier and T Knaap, 'Who Supported the Deutsche Bundesbank? An Empirical Investigation' (2002) 24 *Journal of Policy Modeling* 834; Moser (n 5) 1569–93. Both Lohmann and Moser focus on the federal nature of the German state as a guarantee of the independence of the Bundesbank. They seem to assume that the Bundesrat could hinder the repeal or amendment of the Bundesbank Act, whereas Stern is of the opinion that the Bundesrat would not be involved. See Stern (n 8) 473.

[29] As quoted in Marsh (n 15) 256.

[30] A German central banker, as quoted by Goodman in Berger and De Haan (n 5) 22: 'From 1948, we made a very deliberate policy of getting the public on our side. We attempted through all our publications and our speeches to explain our policies to the public and to convince them. By explaining everything and making a very deliberate effort, we never came to a situation where a major party has ever attempted to touch our autonomy.' Also see Amtenbrink (n 1) 177

the Bank Deutsche Länder (BDL, the predecessor of the Bundesbank) and later in 1957, was a result of public support.[31] The defeat of Chancellor Adenauer, who wanted to rein in the power of the central bankers, came only after highly public disagreements between the BDL and the Chancellor in both 1950 and 1956, in which the Chancellor had to back down, due to lack of public support. When in 1967 the Stability Act (Stabilitätsgesetz) was introduced with the aim of laying down the general economic objectives of the whole government, there were politicians who wanted to reduce the independence of the Bundesbank to better co-ordinate policies. Again, they were swimming against the tide of public opinion.[32] But not only has the legislation rested on a widespread support of the public for the independence of the Bundesbank, the Bundesbank itself has made it no secret that it has tried to engage the public on the issue of monetary policy. This, of course, includes a communication strategy to warn the public against inflation, but it also meant that in conflicts with the government, the Bundesbank acted strategically to avoid getting blamed for either a recession or high inflation.[33] Support by the public and by special interest groups have been found to be explanatory factors for the monetary policy of the Bundesbank, suggesting that it has kept a close eye on these societal actors.[34] Lohmann also found that whether or not the Bundesbank would give in to demands of the government was indeed a function of public support, but not for the Bundesbank, but for the government.[35] The more popular the government, the less inclined the Bundesbank was to go against it.

III. THE ECB (PRE-CRISIS)

The exercise of monetary policy at the European level after the introduction of the euro required the creation of a new European body, the ECB. National central banks continued to exist and retained their legal personality, but they became part of the European System of Central Banks (ESCB), which is governed by the decision-making bodies of the ECB. European monetary policy is thus decided upon centrally, but executed in a decentralized manner. The competence of the ECB to set monetary policy is flanked by other competences to secure the effectiveness of that policy. The Council, the Commission and the European

[31] Berger and De Haan (n 5) 23–27; J Bibow, 'On the Origin and Rise of Central Bank Independence in West Germany' (2009) 16 *European Journal of the History of Economic Thought* 155, 164 and 181. Bibow describes the political game, played by the BDL, during the transition from Allied rule to secure independence. Nevertheless, he mentions public support in the early 1950s as a factor for creating BDL independence, which was then carried over to the Bundesbank.

[32] Holtfrerich (n 12) 149. Also see Sturm (n 12) 3.

[33] For the conflicts between the BDL/Bundesbank and the federal government in 1951, 1956 and 1961, see Berger (n 5). For conflicts in 1959, 1966, 1969 and 1972, see Holtfrerich (n 12). For the conflict in 1980, see Kennedy (n 21) 40–54. Also see Marsh (n 15) 76.

[34] Maier and Knaap (n 28). Also see Maier, Sturm and De Haan (n 25) on political pressure and support from the financial sector.

[35] Lohmann (n 12) 5.

Parliament have supportive roles with regards to the technicalities of the execution of monetary policy within the eurozone, through the adoption of secondary legislation. Externally, the Council may conclude international agreements on exchange rate systems, as well as formulate general orientations in the absence of such a system, without prejudice to the objective of the ESCB to maintain price stability.[36] Given that it is unlikely that the euro will become part of an exchange rate regime and that the ECB can easily discard the general orientations (whilst still being bound by them), external monetary policy is a lot less constrained for the ECB than for the Bundesbank. The external representation of the euro area in international organizations is a rather complicated matter, due to the overlay of economic and monetary policy, the ambiguous position of the EU in the international community and the resistance of some Member States, resulting in a less than uniform representation.[37]

The decision-making bodies of the ECB are the Governing Council and the Executive Board. The latter consists of six members, including the president and the vice-president. The procedure for their appointment is regulated in the EU treaties, with the final decision reserved for the heads of state of the governments of the participating Member States, on recommendation of the Council, after consulting with the European Parliament. In practice, certain seats are reserved for the bigger eurozone countries, with the rest of the seats rotating amongst the other countries.[38] The Governing Council consists of the members of the Executive Board and the governors of the central banks of the participating Member States of the euro. The latter are appointed according to national procedures.[39] The division of labour between the Executive Board and the Governing Council is regulated in the Statute, as are the voting modalities of both bodies.[40]

Compared to other central banks, the ECB has been granted a high degree of independence in setting monetary policy. If the four most common indicators for independence of a central bank (institutional, functional, personal, financial) are taken into consideration, the ECB scores rather high on all four counts. Also the economic branch of EMU is, in part, concerned with the independence of the ECB, albeit not in the legal, but in the economic-political sense. The prohibition on the monetary financing of government debts (which is located in TFEU in the chapter on 'Economic Policy') is an obvious example. If the ECB could directly buy government bonds, it might be pressured by governments to do so, thereby endangering its independent decision-making. The prohibition (with its obvious loophole that allows the buying of government bonds on the

[36] Formerly Art 109 EC Treaty, now in part in Art 219 TFEU.

[37] R Smits, 'International Representation of Europe in the Area of Economic and Monetary Union: Legal Issues and Practice in the First Ten Years of the Euro' (2009) 2 *Euredia* 297.

[38] This created a problem when Mario Draghi was appointed President, as there were two Italians on the Executive Board. Lorenzo Bini Smaghi resigned after strong political pressure, to allow for the appointment of a French central banker to the Executive Board.

[39] Governors of national central banks shall be appointed for a period of at least five years. Art 14 Statute of the ESCB and of the ECB.

[40] Arts 10–13 Statute of the ESCB and of the ECB.

secondary market) thus serves the purpose of protecting ECB independence. In a similar vein, the excessive deficit procedure in the Maastricht Treaty, the Stability and Growth Pact, and more recently, the six-pack, the two-pack and the Fiscal Compact, also partially serve the function of protecting the independence of the ECB by ensuring that—or at least trying to ensure that—Member States will not entertain unsustainable deficits and debts, which might have to be 'monetarized' by the ECB. As noted, the word 'independence' has a different meaning in this context. Here it does not refer to the ability of the ECB to take decisions without interference from other actors, but to the dominance of monetary policy over fiscal policy.[41] In this sense, the independence of the ECB is restricted if the fiscal policymakers can create such circumstances that would force the ECB to take actions it would—in other circumstances—prefer not to take. This does not mean that the decision-makers are unduly influenced or that it is irrational to take such a decision. It only means that fiscal policy has created a situation in which the ECB feels obliged to act.

What sets the ECB apart from other independent central banks is the fact that its independence is regulated in detail in the EU treaties and thereby constitutionalized. This makes the relations the ECB has with other institutions and players in the EU radically different from the interactions between the Bundesbank and the German body politic.

With regards to economic policymakers, there is no central, Europeanised economic decision-maker. The ECB has no economic policy partner.[42] Although this is, of course, a result of the particular form of EMU, it is of importance for the constitutional position of the ECB. In Germany, the independent exercise of monetary policy was carved out of the general responsibility of the government for economic policy (in the broad sense). Interactions between the Bundesbank and the government were a game of equals.[43] Both institutions have their domain of influence, but recognise the existence and functions of the other. The position of the ECB in the Union's constitutional construct is therefore relevant, not in the sense that it has a strongly enshrined legal position, but in that it is the only economic player with such a position. With equal partners and a development of monetary and economic policy side-by-side, there is the assumption of an ongoing dialogue. This was, at least, what the German Minister of Economics Erhard had in mind when he defended Bundesbank independence from attacks by Chancellor Adenauer.[44]

Even if the co-ordination of Member States' economic policies can be regarded

[41] J Yiangou, M O'keeffe and G Glöckler, "Tough Love': How the ECB's Monetary Financing Prohibition Pushes Deeper Euro Area Integration' (2013) 35 *Journal of European Integration* 223.

[42] G Majone, 'Rethinking European Integration after the Debt Crisis', University College London Working Paper 3/2012 (2012) 14–16: I exclude the Eurogroup because it has not formal decision-making power.

[43] There is a difference from a strictly legal perspective. The Bundesbank is not a *Verfassungsorgan*, but another high federal body. This difference is not relevant in relation to the exercise of monetary and econonomic competences, as described above. See Stern (n 7).

[44] Bibow (n 31) 179.

as European economic policy, there is no viable partner for the economic/monetary debate that characterized the relation between the Bundesbank and the German government because of the fragmented nature of the process of co-ordination. For the ECB, not only is there no such partner, but all EU institutions and Member State governments are forbidden from trying to influence the ECB decision-makers. There is no European government or European finance ministry.[45] Naturally, one may expect the ECB to create and maintain constructive relationships with all the eurozone Member States, especially the bigger Member States. Nonetheless, such interactions are of a fundamentally different nature to the interactions between, for example, the Bundesbank and the German Federal Government: individual Member States cannot sway economic policy in the eurozone to such an extent as to force the ECB to change its monetary policy, or the other way around. Monetary policy is to a very large extent to be set for the entire eurozone. Monetary policy in a single currency area can hardly be differentiated. As a consequence, the ECB cannot credibly use its monetary policy to demand an individual Member State change its fiscal policy, because that Member State knows the ECB has to set monetary policy for the entire eurozone.

One of the initial complaints about the Bundesbank's independence was its undemocratic character. Chancellor Adenauer even stated that it would be unconstitutional.[46] Similar complaints have been voiced for the ECB.[47] To counter this problem, much emphasis is placed on the role of the European Parliament in holding the ECB accountable.[48] At first glance, the relation between the ECB and the European Parliament seems to reflect an improved form of interaction, compared to the relation between the Bundesbank and the Bundestag, the latter being almost non-existent in day-to-day politics.[49] This is misleading, because of the strong, but indirect, democratic legitimacy of the German government. In effect, the Bundesbank's interaction and constant negotiation with the government provided for a better form of accountability than the European Parliament can, given the current shape and nature of EMU. The accountability relationship between the European Parliament and the ECB is flawed, due to the constitutionally enshrined competences of both institutions. Without going into much detail, it can furthermore be expected that parliaments are in an institutionally weak position to hold a central bank accountable. Monetary policy is a highly technical field of policy and heavily intertwined with other aspects of economic policy. Given the dominance of the executive in economic policy and a general lack of expertise in parliament, the latter is a second-best

[45] Majone (n 42) 14. The term 'institutional loneliness' is from Padoa-Schioppa, as quoted in F Torres, 'The EMU's Legitimacy and the ECB as a Strategic Political Player in the Crisis Context' (2013) 35 *Journal of European Integration* 287, 294.

[46] Bibow (n 31) 181.

[47] See eg Gormley and De Haan (n 1); P Brentford, 'Constitutional Aspects of the Independence of the European Central Bank' (1998) 47 *International & Comparative Law Quarterly* 75.

[48] Gormley and De Haan (n 1) call the European Parliament the 'appropriate body' for holding the ECB accountable.

[49] Amtenbrink (n 1) 304.

candidate to ensure accountability from a comparative point of view. This holds true for the European Parliament. It has no active role in the co-ordination of national economic policies and consequently lacks the economic information and bargaining position to hold a meaningful debate with the ECB. Moreover, the tools available for the European Parliament to hold the ECB accountable are weak, not least because the European Parliament cannot, in any way, sanction the ECB or dictate its policy.[50] The ECB merely has the duty to provide a report on its activities, and the president of the ECB has a duty to show up in the European Parliament. He may be asked questions, but he is under no obligation to provide substantive answers. The European Parliament's role in the appointment procedure of the members of the decision-making bodies of the ECB is as close to non-existent as possible. This would not be problematic if the EP had the ability to give itself the competence, through secondary legislation, to sanction the ECB. The mere threat of legislative change might in that case be enough to create a true relationship of accountability, as is the case in the relationship between the Federal Reserve Bank and the US Congress.[51] The exhaustive constitutionalization of the marginal relationship between the European Parliament and the ECB restricts such a possibility. Put simply, the ECB has nothing to fear from the European Parliament. The fact that intricate interactions exist between the ECB and the European Parliament, or that both the ECB and the European Parliament have dubbed their interactions a 'monetary dialogue', does not counter the central claim that the European Parliament is powerless with regards to the monetary policy of the ECB. One can hardly expect a dialogue if one of the two partners is obliged to refrain from trying to influence the other. Hence, it is exactly because of the powerlessness of the European Parliament that the ECB is willing to indulge such interactions. It gives it an aura of democratic legitimacy, whilst allowing it to avoid external influence.

In his work on the democratic accountability of central banks, Amtenbrink posed the question whether democratic accountability and independence of a central bank are mutually exclusive. He argues that that is not necessarily the case: 'It makes sense to remove monetary policy from short-term political consideration, but at the end of the day it is the electorate which must have the basic choice between different alternatives.'[52] This leaves open the question through which process the electorate and its representatives can make this choice between different alternatives. Should it be through ordinary law (secondary legislation) or through constitutional law (EU primary law)? And more importantly, what are the determining factors in deciding this question? In other words, what kinds of arguments are acceptable in this debate? The difficult relation of accountability between the ECB and its subjects—the eurozone peoples—must be explained as resulting from the position of the ECB in the EU treaties. Whereas the legitimacy of the Bundesbank was derived continuously from the Bundesbank Act

[50] Gormley and De Haan (n 1) 108.
[51] Ibid 109. Also see Amtenbrink (n 1) 287.
[52] Amtenbrink (n 1) 380 and 59–61.

of 1957—which the German legislator could change at any time—the legitimacy of the ECB is of a different character. The EU treaties derive their legitimacy from the ratification of all Member States in accordance with their constitutional requirements. This creates, in theory at least, a high level of democratic legitimacy, but with a limited shelf-life.

Whereas the decision-making by the ECB is to a large extent shielded from political influence, the institution is still bound by the rule of law. The argument here focuses on two elements of the basic agreement concerning the establishment of the ECB: the independence and its mandate. As Issing (a former member of the ECB Executive Board) has pointed out, these two elements are 'mutually dependent'.[53] They are two sides of the same coin. Setting the priorities of monetary policy is a genuinely political decision and therefore ought not to be taken by an independent organization. Hence, in the Maastricht Treaty the goal of a Europeanized monetary policy was set: maintaining price stability. The ECB was given independence in order to secure this goal and it was the consensus at the time that *only* an independent central bank could fulfil that goal. Therefore, independence requires a strict mandate and the mandate in the Maastricht Treaty required independence. And this is where the CJEU comes in. As noted above, the other institutions of the EU are prevented from interfering with ECB policy because of the prohibition on trying to influence the ECB, the lack of centralized economic policy and the overall constitutional enshrinement of the institutional relations. As a result, it falls to the CJEU to determine the legal meaning of the independence of the ECB and the limitations on the exercises of its competences, most notably the mandate. With regards to the independence of the ECB, the CJEU is in a fairly good position to assess and protect it.[54] Even before the Maastricht Treaty, the CJEU had been active in protecting and sometimes redrawing the lines of institutional balance. As long ago as *Meroni*, in 1958, the Court showed that it was willing to intervene in the way in which institutions and bodies exercise (in this case through delegation) their competences. The struggle of the European Parliament for its place amongst the European institutions was, in no small part, fought before the CJEU.[55] The ECB lacks the general qualification to bring cases to the Court on the basis of a treaty infringement, but it may do so to protect its prerogatives.[56] This certainly includes possible intrusions into the independence of the ECB (and of the national central banks in the ESCB).[57] In such cases, it is up to the CJEU

[53] O Issing, *The Birth of the Euro*, trans N Hulbert (Cambridge, Cambridge University Press, 2008) 58. Also see European Central Bank, 'The ECB's Relations with European Union Institutions and Bodies—Trends and Prospects' [January 2010] *ECB Monthly Bulletin* 73.

[54] Case C-11/00 *Commission v ECB* [2003] ECR I-7147.

[55] Dutzler (n 27) 134–40.

[56] Formerly Art 173 EC Treaty (now Art 263 TFEU) and Art 35 of the Statute of the ESCB and of the ECB. See P Craig, 'EMU, the European Central Bank and Judicial Review' in PR Beaumont and N Walker (eds), *Legal Framework of the Single European Currency* (Oxford, Hart Publishing, 1999).

[57] Formerly Art 180(d) EC Treaty (now Art 271(d) TFEU). R Smits, *The European Central Bank: Institutional Aspects* (The Hague, Kluwer Law International, 1997) 109. Also see Craig (n 56) 113.

to decide on the scope and goal of central bank independence. The Court also plays a significant role as regards the personal independence of the members of the decision-making bodies of the ECB. Members of the Executive Board can be compulsorily retired only by the CJEU, and removal of a national governor can be directly appealed to the Court.[58]

The possibilities for the CJEU to guard and/or limit the independence of the ECB are disconnected from its ability to effectively control the exercise of competences by the ECB in light of its mandate, for three reasons. Firstly, the mandate of maintaining price stability is conceptually weak in the sense that it provides few easy clues for the Court to assess the conduct of the ECB. Although 'maintaining price stability' is a more precise concept than the German mandate for the Bundesbank (safeguarding the currency because it more clearly refers to the internal value of the currency), it still leaves much room to the ECB to choose what it thinks it should mean. Smits refers to the supposedly limitless discretion of the ECB to determine the goal of monetary policy as 'auto-interpretation'.[59] The only real clue to its meaning is that both inflation and deflation should be prevented. There are good economic reasons to fear deflation more than inflation, legitimating the ECB's current interpretation of its mandate as aiming for inflation below, or close to, 2 per cent in the medium term,[60] but there is nothing in the EU Treaties that would suggest that, for example, a goal of 3 per cent inflation would not also fall under its mandate. The fact that the mandate is vague is not the biggest problem: it is also inherently forward-looking and therefore practically impossible to enforce. This becomes clear when the relation between the primary mandate and secondary mandate is discussed. Besides the objective of maintaining price stability, the ECB (as part of the ESCB) is bound by a multitude of other objectives. Without prejudice to the primary objective of maintaining price stability, the ESCB is obligated to support the general economic policies of the EU. The ESCB is furthermore obligated to act in accordance with the principles of an open market economy and free competition.[61] The activities of the EU in the field of economic and monetary policy should also comply with the principles of stable prices, sound public finances and monetary conditions, and a sustainable balance of payments. The general objectives of EU are also applicable to the ECB, such as a high level of employment, the quality of life and economic and social cohesion.[62] To determine the relation between the primary and secondary objectives, it is paramount to evaluate the particular nature of the primary objective. What is meant exactly by 'maintaining price stability'? Economic theory guides the interpretation here. When economists and

[58] Arts 11.4 and 14.2 Statute of the ESCB and of the ECB.

[59] Smits (n 57) 186.

[60] Decision of the Governing Council of the European Central Bank of 13 October 1998: 'Price stability shall be defined as a year-on-year increase in the Harmonised Index of Consumer Prices (HICP) for the euro area of below 2%.' The phrase 'or close to' was added later.

[61] Formerly Art 105 EC Treaty, now Art 127 TFEU.

[62] C Zilioli and M Selmayr, *The Law of the European Central Bank* (Oxford, Hart Publishing, 2001) 35.

central banks are concerned with inflation, they generally mean future inflation.[63] Monetary policy cannot—or at least should not—be concerned with offsetting the negative effects of past inflation, but with the expectations of future inflation. The primary objective of the ECB clearly reflects this by emphasizing that price stability must be *maintained*.[64] The primary objective of the ECB is never fulfilled: inflation might be just around the corner. As a result, the obligation to support the general economic policies of the EU without prejudice to the primary objective is quite insubstantial. The secondary objective can hardly ever play a role in limiting the discretion of the ECB to set monetary policy because the primary objective is never achieved.[65] The inherently forward-looking nature of the mandate also makes it difficult to apply as a legal standard for reviewing the actions of the ECB.

Secondly, the exercise of monetary competences is a rather technical discipline, one in which the CJEU will be hesitant to intervene. Smits expected that the Court would apply similar restraint in assessing the actions of the ECB as it does to economic policy actions by other institutions, or even more so, because of the independence of the ECB.[66] However, it would be inappropriate to compare the ECB in this sense with the other institutions, and their discretion to set economic policy. For those institutions, judicial control comes only after political control; with almost all actors of the EU being responsible (in some way) to a democratically elected body. For the ECB, that political accountability is lacking, thereby changing the role of the judiciary.[67] An example shows the difficulty the CJEU faces in using the mandate of price stability to review the actions of the ECB. As mentioned, the EU treaties prohibit the buying of government bonds on the primary market, but do not prohibit buying them on the secondary markets. Many have argued that it would also be illegal for the ECB to buy bonds on the secondary markets, if the goal is indirectly to bail out a Member State.[68] Hence, were the issue to come before the CJEU, the judges

[63] Issing (n 53) 65.

[64] But see Smits (n 57) 184.

[65] For the relationship between inflation and employment and the role of the ECB, see Issing (n 53) 65. Dutzler states that only the ECB can decide whether to pursue its second objective. Dutzler (n 27) 207.

[66] Smits (n 57) 110. Smits sees a role for the Court in 'determining whether the level of price stability achieved is within the limits of the law'. The focus by Smits is thus on the achieved level, not on future levels of inflation. Such an analysis is, I believe, incongruent with the treaties, which are inherently forward looking. Also see Dutzler (n 27) 113. She makes a similar mistake, saying that the 'obligation to maintain price stability is not a justiciable benchmark, as the ECB's acts are not illegal if its objective is not fully met'. Craig (n 56) 111 expects the CJEU to scrutinize actions of institutions 'less intensively where the subject matter involves complex economic determinations'.

[67] For a similar argument, but a very different context, see SP Croley and JH Jackson, 'WTO Dispute Procedures, Standard of Review, and Deference to National Governments' (1996) 90 *American Journal of International Law* 193, 207–09 about whether the level and structure of deference to administrative agencies in the US is also appropriate for the WTO. They argue that, since the administrative agencies are embedded in a constitutional, democratic environment, deference is due. In case of the WTO, such a democratic embedding (to the WTO community as a whole) was lacking and hence a different level of deference to national governments is appropriate.

[68] Not in the least the Bundesverfassungsgericht. BverfG, 2 BvR 1390/12.

would have to assess the credibility of the claim by the ECB that the bond-buying actually serves the purpose of maintaining price stability. To do so, it would have to analyse the effects, intents and alternatives of monetary policy—a highly contentious task, from which the judges are likely to shy away.

Thirdly, only a limited number of actors have the possibility to challenge acts by the ECB that violate its mandate.[69] Individuals will rarely have standing before the CJEU to pursue a complaint against the ECB, and the other EU institutions will lack incentives to do so, at least in case of a crisis in which the ECB is the only institution capable of acting forcefully.

To conclude the comparison: the position of the ECB vis-à-vis other actors in the EU is entirely different from the relations the Bundesbank had with the German body politic. The difference between the two is mainly due to the different nature of the legal instruments that regulate their independence. The difference is then amplified by the particular setup of EMU in which economic policy remains decentralised, as a result of which no economic government could function as a counterweight to the ECB.

IV. THE ECB (POST-CRISIS?)[70]

The analysis above has highlighted the factors that determined the position of the ECB in relation to the other EU players: the institutions and the Member States. Now follows a brief and non-exhaustive summary of the developments of the euro crisis that have significantly affected the position of the ECB, and which will consequently affect the way in which the budgetary restraints function. Firstly, it is important to reiterate that before the crisis the ECB had few options to influence policy on the Member State level, both in terms of competences (it was not involved in the excessive deficit procedure) and in terms of the dynamics of monetary and fiscal policy (it did not have the bargaining power in relation to individual Member States to coerce them). The crisis has provided the ECB with more options to differentiate its policies for the different Member States in the eurozone, thereby changing its relationship with the individual Member States.[71] The ECB has bought, in substantial amounts, government bonds of Member States that were in financial trouble. Although these purchases occurred on the secondary market, since directly buying them on the primary market is forbidden, this has provided the ECB with leverage over the governments of these Member States. Buying government bonds on the secondary market lowers the interest rates at which governments can borrow. These purchases by the ECB also reduce the risk of a downward spiral, where the interest rate

[69] Craig (n 56) 103.

[70] The role of the ECB in the euro crisis is described in more detail in the next chapter by Prof Baroncelli.

[71] The ECB already had the legal capacity to buy government bonds before the crisis, but only started using it on a large scale during the crisis.

increases, reducing the sustainability of government finances, thereby increasing the interest rates. Although anecdotal, the letter sent to the Italian government in August 2011 by the ECB, urging it to implement a 'golden rule' in its constitution, proves that the ECB is no longer afraid of interfering with the domestic politics of Member States. The deferential reaction of the Italian government at that time shows the strength of the voice of the ECB.[72]

Secondly, representatives of the ECB had to appear in court to defend the legality of Outright Monetary Transactions (OMT), although in a different court than many considered opportune: the German BVerfG. The OMT is a programme that promises to buy government bonds of countries that have also asked the ESM for assistance, and are therefore receiving aid 'under strict conditionality'. The case before the BVerfG is, amongst other things, about whether the ECB acts ultra vires.[73] Naturally, it has been controversial whether the BverfG is the appropriate forum to discuss such matters.[74] However, there is a case before the CJEU that involves a rather similar question, yet it is likely to fail the test of admissibility.[75] Leaving aside whether the BverfG ought to refer the question to the CJEU, the relevant fact here is that *a* court is examining the boundaries of the discretion of the ECB to act, thereby enforcing the original 'constitutional agreement' of the Maastricht Treaty.

Thirdly, the steps being taken to establish a 'banking union' will bring the ECB in closer contact with the EU legislature and into the political arena. A 'firewall' is supposed to protect decision-making in monetary policy from pressure from, and on, the prudential supervisor, but already the fact that prudential supervision is exercised in close proximity to monetary policy will alter the current institutional landscape. Although the relationship between the ECB and the other actors in the EU in this construction will still be quite different from the 'normal' relationship between a central bank and its Ministry of Finance, the setup of the banking union through secondary legislation is a step towards a different kind of accountability of the ECB.

Fourthly, the reinforcement of the rules on national budgetary deficits can be seen as an attempt to reinstate the dominance of monetary policy over fiscal policy.[76] By strengthening the rules and increasing their enforceability on budgetary deficits and limiting the discretion Member States have in setting economic policy, the chances that the ECB will be forced to use its monetary tools to save the euro (if the underlying presumptions of economic growth hold, that is) are

[72] See the statement of former Italian Prime Minister, M Monti on 9 May 2013: www.stateoftheunion.eui.eu.

[73] At the time of writing, no decision had been announced. For an account of the proceedings, see M Steinbeis, 'Die EZB vor dem Bundesverfassungsgericht', Verfassungsblog, 11 June 2013, www.verfassungsblog.de/de/die-ezb-vor-dem-bundesverfassungsgericht-teil-1.

[74] C Eckes, 'To Rule or Not to Rule? Should the German Constitutional Court Have the Last Word in the Eurocrisis?', ACELG Blog, 18 June 2013, www.acelg.blogactiv.eu/2013/06/18/to-rule-or-not-to-rule-should-the-german-constitutional-court-have-the-last-word-in-the-eurocrisis.

[75] Case T-492/12 *Von Storch and Others v ECB*, nyd.

[76] Yiangou, O'Keeffe and Glöckler (n 41).

reduced. From this perspective, the independence of the ECB during the crisis was ambiguous. On the one hand, it was hailed as the only institution capable of acting forcefully, and ECB President Draghi was the man of the hour. On the other hand, monetary policy during the crisis, including OMT, can be seen as the defeat of independent central banking in the EU. Monetary policy in the crisis was forced to respond to the situation created by fiscal and economic policy. Fiscal policy dominated monetary policy.

V. CONCLUSIONS—ON ECONOMIC CONSTITUTIONALISM

The focus of this chapter was on the Treaty of the Maastricht, not on the euro crisis. Instead of showing the peculiar nature of the institution of the ECB *in or after* the crisis, this chapter aimed to show how fundamental characteristics of the EU's constitutional construct have allowed the ECB to take on such an idiosyncratic role. My argument is that the separation between the economic and monetary branches of the EU and the detailed constitutionalization of the position of the ECB vis-à-vis the other public actors on the European level contributed to the 'institutional loneliness' of the ECB. By artificially severing the ties between economic and monetary policy, there is no counterweight to keep the ECB in check. No institution can fill this gap, due to the detailed regulation of the independence of the ECB in the EU treaties.

What does the position of the ECB in the EU's constitutional construct teach us about economic constitutionalism? I argue that three lessons are of value here. Firstly, it is possible to successfully construct new institutions through treaty amendment. Many doubted whether it was possible to create a European Central Bank that would be just as independent as the Bundesbank. If the 'myth of the Bundesbank' is punctured and its operations objectively assessed, it was not significantly more independent than the ECB is now. The institutional engineering of the Maastricht Treaty has—in this sense—succeeded, in no small part due to the strength of EU constitutional law. Secondly, limiting the discretion of economic (in the wider sense, thus including monetary and fiscal) policymakers through ambiguous legal mandates or prohibitions is likely to be unsuccessful. European constitutional law is doctrinally not equipped to deal with questions of economic policy of this kind. Relying on courts to enforce the (constitutional) prohibitions of EMU is naïve, because of the enormous financial and political pressures that exist within the system. If new limits or mandates are introduced, the broader implications for the constitutional framework must be assessed. Pressure to comply should be built into the structure and enforcement should not be reliant only on the strength of the rule of law. Thirdly, using constitutional law to accomplish economic objectives raises, almost by definition, questions of democratic legitimacy. Although constitutions serve multiple functions or roles, they are always counter-majoritarian, and thus, in a way, undemocratic. Although, of course, certain topics are of such importance that they ought to be outside the scope of majoritarian decision-making, it remains doubtful whether economic topics are amongst these. Even before the question of how economic topics can be integrated into constitutional law, the question must be asked whether the principle of democracy would permit such a turn of events.

7

The Independence of the ECB after the Economic Crisis

STEFANIA BARONCELLI

I. INTRODUCTION

UNDER THE MAASTRICHT Treaty, the European Central Bank (ECB) was charged with the primary goal of ensuring price stability. This objective has been enshrined in primary law, and has been identified with the maintenance of a low rate of inflation, which has in turn been defined by the ECB itself as 'below 2 per cent of the Harmonised Index of Consumer Prices'.[1] This definition is a clear indication of the discretion enjoyed by the ECB in interpreting its mandate and makes it clear that not only inflation above 2 per cent, but also deflation (identified in a decline of price level) in the eurozone is inconsistent with the concept of price stability.[2] The possibility of a deflationary spiral, although theoretically possible when the European Monetary Union (EMU) was established, has only recently emerged as a highly probable consequence of the financial crisis, due to the ECB's tight monetary policy.[3] Indeed, to define the concept of 'price stability' and the source of such a definition is not a pointless theoretical exercise, as the actions carried out by the central bank in order to save the euro may be legitimized on this basis, thereby establishing the outer limits of the ECB's powers. Indeed, the definition of 'price stability' may be used as a basis for inferring whether the ECB has exceeded its mandate acting ultra vires.

During the initial part of the economic and financial crisis, the ECB took a rather passive approach and refused to adopt more aggressive measures in order

[1] The concept of price stability was already defined by the Governing Council of the ECB when it started to function. According to the decision of 13 October 1998 'Price stability is defined as a year-on-year increase in the Harmonised Index of Consumer Prices (HICP) for the euro area of below 2%'.

[2] M van der Sluis, 'Maastricht Revisited: Economic Constitutionalism, the ECB and the Bundesbank', Chapter 6 in this book.

[3] H Schmieding, *The Economist*, 17 June 2013. According to *The Economist*, in the wake of the post-Lehman recession, the Federal Reserve and the Bank of England have bought bonds worth 19% and 25% of their country's GDP, respectively. Asset purchases by the European Central Bank remain at only 3% of GDP.

to limit the damage caused by flaws inherent within the EMU system, which was threatening the entire European construction. However, subsequently, after the crisis had spread throughout Europe, it changed its attitude and became the 'defender' of European integration. In fact, it emerged as the only EU institution that was capable of reassuring the financial markets. Moreover, it also proved to be capable of mitigating the antagonisms between the various groups of states, identified as the creditors (first and foremost Germany, but also other smaller states such as Finland and the Netherlands), and the debtors (mainly Ireland and Spain, but also other states), due to their different economic conditions and priorities. However, this growing role of the ECB as an institution within the European context has given rise to mounting criticism from academics, media and politicians, who stress that there is no clear legal basis in the EU treaties. This negative attitude also resulted in a challenge before the German Constitutional Court of the measures taken by the ECB in relation to the sovereign debt crisis, which has yet to be decided.[4] According to this line of thought, the new 'activist' ECB implies a rejection or, at least, a silent redefinition of the model agreed upon in Maastricht. With the future creation of the European Banking Union, the role of the ECB is due to grow even further. What repercussions will this process have on the governance of the ECB and its independence? Will this encroach upon the original tasks of the ECB?

After highlighting the concept of the independence of the ECB as linked to the concept of 'price stability' along with its evolution over the years (Section II), we shall analyse how it has been stretched during the current economic and financial crisis, following the ECB's acquisition of a new central role within the EU system with the adoption of unconventional measures (eg Outright Monetary Transactions (OMT)) (Section III) and the establishment of the European Banking Union (Section IV). Finally, some conclusions will be drawn regarding the repercussions of these developments on the independence of the ECB and its legitimacy (Section V).

II. THE REASONS UNDERPINNING CENTRAL BANK INDEPENDENCE

The most important institutional feature of the ECB as a legal entity is its independence. This is a multifaceted concept, which includes an institutional dimension—entailing longer appointments of the members of its board and their protection from removal on political grounds—and a budgetary guarantee. In addition to these, which are granted by the EU treaties, a functional independence has been acknowledged to the ECB, consisting in the power to pursue its objectives free from political pressures. As stated above, this objective is laid down by Article 127 TFEU as the goal of price stability; once this objective has

[4] In the case of the 'ESM/EZB' principal proceedings, the Second Senate of the Federal Constitutional Court conducted an oral hearing on 11 and 12 June 2013.

been achieved, the European System of Central Banks (ESCB) shall support the general economic policies in the EU, in order to contribute to the attainment of the objectives of the EU as laid down by Article 3 of the Treaty on European Union (TEU). While the main goal of independence is to keep politics out of the decision-making at the ECB, it also ensures that the balance of powers between the Member States as agreed in the Maastricht Treaty and reflected in the rules governing ECB Governing Council decision-making remains unchanged.

While Germany and other smaller European countries such as the Netherlands were accustomed to having a central bank that is independent from the government, others such as France, the United Kingdom or Italy operated centralized systems where monetary policy is managed by their respective treasuries and, ultimately, by the government.[5] Central banks in these countries used to respond to the short-term requirements of governments, which were identified with different policy objectives, depending on the necessities of the day.

With the creation of the ECB by the Maastricht Treaty, the countries participating in EMU made a decisive step by acknowledging the model of an independent central bank charged with a single objective. This decision was based predominantly on the German Bundesbank model, although this bank enjoys less autonomy than the ECB, as it is fully integrated into the constitutional system of checks and balances established by the Federal Constitution. The reasons behind the adoption of such a model in Germany derive from the collective belief expressed by the elite, the main political parties and the population at large that a prosperous economic and social system is based on a series of legal and economic principles. Such beliefs, including the concept of the social market economy enshrined in the German Constitution, have been influenced by ordoliberal ideas which were already being disseminated in Germany by economic scholars at the time the Federal Republic of Germany was founded.[6]

Ordoliberalism differs from other schools of liberalism such as the Anglo-Saxon neoliberalism because it emphasizes the prevention of cartels and monopolies. In addition, it opposes intervention in the normal course of the economy. For instance, it rejects the idea that monetary or fiscal policies can be used to stabilize the business cycle during an economic crisis.[7] Ordoliberal ideas were thus reflected in the legislation adopted after the World War II and until the end of 1960s, which limited competition and regulated the Bundesbank, creating an environment that facilitated Germany's reconstruction and the rapid increase in living standards. These ideas remained within the people's minds as a cultural legacy, although ordoliberalism was no longer an important school of thought. In fact, they still play an important role in the attitude shown by Germany towards

[5] For a comparison between the Bundesbank and the ECB from an institutional point of view, see van der Sluis (n 2).

[6] Art 20 of the German Constitution: 'Die Bundesrepublik Deutschland ist ein demokratischer und sozialer Bundesstaat'.

[7] See S Dullien and U Guerot, 'The Long Shadow of Ordoliberalism: Germany's Approach to the Euro crisis', www.ecfr.eu/page/-/ECFR49_GERMANY_BRIEF_AW.pdf.

the European construction.[8] This is especially true for the euro crisis, as such attitudes influence the views expressed not only by the Bundesbank, but also by the main political parties such as the CDU led by Angela Merkel, the CSU, the liberals (Free Democratic Party) and also, though to a lesser extent, the SPD.[9] In particular, the fact that the Bundesbank hires mainly from German universities, where economic courses are taught by liberal economists, has been identified as one important factor affecting the German approach to the euro crisis.

The German model of an independent central bank was chosen for EMU because the Bundesbank had proved successful in the fight against inflation. However, this result was based more on the anti-inflationary bias of the electorate and on ordoliberal ideas which permeated the programmes of the coalition parties than on a strong legal basis, which remained rather fragile.[10] Indeed, prior to the amendments required in order to ratify the Treaty of Maastricht, the German Constitution did not make any reference to the concepts of price stability and independence. It stated only the obvious fact that 'a central bank has the task of managing monetary policy' while the principles of independence and price stability were enshrined in the law establishing the central bank, and could consequently be easily changed by the political majority. The fact that this did not occur is usually explained by the widespread consensus shared by policymakers and the electorate on the success of such concepts in keeping inflation under control whilst enabling sustained economic growth.

Another reason in favour of the model of an independent central bank can be found in the near-universal acceptance of this model by the economic literature from the 1990s, in both theoretical terms and empirically.[11] According to the monetarist-neoclassical school, in fact, independence should facilitate an anti-inflationary policy and, at the same time, generate economic growth in the medium term.[12] The opposite Keynesian theory, which sought to legitimize a

[8] C Joerges, 'What Is left of the European Economic Constitution?', EUI Working Papers, Law 2004/13.

[9] See Dullien and Guerot (n 7) 6.

[10] See also van der Sluis (n 2).

[11] See, amongst the numerous empirical studies: A Alesina, 'Politics and Business Cycles in Industrial Democracies' (1989) 8 *Economic Policy* 58; A Cukierman, *Central Bank Strategy, Credibility and Independence* (Cambridge, MA, MIT Press, 1992); A Alesina and LH Summers, 'Central Bank Independence and Macroeconomic Performance: Some Comparative Evidence' (1993) 25 *Journal of Money, Credit and Banking* 151. For the theoretical studies, see FE Kydland and EC Prescott, 'Rules rather than Discretion: The Time Inconsistency of Optimal Plans' (1977) 85 *Journal of Political Economy* 473; R Barro and R Gordon, 'Rules, Discretion and Reputation in a Model of Monetary Policy' (1983) 12 *Journal of Monetary Economics* 101; and A Alesina and V Grilli, 'The European Central Bank: Reshaping Monetary Policies in Europe', Discussion Paper 563, Centre for Economic Policy Research, London (1991).

[12] According to the economic doctrine associated with the monetarist school, an independent central bank with low inflation preferences should be seen as the necessary precondition for maintaining a low level of inflation; this result, in addition, should be considered as an important factor in ensuring a high and sustained growth. This phenomenon is described by the term 'vertical long-term Phillips curve', which implies that price stability can be achieved without sacrificing employment, at least in the long term, and with the concept of 'political business cycle'. For a critical study on the economic literature underlying the independence of central banks, see M Baimbridge, 'The

democratically accountable central bank, was in fact no longer in vogue among economists at the time. It implies that governments should control monetary policy in order to pursue the goals of full employment, rising living standards, social solidarity and sustained economic growth. Central bank independence was thus mainly associated with the single objective of price stability, while a multiplicity of goals was commonly identified with a lesser degree of independence. In the debates on the future institutional structure of the monetary union reference was often made to the Delors Report adopted in 1989, which proposed a new system endowed with the status of a full independent institution committed to the objective of price stability.[13]

The multiple-objectives system is still adopted by the most important central bank in the world, ie the US Federal Reserve System (Fed), which is obliged by law (the Federal Reserve Act) to promote effectively the goals of 'maximum employment, stable prices, and moderate long-term interest rates' and, as a secondary objective, to sustain the general economic policies of the government.[14] Even though the Fed's mandate includes three primary goals, it is commonly referred by economists as a dual mandate, including only maximum employment and stable prices. This institutional configuration makes the Fed a flexible independent agency within the federal government which is vested with discretionary power and can react and adapt depending upon whether the economy is in a growth or recessionary phase. At the same time, it maintains a high level of institutional independence, given that its governor has a life mandate and cannot be dismissed by the US President for his or her conduct.[15]

Recently, however, mounting criticism has been expressed also in the US regarding the excessive discretion enjoyed by the Fed. In the past two decades bills have been introduced in Congress to change the Fed's dual mandate into a single objective based on price stability.[16] Such criticism has increased following the Fed's accommodating stance during the financial crisis and the economic recession. This current of thought blames the US central bank for not reacting swiftly and correctly to the economic downturns, for bailing out the banks,

ECB in Theory and Practice' in P Whyman, M Baimbridge and B Burkitt (eds), *Implications of the Euro. A Critical Perspective from the Left* (London, Routledge, 2006) 77. This author criticizes the assumptions underlying central bank independence, suggesting that a continued independence of the central bank will block the establishment of a true economic policy, because it would be based more on financial data than on the real economy.

[13] See Committee for the Study of Economic and Monetary Union, 'Report on Economic and Monetary Union in the European Community', Office for Official Publications of the European Community, Luxembourg (1989) (hereafter the Delors Report). According to this Report, uncoordinated budgetary policies would undermine monetary stability and cause imbalances in the real and financial sectors. See J Mortensen, 'Economic Policy Coordination in the Economic and Monetary Union', CEPS Working Document 381 (August 2013) 4.

[14] Section 2A of the Federal Reserve Act, 12 USC 225a.

[15] On the objectives of the Fed compared with those of the ECB, see S Baroncelli, *La Banca centrale europea: profili giuridici e istituzionali. Un confronto con il modello americano della Federal Reserve* (Florence, European Press Academic Publishing, 2000).

[16] M Labonte, 'Changing the Federal Reserve's Mandate: An Economic Analysis', CRS Report for Congress (12 August 2013) 2.

and inflating the housing bubble. More specifically, they criticize the Fed for increasing liquidity within the system through unconventional measures of quantitative easing (QE) in order to boost growth and improve the employment rate, which, according to them, can lead to high inflation. For this reason, a proposal has been passed to repeal the dual mandate with a single one, striking 'maximum employment' from the mandate and maintaining only the 'stable prices' objective.[17] In addition, the bill requires that the Fed establish an inflation target ex ante to promote price stability. This goal, coupled with the ability to dismiss the Fed's governor should he/she fail to achieve the target, would boost the degree of accountability of the central bank towards Congress, and increase the degree of transparency towards citizens and financial markets.

While monetary policy is difficult to scrutinize, given the different goals that can be pursued by a central bank (as for the Fed) or the ambiguity of the concept of price stability (as for the Fed and ECB), the essence of which is set by the central bank itself, the establishment of an inflation target ex ante would increase the degree and quality of parliamentary oversight, whilst also dampening the expectations of the financial markets. On the other side, such a solution may be a source of rigidities hampering the proper operation of the system, especially in times of emergency.[18]

Central bank independence challenges the legal and political concepts which underlie parliamentary systems. However, this trend is not entirely new. National administrations tend to delegate specific technical tasks with increasing frequency to independent bodies which lack full political accountability.[19] What is distinctive in the transfer of monetary power to the ECB is the extent of such powers, the repercussions of which are not clearly identifiable by citizens and political bodies: money is the measure of all commodities, and monetary policy can influence the value of many economic variables.

III. THE LEADING ROLE OF THE ECB IN THE FINANCIAL CRISIS: TOWARDS NON-CONVENTIONAL MEASURES

The financial crisis and the following economic recession made the peculiar features of the ECB stand out in comparison to those of other central banks. In fact, primary law does not vest the ECB with the power to finance Member State deficits (known as the 'no-bailout clause', Article 125 TFEU) and does not allow it to act as a lender of last resort for eurozone banks.[20] The limited role of the ECB is apparent when compared with the Fed's powers and tools. Indeed,

[17] 113th Congress, HR 215.

[18] As for the ECB inflation target, see n 2. As for the Fed, see M Labonte, 'Changing the Federal Reserve's Mandate'.

[19] P Magnette, 'Towards "Accountable Independence"? Parliamentary Controls of the European Central Bank and the Rise of a New Democratic Model' (2000) 6 *European Law Journal* 326.

[20] P De Grauwe, 'The Governance of a Fragile Eurozone', CEPS Working Document 346 (May 2011) 2.

the Fed functions as the central bank for all the banks in the US and for the US federal government.[21] The underlying reason for this difference may be found in the uncertain institutional characteristics of the EU: not yet a political union or federation, but already an economic union or quasi-federal union, without a legitimized economic government. It is not by chance that economic policies are adopted primarily at the Member State level, with some power of co-ordination reserved to the European Commission, although a growing degree of harmonization is occurring within the EU, mostly in the field of fiscal policy through the adoption of the broad economic policy guidelines,[22] along with the Treaty on Stability, Coordination and Governance (Treaty on Stability, Coordination and Governance in the Economic and Monetary Union, or Fiscal Compact)[23], which requires ex ante co-ordination of national reforms.[24]

The reason why EMU had lacked institutional mechanisms for fiscal transfers to Member States suffering from exceptional economic shocks probably lay in the optimistic view that there would be no crises, or at least no crises as intense as the current one.[25] In addition, it was thought that the Fed would continue to perform the function of the world's central bank, as it had been doing for the last 50 years. However, the EU took a significant risk in failing to provide for a mechanism of fiscal transfers towards Member States suffering from country-specific shocks. The need to provide for such a feature was already stated in the Delors Report. However, this proposal was not implemented as it contrasted with the political will of the Member States, which chose not to establish any mechanism as they believed that economic convergence would be ensured through other softer means.[26]

Governance of EMU was thus the result of a compromise. Because the Bundesbank, the conservative electorate and anti-European political parties opposed the cession of German monetary sovereignty to the ECB, the range of tasks entrusted to the new central bank in Frankfurt am Main were intentionally weakened. In addition, the ECB was established as independent of the political power of the EU institutions and the Member States, whilst its mandate was limited to the pursuit of price stability. Germany was, however, forced to accept the rule that the ECB decision-making body—the Governing Council—is to be comprised not

[21] The Fed's primary function is to control inflation and promote full employment. In addition, it supervises the federal banking institutions, and functions as the central bank for other banks, the US government and foreign banks.

[22] Art 121 TFEU.

[23] Art 11 of the Treaty on Stability, Coordination and Governance (TSCG): 'With a view to benchmarking best practices and working towards a more closely coordinated economic policy, the Contracting Parties ensure that all major economic policy reforms that they plan to undertake will be discussed ex-ante and, where appropriate, coordinated among themselves. Such coordination shall involve the institutions of the European Union as required by European Union law.'

[24] Treaty on Stability, Coordination and Governance in the Economic and Monetary Union, 1–2 March 2012, http://european-council.europa.eu/media/639235/st00tscg26_en12.pdf.

[25] See H Guaino and D Kessler, 'L'avenir de l'euro et de la BCE', Institut Diderot, Les Carnets des Dialogues du Matin (2013) 8.

[26] See D Gros and N Thygesen, *European Monetary Integration. From the European Monetary System to European Monetary Union* (London, Longman, 1992) 480.

according to criteria of economic strength but rather of legal equality, whereby small countries such as Austria or Luxembourg have the same power of bigger countries, according to the rule of one country–one vote.[27]

With the outbreak of the crisis these constitutional weaknesses came to the fore. While the Fed launched its liquidity and credit programmes and other monetary policy tools in response to the financial crisis which broke out in the summer of 2007,[28] the European Union lacked the expertise and experience necessary in order to fight the recession. Not only was the ECB a recent creation with few tasks, but the most important central bank of the ESCB—the Bundesbank—along with German public opinion opposed any active intervention by the EU, in accordance with the prevailing economic and political theories, and on the basis of the no-bailout clause enshrined in the Treaties.

Thus, instead of granting the ECB powers to intervene, thus making it a true central bank like the Fed, the solution chosen involved the establishment of new instruments, such as the European Financial Stabilisation Mechanism (EFSM),[29] which was created in May 2010 and subsequently transformed into a permanent rescue fund, the European Stability Mechanism (ESM).[30] Although these funds have different legal foundations and are subject to different regimes, they all imitate on a weaker scale the functioning of the International Monetary Fund, operate through devices typical of international and private law, and have different degrees of compatibility with EU law.[31] This is also the case for the Fiscal Compact, an intergovernmental treaty aimed at strengthening fiscal discipline in the eurozone Member States through a balanced budget rule and automatic corrective mechanisms. At the same time, some other measures continue to be adopted on the basis of the EU method, such as the six-pack proposal and the future European Banking Union.

Despite this poor institutional background, the ECB emerged as the leading institution during the crisis. However, this result was achieved gradually, and at the cost of serious differences of opinion between the members of the Governing Council. During the first part of the crisis, as the economic situation in Greece deteriorated, the ECB proved to be incapable of anticipating the Member States, and its action was blocked due to opposing views as to which stance should be adopted. Its passive position was based on the view that the EU Treaty articles on state financing prevented it from taking the initiative. Articles 123 and 125 TFEU were thus to be construed literally. This was the only way in which the ECB was able to maintain the objective of price stability

[27] Art 10.2 of the Statute of the European System of Central Banks and of the European Central Bank.

[28] www.federalreserve.gov/newsevents/reform_transaction.htm.

[29] Council Regulation (EU) 407/2010 of 11 May 2010 'establishing a European financial stabilisation mechanism' [2010] OJ L18/1. The act is based on Art 122(2) TFEU.

[30] www.esm.europa.eu/.

[31] G Bianco, 'The New Financial Stability Mechanisms and their (Poor) Consistency with EU Law', EUI Working Papers, RSCAS 2012/44.

whilst also justifying its position of independence. The result was a dramatic fall in the financial markets.[32]

In 2010, however, the ECB began to use its powers in a pragmatic way, with the goal of reassuring the markets and ensuring the survival of the eurozone. A salient example has been the purchase of government bonds issued by the Member States of the eurozone through the Securities Market Programme (SMP), which permitted the central banks of the Member States to buy government bonds issued by eurozone Member States on the secondary market.[33] This decision was taken after the Member States of the eurozone had launched a plan involving bilateral loans to shore up government bonds offered by Greece. In doing so, the ECB agreed to accommodate the Member States' actions, helping them to reach the agreed objectives.[34] It justified its action by stating that it had taken this decision in full independence and that it was necessary in order to re-establish the transmission of monetary policy throughout the eurozone. It thus fell within the limits of the ECB mandate pursuant to Article 127(2) TFEU, and did not infringe the principle of price stability. Nonetheless, the SMP was subject to a wave of criticism by economists, who maintained that it ran contrary to the no-bailout principle, an outcome that is also forbidden under primary law.

However, the most important extraordinary measure taken by the ECB was announced in the informal speech given by the President of the ECB, Mario Draghi, at the Global Investment Conference held in London on 26 July 2012. On this occasion he declared that the euro was irreversible. To ensure this irreversibility 'the ECB is ready to do whatever it takes to preserve the euro. And believe me, it will be enough.'[35] With this talk, the ECB took a stance in favour of the principle of the irreversibility of the euro, giving short shrift to the various economic theories that favoured (and still favour) the division of the eurozone in different blocks, drawing a line between the strong and the weak Member States, and leaving the two blocks with different currencies. It also sent a signal to the various anti-European political movements on the rise throughout the EU, which are calling for the return to the old currencies.

On 6 September 2012 the ECB acted on its promise and adopted Outright Monetary Transactions (OMTs) as a supplementary monetary tool. OMT transactions involve unlimited purchases of government bonds without pre-established quantitative limits and without any time limits. This enables the ECB to transact directly in secondary markets on which the government bonds of eurozone Member States are traded. The ECB specified that any purchase would

[32] With the result of making the return of Italian treasury bonds as high as 7%, and causing the collapse of the Italian Stock Exchange. G Tabellini, 'La Bce può fare meglio e di più', *Il sole 24 ore*, 9 December 2011, 1.

[33] ECB, Decision of 14 May 2010 (Bce/2010/5).

[34] See G Napolitano, 'La crisi del debito sovrano e il rafforzamento della governance economica europea' in G Napolitano (ed), *Uscire dalla crisi. Politiche pubbliche e trasformazioni istituzionali* (Bologna, il Mulino, 2012) 405.

[35] Speech by Mario Draghi, President of the European Central Bank, at the Global Investment Conference in London, 26 July 2012, www.ecb.int/press/key/date/2012/html/sp120726.en.html.

be offset in full by removing an equivalent amount of money from circulation (ie sterilized), in order to avoid inflation.[36] Because the liquidity created through OMTs will be fully sterilized, these transactions differ from unconventional easing policies undertaken by the Bank of England, the Fed, the Bank of Japan and other central banks. In addition, OMTs are conditional upon a specific request by a Member State for EFMS/EMS assistance and strict monitoring of agreed fiscal policies and structural reforms associated with the programme, subject to the penalty of termination in the event of non-compliance.[37] The ability to engage in OMTs was established without changing the EU Treaties.

Through this development, the President of the ECB was able to transform an institution, the main aim of which was to keep inflation low, into a lender of last resort which is ready to buy the distressed eurozone sovereign debt of distressed states such as Portugal, Spain, Greece or Italy, thereby ensuring the survival of the euro. However, this development has occurred without any formal amendment of the text of the EU Treaties, including specifically the articles that forbid the bailout of Member States, markets and banks (Articles 123 and 125 TFEU). Instead, the ECB justified OMTs as a new non-standard monetary policy instrument which is necessary in the exceptional circumstances where the efficacy of standard monetary policy measures has been reduced by market dysfunctions impairing the transmission mechanism.[38] As such, OMTs can be justified by construing Article 127(2) TFEU on the basis of the 'effet utile' principle: when standard monetary measures are not working, new instruments may be created in order to achieve the goal of price stability established in the TFEU effectively. Moreover, OMTs are explicitly provided for by Article 18(1) of the ESCB Statute, in relation to open market and credit operations.[39]

Interestingly enough, OMTs are not unique but form part of a global

[36] ECB press release, 'Technical Features of Outright Monetary Transactions' (2012).

[37] 'In order to address severe distortions in the pricing of sovereign debt in some euro area countries, the Governing Council announced its readiness to undertake Outright Monetary Transactions (OMTs) in secondary markets with regard to sovereign bonds in the euro area. These were first announced in August 2012, with further details on the modalities being provided in September. 2. At the same time, the ECB announced that it would terminate the Securities Markets Programme which had been introduced in May 2010. OMTs have not yet been activated but the Eurosystem is ready to undertake them under certain conditions. … The Governing Council will independently consider conducting OMTs to the extent that they are warranted from a monetary policy perspective in the event of market fragmentation. OMTs are aimed at supporting the transmission mechanism in all euro area countries and the singleness of the monetary policy. They provide a fully effective backstop to avoid destructive scenarios with potentially severe challenges for price stability in the euro area. The announcements about OMTs helped to alleviate tensions in financial markets and reduced tail risks and uncertainty in the second half of 2012. They contributed to an overall improvement in financing conditions, which was evidenced, for example, by a decline in the government bond yields of countries under stress … and the issuance of new bonds by banks, companies and sovereigns which for some time had not had access to markets. However, the situation remains fragile as long as the root causes of the current crisis are not fully addressed. This can only be done by governments, which need to ensure sustainable public debt, make their economies more competitive, strengthen the resilience of their banks, and continue to improve the institutional setting of EMU.' ECB, Annual Report (Frankfurt-am-Main, 2012) 16. See www.ecb.eu/pub/pdf/annrep/ar2012en.pdf.

[38] ECB Monthly Bulletin (October 2012) 9.

[39] Art 18(1) Statute of ESCB.

trend which emerged during the financial crisis when the so-called 'non-standard monetary policy measures' adopted by central banks became widespread throughout the world. Although there is no list as such of non-standard measures, such instruments have been identified in the different tools used by the central banks on the basis of their specific institutional and economic circumstances and include enhanced credit support, credit easing, QE, intervention in foreign exchange and securities markets, and the provision of liquidity in foreign currency.[40] While the Fed and the Bank of England began large-scale asset purchases or QE in 2009,[41] as we have seen the ECB only launched measures with a similar effect to QE at a later date.[42]

The distinguishing feature of OMTs is that they involve the purchase of government bonds by central banks on the secondary market, although not participation in the government's issuing auctions. However, the context in which purchases are made implies an agreement between the government and the central bank, where the Member State is making large issues in the primary market on the assumption that the central bank will subsequently buy them on the secondary market. In addition, according to many economists, the purchase of debt by the central bank may enable the government's fiscal deficit to be refinanced.[43]

These reflections show that there is a current trend towards the establishment of a certain level of co-ordination between the government and the central bank, which departs from the standard situation where the central bank has the sole objective of establishing an inflation target and setting interest rates. From an institutional point of view, a closer relationship of this kind between the ECB and the government of the type required by OMTs involves calling into question the concept of the independence of the central bank. Also, the idea of independence justified as a necessary precondition for achieving growth over the medium term seems to be losing ground, in view of the recession and the high rate of unemployment reached in many eurozone countries despite the low inflation rate.

In addition, the model of the ECB as impartial and immune to political influences has also been weakened. The fact that two members of the ECB Governing

[40] J-C Trichet, 'Unconventional Monetary Policy Measures: Principles—Conditions—Raison d'etre' (2013) *International Journal of Central Banking*, January, 230.

[41] Quantitative easing (QE) is an unconventional monetary policy where the central bank creates money to buy government debt. It is used to stimulate the national economy when standard monetary policy has become ineffective. A central bank implements QE by buying up financial assets from commercial banks and other private institutions, thus increasing the monetary base. This is distinguished from the more usual policy of buying or selling government bonds in order to keep market interest rates at a specified target value. See Bank of England, 'Quantitative Easing Explained. Putting More Money into our economy to Boost Spending', www.bankofengland.co.uk/monetarypolicy/Documents/pdf/qe-pamphlet.pdf.

[42] See C Bordes and L Clerk, 'The ECB's Separation Principle: Does it "Rule OK"? From Policy Rule to "Stop-and-Go" Policy' (2012) Suppl 1 *Oxford Economic Papers* 66; D Cobham, 'The Past, Present, and Future of Central Banking' (2012) 4 *Oxford Review of Public Policy* 737.

[43] The financing of the government's fiscal deficit is a consequence of the increase of bank reserves and the banking deposits of the private sector—both elements of the definition of the money stock—caused by the purchase of debt. See for the explanation, Cobham (n 42) 741.

Council resigned following the adoption of SMP has brought to light the fact that political divisions between the eurozone Member States have been reproduced within the Governing Council of the ECB. Since then, the governor of the Bundesbank has publicly stated his dissenting opinion, showing his disagreement with the position expressed by the German member of the Executive Board appointed by the German government.

Such a contrast resulted in a recent challenge of OMTs before the German Constitutional Court, which has held a public hearing and heard the expert opinion of two members of the ECB Governing Council. On the one side, Bundesbank President Weidmann exemplified the position of the German Central Bank that the purchase of government bonds under the OMT programme runs the risk of being strongly influenced by fiscal policy considerations. This, in turn, may be detrimental to the main ECB goal of the maintenance of stable prices. On the other side, one member of the ECB Executive Board, Jörg Asmussen, clearly stated that the independence of the ECB when purchasing government bonds on the secondary market is one of the instruments available to the central bank in order to ensure the smooth operation of monetary policy.[44] In addition, he stressed that the ECB's decision was justified on the basis of a state of necessity, in order to ensure the survival of the euro, which risked breaking up. The introduction of the OMT programme was thus necessary in order to ensure price stability within the eurozone. After all, according to Asmussen, 'a currency can only be stable if its continued existence is not in doubt'.[45]

The final judgment has still to be delivered. However, the tension described between the Bundesbank and part of the German electorate on the one hand and the ECB on the other in the pending OMT case mirrors the tensions and differing priorities both of the EMU countries (creditor/debtor countries) and within the German institutional framework (the German central bank and part of the German electorate on the one hand and the Chancellor and European Council on the other hand).

As we have seen, the ECB took on a leading role during the crisis. Following an initial stage in which it did not react, it developed certain measures aimed at sustaining the initiatives launched by the Member States through intergovernmental arrangements (SMP). More recently, it embarked upon non-standard measures independently of the Member States (OMTs), thus de facto acquiring a fiscal role. In fact, we cannot deny that such interventions have had an impact on the wealth of the Member States as well as on domestic social and economic choices. On the other hand, the ECB has managed to limit and justify such measures by construing the primary provisions on monetary tools extensively, using the 'effet utile' principle and taking advantage of its independent position vis-à-vis the political powers. This is true especially for the European Council, which is blocked by differing visions and the veto power of the Member states.

[44] See J Asmussen, Member of the Executive Board of the ECB, Introductory Statement by the ECB in the proceedings before the Federal Constitutional Court, Karlsruhe, 11 June 2013.

[45] Ibid.

More generally, we have also noted that the stabilizing role acquired by the ECB is in keeping with the more active role played by central banks around the world during the crisis. As the Fed's history shows, the powers of central banks are often stretched and transformed during a serious crisis, in order to restore a smooth functioning to the market.

In this vein, we should not forget that price stability is not the only objective which must be pursued by the ECB. Once this goal has been achieved, the ECB is free to support the general economic policies of the EU. It is thus open to question how long it will be possible to base non-conventional measures on monetary policy discretion and price stability, considering that the most important central banks in the world are also playing a more active role with the aim of raising the level of employment and stimulating growth instead of limiting themselves to keeping inflation low.

IV. THE STRENGTHENED ROLE OF THE ECB IN THE EUROPEAN BANKING UNION: FROM MONETARY TO FINANCIAL STABILITY

In September 2012, the European Commission published its proposals for the transfer of supervisory responsibilities to the ECB under Article 127(6) TFEU.[46] These rules must be approved according to a special procedure, under which, after obtaining the opinion of the European Parliament and the ECB, the Council may unanimously vote to 'confer specific tasks upon the European Central Bank concerning policies relating to the prudential supervision of credit institutions'. The Commission proposal has been conceived as a first step toward the creation of a European Banking Union, to be followed and supplemented by European deposit insurance and crisis management, including 'resolution procedures'. These three functions are closely interconnected within the EU, since only their joint management can reduce or even eliminate the expectation of Member State bailouts within the internal market and create incentives against reckless risk-taking by banks.[47]

The Commission proposal covers bank supervision in providing for a Single Supervisory Mechanism (SSM) and for some degree of crisis management, although not deposit insurance and resolution. The reason must be found in the legal basis: Article 127(6) TFEU targets only supervisory functions requiring unanimity within the Council. By contrast, the legal basis for deposit insurance instead continues to be Article 114 TFEU, and therefore decisions must be taken according to ordinary legislative procedures. The banking union is thus

[46] European Commission, Proposal for a Council Regulation conferring specific tasks on the European Central Bank concerning policies relating to the prudential supervision of credit institutions, Brussels, 12.9.2012 COM(2012) 511 final.

[47] See G Ferrarini and L Chiarella, 'Common Banking Supervision in the Eurozone: Strengths and Weaknesses', ECGI, Law Working Paper 223/2013, 60.

emerging as a work in progress, where the different pieces of the puzzle are still missing, and the final drawing remains to be seen. In spite of this, it is possible to discern some general principles on the basis of the draft regulation approved by the Ecofin Council in April 2013, with the agreement of the European Parliament (hereinafter the draft regulation on prudential supervision).[48] This text was approved by the European Parliament plenary on 12 September 2013.[49]

The main reason for the creation of a banking union was stressed unanimously by representatives of the ECB, specifically President Mario Draghi and Yves Mersch, member of the Executive Board. In their view, the advantage of a banking union lies in the fact that it can delink sovereigns from banks, fostering the reintegration of financial markets. Another advantage is said to lie in the avoidance of national preferences and protectionist mechanisms within banking supervision, which also has the central effect of restoring the proper transmission of monetary policy.[50] The importance of preventing sovereign problems from spreading to banks, and vice versa (avoiding banking problems from spreading to sovereigns) is something that policymakers and central bankers have learnt from the economic and financial crisis. If a government decides or is expected to bailout banks due to financial difficulties or a lack of capitalization, the government's borrowing will increase, and the bank's funding costs will also substantially increase. This result affects the budgetary capacity of the state and limits its efforts to establish financial sustainability, especially for eurozone Member States.

The fragmentation of the eurozone banking system along national lines, as a result of pressures within the lending and funding markets, has led to an increase in banks' funding costs and governments' borrowing costs, especially in the economically weaker countries. When a country loses the confidence of the market, it becomes more dependent on internal sources of financing, due to an outflow of externally held capital, and is less responsive to monetary policy decisions. At the same time, the division of the banking systems along national lines results in differences in funding conditions within the banking sector, and thus to a rise in differences in lending conditions for households and firms from different countries, which become tighter in peripheral countries and create inefficiencies in the transmission of monetary policy in the eurozone financial system. In short, in Mersh's view 'The establishment of a banking union would help to break this negative feedback loop between sovereign and banks.'[51] In order to overcome these difficulties, the experience of co-ordination among the

[48] On 19 March 2013, the Permanent Representatives Committee agreed with the European Parliament on the text of the Regulation conferring supervisory tasks on the European Central Bank (7776/1/13). The text was recently approved by the plenary of the European Parliament on September 12. On March 19, the draft regulation 7775/13, modifying regulation 1093/2010 establishing the European Banking Authority, was also approved.

[49] Council Regulation (EU) conferring specific tasks on the European Central Bank concerning policies relating to the prudential supervision of credit institutions, 9044/13, not yet published.

[50] A Sapir and G Wolff, 'The Neglected Side of Banking Union: Reshaping Europe's Financial System', note presented at the informal Ecofin meeting, 14 September 2013, Vilnius, Bruegel, 2.

[51] Y Mersch, 'The Banking Union—A European Perspective: Reasons, Benefits and Challenges of the Banking Union', speech at the seminar 'Auf dem Weg zu mehr Stabilität—ein Dialog über

Member States' banking authorities chosen by the EU as a complement for the internal market has proved to be ineffective and incomplete, especially in relation to cross-border banking or banks with subsidiaries in the eurozone due to the poor functioning of the principle of home country control on which it relies.[52]

The first element of the European Banking Union is an SSM, a network without legal personality comprised of the ECB and the national authorities of the participating Member States. This is a system of financial supervision for all eurozone banks and is open to all Member States willing to participate in the arrangement. The power of prudential supervision of credit institutions is vested in the ECB, with a view to attaining the 'safety and soundness of credit institutions and the stability of the financial system within the Union and each Member State'.[53] As a consequence, the ECB is the institution responsible of the effective and consistent functioning of the SSM. In order to ensure the smooth functioning of the mechanism, the ECB and national authorities are under a duty to co-operate in good faith; this implies in the first place an obligation to exchange information.[54]

A consequence of the above is that the ECB has been entrusted with some supervisory powers that national authorities currently enjoy under EU banking legislation. Thus, pursuant to Article 4 of the draft regulation on prudential supervision, it has the exclusive competence to authorize the opening of all new banks in the eurozone and withdraw their authorizations. It may also assess notifications of the acquisition and disposal of qualifying holdings in credit institutions and carry out the tasks allocated under EU law to the authority of the home Member State where a credit institution established in a participating Member State wishes to establish a branch or provide cross-border services in a non-participating Member State.[55] In short, the ECB will acquire all powers associated with the classification of 'home' and 'host' under EU legislation.

In addition, the ECB has also been granted wider direct supervisory powers over the credit institutions deemed to be of greater relevance on a consolidated basis, according to the criteria laid down by Article 6(4) of the draft regulation. The significant relevance of a credit institution is evaluated on the basis of its size, its importance to the economy of the EU (or of a participating Member State), and the importance of its cross-border activities.[56] All the other banking institutions are subject to the supervisory powers of the national authorities. The size of banks subject to the ECB prudential supervision is an important issue and,

die Ausgestaltung der Bankenunion zwischen Wissenschaft und Praxis' organized by Europolis and Wirtschaftswoche, Berlin, 5 April 2013.

[52] See especially M Mancini, 'Dalla vigilanza nazionale armonizzata alla Banking Union', Banca d'Italia, Quaderni di Ricerca giuridica no 73 (September 2013) 7.

[53] See Art 1 of the draft regulation on prudential supervision.

[54] See Art 6 of the draft regulation on prudential supervision.

[55] See Art 4(a)–(c) of the draft regulation on prudential supervision.

[56] In more detail, a bank is to be considered as relevant if the value of its assets is more than €30 billion, and if the ratio of its assets over the GDP of the Member State where it is established is more than 20% (unless the total value of its assets is less than €5 billion).

whilst some countries such as Germany favoured insulating its *Ländesbanken* and saving banks from the SSM, other countries supported the idea of placing all banks under the umbrella of the ECB. Whilst thus far it has been chosen to differentiate between banks that are significant (approximately 150 European banks) or insignificant on a consolidated basis, it is noteworthy that banks for which public financial assistance has been requested or received directly from the EFSF or the ESM will not be regarded as less significant and are thus supervised by the ECB.

In order to fully perform its supervisory role, the ECB has been vested with new exclusive investigatory powers, such as access to necessary and relevant information, along with the right to examine the books and records, to obtain written or oral explanations, and to conduct onsite inspections.[57] These are new tools, which have been added to the liquidity lever, ie the power to set interest rates, which is currently the main one available to the ECB.

An issue that has still to be fully clarified is the division of powers between the ECB and the national authorities.[58] Most commentators agree that in order to ensure an efficient system of supervision, the European authority should have the final say.[59] This is not least because national authorities often attempt to conceal national banking institutions in distress, and also because small and local saving banks (such as, for example, the Spanish *cajas*) had a impact on the economic crisis.[60] On the other hand, however, the national authorities have the benefit of access to more information and data on the basis of which day-to-day control may be exercised over national and local banks. In addition, they speak the language of the country and have significant resources at their disposal. Thus their role has to be recognized, not only for practical reasons but also in accordance with the principle of subsidiarity, at least in cases where the ECB's competence is not exclusive.

The solution adopted by the Commission was to allocate all decision-making powers in relation to all EU banks to the ECB, limiting the national authorities to essentially auxiliary tasks. However, the draft text adopted by the Council has been adapted to the political compromise that was necessary in order to meet the Member States' requests, and is less clear in defining the relationship between the European supervisor and the national authorities. For instance, both preparatory action and implementation of the acts adopted by the ECB are

[57] See Arts 10, 11 and 12 of the draft regulation on prudential supervision.

[58] See J-V Louis, 'Éditorial: Vers l'Unione bancaire' (2012) 3 *Cahiers de droit européen* 300.

[59] The creation of a supranational authority in the EU financial market has been proposed by the de Larosière group of experts, while the opposite thesis, advocating a strengthening of the national authorities of the host countries for the regulation and supervision of cross-border banks, has been advocated by the Turner Review. See Financial Services Authority, 'The Turner Review. A Regulatory Response to the Global Banking Crisis' (March 2009) 96.

[60] For an analysis of the different forms of centralization in the financial sector, see Ferrarini and L Chiarella (n 47) 15, 20. These authors, after analysing the different models of centralization in the EU (enhanced co-operation and co-ordination among authorities in different Member States, lead home supervisor, and supranational authority) favour strong co-ordination via a supranational authority not only in banking supervision but also in early intervention and resolution.

required on the part of the national authorities even where the European bank exercises its exclusive powers under Article 4 of the draft regulation.[61] In this respect, the national authorities will act as agents of the ECB, and the procedure will be subject to European administrative rules, and will thus be subject to appeal to the CJEU. Where powers are vested in the national authorities, as in the event of banks of less significant relevance on a consolidated basis, the ECB still retains the power to issue regulations, guidelines or general instructions to national competent authorities.[62] More importantly, the ECB retains the power to decide whether to exercise directly all the relevant powers over specific credit institutions, even though such powers in principle lie with the national authority.[63] This also includes cases in which financial assistance has been requested or received indirectly from the EFSF or the ESM.

To summarize, it may be concluded that the powers of the ECB have been significantly strengthened by the acquisition of powers of prudential supervision. This holds true for the supervisory powers exercised over cross-border banks and banks of significant relevance, including those for which public assistance has been requested. The ECB also performs a role of supremacy vis-à-vis banking institutions of less significant relevance, as it may exercise a normative power and authorize the opening of new banks or withdraw authorizations. Although many pieces of the final puzzle are still missing, it may be concluded that the ECB has been vested with new legislative, supervisory and control powers, which make it an important political player within the European framework.[64]

V. THE SOVEREIGN DEBT CRISIS AND ITS REPERCUSSIONS ON THE CONCEPT OF ECB INDEPENDENCE

The concept of the independence of the ECB has acquired a new dimension in the light of developments in the sovereign crisis. The concentration in the hands of the ECB of both the tasks of (active) monetary policy and prudential supervision entrusts this institution with a powerful set of instruments not only in the monetary but also in the financial field. This duality of tasks may represent a potential source of conflict between the different objectives that the bank must pursue. In order to preserve the integrity of the different functions it is thus important to ensure a proper separation between the monetary and microsupervisory functions of the ECB.

According to the draft regulation on prudential supervision, the tasks vested

[61] Art 6 of the draft regulation.

[62] Art 6(5)(a) of the draft regulation.

[63] Art 6(5)(b) of the draft regulation.

[64] See Mancini (n 52) 27. But see Ferrarini and Chiarella (n 47) 51. According to these authors, the scheme of banking supervision in the eurozone represents a semi-strong form of centralization. In fact, co-operation mechanisms tend to fail a crisis scenario, while delegation suffers from information asymmetries, which makes the national authorities use the information at their disposal for their own advantage.

in the ECB will be performed by a new Supervisory Board.[65] It will be headed by a Chair appointed for a five-year term (non-renewable) through a selection open to individuals of recognized standing and experience in banking and financial matters who are not members of the Governing Council of the ECB. The Vice-Chair will be a member of the ECB Executive Board, in order to establish a permanent link and co-ordination with the body entrusted with monetary policy. Both the Chair and the Vice-Chair will be appointed by the Council, acting on a proposal by the ECB and following approval by the European Parliament. The other members will be four representatives of the ECB who do not perform direct monetary functions and are appointed by the ECB Governing Council. Of course, there will also be one representative of the competent national authority for each participant Member State.[66]

In contrast to the Commission proposal, the draft regulation provides for an independent Council with general responsibility over the preparation of draft decisions on supervision, which will be then adopted automatically by the Governing Council of the ECB unless an objection is raised due to monetary concerns within a period not exceeding ten working days. The formal decision then will be taken by the Governing Council, but must state the reason in writing with reference with monetary issues, while the fulcrum of decision-making will be the Supervisory Board.[67] Such a system has been designed to avoid the possibility that decisions of prudential character affect negatively the objective of price stability. This, in turn, is necessary to preserve the rationale underlying the ECB's independence. We may wonder, however, who will be the four representatives of the ECB who are not directly involved in monetary policy, considering the vagueness of such definition.

As noted above, the concept of independence is not a value in itself, but has been established in order to ensure that the ECB is able to achieve price stability. This has been clarified in the first place within the economic literature, which defines independence as a necessary tool in order to enable the central bank to achieve a low level of inflation. The functionalization of the concept of independence has also been endorsed by the CJEU. In the milestone Case C-11/00, *Commission v ECB*, decided in 2003,[68] the Court made it clear that

[65] Art 26 of the Draft Regulation.

[66] If the national authority is not a central bank, a member of the country's central bank may also be invited.

[67] An alternative proposal has been made by Carmassi, Di Noia and Micossi. They suggest establishing an Executive Board of nine members (six appointed by the EU Council, plus the Vice-President of the ECB, the chairs of EBA, and ESM) and the presidents of national supervisory bodies. According to this proposal, such an institutional arrangement would render the microsupervision and monetary policy independent, although interlinked through the Vice-President of the ECB. J Carmassi, C Di Noia, and S Micossi, 'Banking Union: A Federal Model for the European Union with Prompt Corrective Action', CEPS policy brief 282 (17 September 2012).

[68] Case C-11/00 *Commission v European Central Bank* [2003] ECR I-7147. For a comment on this decision, see F Elderson and H Weenink, 'The European Court of Justice Redefined? A Landmark Judgment of the European Court of Justice' [2003] *Euredia* 273 and S Baroncelli, 'The EMU model and its Aftermath: Back to Maastricht or Far from Maastricht?' in S Baroncelli, C Spagnolo and LS

independence is not an all-purpose function, but is intended to enable the ECB to perform the functions enshrined in Article 127 TFEU. In doing so, the ECB should co-operate with the institutions of the EU, because it constitutes part of the EU framework. Article 130 TFEU (on ECB independence) must accordingly be considered as *lex specialis* and construed narrowly. In fact, Article 130 TFEU shields 'the ECB from all political pressure in order to enable it effectively to pursue the objectives attributed to its tasks, through the independent exercise of the specific powers conferred on it for that purpose by the EC Treaty and the ESCB Statute'.[69] After the judgment was enacted, the Lisbon Treaty recognized the ECB as having the status of an 'EU institution' and imposed an obligation upon it to respect the principle of loyal co-operation with the other EU institutions.

In order to guarantee the principle of independence, a major division should be imposed within the ECB organizational structure between the departments and staff who deal with banking supervision and those dedicated to monetary policy. If this were to be done, the question then arises as to what kind of independence should be granted to the ECB when performing its supervisory role. According to CJEU case law, independence should be interpreted restrictively. However, the status of independence has been allocated by the Treaty to the whole ECB, and not to single parts. The fact remains that central bank members of the ESCB should be independent under primary legislation (Article 130 TFEU), although the same is not true of the supervisory authorities of the Member States. In addition, according to the economic literature, autonomy serves the purpose of ensuring price stability, but the same principle does not apply to the prudential supervision field.[70] However, according to the draft regulation on banking supervision, not only the ECB, but also the competent national authorities acting within the SSM must act independently without taking any instructions from the institutions or bodies of the EU or from the Member States.[71] It remains to be seen, then, to what extent the provisions on the ESCB can be applied to the SSM's organizational structure.

In addition, the ECB should heed the risk of its reputation being dented, as negative conduct in relation to banking supervision may have a bad influence on the perception of its reputation as an inflation buster. In addition, the independence of the ECB may be jeopardized by its entry into the political fray when it is required to sanction or steer banks in danger of failing. This was the main

Talani (eds), *Back to Maastricht. Obstacles to Constitutional Reform within the EU Treaty (1991–2007)* (Cambridge, Cambridge Scholars Press, 2008) 121.

[69] Case C-11/00, para 134.

[70] According to the ECB, it 'should remain independent in carrying out all its tasks'. ECB, 'Opinion of the European central bank on a proposal for a Council Regulation conferring specific tasks on the European Central Bank concerning policies relating to the prudential supervision of credit institutions and a proposal for a regulation of the European Parliament and of the Council amending Regulation (EU) No 1093/2010 establishing a European Supervisory Authority (European Banking Authority)', CON/2012/96, 2013/C 30/05, para 1.4.

[71] Art 19 of the draft regulation.

reason why the de Larosière Report strongly argued against granting supervisory powers to the ECB. [72]

Furthermore, once it has been entrusted with these multiple tasks, it will be difficult to control the ECB's behaviour. First, the Governing Council and the members of the Executive Committee of the ECB are essentially exempt from any negative consequences of their actions, as they can only be discharged from their duties by the CJEU in extremely serious cases. In addition, the ECB is not very open about publicizing its procedure, actions and interventions. Finally, the quarterly dialogue with the European Parliament also does not offer many positive results in terms of collaboration between the two institutions, at least in the definition of its objectives.

If the lack of accountability on the part of the ECB before the European Parliament when charged with monetary policy only is already questionable, it would appear to be completely unacceptable for an institution that has the political power to supervise banking institutions to evade democratic control. In fact, the closure of banks entails the ability to reassign property rights and impinges on the rights of creditors and small savers. That is why a careful communication channel with the European Parliament should be kept open. Some tools for communicating with the national parliaments and with the European Council should also be put in place.

This is why the European Parliament and the ECB signed an inter-institutional agreement in September 2013 laying down certain specific principles of co-ordination between the two institutions in relation to the exercise of powers in the area of prudential supervision.[73] This important document sets out very detailed provisions which are intended to ensure that the ECB remains accountable, taking into account its independent status. In particular, the Chair of the Supervisory board of the ECB may participate in a hearing before the committees of the European Parliament, either openly or confidentially. The rules on selection procedures are extremely detailed, and the European Parliament even has a veto power over the Chair proposed by the ECB. Specific rules also apply for the adoption of acts by the ECB, involving the establishment of a communication channel with the European Parliament in relation to the public consultation procedure. Similar procedures have been also envisaged for the national parliaments and the Council within the draft regulation on prudential supervision.[74]

However, in order to establish fruitful co-operation with the democratic insti-

[72] 'Report of the High-Level Group on Financial Supervision in the EU Chaired by Jacques de Larosière', Brussels, 25 February 2009.

[73] European Parliament, Committee on Constitutional Affairs, 'Report on the conclusion of an Inter-institutional Agreement between the European Parliament and the European Central Bank on the practical modalities of the exercise of democratic accountability and oversight over the exercise of the tasks conferred on the ECB within the framework of the Single Supervisory Mechanism', session document, 30 September 2013.

[74] These procedures have been envisaged in the following: submission of the annual report; reply in writing to observations or questions submitted to the ECB; invitation of the Chair or a member of the supervisory body to participate in an exchange of views in relation of the supervision of credit institutions in that Member State along with a representative of the national competent authority.

tutions, we may wonder whether it would be useful for the ECB to establish a set of pre-established conditions and criteria on the basis of which it will act. Such criteria, in fact, would not only increase the ECB's accountability, but also create a channel for communication with the financial markets, which is able to inform them ex ante whether the ECB will intervene.

There is an additional aspect, which must also be taken into account in the analysis of the democratic accountability of EMU, and which addresses the wider dimension of this union. Although monetary powers are defined as 'exclusive' by the Treaty of Lisbon (Article 3.1(c) TFEU), the very existence of EMU depends on the proper functioning of the economic union. This, in turn, entails a co-ordination of policies, which, however, continue to be set on national level.[75] This means that even if a proper set of institutional tools are adopted and implemented in order to ensure the democratic accountability of the ECB, the existence and sustainability of the common currency will nonetheless remain dependent on the proper functioning of the rules and parameters of the Stability and Growth Pact and the Fiscal Compact. The implementation of such acts is assigned to the European Commission and the Council of Ministers (Article 5 TSCG), while the surveillance process remains in the hands of the national governments.

The predominance of the role played by executives and technocratic bodies such as the European Commission and the ECB in this respect undermines not only the role of the European Parliament, but also that of national parliaments, which remain largely excluded from any ability to exercise a positive influence on decision-making processes. In fact, the predominance of the executives in this respect—so-called 'executive federalism'—not only reduces the scope for activating a political debate that is open to different players on European level, but also increases the weight of bigger and wealthier states—ie the creditor states of the EU.[76] The parliaments and constitutional courts of these countries, such as Germany and France, will increase their importance and capacity to exert pressure within the EU decision-making system, with the final result of undermining the principle of equality between the Member States and their right to self-government, enshrined in primary law (Article 4.2 EU Treaty). This is reinforced by the fact that debtor countries do not have any real alternative. In fact, the choice of exiting the eurozone is not a credible one, given the enormous costs associated with such an option. This became apparent in the Greek saga in November 2011, when the Prime Minister backtracked on the decision to hold a referendum on acceptance of the EU loan and the conditions attached to it.[77]

[75] F Allemand and F Martucci, 'La nouvelle gouvernance économique européenne' (2012) 1 *Cahiers de droit européen* 18.

[76] On the notion of executive federalism, see B Crum, 'The Democratic Dilemma of Monetary Union', paper presented at the 2012 EUDO Dissemination Conference 'The Euro Crisis and the State of European Democracy', European University Institute, Florence, 22–23 November 2012.

[77] For an account on the Greek situation, see Chapter 11 in this book.

VI. CONCLUSIONS

The financial crisis in Europe has not only been a stress factor for all EU institutions, but has also resulted in the creation of new legal entities with an international and private character. It has also gradually transformed the role of the ECB into a more powerful institution. The ECB has not only managed to stem the sovereign debt crisis through the establishment of OMTs, but it will in future be entrusted with the task of supervising the eurozone banks. As a result, the connection between the ECB and the Member State governments has been increased, with some repercussions on the concept of the independence of the ECB, which has been transformed into a more complex and differentiated institution.

In order to justify the new non-conventional measures, the mandate of the ECB has formally remained that written in the EU Treaties but it has been interpreted widely, according to an 'effet utile' construction. In fact, the ECB has always preferred to justify the adoption of its new tools on the basis of the need to act to preserve the stability of the currency, and the existence of the euro itself. However, some commentators argue that this position is hypocritical. They favour a formal alteration of the objectives of the ECB, and the introduction of the obligation to sustain economic growth alongside the duty to fight inflation and maintain financial stability. They claim that it is paradoxical for the ECB to stick to the ordoliberal paradigm of non-intervention during the crisis, when the trend at global level is towards more active central banks, such as the Fed and the Bank of Japan. Even if the ECB has managed to find its role during the economic crisis, wasn't this just due to the personality of its President, who has managed to justify the new tasks? What if the independence of central bank were to fall prey to international exchange rate pressures?

The new proposal for a European Banking Union implies the assignment of prudential supervision of credit institutions to the ECB. These new powers need to be carefully accommodated within the ECB's institutional design in order to provide the ECB with the level of independence necessary in order to achieve monetary stability. Steps are being taken to introduce a higher degree of accountability of the ECB towards the European Parliament, the Eurogroup, and the national parliaments when acting as the controller of the SSM. This is why an inter-institutional agreement between the ECB and the European Parliament has been approved, containing specific provisions on reporting, the exchange of opinions and data, and procedures for the appointment or removal of members of the new Supervisory Boards. At the same time independence has also been granted to the new organs and authorities operating under the SSM.

Although these decisions are an important step in order to enhance the parliamentary oversight of the ECB, it remains to be seen what are the actual influences the Member States exert on this institution, and in particular what will be the weight of the larger Member States within the Supervisory Board of the ECB, and how the balance of powers within the Governing Board will influence the decisions taken in the field of banking supervision. The eurozone Member States have already tied their hands by renouncing their currency, and thus have limited their power to protect their own financing. This situation has led to the creation of a differentiated EU, formed of creditor and debtor states, each one with different priorities and necessities. Although the banking union has been created in order to reduce and eliminate such fragmentation, the risk exists that states become no longer capable of interacting efficiently with their own credit institutions, with the effect of blocking the economic growth of some areas of the EU, and the final result of undermining the principle of equality between the Member States and their right to self-government, enshrined in primary law (Article 4.2 EU Treaty).

The problem is also exacerbated by the predominance of the executives in this respect, which not only reduces scope for activating a political debate that is open to different actors and citizens on European level, but also increases the weight of the bigger and wealthier EU states. The parliaments and constitutional courts of these countries, such as Germany and France, are already increasing their importance and capacity to exert pressure within the EU decision-making system. The case on OMTs to be decided by the German Constitutional Court is a good example of this trend. This result is reinforced by the fact that debtor countries do not have any real alternative. In fact, the choice of exiting the eurozone is not a credible one, given the enormous costs associated with such an option.

Part 2

The Constitutionalization of European Budgetary Constraints: Comparative Experiences

8

(Un)Balanced Budget Rules in Europe and America

PIETER-AUGUSTIJN VAN MALLEGHEM

I. INTRODUCTION

THE SOVEREIGN DEBT crisis shook the eurozone to its very foundations. Ever since Greece's government announced that it had gravely underestimated its deficit figure in October 2009, financial markets have been wary of the sovereign debt of eurozone countries. In a matter of months, the yields on Irish, Portuguese, Spanish and Italian bonds rose rapidly. Fears of further contagion to core eurozone countries, such as France, grew and the eurozone failed to recover from the recession it had entered into with the start of the global financial crisis. Unemployment rates grew dramatically throughout the EU, especially for the younger generation. Politicians increasingly became aware that there was more to the situation than financial speculation: the very existence of the eurozone, if not the EU, was under threat.

Paradoxically, the policy response to the crisis might be even more threatening to the survival of the eurozone and, indeed, the EU as a whole. On the brink of disaster, politicians and EU institutions took unprecedented action to safeguard the euro.[1] The European Financial Stability Facility (EFSF), the European Financial Stabilization Mechanism (EFSM) and later the European Stability Mechanism (ESM) were created to bailout eurozone countries who could not find financing on capital markets. Simultaneously, measures were taken to strengthen budgetary oversight in the EU. The six-pack and two-pack, alongside the Fiscal Compact, sought to avoid the unsustainable fiscal positions of some Member States. Finally, the European Central Bank took unprecedented action by ensuring long-term financing for financial institutions and by intervening on secondary markets for government bonds.[2]

The crisis brought fundamental changes to the legal architecture of the Economic and Monetary Union (EMU). The Treaty on Stability, Coordination and Governance in the Economic and Monetary Union (TSCG or Fiscal

[1] See also the contribution of P Craig in this volume (Chapter 2).
[2] See also the contribution of S Baroncelli in this volume (Chapter 7).

Compact) concluded on 2 March 2012, is a major component of the European policy response. It established new rules concerning fiscal sustainability, as well as a new institutional framework for the governance of the eurozone. However, it was the requirement for the Contracting Parties to implement a balanced-budget rule (BBR) in their constitutions, or any equivalent legal instrument, that made newspaper headlines.

The policy response to the crisis can be captured in the tension between austerity and growth. Some have argued that only calling a halt to fiscal profligacy and implementing structural reforms could ensure the viability of the eurozone. Others have responded that fiscal austerity and internal devaluations are a recipe for disaster, had have instead called for investments in future European growth. The policy response of European leaders should be read in this light.

This paper addresses the role and effects of the TSCG within the EMU. It hopes to answer some crucial questions concerning the implementation of this Treaty. Will the TSCG be able to deliver on its promise of balanced budgets and fiscal sustainability? Does the Fiscal Compact translate political pleas for fiscal austerity into the *dura lex* of monetary union? Is the TSCG an obstacle to policies for growth in Europe?

This chapter aims to respond to these questions by means of a comparative analysis between the BBR implemented in the TSCG and the BBRs that were adopted by the different US states. It starts from the premise that a sound understanding of a legal rule can only be achieved through an analysis of similarities and differences with comparable rules in other legal systems. A comparison of the TSCG with US laws appears natural. According to most accounts, 49 of the 50 US states have enacted some form of BBR. Furthermore, most of these rules were enacted some 150 years ago, giving us access to considerable scholarship on the topic. This chapter attempts therefore to draw some lessons from the US experience.

The methodology adopted here is one of comparative law and economics. It relies upon economic theory and evidence in order to shed light on similarities and differences between BBRs in Europe and the United States, both from a descriptive and a normative perspective. This is a sound approach for several reasons. First, the subject lends itself particularly well to economic analysis given its nature. Second, the literature developed overseas on this particular subject relies extensively on economic analysis.

The chapter is structured as follows. First, I shed some light on the origin and typology of BBRs in the United States and the EU (Section II). Second, I analyse the US experience with the implementation and enforcement of BBRs and attempt to draw insight on their expected effectiveness in the EU (Section III). Then, I compare Europe's and America's BBRs within the context of their respective systems of fiscal federalism (Section IV). Section V presents my conclusions.

II. UNDERSTANDING BALANCED-BUDGET RULES

In order to gain an understanding of BBRs, one should take their historical development and their taxonomy into account. In the first sub-section I examine the origins of BBRs in the US states and highlight similarities and differences with the emergence of BBRs in contemporary Europe. In the second sub-section I map the varieties of BBR existing in the US states and contrast them with the fairly harmonized model of BBRs mandated by the Fiscal Compact in the EU today.

A. Balanced Budget Rules in Historical Perspective

In the United States, BBRs emerged progressively in the nineteenth century. They came into being as a result of a series of economic and fiscal crises, combined with a 'no-bailout' policy enforced by the US federal government.

In the beginning there were no BBRs in the laws of the US states, nor did the federal government enforce a 'no-bailout' policy. In fact, the adoption of the US Constitution virtually coincides with a massive bailout of the states. By 1788, the finances of the thirteen US states had been crippled as a consequence of the massive debts incurred by the American Revolutionary War. In 1790, Alexander Hamilton, a founding father and the first US Secretary of the Treasury, made a controversial proposition: to assume the debts of the states.[3] Although the debt would be partly restructured,[4] this implied that the more solvent states would contribute to the repayment of the debts of the more profligate states. The controversy led to the compromise of 1790: the debts of the states would be assumed, but in return, the capital of the United States would be established along the Potomac River. The compromise ensured reliable access to financial markets for the United States as a whole.

It is only some fifty years afterwards that a 'no-bailout' policy and BBRs would make their appearance in the US legal system. During the 1820s and 1830s, the US economy was undergoing a profound transformation as a result of the industrial revolution. Roads, railways, harbours and canals could potentially render transport dramatically easier. But this economic metamorphosis required capital investment on a scale that was unheard of. As private undertakings did not have access to this sort of money, public authorities stepped in to ensure that these new infrastructures were created.

Public intervention could easily be justified, as the economic benefits of these investments would be widely shared among the general population. But only the

[3] A Hamilton, 'Report Relative to a Provision for the Support of a Public Credit' in H Syrett, J Cooke (eds), *The Papers of Alexander Hamilton*, vol 6 (New York, Columbia University Press, 1961–87) 66.

[4] CR Henning and M Kessler, 'Fiscal Federalism: US History for Architects of Europe's Fiscal Union' Peterson Institute for International Economics Working Paper Series, WP 12-1, 4.

states had access to the kind of funding that was called for. States did not use taxation to finance these public investment projects partly because that would have been unpopular, and partly because of the belief that these investments would eventually pay for themselves.[5] The means governments used to finance these projects were incredibly diverse, ranging from subsidies over guaranteed loans to outright debt financing.[6]

An excellent example is the Erie Canal, built with funding from the State of New York. The Erie Canal was built between 1817 and 1825 and provided for a connection between the Atlantic Ocean and the Great Lakes. It was largely financed through bonds issued by the State of New York and was the first example of a public investment on a large scale in the United States.[7] The investment was a huge success. The canal quickly became an extraordinarily important means of transportation, substantially lowering the cost for the delivery of goods in the Mid-West. The project was a turning point for the economic development of several cities in the state, and helped to put New York on the map as a leading state.

The success of the Erie Canal triggered a boom. Other states followed New York's lead and engaged in similar projects, lured by the profits to which such projects could give rise. Ten years after the opening of the Erie Canal, most US states had contracted debt in one way or another to finance infrastructure projects.[8] Unfortunately, many of these projects were significantly more costly or turned out to be less lucrative. While the boom was a motor for the infrastructure development of the United States, it quickly led to the accumulation of unseen levels of public debt. While state debt only amounted to a couple of millions in 1820, it had exploded to $200 million in 1841.[9]

In 1837, the US economy was struck by a banking crisis that eventually caused an economic recession that would last seven years. The combination of sometimes unwise public investments with a banking and economic crisis proved lethal. By 1843, eight states plus the Territory of Florida, which had not yet become a state, had defaulted on their debt.

The default of these eight states occurred despite widespread belief that financially troubled states would be bailed out by the federal government. After all, Alexander Hamilton had done just that at the end of the eighteenth century. But the federal government had grown aware of the problem of moral hazard: given their expectation to be bailed out by the federal government, US states had a perverse incentive to engage in unsustainable borrowing.[10] The firm refusal

[5] SE Sterk and ES Goldman, 'Controlling Legislative Shortsightednesse: The Effectiveness of Constitutional Debt Limitations' (1991) *Wisconsin Law Review* 1301, 1307.

[6] Ibid.

[7] HN Scheiber, 'State Law and "Industrial Policy" in American Development, 1790–1987' (1987) 75 *California Law Review* 415, 420–21.

[8] Sterk and Goldman (n 5) 1308.

[9] J Wallis, 'Constitutions, Corporations and Corruption: American States and Constitutional Change, 1842 to 1852' (2005) 65 *Journal of Economic History* 211, 216.

[10] *Cf* J Rodden, *Hamilton's Paradox: The Promise and Peril of Fiscal Federalism* (Cambridge, Cambridge University Press, 2006).

of the federal government to bailout the states during the 1840s is the origin of the United States' 'no-bailout' commitment. Although it was never legally enshrined, the 'no-bailout' rule is still considered to be the cornerstone of US fiscal federalism.

The banking crisis of 1837, and the resulting economic and fiscal crises, were the proximate cause of the adoption of a first wave of BBRs. The crisis had created awareness that legal action had to be taken in order to ensure fiscal sustainability. The results were tangible: before 1840, none of the US states had a BBR; by 1855, 19 states had adopted some type of rule to keep the budget balance in check.[11]

The Civil War and the subsequent Reconstruction Era provided further impetus for the adoption of BBRs. The Civil War had left the southern US states in a dire state. Labour markets underwent an important shock: the emancipation of slaves and a significant number of wartime casualties led to a shortage in the supply of labour. Southern states had amassed large quantities of debt in order to finance the war. Finally, as southern infrastructure had been targeted during the war, many roads and bridges were in need of repair. Under the command of Washington DC, southern governments authorized further issuance of bonds in order to rollover existing debt and progressively repair existing infrastructure. Over the entire period, the debt of southern states more than doubled.[12] Corruption was widespread and public money often disappeared into private pockets.[13] Because the massive increase in debt was considered to be the result of corrupt politics, many states eventually repudiated Reconstruction debt. The episode further raised awareness of the importance of fiscal sustainability and encouraged southern states to impose limits on state budgets.

The emergence of BBRs in the United States points to a number of similarities and differences with their emergence in Europe. It is remarkable to note that BBRs first emerged in the United States after the financial crisis of 1837, which would lead to a prolonged economic slump. Similarly, the TSCG was adopted after the grave financial crisis that started in 2007 and lead to a protracted economic slump in Europe. In the view of some, it is important to adopt BBRs in Europe today in order to combat imprudent fiscal politics and, sometimes, the corruption that pervades democratic politics. This narrative echoes to some extent the US emergence of BBRs.

In addition, BBRs emerged as an afterthought to the currency union, both in the United States and Europe. In the United States, it took more than fifty years before the first BBRs made their appearance. In Europe too the first genuine BBRs would only emerge a decade after the creation of the euro. This view must be nuanced, however. Unlike the United States, the EU adopted a framework for fiscal supervision, the Stability and Growth Pact, at the inception of the common currency area. In that light, the significance and the objective of the TSCG's

[11] Sterk and Goldman (n 5) 1309.
[12] Henning and Kessler (n 4) 7.
[13] Sterk and Goldman (n 5) 1311.

BBR is broader than that of comparable BBRs in the United States: whereas all these rules were designed to restrain the fiscal profligacy of governments, the TSCG has the additional goal of reinforcing the effectiveness of the reinforced Stability and Growth Pact through independent national rules. A policy intended to increase 'the national ownership of the Union surveillance framework'.[14]

Further differences between the US and European experience are perhaps even more striking. First, the mechanism through which BBRs were adopted is substantially different in Europe and in the United States. The BBRs that were adopted in the United States were the result of a creative frenzy of state legislatures, without any involvement of the federal government. Several states adopted rules with a very similar aim without co-ordinating their respective approaches. In Europe, on the other hand, the BBR came into existence by means of an inter-governmental treaty, the TSCG. It results from a top-down approach: a co-ordinated effort by different Member States and European institutions to bring about a legal regime that is significantly harmonized across the Member States of the EU.[15]

Only Germany and Spain had adopted a BBR prior to and outside of the framework set out by the TSCG. In fact, the German BBR is recognised as the primary model for the BBR enshrined in the TSCG. Germany reformed its fiscal constitution in 2009 based upon its experience with a previous constitutionally enshrined BBR.[16] Similarly, Spain adopted a BBR in its constitution in 2011, prior to the conclusion of the TSCG.[17] It did so amidst a sovereign-debt crisis, in the hope of reassuring the markets and other EU Member States. Both BBRs do, however, explicitly refer to the European framework for fiscal supervision of the Member States.

Secondly, the economic context to which BBRs in Europe and the United States respond differs significantly. The US BBRs were adopted as a result of a series of state defaults. BBRs were designed to prevent this from occurring again. By contrast, the TSCG emerged as a result of several bailouts of eurozone Member States. They were designed to mitigate the risk of moral hazard resulting from the provision of such bailouts. In Europe, there is a widespread perception that the default of a single eurozone country might be contagious and result in financial instability for, and potentially even the dissolution of, the eurozone as a whole. In the United States, the possibility of state defaults did not create fears that the dollar as a whole would collapse.

This divergence is closely related to the different realities associated with the 'no-bailout' policies in Europe and the United States. In the latter, the BBRs that emerged progressively since the nineteenth century were the consequence of the

[14] European Commission, 'Common Principles: Common Principles on National Fiscal Correction Mechanisms', 3.

[15] With the important exceptions of the United Kingdom and the Czech Republic, who did not sign the Treaty.

[16] *Cf* the contribution of G Delledonne in this volume (Chapter 9).

[17] Ibid.

strict enforcement of a 'no-bailout' policy by the US federal government that remains in force up to this day. By contrast, the adoption of the Fiscal Compact coincides with the weakening of the comparable rule laid down in the Treaty on the Functioning of the European Union. Since the beginning of the sovereign debt crisis, the Member States and the European institutions have provided bailouts for several troubled eurozone Member States. Indeed, the EFSM, EFSF and ESM are vehicles through which Member States effectively bailout peers who cannot sustainably refinance themselves on the financial markets. The ESM Treaty relies upon the BBR contained in the Fiscal Compact.[18] In the *Pringle* judgment, the CJEU interpreted the EU's 'no-bailout' provision strictly and literally, and ruled that bailouts did not necessarily constitute a violation of that provision.[19] BBRs were therefore adopted in Europe in order to guarantee fiscal sustainability in a legal climate that *does* provide financial support for eurozone Member States on the verge of default.

B. Balanced Budget Rules: A Taxonomy

The experience of unsustainable public debt and fiscal crisis made it clear that the fiscal positions of state and local governments had to be kept in check. BBRs are now virtually omnipresent in the laws of the United States. Most authors agree that 49 out of 50 US states have some form of BBR,[20] Vermont usually being cited as the exception. There is a vigorous debate as to whether such a rule ought to be incorporated in the US Federal Constitution.

But the label 'BBR' is deceptively simple, and covers a wide array of heterogeneous legal rules. While the concept of 'BBR' in the literature does refer to legal rules designed to keep expenditures in check, it does not necessarily relate to a balance between revenues and expenditures. Different types of BBRs can be identified. One type of rule is the so-called 'public purpose' requirement. This limits the ability of governments to invest in private enterprises.[21] Other instru-

[18] Preamble to the ESM Treaty, recital 5.

[19] CJEU, Case C-370/12 *Pringle*, nyr, paras 129–47. The Treaty's 'no-bailout' provision (Art 125(1) TFEU) stipulates that: 'The Union shall not be liable for or assume the commitments of central governments, regional, local or other public authorities, other bodies governed by public law, or public undertakings of any Member State, without prejudice to mutual financial guarantees for the joint execution of a specific project. A Member State shall not be liable for or assume the commitments of central governments, regional, local or other public authorities, other bodies governed by public law, or public undertakings of another Member State, without prejudice to mutual financial guarantees for the joint execution of a specific project.'

[20] Though different methodologies lead to significantly different results. Not everybody agrees that 49 states do have such a rule. *Cf* National Conference of State Legislatures, 'NCSL Fiscal Brief: State Balanced Budget Provisions' (2010); Y Hou and D Smith, 'A Framework for Understanding State Balanced Budget Requirement Systems: Reexamining Distinctive Features and an Operational Definition', (2006) 26 *Public Budgeting and Finance* 22; United States General Accounting Office, 'Balanced Budget Requirements: State Experiences and Implications for the Federal Government' (1993).

[21] R Briffault, 'Foreword: The Disfavored Constitution: State Fiscal Limits and State Constitutional Law', 34 *Rutgers Law Journal* 907, 910. Art VIII §8(1) of the New York Constitution provides an

ments used by legislatures are tax and expenditure limitations. These provisions restrict tax rates or limit the uses to which such resources may be put.[22] A third type of provision adopted are debt limitations. While these provisions do restrict the possibility of legislatures to incur debt, these rules are not necessarily formulated as a requirement to balance the budget. Some states cap the amount of debt a state can incur, either to a specific dollar amount or to some fraction of state income.[23] A fourth type of provision is the 'rainy day fund', a rule that typically requires states to save money in good fiscal years, giving them some breathing room in times of recession.[24] A final type of rules is the BBR sensu stricto: it requires a balance to be achieved between expenditures and revenues, net of borrowing.[25] These different types of rules work together, in the consti-

example: 'The money of the state shall not be given or loaned to or in aid of any private corporation or association, or private undertaking; nor shall the credit of the state be given or loaned to or in aid of any individual, or public or private corporation or association, or private undertaking, but the foregoing provisions shall not apply to any fund or property now held or which may hereafter be held by the state for educational, mental health or mental retardation purposes.' §8(2) and (3) stipulate several exceptions.

[22] Art 13A, s 1(a) of the Californian Constitution provides an example: 'The maximum amount of any ad valorem tax on real property shall not exceed one percent (1%) of the full cash value of such property.'

[23] The Arizona Constitution, for instance, caps the total amount of outstanding debt to $350,000. Art IX, s 5 provides that:

> The state may contract debts to supply the casual deficits or failures in revenues, or to meet expenses not otherwise provided for; but the aggregate amount of such debts, direct and contingent, whether contracted by virtue of one or more laws, or at different periods of time, shall never exceed the sum of three hundred and fifty thousand dollars; and the money arising from the creation of such debts shall be applied to the purpose for which it was obtained or to repay the debts so contracted, and to no other purpose.
>
> In addition to the above limited power to contract debts the state may borrow money to repel invasion, suppress insurrection, or defend the state in time of war; but the money thus raised shall be applied exclusively to the object for which the loan shall have been authorized or to the repayment of the debt thereby created. No money shall be paid out of the state treasury, except in the manner provided by law.

[24] Art 13B, s 5 of the Californian Constitution provides an example: 'Each entity of government may establish such contingency, emergency, unemployment, reserve, retirement, sinking fund, trust, or similar funds as it shall deem reasonable and proper. Contributions to any such fund, to the extent that such contributions are derived from the proceeds of taxes, shall for purposes of this Article constitute appropriations subject to limitation in the year of contribution. Neither withdrawals from any such fund, nor expenditures of (or authorizations to expend) such withdrawals, nor transfers between or among such funds, shall for purposes of this Article constitute appropriations subject to limitation.'

[25] Art 4, s 12(a) of the Californian Constitution provides that 'Within the first 10 days of each calendar year, the Governor shall submit to the Legislature, with an explanatory message, a budget for the ensuing fiscal year containing itemized statements for recommended state expenditures and estimated state revenues. If recommended expenditures exceed estimated revenues, the Governor shall recommend the sources from which the additional revenues should be provided.' In 2004, California approved of Proposition 58, which introduced s 12(g): 'For the 2004–05 fiscal year, or any subsequent fiscal year, the Legislature may not send to the Governor for consideration, nor may the Governor sign into law, a budget bill that would appropriate from the General Fund, for that fiscal year, a total amount that, when combined with all appropriations from the General Fund for that fiscal year made as of the date of the budget bill's passage, and the amount of any General Fund moneys transferred to the Budget Stabilization Account for that fiscal year pursuant to Section 20

tutions of the US states, in order to build a framework of rules that can keep the budget in balance.[26]

Further important distinctions between BBRs exist. BBRs are often distinguished according to their statutory or constitutional nature.[27] Whereas a BBR of statutory nature has the same legal rank as a budget voted into law, a BBR of a constitutional nature is hierarchically superior to such a budget. In case of conflict, a budget in deficit will be considered an exception to the statutory BBR, but a violation of the constitutional provision. In the latter case, the conflict can therefore be resolved by declaring the budget to be unconstitutional or by amending the constitution.

A second distinction is often made between ex ante and ex post BBRs. Ex ante BBRs require governments to submit a balanced budget in accordance with projected revenues for a given fiscal year.[28] Ex post BBRs require governments to balance their budgets at the end of the given fiscal year, ie in accordance with the fiscal revenue that has effectively been collected.[29] This distinction is particularly useful because it directs us towards the crucial importance of economic projections for the creation of a balanced budget.

Finally, BBRs are distinguished on the basis of their substantive or procedural nature. Substantive BBRs are rules that materially limit a government's possibility of incurring debt. Procedural BBRs cannot be considered as BBRs stricto sensu, as they do not outlaw a budgetary deficit as such. Rather, they impose additional procedural hurdles when a budget is not balanced. In the United States, procedural BBRs take three major forms. Some states require a supermajority[30] to pass

of Article XVI, exceeds General Fund revenues for that fiscal year estimated as of the date of the budget bill's passage. That estimate of General Fund revenues shall be set forth in the budget bill passed by the Legislature.'

[26] Hou and Smith (n 20) 44.

[27] Massachusetts has a statutory BBR. Chapter 29, s 6E of the Massachusetts General Laws provides: 'The governor shall recommend, the general court shall enact and the governor shall approve a general appropriation bill which shall constitute a balanced budget for the commonwealth. No supplementary appropriation bill shall be approved by the governor which would cause the state budget for any fiscal year not to be balanced.' The California Constitution, cited above (n 22) is an example of a constitutional BBR.

[28] Art X, s 7, second paragraph, for instance, provides: 'Other than as may be provided for in the debt provisions of this Constitution, the Governor, subject to such criteria as may be established by the General Assembly, shall ensure that no expenses of the Commonwealth be incurred which exceed total revenues on hand and anticipated during a period not to exceed the two years and six months period established by this section of the Constitution.'

[29] In the United States, ex post BBRs often take the form of a prohibition to carry over a deficit from one fiscal year to another. The Louisiana Code Title 39, s 76, for instance, provides that '[i]f a deficit exists in any fund at the end of the fiscal year, that deficit shall be eliminated no later than the end of the next fiscal year'.

[30] The Delaware Constitution, Art VIII, §3 provides that: 'No money shall be borrowed or debt created by or on behalf of the State but pursuant to an Act of the General Assembly, passed with the concurrence of three fourths of all the members elected to each House, except to supply casual deficiencies of revenue, repel invasion, suppress insurrection, defend the State in war, or pay existing debts; and any law authorizing the borrowing of money by or on behalf of the State shall specify the purpose for which the money is to be borrowed, and the money so borrowed shall be used exclusively for such purpose; but should the money so borrowed or any part thereof be left after the

a budget that has not been balanced, others require a referendum[31] to approve of such a budget and still others require a combination of both.[32]

Different attempts to categorize states' BBRs have lead to efforts to rank different BBRs according to their stringency.[33] Such a ranking typically takes the following form:

- the Governor must propose a balanced budget;[34]
- the legislature must pass a balanced budget;[35]
- a limit on the amount of debt;[36]
- the governor must sign a balanced budget;[37]
- controls during the ongoing fiscal year to keep the budget in check;[38]

abandonment of such purpose or the accomplishment thereof, such money, or the surplus thereof, may be disposed of according to law.'

[31] The Pennsylvania Constitution provides in its Art VIII, §7(a): 'No debt shall be incurred by or on behalf of the Commonwealth except by law and in accordance with the provisions of this section. … (3) Debt may be incurred without limit for purposes specifically itemized in the law authorizing such debt, if the question whether the debt shall be incurred has been submitted to the electors and approved by a majority of those voting on the question.'

[32] Art IX, §15 of the Michigan Constitution provides that: 'The state may borrow money for specific purposes in amounts as may be provided by acts of the legislature adopted by a vote of two-thirds of the members elected to and serving in each house, and approved by a majority of the electors voting thereon at any general election. The question submitted to the electors shall state the amount to be borrowed, the specific purpose to which the funds shall be devoted, and the method of repayment.'

[33] See eg n 20.

[34] The Rhode Island Code, Title 35, ch 3, s 13 provides that: 'The governor shall submit the budget and the appropriation bill or bills for the fiscal year to the general assembly, which may increase, decrease, alter, or strike out the items contained therein; provided, that no action on its part shall be taken which will cause an excess of appropriations for revenue expenditures over expected revenue receipts. If additional appropriations are deemed necessary by the general assembly, it shall not make the appropriations unless it shall provide the necessary additional revenue therefor.'

[35] The Delaware Code, Title 29, ch 63, s 6337 provides that: 'The General Assembly may increase, decrease or eliminate items in the Budget Appropriation Bill in any way that is not contrary to the Constitution of the State, except as hereinafter provided, but neither House shall consider further or special appropriations, except in case of emergency, which fact shall be clearly stated in the appropriation bill therefor, until the Budget Appropriation Bill shall have been finally acted upon by both Houses. No items providing for appropriations for payment of interest or principal due on state debt shall be decreased or eliminated. The total budget appropriation items may not be increased in the aggregate to a point where they would exceed the state revenue from all sources as estimated in the budget.'

[36] *Cf* the Arizona Constitution (n 23).

[37] The Massachusetts Code (n 27) provides a good example. In reality, the Massachusetts provision simultaneously imposes an obligation on the governor to propose, the legislature to enact, and the governor to sign into law a balanced budget.

[38] The Louisiana Code, Title 39, s 72(A) provides:

> The division of administration shall, prior to the first day of each quarter of the fiscal year:
>
> (1) Review the progress of the collection of revenues, consider the condition of the treasury, forecast the receipts of the treasury for the next ensuing quarter, and estimate the total cash resources of the period that will be available for expenditures.
>
> (2) Estimate the probable cash requirements for expenditures to be made in the period, by categories as follows: …
>
> (3) Confirm or revise any allotments previously made and make any additional allotments for

- the prohibition to carry over a deficit.[39]

The comparison with the elaborate BBRs of the United States is enlightening for the BBR enshrined in the TSCG. The BBR contained in Article 3(1) TSCG deserves to be quoted in full:

> 1. The Contracting Parties shall apply the rules set out in this paragraph in addition and without prejudice to their obligations under European Union law:
>
> (a) the budgetary position of the general government of a Contracting Party shall be balanced or in surplus;
>
> (b) the rule under point (a) shall be deemed to be respected if the annual structural balance of the general government is at its country-specific medium-term objective, as defined in the revised Stability and Growth Pact, with a lower limit of a structural deficit of 0.5 gross domestic product at market prices. The Contracting Parties shall ensure rapid convergence towards their respective medium-term objective. The time-frame for such convergence will be proposed by the European Commission taking into consideration country-specific sustainability risks. Progress towards, and respect of, the medium-term objective shall be evaluated on the basis of an overall assessment with the structural balance as a reference, including an analysis of expenditure net of discretionary revenue measures, in line with the revised Stability and Growth Pact;
>
> (c) the Contracting Parties may temporarily deviate from their respective medium-term objective or the adjustment path towards it only in exceptional circumstances, as defined in point (b) of paragraph 3;
>
> (d) where the ratio of the general government debt to gross domestic product at market prices is significantly below 60% and where risks in terms of long-term sustainability of public finances are low, the lower limit of the medium-term objective specified under point (b) can reach a structural deficit of at most 1.0% in the event of significant observed deviations from the medium-term objective or the adjustment path towards it, a correction mechanism shall be triggered automatically. The mechanism shall include the obligation of the Contracting Party concerned to implement measures to correct the deviations over a defined period of time.

the next ensuing quarter under each of the categories listed under Paragraph (2) of this Subsection. The allotments of each category shall be dealt with separately, in succession. In the case of each category after the first, the action shall be based upon consideration of the estimated cash resources available after allowing for the allotments already confirmed, revised or made under the preceding category or all the preceding categories, with a view to promotion of economical spending and to keeping the total of all the allotments for the quarter within the amount of the available cash resources of the quarter, and avoiding incurrence of a cash deficit.

(4) In accordance with Subsection B of this Section, make allotments, or confirm or revise allotments previously made, for ordinary recurring expenses for each succeeding quarter of the fiscal year, and for each extraordinary expense and capital outlay or project for each succeeding quarter year until the purpose or project is completed, or the equipment or other property has been acquired.

[39] The Montana Code, Title 17, ch 7, s 131(2) provides: 'The adopted budget must be limited so that a positive ending general fund balance exists at the end of the biennium for which funds are appropriated.'

Article 3(2) TSCG further provides that this BBR shall be implemented in national law 'through provisions of binding force and permanent character, preferably constitutional, or otherwise guaranteed to be fully respected and adhered to throughout the national budgetary processes'.

When compared with US BBRs, a number of deficiencies in the TSCG become quickly apparent. Which budget should be in balance: the proposed budget, the budget adopted by the legislature or the budget that is eventually signed into law? Does the TSCG envisage a constitutional BBR, or a statutory one? What is the meaning of the clause that the BBR's implementation in national law should be 'guaranteed to be fully respected and adhered to throughout the national budgetary processes'? Is the BBR an ex ante or ex post rule? On none of these points does the TSCG offer conclusive answers.

The primary distinguishing feature of the European BBR is undoubtedly its relationship with existing EU fiscal supervision rules. Crucially, the BBR is really a rule to keep the structural budgetary position 'at its country-specific medium-term objective,'[40] a concept derived from the Stability and Growth Pact. The substantive content of the BBR therefore originates in the existing framework for the fiscal supervision of EU Member States. The TSCG repeatedly refers to provisions of Union law.[41] Furthermore, the TSCG aims at reducing the debt of Member States whose debt-to-GDP ratio exceeds the 60 per cent reference value, as was the intention of the Stability and Growth Pact.[42]

Two further characteristics set the TSCG apart from many of its American counterparts. First, the European BBR aims to balance the structural, rather than the nominal budget. The TSCG itself construes the 'annual structural balance of the general government' as meaning 'the annual cyclically-adjusted balance net of one-off and temporary measures.'[43] The structural balance makes abstraction of the economic cycle of booms and busts, as well as possible fiscal gimmicks in the shape of one-off measures. But calculating the structural balance, by making abstraction of the economic cycle of booms and busts requires a controversial economic value judgment: where does the boom-and-bust cycle start and end? Likewise, who is to decide which measures are temporary? The TSCG itself is unclear as to who should make these determinations.

Second, the TSCG provides that the Member States may deviate from their medium-term objective in case of exceptional circumstances[44] defined as

> an unusual event outside the control of the Contracting Party concerned which has a major impact on the financial position of the general government or to periods of severe economic downturn as set out in the revised Stability and Growth Pact,

[40] Art 3(1)(b) TSCG.
[41] Especially Art 3(3) TSCG.
[42] Art 4 TSCG.
[43] Art 3(3)(a) TSCG.
[44] Art 3(1)(c) TSCG.

> provided that the temporary deviation of the Contracting Party concerned does not endanger fiscal sustainability in the medium-term.[45]

But, once again, the TSCG itself is unclear who should determine whether we are in the presence of an unusual event outside the control of a Contracting Party, or in a period of severe economic downturn.

Most importantly, the TSCG's BBR really is not a BBR in the strict sense of the word. The budget is deemed in balance when it achieves the balance defined by the country's specific medium-term objective. The BBR does, however, set a lower limit for the budgets of the Member States: a structural deficit of 0.5 per cent of GDP. This lower limit is more stringent than the existing limit of 1 per cent provided for by the revised Stability and Growth Pact.[46]

A summary comparison between US and European BBRs reveals that Europe has not necessarily learnt the lessons from the American experience. One can regret the TSCG's lack of clarity in terms of what budget should be balanced (proposed, adopted, signed into law?), when it should be balanced (ex ante or ex post) and how this should be done (implementation by means of procedural requirements?). The same goes for its specific characteristics (a structural BBR, a provision for exceptional circumstances). Perhaps the existing EU framework for budgetary supervision can remedy these shortcomings. But then we are left with a puzzling question: what is the added value of the TSCG in the first place? Where was the existing EU framework insufficient and how does the Fiscal Compact reinforce it? To these questions, the TSCG does not offer a straightforward answer.

III. HOW EFFECTIVE ARE BALANCED BUDGET RULES?

Beyond the analytical clarity that an exercise of comparative law can provide, an analysis of US BBRs is useful because it gives access to empirical studies on

[45] Art 3(3)(b) TSCG.

[46] The new Art 2a of Regulation 1466/97 reads:

> Each Member State shall have a differentiated medium-term objective for its budgetary position. These country-specific medium-term budgetary objectives may diverge from the requirement of a close to balance or in surplus position, while providing a safety margin with respect to the 3% of GDP government deficit ratio. The medium-term budgetary objectives shall ensure the sustainability of public finances or a rapid progress towards such sustainability while allowing room for budgetary manoeuvre, considering in particular the need for public investment.
>
> Taking these factors into account, for participating Member States and for Member States that are participating in ERM2 the country-specific medium-term budgetary objectives shall be specified within a defined range between −1% of GDP and balance or surplus, in cyclically adjusted terms, net of one-off and temporary measures.
>
> The medium-term budgetary objective shall be revised every 3 years. A Member State's medium-term budgetary objective may be further revised in the event of the implementation of a structural reform with a major impact on the sustainability of public finances.

Cf Regulation (EU) No 1175/2011 of the European Parliament and of the Council of 16 November 2011 amending Council Regulation (EC) No 1466/97 on the strengthening of the surveillance of budgetary positions and the surveillance and coordination of economic policies [2011] OJ L306/12.

the effectiveness of BBRs. A wide literature exists in the United States dealing with the effects of BBRs for the fiscal policy of US state governments. In particular, the possibility of adopting a federal constitutional amendment requiring a balanced budget and the emergence of EMU has spurred an interest in the effects of these rules.

A. The Importance of Specific Characteristics

Empirical research suggests that BBRs are effective at limiting the frugality of states. BBRs are likely to reduce significantly the per capita debt and the debt-to-income ratio of states.[47] Other research indicates that BBRs can 'dramatically limit the issuance of debt to which they pertain'.[48] This view is confirmed by the fact that the average overall debt level of US states is significantly lower than that of eurozone Member States.

The specific characteristics of BBRs are a crucial determinant of their effectiveness. A first significant distinction is that between BBRs of statutory and of constitutional nature. Legally speaking, it seems likely that BBRs of a statutory nature are but a weak constraint for the legislature wishing to pass a budget into law. In a legal system that puts great emphasis on the power of judicial review, it seems plausible that constitutionally enshrined BBRs are significantly more effective than statutory BBRs. Nevertheless, at least one empirical study has found that the legal status of BBRs did not have a statistically significant effect.[49]

This empirical result can be explained by drawing upon a second distinction, between procedural and substantive BBRs. The constitutional restraints on government borrowing are merely as strong as the procedural obstacles to amend the constitution.[50] In several US states, eg Texas, debt is routinely issued as a result of constitutional amendment.[51] It is widely recognised, however, that procedural requirements are not always effective in reducing state debt. Super-majority requirements, for instance, are associated with higher than average state debt.[52] That is different for the referendum requirement. Although there are outliers, most states that impose referenda for issuing debt amass lower levels of debt.[53] The stringency of a constitutionally enshrined BBR therefore depends on the stringency of the procedural constraints on constitutional amendments.

A third and final important distinction is that between rules that require

[47] J Von Hagen, 'A Note on the Empirical Effectiveness of Formal Fiscal Constraints' (1991) 44 *Journal of Public Economics* 199, 205.

[48] DR Kiewiet and K Szakaly, 'Constitutional Limitations on Borrowing: An Analysis of State Bonded Indebtedness' (1996)12 *Journal of Law, Economics & Organization* 62, 63.

[49] H Bohn and RP Inman, 'Balanced Budget Rules and Public Deficits: Evidence from the US States', (1996) 45 *Carnegie-Rochester Series on Public Policy* 13, 43. This result might be due to the very small sample size (three states).

[50] Briffault (n 21) 916–17.

[51] Kiewiet and Szakaly (n 48) 68. In Texas, this is required by Art 3, s 49(b) of the Constitution.

[52] Ibid, 76.

[53] Ibid, 79.

a balancing of the budget ex ante and those that require a balance ex post. Whereas the former require a budget to be balanced in accordance with projections of tax revenue (a function of economic growth), the latter require a budget to be balanced in effect, ie in accordance with actual tax revenues collected by government per fiscal year. By manipulating projections of economic growth, governments can balance budgets ex ante, though they might not realistically be able to balance them in practice. Studies have found that states who adopt an ex post rather than an ex ante BBR reduce the probability of running a deficit from 26 per cent to 11 per cent.[54] Ex post BBRs are therefore significantly more effective than their ex ante counterparts.

In order to predict the effectiveness of the BBR enshrined in the TSCG, it is therefore crucial to consider its specific characteristics. In that regard, an analysis of the TSCG is disappointing. First of all, the effectiveness of a BBR crucially depends on whether it applies ex ante or ex post. The TSCG remains silent in this regard. Everything will depend, therefore, on the specific transposition of this rule into national law, or on the interpretation given to these rules by the appropriate authorities. Perhaps we are to think that the Stability and Growth Pact, which does require budgets to be balanced ex ante and ex post through its preventive and corrective arms, respectively, can remedy this deficiency of the TSCG. But what, then, precisely is the added value of the TSCG when compared with a world where only the existing EU framework for fiscal supervision would exist?

Originally, the draft TSCG provided for a BBR to be implemented in the constitutions of the Member States. That requirement did not make it into the final wording of the Treaty. However, the US experience calls into question whether the constitutional nature of a BBR is that important in the first place. Indeed, a constitutional provision is only as strong as the procedural requirements that stand in the way of constitutional amendments. The US states that have made use of the possibility to amend the constitution to circumvent such constitutional obligations are a patent demonstration thereof. A fortiori, there is room for doubts about the effectiveness of other rules 'of binding force and of permanent nature … otherwise guaranteed to be fully respected and adhered to throughout the national budgetary processes'. Enshrining a BBR into a document of constitutional or equivalent rank seems more of a symbolic gesture to appease markets than an effective means of preventing excessive fiscal deficits. Are we to understand that the added value of the TSCG is merely symbolic?

B. The Effectiveness of BBRs: Some Controversy

Although a series of authors have argued that BBRs may be effective at reducing overall state debt levels, there is considerable controversy in the literature about

[54] Bohn and Inman (n 49) 6.

the question of whether or not BBRs are effective at restraining government borrowing. To that extent, many authors are sceptical about the overall results of BBRs. Their view is that governments have systematically sought to evade BBRs through circumvention and obfuscation.

Some sceptical authors describe the effects of BBRs at a macrolevel. They argue that the emergence of the first BBRs had the unexpected effect of shifting government borrowing to the level of local government. Whereas local government debt amounted to one-eighth of US state government debt in 1840, local government debt was eight times as high as state government debt by 1902.[55] When an ulterior set of BBRs regulated that type of government borrowing as well, governments created 'special districts' or 'special purpose governments' specifically for the purpose of borrowing, thereby circumventing existing legal limits.[56]

Other authors make similar arguments at a microlevel, where law plays a more visible role. Their narrative typically relies upon the notion of 'full faith and credit' debt. Limitations on the issuance of debt by governments are typically restricted to 'full faith and credit' debt, ie debt backed by a state or local government power to raise taxes in order to satisfy its obligations.[57] These requirements were often held not to apply to debt forms to which states did not pledge 'full faith and credit'.[58] The scope of application of the BBR therefore depends crucially on the legal qualification of debt instruments as pledging 'full faith and credit' or not.

Circumvention attempts can take different shapes and forms. Historically, one can recognize several examples. One form was the project finance bond. Public authorities issued project finance bonds for the purpose of the financing of a specific project. The terms of the bond issuance provided explicitly that the revenues generated by the project would allow future repayment of the debt. For instance, a bond could be issued to build a bridge. By providing that a toll would be imposed on any traffic crossing the bridge, future repayment of the debt could be ensured. Because bridges could attract and even increase traffic in a given region, such a justification was plausible. Over time, however, the relation between the mechanism for repayment and the project itself would become less obvious. A project bond could be created for the building of a highway, for instance, whereas repayment for such bonds could be ensured through increased tax revenue from car and fuel usage.[59] This type of government borrowing could

[55] Wallis (n 9) 245.

[56] I Rodriguez-Tejedo and J Wallis, 'Fiscal Institutions and Fiscal Crisis' in P Conti-Brown and D Skeel (eds), *When States Go Broke: The Origins, Context and Solutions for the American States in Fiscal Crisis* (Cambridge, Cambridge University Press, 2012), 24.

[57] Briffault (n 21) 918.

[58] R Briffault, 'Courts, Constitutions and Public Finance' in E Garrett, E Graddy and H Jackson (eds), *Fiscal Challenges: An Interdisciplinary Approach to Budget Policy* (Cambridge, Cambridge University Press, 2008) 424.

[59] Briffault (n 21) 918–19.

escape the scrutiny of BBRs because the revenue of one specific project rather than the general power of public authorities to tax backed these bonds.

The scrutiny of BBRs could further be avoided by ensuring that bonds are not so much issued by public authorities, but rather by other entities. These entities could either be private or public undertakings, as long as they did not form part of the government stricto sensu. The trick would then consist in having the government contracting with the entity, ensuring that sufficient payments are made to allow interest and capital of any given bond to be refunded.[60] In economic terms, such bonds were indeed funded by the government and the tax revenues behind it. Nevertheless, legal gimmicks could prevent the application of BBRs.

There is empirical support for the thesis that circumvention and evasion is an important side effect of BBRs. Wallis and Weingast summarize it succinctly: 'Paradoxically, the effect of fiscal restrictions over time has been to produce more borrowing and larger governments.'[61] Some suggest that BBRs are not effective by themselves, but do have effects when combined with supermajority voting requirements.[62] Others believe that BBRs lead to devolution of debt to lower levels of government.[63] Still others argue that strong or weak BBRs do not have an effect on excessive budget deficits or debt levels.[64] Worryingly, BBRs might lead governments to reduce pension funding in times of fiscal stress.[65] One author came to the conclusion that the 'most significant effect' of BBRs is 'to induce governments to substitute nonrestricted for restricted debt instruments, thereby reducing the relevance and clarity of data on government debt'.[66]

Doubts about the effectiveness of BBRs have been corroborated by recent events. Both California and Illinois were on the brink of bankruptcy at the beginning of the twenty-first century. The Illinois state comptroller was particularly direct about the effectiveness of these rules, calling them 'a sham'. 'It isn't balanced, it's never balanced, … there's always ways to have things off budget.'[67] More worryingly, the stringent constitutional BBR adopted by California in 2005, Proposition 58,[68] has not been able to reduce California's debt woes. Half a decade later, the state was still on the verge of bankruptcy, often being considered the United States' Greece.[69]

[60] Ibid, 920.

[61] J Wallis and B Weingast, 'Dysfunctional or Optimal Institutions?' in Garrett et al (n 58) 332.

[62] D Bails and MA Tieslau, 'The Impact of Fiscal Constitutions on State and Local Expenditures', 20 *Cato Journal* 255, 271.

[63] Kiewiet and Szakaly (n 48) 91. See also Sterk and Goldman (n 3) 1312.

[64] F Canova and E Pappa, 'The Elusive Costs and the Immaterial Gains of Fiscal Constraints' (2006) 90 *Journal of Public Economics* 1391.

[65] BA Chaney, PA Copley and MS Stone, 'The Effect of Fiscal Stress and Balanced Budget Requirements on the Funding and Measurement of State Pension Obligations' (2002) 21 *Journal of Accounting and Public Policy* 287, 307.

[66] Von Hagen (n 47) 209.

[67] 'State Comptroller Untangles Illinois' Debt Woes', *Financial Times*, 4 November 2011.

[68] Proposition 58 introduced Art IV, s 12(g) into the Constitution. *Cf* n 22 above.

[69] *Cf* P Krugman, 'A Money Too Far', *New York Times*, 6 March 2010.

This analysis leads to further doubts about the effectiveness of the golden rule enshrined in the Fiscal Compact. Not that the unfortunate consequences of US BBRs apply without further justification to European BBRs. It is true, for instance, that statistics for government debt exclude any kind of commercial operations in which the government is involved in Europe as well.[70] Nevertheless, state support for private undertakings will fall within the scope of application of the state aid rules[71] and is likely to be found to be illegal.

However, there might be substantial scope for creative accounting measures in Europe. The strength of Europe's budgetary rules has been identified a long time ago as the weak element in the foundation of the Stability and Growth Pact.[72] In fact, the proximate cause of the European sovereign debt crisis may have been the creative accounting that put Greece's deficit figure into doubt.[73] It is true that the EU has attempted to reinforce the solidity and uniformity of European accounting figures through one of the legislative measures in the six-pack.[74] However, it can be doubted whether this Directive can definitively call a halt to creative accounting by EU Member States. And once more, it becomes apparent that a decisive feature of Europe's fiscal sustainability depends not on the TSCG or its BBR, but rather on an instrument of EU law. If so, what is the added value of enshrining binding BBRs in the national laws of the Member States?

Furthermore, the requirement of achieving 'annual structural balance'[75] crucially depends on the inherently uncertain exercise of economic forecasting. Determining the structural budget figures of the Member States depends upon the estimates of the potential GDP that can be achieved by a Member State and how much deviations from the potential GDP will affect a Member State's budget. Optimistic forecasts have been known, certainly across the Atlantic, to be a means of circumventing BBRs.[76] Furthermore, the structural balance makes abstraction of one-off and temporary measures, defined as 'measures having a transitory budgetary effect that does not lead to a sustained change in the intertemporal budgetary position'.[77] Such estimates are inherently unreliable and

[70] Art 1(2) of Council Regulation (EC) No 479/2009 of 25 May 2009 on the application of the Protocol on the excessive deficit procedure annexed to the Treaty establishing the European Community [2009] OJ L145/1.

[71] Arts 107 and 108 TFEU.

[72] *Cf* B Dafflon and S Rossi, 'Public Accounting Fudges towards EMU: A First Empirical Survey and Some Public Choice Considerations' (1999) 101 *Public Choice* 59.

[73] 'EU Casts Doubt on Greece Economic Figures', *BBC News*, 13 January 2010.

[74] *Cf* Council Directive 2011/85/EU of 8 November 2011 on requirements for budgetary frameworks of the Member States [2011] OJ L306/41.

[75] Art 3(1)(b) TSCG.

[76] R Briffault, *Balancing Acts: The Reality Behind State Balanced Budget Requirements* (New York, The Twentieth Century Fund Press, 1996) 19.

[77] European Commission, 'Specifications on the Implementation of the Stability and Growth Pact and Guidelines on the Format and Content of Stability and Convergence Programmes', available at http://ec.europa.eu/economy_finance/economic_governance/sgp/pdf/coc/code_of_conduct_en.pdf, 4.

prone to significant measurement errors.[78] The TSCG does not define who is to make these determinations. There is certainly room for divergences between different determinations. Especially when Member States adopt figures favourable to them, which are later contested by EU institutions, the effectiveness of the BBRs enshrined in national law can be called into question. That might well endanger the effectiveness of the BBR contained in the TSCG.

C. The Importance of Courts

Given the importance of BBRs in ensuring the fiscal sustainability of states, it seems reasonable to believe that courts would vigorously enforce BBRs. One might think that courts would attach great importance to containing the negative side-effects of democratic politics for its budgets. Such a view is clearly denied by the US experience with BBRs. There, at least, courts have played an active role in undermining the effectiveness of BBRs. One author called these provisions the 'disfavored constitution' of the US states.[79]

Certainly, the courts did actively step in when it came to interpreting BBRs. Since the panic of 1837, the courts' interpretation of BBRs has been decisive for the development of this field of the law. At decisive turning points, courts had the power to enforce BBRs stringently, but chose not to do so. On the contrary, as scholars have argued, courts were actively involved in the progressive erosion of the constraint imposed by BBRs over the past 150 years.[80]

Two examples can illustrate this. The first concerns project finance bonds. Initially, project finance bonds exclusively concerned situations where the revenues generated by the project financed by a bond would be used in order to repay the debt. For instance, a project bond issued to finance a bridge would be paid back by revenue raised by imposing a toll on the bridge concerned. Under the 'special fund doctrine', state courts were quick to endorse the view that these bonds were not debt in the meaning of BBRs to the extent that states would not use any other revenue to repay the bonds.[81] Nevertheless, courts allowed the nexus between the financed project and the revenues used to pay back the bonds to be progressively loosened.[82] Project bonds used to finance highways could be paid back by anticipated increases in revenues from additional usage of cars or fuel taxes. The theory was that building highways would lead to increased traffic,[83] though the tax was far from exclusively linked to one specific project. Similarly, a project bond for the construction of a convention centre

[78] L Reiss, 'Structural Budget Balances: Calculations, Problems and Benefits' (2013/Q1) *Monetary Policy and the Economy* 12, 27.

[79] Briffault (n 21).

[80] Sterk and Goldman (n 5) 1316.

[81] Briffault (n 76) 44.

[82] Briffault (n 14) 919.

[83] Eg *In re Okla Capitol Improvement Auth*, 958 P2d 759 (Okla 1998).

could be financed by an increase in hotel taxes.[84] Such practices were allowed on the theory that convention centres would attract additional visitors. But the link between the project that was financed and the means to repay bondholders became ever more remote.

The second example concerns bond issues that were done by public or private entities. These entities were so designed that they were relatively independent of state government, thereby falling outside the scope of application of BBRs. Initially, such an entity would issue bonds to finance some form of infrastructure. That entity could later lease the infrastructure to the government, against a price covering the repayment of the bonds. Progressively, courts relaxed these requirements. From what was originally known as the lease financing model emerged a new model, called 'subject-to-appropriation' debt.[85] Governments were no longer required to lease back any infrastructure built up by the entity. Rather, the government could simply contract with the entity and promise to cover the necessary costs for annual debt service. This form of debt 'dramatically expand[ed] the opportunities for evasion'[86] and is now used in thirty-two states.[87]

Empirical studies confirm that courts may be important for the enforcement of BBRs. When assessing the importance of a BBR, differences between courts appointed by a state's governor or legislature rather than directly elected by voters have dramatic effects. On average, a state budget in a state with an elected supreme court will carry a surplus of some $155 per capita, whereas a state with an appointed supreme court will only carry a surplus of some $59 per capita.[88] Those results might indicate that courts directly influence the enforcement of BBRs, irrespective of the literal wording of the rules they are enforcing.

Similarly, the TSCG prompts an important role for national courts. If the goal of the TSCG is to reinforce 'the national ownership of the Union surveillance framework',[89] national rules should also have some teeth. This ought to be translated into a capacity for enforcing these rules at the national level. Implementing these rules in constitutional law, for instance, might allow constitutional courts to strike down a budget that violates a BBR. Several authors have argued that the constitutionalization of budgetary rules might strengthen the rule of courts in the enforcement of fiscal discipline, at least in some Member States.[90] In light of the US experience, it appears doubtful that national courts will be efficient enforcers of national BBRs. As in the United States, courts might progressively relax the requirements associated with these rules; and as in the

[84] Eg *Convention Ctr Auth v Anzai*, 890 P2d 1197 (Haw 1995).
[85] Briffault (n 21) 918–20.
[86] Ibid, 920.
[87] *Lonegan v State*, 819 A2d 395, 404 n2 (NJ 2003).
[88] Bohn and Inman (n 49) 54.
[89] European Commission, 'Common Principles' (n 14) 3.
[90] *Cf* F Fabbrini, 'The Fiscal Compact, the "Golden Rule", and the Paradox of European Federalism' (2013) 36 *Boston College International & Comparative Law Review* 1, 21 as well as the contribution of G Delledonne in this volume (Chapter 9).

United States, they might restrict the scope of these rules, giving ample margin to circumvent them.

Are these concerns not alleviated by the TSCG's creation of the automatic correction mechanism[91] it provides for? It is true that automatic correction mechanisms do not appear to require intervention by national courts. However, the triggering of the automatic correction mechanism occurs only 'in the event of significant observed deviations from the medium-term objective'.[92] The notion of a significant deviation is not clearly defined. Likewise, it remains vulnerable to the inherent difficulties in assessing the structural deficits of the Member States, as well as the possibility of Member States making use of creative accounting.

If national courts were to fail to uphold the TSCG's strict BBRs, another enforcement authority might play an important role. The Member States are to create independent institutions at the national level for the monitoring of compliance with the BBRs enshrined in the TSCG.[93] These institutions are to

> support the credibility and transparency of the correction mechanism' by providing 'public assessments over: the occurrence of circumstances warranting the activation of the correction mechanism; of whether the correction is proceeding in accordance with national rules and plans; and over the occurrence of circumstances for triggering, extending and exiting escape clauses.[94]

However, neither the TSCG nor the Common Principles set out by the Commission make it clear how inconsistencies between national and supranational authorities are to be dealt with. If national authorities are simply overruled by a stricter supranational finding, what is the added value of national authorities in the first place? Furthermore, politicians can simply set aside the assessment made by national authorities. Indeed, '[t]he concerned Member State shall be obliged to comply with, or alternatively explain publicly why they are not following the assessments of these bodies.'[95] Is naming and shaming the most appropriate sanction in these circumstances?

Or perhaps the effectiveness of these rules will be ensured by the European Union? Both the European Commission and Contracting Parties to the TSCG are entitled to bring an action before the CJEU when they find that a Contracting Party has not complied with its obligations under Article 3(2) TSCG. That provision requires transposition of the TSCG's BBR into national law as well as the enactment of an automatic correction mechanism. Nevertheless, it remains unclear whether that provision allows for an action to be brought before the CJEU when a Contracting Party has enacted both a BBR and an automatic correction mechanism, but these mechanisms did not prevent a violation of the TSCG's BBR. And to the extent that true deviations are sanctioned by the

[91] Art 3(1)(e) TSCG.
[92] Ibid.
[93] Art 3(2) TSCG.
[94] European Commission, 'Common Principles' (n 14) 7.
[95] Ibid.

reinforced Stability and Growth Pact, the consequence remains puzzling: what, then, is the added value of the TSCG?

In conclusion, the US experience with BBRs and the legal and economic literature it has inspired leave us with significant questions about the effectiveness of European BBRs. Importantly, these questions rely upon the comparability of the US and European BBRs. We have already noted that the European BBRs differ to a very significant extent from their US siblings to the extent that, in Europe, these rules work alongside the existing Stability and Growth Pact. At several junctures of our analysis, we have noted that the added value of the TSCG with respect to the existing European framework of fiscal supervision is unclear. However, even if BBRs enshrined in the national laws of EU Member States might be ineffective *on their own*, that does not necessarily imply that they cannot bring *any* added value to Europe's existing framework of budgetary supervision. What if the whole is greater than the sum of its parts? In the following section, that hypothesis is taken seriously.

IV. ON BALANCED BUDGET RULES AND FISCAL FEDERALISM

Rules need to be understood in context. BBRs cannot be understood without reference to the macroeconomic background against which they can be understood and the system of fiscal federalism in which they operate. The interaction between fiscal policy at federal and decentralized levels is essential to understand the importance of BBRs in context. A comparative legal and economic methodology has double significance here: at a descriptive level, it allows to clarify important differences between the US and European legal systems, and at a normative level, it can be of help in making policy prescriptions.

A. Macroeconomics and Countercyclical Economic Policy

The aftermath of the Great Depression saw the emergence of a revolution within economic thought: the emergence of macroeconomics. John Maynard Keynes single-handedly brought about this revolution. Keynes's ideas challenged the view that economic recessions are natural consequences of the market mechanism over which humans have no control. His doctrines introduced the idea that, on the contrary, the macroeconomic boom and bust cycle could be managed by means of proper policy.

Keynes believed that government budgets ought to run a surplus in good years, and a deficit in times of recession.[96] His insight stemmed from the belief that recessions were caused by a deficiency in aggregate demand. That could lead

[96] JM Keynes, *The General Theory of Employment, Interest and Money* (London, Macmillan, 1936).

the economy into a suboptimal equilibrium with high unemployment and output short of its full potential. In these circumstances, countercyclical economic policy could stimulate demand, bringing the economy back on track towards its natural output level. Because the economy was stuck at a suboptimal level, the additional investment would result in a more than proportionate stimulus for the economy as a result of the multiplier effect. Keeping the budget balanced, on the other hand, was potentially disastrous: the decrease in fiscal revenue due to the recession meant that the government would have to cut back on expenses. Such procyclical fiscal policy would further decrease aggregate demand in the economy, worsening the economic slump. This led Keynes to the counterintuitive conclusion that government borrowing in bad economic times could be a good thing.

Keynes's thoughts were prompted by the Great Depression. In fact, President Roosevelt's New Deal policies can be considered as an example *avant la lettre* of Keynesian theory put into practice.[97] Roosevelt created the building blocks of America's social welfare state by enacting programs for the unemployed and the poor. In addition, he made several efforts to stimulate the economy. The Keynesian ideas of countercyclical fiscal policy could only be implemented through the federal government, because the BBRs adopted by the states rendered countercyclical fiscal policy at the state level impossible. Therefore, only the federal government had the capacity to intervene.

The New Deal was not just an economic, but also a legal revolution in the United States. The majority of Roosevelt's policies were previously thought to be beyond the powers of the US federal government. Yet the states did not have the financial means to adopt similar policies. These issues lead to the demise of the 'dual' model of fiscal federalism in favour of an alternative 'co-operative' model.

At its inception, the United States adhered to a 'dual' model of fiscal federalism. According to this model, both the federal government and state governments were sovereign and equal in their respective spheres.[98] Both federal and state governments had broad power to tax, each in their own sphere. However, both levels of government would avoid interfering with each other's respective powers.

This model provided the theoretical basis for the 'no-bailout' rule enforced by the US government since the 1840s. In fact, according to a strict reading of the dual model, the original post-Revolutionary War assumption of state debt is to be condemned. Rather, the federal government should have resisted any temptation to interfere with state affairs. Only the state ought to be responsible for fiscal failures within its sphere of power. That was thought to bring about durable fiscal discipline.

The adoption of the Roosevelt's New Deal policies led to the emergence of a

[97] Though there is some controversy in the economic literature as to whether Roosevelt's policies were truly Keynesian.

[98] E Corwin, 'The Passing of Dual Federalism' (1950) 36 *Virginia Law Review* 1, 4.

new model of fiscal federalism called 'co-operative federalism.'[99] Legally, the New Deal programmes were the product of co-operation between the federal government and state and local governments. The money for these programmes came largely from the federal government, but the programmes were mostly administered by the state. As a consequence, the foundations of the 'dual federalism' model collapsed. Transfers between the federal government and state and local governments became commonplace, and federal government started to interfere in the political sphere of the states when it attached conditions to the grants of federal money.

The new model of 'co-operative federalism' flourished. After the World War II, many federal programmes granted aid to the states. Medicare and Medicaid are but two famous examples of this development. During the financial crisis of 2008, the federal government enacted a stimulus bill that, for an important part, reinforced federal grants administered by the states, in accordance with this model of 'co-operative federalism'.

B. Fiscal Federalism and Countercyclical Fiscal Policy

But what level of government of government is the most appropriate to enact countercyclical fiscal policies? Roosevelt's New Deal policies were made into law at the level of the federal government. But was that merely a historical contingency, or can we draw a normative conclusion from this example? That is a matter of fiscal federalism. At heart, the fiscal federalism literature deals with the question: which functions should be assigned to which levels of government?[100] The literature on fiscal federalism seeks to answer that question by relying upon the tools of economic science. An important conclusion of this literature on fiscal federalism is that countercyclical fiscal policy ought to be enacted at the federal level, the path the United States chose in the 1930s.

A central doctrine of fiscal federalism is that the central government ought to have the role of macroeconomic stabilization and income redistribution. Doing otherwise would be counterproductive. In a federal state, monetary policy is by definition assigned to the central government. Decentralized entities therefore have no control over a crucial tool for the stabilization of their economies. Any attempt by decentralized governments to enact fiscal stimulus in order to achieve macroeconomic stabilization would be largely ineffective. In a federal structure the market is (at least) as large as the federal state. Hence, local fiscal stimulus will quickly spill over to neighbouring regions, diminishing the effect of the stimulus on the population that enacted it in the first place. Moreover, this leads to a free-rider problem: local governments have no incentive to enact fiscal stimulus packages, because waiting for a neighbouring government to do

[99] MS Greve, 'Our Federalism Is not Europe's. It's Becoming Argentina's' (2012) 7 *Duke Journal of Constitutional Law & Public Policy* 17, 26.

[100] WE Oates, 'An Essay on Fiscal Federalism' (1999) 37 *Journal of Economic Literature* 1120, 1121.

so will lead to similar effects at lower cost. Finally, macroeconomic stabilization creates the risk that the budgets of decentralized governments become unsustainable and thereby endanger the macroeconomic stability that was sought after in the first place.[101] Similarly, redistributive policies are most effective at the central level. If a decentralized government were to attempt to enact a favourable redistributive policy, a mobile population would lead to an influx of poor people and drive away the wealthy, undermining the resources of the decentralized government.[102] Just like federal states, monetary unions require a form of budgetary union in order to prevent asymmetric shocks from threatening the economic stability of member countries.[103]

This normative argument of fiscal federalism collides to some extent with the rationale of BBRs. In the absence of countercyclical policy at the level of central government, BBRs force local government to engage in procyclical fiscal policy. Irrespective of the functions assigned to decentralized government, in times of recession their fiscal receipts will diminish. As a consequence, they will spend less and exacerbate the business cycle. This procyclical policy thereby runs counter to the objectives of macroeconomic stabilization. Moreover, when a central government does enact countercyclical fiscal policy, BBRs are still counterproductive: the negative effects of states' procyclical fiscal policy could absorb the positive effects of federal stimulus. There is conflicting empirical evidence in this regard. While one author finds that BBRs exacerbate the business cycle, especially in large states,[104] another study comes to the opposite conclusion.[105]

To the extent that BBRs do run counter to the objective of macroeconomic stabilization, the presence of BBRs thereby increases the pressure on a system of fiscal federalism. When governments do wish to stabilize their economies, they are confronted with a choice. They can either reinforce the macroeconomic stabilization function of the central government, ensuring that it has the capacity to overcome the opposite tendency of procyclical fiscal policy at lower levels of government. Or they can simply set aside BBRs. When decentralized governments, legislatures or courts realize that the central government is attempting to stabilize the economy, and that their own BBRs counteracts this policy of the central government, they may have an incentive to circumvent these rules.

[101] B Dafflon, 'The Assignment of Functions to Decentralized Government: From Theory to Practice' in E Ahmad and G Brosio (eds), *Handbook of Fiscal Federalism* (Cheltenham, Edward Elgar, 2006) 275–76.

[102] Ibid, 278.

[103] P De Grauwe, *The Economics of Monetary Union*, 9th edn (Oxford, Oxford University Press, 2012) 14.

[104] A Levinson, 'Balanced Budgets and Business Cycles: Evidence from the States' (1998) 51 *National Tax Journal* 715, 730.

[105] A Alesina and T Bayoumi, 'The Costs and Benefits of Fiscal Rules: Evidence from US States', NBER Working Paper Series, Working Paper 5614 (June 1996) 8.

C. The Fiscal Compact's Chiastic Structure

For a monetary union, one can identify the broad strokes of two alternative institutional models of fiscal federalism. A first viable model combines strong fiscal centralization with the adoption of BBRs at a decentralized level. This is the model that has been chosen by the United States. It conforms to the prescriptions of the fiscal federalism literature. A second model combines weak fiscal centralization with the absence of balanced budget rules. This is the model Europe opted for prior to the sovereign debt crisis at least to the extent that one considers that the Member States did have the capacity to adopt countercyclical fiscal policies to the extent that the Stability and Growth Pact was 'dead'.[106] Moral hazard concerns were thought to have been dealt with by means of the strict enforcement of a 'no-bailout' provision (Article 125 TFEU) and the corrective and preventive arms of the Stability and Growth Pact. This second institutional model of fiscal federalism is suboptimal, as it ignores the argument of the fiscal federalism literature that macroeconomic stabilization ought to be dealt with at the central level.

By adopting the TSCG and the Stability and Growth Pact, Europe opted for neither of those alternatives. Instead it chose to undertake a radical institutional experiment, thereby endangering their capacity to stabilize their economies. With the Fiscal Compact, a new model of fiscal federalism was adopted. The Member States of the eurozone picked features of both models in order to come to a new, hybrid form of fiscal federalism. The structure of this model is chiastic: it combines the BBRs of the first model with the absence of fiscal centralization proper to the second model. The Member States imposed on themselves obligations that were previously thought of as incompatible: BBRs on the one hand, and ensuring macroeconomic stabilization on the other hand. Whether this model is viable remains an unanswered question. The adoption of this novel institutional arrangement was thought to be necessary as fiscal sustainability was under threat. Indeed, the CJEU had severely restricted the scope of, if not set aside entirely, the 'no-bailout' clause contained in Article 125 TFEU,[107] removing a cornerstone of Europe's model of fiscal federalism.

As a result, the Fiscal Compact suffers from being torn between two conflicting imperatives: on the one hand, it is designed to restrain government borrowing as much as possible, and on the other hand, it is designed to allow for government borrowing in order to accommodate countercyclical fiscal policy. This is reflected in the implementation of the Compact's golden rule. In this regard it is significant that the TSCG aims not at a nominal balance of the budget but at an 'annual structural balance',[108] understood as the 'annual cyclically-adjusted

[106] *Cf* P Leblond, 'The Political Stability and Growth Pact Is Dead: Long Live the Economic Stability and Growth Pact' (2006) 44 *Journal of Common Market Studies* 969.

[107] Case C-370/12 *Pringle*, nyr, paras 129–47.

[108] Art 3(1)(b) TSCG.

balance'.[109] Second, deviations from this general rule are possible in 'exceptional circumstances',[110] defined as any

> unusual event outside the control of the Contracting Party concerned which has a major impact on the financial position of the general government or to periods of severe economic downturn as set out in the revised Stability and Growth Pact, provided that the temporary deviation of the Contracting Party concerned does not endanger fiscal sustainability in the medium-term.[111]

This accommodates the needs of macroeconomic stabilization in a system of fiscal federalism. The decisive question in the analysis of the Fiscal Compact is how the dynamic between the golden rule and its limits will be shaped in the practice of the enforcers of the Compact.

This sheds new light on the issue of the potential ineffectiveness of the Fiscal Compact. The chiastic logic of the Fiscal Compact emphasizes balanced budgets on the one hand, and the imperative of macroeconomic stabilization on the other. The 'escape routes' inherent in the Fiscal Compact's BBR almost seem like structural features designed to allow for government spending, rather than preventing it. The TSCG risks death by tautology: the budget has to be balanced, except when it cannot be balanced. It might well undergo the same faith of the first Stability and Growth Pact, which was eventually set aside by the Member States themselves.[112]

Alternatively, the TSCG's BBR might be strictly enforced. In that case Europe would find itself incapable of managing economic crises. Paradoxically, its policy response to the sovereign debt crisis would therefore be a commitment not to manage economic crises in the future. Such an outcome would be disastrous for the eurozone, if not for the EU as a whole. Prolonged self-imposed austerity measures would then stall growth. Rather than reassuring the financial markets that outstanding debt will be paid back, lack of economic growth might alert them that the fiscal positions of the Member States are not sustainable after all. The economic woes of the sovereign debt crisis could then well return. To the extent that the EU finds public support in its output legitimacy, the news is even more disheartening. The EU, once thought of bringing economic prosperity to all by virtue of the internal market, would now bring the very opposite. When the benefits of the EU disappear, and its costs appear to be continuously increasing, how long can the project of European integration remain viable?

While the systemic contradictions of Europe's fiscal federalism have long been recognized, the Fiscal Compact now significantly exacerbates them. To the extent that they existed within the Stability and Growth Pact, they have now reached a critical level. Europe now confronts a dilemma. First, the Fiscal Compact could be rigidly enforced. The design flaws of the Fiscal Compact would then lead to

[109] Art 3(3)(a) TSCG.
[110] Art 3(1)(c) TSCG.
[111] Art 3(3)(b) TSCG.
[112] As exemplified by Case C-27/04 *Commission v Council* [2004] ECR I-6649.

the perpetuation of systemic crisis. That would work to the detriment of the Compact's legitimacy, and the EMU's and the EU's chances of survival. Second, the golden rule might fall prey to systemic circumvention. That would reflect the insight that Europe's model of fiscal federalism is untenable, and that the golden rule is unenforceable in practice.

E. A Fiscal Capacity for the European Union

Or perhaps a third way can be imagined: if the EU were to dispose of an economically significant fiscal capacity, the dilemma could be avoided.[113] At the moment, the EU only disposes of very limited fiscal capacity (of the order of 1–2 per cent of GDP), a decisive difference with the United States. Whereas the US federal government has substantial fiscal firepower, in the EU the bulk of fiscal capacity remains with the Member States.

Since its inception, prominent scholars have argued that the project of EMU was only viable when enacted within the framework of a broader political union,[114] implying that the EU would need an economically significant budget. The MacDougall Report recognized as long ago as 1977 the importance of fiscal centralization for the project of the monetary integration.[115] Some ten years later, the Delors Report would do the same.[116] When EMU eventually became a reality, the fiscal discipline that was enforced through the Stability and Growth Pact was thought to 'aggravate the very problem it is designed to avert'.[117] Rather than leading to fiscal sustainability, it was argued that Member States would put pressure upon the EU to increase its fiscal powers.[118]

Until the sovereign debt crisis erupted, there is little indication that Member States exercised that kind of pressure, or at least that Brussels gained important fiscal powers. But to what extent can it be said that the eurozone area, in 2013, has no supranational fiscal capacity allowing Member States to manage the cycle of economic booms and busts? Since the eurozone sovereign debt crisis, the euro area has witnessed the appearance of the EFSM,[119] the EFSF[120] and

[113] On the importance of such fiscal capacity, see also the contribution of F Fabbrini in this volume (Chapter 19).

[114] M Feldstein, 'The Case Against EMU', *The Economist*, 13 June 1992.

[115] Commission of the European Communities, 'McDougall Report ofthe Study Group on the Role of Public Finance in European Integration' (1977).

[116] Committee for the Study of Economic and Monetary Union, 'Report on Economic and Monetary Union in the European Community', Official Publications Office of the European Communities, Luxembourg (1989).

[117] J Von Hagen and B Eichengreen, 'Federalism, Fiscal Restraints, and European Monetary Union', 86 *American Economic Review* 134, 137.

[118] Ibid.

[119] Council Regulation (EU) No 407/2010 of 11 May 2010 establishing a European financial stabilisation mechanism, [2010] OJ L118/1.

[120] Council of the European Union, 9/10 May 2010, press release 9596/10 (available at http://register.consilium.europa.eu/pdf/en/10/st09/st09614.en10.pdf).

the ESM.[121] These mechanisms have provided substantial financial support for Greece, Ireland, Portugal, Spain and Cyprus. But these mechanisms for financial support have the limited goal of bridging times during which Member States are unable to refinance themselves sustainably on the financial markets. Their aim is to provide states with enough financial support to avoid default, while stopping short of providing the necessary (but expensive) fiscal stimulus that would be appropriate from the point of view of countercyclical economic policy. In addition, these loans come with economic conditionality attached to them. Loans from the ESM, for instance, are subject to 'strict conditionality'.[122] In economic terms, these conditions implement austerity policies rather than countercyclical fiscal policies Keynes would have pleaded for. The existing infrastructure is therefore inappropriate for implementing countercyclical macroeconomic policies.

Recent policy proposals have attempted to revive projects for a genuine fiscal capacity for Europe. The Four Presidents Report, for instance, pleads for the 'establishment of a fiscal capacity to facilitate adjustment to economic shocks'.[123] A more detailed analysis of this proposal, however, reveals that the stress remains upon the temporary, shock-absorbing nature of such a fiscal capacity, designed to avoid contagion of economic crises across the EU rather than countercyclical fiscal policy.[124] The system is designed as an insurance mechanism rather than a mechanism incorporating genuine redistribution between rich and poor eurozone members. It, too, stops short of genuine countercyclical policies designed to bring about growth rather than avert crisis.

The Commission proposal[125] for 'a full fiscal and economic union' with a 'central budget as its own fiscal capacity' comes closer to the idea of a genuine fiscal capacity that allows for genuine countercyclical fiscal policy.[126] It would support adjustment to economic shocks and facilitate the convergence of the eurozone economies, and could even incorporate funding for the Member States earmarked for specific purposes, such as unemployment benefits. But even the Commission's blueprint refuses in principle the idea of 'permanent transfers' between countries, thereby undermining the solidarity necessary for a genuine European supranational democracy that has the capacity to overcome future crises.[127]

[121] Treaty Establishing the European Stability Mechanism, 2 February 2012, available at http://www.european-council.europa.eu/media/582311/05-tesm2.en12.pdf.

[122] *Cf* Recital 2 to the ESM Treaty.

[123] H Van Rompuy in close collaboration with J M Barroso, J-C Juncker and M Draghi, 'Towards a Genuine Economic and Monetary Union', 5 December 2012, www.consilium.europa.eu/uedocs/cms_data/docs/pressdata/en/ec/134069.pdf, 9–10.

[124] Ibid, 10.

[125] Commission Communication, 'A Blueprint for a Deep and Genuine EMU: Launching a European Debate', 28 November 2012, COM(2012) 777 final.

[126] Ibid, 32.

[127] J Habermas, 'Democracy, Solidarity and the European Crisis', lecture delivered on 26 April 2013 at KU Leuven.

V. CONCLUSION

The sovereign debt crisis has threatened the eurozone and indeed the very existence of the EU as a whole. Paradoxically, the policy response to this crisis may be even more dangerous. By compelling the contracting parties to the TSCG to enact golden rules in their constitutions (or equivalent legal instruments), the Fiscal Compact is widely considered to be a reflection of the EU's turn towards austerity. This chapter has argued that there are grounds for scepticism that the Fiscal Compact will succeed in bringing such a turn to austerity, but that if it were to succeed it might cause systemic crisis in the eurozone.

Although BBRs are thought by many to be effective instruments in the attempt to restrain decentralized governments in the issuance of debt, a comparison with the US experience suggests some caution. The recent examples of fiscal crisis in California and Illinois demonstrate that these rules have not always been effective at ensuring fiscal sustainability. Empirical literature has specifically called into question the incorporation of these rules into state constitutions. The US experience shows that even constitutional rules are often circumvented. This begs the question whether the legal status of such rules is at all relevant. The TSCG could also be considered an effective instrument to restrain the spendthrift of European states because domestic courts will now be able to enforce a golden rule. However, the EU experience shows that here too, some caution is advised. The actions of US courts seem to have precipitated, rather than halted, the progressive erosion of BBRs in the laws of the United States.

Moreover, the Fiscal Compact is torn between two conflicting policy imperatives. A comparative analysis of fiscal federalism in the United States and Europe shows why the Fiscal Compact is a double-edged sword. On the one hand, Member States are expected to balance their budgets. On the other, they have the responsibility to stabilize their economies and provide redistributive services. While the provisions of the Fiscal Compact accommodate these conflicting imperatives, the Compact cannot hope to achieve both objectives simultaneously. In the worst-case scenario, the Fiscal Compact will be rigidly enforced, to the detriment of macroeconomic stabilization and redistributive policies. Because that would exacerbate the systemic tensions already present in EMU, it could plausibly lead to a breakup of the eurozone.

Given the architecture of European fiscal federalism, alternative scenarios may exist. In line with several policy proposals, the EU (or the eurozone) could finally adopt an economically significant fiscal capacity. The EU would then be capable of enacting countercyclical fiscal policies benefiting economically troubled Member States. Only then could the TSCG's BBR be rigidly enforced without endangering the prosperity of the eurozone as a whole.

9

A Legalization of Financial Constitutions in the EU? Reflections on the German, Spanish, Italian and French Experiences

GIACOMO DELLEDONNE

I. INTRODUCTORY REMARKS

THIS CHAPTER EXAMINES the recent constitutional transformations that have led to wide-ranging reform in financial constitutional law in four Member States of the European Union (Germany,[1] Spain,[2] Italy[3] and France[4]) in light of the new Treaty on Stability, Coordination and Governance in the Economic and Monetary Union (TSCG). Those reforms have prompted the constitutional (or, more ambiguously, supralegislative) entrenchment of balanced-budget clauses or 'golden rules' in most EU Member States. More specifically, balanced-budget clauses have been constitutionally entrenched in Germany, Spain and Italy. In France, after lengthy discussion, the Parliament approved an organic law providing for a more flexible approach to the objective of balancing public budgets. In March 2012, twenty-five EU Member States signed the TSCG, which requires them to entrench balanced-budget clauses in their constitutions or to ensure otherwise their respect throughout the budgetary process. All these clauses, albeit to different degrees, give cause for uncommon limitations of the political process.

This chapter interprets this reform pattern as a possible shift from a (prevailingly) *political* to a (would-be) *legal* notion of financial constitutions. It looks into the respective roles of the political branches and other actors (notably, constitutional courts) in dealing with (and possibly enforcing) these 'thicker' regulations

[1] Gesetz zur Änderung des Grundgesetzes (Artikel 91c, 91d, 104b, 109, 109a, 115, 143d) of 29 July 2009.

[2] Reforma del artículo 135 de la Constitución Española, de 27 de septiembre de 2011.

[3] Legge costituzionale 20 aprile 2012, n 1 (Introduzione del principio del pareggio di bilancio nella Carta costituzionale).

[4] Projet de loi constitutionnelle relatif à l'équilibre des finances publiques, approved by the National Assembly on 10 May 2011, and Loi organique no 2012-1403 du 17 décembre 2012 relative à la programmation et à la gouvernance des finances publiques.

of financial constitutional law. Are these reforms announcing a depoliticization of financial issues, to the advantage, inter alia, of courts? Thus, this chapter partially departs from those views that are mainly concerned with the debate about whether to embrace the principles of *fiscal constitutionalism*, which implies some kind of *substantial* (and not just *procedural*) constitutional limitations on the budgetary process, as well as the determination of the balance between public revenues and expenditures.[5] This line of argumentation was implicit in a recent judgment of the German Federal Constitutional Court concerning the compatibility of the TSCG and the ESM Treaty with the domestic constitutional order. On that occasion the Bundesverfassungsgericht recognized that 'it is not anti-democratic from the outset for the budget legislature to be bound by a particular budget and fiscal policy'.[6]

In fact, according to the literal formulation of Article 3(1) and (2) TSCG, the above-mentioned debate might seem to have come to an end. The 'long march' which started in the late 1960s—when the first Grand Coalition in Germany entrenched an earlier version of the Golden Rule in the Basic Law and passed the Stability Law[7]—appears to have ended after some intermediate, compromise steps at both the EU and national levels. The signatories to the TSCG are now required to enact substantial supralegislative (preferably constitutional) limitations on their public budgetary processes.

The second part of Article 3(2) TSCG is also of great interest. This provision of the TSCG—as well as Article 6(1)(b) of Directive No 2011/85/EU—mainly addresses the role of *fiscal councils*, bodies that help reduce the deficit 'while leaving full discretion to the political representatives'.[8] They signal the reduced role of political actors in national budgetary procedures: at the same time, they should be construed in accordance with the prerogatives of those independent institutions primarily entrusted with the enforcement of supralegislative legal rules, ie constitutional courts.

Why is this chapter focusing its attention on Germany, Italy, Spain and France? The principal reason is that they are the four most important members of the eurozone and share some important traits, eg rigid constitutions and well-established systems of constitutional review. Since this analysis is chiefly interested in comparing constitutional developments, the choice of the relevant cases

[5] See eg E Barthet, 'La Constitution n'a pas à définir le contenu des politiques publiques' (interview with Dominique Rousseau), *Le Monde*, 21 May 2010, at www.lemonde.fr/politique/article/2010/05/20/deficit-il-est-dangereux-d-inscrire-dans-la-constitution-une-obligation-qui-ne-pourra-pas-etre-tenue_1360813_823448.html.

[6] German Federal Constitutional Court (Bundesverfassungsgericht), judgment of the Second Senate of 12 September 2012 (2 BvR 1390/12, 2 BvR 1421/12, 2 BvR 1438/12, 2 BvR 1439/12, 2 BvR 1440/12, 2 BvE 6/12), para 224.

[7] Gesetz zur Förderung der Stabilität und des Wachstums der Wirtschaft of 8 June 1967.

[8] X Debrun, D Hauner and MS Kumar, 'Independent Fiscal Agencies' (2009) 23 *Journal of Economic Surveys* 44, 61. See specifically C Fasone and E Griglio, 'Can Fiscal Councils Enhance the Role of National Parliaments in the European Union? A Comparative Analysis' in B De Witte, A. Héritier and AH Trechsel (eds), *The Euro Crisis and the State of European Democracy* (San Domenico di Fiesole, European University Institute, 2013) 264.

is in accordance with a prototypical-case logic.[9] Germany is the main European stronghold of a culture of constitutional, political and financial stability, while Italy and Spain are two southern countries which have been severely hit by the sovereign debt crisis and forced to modify their constitutions in order to cope with pressure coming from European institutions and, interestingly, financial markets. France, in turn, might be seen, to a certain extent, as an outlier. Firstly, unlike the three others, it does not have a parliamentary system of government; secondly, the French political and scholarly environment has been particularly suspicious towards the constitutionalization of a balanced-budget rule; thirdly, the French Conseil constitutionnel is a unique body among constitutional courts.

Why might it be useful to reflect on the virtues (and limits) of political and legal constitutionalism in financial constitutional matters? In my view, public finance is an area of constitutional law where the dialectic confrontation between political and legal features of constitutionalism has been significantly amplified in the last few years.

The chapter is structured as follows: Section II outlines the traditional picture of financial constitutional law and its difficult relationship with judicial review. Sections III and IV compare recent constitutional amendments (or projected reforms) in the four most important Member States of the eurozone. The focus will be at once on the constitutional system of the EU and those of its Member States. This is a necessary effect of the 'undecided balance' which has marked the European system of public finance since 1992, whereby the establishment of the Economic and Monetary Union (EMU) was not followed by a decisive co-ordination of financial policies and budgetary procedures.[10]

Section V examines the US experience, which offers important evidence concerning the *practical operation* of constitutional balanced-budget clauses. From this perspective, comparison with the US (federal and state) constitutional experiences may be particularly useful: 49 out of 50 states have passed balanced-budget constitutional amendments, and the possible introduction of a balanced-budget clause in the Federal Constitution has been the subject of a long-lasting debate. Comparison with the United States is therefore necessary not only because of its relevance to a proper understanding of the dynamics of the European constitution but also because the United States is the main stronghold of fiscal constitutionalism and its constitutional practice provides important evidence of the possibility of effective constitutional entrenchment of the principles of fiscal constitutionalism.

Section VI assesses the results of comparative analysis in the light of the current debate about political and legal constitutionalism, and Section VII discusses their significance to the development of constitutional law in Europe.

[9] See R Hirschl, 'The Question of Case Selection in Comparative Constitutional Law' (2005) 53 *American Journal of Comparative Law*, 125, 142–44.

[10] See V Giomi and F Merusi, 'Politica economica e monetaria' in MP Chiti and G Greco (eds), *Trattato di diritto amministrativo europeo. Parte speciale* (Milano, Giuffrè, 2007) 1454.

II. FINANCIAL ARRANGEMENTS AS PART OF THE LAW OF THE CONSTITUTION

The origins of modern constitutionalism are usually traced back to parliaments struggling with monarchs for control over taxation and public expenditure. In this respect, English constitutional history provides, of course, the best example. Thus, the origins of constitutionalism are closely related to a seminal version of what contemporary scholarship would frame in terms of financial constitutional law.[11] Incidentally, these non-revolutionary roots might be a reason why constitutional charters are often quite elusive with regard to public finance as a fundamental part of the fabric of government.[12]

The underlying assumption was that parliaments—the representative organs of the people—would have normally opposed the executive's need for money (meaning, in most cases, the military expenditure of monarchical states in the early Modern Age). As has been written, 'the executive normally tends to exaggerate the necessity or appropriateness of expenses … whereas legislatures reveal a willingness … to limit the executive action … by preventing or moderating increased expenditures'.[13]

However, there is another founding myth, of equal strength. According to this account, the origins of constitutional *law* are intimately linked with the rise of judicial review in the United States, and a subsequent wave of judicialization of constitutional questions.[14] Under this perspective, the position of financial constitutional law becomes much more disputable. This is an area of constitutional law where there has traditionally been limited room for judicial review.

How can these two narratives be reconciled with each other? Another seminal moment of European constitutional history—the struggle over the Prussian military budget under Bismarck—is even more telling, and allows us to develop a more proper understanding of all the issues involved. That conflict over budgetary decisions ultimately resulted in (and has been interpreted as) a *great compromise* between the legislature and the Chancellor. This fundamental moment in European constitutional history was a landmark in the rise of a German model of 'pure' constitutional monarchy. Meanwhile, financial constitutional issues had been decisively attracted towards the area of tension over the relationship between executive and legislature. As will be shown in greater detail below, constitutional provisions concerning financial issues typically aim at regulating conflicts between these two political branches. The theoretical outcome of that clash in the 1860s—Laband's conception of budget as a law in the formal sense[15]—has left its mark: it is still the case in Germany that public budgets may be reviewed only to a limited extent by the Bundesverfassungsgericht.

[11] See M Fioravanti, 'Constitutionalism' in D Canale, P Grossi and H Hofmann (eds), *A History of the Philosophy of Law in the Civil Law World, 1600–1900* (Heidelberg, Springer, 2009) 263.

[12] See G della Cananea, *Indirizzo e controllo della finanza pubblica* (Bologna, Il Mulino, 1996) 10.

[13] G Ricca Salerno, *Scienza delle finanze* (Firenze, Barbera, 1890) 111.

[14] See M Loughlin, *Foundations of Public Law* (Oxford, Oxford University Press, 2010) 288.

[15] See P Laband, *Das Budgetrecht nach den Bestimmungen der Preußischen Verfassungs-Urkunde unter Berücksichtigung der Verfassung des Norddeutschen Bundes* (Berlin, Guttentag, 1871).

III. MAJOR ASPECTS OF THE RECENT REFORMS

This section contains a contextual presentation of the innovations brought about by recent constitutional amendments in the four most important Member States in the eurozone.

All these reforms have been initiated out of concern over the financial turmoil. However, their geneses are quite different. The German reform was part of a wider, long-standing debate about the internal balance of German federalism: most of all, it aimed at coping with financial instability in some *Länder*, the main manifestation of which was *Land* Berlin's application for bailout, or, more precisely, for a declaration of budgetary emergency.[16] That is why it was called the 'Second Reform of Federalism' (Föderalismusreform II). Since then, it has served as a blueprint for reform throughout Europe, both at the national and international level.

In Italy and Spain, constitutional amendments were hastily approved in the face of pressure from EU institutions *and* financial markets. In August 2011, the retiring President of the European Central Bank, Jean-Claude Trichet, and his designated successor, Mario Draghi, wrote a letter to the then Prime Minister of Italy, in which they stated that a 'constitutional reform tightening fiscal rules would also be appropriate'.[17] After that, 25 out of (then) 27 Member States of the EU signed the TSCG, which requires the contracting parties to constitutionalize a balanced-budget clause or to guarantee otherwise its respect throughout the budgetary process. In France, the executive presented a draft constitutional amendment bill in the wake of the publication of the Euro Plus Pact, in spring 2011. However, the bill could not be approved before the expiration of the French Parliament. By then, the TSCG had been signed. Since a new President and a renewed legislature took office, France has decided to implement the TSCG in its domestic legal order by means of organic and ordinary legislation instead of constitutional amendment—which it had done by December 2012.

A. Germany: Stability as a Guiding Principle

The quest for stability has typified German constitutional and political culture since the end of World War II and the establishment of the Federal Republic.[18] Thus, it should come as no surprise that the regulation of budgetary issues in the

[16] See *Bundesverfassungsgericht*, judgment of the Second Senate of 19 October 2006 (BVerfGE 116, 327).

[17] Full text of the letter available at www.corriere.it/economia/11_settembre_29/trichet_draghi_inglese_304a5f1e-ea59-11e0-ae06-4da866778017.shtml?fr=correlati.

[18] See Bundesverfassungsgericht, judgment of the Second Senate of 16 February 1983 (BVerfGE 62, 1, 40–41). See generally R Schmidt, 'Geld und Währung' in J Isensee and P Kirchhof (eds), *Handbuch des Staatsrechts der Bundesrepublik Deutschland*, vol 5: *Rechtsquellen, Organisation, Finanzen*, 3rd edn (Heidelberg, CF Müller, 2007) 935, 945–49.

Constitution has always been unusually (by European standards) wide ranging and detailed. Indeed, a 'golden rule' was already present in German constitutional law before 2009. In the late 1960s the first Grand Coalition extensively modified the financial part (Finanzverfassung) of the Basic Law (BL) of West Germany. As noted above, this earlier version of the 'golden rule' permitted public debt provided that most of the revenue obtained by means of borrowing be used to finance investment. Meanwhile, the Stability Law proclaimed the so-called 'magic square': price stability, high employment, a sound balance of trade, and steady and adequate economic growth. The 1969 financial constitution was an important model when the EMU was established in Maastricht.[19] According to the text of Article 3a(3) of the Treaty establishing the European Economic Community, as amended in 1992, 'activities of the Member States and the Community shall entail compliance with the following guiding principles: stable prices, sound public finances and monetary conditions and a sustainable balance of payments'.

It should be noted, however, that German constitutional norms basically entrusted political office-holders with achieving the goal of financial stability. The best example is the 'Höpker–Aschoff Clause' at Article 113 BL, which allows the executive to make interventions in the legislative process in order to limit possible parliamentary excesses.[20] This provision has been criticized by commentators because it seems to overlook the real dynamics of the budgetary process in contemporary democracies, where the executive and 'its' parliamentary majority normally tend to seek the very same policy objectives. In fact, this clause has never been applied because it tends to overestimate the possibility of conflicts between the executive and the legislature.[21] If one turns to financial governance in the German federal order, the overall balance of this complex system was overseen by an intergovernmental consultative body, the Financial Planning Council.

Before the 2009 reform, the enforcement of the Finanzverfassung by the German Bundesverfassungsgericht was not impossible. From a procedural viewpoint, however, it was limited to constitutional disputes between federal constitutional organs, or between the Federation and *Länder*, and abstract review of legislation at the request of the *Bund*, *Länder* or parliamentary minorities. There seemed to be no place, in turn, for concrete review of legislation or individual constitutional complaints (*Verfassungsbeschwerden*). This circumstance could be interpreted as a sign of the pre-eminence of those procedures of constitutional review most closely related to the political process and a long-term effect of Laband's theory of budget as a law in the formal sense. Some influential authors

[19] See M van der Sluis in this book (Chapter 6).

[20] According to this provision, 'Laws that increase the budget expenditures proposed by the Federal Government, or entail or will bring about new expenditures, shall require the consent of the Federal Government. This requirement shall also apply to laws that entail or will bring about decreases in revenue.'

[21] See H Siekmann, 'Artikel 113' in M Sachs (ed), *Grundgesetz: Kommentar*, 5th edn (München, CH Beck, 2009) 2257, 2258.

even made a strong case for the limited justiciability of legislative norms under the provisions of the Finanzverfassung. Yet, such hypothesis has been subsequently overhauled by the case law of the Federal Constitutional Court.[22]

As the Bundesverfassungsgericht itself held in 2007, 'the normative program of Art 115(1), second sentence, of the Basic Law [before 2009] has actually turned out not to work efficiently as a constitutional instrument of rational taxation and limitation of the state debt policy'.[23] This judgment has been criticized because it lay (at least) halfway between constitutional interpretation and constitutional politics;[24] in any case, the Bundesverfassungsgericht was ultimately claiming that an approach to financial constitutional issues premised on a distinction between different kinds of borrowing and relying upon the role of political office-holders and the virtues of political process was insufficient. Perusing the reasoning of the court, one could glimpse the message that a thinner constitutional entrenchment of substantial limitations of the budgetary process was no longer sufficient—some kind of thicker entrenchment of the financial constitution was necessary.

In 2009, the second Grand Coalition modified the Finanzverfassung again in order to prevent the emergence of financial crises in the *Länder*. According to the new Articles 109(3) and 115(2), public budgets shall be balanced 'without revenue from credits'. This principle is deemed to be satisfied when revenue obtained by the borrowing of funds 'does not exceed 0.35 per cent in relation to the nominal gross domestic product'. These provisions, also known as the 'debt brake' (*Schuldenbremse*), apply both to the Federation and the *Länder*. The Financial Planning Council was replaced by a Stability Council, another intergovernmental body entrusted with 'the continuing supervision of budgetary management of the Federation and the *Länder*', in order to 'avoid a budgetary emergency'; in the worst scenario, the Stability Council will define the principles for the establishment and administration of programmes for taking care of budgetary emergencies (Article 109a).

B. Spain: The Emergence and Entrenchment of Financial Constitutional Principles

The German emphasis on stability has very little in common with the other legal systems considered in this chapter.

Unlike the German Basic Law—and in spite of its influence on the post-Francoist constituents—the Spanish Constitution (SC) of 1978 was more laconic with

[22] See especially F Ossenbühl, 'Zur Justitiabilität der Finanzverfassung' in *Einigkeit und Recht und Freiheit: Festschrift für Karl Carstens*, vol 2: *Staatsrecht* (Köln, Heymanns, 1984) 743.

[23] Bundesverfassungsgericht, judgment of the Second Senate of 9 July 2007 (BVerfGE 119, 96, 142–43). As has been noted, 'federal indebtedness has risen from approximately 25,7 milliards Euro to more than 1 billion Euro today since the reform of Art 115 of the Basic Law came into force, in 1969' (C Mayer, 'Greift die neue Schuldenbremse?' (2011) 136 *Archiv des öffentlichen Rechts* 266, 268).

[24] See M Herdegen, 'Verfassungsgerichtsbarkeit als *pouvoir neutre*' (2009) 69 *Zeitschrift für ausländisches öffentliches Recht und Völkerrecht* 257, 260.

regard to financial issues. Before 2011, Article 134, the fundamental provision in its 'financial Constitution', was chiefly interested in making the executive the central actor in budgetary processes and enhancing its pre-eminence vis-à-vis the legislature.[25] More particularly, Article 134(6) SC provides that: 'Any non governmental bill or amendment which involves an increase in appropriations or a decrease in budget revenue shall require previous approval by the Government before its passage.' In addition, Article 135 SC contains some prescriptions on public borrowing. If one also considers organic and even ordinary legislation, however, a principle of budgetary stability was already present in the Spanish legal system, and the Constitutional Court recognized its constitutional foundations in a judgment of 2011.[26]

A draft constitutional amendment bill introducing a constitutional balanced-budget clause was presented to the Spanish lower house on 26 August 2011 in order to react to widespread concerns about public finances in the Spanish State and Autonomous Communities. After an exceptionally rapid parliamentary approval, the constitutional reform received royal assent on 27 September 2011. According to the new text of Article 135 SC, 'All Public Administrations shall adapt their actions to the principle of budgetary stability.' Article 135 contains dynamic clauses, referring to deficit and debt limits defined at the EU level. However, the rules on constitutional standing before the Tribunal Constitucional have been left unchanged. This might entail some problems with regard to the justiciability of the new constitutional provisions, as will be explained below.

Subsequently, Article 135 SC has been implemented by organic law no 2/2012.[27] An important role will be played by the Fiscal and Financial Policy Council, an intergovernmental body that can be roughly equivalent to the German Financial Planning Council.

C. Italy: The Weight of Interpretation

The original text of Article 81(4) of the Italian Constitution (now Article 81(3) IC) states that 'Any law involving new or increased spending shall detail the means therefor.' This is one of the most controversial clauses in the Constitution of 1948. Its ambiguity is the outcome of a clash between diverging views at the Constituent Assembly, where some of the constituents advocated for the construction of this constitutional provision as a balanced-budget clause.[28] This ambiguity, however, is also a result of subsequent constitutional developments. The Italian Constitutional Court has made it clear that the quest for a balanced

[25] See L López Guerra et al, *Derecho constitucional*, vol 2: *Los poderes del Estado. La organización territorial del Estado*, 6th edn (Valencia, Tirant lo Blanch, 2003) 118–19.

[26] See Tribunal Constitucional, judgment no 134/2011 of 20 July 2011.

[27] Ley orgánica 2/2012, de 27 de abril, de Estabilidad Presupuestaria y Sostenibilidad Financiera.

[28] This interpretation, however, has never prevailed through the course of Italian constitutional history: see della Cananea (n 12) 93–94.

budget should be seen as a political goal rather than a legal obligation. The Constitutional Court, holding that 'it is clearly possible [for the government] to … make debts in order to provide the means for future spending', has even been said, perhaps with some overestimation of its role, to have paved the way for the current disastrous level of state indebtedness in Italy.[29]

Apart from these claims, the important point is that Article 81(4) IC was not meant to dictate substantial limitations to budgetary processes—rather, its ultimate goal was to limit parliamentary initiatives in the domain of public finance. Thus, it might be seen as part of the Italian model of the rationalization of the parliamentary system. That might also have contributed to the difficult reviewability of laws involving increased spending before the Constitutional Court: Article 81 IC played a role in the relationship between political officeholders rather than in the overall architecture of the legal system.[30] It dealt with political goals rather than legal obligations. The current rules on legal standing before the Constitutional Court are problematic because they seem to restrict, to a considerable extent, the reviewability of ordinary state legislation under the new constitutional balanced-budget clause. Furthermore, the Court of Auditors, which in principle is entitled to challenge the legitimacy of financial laws before the Constitutional Court under Article 81 IC, has not been particularly zealous in exercising this power. It is worth adding, however, that this also happened as a result of the decline of the traditionally understood control function, of which a key element was the legalistic, formalist approach of the Court of Auditors.

Subsequent attempts at improving the effectiveness of Article 81 have usually relied on a rationalization of parliamentary financial procedures. In 2009, Parliament approved a new law on public finance and accountancy, which provides for a more transparent budgetary decision-making process and strengthened parliamentary oversight.[31] However, the reform of Article 81 IC was the precipitous result of European and international pressures, amidst serious concern for Italian public finances and the level of state indebtedness.

The new Article 81(1) and (2) IC provide that 'The State shall balance revenue and expenditure in its budget, taking account of the adverse and favourable phases of the economic cycle. No recourse shall be made to borrowing except for the purpose of taking account of the effects of the economic cycle.' Moreover, Article 5(1)(f) of constitutional law no 1/2012 provides for the establishment, within the Houses of Parliament, of 'an independent body [ie a Fiscal Council] entrusted with analysing and reviewing the performance of public finance and assessing compliance with budgetary rules'. For the first time in Italian consti-

[29] Italian Constitutional Court, sentenza no 1/1966. See G Di Gaspare, 'Innescare un sistema in equilibrio della finanza pubblica ritornando all'art 81 della Costituzione' in G Di Gaspare and N Lupo (eds), *Le procedure finanziarie in un sistema multilivello* (Milano, Giuffrè, 2005) 201.

[30] See V Onida, 'Giudizio di costituzionalità delle leggi e responsabilità finanziaria del Parlamento' in *Le sentenze della Corte costituzionale e l'art 81, uc, della Costituzione* (Milano, Giuffrè, 1993) 19.

[31] Legge 31 dicembre 2009, n 196 (Legge di contabilità e finanza pubblica).

tutional history, these provisions have been implemented by a special 'organic law'.[32]

D. France: Searching for a Golden Rule

French constitutional law has been marked by extensive change in financial procedures during the last decade. These reforms might be seen as a (meaningful) part of a wider movement of reform which was intended to modernize the 1958 French Constitution (FC).

Financial procedures were chiefly disciplined by an organic ordinance of 1959 which, according to constitutional provisions and the Gaullist institutional project, sought to ensure the pre-eminence of the executive in financial procedures.[33] Recent transformations have not affected the existing situation of executive dominance—instead, they have aimed at strengthening parliamentary control over the executive and its financial propositions, thereby improving the final quality of budgetary decisions. This was the aim of the *loi organique* on public budgets of 2001 (LOLF), whose significance was confirmed and strengthened at the highest level of the legal system by the constitutional reform of 2008.[34] On that occasion, another innovation went largely unnoticed: the amended text of Article 34(7) FC provides that 'the multiannual public guidelines for public finances … shall be part of the objective of balanced accounts for public administration'. Therefore, a 'golden rule' was already present in the constitutional text—it remains to be specified what it entails.

The following developments can be summarized as a difficult path towards the entrenchment of a *règle d'or*. The draft constitutional amendment bill initiated in 2011 was based not on a simple balanced-budget rule but on triennial 'frame laws [*lois-cadre*] for balanced public finance', subject to compulsory a priori review by the Conseil constitutionnel.

As a result of the election of President Hollande in 2012, however, Article 3(2) TSCG has been implemented by means of organic legislation. More properly speaking, the organic law finally implements Article 34 FC, as amended in 2008: multiannual Programming Laws (*lois de programmation des finances publiques*) should seek balanced finances in the medium term. As can be seen, France appears committed to a flexible approach (or a difficult adaptation) to the *règle d'or*. Article 11 of the organic law provides for the establishment, within the Court of Auditors, of a High Council of Public Finance, whose mission is to

[32] See Arts 16–19 of the Constitution-implementing Legge 24 dicembre 2012, n 243 (Disposizioni per l'attuazione del principio del pareggio di bilancio ai sensi dell'articolo 81, sesto comma, della Costituzione).

[33] Ordonnance no 59-2 du 2 janvier 1959 portant loi organique relative aux lois de finances.

[34] See eg Art 24(1) FC, as modified in 2008: 'Parliament shall pass statutes. It shall monitor the action of the Government. It shall assess public policies.' See also Art 47-2(1) FC (added in 2008).

elaborate forecasts and give advice with regard to Programming Laws and annual public budgets.

IV. QUESTIONABLE FEATURES OF NATIONAL CONSTITUTIONAL REFORMS IN THE EUROZONE

These recent constitutional reforms are not immune from interpretive and functional problems. With some noteworthy exceptions, they contain a probably dysfunctional blend of legal and economic concepts, and provide detailed regulation of issues which do have not a properly constitutional substance.[35] Moreover, financial constitutions have often been modified without taking into account their necessary co-ordination with other 'structural' aspects of constitutional orders. In this section, enforceability and derogations will be examined in order to make some points on the magnitude of these transformations.

A. Enforcing Balanced-Budget Clauses

The first issue that should be considered is the actual enforceability of the new constitutional clauses, which is by now (implicitly or not) required by the TSCG. In fact, the TSCG offers an alternative for the implementation of Article 3(1) because some EU Member States (eg the Netherlands)[36] have not established a system of constitutional adjudication: thus, justiciability of national balanced-budget constitutional clauses before constitutional courts was a really urgent issue for the drafters of the TSCG.[37] The new constitutional norms lay down more precise normative frameworks, with which legislators are supposed to comply when drafting the annual budget. Thus, the role of those bodies whose primary mission is judicial review of legislation, ie constitutional courts, is inevitably addressed. Furthermore, courts will have to cope with national constitutional provisions, and not merely with 'pure' EU law, which, in general terms, is not a parameter of legitimacy in national constitutional adjudication.[38] When it comes to the future role of courts, the picture is mixed, and uncertainty is not merely a result of the inevitable ambiguity of concepts whose defining core lies somewhere between economics and law.

What can be said with regard to national constitutional courts?

[35] See discussion by N Lupo, 'La revisione costituzionale della disciplina di bilancio e il sistema delle fonti' in V Lippolis, N Lupo, GM Salerno and G Scaccia (eds), *Costituzione e pareggio di bilancio* (Napoli, Jovene, 2012) 89, 103–105.

[36] See M Diamant and M van Emmerik, in this book (Chapter 12).

[37] See discussion by JV Louis, 'Un traité vite fait, bien fait? Le traité du 2 mars 2012 sur la stabilité, la coordination et la gouvernance au sein de l'Union économique et monétaire' (2012) 48(2) *Revue trimestrielle de droit européen* 5.

[38] See eg V Ruiz Almendral, 'Estabilidad Presupuestaria y Reforma Constitucional' (2012) 11(41) *Revista Española de Derecho Europeo* 33, 84.

In the case of Germany, the constitutional parameters of legitimacy look more precise than they used to be before 2009—thus, their justiciability should 'have improved':[39] the new wording of Article 115 BL is much more detailed than it once was. Looking at the procedures by which an action might be brought before the Bundesverfassungsgericht, however, one would barely recognize any major innovations. The admissible procedures appear to be limited to abstract review, conflicts among constitutional organs, or conflicts between *Bund* and *Länder*. Concrete review or individual complaints are probably excluded. Thus, even if the new constitutional norms provide a much more analytical framework of legitimacy for judicial review, their actual justiciability still largely depends on politically prompted procedures.

The same might be said of Spain.[40] The current organization of the system of constitutional review in Spain makes it quite difficult to challenge the constitutional legitimacy of (state) public budgets before the Tribunal Constitucional. In fact, such a procedure might only be initiated by parliamentary minorities or, possibly, the national ombudsman (Defensor del Pueblo) (Article 162(1) SC). The possibility that the Court of Auditors will go before the Tribunal Constitucional is quite limited. Conversely, the state might challenge the legitimacy of public budgets of the Autonomous Communities much more easily—even in this regard, however, the recent reform has not brought about any changes.

As already observed, there is quite limited room for judicial review of (state) budgets before the Constitutional Court in Italy.[41] An early draft of the Italian balanced-budget constitutional amendment empowered the Court of Auditors to 'request a ruling on constitutional legitimacy for violation of the financial coverage requirement referred to in the third paragraph of Art 81', thus providing the Court of Auditors with more standing before the Constitutional Court. Be that as it may, such provision has disappeared in the most recent version of the amendment—there, in turn, the establishment 'of an independent body within the Houses of Parliament' was announced, whose task is to monitor and check public finance trends and compliance with budgetary rules. This choice has been sharply criticized by the Italian Court of Auditors itself in its advisory opinion on the proposal of the balanced-budget amendment.[42] It might be added, on the other side, that the role of the national Court of Auditors has been 'forgotten' in Spain too.[43]

Whereas in Germany, Spain and Italy courts have not traditionally played a

[39] Mayer (n 23) 301.

[40] See C Fasone, 'La giustiziabilità della clausola sul pareggio di bilancio in Spagna. Quali indicazioni per il caso italiano?' in C Decaro, N Lupo and G Rivosecchi (eds), *La 'manutenzione' della giustizia costituzionale. Il giudizio sulle leggi in Italia, Spagna e Francia* (Torino, Giappichelli, 2012) 221.

[41] See especially G Scaccia, 'La giustiziabilità della regola del pareggio di bilancio' in Lippolis et al (n 35) 211, 215–16.

[42] See Corte dei conti (Italian Court of Auditors) (sezioni riunite in sede consultiva), advisory opinion no 3/2011 (13 December 2011), at www.corteconti.it/export/sites/portalecdc/_documenti/controllo/sezioni_riunite/sezioni_riunite_in_sede_consultiva/2011/delibera_3_2011_cons.pdf.

[43] See Ruiz Almendral (n 38) 85–87.

relevant role in fiscal affairs, in France, on the contrary, constitutional review of financial laws has been in place for many years, and constitutional judges have been developing vast and significant case law concerning financial issues.[44] The French Conseil constitutionnel even declared the constitutional illegitimacy of a public budget in the late 1970s.[45] Furthermore, Article 40 FC, seeking the limitation of parliamentary profligacy, has always been effectively enforced.[46]

However, the French exception is a rather complicated one. As far as its genesis, functions, composition and procedural features are concerned, the Conseil constitutionnel has had a unique history among constitutional courts. Moreover, the French Constitution and organic legislation contain highly analytical rules on financial procedures, and the Conseil was entrusted with their enforcement in order to preserve the respective domains of action of the executive and legislative branches. Indeed, this is a reflex of the original role of the Conseil as a keeper of the constitutional prerogatives of the executive in the face of much-feared exorbitant claims of the legislature. It was a paradoxical reversal of the earlier meaning of (political) financial constitutionalism: by the mid-1950s, the executive was supposed to control Parliament and its alleged tendency to profligacy.[47] Before the introduction of the *question prioritaire de constitutionnalité* in 2008—which should not have any particular effects in this field—legislative deliberations could be reviewed exclusively at the request of legislative or executive office-holders. The above-mentioned provision of Article 40 of the Constitution, limiting parliamentary financial initiatives, was just another component of this constitutional strategy.

As noted above, French constitutional law has been marked by an extensive reform of financial procedures in the last decade. The proposed constitutional amendments on the *règle d'or* laid the ground for compulsory a priori review of frame laws and annual budgetary laws by the Conseil constitutionnel, which should prevent subsequent challenges of their legitimacy under the *question prioritaire de constitutionnalité*. The more recent organic law concerning financial planning and governance no longer provides for a compulsory a priori review by the Conseil constitutionnel—this, however, is a modification of ultimately little significance, for there is already no particular difficulty for parliamentary minorities wishing to challenge public budgets before the Conseil. With care to preserve the *marges de manœuvre* for political office-holders, France continues to go its own way in the management of financial constitutional issues.

[44] See A Mangiavillano, 'La saisine parlementaire et le contrôle de constitutionnalité des lois de finances' (7th French Congress of Constitutional Lawyers, Paris, September 2008, www.droitconstitutionnel.org).

[45] Conseil constitutionnel, Decision no 79-110 DC of 24 December 1979 (Loi de finances pour 1980).

[46] 'Private Members' Bills and amendments introduced by Members of Parliament shall not be admissible where their enactment would result in either a diminution of public revenue or the creation or increase of any public expenditure.'

[47] See J Barthélemy, 'Le procès de la Commission des finances' in *Mélanges Carré de Malberg* (Paris, Sirey, 1933) 243, 265.

B. Derogations: Majoritarian Parliamentary Politics Taking its Revenge?

The other side of this issue is whether and when derogations to basic provisions of financial constitutions are admitted, or, in other words, how constitutional legislators shape the certain amount of flexibility which the TSCG itself sees as inevitable (Article 3(3)(b)). This point does not necessarily concern the relationship between legislatures and courts; however, the ability of parliaments to evaluate the existence of exceptional circumstances and permit derogation to fiscal constitutional limits should be assessed in order to understand how deep the wave of depoliticization of budgetary issues has gone. If legislative supermajorities are required in order to determine the existence of a cause of derogation, this would be another sign of a decisive shift in the internal balance of financial constitutional law. Nevertheless, national legal systems are quite suspicious about taking this step.

In Germany, for instance, during the elaboration of the 'second federal reform' there was some debate about a provision requiring a two-thirds majority of members of the Bundestag in order to recognize an emergency situation allowing for departure from the debt brake: 'If so, the principle of parliamentary legitimacy with regard to majoritarian decisions and responsibility would [have been] severely affected in one important aspect.'[48] Eventually, however, an absolute majority of Bundestag members (ie in most cases, a 'Chancellor majority') was seen as sufficient (Article 115(2) BL)[49]. The same has recently happened in the amended Spanish (Article 135(4))[50] and Italian (Article 81(2))[51] constitutions.

This is perhaps a sign that there is a need for flexibility—and, what is more, flexibility clauses are seen as an occasion for parliamentary majorities (and the executives which they support) to regain some ground. An absolute majority is obviously more than a mere plurality, which is the usual quorum required for parliamentary deliberations. Nevertheless, present-day electoral rules and party systems shape the real meaning of an absolute majority requirement in all these countries. National executives generally command strong and quite cohesive majority support within the legislature. Furthermore, it is far from self-evident whether constitutional courts will chose to engage in a difficult, controversial scrutiny of the degree of 'extraordinariness' of the economic situation after a parliamentary vote. With specific regard to the Italian case, however, it has been

[48] I Härtel, 'Föderalismusreform II. Bund-Länder Finanzbeziehungen im Lichte aktueller Ordnungsanforderungen' (2008) 58 *JuristenZeitung* 437, 441.

[49] 'In cases of natural catastrophes or unusual emergency situations beyond governmental control and substantially harmful to the state's financial capacity, these credit limits may be exceeded on the basis of a decision by a majority of the members of the Bundestag.'

[50] Making reference to 'natural disasters, economic recession or extraordinary emergency situations that are either beyond the control of the State or significantly impair the financial situation or the economic or social sustainability of the State'. See critical assessment by F de Carreras Serra, in 'La reforma del artículo 135 CE' (2011) 31(93) *Revista Española de Derecho Constitucional* 159, 187.

[51] Mentioning the necessity of 'taking account of the effects of the economic cycle, or exceptional circumstances'.

observed that the Italian Constitutional Court has a history of implementing (to a certain extent at least) seemingly undetermined constitutional clauses.[52]

Such a situation might change, however, if the CJEU acquired a leading role in enforcing the obligation not only to enact, but also to respect the constitutional golden rule in national budgetary procedures:[53] this might be an important incentive for national constitutional courts to engage more actively in constitutional review in the light of balanced-budget clauses. Among the violations which the CJEU might be asked to examine under Article 8(1) and (2) TSCG, there may well be imperfect national compliance with the TSCG at the constitutional level. This would be a fundamental innovation: suffice it to make a comparison with the well-known decision of the CJEU in *Commission v Council*, which eventually justified the decision of the Council not to follow recommendations from the Commission under the Stability and Growth Pact.[54]

When asked to assess the compatibility of the TSCG with the German constitutional order, the Bundesverfassungsgericht took the trouble to specify that the competence of the CJEU under Article 8(1) TSCG 'is just limited to the codification of these instruments but does not extend to their concrete application'.[55] Likewise, the Conseil constitutionnel, while reaffirming its constitutional mission of reviewing *lois de finances*, underlined that the TSCG does not necessarily enable the CJEU to assess whether French constitutional law is compatible with the TSCG. This is made possible by the formulation of Article 3(2) TSCG, which allows for supralegislative transposition of the balanced-budget rule[56].

V. LESSONS FROM THE UNITED STATES

Comparison with the US constitutional experience is useful because it shows the difficulties of the practical implementation of the principles of fiscal constitutionalism. Reliance on judicial review and distrust towards the mechanisms of representative democracy—at least at the state and municipal level—have a longer history in the United States.[57]

Subsequent waves of constitutional reforms have entrenched principles of fiscal constitutionalism at the state level in the United States. Scholars distinguish

[52] See Scaccia (n 41) 234; M Luciani, 'Costituzione, bilancio, diritti e doveri dei cittadini' (2012) 31 *Questione giustizia* 92, 126–127.

[53] See F Fabbrini, 'The Fiscal Compact, the "Golden Rule" and the Paradox of European Federalism" (2012) 36 *Boston College International & Comparative Law Review* 1, 25. If one relies on the preparatory works of the TSCG, a more minimalist interpretation should be correct (Louis (n 37)).

[54] CJEU, Case C-27/04 *Commission v Council* [2004] ECR I-6649.

[55] Bundesverfassungsgericht, judgment of 12 September 2012 (n 6) para 316.

[56] Conseil constitutionnel, Decision no 2012-653 DC of 9 August 2012 (Traité sur la stabilité, la coordination et la gouvernance au sein de l'Union économique et monétaire) paras 29–30. With regard to fiscal councils, the *Conseil* also held that '[it] is entrusted with reviewing budget laws, and it will have to exercise such review taking into account the advice of those independent institutions which will have preliminarily been established' (para 27).

[57] See RC Schragger, 'Democracy and Debt' (2012) 121 *Yale Law Journal* 860, 864.

between public purpose requirements, limiting the authority of state governments to providing financial assistance to private enterprises and dating back to the pernicious effects of state assistance to private firms in the 1820s and 1830s; debt limitations, including balanced-budget clauses, which were entrenched as a result of the wave of tax increases adopted to pay off the state debts accumulated during the canal and railroad boom; and tax and expenditure limitations, which have been developing since the late 1970s as part of a wider 'tax revolt'.[58]

Interestingly, balanced-budget clauses do not normally allow debt to be contracted without the approval of a *supermajority* in the legislature, of voters in a referendum, or both: thus, for instance, Article IX(15) of the Constitution of Michigan provides that

> The state may borrow money for specific purposes in amounts as may be provided by acts of the legislature adopted by a vote of two-thirds of the members elected to and serving in each house, and approved by a majority of the electors voting thereon at any general election.[59]

However, scholars are often very sceptical about the merits of entrenching financial policies in constitutional texts: states facing balanced-budget requirements often seek to move as much spending off-budget as possible. Moreover, incentives to use accounting strategies to hide overruns are created: this is at least paradoxical if you compare it with the European situation and the reasons—eg misrepresentation of data in public budgets—which have led to the elaboration of the TSCG. More interestingly, the link between constitutionally entrenched fiscal discipline and the overall economic health of a state is questionable.[60] Apart from this, it seems that political office-holders are neither strongly nor properly influenced by financial constitutional provisions.

Furthermore, US courts have been remarkably shy in constructing and enforcing those clauses. There might be three main reasons for this: first, courts tend to treat fiscal limits not as 'truly' constitutional issues (like, for example, fundamental rights) but rather as ordinary legislation. Secondly, judges, who (contrary to what occurs in Europe) are often directly elected, might share programmatic orientations with political office-holders;[61] and thirdly, courts may be influenced by the degree to which the provisions reflect current political values and enjoy political support.[62]

All these circumstances might have contributed to undermining the authority

[58] See R Briffault, 'Foreword: The Disfavored Constitution: State Fiscal Limits and State Constitutional Law' (2003) 34 *Rutgers Law Journal* 907; PA Van Malleghem, in this book (Chapter 8).

[59] See above at Section IV.B.

[60] Schragger (n 57) 872.

[61] It has been suggested, however, that elected judges, rather than those nominated by the governor and confirmed by the legislature, might be more willing to enforce fiscal constitutional rules effectively (see H Bohn and RP Inman, 'Balanced Budget Rules and Public Deficits: Evidence from the US States', National Bureau of Economic Research Working Paper no 5533, April 1996, available at www.nber.org/papers/w5533).

[62] Briffault (n 58) 939–44; see also DB Tobin, 'The Balanced Budget Amendment: Will Judges Become Accountants? A Look at State Experiences' (1996) 12 *Journal of Law and Policy* 153.

of state constitutions in the United States. This is all the more convincing if one considers that the Federal Constitution has very little to say about the financial aspects of constitutional law, except for conferring some powers on the Congress or setting procedural requirements for public expenditure.

The US experience shows that fiscal constitutional provisions raise many important questions. To summarize, a balanced-budget amendment should be enforceable, 'it should nevertheless permit carefully delimited degrees of flexibility in its application' in order to meet possible economic emergency, and it should be politically neutral.[63]

VI. ASSESSING TRANSFORMATIONS

How can reforms throughout Europe be interpreted? Are we facing some kind of transformation of the way in which constitutional law deals with financial issues? This section will discuss the results of comparative analysis in the light of two alternative narratives. The first one is mainly focused on the respective merits of procedural and substantial approaches to financial constitutional issues; the second one, in turn, is more interested in evaluating the balance between political and legal features in the recent wave of reforms.

A. The Procedural vs. the Substantial

The most important studies of financial constitutional law tend to analyse the rise and transformations of 'financial constitutions' from two alternative perspectives.[64] A first constitutional politics approach relies on *procedural* aspects of budgetary decision-making processes in order to improve the operation of the financial constitution. This scholarship is mostly interested in the allocation of powers as an aspect of the relationship between the executive and the legislature. From the viewpoint of constitutional legal scholarship, therefore, this trend of legislative and constitutional reform can be seen as another step forward in the rationalization of political power.[65] Classical examples of the procedural option are those constitutional provisions which allow the executive to limit those parliamentary initiatives that may have financial implications.[66] Those clauses, however, have been criticized for failing to encompass the actual operation of relationships between the executive and the legislature. They seem to envisage a latent conflict between these two branches of government, thus downplaying

[63] TP Seto, 'Drafting a Federal Balanced Budget Amendment That Does What It Is Supposed to Do (And No More)' (1997) 106 *Yale Law Journal* 1449, 1456.

[64] See eg G Rivosecchi, *L'indirizzo politico finanziario tra Costituzione italiana e vincoli europei* (Padova, Cedam, 2007) 36–37.

[65] As meant by B Mirkine-Guetzévitch, *Les nouvelles tendances du droit constitutionnel* (Paris, Marcel Giard, 1931).

[66] See above at Section III.

the osmotic relationship between the executive and *its* parliamentary majority and the possibly collusive effects of such co-operation.[67]

In the last three decades, the success of procedural financial constitutionalism has been due to a wave of administrative reforms (eg New Public Management)[68] in most Western countries, and an increasing consciousness that institutional arrangements for public budgeting do matter.[69] The principal support of procedural financial constitutionalism comes from various international organizations (eg the International Monetary Fund or the Organisation for Economic Co-operation and Development), which promote, among other things, transparency of budget documents, multiannual budgeting, strengthened ex-post scrutiny, etc.[70] The most elaborated legal output of this trend is perhaps the 2001 French LOLF, whose inspiring principles were partially constitutionalized in 2008.[71] The same could be said of Italian law No 196/2009, containing a comprehensive reform of public finances and accounting. The preamble of Directive No 2011/85/EU, which seeks greater homogeneity among national budgetary processes, is particularly eloquent on this respect: it stresses the importance of 'the availability of fiscal data', the damage brought about by 'biased and unrealistic macroeconomic and budgetary forecasts', and the crucial role of transparency 'in ensuring the use of realistic forecasts for the conduct of budgetary policy'.

A second approach—*fiscal constitutionalism* in the proper sense, heavily influenced by the Public Choice School—is more interested in the constitutional entrenchment of substantial limitations to budgetary decisions. The focus here is more on the *content* of financial decisions than on procedures. The most common (and discussed) manifestations of this trend are balanced-budget constitutional amendments. The chief goal of fiscal constitutionalism is to obtain (by means of formal constitutional entrenchment) something that was originally an unwritten constitutional principle (or 'an old-time fiscal religion') before the fundamental turning point of the establishment of post-war welfare states.[72]

According to the letter of Article 3(1) TSCG and of many of the new national balanced-budget clauses throughout the EMU, substantial fiscal constitutionalism is undoubtedly having one of its finest hours.

[67] See generally A Wildavsky, *Budgeting: A Comparative Theory of Budgetary Processes* (New York, Little, Brown & Co., 1975).

[68] See S Cassese, 'The Rise of the Administrative State in Europe' (2010) 60 *Rivista trimestrale di diritto pubblico* 981, 1002-08.

[69] See A Alesina and R Perotti, 'The Political Economy of Budget Deficits', International Monetary Fund Staff Papers (1995) 1.

[70] See eg the OECD Best Practices for Budget Transparency (www.oecd.org/gov/budgeting/Best%20Practices%20Budget%20Transparency%20-%20complete%20with%20cover%20page.pdf), and general discussion by G Pisauro, 'La valutazione della spesa e il processo di bilancio' (2010) 16 *Giornale di diritto amministrativo* 684.

[71] See eg Art 47-2(2) FC (introduced in 2008): 'The accounts of public administrations shall be lawful and faithful. They shall provide a true and fair view of the result of the management, assets and financial situation of the said public administrations.'

[72] See JM Buchanan and RE Wagner, *Democracy in Deficit: The Political Legacy of Lord Keynes* (San Diego, CA, Academic Press, 1977) ch 2.

This chapter, however, does not follow in the path of the studies that rely on this classic distinction (procedural vs substantial approach). In my opinion, the most interesting aspect in the constitutional reforms since 2009 is how financial constitutions work and how they are enforced, if at all. The relevant question is not the *what* (ie whether financial constitutions take the shape of procedural arrangements or substantial requirements) but the *how* of financial constitutional law. This distinction might be useful to explain the ongoing transformations in the EU. In the next subsection, the constitutional transformations taking place in Europe will be addressed from the viewpoint of the relationship between 'political' and 'legal' constitutionalism, notions that have been coined in order to interpret the internal tensions characterizing present-day constitutional life in Anglo-Saxon countries.

Furthermore, it is necessary to draw a clear distinction between the ongoing debate about the financial constitution of the EU and the conceptual categories of US fiscal constitutionalism. The quest for financial (and, supposedly, economic and political) stability is much more important to the European debate than public-choice-inspired projects of constitutional reform. Fiscal constitutionalism appears to be related to an American line of thought—ultimately arguing for a reduction in the size of government—which cannot be easily recognized in present-day European debates. German ordoliberalism is much more relevant to the current German (and European) constitutional landscape, which is characterized by a complex redefinition of the role of government.[73]

B. The Political vs the Legal

Theories of political constitutionalism—and the political constitution—state that political office-holders 'are held to constitutional account through political means, and through political institutions (for example, Parliament)'.[74] A legal constitution, on the other hand, 'imagines that the principal means, and the principal institution through which the government is held to account is the law and the court-room'.[75] Political constitutionalism defends the democratic process against judicial review 'not on the ground that democracy is more important than constitutionalism, rights or the rule of law, but because democracy embodies and upholds these values'.[76] Political constitutionalism can be said to have developed as a democratic reaction against a perceived hyperjudicialization of constitu-

[73] See S Cassese, 'La nuova costituzione economica' in S Cassese (ed), *La nuova costituzione economica*, 5th edn (Roma and Bari, Laterza, 2012) 324. As for German ordoliberalism and US neoliberalism, see M Foucault, *Nascita della biopolitica. Corso al Collège de France (1978–1979)* (Milano, Feltrinelli, 2005) 176–80.

[74] A Tomkins, *Public Law* (Oxford, Oxford University Press, 2003) 18–19.

[75] Ibid.

[76] R Bellamy, *Political Constitutionalism: A Republican Defence of the Constitutionality of Democracy* (Cambridge, Cambridge University Press, 2007) 260.

tional issues.[77] Therefore, it tries to rehabilitate the virtues of the political process as a fundamental component of contemporary constitutionalism.

For the purposes of this chapter, the most evident practical difficulty about political constitutionalism—and its concrete outcomes in the contemporary constitutional landscape—is the actual weakness of contemporary parliaments. Such weakness is particularly serious when it comes to the legislature exercising its scrutiny function vis-à-vis the executive. Concisely speaking, 'the political constitution relies on the rigour and vigour of the political process. The more open, transparent, participatory, representative and deliberative politics is, the better the model will work in practice.'[78] However, the rise of strongly centralized executives since the 1980s has led to an apparent marginalization of parliaments.[79] This situation seems particularly serious when it comes to holding the executive to account[80]. As has been observed:

> [V]arious measures, arising in different political cultures and affecting different institutional mechanisms, may reflect a need to redress what has become an increasingly unbalanced relationship between parliament and government: but we cannot be confident that those who wiled executive power will willingly expose themselves to the prospect of more effective and transparent political challenge.[81]

The importance of this point is particularly striking when financial issues are concerned: as noted above, attempted reforms in many countries have tried, not so much to alter the balance of power between the legislative and executive branches (thereby opposing an arguably inevitable trend in favour of the latter), as to strengthen parliamentary oversight in order to obtain healthier public finances and a more transparent and effective implementation of public policies. Nowadays, oversight is supposed to be the main parliamentary activity in semi-presidential systems or those parliamentary systems where the executive can rely on strong and docile majorities. Here lies the most serious structural problem of any financial constitution, no matter what it provides for, ie the desirable vigour of the political process, and the actually limited capacity of representative assemblies effectively to exercise their functions—be they of policy co-determination or of oversight—vis-à-vis the executive. In light of this broad context, what changes can be discerned in the respective positions of the branches involved in the management of day-to-day business?

On the side of parliaments, the failure of legislatures to affirm their role in

[77] See M Goldoni, 'Il ritorno del costituzionalismo alla politica: il *"Political"* e il *"Popular" Constitutionalism*' (2010) 30 *Quaderni costituzionali* 733.

[78] Tomkins (n 74) 20.

[79] See eg T Poguntke and P Webb (eds), *The Presidentialization of Politics: A Comparative Study of Modern Democracies* (Oxford, Oxford University Press, 2005).

[80] See A Tomkins, 'What Is Parliament For?' in N Bamforth and P Leyland (eds), *Public Law in a Multi-Layered Constitution* (Oxford, Hart Publishing, 2003) 53; P Craig and A Tomkins (eds), *The Executive and Public Law: Power and Accountability in Comparative Perspective* (Oxford, Oxford University Press, 2006).

[81] AW Bradley and C Pinelli, 'Parliamentarism' in M Rosenfeld and A Sajó (eds), *The Oxford Handbook of Comparative Constitutional Law* (Oxford, Oxford University Press, 2012) 650, 668–69.

budgetary matters has been relentlessly observed. In Germany, scholars have claimed that a 'deparliamentarisation' (*Entparlamentarisierung*) of the budget is taking place.[82] Discussion of budget plans was said to be a 'pointless rite' four decades ago.[83] Recent attempts to reinvigorate parliamentary oversight were apparently unsuccessful in the short term. Legislators in continental European jurisdictions are not particularly interested in controlling the execution of budgets, due partly to a lack of political incentives.[84] Meanwhile, strong executives have acquired extensive control over the budgetary process.

Thus, the case for a (prevailingly) political understanding of financial constitutional issues might not be so strong as long-standing legal traditions might suggest. So what about a *legalization* of this part of the law of the constitution? What kind of judicial review will European constitutional courts be willing to perform when dealing with considerably 'thicker' financial constitutions?

In the debate about political constitutionalism the greatest emphasis has been placed on judicial review when it assesses the compatibility of legislation with constitutional rights. However, the challenge of legal constitutionalism is no less ambitious when it comes to the review of power-related or 'structural' constitutional provisions[85]. Some authors have attempted to engage with this issue by relativizing the *summa divisio* of constitutional provisions. They claim that some kinds of structural review are distinguishable from rights review and are not susceptible to democracy-based objections. Goldsworthy, for instance, includes among those clauses: provisions dividing powers within a federation; 'manner and form' requirements governing the composition, powers and procedures of the legislature and its houses; requirements that only independent courts may adjudicate legal disputes concerning the rights and duties of the litigants; and provisions forbidding states or provinces within a federation from discriminating against the residents or businesses of other states or provinces.[86]

What may this mean with regard to national constitutional courts in the EMU? One might expect, for instance, that they will engage in a stricter scrutiny of constitutional procedural guarantees of the budgetary process than they used to do before.[87] The great question, however, is still how far they will go in reviewing

[82] C Waldhoff, 'Grundzüge des Finanzrechts des Grundgesetzes' in Isensee and Kirchhof (n 18) 813, 898.

[83] S Cassese, 'Controllo della spesa pubblica e direzione dell'amministrazione' (1973) 4 *Politica del diritto* 39, 40—41.

[84] See eg G Carcassonne, 'La LOLF et le renouveau du contrôle' (2007) 25(97) *Revue française de finances publiques* 77, 81.

[85] See A Stone, 'Judicial review without Rights: Some Problems for the Democratic Legitimacy of Structural Judicial Review' (2008) 28 *OJLS* 1; E Cloots, 'The European Court of Justice and Member State Federalism: Balancing or Categorisation' in E Cloots, G De Baere and S Sottiaux (eds), *Federalism in the European Union* (Oxford, Hart Publishing, 2012) 322.

[86] See J Goldsworthy, 'Structural Judicial Review and the Objection from Democracy' (2010) 60 *University of Toronto Law Journal* 137, 153–54.

[87] There is some evidence, for example, that the Italian Constitutional Court has been stressing more effectively the nexus between Art 81(3) Const and financial stability in the last few months: see C Buzzacchi, 'Copertura finanziaria e pareggio di bilancio: un binomio a rime obbligate?' (2012) 2 *Rivista AIC* no 4.

legislation under the new, substance-focused constitutional clauses. To sum up, within the EMU an undeniable trend towards legalisation will have to cope with a constitutional framework of constitutional litigation which has remained largely unaffected after the recent reforms. On the other hand, possible competition with the CJEU may turn out to be a powerful incentive for national courts.

Perhaps the most plausible path of the legalization of financial constitutions is related to the (still vague) emergence of *new* constitutional goods, eg responsibility towards future generations, which lies, almost inevitably, beyond the scope of incumbent representative assemblies (and the executives that they support). In the words of the Constitutional Court of the German *Land* of North Rhine-Westphalia, declaring the illegitimacy of a budgetary law, 'citizens and parliaments in the future have to be protected against the risk of losing their necessary possibilities of financial action (according to their criteria) to cope with problems of the day'.[88] The actual significance of often-invoked 'responsibility towards future generations' lies outside the scope of this study;[89] what is interesting, in turn, is to consider how courts have tried to elaborate this principle, thereby establishing a link with the political process itself. In its preliminary judgment on the ESM Treaty, for example, the Bundesverfassungsgericht also resorted to a similar argument but it linked it more convincingly with the preservation of a sound political process. The Court stated that:

> [A] constitutional commitment on the part of the parliaments and thus a palpable restriction on their budgetary power to act may be necessary precisely in order to preserve the democratic power to shape affairs for the body politic in the long term. … Even if such a commitment restricts democratic legislative discretion in the present, it serves at the same time to guarantee it for the future[90].

VII. CONCLUDING REMARKS

In light of the above discussion, it appears that the current European scene is contradictory and not exempt from paradoxical traits.

First, there is an evident paradox. On the one hand, the Bundesverfassungsgericht has been strenuously defending the sovereignty of German constituent power and 'the political formation of the economic, cultural and social living conditions' at the national level, among which 'fundamental fiscal decisions on public revenue and public expenditure'[91] occupy a central place. On the other hand, a 'Europe that is speaking German' would like to drive Member

[88] Constitutional Court of NRW, judgment of 15 March 2011 (VerfGH 20/10).

[89] See eg critical assessment by M Luciani, 'Generazioni future, distribuzione temporale della spesa pubblica e vincoli *costituzionali*' (2008) 36 *Diritto e società* 145.

[90] Bundesverfassungsgericht, judgment of 12 September 2012 (n 6) para 224.

[91] Bundesverfassungsgericht, judgment of the Second Senate of 30 June 2009 (BVerfGE 123, 267, 356–59).

States to incorporate the golden rule in their constitutions, thereby limiting the political process.[92]

Secondly, there is a seemingly unstoppable push towards the normative entrenchment of some kind of fiscal constitutionalism—this trend, however, is perhaps just the last stage (in Europe, at least) of a transnational movement of constitutional politics.[93] However, I think that the other, perhaps more dramatic shift towards legal constitutionalism has not yet completely manifested itself.

Even if the TSCG states that it will 'fully respect the prerogatives of national Parliaments' (Article 3(2)), its more innovative provisions clearly represent a corrosion of political decision-making at the national level. It is not clear, however, the extent to which such corrosion would take place and financial constitutional laws will be *legalized*. In fact, the (cautiously limited) room for constitutional review of legislation under those clauses in France, Germany, Italy and Spain looks more like Germanic *Staatsgerichtsbarkeit*—a kind of review deeply rooted in the political process. Be that as it may, this is perhaps another chapter in the long history of constitutional conflicts within federal (or, more broadly, compound) legal systems and the perceived, incremental trend towards the quest for judge-made (instead of political) solutions.[94]

According to a recent major account of the foundations, transformations and possible decline of Western public law, the present age is marked by the rise of the so-called ephorate: '[A] new branch of government comprising office-holders who possess the type of expertise and specialised knowledge that has become the basis of effective governmental decision-making … [it] expresses a new phase in the development of government'.[95] Financial issues are the area where this trend towards depoliticization is most evident. Is that hypothesis correct when recent constitutional transformations within the EU are taken into account? In my opinion, the answer should be slightly nuanced: even the apparent victory of a substantial approach to financial constitutional issues—with the constitutional entrenchment of balanced-budget clauses—may not result in their complete depoliticization. The answer depends on the cleavage between a political and a legal understanding of constitutionalism, and how deep the shift towards the latter has been so far.

As noted above, preservation of the *political* aspects of financial constitutions in the future might provide the most plausible justification for their actual *legalization* in the present. According to Miguel Maduro's phrasing, the limitation of 'outbounded democratic externalities' might provide courts with tempting

[92] See Editorial, 'The Fiscal Compact and the European Constitutions: "Europe Speaking German"' (2012) 8 *European Constitutional Law Review* 1.

[93] See R Bifulco, 'Il pareggio di bilancio in Germania: una riforma costituzionale postnazionale?' (2011) 1 *Rivista AIC* no 3.

[94] See H Kelsen, 'Die Bundesexekution. Ein Beitrag zur Theorie und Praxis des Bundesstaates, unter besonderer Berücksichtigung der deutschen Reichs- und der österreichischen Bundes-Verfassung' in *Festgabe für Fritz Fleiner zum 60. Geburtstag* (Tübingen, Mohr Siebeck, 1927) 127; C Schmitt, *Verfassungslehre* (Berlin, Duncker & Humblot, 1928) 112 et seq.

[95] Loughlin (n 14) 450.

arguments when asked to review budgetary laws.[96] It remains for constitutional courts to determine an appropriate balance between these two essential components of constitutionalism when adjudicating cases under the new balanced-budget clauses.

[96] See MP Maduro, 'Three Claims of Constitutional Pluralism' in M Avbelj and J Komárek (eds), *Constitutional Pluralism in the European Union and Beyond* (Oxford, Hart Publishing, 2012) 67.

10

*Fiscal Stability Rules in Central European Constitutions**

MAREK ANTOŠ

I. INTRODUCTION

THE IDEA OF having rules that are intended to limit the freedom of parliaments and governments when creating state budgets, resulting in the long-term sustainability of public finances, is not a new one. The reasons for their adoption are various. Sometimes it may be a recognition of the weakness of political actors, who are well aware that they could forsake good resolutions and prefer a short-term goal over long-term one—for instance to increase expenditure or to decrease taxes at the expense of budget discipline in order to be re-elected. Recalling the Jon Elster's famous theory of precommitment,[1] we can see that while Odysseus had himself tied to the mast of his ship in order to resist the temptation of the Sirens, politicians today are trying to tie themselves as well as their followers to the mast of fiscal rules in order to prevent state indebtedness. However, it is not always about being tied firmly. The reason can be also symbolic: governments try to show their attempts to create healthy public finances both to their own citizens, who then accept some unpopular measures more easily,[2] but also towards financial markets. The latter have, at least lately, become the key actors. The confidence of the financial markets determines the interest rates at which the states can borrow money to cover their expenditures

* I am indebted to all participants at the conference in Tilburg who provided helpful comments on and criticism of this paper, most notably to Federico Fabbrini, Peter Lindseth, Alexandre de Streel and Pieter-Augustijn Van Malleghem. I would also like to express my deepest gratitude to Renata Uitz, not only for her very valuable feedback on the previous version of this paper, but also for all her tremendous support during my stay at the Central European University, Budapest. Last but not least, I would like to thank the Czech Scientific Foundation for its generous support (project no P408/11/P366). All errors of course remain my responsibility.

[1] J Elster, *Ulysses and the Sirens: Studies in Rationality and Irrationality* (Cambridge, Cambridge University Press, 1979) 36.

[2] For a closer analysis of these factors see X Debrun and M S Kumar, 'Fiscal Rules, Fiscal Councils and All That: Commitment Devices, Signaling Tools or Smokescreens?' in Banca d'Italia (ed), *Fiscal Policy: Current Issues and Challenges*, papers presented at the Banca d'Italia workshop held in Perugia, 29–31 March 2007, 479–506.

and, as the examples of Italy and Greece show, these markets can have a critical influence on the duration and composition of governments.

However, according to Ayuso-i-Casals et al, who explored the development of fiscal rules in EU Member States in the years 1990–2005, international (and European) obligations are by far the strongest factor determining the introduction of budget constraints at the national level. Over the past few decades, the number of these obligations has increased almost four times as a direct result of the adoption of the Maastricht Treaty (1992) and the Stability and Growth Pact (1997, revised in 2005).[3] The adoption of the Fiscal Compact (2012) is going to have an even more distinctive effect in this respect since it directly requires contracting parties which are members of the Eurozone or which decide voluntarily for a so-called 'opt-in' (Article 14) to have incorporated the Treaty's fiscal rules into national law 'through provisions of binding force and permanent character, preferably constitutional' (Article 3(2))[4] at the latest by 1 January 2014.[5] Although the rules are quite detailed, especially in terms of the designated goals, they leave certain room for the states to choose the means. Manifestations of constitutional engineering bringing different results in different countries can be monitored throughout Europe. In this chapter I am going to focus on the constitutional arrangements in Germany, Poland, Hungary and Slovakia. The choice of the countries is largely based on both substantial similarities and substantial differences among them. All of them belong to the same legal family. The latter three (together with the Czech Republic) form the so-called 'Visegrad group' of countries which have a shared communist past and co-ordinated their efforts to join the European Union. While Germany and Slovakia are members of eurozone, and therefore the Fiscal Compact applies in full to them, Poland and Hungary are not. However, I will demonstrate that the approaches of all these countries differ in such a substantial way that in fact they represent four specific models of the constitutionalization of fiscal rules.

I analyse these models of the constitutionalization of fiscal rules on the basis of four evaluation criteria. The first criterion is effectiveness, meaning a degree of probability that the budget rules are going to have a positive influ-

[3] J Ayuso-i-Casals et al, 'Beyond the SGP—Features and Effects of EU National-level Fiscal Rules', in *The Role of Fiscal Rules and Institutions in Shaping Budgetary Outcomes: Workshop* (Brussels, European Commission, 2007) 663 and 678.

[4] Unlike the original proposal directly requesting anchoring at the constitutional level, a looser formulation enabling also other ways (eg the form of organic law in France) was in the end chosen. The reason was the opposition of several Member States (see M Kusák, L Pítrová et al, 'Právní aspekty Smlouvy o stabilitě, koordinaci a správě v hospodářské a měnové unii' (2012) 1 *Acta Universitatis Carolinae— Iuridica* 51). Another explanation may be also the rigidity of some constitutions (eg Belgian, Danish or Dutch) which, in order to accept any change need to be approved not only by current parliament but also by parliament elected in the next elections, which would have been a lengthy and uncertain procedure (see Editorial, 'The Fiscal Compact and the European Constitutions: "Europe Speaking German"' (2012) *European Constitutional Law Review* 3).

[5] Art 3(2) sets a time limit for their adoption—one year from the moment when the Treaty comes into force which happened on 1 January 2013 (see Council of the European Union, 'Fiscal Compact Entered into Force on 1 January 2013', *Consilium*, 1 January 2013). The term is, however, calculated on an individual bases in the states which have ratified it after this date.

ence on the development of public finances, which is closely connected with their enforcement mechanisms. The second criterion is their democratic legitimacy and compatibility with a classical notion of parliamentarianism which considers the "power of the purse" to be one of the very basic powers of parliament. The third criterion is their flexibility in relation to the economic cycle, in particular whether they have either procyclical or countercyclical design. It must be admitted, however, that these criteria, in particular the first two, are to some extent conflicting, and therefore all three cannot be fully met at once. For instance, an introduction of an independent non-elected fiscal council empowered with strong budgetary powers might surely be an effective and countercyclical measure, but not a very democratic one. On the other hand, for example, a vague constitutional limitation of budgetary deficit, albeit binding for parliament but with no enforcement mechanism, might be very democratic, arguably also flexible, but not very effective. Therefore, an effort to find a proper design of constitutional fiscal rules means rather an optimization exercise than a strict focus on any single one of these three criteria.

To some extent, although it intentionally leaves a certain discretion as to whether national authorities that should implement it in their national legal order, the Fiscal Compact itself is a result of such an optimization exercise and tries to reconcile these three criteria. And as the countries analysed here have all signed the Compact, the fourth criterion of my analysis is their compliance with the requirements established therein.

II. THE FISCAL POWER OF PARLIAMENT AND ITS LIMITATIONS

Traditional parliamentary powers include the right to approve the state budget. Historically, this power is derived from the Magna Carta, passed in 1215, in which the English king bound himself not to levy taxes without the consent of the nobility (Articles 12 and 14). However, as Wehner notes, the kings tended to circumvent this limitation by covering their expenses through indebtedness, relying on the fact that parliament would in the end have to agree to the deductions necessary to pay off these expenses. Therefore, over centuries parliament gradually gained also the right to approve expenses, which was confirmed by the adoption of the Bill of Rights in 1689.[6] While budgetary power has been shifted to parliament it also became democratized when the non-elected House of Lords gradually lost the right of veto over financial laws. At first, this was ensured by a constitutional convention, but later—after a conflict with the House of Commons which resulted in the adaptation of the Parliament Act of 1911—was also expressed in written law.[7]

[6] J Wehner, *Legislatures and the Budget Process: The Myth of Fiscal Control* (New York, Palgrave Macmillan, 2010) 3.

[7] Ibid, 6.

Therefore it can be assumed that parliamentary control over the budget has two basic functions, at least from a historical point of view. First, it represents a democratic control of the handling of public resources and a manifestation of the principle 'no taxation without representation'. Secondly, it offers a protection against indebtedness and a guarantee of fiscal discipline. The latter function was been fulfilled successfully in most countries until World War II, especially due to the fact that the state played a limited role in the economy, with the result that deficits were not considered normal except in extraordinary periods. However, this idea perished: primarily because of the invention of the welfare state and the expanding role of the state in the economy under the influence of Keynesianism, but also as a consequence of neoclassical economic theory which enforces a constant tax rate even at the cost of a temporary state budget deficit.[8] Such deficits have become a new standard which, as of the 1970s, has led to a steep increase in state indebtedness in most developed countries.[9]

The reason for this behaviour is the so-called 'deficit bias', which is 'a tendency to run fiscal deficits that are not consistent with medium-term fiscal sustainability'.[10] Above all, this is caused by the fact that governments often prefer short-term objectives, such as re-election, to long-term ones, such as creating sustainable public finances.[11] Moreover, public finances suffer from a 'common pool' problem, the result of which is that not only the government, but rather each individual or interest group in a society tries to maximize its own benefit regardless of the common costs, especially as these are only revealed in a long-term perspective.[12] Furthermore, fiscal policy is often procyclical, which means that it is loose in good times and tight in bad times, whereas economic theory recommends quite the opposite.[13]

How is it possible to avoid deficits if parliamentary safeguards have ceased to function and the logic of political competition rather supports them? One possibility is a strong social consensus across the political spectrum which is often achievable when the financial situation reaches an unbearable state. Examples of such consensus include Denmark, which reduced its state debt from 60 per cent to 36 per cent of GDP in 1997– 2005, and Ireland, where the debt was reduced from 120 per cent to 27 per cent of GDP from the beginning of the 1980s to 2005. Wrobel, on the basis of these examples, argues that it is widely estab-

[8] RM Wrobel, 'Balanced Budget Rules in Europe: A Comparative Institutional Analysis' (2008) *International Area Studies Review* 156.

[9] According to the OECD, 'Gross general government debt as a share of GDP for the OECD area has been gradually on the rise since the 1970s, reaching a record level of nearly 100% in 2010' (OECD, 'Government Debt', in *OECD Factbook 2011–2012: Economic, Environmental and Social Statistics* (OECD Publishing, 2011), http://dx.doi.org/10.1787/factbook-2011-91-en).

[10] A Corbacho and G Schwartz, 'Fiscal Responsibility Laws', in MS Kumar and T Ter-Minassian (ed), *Promoting Fiscal Discipline* (Washington, DC, International Monetary Fund, 2007) 59.

[11] Ayuso-i-Casals et al (n 3) 655.

[12] A Fölscher, 'A Balancing Act: Fiscal Responsibility, Accountability and the Power of the Purse' (2006) 6(2) *OECD Journal on Budgeting* 139.

[13] See F Balassone and M S Kumar, 'Cyclicality of Fiscal Policy,' in MS Kumar and T Ter-Minassian (eds), *Promoting Fiscal Discipline* (Washington, DC, International Monetary Fund, 2007) 19–35.

lished consensus of this nature which brings the best results.[14] A second possibility consists of introducing fiscal rules which respond to the disfunctionality of parliamentary control by limiting the powers of parliament. These rules may be divided into three groups: procedural, numeric and institutional.

The first group, procedural rules, includes measures strengthening the government's position (or the minister of finance's position) vis-à-vis parliament in the budgetary process, for instance by giving it the right of veto against amendments as parliament negotiates the budget. The government can have the right of veto also against bills proposed by MPs which would increase cost or decrease incomes, as in Germany or France. It includes also a time limit for the negotiation of the state budget or hierarchy negotiation, meaning that first the total balance of the budget is set and all changes can then only be made within this framework.[15] The last mentioned rule, however, can be circumvented easily: the members of parliament only virtually reduce the mandatory expenses and then transfer the means 'spared' in this way into another chapter, which actually means extra expenses for the budget.

The second group consists of numerical rules having a form of a certain ceiling set for the overall state (or public) debt or for the state (public) budget deficit. The ceilings can be determined by an absolute amount of money; however, a relative specification in terms of the share of GDP is more typical. Their procyclical influence may be a disadvantage of these rules. As GDP is reduced during a recession, a government is forced by the rules to limit expenses so that the state budget deficit is maintained within the specified tolerances which lead subsequently to further deepening of the recession. And conversely, in a period of boom, increasing GDP enables the government–expressed in absolute numbers—to spend more and more since relative indebtedness or a deficit in relation to GDP decreases. The solution is a construction of numerical rules which take into account the economic cycle, for instance by looking at the so-called 'structural deficit' instead of the overall state budget deficit. On the other hand, rules designed in this way considerably increase room for different interpretations and circumventions, since unlike the account balance, the structural deficit is not a variable determinable unambiguously and exactly. The other problem consists in the enforceability of these rules, not only at the national, but also at the supranational level. This is testified by the fact that the two largest economies of the Eurozone—Germany and France—broke the numeric rules anchored in the Stability and Growth Pact for a long time without the sanction mechanism being applied.[16]

Finally, the third group consists of rules which establish independent institutions (fiscal councils) to supervise and influence budgetary policy. They usually do not have the right to veto the decisions of government or parliament, or even

[14] Wrobel (n 8) 157–161.

[15] See generally Fölscher (n 12) 147–148.

[16] See L Schuknecht et al, 'The Stability and Growth Pact: Crisis and Reform', European Central Bank Occasional Paper Series (September 2011) 9–10.

to decide independently, but work rather as advisory bodies. However, their informal influence can be considerable. The reason why they are not entrusted, with a few exceptions, with the right of veto is not only the concern that a possible conflict between the budgetary council and parliament or government could lead to 'a considerably suboptimal result',[17] as Schneider explains laconically, but also their lower democratic legitimacy. However, it cannot be overlooked that even central banks which have been entrusted with a range of important powers in the monetary policy by modern institutions have a similarly low democratic legitimacy, and an establishment of a similar institution limiting parliament in the fiscal area therefore cannot be a priori excluded as inadmissible.

There is a relatively extensive economic literature evaluating the effects of all three types of fiscal rules, unfortunately without leading to clear conclusions. Not only the empirical findings (ie whether a certain rule introduced in different countries correlates with the fact that these countries achieve better fiscal results) but also their evaluation differ. The causality is not obvious, neither is its direction: does the introduction of fiscal rules cause bigger responsibility of governments and therefore better management? Or is the introduction of fiscal rules one of the consequences of the fact that the governments decide such responsibility?[18] While this dispute is reminiscent of the chicken-and-egg problem, it actually highlights an important issue: if the second claim was valid, the rules would actually be useless since only the political decision would be decisive.

The current state of knowledge suggests that social consensus about the need of healthy public finances contributes to their achievement much more than any legally or constitutionally anchored rules. Nonetheless, if some rules are to be anchored, the institutional rules establishing independent fiscal councils or strengthening the powers of finance ministers have the biggest impact.[19] Therefore one can agree with the conclusion that the fiscal rules are 'primarily the demonstration of an implicit contract with the electorate. … The adoption of the rules reflects a conscious commitment to fiscal discipline rather than an attempt to suppress discretion and reduce its potentially injudicious use.'[20]

[17] O Schneider, *Rozpočtové instituc—evropské zkušenosti a aplikace na Českou republiku* [*Fiscal Institutions—European Experiences and their Application on the Czech Republic*] (Praha: Národohospodářský ústav AV ČR, 2012) 8.

[18] See eg Debrun and Kumar (n 2) 481, 485–506; Schneider (n 17) 11 or Ayuso-i-Casals (n 3) 671 and 679. An interesting literature review is also provided by A Geršl, 'Political Economy of Public Deficit: Perspectives for Constitutional Reform' (2007) *Acta Universitatis Carolinae—Oeconomica* 67–86.

[19] See L Helland, 'Fiscal Constitutions, Fiscal Preferences, Information and Deficits: An Evaluation of 13 West-European Countries 1978–95' (2000) *ZEI Studies in European Economics and Law* 129; C Mulas-Granados, J Onrubia and J Salinas-Jiménez, 'Do Budget Institutions Matter? Fiscal Consolidation in the New EU Member States' in Banca d'Italia (n 2) 641.

[20] Debrun and Kumar (n 2) 506.

III. FISCAL RULES IN THE FISCAL COMPACT AND THEIR REQUIRED NATIONALIZATION

The Fiscal Compact, which forms the essential Title III of the Treaty on Stability, Coordination and Governance in the EMU, enshrines a set of fiscal rules which should be obeyed by the states and transformed into their national laws. As its point of departure it stipulates that 'the budgetary position of the general government … shall be balanced or in surplus' (Article 3(1)(a)). According to further provisions, this means that the annual structural deficit of public budgets shall—generally–not exceed 0.5% of GDP, or 1% of GDP if the governmental debt is 'significantly below 60% and … risks in terms of long-term sustainability of public finances are low' (Article 3(1)(d)).

An escape clause provides for temporary deviation from this rule (and/or the path to its achievement) in case of exceptional circumstances, which are defined as 'the case of an unusual event outside the control of the Contracting Party concerned which has a major impact on the financial position of the general government or to periods of severe economic downturn' (Article 3(3)(b)). Should be any other deviation be observed, outside of the scope of exceptional circumstances, the Compact requires a 'correction mechanism … [to] be triggered automatically' (Article 3(1)(e)). The Treaty does not provide any details of how such a correction mechanism should be designed and how should it operate. Instead, the European Commission was entrusted with the task of proposing common principles thereof which are to be followed by the states when implementing the rules in their national law.

Consequently, the Commission has published seven principles which should be observed by Member States when they design their national fiscal correction mechanisms.[21] According to these principles, the mechanism should 'rely closely on the concepts and rules of the European fiscal framework', especially when it comes to deficit targets and escape clauses. Importantly, 'both *ex ante* mechanisms that set budgetary objectives preventing the materialization of deviations and *ex post* mechanisms that trigger corrections in reaction to prior deviations, may fulfil the requirements'. Accordingly, and although the language of the Treaty itself might suggest otherwise, national rules are not required to enshrine any automatic expenditure cuts or tax increase measures, and thus parliament retains discretion as to how it deals with a particular budget deficit. One of the principles also deals with the role and independence of monitoring institutions, eg fiscal councils. They should be provided with a sufficient level of independence, or at least 'functional autonomy' and provide public assessments concerning the correction mechanism. Interestingly, a 'comply or explain' principle is enshrined here: in the event that government or parliament does not comply with the assessment of the independent institution, it must give a public explanation

[21] European Commission, 'Common Principles on National Fiscal Correction Mechanisms', COM(2012) 342 final.

thereof. This is clearly inspired by German system (see below) where it serves as a part of the enforcement mechanism.

According to Article 14(5) of the Treaty,[22] these rules and principles are binding for eurozone Member States, and for other signatories if they voluntarily opted-in. The same applies to the duty to transform these rules into national law, preferably into their constitutions.

IV. CONSTITUTIONAL ANCHORING OF FISCAL RULES IN THE CENTRAL EUROPEAN COUNTRIES

A. Germany

'Once again German will be spoken in Europe.' With these words, the then draft Fiscal Compact was greeted by one of the leaders of Germany's governing CDU party.[23] The final version of the treaty confirms his statement: despite some partial or parametric differences, Germany has basically managed to get through its own constitutional arrangement which was adopted with effect from 1 August 2009.[24]

The core of the debt brake in Germany is a new wording of Article 109(3) of the Basic Law, according to which the federal budget as well as states' budgets shall 'in principle be balanced without revenue from credits'.[25] In particular, in the case of federal budgets a maximum deficit 0.35 per cent of GDP is admissible. However, this is a structural deficit: if the economy deviates from its normal development, Article 115 provides that the maximum deficit also shall be adjusted accordingly, in both directions. Debts that have arisen in this way must be settled in the course of the economic cycle. Exceptions are allowed in the case of 'natural catastrophes or unusual emergency situations beyond governmental control and substantially harmful to the state's financial capacity' to be approved by an absolute majority of the members of the lower house of parliament. A so-called Stability Council has been established composed of both federal and state government representatives whose task is to supervise continuously the budgetary management and to prevent budget crises (Article 109a).[26]

[22] 'This Treaty shall apply to the Contracting Parties with a derogation, as defined in Article 139(1) of the Treaty on the Functioning of the European Union, or with an exemption, as referred to in Protocol (No 16) on certain provisions related to Denmark annexed to the European Union Treaties, which have ratified this Treaty, as from the date when the decision abrogating that derogation or exemption takes effect, unless the Contracting Party concerned declares its intention to be bound at an earlier date by all or part of the provisions in Titles III and IV of this Treaty.'

[23] LEM Besselink and JH Reestman, Editorial, 'The Fiscal Compact and the European Constitutions: "Europe Speaking German"' (2012) 8 *European Constitutional Law Review* 2.

[24] See also G Delledonne, in this volume (Chapter 9).

[25] 'Basic Law for the Federal Republic of Germany' (2012) www.gesetze-im-internet.de/englisch_gg/englisch_gg.html.

[26] See also F Zipfel, *Stability Council: Financial Inspector of Germany's Länder* (Frankfurt, Deutsche Bank Research, 2011).

In addition the Economic Expert Council (the so-called 'Wise Persons Council') advising the government on economic and fiscal policy is still functioning. It only has an advisory vote but if the government decides to ignore its recommendation, it must give a public explanation for doing so.[27] The constitutional anchoring of the budget rules also comes with the possibility for the budget to be reviewed by the Federal Constitutional Court.

The entry into force of the new rules has been postponed so that both the federal budget and the state budgets can adapt to them gradually. Under the temporary provision in Article 143d, they become fully effective in regards to the federation only as of 1 January 2016 and in regards to the states as of 1 January 2020.

B Poland

Poland is among the 25 EU Member States which have signed the Fiscal Compact; however, it has not yet completed the ratification process.[28] The duty to meet the fiscal rules and to transpose them into its legal order will not apply to it until it becomes a member of the eurozone or decides for a voluntary opt-in. However, the Polish Constitution has contained budgetary limitations since its adoption in 1997. Under Article 216, it is 'neither permissible to contract loans nor provide guarantees and financial sureties which would engender a national public debt exceeding three-fifths of the value of the annual gross domestic product'.[29] The constitution also contains a procedural limitation: only the government has the right to propose the state budget (Article 221) and the Sejm (the first chamber of parliament) shall not make any changes that would lead to an increase in the budget deficit (Article 220). If the budget is not approved with four months of being presented, the President of the Republic can dismiss the Sejm. The President of the Republic has also the right to submit the adopted budget for review by the Constitutional Tribunal (Article 224).

The Public Finance Act setting out two state debt safety limits follows the constitutional arrangement.[30] If the state debt reaches between 50 and 55 per cent of GDP, the government shall not submit a state budget proposal

[27] Schneider (n 17) 7.

[28] See 'Table on the Ratification Process of Amendment of Art 136 TFEU, ESM Treaty and the Fiscal Compact' (European Parliament, 21 February 2013) www.europarl.europa.eu/webnp/webdav/site/myjahiasite/users/fboschi/public/esm%20tscg/art.%20136%20ESM%20fiscal%20compact%20ratprocess.pdf and 'Press release after the hearing concerning the Act on the ratification of the European Council Decision of 25 March 2011 amending Article 136 of the Treaty on the Functioning of the European Union with regard to a stability mechanism for Member States whose currency is the euro (2011/199/EU)' (Polish Constitutional Tribunal, 26 June 2013) www.trybunal.gov.pl/eng/press_releases/k3312.htm.

[29] The Constitution of the Republic of Poland' (1997) www.sejm.gov.pl/prawo/konst/angielski/kon1.htm.

[30] See A Rutkowski, 'Ceilings and Anchors: Fiscal Rules for Poland' (2007) 4 *ECFIN Country Focus* 1–6.

with a higher deficit than in the previous year. If the debt reaches between 55 and 60 per cent of GDP, the state budget is to be proposed in such a way that the debt ratio to GDP is not increased. And finally, if the debt exceeds 60 per cent, the constitutional rule, according to which the state budget must be balanced or in surplus, shall be applied. Moreover, legal limits (the so-called 'Belka's rule')[31] were adopted in 2011, according to which non-mandatory and newly approved state budget expenses shall not increase year-on-year by more than 1 per cent in real terms (ignoring inflation).[32]

According to OECD methodology, the total level of state debt reached 57 per cent in 2011 which means that the 55 per cent threshold triggering the debt increase prohibition has been exceeded and certain measures should have been activated. In fact this did not happen since the government has transferred infrastructural project financing to BGK, a state-owned development bank, the obligations of which do not count as state debt according to national methodology, which means a decline of about 3.5 per cent.[33]

C. Hungary

In terms of the Fiscal Compact, Hungary is in a similar situation to Poland: it has signed it but not yet ratified it,[34] and in any case the fiscal rules anchored in it do not apply to Hungary until it enters the eurozone or unless it decides for a voluntary opt-in. The new Hungarian Fundamental Law adopted in March 2011 and effective as of 1 January 2012, ie before the completion of the Fiscal Compact, contains, however, strict fiscal stability rules. The starting point is Article N in the basic provisions of the Constitution, according to which:

> Hungary shall enforce the principle of balanced, transparent and sustainable budget management. Parliament and the Government shall have the primary responsibility. … [However,] in the course of performing their duties, the Constitutional Court, courts, local governments and other state organs shall [also] be bound to respect the principle.[35,36]

[31] The rule is named after former Vice-Premier Marek Belka who proposed it in 2001, though it was not adopted at that time.

[32] A Schaechter et al, 'Fiscal Rules in Response to the Crisis—Toward the "Next-Generation" Rules. A New Dataset', IMF Working Paper (July 2012) 43.

[33] OECD, *Poland*, OECD Economic Surveys (March 2012) 13.

[34] Table on the Ratification Process of Amendment of Art 136 TFEU, ESM Treaty and the Fiscal Compact.

[35] The Fundamental Law of Hungary (2011) http://mkab.hu/rules/fundamental-law.

[36] It is remarkable that courts too should be concerned about sound public finance. Most strikingly this applies to the Constitutional Court the powers of which are limited by the well-known Art 37(4) of the Fundamental Law:

> As long as the level of state debt exceeds half of the Gross Domestic Product, the Constitutional Court may, within its competence pursuant to points b) to e) of paragraph (2) of Article 24, review the Acts on the central budget, on the implementation of the budget, on central taxes, on duties and on contributions, on customs duties, and on the central conditions for local taxes as to their conformity with the Fundamental Law exclusively in connection with the rights to life

This principle is followed by Article 37, which stipulates a debt ceiling 50 per cent of GDP, i.e. about 35 percentage points less than the current state.[37] No state budget can increase the state indebtedness level over this limit (Article 36(4)); and as long as the debt level is over the 50 per cent limit it is required that each state budget reduces the relative indebtedness in relation to GDP (Article 36(5)). Exceptions are admissible only in case of a 'special legal order' or during 'a significant and enduring national economic recession, to the extent necessary to restore the balance of the national economy' (Article 36(6)).

In order to enforce these rules, the Constitution has established the Budget Council (Article 44) consisting of the President of the Budget Council appointed by the President of the Republic (without countersignature) for the period of six years, and of two ex officio members. These are the Governor of the National Bank of Hungary appointed by the President of the Republic—with countersignature of a member of the Government—for a 6-year term, and the President of the State Audit Office elected by the Parliament by two-thirds majority for a 12-year term. At first sight, the Council has a predominantly advisory character: it is a body 'supporting the legislative activity of the Parliament; it shall examine whether the central budget is well-founded … [and] … take part in the preparation of the Act on the central budget' (Article 44). In fact, however, its position is extraordinarily strong since its ex ante approval that the balanced or surplus budget requirement has been fulfilled is needed for the adoption of the state budget: it thus has the right of absolute veto. If the Parliament passes the budget despite the Budget Council opposition, it can be cancelled by the Constitutional Court for breach of procedural rules (Article 37(4)).

This provision can lead in practice to an essential conflict of institutions and result in early elections: under Article 3(3), if the state budget is not approved by March 31 of a given year, the President of the Republic can dissolve parliament. Moreover, one can imagine, theoretically, a situation in which even a newly elected parliament cannot reach agreement with the Budget Council, and thus the constitutional crises will be prolonged. This constitutional provision is subject of justified criticism not only for the conflict with democratic values (the three-member council appointed for a long term can block the functioning of the parliament with much bigger democratic legitimacy) but also for imprudence (such a crisis could have a worse impact on the state economy than a budget deficit).[38]

and human dignity, to the protection of personal data, to freedom of thought, conscience and religion, or in connection with the rights related to Hungarian citizenship, and it may only annul these Acts for the violation of these rights. The Constitutional Court shall have the right to annul without restriction Acts governing the above matters if the procedural requirements laid down in the Fundamental Law for the making and publication of such Acts have not been observed.

[37] OECD, *Hungary*, OECD Economic Surveys (March 2012) 4.

[38] M Varju, 'Governance, Accountability, and the Market' in GA Toth (ed), *Constitution for a Disunited Nation: On Hungary's 2011 Fundamental Law* (Budapest and New York, Central European University Press, 2012) 316.

D. Slovakia

Slovakia is a member of the eurozone and ratified the Fiscal Compact on 17 January 2013, which means that the fiscal rules set out were to be implemented at the latest by 1 February 2014. In reality, the constitutional Act on Budget Responsibility, effective as of 1 March 2012 (in some parts as of 1 January 2015) was passed already on 8 December 2011, thus before signature of the Final Compact.[39] A debt ceiling of 50 per cent of GDP, i.e. about 7 percentage points under the current level,[40] was set by this constitutional act. The basis for the debt's assessment shall be European Commission (Eurostat) official statistics rather than domestic statistics (Article 5(2)). At the same time, the Act lays down in a great detail the gradually escalating provisions leading to the decrease of debt which are triggered automatically when the debt exceeds 40 per cent. If the debt is between 40 and 43 per cent of GDP, the Ministry of Finance should submit to the National Council (the parliament) a written justification and a proposal for measures to decrease it. Further, in the interval between 43 and 45 per cent the salaries of the members of the government are lowered to the level of the previous year if there has been an increase in the meantime.

If the debt reaches the interval between 45 and 47 per cent, the measures continue in such a way that the Ministry of Finance is obliged to hold 3 per cent of state budget expenses in the given year (calculated without the debt-servicing expenses, monies from the EU and monies intended for co-financing, payments to the EU budget), social insurance company expenses and expenses for the liquidation of damages incurred by disasters. Moreover, an expense ceiling is applied which means that the government must not propose a state budget which would contain—in nominal expression—expenses higher than the previous state budget, with the exception of the above-mentioned budget chapters. Local and regional self-governing units are required to manage with balanced budgets, and the government shall not draw from its budgetary reserve. The measures escalate even further: in the interval of between 47 and 50 per cent, the government must not submit a state budget in deficit, and if the threshold of 50 per cent is exceeded, it must ask for a vote of confidence. However, the measures described in this paragraph apply neither during 'the period of 24 months … after the day when the governmental program declaration has been approved and the government has won the vote of confidence' (Article 5(10)) nor during a period of serious economic recession which is defined by a change in the GDP development by more than 12 per cent (Article 5(11)).[41] Neither shall it be applied

[39] Ústavný zákon č 493/2011 Zb, o rozpočtovej odpovědnosti [Constitutional Act on Budget Responsibility] (2011).

[40] OECD, *Slovakia*, OECD Economic Surveys (December 2012) 6.

[41] Art 5(11)(a) is somewhat less understandable for a lawyer in this respect. It seems that the crucial criterion is not directly an expression of GDP decline but a change of trend. It is better illustrated by an example: GDP grows by 7% in the first year while it decreases by 6% in the second year. The total difference amounts to 7—(–6) = 13 percentage points, and the constitutional condition has therefore been met.

when there are increased governmental expenses exceeding 3 per cent of GDP, necessary because of bank crises, disasters or international obligations, as well in time of war (Article 5(11)(12)).

Furthermore, these rules will not be fully applicable until the budgetary year 2028, i.e. 16 years after the constitutional act has been passed. Until then, there is time left for gradual adapting, which is demonstrated by a gradual decline in the debt ceiling. The debt ceiling from now until the end of 2017 amounts to 60 per cent of GDP, ie 10 percentage points more, and other intervals for the measures to be taken are adjusted in the same way. In the period from 2018 until 2027, all the limits will be gradually decreased by 1 percentage point per year (Article 12).

The Council for Budgetary Responsibility has been established by constitutional act. All three members thereof are elected and removed by parliament: one upon the proposal of the government by a three-fifths majority of the members of parliament, the second upon the proposal of the President of the Republic by a simple majority, and the third upon the proposal of the Governor of the National Bank of Slovakia also by a simple majority. The competences of the Council, as specified in Article 4 of the Constitutional Act, have an advisory character: the Council prepares a report on long-term sustainability and on the fulfilment of the budgetary responsibility rules, on its own initiative or at the request of a parliamentary political group, expresses its opinion on the presented draft laws, etc. However, it does not have any power of decision, nor it can block the adoption of the state budget.

V. ANALYSIS

A. Rules Categorization

Despite several differences, the four countries described above have something in common: their debt brakes work with the combination of all three types or rules discussed in Section II, ie with numerical, institutional and procedural rules. However, they differ somewhat in terms of emphasis: all of them rely on numerical rules but Slovakia and Poland rely mostly on them while Germany combines them more with procedural rules and Hungary with institutional enforcement. If we take into consideration the results of the above-mentioned empirical studies, the attitude of the latter two countries can be considered more suitable in terms of effectiveness. Let us remember that those countries with a strong position of government relative to the parliament and of ministers of finance within government were better able to deal with the budget deficit.

B. Criterion for the Debt Brake

A substantial difference can be observed in the selection of the central criterion. While in Germany, it is the amount of structural deficit, in all other countries it is primarily total state indebtedness expressed relative to GDP. Only once this debt ceiling has been broken or when the debt ceiling is being approached do state budget deficits start to be monitored. Slovakia is then required to have a balanced or surplus budget, ie the sum of expenses has to be no higher than the level of income. In Poland and Hungary the construction is more complex since their constitutions require the state budget not to increase (or directly decrease) the level of indebtedness relative to GDP. If GDP grows, this condition is met even in the case of a (slight) deficit, while if the GDP declines, even a (slight) surplus may not meet the condition. Apart from that, none of these countries—except Germany—monitors the amount of *structural deficit*, which takes into account the phase of the economic cycle. While Poland does not provide for an escape clause, some exceptions are possible in the other countries, eg in case of economic recession; however, these are not very explicit and can tempt abuse or dispute over their interpretation which would limit their effectiveness.

Using debt as the central criterion might seem like a sound idea at first sight as it goes to the core of the problem: the state budget may be in deficit from time to time, especially during economic downturns, but the overall debt should be kept within some reasonable limits. There are two problems, however. The first one is that as there is no universal or scientific view as to the appropriate level of indebtedness—any rule is inevitably regarded as arbitrary. This is particularly well illustrated by the 60 per cent of GDP debt limit set by Maastricht Treaty, which was not the result of any expert assessment, but rather a matter of coincidence as it simply corresponded to the average level of debt of the then European countries on the day the Treaty was finalized.[42] But this is not only the case for the EU: as we will see later, even when the debt limit is set domestically, it is largely influenced by the present situation which it aims either to preserve or improve. Constitutional provisions, however, should be designed on a more abstract basis with the view that they will persist for a long time.

The second problem is that the debt rule does not work properly. In good times, when the actual debt is well below the limit, it does not restrain governments at all. In fact, given the method of calculation, when the GDP grows, the government may run a deficit and still the ratio of debt to GDP remains the same. This is illustrated by Table 1: if we assume a debt level of 60 per cent and economic growth at, for example, 5 per cent, then the budget deficit may be up to almost 3 per cent GDP and the level of indebtedness remains the same. But it works both ways: in bad times of economic recession the level of debt grows automatically even if the budget is balanced, which means that if a govern-

[42] C Wyplosz, 'Fiscal Policy: Institutions vs Rules', HEI Working Paper 03/2002 (Geneva, The Graduate Institute of International Studies, 2002) 79.

Table 1. Simulation of debt-neutral deficit depending on level of GDP growth

	GPD growth (%)	GDP	Debt	Deficit	% Deficit
Previous year		1000	600	0	
Current year	5	1050	630	−30	−2.9
	4	1040	624	−24	−2.3
	3	1030	618	−18	−1.7
	2	1020	612	−12	−1.2
	1	1010	606	−6	−0.6
	0	1000	600	0	0.0
	−1	990	594	6	0.6
	−2	980	588	12	1.2
	−3	970	582	18	1.9
	−4	960	576	24	2.5
	−5	950	570	30	3.2

ment wanted to comply with the rule, it would actually need to run a surplus. Governments do not need rules to be motivated to spend during expansion and save during recession; they can do it themselves: but it is exactly counter to the desired objective.

'Belka's rule', applied in Poland, in addition, limits the state budgetary expenditure by allowing year-on-year increases in expenses of at most 1 per cent. If this limit were to be sustained, it would have an obviously positive influence on the state budget development from a long-term point of view. Therefore, it can be deemed positive in terms of effectiveness though I have doubts about its enforcement since it has no constitutional basis. And even if it was institutionalized in the future, it might well prove too big an interference with the democratic principles when the state reallocation level which should be a subject of political process is de facto stipulated. It is one thing to say that states can be constitutionally prevented from spending more than they collect, but it is another to say that parliament cannot considerably increase expenditure should it acquire additional income to cover this, eg from higher taxes.

As regards the Fiscal Compact, all the countries except for Poland seem to comply with its requirements. The Polish provisions are problematic as they are concerned solely with the debt and not with the deficit, which may be easily explained by the fact they were adopted in 1997, long before the Fiscal Compact, and since Poland is not a member of eurozone, it is not required to comply with these requirements.

C. Enforceability

The above-mentioned empirical studies imply that the fiscal rules can achieve the best results if they reflect a wider consensus. In such case it is not necessary to look for external means to enforce them since the political actors will abide by them voluntarily, eventually under the pressure of public opinion, and also under pressure from the financial markets.

In the past, economists thought that the market would provide the best solution. If a government runs a deficit, it must acquire the shortfall in funds from somewhere. One possibility would be to borrow from the central bank, but as this comes with a high risk of moral hazard, it is forbidden in most countries. The second possibility is to turn to the markets and borrow there, eg by issuing state bonds. Investors can then assess the risk based on the state's fiscal policy. If its public finances are not sustainable, the investors, banks, etc, will not buy its bonds, or at least will require a risk premium, motivating the government to make reforms. Unfortunately, it has been demonstrated that this theory does not work in practice. During periods of economic expansion, the market actors actually encourage states to incur debts as this is the source of their profits, while during downturns financial sources suddenly become unavailable.[43] Once again, it is not an effective constraint and it is procyclical.

Drawing on these findings, Kelemen and Teo have proposed another theory. They assume that the failure of market enforcement of sustainable fiscal policy is partly based also on the variety of market participants who 'often hold different views which makes coordination challenging and decentralized punishment difficult'.[44] In this setting, fiscal rules can serve as a unifying focal point that gives a clear guidance to the market, and the market itself can then enforce them.[45]

It seems that the constitutional arrangements in Germany and Poland are based predominantly on this 'soft' approach to enforcement. These countries set a certain goal and emphasize transparency and public control rather than detail ways how to achieve this. In addition, the process in Germany is supported by an institution of independent experts, whose advice, which has a strong influence on public opinion, the government is obliged to consider. To a considerable extent, a degree of effectiveness depends on the electorate—a solution with considerable democratic legitimacy.

In terms of particular steps which need to be done (especially) by the government in case of negative developments, the Slovak arrangement is much more specific. If we look closer, however, we see that in fact these are relatively harmless and less effective tools. Take, for instance, the duty of the government to ask for a vote of confidence if the debt exceeds 50 per cent of GDP: if the government has a majority in parliament, this presents no obstacle to it. But even if we assume that this is not always the case, it is a sanction without much rationale, since it does not affect those governments that previously ran the state into debt but only the one that has the bad luck of being in power at the moment the debt exceeds the set limit, eg as a consequence of economic recession. And if it turns out that the government does not have a majority in a

[43] RC Schragger, 'Democracy and Debt' (2012) 121 *Yale Law Journal* 864.

[44] RD Kelemen and TK Teo, 'Law and Eurozone Crisis', paper prepared for the American Political Science Association Annual Convention, 30 August–2 September 2012, 5 and 10.

[45] Ibid 21–22.

vote of confidence, the state, in addition to indebtedness and economic recession, then also faces a constitutional crisis, which can be hardly considered to be the best recipe for enhancing the situation. This solution thus does not appear to be effective; furthermore it can have a procyclical effect based on the fact that a possible governmental crisis creates uncertainty in the financial markets and thereby deepens the economic recession even further.

In terms of enforceability, the strongest model is the Hungarian arrangement, which gives the independent Budget Council the right of absolute veto over any budget that does not meet the numerical rules stipulated in the Constitution. This solution may clearly be effective at enforcing strict compliance with budget rules; its democratic legitimacy, however, is doubtful.

The constitutional basis of numerical rules also creates space for constitutional review, which can be viewed as an invitation to involve constitutional courts in an area that they have previously tended to avoid.[46] This possibility cannot immediately cure all possible faults (what is going to happened after the constitutional court cancels the state budget because the deficit is too high?) but it can have a preventive role. The difficulty is at the practical level: despite some claims to the contrary, economics is not an exact science but a social science. The courts can assess whether the procedures or, for instance, the accounting regulations have been maintained, but these procedures will not determine the right economic policy, how high the structural budget should be, etc. Not to mention the fact that lawyers, not economists, usually become the constitutional judges.[47]

Concerning compliance with the Fiscal Compact, the result of the assessment is the same as in the previous section of this chapter concerning the criteria of the debt brakes. Except for Poland, which is not yet bound by the Compact, all the countries comply with its requirements. Most importantly in this respect, they all provide for an independent fiscal council which is required by the common principles set by the Commission.

VI. CONCLUSION

From the comparative analysis made above of the constitutionalization of budgetary rules in Germany, Poland, Hungary and Slovakia, it can be deduced that less can be sometimes more: instead of a very detailed arrangement introducing particular procedural steps for controlling budgets, enhancement of fiscal discipline can be achieved by anchoring the basic principles. I find targeting a very important factor: it is better to limit the state deficit rather than the state debt—this approach reveals the problem early enough and can in time solve it. In addition, it is necessary to take into account the economic cycle, and to construe the rules so that the state is forced to save in the time of boom, while helping

[46] See G Delledonne in this volume (Chapter 9).

[47] See also F Fabbrini, 'The Fiscal Compact, the "Golden Rule" and the Paradox of European Federalism' (2013) 36 *Boston College International & Comparative Law Review* 22.

to damp an economic downturn in time of recession. Not even in times of economic crises should we forget democratic values, and just as the threat of terrorism was not a reason to justify the removal of basic rights, state debt should not justify the removal of key fiscal powers from the hands of representative bodies and entrusting them to independent councils without sufficient legitimacy. The proper solution should support rather than replace the political process.

In my view, the rules set by the Fiscal Compact itself are reconcilable with these requirements, and moreover they leave states with a degree of discretion as to how they should be implemented in national law. However, this implementation is crucial, and something to which Member States should pay careful attention. As I argued above, the German arrangement is the most suitable in terms of the criteria that I have chosen for the evaluation of debt brakes in four EU Member States of Central Europe, whereas the constitutional provisions in the other three countries are less appropriate in terms of effectiveness (Poland, Slovakia) or also of legitimacy (Hungary).

11

Can Constitutional Rules, Even if 'Golden', Tame Greek Public Debt?

LINA PAPADOPOULOU[1]

I. SETTING THE SCENE

GREECE HAS STOOD at the epicentre of the ongoing public debt crisis since its outburst. The country's attempts during the last three years to rein in the deficit in its public accounts reflect a belated recognition for its huge debt being an issue, born out of concern in the face of state default. The pernicious effects of repeated borrowing are only now becoming obvious, prompting the population to undergo a process of self-knowledge.[2] The following quotation effectively captures the issue at hand: '[T]he agony of a pensioner who cannot live with 350 Euros per month is opposed to the agony of Greece who cannot live with 350 billion of debt.'[3]

The crisis is constantly evolving, not only creating new financial, political and social challenges but also fostering transformations in the constitutional architecture both at national and European level. New European institutions and legal measures emerge and significantly alter the substance of economic governance, as well as the political systems of both the EU and its Member States. Constitutions are called upon to regulate the economic and fiscal behaviour of the respective states in several ways, predominantly through the incorporation of budgetary constraints. Greece has needed to adapt radically, almost violently, to the new facts; and a hurricane of parliamentary acts and case law confirm this radical change. Although the Greek written constitution has not undergone any formal revision due to political and technical reasons that will be explained below, the Greek living constitution has already experienced a profound transformation.

This chapter intends to contribute to the ongoing discussion concerning

[1] Many thanks to Federico Fabbrini for revising this paper, as well as to Xenofon Kontargyris, Eva Tsoukalidou and Victoria Brooks for linguistically editing it.

[2] A Doxiades, 'The Real Greek Economy: Owners, Rentiers and Opportunists', www.constitutionalism.gr/html/ent/733/ent.1733.asp (accessed 10 May 2013).

[3] Y Drossos, 'The Memorandum as a Turning Point to the Form of Government' (2011) 6 *The Book's Journal* 42 (in Greek).

the 'Greek case' with respect to the role of the constitution in coping with the economic and fiscal crisis. In particular, it aims to explore the strengths and weaknesses of the constitution as a device to deal with the current situation and also prevent future fiscal crises, with a focus on the Greek experience. The enquiry proceeds in three steps, which are built upon three claims.

Firstly (Section II), before delving into the constitutional discussion and in order to place it in a wider context, the course that brought Greece to today's critical situation shall be traced. This will also provide a brief historical review as to why Greece, a small peripheral member of the EU, has proven to be the weakest link of European Monetary Union (EMU) and how it arrived at the present impasse. The claim, upon which this section is built, is that, 'the Greek case' is partly an exception and partly an inevitable consequence of the incomplete European economic governance. Specifically, although Greece may appear as an exception in some respects, it is but a typical example of the lack of a common European economic policy, as well as the evidence that facing the national debt crisis demands supranational measures and further steps towards a more enhanced political Union. The second claim is that the particularities of Greece's constitutional system render a constitutional balanced budget amendment improbable—at least in short term—and yet rather redundant. In order for this to be proven, the particularities of the Greek constitution will be considered closely, with the aim of explaining why the constitutionalization of a 'golden rule' may be close to impossible in the near future. The fact that this amendment is so unlikely to be implemented does not undermine the rule's normative power (if there is such) since its incorporation into national law has already taken place through the ratification of the Fiscal Compact (Section III). This is supplemented by a third and more general claim concerning the limited strength of every constitution actually to frame and shape economic and fiscal matters in an independently normative way. Hence, the constitutional nature and efficacy of the balanced budget constitutional rule shall be examined (Section IV). Lastly (in Section V), some preliminary conclusions are drawn.

II. GREECE: AN EXCEPTION OR THE RULE?

A. The Greek 'Exception'

For 20 years after World War II and the Greek civil war between left and right (1946–49), Greece presented an impressive economic performance, enjoying rapid growth, high investment and low inflation. The pre-1974 regime, however, was politically illiberal, autocratic and eventually degenerated into a military dictatorship (1967–74). After a relatively smooth transition from dictatorship to democracy, the prevailing ideological climate was such that both governing parties, New Democracy (ND) (1975–81) and then later the Panhellenic Socialist Movement (PASOK) (1981–89) accommodated the popular demand for an expanded role of the state, and for redistribution. Both would only become possible through borrowing.[4]

Greece applied to join the European Economic Community (EEC) in June 1975 and eventually joined in 1981, based on a political bargain with the nine existing Member States. This was achieved, in part, as a consequence of Europe's collective guilt concerning its passive stance toward the dictatorship, and despite the fact that the country's economic development lagged behind that of other members.[5] Thus, Greece's entry (and the same applies in respect of Spain's and Portugal's entry five years later) was equally justified on political as well as economic grounds. Furthermore, entry to the EEC was intended to act as a safeguard of the country's recently restored democratic institutions.[6]

One of the basic faults was that the country entered the common market without having first addressed its structural economic deficiencies, mainly consisting of a restricted productive base, a rather strong—but dispersed in small properties—agricultural sector, an emerging manufacturing industry which proved unready for an open competition, and an underdeveloped service sector, mostly restricted to the emerging tourist industry. Following the second oil shock and its admission to the EEC, Greece entered a period of persistent stagflation: Greek manufacturing declined,[7] while public sector deficits and debts exploded.[8] Not using debt for domestic public investment which would have encouraged growth, but rather for subsidizing private businesses and income redistribution in favour of the medium and lower strata, pushed both government and private consumption upwards.[9]

During the 1990s, generous financial support from the Community for economic and social cohesion helped to change the climate for the better: it reduced the external imbalance, high rates of growth were sustained, a successful ten-year macroeconomic stabilization programme was executed, and a number of economic distortions began to be corrected. Also, at the time, monetary financing of the fiscal deficit had been reduced in compliance with the provisions

[4] For a brief review, see also R McDonald, 'The Greek Deficit and Debt Crisis: An End or a Beginning?', lecture for the Athens Centre delivered on 23 May 2011, www.economia.gr/index.php?dispatch=pages.view&page_id=1541 (accessed 17 April 2013). He recalls that after World War II and under 'the Truman doctrine Greece received some $300m, under the Marshall Plan $376m and under various Foreign Military Assistance programmes during the 1970s, 1980s and 1990s, a total of some $6bn. These sums may not sound like much in today's prices but they were significant at the time.'

[5] E Oltheten, G Pinteris and Th Sougiannis, 'Greece in the European Union: Policy Lessons from Two Decades of Membership' (2003) 43 *Quarterly Review of Economics and Finance* 774, 780.

[6] Ibid, 775 et seq. According to the authors, at the time of entry Greece's per capita GDP was 68% of the EU average, higher only than Ireland's.

[7] Ibid, 784 et seq.

[8] For a detailed account, see G Alogoskoufis, 'The Two Faces of Janus: Institutions, Policy Regimes and Macroeconomic Performance in Greece' (1995) 10 *Economic Policy* 149, 150 et seq.

[9] According to Alogoskoufis (ibid, 173) 'the deterioration in Greece's balance of payments, despite the drop in investment spending, is attributable to lower national saving after the rise in public deficits and debts, rather than to a deterioration in Greece's competitiveness following the rise in relative unit labour costs or EC entry'.

of the Maastricht Treaty, in order to fulfil the fiscal and monetary 'Convergence Criteria'.[10] In this way, EC transfers contributed to Greece's welfare. However, as a result of being largely unconditional, they did not create incentives to counteract the relaxation of the external constraints, but rather masked the underlying structural problems,[11] making necessary adjustments less pressing to the political elites and almost invisible to the public. So, when it entered the EMU in 2001, Greece still lagged behind in terms of infrastructure as well as technological and institutional development in relation to most of its monetary partners. In addition, the country had not adjusted the competitiveness of its economy, in order to face the challenges. This would have minimized the pressure which resulted from the introduction of the common currency.[12] Moreover, tax authorities lost their credibility and tax evasion was taking place on an immense scale.[13]

Until recently, Greek politics used to be heavily majoritarian, dominated by one governing party, with the phenomenon of partitocracy affecting the whole state apparatus. Partitocracy, together with political short-terminism and the weakness of civil society, were the main particularities of Greece compared with its fellow partners in the EU. During the last 35 years, budget deficits and debt accumulation have served to redistribute income in favour of the lower and middle classes, to finance private enterprises, and to ensure the alternation of the two governing parties in power. The stronger presence (compared to other European democracies) of political polarization might have also contributed to the government's tendency to over-issue public debt.[14]

In 2004, Greece was placed under surveillance by the European Commission under the excessive deficit procedure, but sanctions were never applied. As a result, imprudent government spending continued, raising the budget deficit in 2009 to 15.4 per cent[15] and general government debt to 127.1 per cent of GDP.[16] The European Commission rightly reacted and in March 2009, the Economic

[10] From 1994 to 2001 the budget was in surplus. The criteria for the EMU included basic rules that deficits should be no more than 3% of GDP and debt should be equivalent to, or headed towards, 60% of GDP. See also Oltheten, Pinteris and Sougiannis (n 5) 776.

[11] Alogoskoufis (n 8) 161, 177. The same (181) also notes that '[persistently] Greece failed to make the necessary adjustments to allow its participation in the Exchange Rate Mechanism of the EMS'.

[12] In 1998 Greece wanted to join but with a deficit at 4.6% of GDP and a debt at 108.5% of GDP did not qualify. Through the use of accounting practices then sanctioned by Eurostat but later heavily criticized by the conservative party Nea Dimokratia when it came to government, the Pasok government of the day reduced the government budget deficit and debt squeezed the inflation through a series of administrative measures. So, in March 2000 Greece was declared to have met the membership targets and on 1 January 2001 it became the 12th member of the EMU. According to later calculations, however, it is purported that Greece had never met the criteria for EMU membership. See McDonald (n 4).

[13] See M Mitsopoulos and T Pelagidis 'The Real Cause of Greek Debt: Taxation and Labour Market Distortions in Greece' (2011) 46 *Intereconomics* 112; G Kaplanoglou and V Rapanos 'Tax and Trust: The Fiscal Crisis in Greece' (2012) 17 *South European Society and Politics* 1.

[14] *Cf* A Alesina and G Tabellini, 'A Positive Theory of Fiscal Deficits and Government Debt' (1990) 57 *Review of Economic Studies* 403, 412.

[15] Euroindicators, Eurostat, 60/2011, 26 April 2011. The average in the EU27 was 6.8% and in the eurozone (of 17 Member States) 6.3%.

[16] Nearly 70% above the EU average, which in the EU27 was 74.4% and in the eurozone 79.3%.

and Finance Minister's Council (Ecofin) placed Greece under the excessive deficit procedure again. No further measures were taken, given that the governing party and the then Prime Minister cared more about the results of the approaching elections rather than the medium- or long-term effects of their policy.

After the elections in October 2009, when Greece was no longer able to meet its debt obligations at a sustainable market price, and thus faced bankruptcy, it asked for financial assistance.[17] As a result, the first rescue plan, in the form of an 'Economic Adjustment Programme for Greece'[18] was signed in May 2010, containing, inter alia, a Memorandum of Understanding (MoU). The agreement launched an economic recovery programme, consisting of both fiscal and structural reforms, in order to render Greece eligible to receive a uniquely large loan facility from the EU and the International Monetary Fund (IMF).[19] 'Greece is assisted, because the Euro had to be assisted.'[20] Internal devaluation was supposed to be the most economically sensible solution; instead what has resulted is unprecedented economic recession, comparable to that of a war, and a dramatic increase in unemployment.

The loan was to be paid in 13 tranches under the IMF's model of 'strong conditionality': the payment of each one depended (and still depends) on an evaluation of the progress made in relation to the reform programme, made by a team comprising the European Commission, the European Central Bank and the IMF—known as the 'Troika'—with the final decision to be taken by the board of the IMF and the Ecofin. Should the Government's performance be evaluated as not fulfilling its obligations, instalments would be withheld. The loan is definitely cheaper than any form of financing Greece could have obtained from the markets but also lucrative for the creditor states,[21] which allowed the anti-memorandum side to accuse the EU borrowing partners, especially Germany, of taking advantage of the situation. This accusation—combined with stereotypical prejudices across the continent—ignited anti-EU as well as anti-German feelings and inspired massive popular protests, especially in summer 2011, when a mass of people occupied Syntagma Square just opposite the parliament building.

However, because the first rescue plan turned out to be insufficient to tackle the Greek fiscal challenges, a new joint rescue package from the European Financial Stabilisation Mechanism (EFSM), the European Financial Stability Facility (EFSF) and the IMF was negotiated with Greece and decided in June 2011 by the European Council. The second rescue plan included 'voluntary private sector

[17] See also A Antoniadis, 'Debt Crisis as a Global Emergency: The European Economic Constitution and Other Greek Fables', in A Antoniadis, R Schütze, E Spaventa (eds), *The European Union and Global Emergencies: A Law and Policy Analysis* (Oxford, Hart Publishing, 2011), available at SSRN: http://ssrn.com/abstract=1699082.

[18] Available at http://ec.europa.eu/economy_finance/publications/occasional_paper/2010/op61_en.htm.

[19] Total worth of the loan was €110 billion out of which €80 billion was to be provided by the EU and €30 billion by the IMF.

[20] Y Drossos, 'Greece—The Sovereignty of the Debt, the Sovereigns over the Debts and Some Reflections on Law', www.constitutionalism.gr, 4.

[21] Ibid, 9.

involvement (PSI)[22] in the form of informal and voluntary roll-overs of existing Greek debt at maturity'.[23] On 14 March 2012, the Ecofin approved the Second Economic Adjustment Programme for Greece,[24] which is financed by the EFSF, as opposed to the first, which was based on bilateral loans.

The government of Georgios Papandreou surrendered power to a coalition government; after his proposal for a referendum on the measures following the decision on restructuring the Greek debt was not backed up by the Deputies of the governing party, Papandreou resigned. A multiparty parliament emerged from the double elections in May and June 2012.[25] Besides the near political extinction of the once powerful PASOK, the most impressive and alarming outcome of the election is the rise of an ultra-right, nationalist party with neo-nazi features and a mode of behaviour that threatens anyone in disagreement with it, and ultimately, democracy itself.

B. Greece as a Rule

Notwithstanding the above, Greece's unbearable public debt is not only due to imprudent domestic economic and fiscal policy but also to the notorious asymmetries in the design of EMU. Since Maastricht, EMU has favoured monetary integration at the expense of economic integration and has failed to take into account the imbalance between developed and peripheral economies. Thus, it comes as no surprise that the so-called 'PIIGCS'[26] are increasing in number and there is a growing fear that France may soon join the Mediterranean camp.

As already implied, deficient fiscal surveillance in the context of the EMU, as well as the continuing lack of institutional mechanisms on its behalf to restrain the choices of Greek policymakers are also equally to blame. Not only have sanctions never been applied under the excessive deficit procedure, but the relevant surveillance of Greece was lifted in June 2007.[27] Although the Greek economy had not recovered, the rules of the Stability and Growth Pact had meanwhile changed in 2005, in order to accommodate France's and Germany's

[22] The voluntary private sector involvement (PSI) was initially set at a level of 21% restructuring and resulted in a 50% 'haircut' at the Euro Summit on 26 October 2012.

[23] *Cf* Statement by the Eurogroup of 20 June 2011, available at: www.consilium.europa.eu/uedocs/cms_data/docs/pressdata/en/ecofin/122908.pdf (accessed 04 May 2013), followed by European Council of 23/24 June 2011, Conclusions, Doc EUCO 23/11, para 15. See also M Ruffert, 'The European Debt Crisis and European Union law' (2011) 48 *Common Market Law Review* 1777, 1781–82.

[24] It included the undisbursed amounts of the first programme (Greek loan facility) plus an additional €130 billion for the years 2012–14.

[25] The second election took place as the first did not result in a governing majority.

[26] Portugal, Italy, Ireland, Greece, Cyprus and Spain.

[27] The deficit was reported in 2006 to be equal to 2.6% of GDP, a figure that was also revised later by Eurostat—when it finally finished checking Greek accounts (in 2009)—to 5.7%! Some political analysts have suggested that Greece's exit from surveillance in 2007 was based on political grounds, ie the political affinity between the conservative Prime Minister Kostas Karamanlis and the Commission's President Manuel Barroso, in order for the former to win the preterm elections in 2007.

failure to comply with the original rule of the Pact. As a result, Greece exited the surveillance status and even during the 2008 global financial crisis[28] the (then) conservative government insisted that the country was insulated from its worst effects and hence continued spending and raising the debt.

As noted above, EMU was born with a genetic flaw: monetary union was achieved, yet economic union was far from real; fiscal policies remained completely uncoordinated.[29] By prohibiting the new European Central Bank from bailing out a country with an excessive deficit by lending money directly to governments and yet not foreseeing a euro-exit process, the EU Treaties completed the chronicle of a fiscal crisis foretold. Some economists[30] had long ago foreseen the adverse economic consequences of a common currency for a highly heterogeneous group of countries, including the sovereign debt crises and large trade deficits that now plague most eurozone countries, the fragile condition of major European banks and high levels of unemployment across the eurozone. It is worth noting that the measures taken ex nihilo, firstly exclusively for Greece and under the fear that the 'patient' might infect other vulnerable states and lead to the demise of the euro,[31] paved the way for the design of new institutional mechanisms at European level (such as the emergency and temporary mechanisms of the EFSM and EFSF and the permanent European Stability Mechanism (ESM)[32]) and further national rescue plans that then served for more vulnerable eurozone economies (eg Portugal, Ireland, Spain and Cyprus).[33]

Although Greece has indeed proven to be the weakest link, this is definitely not merely a Greek crisis; it is rather a severe EU crisis with many facets such as the rise of Euroscepticism, tendencies to renationalize competences even in breach of EU law,[34] and uncertainty about the future of the euro. The debris of the economic, political and constitutional earthquake that has shaken Greece may only be recovered via a combined strategy to be followed by Greece, the EU and all the Member States. Neither the economic nor the constitutional architecture can be exclusively national in character. Renationalization will prove to be disastrous. The only way is to proceed with the Europeanization of the constitution, including the economic constitution, and the constitutionalization of Europe.

[28] *Cf* G Pagoulatos and Chr Triantopoulos, 'The Return of the Greek Patient: Greece and the 2008 Global Financial Crisis' (2009) 14 *South European Society and Politics* 35, 43 et seq.

[29] Critically J. Habermas, 'Die Krise der Europäischen Union im Lichte einer Konstitutionalisierung des Völkerrechts –Ein Essay zur Verfassung Europas' (2012) 72 *ZaöRV* 1, 2–3.

[30] See eg M Feldstein, 'EMU and International Conflict' (1997) 76 *Foreign Affairs* 60 et seq, available at: www.nber.org/feldstein/fa1197.html.

[31] *Cf* N Ferguson, 'The End of the Euro', *Newsweek*, 6 May 2010, www.thedailybeast.com/newsweek/2010/05/07/the-end-of-the-euro.html.

[32] See P Craig in this volume (Chapter 2).

[33] For the entire series of measures taken, see European Commission, Economic and Financial Affairs, EU Response to the Economic and Financial Crisis, at: http://ec.europa.eu/economy_finance/focuson/crisis (accessed 20 May 2013). See also AG Merino, 'Legal Developments in the Economic and Monetary Union During the Debt Crisis: The Mechanisms of Financial Assistance' (2012) 49(5) *Common Market Law Review* 1613 et seq.

[34] Ruffert (n 23) 1777.

C. Economic Policy Constraints and Memoranda of Understanding

As mentioned above, the legal framework currently in place in Greece to deal with the fiscal emergency is based on the MoUs. The MoUs contain measures concerning fiscal, tax, social and social security policies, such as reform of the pension schemes including pension and salary cuts, bold tax increases, including housing taxes, loosening of labour law protections, as well as deep structural reforms towards a more competitive economy and fiscal sustainability with the aim of regaining the confidence of the markets. The parliamentary acts adopted to materialise the latter have been based on a legal framework of a multiple and overlapping nature, including international, European, national and also private laws. The content of instruments of international law was repeatedly copied verbatim in EU or national acts. Specifically, the MoU,[35] signed on 3 March 2010 between Greece and the Commission, has been accorded a distinctive status, owing to its linkage with different legal measures of the international, EU and Greek legal order.[36] Firstly, it has been incorporated into Greek law, since it has been attached as an annex to Law 3845/2010, containing measures for the application of the support mechanism.[37] Secondly, the Loan Facility Agreement,[38] technically a contract under international law between Greece and its foreign lenders, refers to the MoU as a condition for the release of the loan tranches. Thirdly, the main commitments laid down in the MoU were copied in the Council Decision 320/2010/EU.[39]

For the last three years, the MoU has been the main keyword in public discourse. Not only has it caused a civil division and a new kind of political cleavage between camps, consisting of parties from both the right and the left, but it has also become the object of legal controversy. To be more precise, the political debate was eventually legalized and a vast number of cases concerning the compatibility of the MoU with Greek, EU and international law were brought

[35] The MoU consists of three parts: (a) The Memorandum of Economic and Financial Policies (MEFP), (b) the Memorandum of Understanding on Specific Economic policy conditionality (SEPC) and (c) the Technical Memorandum of Understanding (TMU).

[36] I Vlachou, *Memoranda sunt servanda?—The Legal Status of the Memorandum of Understanding of the Greek Bailout in the Hellenic, European and International Legal Order*, LLM master's thesis, University of Leiden Faculty of Law (October 2012) available at: http://studentthinktank.eu/wp-content/uploads/2012/11/THESIS_I.Vlachou-11.pdf, 14.

[37] Law 3845/2010, 'Measures for the application of the support mechanism for the Greek economy by euro area Member States and the International Monetary Fund', Official Gazette A′ 65/ 06.05.2010. The MoU has also been connected to the standby arrangement, constituting a condition for IMF financing.

[38] The Agreement was signed on 8 May 2010 by Greece on the one hand and the rest of the Member States on the other, except from Germany, on behalf of which the German Kreditanstalt für Wiederaufbau signed it. Art 1(1) of the Loan Agreement provides that: 'The Lenders make available to the borrower a loan facility … subject to the terms and conditions of the MoU and this Agreement.'

[39] Council Decision 320/2010/EU, EE L 145, 11 June 2010, 6–11, 'addressed to Greece with a view to reinforcing and deepening fiscal surveillance and giving notice to take measures for the deficit reduction judged necessary to remedy the situation of excessive deficit' (based on Arts 126(9) and 136 TFEU), later revised by Council Decision 2011/57/EU of 20 December 2010.

before the competent courts. Human dignity, the right to property, protection of labour, and social rights in combination with the principles of proportionality, legal certainty, the rule of law, and national sovereignty itself have been invoked in these legal challenges.[40]

Austerity measures imposed through the first MoU and its related laws (especially Law 3845/6.5.2010, A′ 65) have been challenged before the courts, especially the highest administrative court, the Council of the State (Symvoulio tis Epikratias) triggering a debate on the constitutionality of the MoU.[41] It is worth noting that that Greece does not have a constitutional court. Review of constitutionality is diffuse, being exercised by all courts.[42] However, the highest administrative court, the Council of the State, effectively concentrates on constitutional review.[43] With its Decision 668/2012, the Council of State dismissed the case of the alleged unconstitutionality of the measures. The Strasburg Court also denied their unconventionality, coming to the conclusion that salary cuts do not violate Article 1 of the 1st Additional Protocol to the European Convention on Human Rights (ECHR)[44] and it thus rejected the relevant application as 'manifestly ill-founded' (Article 35(3) and (4) ECHR).

III. BALANCED-BUDGET AMENDMENT IN THE GREEK CONSTITUTION

The tendency within the course of constitutionalism is to enhance the 'economic'[45] and/or 'fiscal' constitutionalism both at national, supranational[46] and

[40] *Cf* A Pottakis, 'Greece—In Search of a Modern Deus ex Machina: Towards an Orderly Bankruptcy of European Legal Orders' (2011) 17 *European Public Law* 187; Y Kouzis, 'The Impact of the Crisis on Labour Relations and Collective Agreements in Greece—Towards a Sustainable Recovery: The Case for Wage-Led Policies', (2011) 3 *International Journal of Labour Research* 245, as well as abundant Greek literature.

[41] *Cf* X Contiades and I Tassopoulos, 'The Impact of the Financial Crisis on the Greek Constitution' in X Contiades (ed), *Constitutions in the Global Financial Crisis: A Comparative Analysis* (Surrey, Ashgate 2013) 195, 201 et seq.

[42] See Art 93(4) GrC: '4. The courts shall be bound not to apply a statute whose content is contrary to the Constitution.' In such a diffuse system, any court exercises a specific review, ie of the application of the law in the very specific case before it. When a court finds that the legal provision as applied in the specific case is unconstitutional, it misapplies it, but id may not annul it (with the exception of the Highest Special Court, called to judge in specific cases).

[43] This is mainly due to hierarchical structure of the judicial system, which allows for repeal of the decisions taken at first instance. Lower courts tend to adjust to the higher courts' decisions, even though they are not legally obliged to do so. See also Art 100(5) GrC: 'When a chamber of the Council of State or of the Supreme Civil and Criminal Court or of the Court of Audit judges a provision of a statute to be contrary to the Constitution, it is bound to refer the question to the respective plenum, unless this has been judged by a previous decision of the plenum or of the Special Highest Court of this article. The plenum shall be assembled into judicial formation and shall decide definitively.'

[44] See judgements 57665/12 and 57657/12, Ioanna Koufaki c la Grèce and ADEDY c la Grèce, 7 May 2013, available at: http://hudoc.echr.coe.int/.

[45] G Beaucamp, 'Grundzüge der Finanzverfassung' (1998) 30 Juristische Arbeitsblätter 774; R Zippelius and M Wurtenberger, *Deutsches Staatsrecht* (Munich, Beck, 2005) 467 et seq.

[46] A look at the agenda of European Council Meetings during these last three years reveals that most of the topics focus on the reformation of the economic constitution of the EU.

international level.[47] The global financial crisis and the subsequent European sovereign debt crisis mark—although not exclusively—the peak of this tendency. One could reasonably argue that the strengthening of global markets is the environment to which legal regulations need to adapt. This creates the need for the adoption of common economic policies, the efficacy of which is ensured through their entrenchment in national, European and international law. A question then arises as to the relationship between this new type of economic and fiscal constitutionalism and the classic, liberal and democratic constitutionalism as we used to know it.

Returning to the case of Greece—and combining the international with the national arena—one could arguably reach the conclusion that, if the flaw in the design of Greek economic policy is structural, then changing the basic law, the Constitution, could help the state face the current fiscal crisis or prevent the next one from hitting shortly afterwards. In other words, should the necessary structural correction start from the fundamental law of the state? Will imposed constitutional constraints effectively change the basic rules of the fiscal game? The constitutional agenda on this point has been set Europe-wide by the Fiscal Compact, which demands the incorporation of the 'golden rule' in the national legal apparatus, preferably at constitutional level. This section will focus on the legal merits and flaws of introducing the 'balanced-budget rule' into constitution, and especially into the Greek Constitution.

A. The 'Golden Rule' Amendment

(i) The Requirements of the Fiscal Compact

The Treaty of Maastricht has already set the goal of maintaining price stability and preventing high inflation.[48] Article 126(1) TFEU (in its post-Lisbon version) states that 'Member States shall avoid excessive government deficits' while monitoring by the Commission based on specified criteria is foreseen in the second paragraph. This monitoring possibly counterbalances the fact that economic policy remains a national competence.[49] In the same vein, the Treaty on Stability, Coordination and Governance (TSCG) was signed with the aspiration, according to its Preamble, 'to promote conditions for stronger economic growth in the European Union and, to that end, to develop ever-closer coordination of economic policies within the euro area'. In the same Preamble the contracting parties explicitly recognize that

> the need for governments to maintain sound and sustainable public finances and to prevent a general government deficit becoming excessive is of essential importance

[47] The number of G8 and G20 meetings has substantially increased over time.
[48] See also Art 119(2) and Art 127(1) TFEU as well as Art 3(3) TEU.
[49] See C Hillgruber, 'Disziplinlosigkeit oder Vertragsbruch?' [2004] *Juristenzeitung (JZ)* s 166–72.

to safeguard the stability of the euro area as a whole, and accordingly, requires the introduction of specific rules, including a 'balanced budget rule' and an automatic mechanism to take corrective action.

The main commitment that Member States undertake with regards to the new Treaty is to introduce—within one year of the Treaty coming into force (1 January 2013)—into their national legal system the so-called 'golden rule', or 'balanced-budget rule', ie a legal prohibition of deficit government spending.[50] More specifically, Article 3(2) TSCG imposes on Member States the duty to incorporate the 'golden rule' at national level by means of 'provisions of binding force and permanent character, preferably constitutional, or otherwise guaranteed to be fully respected and adhered to throughout the national budgetary processes'. This is the first time that an EU treaty has imposed on Member States an explicit constitutional amendment, rather than just causing implicit changes, as most such treaties have done until now. Moreover, Article 8(1) TSCG[51] allows the CJEU to be called upon to judge if a Member State has failed adequately to incorporate the 'golden rule' in its national legal apparatus.

(ii) Why in the Constitution?

Inserting budgetary constraints into Member State constitutions is intended to guarantee legal certainty and effectiveness. If the effectiveness of legal provisions is closely linked with enforceability, then in order for the 'golden rule' normatively to command any disobedient budget legislator, it needs to be justiciable. Thus, courts are invited into the game. In this light, one could easily understand the regulation on competence of the CJEU, which may be called upon by any Member State in order to adjudicate whether another Member State has not been applying the fiscal rules. It then becomes unclear why it is necessary for the balanced-budget amendment to be introduced into national law. Besides, by remaining a provision of EU law, the 'golden rule' acquires the same force by being adjudicated upon in the CJEU.

One answer to the question why the constraints should be transposed into national legal order is the fear that national constitutional courts might develop a stance of 'judicial disobedience' towards the Fiscal Compact and probably CJEU

[50] For the 'golden rule' in the Fiscal Compact, see F Fabbrini, 'The Fiscal Compact, the "Golden Rule," and the Paradox of European Federalism' (2013) 36 *Boston College International & Comparative Law Review* 1, 4.

[51] 'The European Commission is invited to present in due time to the Contracting Parties a report on the provisions adopted by each of them in compliance with Article 3(2). If the European Commission, after having given the Contracting Party concerned the opportunity to submit its observations, concludes in its report that such Contracting Party has failed to comply with Article 3(2), the matter will be brought to the Court of Justice of the European Union by one or more Contracting Parties. Where a Contracting Party considers, independently of the Commission's report, that another Contracting Party has failed to comply with Article 3(2), it may also bring the matter to the Court of Justice. In both cases, the judgment of the Court of Justice shall be binding on the parties to the proceedings, which shall take the necessary measures to comply with the judgment within a period to be decided by the Court of Justice.'

rulings.[52] That they would, in other words, declare a European 'golden rule' inapplicable in national fiscal matters either as unconstitutional vis-à-vis their own national constitution or outside of EU competence (ultra vires). The inadequacy of available legal bases might have after all compelled the European political elite to design the Fiscal Compact as an international treaty and not as an EU law instrument. The fact that an international treaty needs to be transformed into national law—independent of the self-executing nature of international law (or the lack thereof)—helps overcome the impediment of economic policy remaining at national level.

The alternative to constitutional incorporation, namely a regulation based on Article 136 TFEU,[53] would run the risk of being declared by a national court as violating a national constitution or even being ultra vires. Thus, such an alternative would not necessarily guarantee the higher legal value that the drafters of the Fiscal Compact had wished to safeguard.[54] Their discomfort reflects the uncertainty of EU law when it faces national constitutional law, as well as their fear that the principle of supremacy might be undermined in its full application by national constitutional courts.

B. The Greek Particularities

(i) The Balanced-Budget Amendment Is Improbable

Greece's fiscal constitution[55] does not contain any provisions concerning public borrowing. Hence, if the 'golden rule' were to be inserted into the Greek Constitution (GrC), then the latter would have to be formally amended. The revision procedure of the relatively rigid Constitution is foreseen in Article 110.[56] A

[52] *Cf* Czech Constitutional Court, judgment of 31 January 2012, Pl ÚS 5/12, R Zbíral, 'Case Note: A Legal Revolution or Negligible Episode? Court of Justice Decision Proclaimed *Ultra Vires*' (2012) *Common Market Law Review* 49, 1475.

[53] According to a convincing opinion, Art 136 TFEU is not a substantive legal basis as such but rather the basis for enhanced co-operation between eurozone members, and thus it requires an international compact—eg it has been utilized to adopt the 'two-pack' of regulations. For this view see Ruffert (n 23) 1777.

[54] See A Dimopoulos in this book (Chapter 3).

[55] Section III: Parliament, Chapter Six: Taxation and fiscal administration, Arts78–80 GrC, or Art 75 'Bills resulting in burdening the State budget'.

[56] Art 110 GrC:

1. The provisions of the Constitution shall be subject to revision with the exception of those which determine the form of government as a Parliamentary Republic and those of articles 2 paragraph 1, 4 paragraphs 1, 4 and 7 , 5 paragraphs 1 and 3, 13 paragraph 1, and 26.

2. The need for revision of the Constitution shall be ascertained by a resolution of Parliament adopted, on the proposal of not less than fifty Members of Parliament, by a three-fifths majority of the total number of its members in two ballots, held at least one month apart. This resolution shall define specifically the provisions to be revised.

3. Upon a resolution by Parliament on the revision of the Constitution, the next Parliament shall, in the course of its opening session, decide on the provisions to be revised by an absolute majority of the total number of its members.

balanced-budget amendment is in principle not excluded by the 'eternity clause' of Article 110(1) GrC. The argument that such a rule poses too wide a restriction on a government's framework to design and execute its policy and hence runs counter to the principle of democracy is not very convincing here, since it ignores the constitutional character of Greek democracy, which allows for a binding frame within which decisions are allowed. Furthermore, it has been proposed that fiscal irresponsibility cannot be laid at the feet of particular politicians or parties, since the expectation that, 'with electoral rotation, those who stand for fiscal integrity might eventually replace those who are fiscally profligate' is utopian since there is a fault not 'in ourselves, as participants in the ordinary politics of modern majoritarian democracy, but in the structural rules within which this politics takes place'.[57]

In any case, in order formally to revise the Constitution, the Parliament must approve with qualified majorities the amendment in two subsequent periods. Given the requirement for a qualified majority (ie three-fifths of the total number of MPs, see Article 110(4) GrC), inserting a 'golden rule' into the Constitution presupposes that different political parties have to agree on the basics of future economic policies and on a set of contingencies that would only provide them with little room to deviate from a balanced budget when in office. Given the current political situation, a balanced-budget amendment is unlikely to be supported by the necessary three-fifths majority (180/300 MPs). Moreover, for the amendment procedure to be properly completed, an absolute majority of MPs in the next parliamentary period after the elections is required.[58] Not only does this result in a delay, but it also risks annulment of the forthcoming amendment, in the event of a possible radicalization of voters and/or a change in government in favour of opposition parties. Thus, amending the Constitution of Greece in order to incorporate the 'golden rule' is not only technically difficult and time consuming but politically complex as well. Furthermore, such a change would face the accusation that it was causing a further loss of sovereignty.[59]

4. Should a proposal for revision of the Constitution receive the majority of the votes of the total number of members but not the three-fifths majority specified in paragraph 2, the next Parliament may, in its opening session, decide on the provisions to be revised by a three-fifths majority of the total number of its members.

5. Every duly voted revision of provisions of the Constitution shall be published in the Government Gazette within ten days of its adoption by Parliament and shall come into force through a special parliamentary resolution.

6. Revision of the Constitution is not permitted before the lapse of five years from the completion of a previous revision.

[57] J Buchanan, 'The Balanced Budget Amendment: Clarifying the Arguments' (1997) 90 *Public Choice* 117, 120-21.

[58] For a similar revision procedure see M Diamant and M van Emmerik in this volume (Chapter 12).

[59] Contiades and Tassopoulos (n 41) 214.

(ii) The Balanced-Budget Amendment Is Legally Unnecessary

If Greece does not succeed in completing a constitutional amendment due to the technical and political reasons explained above, the question arises whether it should expect to be brought before the CJEU accused of not implementing Article 3(2) TSCG, pursuant to Article 8(1) TSCG. A possible line of defence in such a case—which at the same time provides a profound and solid ground for proving that a balanced-budget amendment is not necessary for the rule to be eventually enforced—lies with the legal status of international treaties in the Greek legal order.

Within the context of a mixed model (monist and dualist[60]), international law—such as the TSCG—after its incorporation into national law, acquires a legal position higher than formal laws, ie laws voted upon by the Parliament, including the law on state budget. The TSCG has already been ratified and incorporated into Greek legal system through Law 4063/2012.[61] In this way, the Fiscal Compact (Article 3 TSCG) has become part of the Greek legal order (due to the monist effect of the incorporation of international law according to Article 28(1) GrC) and has acquired higher legal validity than any contrary provision of law.

Consequently, Greece's obligation resulting from Article 3(2) TSCG to give effect to the rules of Article 3(1) TSCG 'in the national law through provisions of binding force and permanent character … guaranteed to be fully respected and adhered to throughout the national budgetary process', although not on a constitutional level (something not necessarily demanded by the TSCG), has already been formally fulfilled.

The legal status of the Fiscal Compact as an international treaty is higher than that of formal laws, but below the Constitution. Theoretically speaking, this allows a court to undertake a constitutionality review of the 'golden rule' based on the assumption that it contravenes both fundamental principles, such as democracy (Article 1 GrC) and the social state (Article 25(1) GrC), as well as specific social rights. Such a development, however, leading to Greek courts restricting the executive as regards the execution of its budgetary obligations ,is highly improbable in light of the judicial experience to date.

(iii) Executive Unbound?

Since the signing of the MoU, Greek legislative and executive institutions have functioned under the auspices of the Troika, which has taken charge to fix not

[60] The dualist element is the requirement of incorporation whether the monist elements consists in the incorporation of the international law into the Greek legal order. *Cf* Art 28(1) GrC: 'The generally recognised rules of international law, as well as international conventions as of the time they are sanctioned by statute and become operative according to their respective conditions, shall be an integral part of domestic Greek law and shall prevail over any contrary provision of the law. The rules of international law and of international conventions shall be applicable to aliens only under the condition of reciprocity.'

[61] Art 3 of Law 4063/2012, Official Journal of the Government (FEK) A′ 71/30.03.2012. The same law ratified the amendment of Art 136 TFEU (Art 1) and the ESM Treaty (Art 2).

only the nation's finances but the entire Greek administration. Although the members of the Troika are simply high-ranking officials of the organizations in which they work, they negotiate with ministers—though the word 'negotiation' might be considered a euphemism for predetermined decisions imposed on the Greek government.[62] It is actually the Troika that sets the political agenda, since it delivers the report on which the release (or not) of the next loan instalment depends.

As a result, the constitutional regime during the crisis is mainly marked by an intensification of the tendency for an 'unbound executive' along with a diminishing capacity for supervision both by Parliament and by the courts when it comes to economic issues. Executive power itself is dichotomized between politically accountable ministers and the heads of the parties supporting the government, and the Troika, who are politically unaccountable, supported by a large number of publicly unknown but powerful 'ephorate', 'a new branch of government comprising office-holders who possess the type of expertise and specialised knowledge that has become the basis of effective governmental decision-making'.[63] Such an evolution with regards to the Troika's role and the transfer of a substantial amount of political power to this kind of transnational 'ephorate' exemplifies a new phase in the development of government.[64] However, this is also the government's fault to the extent that no plan for national reforms was being prepared to maintain and promote the country's comparative advantages within the EU and/or at a global level. Two coinciding trends of depoliticization may be observed and financial issues are a domain par excellence in which to observe these trends: first, the transfer of economic decision-making to the EU, only partially legitimized by the citizens, since power is exercised mainly by the Council (on which representatives of the executive sit); and second, the strong role played by professional executives—a new 'ephorate', represented par excellence by the Troika. In this context, the commitment imposed by Article 3(2) TSCG to 'fully respect the prerogatives of national Parliaments' sounds like a euphemism. Where financial issues are concerned, not only courts but even parliaments seem to lose their say and executive power, old and new, appears more unbound in all respects.

A further trend of depoliticization is reflected in the 'judicialization of mega-politics'.[65] In this vein, an unprecedented recourse to the Greek courts has harboured hollow hopes that the MoU's austerity policies will be defeated in courtrooms. Moving between technocratic decisions taken by the executive (and merely endorsed by the Parliament) and judicial judgments proves to be a 'no-win situation' for politics. Nevertheless, Greek judicial practice from previous

[62] *Cf* Drossos (n 20) 11.

[63] M Loughlin, *Foundations of Public Law* (Oxford, Oxford University Press, 2010) 450.

[64] Ibid.

[65] R Hirschl, *Towards Juristocracy: The Origins and Consequences of the New Constitutionalism* (Boston, MA, Harvard University Press 2004) 169–70; R Hirschl, 'The Judicialization of Mega-Politics and the Rise of Political Courts' (2008) 11 *Annual Review of Political Science* 93, available at ssrn.com/abstract=1138008.

years asserts the general observation that, with a few exceptions, '[i]n matters of broad economic and social policies, the courts have generally been less active' since such issues 'require wider state intervention and changing public expenditure priorities'.[66] As mentioned above, Greek courts (with the exception of few decisions mainly taken by lower courts) have been hesitant to intervene in this field since they are inadequately equipped to convincingly overturn economic decisions taken by the executive power and endorsed by the Parliament. The most they could possibly ask for from the latter—in practice from governmental officials—is a detailed cost–benefit analysis report justifying the necessity of the measures.[67]

However, there is a caveat to the above evaluation concerning the courts' reduced capacity to administer the economy through the rule of law: given the fact that a constitutionally embedded 'golden rule' sets a procedural limit,[68] a prohibition, the enforcement of a 'golden rule' merely presupposes that the courts exercise their function of ideal type, which is negative legislating. This is more apt to their nature, as opposed to the implementation of social rights that implies the exercise of positive legislation.[69] Thus, courts might be expected to be less reluctant to reinforce the 'golden rule' than they are to reinforce social rights and distributive justice. This argument, however, ignores the fact that the very nature of constitutionalization and the corresponding expansion of judicial adjudication is a political, rather than a juridical, phenomenon.[70] In this context, judicial decisions are hardly likely to resist governmental decisions, especially given the fact that the 'golden rule' foresees a wide range of exceptions, making it susceptible to breaches masked as normatively prescribed for 'exceptional circumstances'. If the hypothesis that courts, especially in economic matters, are inclined to withhold decisions of the executive, then by legalizing and constitutionalizing budgetary constraints the real power is rather being transferred to the new 'ephorate'—bureaucrats and economists, executives and lobbyists. On the other hand, if the political community through a constitution-amending majority decides to impose such a rule as an exercise in self-command,[71] meaning an effort to 'overrule one's own preferences',[72] they will already have shown the second-order political will to obey to such a rule. The latter could provide a legitimate excuse

[66] R Hirschl, 'Constitutionalism, Judicial Review, and Progressive Change: A Rejoinder to McClain and Fleming', (2005) 84 *Texas Law Review* 471, 475.

[67] See Council of State judge's Karamanof dissenting opinion in three judgements of the Court: (a) 668/2012 (Plenum), para 33.Γ, (b) 1972/2012 (Plenum), para 17.B and (c) 38/2013 (Plenum), para 7.

[68] Buchanan (n 57) 126.

[69] *Cf* H Kelsen, 'Judicial Review of Legislation: A Comparative Study of the Austrian and American Constitution' (1942) 4 *Journal of Politics* 183.

[70] Hirschl, *Towards Juristocracy* (n 65) 12.

[71] W Keech, 'A Theoretical Analysis of the Case for a Balanced Budget Amendment' (1985) 18 *Policy Sciences* 157, 158.

[72] TC Schelling, 'Self-command in Practice, in Policy and in a Theory of Rational Choice' (1984) 74 *American Economic Review* 1. Schelling develops this concept in the context of theories of rational choice on the individual level, such as consumer behaviour.

for the government to avoid spending, as long as it decides to do so and not rely on the exceptions foreseen by the rule itself.

A further argument used by some proponents[73] of a balanced-budget amendment builds on the analogy that the government is like an alcoholic, drunk on deficits and unable to achieve the sobriety of balanced budgets without a constitutional constraint. This argument does not hold for Greece nowadays either, since the country has ran out of alcohol anyway! Having already signed MoUs with its creditors, Greece does not even need to proceed formally to a constitutional amendment in order to respect budgetary constraints. The MoUs—although they are not legal texts, according to decision 668/2012 of the Council of State discussed above, but merely political agreements—are enough to guarantee Greece's obedience to the substance of the 'golden rule'. Tight fiscal surveillance under the EU deficit procedure and the Troika guarantee this result better and more effectively than a constitutional provision in a country without a constitutional court. Thus, the normative power of the facts themselves—'die normative Kraft des Faktischen'—in harmony with the 'state of emergency' largely evoked by the courts, seem to overrule the normative Constitution and render a balanced-budget amendment redundant—at least for the time being.

IV. DOES THE 'GOLDEN RULE' BELONG TO THE CONSTITUTION?

The previous comment opens a Pandora's box. Apart from the practical difficulties of a political nature that amending the Greek Constitution would nowadays involve, a more general, theoretical question arises: even if agreement is reached on the substance of the 'golden rule', should this politico-economic policy be dressed in a constitutional cloak, and thus frozen, thereby binding future parliamentary majorities? In this respect, considerations of constitutional theory and politics come to the fore. The question is whether the constitution is the suitable legal topos for a balanced-budget rule.

A. About the Constitutional Fabric

At this juncture, it is worth posing three distinct questions that might undermine the first-order belief that a balanced-budget rule should be inserted into the Constitution. Firstly, does economic policy belong in the content of a constitution? Secondly, to go a step further, who is to decide the eligible content of constitutions? Here, the grammar of constitutionalism is called upon. The demand for constitutionally setting the budget framework raises questions concerning the very existence and function of a constitution. These are ques-

[73] J Buchanan and RE Wagner, *Democracy in Deficit* (New York, Academic Press, 1977) 159.

tions with difficult, uncertain, debatable and labile answers. Thirdly, if the constitution 'is there everlastingly to depend upon, and to relieve us from the necessity of facing and settling matters of principle',[74] one would ask whether the balanced budget is such a matter of principle or it should rather be inserted as 'a check upon the experimental spirit which is the natural corollary of democratic theory'.[75]

Constitutions were conceived as written declarations aiming to restrain political power over the citizenry and originally the bourgeoisie, concerning primarily taxation, private ownership and religious tolerance. In terms of taxation, one can already distinguish the seeds of a fiscal and financial constitutionalism in this early constitutional setting. This kind of financial constitutionalism, however, was confined to procedural guarantees protecting the emerging bourgeois class from the monarch's omnipotence. Parliament, as a representative organ of the bourgeois citizens, had a veto over the monarch's prerogative to impose new taxes upon them and is still maintains competence to decide upon the budget. Today, however, democratically elected representatives tend to approve the executive's proposals for higher spending even at the expense of the public debt, since they are also concerned about their functional legitimacy—to term it benevolently—or, they tend to resort to clientelism (which is more the case in the Greek context) in order to be re-elected.

Opponents of constitutional budgetary constraints say that economic policy has to be decided upon by each legislative majority and government, according to the results of elections. Political parties must be free to propose their programmes and design their prospective policies, even if these are based on borrowing. This is why a balanced-budget constitutional rule would violate democracy and its indispensable ingredient, political pluralism, as the guiding principle of a constitutional state, and would excessively narrow 'political manoeuvring in matters of public finance and fiscal policy, inscribing into the Constitution neo-liberal economic policies'.[76] However, setting a constitutional boundary to governmental power is always a boundary to democracy if the latter is conceived only in procedural terms. The balanced-budget amendment governs the process and 'lays out a new rule for making fiscal choices; it does not lay down guidelines for what these choices might be'.[77] Fundamental rights do nothing less than that, namely setting boundaries. Yet according to the more convincing perception with regards to their nature, fundamental rights should not be conceived as principles contradicting popular sovereignty, but rather as mutually interdependent and unbreakable corollaries.[78] Constitutional democracy, as a mixed

[74] AK Rogers, 'Constitutionalism' (1930) 40 *International Journal of Ethics* 289, 289.
[75] Ibid.
[76] Contiades and Tassopoulos (n 41) 214.
[77] Buchanan (n 57) 126.
[78] J Habermas, 'Human Rights and Popular Sovereignty: The Liberal and Republican Versions' (1994) 7 *Ratio Juris* 1, 13.

regime, is based on multiple modes of legitimacy, namely popular election of political representatives and the rule of law.

The question then arises as to what extent, if at all, is the prohibition of excessive sovereign debt different to a fundamental right, eg the prohibition of compulsory work (Article 22(4) GrC).[79] The need for exceptions and for flexibility and change in economic policy apply to both cases. Compelling people to work would probably help the economy to flourish. Yet, nowadays in Europe this is seen (rightly so) as totally excluded and beyond any notion of constitutionalism. Unlike human rights, balanced budgets are not first principles or ends in their own right; rather deficits are opposed for instrumental reasons relating inversely to other implicitly higher goals such as price stability, capital formation, and, by extension, long-term growth.[80] Thus, from a constitutional theory point of view, the legitimacy and acceptance of a constitutionally based balanced-budget rule depends on the elaboration of a theoretical account combining the diminution of debt with constitutional principles which the 'golden rule' serves, beyond pure economic necessity. Such a theoretical account will be explored below.

B. Balanced Budget as a Prerequisite for a Democratic Government

Only if it can be proven that the cutting of fiscal deficits is a prerequisite for democratic governance and/or the rights of the individuals can its insertion be accepted under the principles of constitutionalism. Such an account may be elaborated around three axes.

(i) Sovereign debt vs popular sovereignty

The first axon is the emergence of a bipolarity composed of the states as public spaces, and international private interests that supersede states in economic strength. The functioning of rating agencies and the catalytic repercussions that their credit ratings may have on national economies[81] are pieces of a puzzle that in its totality may prove that the states' relative independence from the 'markets' is the indispensable background for any level of self-government. This argument implies that there is an inverse relationship between sovereignty, either national

[79] Art 22(4) GrC: 'Any form of compulsory work is prohibited. Special laws shall determine the requisition of personal services in case of war or mobilization or to face defence needs of the country or urgent social emergencies resulting from disasters or liable to endanger public health, as well as the contribution of personal work to local government agencies to satisfy local needs.'

[80] Keech (n 71) 159.

[81] *Cf US v McGraw-Hill Companies Inc, and Standard & Poor's Financial Services LLC* (available at www.justice.gov/iso/opa/resources/849201325104924250796.pdf). In this civil lawsuit against Standard & Poor's the US government is seeking $5 billion, accusing the ratings service of defrauding investors.

or popular, and sovereign debt. Thus if a constitution legitimately guarantees the former, it should necessarily prevent the latter.

This analysis is framed by the suggestion that a sustainable notion of democracy presupposes its relative restriction in the present. This argument may be found in a judgment of the German Federal Constitutional Court.[82] Responding to the criticism that a constitutional debt-brake violates the principle of democracy, the Court underlined that such a constraint 'may be necessary precisely in order to preserve the democratic power to shape affairs for the body politic in the long term'.[83] Just as liberty, to be sustainable, may demand some restrictions (eg prohibition of hate speech), democracy needs to be protected against its own excesses too. One can also draw a comparison with rules governing free economic competition. Leaving competition totally free and unregulated will definitely result in a concentration of economic power. Thus, the sustainability of the free competition principle depends upon its procedural limitations. At this juncture, attention may also be drawn to the openness of the democratic process. The same logic that allows for budgetary restrictions in order to preserve the sustainability of popular sovereignty, would also dictate the outlaw of political parties that jeopardized democracy. Hence, the German way of seeing things in budgetary matters is consistent with the notion of *streitbare/wehrhafte Demokratie* that the Republic adopts in order to face its enemies. Although this sounds convincing, it does not correspond with the Greek constitutional philosophy and political culture.[84] By not embracing the philosophy of 'militant democracy', the Greek constitution is thought not to be able to confront by normative means either the debt crisis through the insertion of a 'golden rule' or the democratic crisis posed by an anti-democratic party, such as the Golden Dawn.

[82] Judgment of the German Federal Constitutional Court, BVerfGE 129, 124—EFS of 12 September2012,

[83] Ibid, para 224:

> [I]t is not anti-democratic from the outset for the budget legislature to be bound by a particular budget and fiscal policy' (see BVerfGE 79, 311, 331 et seq; 119, 96, 137 et seq). By putting into specific terms and objectively tightening the rules for borrowing by Federal and *Länder* governments (in particular Article 109 (3) and (5), Article 109a, Article 115 of the Basic Law new, Article 143d (1) of the Basic Law), the constitution-amending legislature made it clear that a constitutional commitment on the part of the parliaments and thus a palpable restriction of their budgetary power to act may be necessary precisely in order to preserve the democratic power to shape affairs for the body politic in the long term (BVerfGE 129, 124, 170). Even if such a commitment restricts democratic legislative discretion in the present, it serves at the same time to guarantee it for the future. Admittedly, even a long-term worrying development of the level of indebtedness is not a constitutionally relevant impairment of the legislature's competence for a situation-dependent discretionary fiscal policy. Nevertheless, it results in a de facto constriction of discretion (see BVerfGE 119, 96, 147). Keeping discretion as broad as possible is a legitimate goal of the (constitutional) legislature.

[84] The whole discussion touches upon the way the Greek political system should face the danger posed by the emergence of the neo-nazi political party called Golden Dawn. It is worth noting here that in Greece there is no legislation for prohibiting political parties.

(ii) Intergenerational Justice

The second axon around which the quality of the 'golden rule' as constitutional fabric may be twined is intergenerational justice. Borrowing today in order to enjoy goods or services results in austerity measures tomorrow, for the next generation.[85] There is an inherent injustice to this scheme, a radical break in the equality and solidarity principle. If this holds, then a constitution as the supreme law, aiming at reversing the unequal way things are naturally and socially structured, may exercise its normative power to try to prevent such an economic and ethical injustice. This thought serves also as a counterargument to the assertion that the 'golden rule' necessarily violates the principle of the social state and the protection of specific social rights. This objection is countered by reference to fact that the obligation of a balanced budget does not prevent a state from redistributing and offering social protection to the poor and weak; it only prohibits deficit spending in excess of revenue, ie funds raised by borrowing, rather than by taxation. Thus it only obliges the government to make the necessary arrangements and save resources for social public expenses through revenues. No governmental outlay, but only high levels of debt-financed public expenses are excluded. The latter seems to enforce solidarity and redistribution more than excessive borrowing and imposes the need for enhanced governance capacity.

(iii) Excessive Borrowing as Unfair Political Competition

The third quality that connects a debt brake with democracy is the need to liberate the political process and party competition from unfair elements. Such an unfair element is the promise to deliver goods to the electorate not based on politics, fostering production, modernizing the administration and redistributing the outcome or through hierarchizing human needs, but rather based on 'cheating'. In this context, suspending the political agents' authority to spend without taxing,[86] and also limiting their borrowing power, prevents them from bribing voters, and corrupting consciences. In this respect, free and fair competition is a principle applying to both the economy and politics. Legal regulation is necessary and applicable to guarantee both, even by limiting the procedural liberty (of governments, political parties and enterprises) in order to safeguard their substance.

The counterargument to the above would be that borrowing in order to invest would be a smart way of reasserting the lost (national and popular) sovereignty.[87]

[85] *Cf* Constitutional Court of North Rhine-Westphalia, Germany, VerfGH 20/10, 15 March 2011, available at www.vgh.nrw.de/pressemitteilungen/2011/05_110315/110315_vgh_Urteil.pdf. The Court states (C.I.1) that the aim is the protection of future generations; more specifically future citizens and parliaments need to be protected from the fact that they will not have the necessary financial framework to face the problems of their time, according to their own criteria. That is why income that burdens future budgets needs to be compensated with spending which benefits the future.

[86] Buchanan (n 57) 121.

[87] Thus the old debt brake in the German Constitution looks more justified than the new one.

Moreover, considerations of economic relevance would come to the fore, which go beyond the subject matter of this discussion. The open-ended character of the discussion, the polarization it provokes and the ambiguity of the whole issue may be a good reason not to adopt such an amendment after all.

C. The Strengths and Weaknesses of a Constitution

Even if the answer to the previous question concerning the constitutional quality of the 'golden rule' is positive, a further question arises as to whether and how effective a national constitutional amendment may prove. In other words, whether incorporation into national law and thus possible enforcement by national courts would enhance the balanced budgetary rule's effectiveness and intensify its normative strength, if compared with its mere embeddedness in the European legal order. The question concerns the real normative ability of a constitution to regulate the economy, beyond the basics (ie basic freedom of economic transactions as a part of personal autonomy). In classical terms, if there is a bipolarity between 'rules and coordination based modes of governance',[88] the former is the more intensive and pressing mode of proceeding, often equated with sanctions, while the latter is looser and may be less efficient. One may convincingly think that Article 3(2) TSCG aims exactly at enhancing this kind of normativity and efficiency.

However, this is not necessarily the case with a state such as Greece, where existing law is not always enforced. As the example of 'Greek statistics', namely the attempt to use creative accounting strategies to hide debts, shows, a single constitutional provision has not the force to guarantee that such creative means will not be used in the future to hide overruns. It is only practices and policies that could prevent this from happening—not a legal norm, no matter how high its placement in the legal hierarchy. Moreover, as already noted above, there is no constitutional court in Greece and the highest administrative court (that may be thought of as quasi-constitutional court, since most cases concerning constitutional review are concentrated in its plenum) hesitates (for reasons explained above) to intervene in economic matters. Therefore, a balanced-budget amendment may be responsible for undermining the authority of state constitutions.

Moreover, and needless to say, the relevant set of contingencies to be included in the escape clauses can be very hard to identify and serious problems of enforcement and monitoring may arise. In this respect, these normative prescriptions lead once again to the well-known policy dilemma of choosing between 'simple rules and discretion'.[89] The existence of wide-ranging derogations[90] proves

[88] *Cf* KA Armstrong in this volume (Chapter 4).

[89] Alesina and Tabellini (n 14) 413.

[90] See: Art 115(2) of the German Basic Law, as modified in 2009; Art 135(4) of the Spanish Constitution, as modified in 2011; Art 81(2) of the Italian Constitution, as modified in 2012.

that drafters are fully aware of this fact. If one excludes natural catastrophes, an unprecedented fiscal crisis such as the current one clearly falls under the terms 'unusual emergency situations' and 'economic recession or extraordinary emergency situations that are either beyond the control of the State or significantly impair the financial situation or the economic or social sustainability of the State' and 'exceptional circumstances' that are foreseen as eligible bases for derogation in the German, Spanish and Italian constitutions. The Fiscal Compact itself foresees in Article 3(1)(c) 'exceptional circumstances'[91] as a legitimate ground for the Contracting Parties to 'temporarily deviate from their respective medium-term objective or the adjustment path towards it'. This clause may counterbalance '[t]he chief drawback of constitutionalisation', which is that it severely limits the ability of governments 'to respond to changes in economic circumstances',[92] but it definitely undermines legal certainty and the normativity of legal texts. It is not unusual that courts, feeling obliged to obey economic necessities, surpass a strict legalistic reading of the normative texts. The famous *Pringle*[93] decision of the CJEU is a typical example of a deviation from the normative content of the constitutional rule.

After all, both constitutionalization and legalization of fiscal discipline reveal a bold distrust of the people's representatives;[94] the same applies for the institutionalization of an independent Fiscal Council. However, the possibility of a deviation being allowed can result in the repoliticization[95] of the otherwise depoliticized fiscal policy.

V. CONCLUSIONS: THE GREEK DEBT BETWEEN RULES AND POLICIES

This chapter leads to the conclusion that the influence exerted on domestic policy by a constitutional provision is limited. A 'thick' constitution is more sensitive to violations and misunderstandings. It would thus be preferable rather to abstain from constitutional ambitions and opt for a 'thinner' constitutional economic framework, limiting government in sectors germane to normative regulation.

[91] See Art 3(3)(b): '"[E]xceptional circumstances" refers to the case of an unusual event outside the control of the Contracting Party concerned which has a major impact on the financial position of the general government or to periods of severe economic downturn as set out in the revised Stability and Growth Pact, provided that the temporary deviation of the Contracting Party concerned does not endanger fiscal sustainability in the medium-term.'

[92] RC Schragger, 'Democracy and Debt' (2012) 121 *Yale Law Journal* 860, 869.

[93] Case C-370/2012 *Thomas Pringle v Government of Ireland, Ireland and The Attorney General*, 27 November 2012. *Cf* B de Witte and T Beukers, 'The Court of Justice Approves the Creation of the European Stability Mechanism outside the EU Legal Order: Pringle' (2013) 50 *Common Market Law Review* 805, 834 and 848, who conclude that 'the Court has given, in Pringle, a well- reasoned judgment expressing a good mixture of legal principle and political pragmatism'.

[94] See also Schragger, 'Democracy and Debt' (n 92) 883.

[95] As G DelleDonne in this volume (Chapter 9), notes: '[I]t is far from self-evident that constitutional courts decide to engage in a difficult, controversial scrutiny of the degree of "extraordinariness" of the economic situation after a parliamentary vote.'

Economic issues can be regulated less by the normative strength of the normative ('die normative Kraft des Normativen'), which means enforceability of rules, and more under the 'normative strength of the factual' ('normative Kraft des Faktischen').[96] The first two attempts to legalize budgetary amendments in the Maastricht Treaty and the Stability and Growth Pact have already shown the boundaries of the normative when not supported by the necessary political will and effective surveillance policies. A constitutional balanced-budget amendment might be defensible in some cases, such as the Greek case, when the political process systematically undervalues a desirable relationship between revenues and expenditures.[97] Yet, even in these cases, or maybe especially in these cases, it is highly debatable as to what extent such a constitutional rule would be effective. Thus it would rather be wiser to 'save' the Constitution from the burden of entanglement within the fiscal crisis, which it cannot carry.

European policies and surveillance, as well as constitutional changes at EU level rather than constitutional changes at national level, can facilitate structural reforms in Greece's economy and administration and the modernization of the system. These policies coming from 'outside' must be continuously evaluated and improved, so that their effectiveness is maximized. At the same time, political circumstances need also to be taken into account in order for the financial crisis not to turn into a political and democratic crisis.[98] This is often the case since austerity measures largely feed populist policies that inhibit any efforts to restore macroeconomic stability and reform the state. In this context, the worst phenomenon is the emergence and strengthening of a neo-nazi party, the Golden Dawn, which is today represented in the Greek Parliament, and, as indicated by the polls, is rising in popularity.

According to the mainstream constitutional ethos in Greece, neither the 'golden rule' in the Constitution nor a prohibition of the Golden Dawn would prove particularly effective. At the same time, social rights were not safeguarded when the hurricane of the fiscal crisis hit the country because they were traditionally enshrined in the Constitution. To develop a theory of social rights in the courts, or to insert a rigid rule such as the one calling for a balanced budget, or to outlaw a popular party as counterdemocratic—all such moves are destined to fail in practice. Moreover, all these three examples are expressions of the limitations to the Constitution's normative strength. Hence, overestimating the normative strength of the latter would rather degenerate and undermine it. The general idea that 'law, in the form of its supreme appearance, is apt to be the warrant to all good things that can be achieved' is a rather 'metaphysical approach'. After all, the Constitution is not sufficient to overcome a crisis it did not cause.[99]

The blurring of distinctions between institutional praxis and legal regulation within the course of EU, international and national law has been so far, and

[96] G Jellinek, *Allgemeine Staatslehre* [1905], 4th edn (Bad Homburg vdH, Berlin, Zürich 1966) 338.
[97] Keech (n 71) 166
[98] Oltheten, Pinteris and Sougiannis (n 5) 774.
[99] Drossos (n 20) 42.

will remain, the main feature of efforts by the EU to address the crisis. These combinations imply and presuppose equilibrium between rule-based governance and policy co-ordination and surveillance. Under the conditions of fiscal and political uncertainty surrounding Greece, Greek citizens and elites maintain a vital role: 'representative democracy—citizens' power to elect fiscally prudent agents and decline to elect fiscally imprudent ones— … [remains] the chief way to control local fiscal behaviour'.[100] Furthermore, reforming the state and the political system is a Sisyphean task and belongs to the Greek people themselves, if we want it to be both effective and democratic. Otherwise no real change can be long lasting.

[100] Schragger (n 92) 865–6.

12

Mandatory Balanced Budget in Dutch Legislation Following Examples Abroad?[1]

MICHAL DIAMANT and MICHIEL VAN EMMERIK

I. INTRODUCTION

ON 2 MARCH 2012, 25 EU Member States (excluding the United Kingdom and the Czech Republic, for the time being) signed what is known as the Fiscal Compact.[2] The objective of this treaty is to tighten budgetary discipline within the EU. This is achieved mainly through the introduction of a 'balanced-budget rule'—the obligation to maintain balance in national budgets. This balanced-budget rule should be incorporated into national law, preferably via a change to the constitution, within one year of the treaty coming into force.[3] This rule introduces actual—substantive—conditions for national budgets. What can be expected as a result of incorporating this balanced-budget rule—also known as the 'golden rule'—into national (constitutional) law?

In this chapter we will explore the issue by considering the case of the Netherlands. The Fiscal Compact was approved by Parliament[4] in the summer of 2013.[5] Furthermore the Wet Houdbare Overheidsfinanciën (Wet HOF, Sustainable Public Finances Bill) is intended[6] to meet the obligation enshrined in Article 3 of the Fiscal Compact: the implementation of the balanced-budget rule in

[1] This chapter was finalized in September 2013. This article is partly based on a previous article by the authors: M Diamant and ML van Emmerik, 'Verplicht begrotingsevenwicht in de Nederlandse (Grond)wet naar buitenlands voorbeeld?' [Mandatory Balanced Budget in Dutch (Constitutional) Law Following Examples Abroad?] (2012) 29 *Nederlands Juristenblad* 2024–31.

[2] Treaty on Stability, Coordination and Governance in the Economic and Monetary Union (the text of the Treaty is available at www.eurozone.europa.eu/media/304649/st00tscg26_en12.pdf (accessed 16 September 2013).

[3] Art 3(2) Fiscal Compact. The Fiscal Compact became effective on 1 January 2013 (Art 14 Fiscal Compact). The balanced-budget rule should thus be implemented by 1 January 2014.

[4] Through an Act of Parliament: [2013] *Staatsblad* (Official Gazette) 290.

[5] Although the Fiscal Compact has been approved by Parliament, up to this point the Netherlands has not yet ratified the Treaty.

[6] The Wet HOF which will implement the balanced-budget rule in Dutch law has not yet been adopted. On 23 April 2013 the Dutch House of Representatives approved the Sustainable Public Finances bill. The bill still has to be approved by the Dutch Senate before it will be adopted.

Dutch law. In this chapter we will consider the implementation of this golden rule in the Wet HOF in light of the Dutch constitutional system and the several challenges that this implementation raises. These challenges relate especially to the specific features of the Dutch constitutional system. Firstly, it is very difficult to change the Dutch Constitution, which is one of the reasons why the balanced-budget rule will be implemented in an Act of Parliament and not in the Constitution. This raises the question whether the balanced-budget rule will have been implemented correctly according to Article 3 Fiscal Compact and the European institutions who will review the implementation. The Wet HOF is not higher in status than a regular budgetary Act, and can thus deviate from the balanced-budget rule. Secondly, if the balanced-budget rule were to be implemented in the Dutch Constitution, this rule cannot be adjudicated because there is no judicial review of legislation. At first sight it would seem that the implementation of the balanced-budget rule in an Act of Parliament is favourable, because the rule can then be adjudicated. However, we will point out in Section III that the national courts are very reserved when it comes to adjudicating budgetary rules. On the other hand the Fiscal Compact, an international treaty that is ratified by the Netherlands, has superior status over domestic law according to Articles 93 and 94 of the Dutch Constitution and is above all directly binding upon the branches of government in the Netherlands (legislator, administration and judiciary). Therefore the national court is allowed, when certain conditions are met, to review the compliance of an Act of Parliament with international treaties. Does this mean that the Netherlands is already in compliance with the Fiscal Compact obligation by ratifying the Fiscal Compact, notwithstanding the implementation of the balanced-budget rule in Dutch law?

In our analysis of the Dutch case we will consider the above questions and challenges. We will further consider the Dutch case by looking beyond the Netherlands and, in particular, towards the United States and Germany. Experiences in the United States and Germany, for example, show that the value of statutory and constitutional measures in controlling the national economy should not be overestimated. In the United States the individual states have a long tradition of various constitutional provisions to curb government spending (debt ceilings, loan prohibitions, balanced-budget rules).[7] These provisions were incorporated from the mid-nineteenth century onwards in state constitutions in response to the economic crisis and financial problems that many states were experiencing at that time, having invested heavily and run up debts for the construction of railroads, bridges, canals, etc. How did these constitutional provisions work out in the end? It would appear that they had little effect on the whole and that the courts were not inclined actually to enforce them. On the one hand we should of course exercise caution when comparing these state practices in the United States to current developments within the EU. On the other hand, however, they do offer some kind of indication of the chances for success of this type of consti-

[7] See also the contribution of PA Van Malleghem in this volume (Chapter 8).

tutional provision. The various proposals to incorporate a balanced-budget rule in the federal US Constitution have come to nothing, but a national statutory debt ceiling does exist. Germany also has more than 40 years' experience with constitutional provisions in the form of debt ceilings.[8] Moreover, the last amendment to the Finanzverfassung in 2009, which introduced a balanced-budget rule into the German Constitution (Grundgesetz (GG)), served as an example for the establishment of a balanced-budget rule in line with the Fiscal Compact.[9] The Dutch golden rule will be assessed in the light of these experiences abroad: what general lessons can we learn from the examples in the United Stated and Germany? And—where possible—certain proposals will be made to ensure that the Dutch golden rule is as effective as possible.

This chapter is structured as follows. After outlining the golden rule in the Fiscal Compact, we will consider the implementation of the balanced-budget rule in the Wet HOF. Hereafter we will consider the specific features of the Dutch constitutional system in which the balanced-budget rule has to operate. We then give an overview of experiences in the United States with regard to the constitutional restrictions in government (particularly state government) spending. We then consider the state of play in this area in Germany. Using these comparative law examples, we draw some general lessons on how balanced-budget rules can be most effective and what can be expected from constitutional obligations in controlling the national economy. Finally, using these general lessons, we will anticipate the effectiveness of the Dutch golden rule in light of the Dutch constitutional system. First we will consider what is the added value, if any, of the implementation of the balanced-budget rule in the Wet HOF. In addition, a number of suggestions will be made to make this golden rule as effective as possible, guided by experiences beyond the borders of the Netherlands, and to ensure the visibility of the balanced-budget rule in Dutch law.

II. THE GOLDEN RULE IN THE EU FISCAL COMPACT

A. Aim

The aim of the Fiscal Compact is to achieve stricter budgetary discipline in the Economic and Monetary Union (EMU) by introducing a fiscal agreement, by establishing rules to strengthen the co-ordination of economic policy and by improving the governance of the eurozone (Article 1 Fiscal Compact). The intergovernmental treaty incorporates many existing rules that have arisen from, for

[8] See also the contribution of G Delledonne in this volume (Chapter 9).

[9] See also F Fabbrini, 'The Fiscal Compact, the "Golden Rule" and the Paradox of European Federalism' (2013) 36 *Boston College International & Comparative Law Review* 1–38, 7–9, http://papers.ssrn.com/sol3/papers.cfm?abstract_id=2096227 (accessed 16 September 2013).

example, what is known as the European Semester,[10] the Euro Plus Pact[11] and the 'six-pack'. The 'six-pack' on governance consists of five Regulations and one Directive to strengthen the Stability and Growth Pact (SGP).[12] With this set of rules, the EU and the eurozone countries have taken a significant step towards establishing a fixed framework for the co-ordination of national economic and budget policy and for stricter budgetary discipline.[13] The added value of the Fiscal Compact lies in the tightening of the existing set of rules and the strict observance of these rules—through the domestication of budgetary rules. In addition, new rules have been established to tighten further the co-ordination of economic policy and convergence. It would seem, therefore, that the Treaty wants to transmit an important political signal with which the eurozone countries effectively declare that they are prepared to introduce stricter budgetary discipline and to enforce this. Above all, in May 2013 the 'two-pack'[14] was adopted; this integrates some of the elements of the Fiscal Compact into EU law[15]—although the 'two-pack' does not duplicate the obligation to put into place a numerical rule of a balanced-budget in national law.[16] The 'two-pack' consists

[10] On 7 September 2010 the Ecofin Council—consisting of all the Ministers of Finance and Economics of the Member States—agreed upon the introduction of an European Semester in line with a proposal from the European Commission http://consilium.europa.eu/uedocs/cms_data/docs/pressdata/en/ecofin/116306.pdf (accessed 16 September 2013). The Commission also expressed the intention to make the European Semester legally binding through a modification of the Regulation 1466/97 on the surveillance of budgetary positions and the surveillance and coordination of economic policies—which has been the case with the introduction of the six-pack.

[11] European Council, Conclusions 20 April 2011, Annex I, www.consilium.europa.eu/uedocs/cms_data/docs/pressdata/en/ec/120296.pdf (accessed 16 September 2013).

[12] Regulation (EU) No 1173/2011 of the European Parliament and of the Council of 16 November 2011 on the effective enforcement of budgetary surveillance in the euro area [2011] OJ L306/1; Regulation (EU) No 1175/2011 of the European Parliament and of the Council of 16 November 2011 amending Regulation (EC) No 1466/97 on the strengthening of the surveillance of budgetary positions and the surveillance and coordination of economic policies [2011] OJ L306/12; Council Regulation (EU) No 1177/2011 of 8 November 2011 amending Regulation (EC) No 1467/97 on speeding up and clarifying the implementation of the excessive deficit procedure [2011] OJ L306/33; Regulation (EU) No 1176/2011 of the European Parliament and of the Council of 16 November 2011 on the prevention and correction of macroeconomic imbalances [2011] OJ L306/25; Regulation (EU) No 1174/2011 of the European Parliament and of the Council of 16 November 2011 on enforcement measures to correct macroeconomic imbalances in the euro area [2011] OJ L306/8; Council Directive 2011/85/EU of 8 November 2011 on requirements for budgetary frameworks of the Member States [2011] OJ L306/41, which were enacted pursuant to Articles 121, 126 and 136 TFEU.

[13] See also F Ambtenbrink, 'Naar een effectievere economische governance in de Europese Unie?' [Towards More Effective Economic Governance in the European Union?] (2011) 10 *SEW* 429–43.

[14] Regulation (EU) No 472/2013 of the European Parliament and of the Council of 21 May 2013 on the strengthening of economic and budgetary surveillance of Member States in the euro area experiencing or threatened with serious difficulties with respect to their financial stability [2013] OJ L140/1; Regulation (EU) No 473/2013 of the European Parliament and the Council on common provisions for monitoring and assessing draft budgetary plans and ensuring the correction of excessive deficit of the Member States in the euro area [2013] OJ L140/11, which were enacted pursuant to Articles 121 and 136 TFEU.

[15] Among which is the obligation to draw up an economic partnership program (Art 5 Fiscal Compact, respectively Art 9 Regulation (EU) No 473/2013) and the obligation of the Member States to report, in advance and in a timely manner, to the Commission on their national debt issuance plans (Art 6 Fiscal Compact, respectively Art 8 Regulation (EU) No 473/2013).

[16] In the first draft of the proposed Regulation (COM(2011) 821 final), Art 4(1) contained the

of two Regulations which further strengthen the economic governance and only apply to the countries in the eurozone.

B. The Golden Rule

One of the rules that is intended to guarantee stricter budgetary discipline is contained in Article 3 of the Fiscal Compact. This rule is twofold: a Member State shall first commit itself to the rule of a balanced budget (Article 3(1)(a) Fiscal Compact). This requirement is met when the Member State satisfies the country-specific structural Medium Term Objective (MTO), which has as its lower limit a structural deficit of 0.5 per cent of GDP at market prices (Article 3(1)(b) Fiscal Compact). Deviating from the limits is temporarily allowed in 'exceptional circumstances' (Article 3(1)(c) Fiscal Compact). In addition, the Member State is to set up a correction mechanism that is automatically triggered in the event of 'significant deviations' and which corrects the deviation (Article 3(1)(e) Fiscal Compact), on the basis of the common principles proposed by the European Commission (Article 3(2) Fiscal Compact).[17] Secondly, these budget rules should be incorporated in national law through 'provisions of binding force and permanent character, preferably constitutional, or should otherwise be guaranteed to be fully respected and adhered to throughout the national budgetary processes'. An independent national institution will monitor compliance with these rules. In the correction mechanisms, the prerogatives of the national parliament will be fully respected (Article 3(2) Fiscal Compact).

According to Article 8 of the Fiscal Compact, the European Commission will assess and monitor whether the Contracting Party has incorporated the golden rule in national law pursuant to Article 3(2) of the Fiscal Compact. If the Commission concludes that a Member State has failed to comply with this provision, the matter will be brought before the CJEU by one or more Contracting Parties.[18] The CJEU can ultimately impose a penalty for the incorrect implementation.

obligation to put in place a numerical fiscal rule (based upon the requirements as set out in the SGP) into national law. After comments from, among others, the French Senate, the obligation was removed and is thus not enshrined in the Regulation (see the contribution by KA Armstrong in this volume (Chapter 4)).

[17] COM(2012) 342 final. The common principles provide recommendations with regard to the nature, the size and the time frame of the correction action and with regard to the role and independence of the institutions responsible at national level for monitoring the observance of the balanced-budget rule.

[18] The rules that apply to bringing a matter to the CJEU pursuant to Art 8 Fiscal Compact are agreed upon in an annex of the Treaty, www.europolitics.info/pdf/gratuit_en/310236-en.pdf (accessed 16 September 2013).

C. Enforcement

Uncertainty exists, however, about the observance of Article 3 of the Fiscal Compact, and more specifically the application of the provision that permits deviations from the limits. After all, how does the Commission or the CJEU monitor and assess whether a Member State has correctly laid down the golden rule in national law?

The text of Article 3 of the Fiscal Compact refers to the incorporation of the golden rule at the national level by means of 'provisions of binding force and permanent character, preferably constitutional, or otherwise guaranteed to be fully respected and adhered to throughout the national budgetary processes'. In our reading, the first part of the sentence—'provisions of binding force and permanent character, preferably constitutional'—seems to refer to statutory law (constitutional or otherwise). The addition of the part 'or otherwise guaranteed to be fully respected and adhered to throughout the national budgetary processes' would seem at first to be superfluous to us, but could for example point towards the existence of parliamentary conventions.[19] We thus consider the first part of the sentence to be alternative to the second part. But the provision can also be interpreted in an alternative way. The first part of the sentence 'provisions of binding force and permanent character' is then leading. In this interpretation 'binding force and permanent character' can be achieved preferably via constitutional change or alternatively via other acts guaranteed to be fully respected in the budget process.

The addition of the second part of the sentence 'or otherwise guaranteed', therefore, creates uncertainty because it can be interpreted in different ways, particularly when assessing whether Article 3 has been correctly enshrined in national law. What is more, in the Netherlands the balanced-budget rule has been laid down in an ordinary legislative Act,[20] which could then be cancelled by a later (budget) Act which is established at the same level. Would the Commission or the CJEU then consider that the rule from the Fiscal Compact has been incorporated in a sufficiently 'binding and permanent' manner?[21] Or does a legislative Act fall under 'otherwise guaranteed'? This 'guarantee' should at least

[19] One possible explanation for including this part of the sentence could be that when the text was drawn up, the possibility still existed that the UK would join the Treaty, or to keep the door open if they decided to join later. The UK, after all, does not have a written Constitution in which such a rule could be incorporated. According to the French Conseil Constitutionnel, in its assessment of the constitutionality of the Fiscal Compact, 'otherwise guaranteed' means that 'adherence to the rules of paragraph 1 Article 3 will not be guaranteed by provisions of "binding force"; that on the one hand, it is for the Member States to determine, for the purpose of ensuring that their commitment is respected, the provisions having the effect required under paragraph 2; that on the other hand, the Treaty stipulates that adherence to the rules laid down in paragraph 1 of Article 3 will not be guaranteed under national law by a provision that is hierarchically superior to legislation', Constitutional Council, Decision, 9 August 2012, no 2012-653 DC, no 22.

[20] See section III.

[21] Editorial, 'The Fiscal Compact and the European Constitutions: "Europe Speaking German"' (2012) 1 *European Constitutional Law Review* 3–4.

ensure that the golden rule will be fully respected and adhered to throughout the national budgetary processes. But should it also be 'binding and permanent'?

In addition, it is unclear whether Article 8 of the Fiscal Compact, which covers compliance with Article 3(2) of the Fiscal Compact—the institutional obligation to incorporate the balanced budget rule in national (constitutional) law—does not also cover compliance with Article 3(1) of the Fiscal Compact—the substantive balanced-budget rule. Craig notes that breaching the fulfilment of the institutional obligation is in itself dependent on a breach of the substantive obligation, though this will not easily be accepted by the Contracting Party.[22] After all, the obligation to incorporate the rule in national law, pursuant to Article 3(2) of the Fiscal Compact, entails that the Member States must guarantee that this obligation is observed and that it is fulfilled during the national budget processes.[23]

A breach of Article 3(2) of the Fiscal Compact will, however, be difficult for the CJEU to establish. For example, it is not clear who will assess whether 'exceptional circumstances' exist as defined in Article 3(3)(b) of the Fiscal Compact, and in which case a Contracting Party may therefore deviate from the limits. According to the European Commission's common principles, the national independent supervisory body (the so-called Fiscal Council)—which provides Member States with advice that may only be disregarded with good reason—should ensure the extension and conclusion of this escape clause.[24] Inherent to the notion 'exceptional circumstances' is that they cannot be categorically defined—for example, reference is made to 'an unusual event which has a major impact on the financial position of the government'. Hence, some margin of assessment and flexibility will always exist when it comes to 'exceptional circumstances' and this can be best filled in by the Member State itself. The common principle, as mentioned above, on the role of a national independent supervisory body in the assessment of the coming into force and conclusion of the escape clause would appear to take this into account. A Member State can thus always argue that the Commission, when it has established a breach, has not taken the 'exceptional circumstances' into account. Besides this, it is also unclear how long it is possible to deviate from the limits. The notion 'temporary' is not further specified, and as a result it is not clear when the provision is actually violated. The provisions will thus be difficult to enforce in practice.

In conclusion: on the one hand, by introducing a balanced-budget rule (a rule defined in figures), a clear, strict rule has been established. On the other hand, it is still unclear how this rule will be enforced at the various national levels and how this will be assessed subsequently by the European institutions.

[22] PP Craig, 'The Stability, Coordination and Governance Treaty: Principle, Politics and Pragmatism' (2012) 37 *European Law Review* 237.

[23] According to the Bundesverfassungsgericht, in its assessment of the constitutionality of the Fiscal Compact, the assessment of the CJEU, pursuant to Art 8, is limited to an assessment of the codification of the instrument and not the actual application. BverfG, 2 BvR1390/12, Abzats-n 316. See also Fabbrini (n 9) 19.

[24] Principle 7, COM(2012) 242 final.

III. PROPOSAL FOR A DUTCH GOLDEN RULE

A. The Wet HOF

The Dutch government has included the European requirements on budgetary discipline, in particular the balanced-budget rule from Article 3 Fiscal Compact, in the legislative bill Wet HOF.[25] This will be, when adopted by Parliament[26], a legislative Act on the basis of Article 81 of the Dutch Constitution,[27] just like the annual budget Acts (Article 105 Dutch Constitution[28]). This Act also establishes that the local and regional authorities must adhere to these European budget requirements.

The Wet HOF fills a void in Dutch legislation: in the Netherlands there was no statutory law on national and/or European budgetary rules. Yet, since 1994 national budgetary rules have existed which are adhered to for the duration of a cabinet (normally four years). These rules are established during the negotiations on the coalition agreement that is drawn up when a new cabinet is formed and will only apply during that cabinet period.

Article 2 (1) and (2) of the Wet HOF codifies the Dutch budget rules (at national level) and the departure points that have to be taken into account when implementing these budgetary rules. It must be emphasized that the Wet HOF only contains the principal features of the budget policy. More specific budget rules are not included, because the actual details depend on the budgetary situation.[29]

The third paragraph of Article 2 Wet HOF contains the national statutory basis for the European budget rules. It establishes that the national budget policy, stated in paragraphs 1 and 2, will be implemented with due regard to the MTO for a structural EMU balance that applies to the Netherlands, and with due regard to the applicable standards within the EU for the actual EMU balance and the actual EMU debt. According to the Explanatory Memorandum, this last reference—'the applicable standard within the European Union'—refers to the 3 per cent and 60 per cent standard, respectively, in the SGP. The first reference to the 'MTO for a structural EMU balance' refers to both the standards in the SGP for a structural balanced budget and to Article 3 of the Fiscal Compact.[30]

[25] *Kamerstukken II* (Dutch Parliamentary Papers) 2012/13, 33 416, no 2.

[26] On 23 April 2013 the Dutch House of Representatives approved the Sustainable Public Finances bill. The Bill still has to be approved by the Dutch Senate. It is expected that the bill will be adopted in the autumn of 2013.

[27] Art 81 Dutch Constitution: 'Acts of Parliament shall be enacted jointly by the Government and the States General' (translation from www.denederlandsegrondwet.nl (accessed 27 June 2013)). For the sake of clarity we also use the term Acts of Parliament, although, in the Dutch context, this is not completely correct.

[28] Art 105(1) Dutch Constitution: 'The estimates of the States revenues and expenditures shall be laid down by Act of Parliament' (translation from www.denederlandsegrondwet.nl (accessed 27 June 2013)).

[29] *Kamerstukken II* (Dutch Parliamentary Papers) 2012/13, 33 416, no 3, p 5.

[30] *Kamerstukken II* (Dutch Parliamentary Papers) 2012/13, 33 416, no 3, pp 29–30.

Paragraphs 4–6 of Article 2 of the Wet HOF stipulate that a correction mechanism (a 'recovery plan') will automatically take effect if the budget policy is not sufficient to achieve the MTO for the structural EMU balance, as assessed either by the Minister of Finance or by the competent European institutions which give a recommendation to correct the deviation. In the latter case the Minister of Finance will immediately take appropriate measures to correct the deviation in a 'recovery plan'. Paragraph 8 stipulates that advice from the Council of State with regard to the 'recovery plan' be heard.

Ultimately, the Wet HOF does not contain any numerical rules and solely refers to the European rules and norms, which are laid down in the SGP and other EU or international agreements. It is noteworthy that the Wet HOF does not mention application of the escape clause—how or when it is triggered and which organ will assess this. In the Explanatory Memorandum the Cabinet states that there is no need or European obligation to include an additional escape clause in Dutch law. According to the Cabinet, this means that the Netherlands is entirely in line with the European rules that stem from the SGP. After all, the Council and the Commission will decide whether or not a recommendation to correct the deviation will be given to the Netherlands.[31] In other words: the Council and the Commission will decide whether or not exceptional circumstances exist. If they decide that no exceptional circumstances exist, the Netherlands should correct the deviation and will be notified of this by a recommendation. But if the Council and the Commission decide that exceptional circumstances *do* exist, no recommendation will be given to the Netherlands and no correction of the deviation will be triggered. For the Netherlands, so the argument goes, it is important only to know when it should correct the deviation. National political institutions—Parliament or Cabinet–play no role whatsoever in the application of the escape clause and thus the assessment of exceptional circumstances.

B. Specific Features of the Dutch Constitutional System

Before discussing whether or not the implementation of the golden rule in Dutch law has any added value, and if (or how) the golden rule can be expected to be effective, it is important to elaborate some more on the possible implementation of the golden rule in light of the specific features of the Dutch constitutional system. This is important to give more context to the possible effectiveness of a golden rule codified in Dutch law.

(i) No Judicial Review of Legislation

The government has not opted to incorporate the golden rule into the Dutch

[31] *Kamerstukken II* (Dutch Parliamentary Papers) 2012/13, 33 416, no 3, p 9.

Constitution. This would have had the advantage that the golden rule would be more difficult to amend, in view of the complicated amendment procedure of the Constitution.[32] As it stands, the golden rule can be cancelled by a subsequent legislative Act.[33] Even if the golden rule were to be enshrined in the Constitution, however, courts would not be able to assess a breach of this rule because of the prohibition on judicial review of the constitutionality of Acts of Parliament.[34] A breach of the golden rule at national level will, after all, usually be the result of a legislative Act, namely the (regular) budget Act or a supplementary budget Act established by Parliament and the government. Breaches of the golden rule as a result of local authority budgets would not be affected by the prohibition of judicial review.

(ii) Political Enforcement of the Golden Rule

In the Netherlands, budget Acts are Acts adopted jointly by the Parliament and the government. Budget acts above all apply between the government and Parliament; citizens cannot derive rights from them directly.[35] This entails that the issue of the legitimacy of budget Acts is predominantly a political issue about which the (ordinary) courts do not want to adjudicate, notwithstanding the question of whether such matters can even be put before such courts. Within the political arena, a judgment will have to be passed on the legitimacy of the budget in the light of the balanced-budget rule. In its role as independent advisor to the government and Parliament, the Council of State will review whether the budget Act is in line with the European budgetary rules, and thus with the balanced-budget rule (Article 2(8) Wet HOF). The Council of State can only issue advice, and the government may only disregard this advice with good reason.

(iii) Direct Effect and Superiority of International Treaties

Although there is no constitutional review in the Netherlands the national courts can review the compliance of these Acts with international treaties and EU law. According to Articles 93[36] and 94[37] of the Dutch Constitution, provisions of

[32] See Art 137 of the Dutch Constitution: two readings, dissolution of the Lower House and new elections, two-thirds majority in second reading.

[33] See also the plea made by Geerten Boogaard to quickly incorporate the golden rule in the Constitution, www.publiekrechtenpolitiek.nl/begrotingsregels-in-de-grondwet (last accessed 16 September 2013) and 'Europe Speaking German' (n 21).

[34] See Art 120 of the Dutch Constitution: 'The constitutionality of Acts of Parliament and treaties shall not be reviewed by the courts' (translation from www.denederlandsegrondwet.nl (accessed 16 September 2013)).

[35] Hoge Raad (Supreme Court of the Netherlands) 5 October 1869, W 1058.

[36] Art 93 Dutch Constitution: 'Provisions of treaties and of resolutions by international institutions which may be binding on all persons by virtue of their contents shall become binding after they have been published' (translation from www.denederlandsegrondwet.nl (accessed 16 September 2013)).

[37] Art 94 Dutch Constitution: 'Statutory regulations in force within the Kingdom shall not be applicable if such application is in conflict with provisions of treaties or of resolutions by inter-

ratified international treaties have direct effect within the Dutch legal order and enjoy a superior status over Acts of Parliament.[38]

This means that all branches of government (legislature, administration, judiciary) in the Netherlands are directly bound by the provisions of a ratified treaty. On the other hand, national courts are only competent to review the compliance of Acts of Parliament with international treaties when the provisions 'may be binding on all persons by virtue of their contents'. This is in essence a matter of justiciability: does the text of the provision provide the courts with judicially manageable standards to decide the case? According to a landmark decision of the Supreme Court of the Netherlands, the justiciability is decided upon in two steps. First: is the legislature obligated to incorporate this specific provision in national law, which will further elaborate on the content and purpose of the provision? Second: is the provision sufficiently clear as to its objective and can it be directly applied by the national courts?[39] There is extensive case law in which the national courts have judged that provisions of human rights treaties, in particular protecting civil and political rights (the European Convention on Human Rights is an important example), are eligible to bind all persons, or to use a different term, are 'self-executing'.[40]

It can, first of all, be argued that the substantive balanced-budget rule as laid down in Article 3(1) of the Fiscal Compact can be separated from the institutional obligation to incorporate the rule into national law as laid down in Article 3(2) of the Fiscal Compact. Therefore it can be defended that the substantive balanced-budget rule as such does not entail the obligation to incorporate the provision into national law (the first requirement to be self-executing). As to the second requirement: is the provision in Article 3(1) of the Fiscal Compact sufficiently clear as to its objective and can it be directly applied by the national courts? It is arguable that this requirement is also met, because Article 3(1) of the Fiscal Compact contains clear requirements as to what the balanced budget rule is and how these requirements are met. The requirements therefore do not have to be further elaborated by the national legislature and can be directly applied by the national courts—it is 'objective law'.

Yet another question is whether the national court will find the action admissible and whether the applicant has standing. How should one demonstrate that it is in his or her own interest to maintain a balanced budget? Consider the case in which an individual applicant might complain of a violation of the balanced-budget rule at a local level (as the Wet HOF also binds local and regional authorities to the European balanced-budget rule) where a municipal council decides

national institutions that are binding on all persons' (translation from www.denederlandsegrondwet.nl (accessed 16 September 2013)).

[38] *Cf* EA Alkema, 'International Law in Domestic Systems', in JHM van Erp and LPW van Vliet (eds), *Netherlands Reports to the Eighteenth International Congress of Comparative Law, Washington 2010* (Antwerp, Oxford, Portland, Intersentia, 2010) 375–401.

[39] Hoge Raad (Supreme Court of the Netherlands) 30 May 1986, NJ 1986, 688 (Spoorwegstaking).

[40] *Cf* J Uzman, T Barkhuysen and ML van Emmerik, '*The Dutch Supreme Court: A Reluctant Positive Legislator?*' in van Erp and van Vliet (n 38) 423–62.

to finance a soccer stadium without the necessary budgetary means. Such an applicant will encounter all kinds of legal difficulties, such as the requirement of relativity (the so-called *Schutz-norm*: is the norm intended to protect the interests of the applicant?)

There is an example to be found in Dutch case law in which the Supreme Court of the Netherlands applied a broad scope to assess whether a case was admissible and whether an applicant had standing. In this case the applicant—a foundation whose aim is to support fundamental and proactive lawsuits to improve the legal status of women—argued that a general interest, namely the elimination of discrimination, was violated because the defendant, the SGP (Reformed Protestant Party), did not allow women to become party members and consequently stand for election to organs of general representation. The court ruled that the case was admissible and the applicant had standing in this case.[41] In line with this example, it might be argued that there is a slight possibility of bringing a suit before the national court where it concerns a general interest (maintaining a balanced budget). On the other hand we should not forget that the elimination of discrimination is something profoundly different to maintaining sustainable public finances. Moreover, it is very unlikely that the national courts will even burn its fingers on questions regarding the enforcement of fiscal provisions and the review of budgetary Acts.

(iii) Assessing the Domestication of the Golden Rule

Although it can be argued, on the grounds set out above, that national courts might be able to review compliance of a budget Act with the balanced-budget rule from the Fiscal Compact, it is rather unlikely that the national courts will do so. Even though the golden rule will be implemented in Dutch law and is (directly) binding upon the Netherlands, the national enforcement of the rule will, almost certainly, remain a predominantly political issue.

Regarding the enforceability of the golden rule at the European level, it remains to be seen if and how the European Commission and the CJEU will assess whether the Contracting Parties have incorporated the golden rule correctly into national law. Will the Commission, in the Dutch case, regard the incorporation of the golden rule in the Wet HOF as sufficiently 'binding and permanent'? The Wet HOF is an ordinary act which, after all, can be annulled by a successive budgetary Act. On the other hand the provisions of the Fiscal Compact enjoy a superior status over Acts of Parliament and are directly binding upon (all branches of government in) the Netherlands, apart from the question of justiciability before the courts. Therefore it can be argued that the Netherlands in any case is in compliance with the—substantive—balanced-budget rule ordained by the Fiscal Compact.[42]

[41] Hoge Raad (Supreme Court of the Netherlands), 9 April 2010, ECLI:NL:HR:2010:BK4549 (SGP).

[42] *Cf* JH Reestman, 'Constitutioneel minimalisme, het Stabiliteitsverdrag in de Nederlandse rechtsorde' (2013) 1 *Tijdschrift voor Constitutioneel Recht* 6–27, 19–20.

IV. EXPERIENCES OUTSIDE THE NETHERLANDS

In this section we will consider very briefly the cases of the United States and Germany. These countries both have long traditions with constitutional provisions to curb government spending. The United States has over 150 years of experience. The German balanced-budget rule in its turn served as an example for the balanced-budget rule in the Fiscal Compact.

A. Experiences in the United States

(i) State Constitutions

The United States has more than a century and a half of experience at state level with constitutional provisions to curb government spending as much as possible. In the first half of the nineteenth century, many states and cities sought their share of the nation's growing economic prosperity. It was the start of industrialization and the period of migration towards the (Mid) West of America. In 1817 a start was made on the construction of the Erie Canal, for which New York State got itself into deep debt. When the canal had been completed, these investments more than proved their worth and many states and cities followed this example. Massive debts were taken on for the construction of toll roads, railways and canals among other things. Many states went bankrupt when the economic crisis hit in the 1830s and 1840s. Discontent among taxpayers about the enormous financial burden of the states led in the 1840s to provisions in various state constitutions which restricted the possibilities for local governments to run up debts. This included a wide range of provisions, such as debt ceilings (often with specific maximum amounts) and even a total ban on concluding loans.[43] One important reason for laying down such provisions in state constitutions was that it was attractive for politicians to spend more money on popular projects, while their successors in office were confronted afterwards with the negative financial consequences.[44]

Broadly speaking, two categories of constitutional provisions can be distinguished. On the one hand, there are conditions under which states may borrow to finance certain projects after receiving approval from the population via a referendum. On the other hand, there are provisions that absolutely prohibit borrowing. In this latter category, states can only borrow if they are specifically authorized for that purpose following an amendment to the (state) constitution.

[43] See for more information AJ Heins, *Constitutional Restrictions against State Debt* (Madison, University of Wisconsin Press, 1963). See also JJ Wallis, 'Constitutions, Corporations, and Corruption: American States and Constitutional Change, 1842 to 1852' (2005) *Journal of Economic History* 211–56.

[44] See D Gamage, 'Preventing State Budget Crises: Managing the Fiscal Volatility Problem' (2000) 98 *California Law Review* 762.

Within this category, many kinds of conditions and exceptions exist. For example, it is possible to borrow in exceptional circumstances such as the defence of the state or to combat an uprising.[45] In a study carried out half a century ago, Heins concluded that it is by no means clear that the constitutional state debt restrictions referred to above have actually contributed towards curbing the burden of debt in the individual states. Since the nineteenth century various states have taken all kinds of roads outside the constitutional highway to borrow money and get round the constitutional obstacles. This usually concerned debts where state public funds were not required to repay these debts. This practice is protected by state courts, since the constitutional debt restrictions are not related to such specific debt instruments.[46]

In a more recent article, Schragger sums up the constitutional provisions introduced in the nineteenth century to curb government spending in the term 'fiscal constitution'.[47] He concludes that this so-called fiscal constitution has not worked, in view of the large number of budget crises that have continued to occur at state and local level since the introduction of such constitutional restrictions. To a large degree, this fiscal constitution limits the possibility for states and local governments to react adequately to economic relapse and results in them trying other, inefficient ways to receive funding. This was also concluded in an extensive study done by Briffault in 1996.[48] He demonstrates that states have known how to get round the strict constitutional 'debt provisions' via all kinds of smart finance constructions. As a result, the costs of borrowing have been pushed up and local administration has become increasingly fragmented (by outsourcing tasks to quasi-government bodies that are not bound by constitutional debt restrictions).[49] States attempt to keep their budget in balance, not so much on account of the constitutional restrictions referred to, but more on the basis of political and economic considerations. In view of these experiences with the fiscal constitution at state level, Briffault clearly advises against including a balance budget rule in the Federal Constitution.[50] Every now and then, it is said that the constitutional debt restrictions have, to some extent, restricted the authority of political actors to enter into debt, though this is not concerned with absolute restrictions.[51] But the prevailing opinion is that the constitutional

[45] Heins (n 45) 9–12.

[46] Ibid, 82–84.

[47] RC Schragger, 'Democracy and Debt' (2012) 121 *Yale Law Journal* 860–86. See for a good and extensive description of the variety of state provisions (from very strict to less strict) a very worthwhile report by the National Conference of State Legislatures, *NCSL Fiscal Brief: State Balanced Budget Provisions* (October 2010), which can be found at www.ncsl.org/documents/fiscal/StateBalancedBudgetProvisions2010.pdf (accessed 16 September 2013).

[48] R Briffault, *Balancing Acts. The Reality Behind State Balanced Budget Requirements* (New York, The Twentieth Century Fund Report,1996). See also R Briffault, 'Foreword: The Disfavored Constitution: State Fiscal Limits and State Constitutional Law' (2003) 32 *Rutgers Law Journal* 907–57.

[49] Briffault (ibid, 1996) 50–51.

[50] Ibid, 63–65.

[51] SE Sterk and ES Goldman, 'Controlling Legislative Shortsightedness: The Effectiveness of Constitutional Debt Limitations' (1991) *Wisconsin Law Review* 1301–67.

restrictions referred to appear to have had little effect. The (state and local) government looks for all kinds of escape routes that are generally protected in the courts. The courts do not appear to want to burn their fingers on political and economic issues. They have certainly no inclination to treat the 'fiscal constitution' in the same way as issues concerning fundamental rights or the structure of the government (horizontal or vertical division of powers).[52] State judges, who are very often directly elected, usually take a positive stance towards government programmes that would perhaps be frustrated by the strict application of constitutional debt restrictions. This is most certainly a task of the administration in consultation with the people's elected representatives.[53] It would appear that the most important means of enforcement is therefore the political 'convention' to keep the budget in balance.[54]

(ii) Federal Constitution

Attempts (particularly by Republicans) to include a balanced-budget rule in the Federal Constitution appear to have been futile up until now.[55] The most successful attempt was a motion in 1995 which fell short of a majority in the Senate by just one vote. The motion proposed that income and spending in a fiscal year had to be in balance, unless a supermajority (three-fifths) of Congress gave special approval for overexpenditure. The debt ceiling of the United States could not be exceeded unless the special three-fifths majority in Congress gave its consent in legislation. In order to prevent these strict restrictions being bypassed, the motion also stipulated that borrowed sums would not be included under income.[56] Briffault was not at all enthusiastic about the effectiveness of a balanced-budget rule in the Federal Constitution. He indicated that it could not be predicted exactly how federal courts would treat such a rule laid down in the Constitution. The rather unsuccessful long-term practice at state level, however, would suggest that the federal courts will also observe restraint in this respect and will not be keen to move to enforce such a balanced-budget rule on the

[52] Briffault (n 48, 2003) 939–40.

[53] Ibid, 941–42.

[54] See eg NCSL (n 47, 2010): states with less strict requirements for the balanced budget are also continually focused on keeping their budget in balance.

[55] It is worth noting that according to Janse de Jonge, the principle of a balanced budget was an important point of departure in the establishment of the Federal Constitution. This all had to do with the vision of a Federal government whose role was limited as far as possible and where it was essential that Federal spending would be covered in full by Federal income from taxation—see eg EJ Janse de Jonge, 'Begrotingstekort, wetgeving en de visie op de federale staat in Amerika' [Budget Deficit, Legislation and the Vision of the Federal State in America], in HAM Backx (ed), *Recht doen door wetgeving, opstellen over wetgevingsvraagstukken* [Administering Justice through Legislation, Essays on Legislative Issues] (Zwolle, WEJ Tjeenk Willink, 1990) 349–62 and 352–54. For more information on the right to approve and amend budget policy of Congress by the same author, EJ Janse de Jonge, *Amerikaans staatsrecht* (American constitutional law) (Nijmegen, Wolf Legal Publishers, 2012) 130–43.

[56] See also Briffault (n 48, 1996) 51–52.

President and the Congress.[57] A more recent Republican proposal can also not expect to receive much enthusiasm from the Democrats.[58]

A statutory debt ceiling does exist at federal level. This ceiling was established by a federal law (not in budget legislation) and can therefore be raised or lowered with a (simple) majority in Congress. This federal debt ceiling sets no limit on entering into new commitments, as the debt level is determined by a previously established tax and spending policy in the annual budget, but it does set a limit on the possibility to fulfil existing obligations. In concrete terms this means that the government fixes income and spending in budget legislation, and afterwards, once the obligations have been entered into, is confronted with the debt ceiling that sets limits on government spending. The result of not raising the debt ceiling is that the government can no longer meet its payment obligations and also that the government has to get into more debt. Once again in 2011, after fierce discussion in Congress, the debt ceiling was raised to more than $16.4 billion.[59] But discussions about this debt ceiling have only a very narrow effect on the prospect of limiting government debt. As a result, the US Government Accountability Office suggests a better adjustment of the budget to the debt ceiling instead of being presented with an accomplished fact afterwards, which is the situation at the moment.[60]

B. Experiences in Germany

Germany has experience going back four decades on constitutional restrictions related to debt ceiling at federal level.[61] This *Schuldenbremse* has been incorporated in the Grundgesetz since the amendments to the Constitution in 1967 and 1969 (former Articles 109 and 115 GG). However, these provisions have not stopped public debt in Germany steadily increasing.[62] Public debate on the effectiveness of the provisions, the increase in the national debt and the realization that these provisions did not meet the requirements of the SGP have led to a new constitutional golden rule, incorporated in the current Articles 109 and 115 GG. The new provisions have been in effect since 1 August 2009.

[57] Ibid, 52–54 and 63–65.

[58] J Steinhauer, 'Republicans Set Sights on Balanced Budget Amendment', *New York Times*, 5 August 2011 5. See also a critical Schragger (n 49) 884–85.

[59] Since 1995 the debt ceiling has been raised 12 times. For more on the debates, see eg http://topics.nytimes.com/topics/reference/timestopics/subjects/n/national_debt_us/index.html (accessed 16 September 2013).

[60] US Government Accountability Office, 'Debt Limit. Delays Create Debt Management Challenges and Increase Uncertainty in the Treasury Market', Report to Congress, February 2011.

[61] A debt ceiling also exists for the *Ländern*. In this chapter, however, we will not consider the rule in relation to the *Ländern*.

[62] LP Feld and T Baskaran, 'Federalism, Budget Deficits and Public Debt: On the Reform of Germany's Fiscal Constitution' (2010) 6 *Review of Law and Economics* 365, 370–72; and E Baumann and C Kastrop, 'A New Budget Rule for Germany', in *Fiscal Policy: Current Issues and Challenges*, Banca d'Italia, Research Department, Public Finance Workshop (2008) 595.

(i) Current Constitutional Provisions[63]

Like the requirements in the Fiscal Compact, Article 109 GG contains a balanced-budget rule. Further details about the federal budget are included in Article 115 GG. This Article sets limits on the sums of money the federal state is permitted to borrow. The structural government deficit over several years can amount to a maximum of 0.35 per cent of GDP with an absolute limit of 1.5 per cent. If this limit is exceeded, an automatic correction mechanism takes effect to reduce the deficit. This mechanism is incorporated in a federal law and only takes effect in times of economic prosperity. In addition, the deficit will not be reduced to less than 0.35 per cent GDP. Because this repayment is spread out, the correction mechanism will take effect when an absolute deficit of 1.0 per cent GDP is reached.[64] Deviating from the limits is permitted in the event of a natural disaster or emergency situation outside the realm of influence of the government and with a large effect on the financial position of the government—a cyclical economic decline is not included here[65]—and this should also be accompanied by a repayment plan.

According to the transition provision in Article 143d GG, Articles 109 and 115 GG will apply for the first time to the federal budget of 2011. There is one exception to this: it is not necessary that the structural government deficit over several years is reduced to a maximum of 0.35 per cent by 2016. Because of this transition provision, it is not yet possible to say what can be expected of the new golden rule. It is therefore worth taking a look at the former *Schuldenbremse* and to consider why this did not have the desired effect and why it is thought (or not) that the current provisions will be effective in reducing government debt.

(ii) Ineffectiveness of the former Schuldenbremse

The old debt ceiling permitted borrowing to the same amount that was required to carry out public investments. A budget Act could deviate from the limits if the legislator deemed that a 'disruption in the economic balance' existed.

Since 1970, almost half the annual budgets have exceeded the debt ceiling.[66] The problems with the old provisions were primarily concerned with the application of the definitions in the provision. It was not clear exactly what expenditure was included in the definition 'public investments',[67] and following on from this, it was therefore not clear what the debt limit was. Moreover, there were no

[63] See also Feld and Baskaran (n 62) 384–86.

[64] Federal Ministry of Finance, Compendium on the Federation's Budget Rule as set out in Article 115 of the Basic Law 2012, 6 and 24 (see www.bundesfinanzministerium.de/Content/DE/Standardartikel/Themen/Oeffentliche_Finanzen/Schuldenbremse/2012-06-14-kompendium-en.pdf?__blob=publicationFile&v=2 (accessed 16 September 2013)).

[65] Federal Ministry of Finance, Compendium on the Federation's Budget Rule as set out in Article 115 of the Basic Law 2012, 6.

[66] Baumann and Kastrop (n 62) 597.

[67] Ibid, 600–01.

clear guidelines to determine whether there was a situation of 'disruption in the economic balance'. Governing politicians were quick to refer to the economic situation as a 'disruption in the economic balance', and with a majority vote in the Bundestag it was relatively easy for them to exceed the limits.[68]

More important, though, is that it was difficult to enforce these provisions during the implementation of the budget and because of this the procedure to establish the budget almost appeared to be a farce. The limit was often exceeded in supplementary budgets, which amended the original budget during the applicable year, and not in the original budget. In addition, there were no direct sanctions in the case of a clear breach of the provisions, only indirectly via the vote of the electorate.[69] Besides, the Bundesverfassungsgericht (German Constitutional Court), which monitors the application of the GG, can only establish if the limits were deviated from incorrectly in retrospect, when an obligation has already been entered into. And it often takes years before a complaint to the Bundesverfassungsgericht results in a decision.

(iii) Assessment by the Bundesverfassungsgericht

The Bundesverfassungsgericht has ruled twice on the application of this *Schuldenbremse* by the legislator. Once in 1989, concerning the budget of 1981; and secondly, in 2007, concerning the budget of 2004, and both times on the initiative of (opposition) members of the Bundestag.[70] On both occasions, the Bundesverfassungsgericht appeared reserved in its assessment of whether the legislator was permitted to deviate from the limits. In both cases the Court explicitly referred to the ineffectiveness of the provisions, but considered it a matter for the legislator to give substance to terms such as 'public investments' and the 'disruption of the economic balance'.

(iv) Towards an Effective Schuldenbremse?[71]

The new provisions set strict limits instead of employing vague concepts. There is now a fixed amount set as the debt limit. As a result, the rule is more precise and provides the courts with more points of reference to enforce these provisions. However, it would (yet again) appear that the Bundesverfassungsgericht will carry out an abstract review, because the review is very much dependent on politically initiated procedures. An assessment of the provision will only take place in the case of a constitutional dispute between federal constitutional organs (*Organstreiten*) or if there is a conflict between the federal *Bund* and *Länder*.[72]

[68] Ibid, 597.

[69] Ibid, 598.

[70] BVerfG 18 April 1989, 2 BvF 1/82 and BVerfG 9 July 2007, 2 BvF 1/04.

[71] See also C Mayer, 'Greift die neue Schuldenbremse?' (2011) 136 *Archiv des öffentlichen Rechts* 266–322.

[72] G Delledonne in this volume (Chapter 9). G Delledonne, 'Financial Constitutions in the EU:

For the constitutional provisions to be effective, it is important that the debt limits can be applied flexibly so as to be able to respond to economic fluctuations. This flexibility is offered, for example, through the possibility to deviate from the limits in an emergency situation. One possible problem with this provision is—besides the fact that the term is not defined—that an emergency situation can already be established in law by an absolute majority in the Bundestag. This would not appear to pose too much of an obstacle to apply this emergency provision.[73] Moreover, the Bundesverfassungsgericht will very likely show restraint in its assessment of whether the application of this emergency rule by the legislator was necessary. After all, a political decision has already been given on whether or not an emergency situation exists.[74]

V. EFFECTIVENESS OF CONSTITUTIONAL DEBT PROVISIONS

After taking a look at various countries' experiences on constitutional debt limitation and/or balanced-budget rules, it is now time to take stock. From the brief analysis of the United States' and Germany's experiences we will now try to draw some general lessons about the effectiveness of constitutional debt provisions. Although it pays to be cautious when comparing such different constitutional systems on the effectiveness of establishing rules in legislation, questions can certainly be raised. For instance, it can be noted that the codification of budgetary rules entails a certain amount of ambiguity. It is necessary that these rules provide a framework within which the budget is to be fixed—otherwise the rules cannot be enforced—and this should be as specific as possible. At the same time, the budgetary rules should offer some form of flexibility to be able to respond to economic fluctuations and in particular to offer an escape clause in an (economic) emergency situation. Inherent to this flexibility is that (at least some) space must be left open for the political process.[75] In Germany and the United States, the courts are permitted to rule on a breach of the provisions incorporated in these countries' constitutions with regard to debt ceilings, but they show restraint in doing so. Perhaps the most important function of these constitutional debt provisions is that they are at least a demonstration of political commitment and serve a signalling function to the financial markets.[76] After all, the financial markets can better predict what the reaction of governments will

From the Political to the Legal Constitution?' (no 5/2012) STALS Research Paper 1–29, 16, http://papers.ssrn.com/sol3/papers.cfm?abstract_id=2180014 (accessed 8 May 2013).

[73] LP Feld, 'Sinnhaftigkeit und Effektivität der deutschen Schuldenbremse' (2010) 11 *Perspektiven der Wirtschaftspoliti* 226, 238l and Feld and Baskaran (n 62) 385 and 387.

[74] See also Delledonne (n 72) 20.

[75] Ibid, 21–22.

[76] See RD Kelemen and TK Teo, 'Law and the Eurozone Crisis', APSA 2012 Annual Meeting Paper, 1–28, 5–6. Available at: http://papers.ssrn.com/sol3/papers.cfm?abstract_id=2107426> (accessed 16 September 2013). Keleman and Teo make the point that it is the bond markets rather than the courts that discipline the violations of fiscal rules by states.

be to statutory standards. It is therefore crucial that the proposal for a national golden rule—within the limits of the Fiscal Compact—fits into the political system, is feasible and can also count on support from national politicians.[77]

VI. EFFECTIVENESS OF THE GOLDEN RULE IN DUTCH LAW

In this section we will consider the effectiveness of the implementation of the golden rule in Dutch law. We will first assess whether the implementation of the golden rule in national statutory law has any added value. We will then formulate some proposals on how the Wet HOF can be as effective as possible in Dutch law in light of the Dutch constitutional system. These proposals try to take into account the lessons that can be learned from the experiences of other countries, as described in section V. In particular that the rule should on the one hand be as specific as possible, but on the other hand should offer some form of flexibility, decided upon by the national political institutions. These proposals also try to advance the visibility and 'domestication' of the balanced-budget rule as is required by the Fiscal Compact.

In the Dutch Senate questions were raised on the necessity and added value of including the European rules on budgetary discipline in national (constitutional) law. The Dutch Minister of Finance replied on behalf of the Cabinet that many of these rules on budgetary discipline are already laid down in EU regulations that apply directly to the Netherlands. The legal necessity also to include these European requirements in Dutch national legislation has now come into existence as a result of the Fiscal Compact. According to the Cabinet, the implementation of the European budget rules in national law can for various reasons have a significant added value, such as the increased visibility of these European budgetary rules at a national level. In addition, this national codification could act as a catalyst for further modifications and reinforcements to national budgetary rules.[78] The Explanatory Memorandum adds to this that the incorporation of European budgetary rules in national legislation will send out a clear message that the Member States are well aware of the urgency and necessity to improve the functioning of the EMU and remove unrest on the financial markets.[79] For that matter, it would be more obvious to include such matters in the Comptabiliteitswet (Government Accounts Act), in which the complete budget procedure is set out in detail.

The introduction of the golden rule in Dutch legislation would at first appear to have little added value, especially with regard to the fact that the Fiscal Compact is already directly binding upon the Netherlands. Introducing more concrete, substantial standards in Dutch law will probably have no particular significance in the Netherlands when it comes to the enforcement of these rules

[77] See also Fabbrini (n 9) 14.
[78] *Kamerstukken I* (Dutch Parliamentary Papers) 2011/12, 33 181, no A, p 11–13.
[79] *Kamerstukken II* (Dutch Parliamentary Papers) 2012/13, 33 461, no 3, p 2.

by the courts, since—as already stated—the courts will not be willing to pass judgment. More specific standards, however, could provide political institutions with clearer direction. Moreover, setting more specific standards could be conducive to political neutrality.[80] Above all, these specific standards will serve a signalling function.[81] The financial markets have an indication of how the government will act. On the other hand, though, in the Dutch provision only a brief reference is made to the European standards. It is understandable that there is no direct reference to the MTO, which is revised every three years.[82] It would, however, definitely be helpful if the Dutch golden rule at the very least referred to the absolute, minimum standards as contained in the Fiscal Compact—the numerical rules—if only for the reason of advancing the promised 'visibility' of European legislation. But there are also more substantive proposals to be made to ensure the effectiveness of the Wet HOF.

First of all, in the Wet HOF a provision could be included that if the golden rule is not met, the budget legislator would face an extra strict obligation to motivate this. It could even be considered to introduce the requirement of an increased majority (two-thirds would seem the most obvious option in the Dutch constitutional system) in Parliament to adopt a budget Act (ordinary or supplementary) which violates the golden rule. This would introduce an extra barrier for the government to overcome if it wants to deviate from the balanced-budget rule. For the latter suggestion, ie the introduction of a requirement for an increased majority in Parliament to adopt a budget Act, an amendment to the Constitution would be required, as it involves a deviation from the ordinary legislative procedure in which an ordinary majority is sufficient (see Article 67(2) in conjunction with Article 81 of the Dutch Constitution[83]).

Secondly, with regard to the definition of significant deviations, the legislator could detail the meaning of this clause. Article 2(4) Wet HOF contains the possibility for different ministers to take budgetary correction measures if the Minister of Finance judges that 'the budget policy is not sufficient to achieve the MTO for the structural EMU balance'. The framework for assessment could be detailed as far as possible for the Netherlands, partly using the criteria referred to in one of the six-pack regulations. These European criteria give some kind of reference point but still remain rather vague. The legislator could make this more specific, geared towards the Dutch situation, and could indicate what the consequences would be in the event of significant deviations, such as an automatic downward adjustment of the budget in the future. The Contracting Parties are, after all, free to include stricter and more detailed requirements. When establishing the significant deviations, the Netherlands Court of Audit could also

[80] Delledonne (n 72) 22.

[81] See Kelemen and Teo (n 76).

[82] Although this is not necessarily a problem now that the rules are laid down in an ordinary Act which can be amended without too much effort.

[83] Art 67(2) Dutch Constitution: 'Decisions shall be taken by majority' (translation from www.denederlandsegrondwet.nl (accessed 16 September 2013).

have a role to play, whereas it currently has no role at all in the application of the correction mechanism.

Thirdly, the golden rule will have to include something on the 'exceptional circumstances' which permit a temporary deviation from the balanced-budget rule. The German example shows that it is extremely difficult to define this kind of emergency situation beforehand. After all, the distinguishing feature of an emergency situation is that it is unpredictable. Flexibility is what is needed to be able to react to exceptional (economic) situations. Constitutional debt provisions can also have a paralysing effect. In view of this, a political assessment is required in the first instance—the courts are less well equipped for this task as we have seen in the US and German examples. As mentioned above in Section III.A, the Wet HOF currently does not provide any role at all for the Dutch Parliament in establishing an emergency situation. In the current German constitutional provisions the Bundestag can establish this kind of emergency situation in an Act with an absolute majority. The Dutch provision could require that this kind of emergency situation be recognized by a two-thirds majority in Parliament in order to create a deterrent to prevent emergency situations being 'proclaimed' too easily. This could be included in the Wet HOF and would not require a constitutional amendment.

VII. CONCLUDING REMARKS

Having considered all these matters, it should not be forgotten that the value of legal remedies (statutory or even constitutional regulation, legally enforceable in the courts, etc) in taking care of a state's financial economic situation should not be overestimated. Even in systems that have constitutional courts, with the special task of monitoring observance of the constitution, it is clear that these courts are reticent when it comes to compliance with the rule on the *fiscal constitution*, certainly in comparison with provisions concerning fundamental (basic) rights.[84] The political arena (at both national and European level) is the principal place for responding best to turbulent economic developments. The law can only provide a framework to ensure that politicians do not exceed the financial limitations too easily. As well as a political commitment, establishing constitutional or statutory limits that force the government to manoeuvre within certain budgetary limits can be beneficial for stability in the financial markets and faith in them. After all, these markets can better predict what the reaction of governments will be to statutory standards.[85]

In addition, the Netherlands has demonstrated in the past that it is politi-

[84] See for more information Fabbrini (n 9) and Delledonne (n 72) who besides the United States and Germany, also look at Spain, France, Italy and Germany.

[85] Feld and Baskaran observe that with the introduction of a balanced-budget rule in Germany in 2009, a signal was sent out to the markets that Germany policymakers were prepared to return to tolerable government spending after the crisis. This may have contributed towards the low interest rate Germany paid to finance its loans. Feld and Baskaran (n 62) 387.

cally committed to achieving budgetary discipline. In 1994, during the first Kok cabinet the Zalmnorm (Zalm Standard, which will now be codified in the Wet HOF) was launched. This standard, to set up a spending ceiling for a period of four years—during which windfall revenue could not be used to compensate setbacks in expenditure—was established during negotiations on the coalition agreement and based on predicted economic developments at that time. This standard was fixed for each new coalition term and so was not laid down in statutory law. The rules, which have to be adhered to by the various ministers who are responsible for the budgets of their departments, were above all strictly supervised by the Minister of Finance, who has a powerful role in maintaining sound public finances. With this in mind, we would agree with Wattel, who concludes that the Netherlands already has its golden rule, and has had for some time, in the shape of the Zalmnorm (and its predecessor, the Zijlstranorm). Neither of these were included in the Constitution or a statutory law and nor was it necessary.[86] Moreover the Netherlands is directly bound to the balanced-budget rule from the Fiscal Compact through the ratification of the treaty. The main function of a golden rule implemented in Dutch law is thus *not* to serve primarily as a signal to Dutch politicians or the financial markets, but to serve as a signal to the European institutions.

[86] P Wattel, 'Schuldenbremse' (2011) 28 *Nederlands Juristenblad* 1857.

13

An Analysis of the Method and Efficacy of Ireland's Incorporation of the Fiscal Compact

RODERIC O'GORMAN

I. INTRODUCTION

ON 31 MAY 2012 the Irish electorate voted by 60.37 per cent to 39.63 per cent to add Article 29.4.10 to the Irish Constitution (Bunracht na hEireann).[1] The new provision permitted domestic ratification of the Treaty on Stability, Coordination and Governance in the Economic and Monetary Union (TSCG, the so-called Fiscal Compact).[2] This was followed by the passing of the Fiscal Responsibility Act 2012 in December of that year. The combination of the constitutional amendment and the legislation were understood as meeting Ireland's obligations under Article 3(2) of the Fiscal Compact, to enshrine the balanced-budget rule (or golden rule)—a commitment that the budgetary position of the government of Ireland would be balanced or in surplus—using 'provisions of binding force and permanent character, preferably constitutional, or otherwise guaranteed to be fully respected and adhered to throughout the national budgetary processes'.[3]

This chapter seeks to analyse the manner in which Ireland has brought the balanced-budget rule and the other provisions of the Fiscal Compact into domestic law. It begins by examining the background of Ireland's constitutional relationship with the EU and suggests that the amendment undertaken cannot be understood to equate with a constitutional-level commitment to the balanced-budget rule. The chapter goes on to look at the manner in which the Fiscal Responsibility Act 2012 was drafted and compares how its provisions

[1] Thirtieth Amendment of the Constitution (Treaty on Stability, Coordination and Governance in the Economic and Monetary Union) Bill 2012.

[2] Ireland was the only state amongst the 25 signatories to the Fiscal Compact to hold a referendum on the Treaty.

[3] Art 3(2), Fiscal Compact. For a comprehensive analysis of the Fiscal Compact, see S Peers, 'The Stability Treaty: Permanent Austerity or Gesture Politics?' (2012) 8 *European Constitutional Law Review* 404.

meet the principles outlined in the European Commission's 'Communication on the Common Principles on National Fiscal Correction Mechanisms'.[4] Here, the potential failure of the domestic legislation to meet the requirements of the Communication regarding the permanency of national measures is highlighted. The approach taken to the correction mechanism is examined and suggestions are made as to how this could have been more effective. A focus is placed on the monitoring institution created under the legislation—the Irish Fiscal Advisory Council (Fiscal Council)—and its ability to positively influence economic planning in Ireland is identified. The chapter concludes by considering the approach taken to the implementation of the Fiscal Compact in certain other signatory states and argues that, comparatively, incorporation will result in strengthened fiscal accountability in Ireland.

II. THE IRISH CONSTITUTION AND EUROPEAN INTEGRATION

As of the Lisbon Treaty in 2009, the constitutional aspects of Ireland's relationship with the EU are provided for across Articles 29.4.2–29.4.9 of the Irish Constitution. These provisions are the result of eight referenda occasioned by the ratification of six separate amendment treaties.[5] Subsequent referenda have resulted in a renumbering and reordering of the relevant Articles. The reason for this complicated process stems from the *Crotty* decision of the Irish Supreme Court in 1987 and directly influenced the decision by the Irish government to undertake a referendum on ratification of the Fiscal Compact.[6] In order fully to comprehend the rationale behind the May 2012 amendment and its legal effect, it is necessary to understand how the *Crotty* judgment constrained successive Irish governments in transferring national sovereignty to the EU.

A. Joining the EEC

Ireland's initial accession to the EEC in the early 1970s required acceptance of the superior role that the institutions of the Community would subsequently

[4] COM(2012) 342 final.

[5] Accession Treaty (1972), Single European Act (1987), Maastricht Treaty (1992), Amsterdam Treaty (1997), Nice Treaty (2001), Lisbon Treaty (2009). The amendments to ratify both the Nice and Lisbon Treaties were rejected the first time they were voted upon by the Irish electorate but subsequently passed on the second attempt.

[6] *Crotty v An Taoiseach & Others* [1987] 1 IR 713. For discussion of the case, see G Hogan, 'The Supreme Court and the Single European Act' (1987) 22 *Irish Jurist* (n.s.) 55; J Temple Lang, 'The Irish Court Case which Delayed the Single European Act' (1987) 24 *Common Market Law Review* 709; J Casey, 'Crotty v An Taoiseach: A Comparative Perspective', in J O'Reilly (ed), *Human Rights and Constitutional Law: Essays in Honour of Brian Walsh* (Dublin, 1992); G Barrett, 'Building a Swiss Chalet in an Irish Legal Landscape? Referendums on European Union Treaties in Ireland & the Impact of Supreme Court Jurisprudence' (2009) 5 *European Constitutional Law Review*, 32.

have. It was necessary to undertake a constitutional amendment in order to ensure that this would not conflict with existing Irish constitutional mandates regarding the sovereignty of the state and the sole lawmaking, executive and adjudicating roles given to the Irish Parliament (Oireachtas), the Government and the Courts.[7] The referendum held in 1972 saw the insertion of what was then Article 29.4.3, which stated:

> The State may become a member of the European Coal and Steel Community (established by Treaty signed at Paris on the 18th day of April, 1951), the European Economic Community (established by Treaty signed at Rome on the 25th day of March, 1957) and the European Atomic Energy Community (established by Treaty signed at Rome on the 25th day of March, 1957). No provision of this Constitution invalidates laws enacted, acts done or measures adopted by the State necessitated by the obligations of membership of the Communities or prevents laws enacted, acts done or measures adopted by the Communities, or institutions thereof, from having the force of law in the State.[8]

As Ireland is a dualist state, the constitutional provision was not, on its own, sufficient to incorporate the existing *acquis communitaire* into domestic law. This was undertaken through section 2 of the European Communities Act 1972.

B. Crotty: The Scope of Ireland's Commitment to the EEC

The full extent of Article 29.4.3 was tested in *Crotty*, a decision of lasting constitutional significance for Ireland's relationship with the EU. The case concerned a challenge to the Irish government ratifying the Single Europe Act (SEA). The plaintiff, a critic of European integration, argued that the Irish Constitution was undermined by provisions of the SEA, including the creation of the Court of First Instance, the move from unanimity to qualified majority voting in certain areas, and the addition of new competences. There was also a concern that Title III of the SEA, concerning the new process of European Political Co-operation in the field of foreign affairs, would constrain the exercise by the Irish government of its constitutional powers in the area of foreign relations.

The applicant's argument had two major strands. He firstly argued that the European Communities (Amendment) Act 1986, which implemented the changes to the existing EC Treaty such as QMV and the Court of First Instance into domestic law, was incompatible with Article 29.4.3. Secondly, he sought to prevent the ratification by the Irish government of the SEA through deposit of the relevant instruments, as this would bind Ireland to the European Political Co-operation contained in Title III. The applicant argued instead that a new amendment to the Constitution was required to allow Ireland to ratify the SEA,

[7] Under Art 46 of the Constitution, the sole manner in which the Constitution can be amended is through a referendum.

[8] The amendment was passed by 83.1% to 16.9% opposed. The two sentences have subsequently been split into two separate subsections and are now entitled Art 29.4.5–6.

which would have to be put to the people via a referendum. The applicant was unsuccessful in the High Court, and appealed to the Supreme Court, which gave its judgment on the two separate aspects.

In order to ascertain the status of the European Communities (Amendment) Act 1986 the Court had to determine whether the licence given by the original insertion of Article 29.4.3 in 1972 extended to permit subsequent amendments to the EC treaties, or whether a constitutional amendment was required in Ireland in order to make any changes to the European treaties constitutionally compatible. To begin, the Court clarified that the proposed amendments contained in the SEA were not 'necessitated' by Ireland's membership of the EEC, and therefore did not already enjoy the protection of the second sentence of Article 29.4.3.[9] As such, the only element relevant to the constitutionality of the Act was the first sentence of the Article. The Court determined that it 'must be construed as an authorisation given to the State not only to join the Communities as they stood in 1973, but also to join in amendments of the Treaties *so long as such amendments do not alter the essential scope or objectives of the Communities*'.[10]

The Court understood the original amendment as providing some degree of flexibility as regards future changes to the EC Treaty, but did not see this as a completely open-ended authority to accept any future changes. In examining whether the elements of the SEA included in the European Communities (Amendment) Act 1986 altered the essential scope or objectives of the Communities, the Court made reference to Articles 2 and 3 of the EC Treaty as well as undertaking an analysis of the relative loss of sovereignty to the Council and the European Court of Justice that had been accepted by the Irish people through the amendment in 1972. In doing so, the Court concluded that the Community was 'a developing organism with diverse and changing methods for making decisions and an inbuilt and clearly expressed objective of expansion and progress'.[11] In light of this, the Supreme Court determined that none of the changes to the EC Treaty mandated by the SEA were outside of the scope of the original authorization given by the Irish people in 1972.[12] Therefore, the Court held that the European Communities (Amendment) Act 1986 was constitutional, in light of Article 29.4.3.

The Court's decision on the second argument concerning the compatibility of Title III has proven to be the most significant aspect of the *Crotty* case. A majority consisting of three of the five Supreme Court justices determined that it would be unconstitutional for the government to ratify it. Walsh J noted how Articles 6, 28 and 29 of the Constitution assigned the executive power of the state to the government.[13] However, he determined that neither the government

[9] Ibid, 767.
[10] Ibid (emphasis added).
[11] Ibid, 770.
[12] The Court did stress, however, that not all changes from unanimity to qualified majority voting would be similarly protected by the original amendment.
[13] *Crotty v An Taoiseach & Others* [1987] 1 IR 713, 777.

nor the Oireachtas could 'free themselves from the restraints of the Constitution or to transfer their powers to other bodies unless expressly empowered so to do by the Constitution'.[14] Article 5 of the Constitution stated that external sovereignty rested with the state.

Having examined what was required of Member States by the provisions of Title III, the majority determined that it would materially qualify the external sovereignty of the state.[15] Therefore, because it was not within the remit of the government to qualify its own constitutionally granted power in this manner, Ireland could only sign up to the provisions of Title III of SEA after a constitutional amendment accepted in a referendum.

C. *Crotty* and the Consequences for the Fiscal Compact

The outcome of the *Crotty* decision is that every subsequent amendment of the European treaties has been put to the Irish electorate and, once passed, has resulted in alterations to the Irish Constitution. At no stage has any Irish government sought to argue that the changes proposed by an amending treaty fall within the essential scope and objectives of the Communities, as per *Crotty*, and therefore relieve the requirement for a vote. Hogan and Whyte have questioned whether, at least as regards the Nice Treaty, it would have been possible successfully to invoke the 'essential scope or objectives' argument.[16]

There is anecdotal evidence to suggest that the consequences of a potential Irish 'no' vote was a factor in the initial negotiations surrounding the Fiscal Compact and that this resulted in a weakening of some of the Treaty's provisions.[17] However, the decision by the British Prime Minister, David Cameron, to veto any proposals to amend the EU treaties in order to include the balanced-budget rule meant that the Fiscal Compact had to be negotiated in the form of a public international law treaty. This prevented the Irish government from arguing that the enshrinement of the balanced-budget rule within the EU treaties fell within the essential scope and objectives of those treaties and thereby avoided the requirement for a referendum.

The Attorney General had to consider whether Ireland's ratification of a non-EU treaty that committed the country to budgetary restrictions which were both defined by and adjudicated upon by a third party (the EU institutions) represented an intrusion on national sovereignty. In light of the prevailing

[14] Ibid, 778

[15] Ibid, 781.

[16] G Hogan and G Whyte, *JM Kelly: The Irish Constitution*, 4th edn (Haywards Heath, Tottel, 2003) 520. See also Barrett (n 6) 45.

[17] See the comments of the German Minister for European Affairs, Michael Link, www.spiegel.de/international/europe/fiscal-pact-referendum-a-decisive-moment-for-ireland-in-europe-a-818313.html (accessed 16 May 12). For further discussion on this point, see D O'Donovan, 'Ireland to Hold Referendum on the Fiscal Treaty', *Human Rights in Ireland*, http://humanrights.ie/constitution-of-ireland/ireland-to-hold-referendum-on-the-fiscal-treaty/ (accessed 16 May 2012).

belief that the Fiscal Compact had been designed in such a way as to avoid the need for a referendum in Ireland, there was some level of surprise when the Attorney General advised the government that a constitutional amendment was necessary.[18] Nevertheless, it is argued here that once the elements of the Fiscal Compact permitting limitations on the state's budgetary powers were stripped of the cover of EU law, there was no other option open to the Attorney General.

D. Article 29.4.10 and the Preferably Constitutional Provision

The referendum on the Fiscal Compact saw the addition of Article 29.4.10 into the Irish Constitution. The provision states:

> The State may ratify the Treaty on Stability, Coordination and Governance in the Economic and Monetary Union done at Brussels on the 2nd day of March 2012. No provision of this Constitution invalidates laws enacted, acts done or measures adopted by the State that are necessitated by the obligations of the State under that Treaty or prevents laws enacted, acts done or measures adopted by bodies competent under that Treaty from having the force of law in the State.

Clearly, the provision bears a striking similarity to the original Article 29.3.4, added on Ireland's accession to the EEC, The interpretation of these provisions is therefore relevant to understanding the new Article 29.10.4.

Barrett notes three critical points in respect of those provisions governing Ireland's relationship with the EU. Firstly, the original amendment in 1972 did not actually achieve Irish membership of the EEC. Rather it removed any existing constitutional barriers to such membership.[19] Nor did it bring the existing *acquis communitaire* into Irish domestic law, as this was done through primary legislation. Finally, Barrett argues that the provision did not enshrine the primacy of Community law over domestic law within the Constitution, but rather sought to avoid such clashes of constitutional norms.

Applying this interpretation to the Fiscal Compact amendment, it is clear that while Article 29.4.10 allows the provisions of the Fiscal Compact to interact within the Irish legal system, it does not equate to giving it constitutional force. The provision is permissive as it authorizes ratification of the Treaty. Therefore, despite the addition of the new provision to the Bunracht na hEireann, it cannot be said that the balanced-budget rule of Article 3(1) of the Fiscal Compact, has come into force in Irish law at a constitutional level, as per the preference indicated in Article 3(2) of the Fiscal Compact.[20] Perhaps surprisingly, this point did

[18] 'Decision to Hold Referendum Surprises Many across EU', *Irish Times*, 29 February 2012; O'Donovan (n 17).

[19] G Barrett, 'The Evolving Door to Europe: Reflections on an Eventful Forty Years for Article 29.4 of the Irish Constitution' (2012) *The Irish Jurist* 132, 133. For more on the constitutional provision, see M Cahill, 'Constitutional Exclusion Clauses, Article 29.4.6, and the Constitutional Reception of European Law', (2011) 34 *Dublin University Law Journal* 74.

[20] The key provisions of the Fiscal Compact were implemented into domestic law via the Fiscal Responsibility Act, 2012 as discussed in Section III.

not feature prominently in the public debate on the amendment during the referendum campaign. A number of witnesses speaking before an Oirechtas subcommittee formed to discuss the Treaty made reference to the fact that the balanced-budget rule was not enshrined in the Constitution.[21] Professor John McHale did flag the possibility that it may be insufficient to meet the requirements of Article 3(2) of the Treaty.[22] However, no one seriously questioned whether adopting the identical approach to making constitutional provision for the EU was appropriate in the context of scope and content of the Fiscal Compact.

This failure of Ireland to put the balanced-budget rule on a constitutional footing is contrasted with the approach adopted in a number of Member States such as, inter alia, Spain, Germany and Poland, all of which have explicit constitutional limitations on deficit spending.[23] Bearing in mind that one of the reasons for the partial flexibility provided for in Article 3(2) of the Fiscal Compact in relation to whether measures are given constitutional status relates to the difficulty in undertaking constitutional amendments in some Member States, it is not feasible for Ireland to seek to rely on such an excuse for not directly enshrining the rule at a constitutional level.[24] The Irish Constitution is in theory straightforward to amend as demonstrated by the 26 amendments made since the document came into force in 1937. While the reality of constitutional amendment in Ireland, particularly in relation to European integration, gives no guarantees as to the success of a proposal, this would represent a poor reason for not proceeding with a direct enshrinement of the rule. It is ironic that after so much effort was expended on the question of whether or not to hold a referendum, it seems that the amendment actually put to the people does not itself conclusively answer the question of Ireland's fulfilment of Article 3(2) of the Fiscal Compact.

D. International Treaties within Irish Constitutional Law

Ireland is not the only Member State to have undertaken incorporation of the Fiscal Compact at a subconstitutional level. However, whereas in states such as the Netherlands public international treaties are treated as being superior to domestic constitutional law,[25] Ireland's position as a dualist state is made clear

[21] *Report of the Sub-Committee*, Sub-Committee on the Referendum on the Intergovernmental Treaty on Stability, Coordination and Governance in the Economic and Monetary Union (May 2012) Prof Gerry Whyte at 77.

[22] Ibid, Prof John McHale at 59.

[23] It should be noted that a number of Member States such as Germany and Poland had constitutional restrictions on deficit spending that pre-dated the Fiscal Compact. See G Delledonne in this volume (Chapter 9); M Antoš in this volume (Chapter 10).

[24] See F Fabbrini, 'The Fiscal Compact, the "Golden Rule" and the Paradox of European Federalism', (2013) 36 *Boston College International and Comparative Law Review* 1, 5–6; Editorial, 'The Fiscal Comact and the European Constitutions: "Europe Speaking German"' (2012) 8 *European Constitutional Law Review* 1, 3; P O'Broin, 'The Fiscal Treaty—An Initial Analysis', Institute of International and European Affairs (2012) 8–9; G Delledonne in this volume (Chapter 9); L Papadopoulou in this volume (Chapter 11).

[25] See M Diamant and M van Emmerik in this volume (Chapter 12).

in Article 29.6 of the Constitution, which states, 'No international agreement shall be part of the domestic law of the State save as may be determined by the Oireachtas.' This has two significant consequences. Firstly, it confirms the wisdom of the Attorney General's advice that a referendum should be held on the Fiscal Compact. The potential risk from a ratification without a referendum, followed by a determination that such ratification was undertaken unconstitutionally, had been outlined by Walsh J in *Crotty*, where he stated:

> If some part or all of the Treaty were subsequently translated into domestic legislation and found to be unconstitutional it would avail the State nothing in its obligations to its fellow members. It would still be bound by the Treaty. Therefore if the ratification of this Treaty under the Irish Constitution requires a referendum to amend the Constitution to give effect to it, the fact that the State did not hold a referendum would not prevent the State from being bound in international law by the Treaty.[26]

The second issue that arises is the status of the Fiscal Compact if a subsequent Oireachtas were to repeal the Fiscal Responsibility Act 2012, the legislation through which the Treaty is incorporated into domestic law as per the requirements of Article 29.6. As the Treaty does not have a constitutional basis, and the provisions of Article 29.4.10 are only permissive, there is nothing in Irish constitutional law to prevent repudiation of the Treaty.[27] While such an event would place Ireland in breach of its obligations under international law, the stricture of supremacy which binds Ireland to comply with devices of EU law does not exist in the case of the Fiscal Compact.

III. THE FISCAL RESPONSIBILITY ACT 2012

The Fiscal Responsibility Act 2012 is the legal device through which the rules in Articles 3 and 4 of the Fiscal Compact take force within Irish domestic law, as per the requirements of Article 3(2) TSCG. The legislation also makes provision for medium-term budgetary objectives, introduces a correction mechanism into Irish law and creates a Fiscal Council. It originated in April 2012 when the Irish Department for Finance published a General Scheme of a Bill to be called the Fiscal Responsibility Bill 2012. This was followed in July 2012 by the publication of the Fiscal Responsibility Bill 2012. The Bill was debated in the Oireachtas and signed into law as the Fiscal Responsibility Act 2012, in December 2012.

A. Fiscal Rules

Section 2 of the Act states that the government shall endeavour to secure both

[26] *Crotty v An Taoiseach & Others* [1987] 1 IR 713, 780.

[27] See the views of Dr Gavin Barrett when he stated 'Ireland can denounce the Fiscal Compact at any time', *Report of the Sub-Committee* (n 21) 72.

the balanced-budget rule and the debt rule arising respectively from Articles 3 and 4 of the Fiscal Compact.[28] The requirements of the balanced-budget rule are set out in detail in section 3, which relies on the text of Article 3 of the Fiscal Compact. It will be met where either (a) the budgetary position of the general government is in balance or surplus (described as the budget condition) or (b) there is convergence of the annual structural budget towards the medium-term budgetary objectives, within the time period set out (described as the adjustment path condition). Section 4, outlining the debt rule, is much more brief, though the provision is merely a restatement of the rules already binding on Ireland as an EU Member State through the regulation on the excessive deficit procedure. Section 5 covers the definition of the budgetary Medium Term Objectives (MTOs), restating much of the language in Article 3(1)(b) and (d) of the Fiscal Compact.

Section 6 deals with the crucial issue of the correction mechanism and how the Irish government proposes to address a breach of the balanced-budget rule. It operates in one of two circumstances. Firstly, if the European Commission issues a warning to the Irish government under Article 6(2) of the 1997 surveillance and coordination Regulation or secondly, if the Irish government itself considers that there has been a failure to comply with the balanced-budget rule and that this equates to a significant deviation for the purposes of Article 6(3) of that Regulation.[29] In either event, the government must prepare and lay before Dáil Eireann (the Irish lower house) a plan setting out what is necessary to secure compliance with the balanced-budget rule. This must be done within two months.

The plan must contain a number of elements. It requires a timetable over which compliance with the balanced-budget rule will be achieved and where such a timetable exceeds a year, annual targets must be included.[30] The plan must set out the size and nature of both revenue and expenditure measures that are to be used to achieve compliance.[31] Further, it must explain how these revenue and expenditure measures will related to subsectors of the general government.[32] Unsurprisingly, the legislation states that the provisions of the plan must be consistent with both the rules of the Stability and Growth Pact and any recommendations made to Ireland under the Pact regarding the period of compliance and the size of measures to be taken.[33] Ireland's specific situation as a country under an economic adjustment programme must also be taken into account.[34]

If the government determines that exceptional circumstances exist for the purposes of Article 3(1)(c) of the Fiscal Compact, then it does not have to

[28] S 2(1)(a) and (b).

[29] Council Regulation (EC) No 1466/97 of 7 July 1997 on the strengthening of the surveillance of budgetary positions and the surveillance and coordination of economic policies [1997] OJ L209/1.

[30] S 6(2)(a) and (b).

[31] S 6(2)(c).

[32] S 6(2)(d).

[33] S 6(3)(a) and (b).

[34] S 6(3)(c).

comply with the elements of its plan. When these exceptional circumstances are, in the view of the government, at an end, the government must within two months present a new plan to the Dáil. This obligation does not apply if there is no longer a failure within the meaning of section 6(1).[35]

The legislation also gives the government the scope to undertake a preventative plan in the event that it feels that a failure to meet the balanced-budget rule is likely. Such a plan has to set out the measures that the government intends to take to avoid this and must be laid before the Dáil within two months.[36]

B. Irish Fiscal Advisory Council

Section 7 establishes a new entity, the Irish Fiscal Advisory Council. The role of this Fiscal Council will be to monitor and provide, at minimum, a yearly assessment of whether Ireland is meeting the balanced-budget rule or if there has been a failure to do so. In the case of a decision by the Irish government or a warning from the Commission that the balanced-budget rule is not being met, the assessment must consider the plan proposed by the government to bring the country back into compliance.[37] Within the assessment, the Fiscal Council must judge whether 'exceptional circumstances' exist or have ceased to exist, within the meaning of the Fiscal Compact.[38] In the event of a plan being in operation to resolve the failure to meet the balanced-budget rule, the assessment must consider whether the government is taking sufficient steps to regain compliance.[39]

The remit of the Fiscal Council is not solely confined to examining compliance with the balanced-budget rule. It gives an assessment of the official forecasts emanating from the Department of Finance and of whether each annual budget is 'conducive to prudent economic and budgetary management'.[40] This assessment should include reference to the Stability and Growth Pact, though it is not limited to just this. The assessment also involves consideration of Ireland's economic adjustment programme.

After providing the government with a copy of the assessment, the Fiscal Council must publish the assessment within ten days.[41] Should the government not accept an assessment by the Fiscal Council, it must lay a statement outlining the reasons for this before Dáil Eireann within two months.[42]

[35] S 6(4).
[36] S 6(5).
[37] S 8(2).
[38] S 8(3)(a).
[39] S 8(3)(b) and (c).
[40] S 8(4)(a) and (b).
[41] S 8(5).
[42] S 8(6).

IV. COMPATIBILITY WITH THE COMMISSION COMMUNICATION

On the basis of Article 3(2) of the Fiscal Compact, the European Commission adopted a Communication designed to set out common principles for the implementation of correction mechanisms across the Member States.[43] This was done 'in view of the general interest of the Union and to contribute to the proper functioning of economic and monetary union'.[44] The Communication is based on a series of seven principles that should be respected by the Member States in designing their correction mechanisms. Within the Communication, these principles are discussed under three general headings: (i) legal status of the rules on the correction mechanisms and relation to the EU Framework; (ii) the substance of correction mechanisms—activation, nature of the correction, operational instruments, escape clauses; and (iii) the role and independence of monitoring institutions. It is relevant to examine the Fiscal Responsibility Act 2012 in relation to both the extent to which it meets with the requirements of the Communication and to demonstrate the significant influence that the Communication has had on certain elements of the Irish legislation.

A. Legal Status of the Rules on the Correction Mechanisms and Relation to the EU Framework

Principle 1 repeats the text of Article 3(2) of the Fiscal Compact in declaring that the correction mechanism shall be enshrined in national law through provisions of binding force and permanent character, preferably constitutional, or otherwise guaranteed to be fully respected and adhered to throughout the national budgetary process. This is further developed by the Communication, which states that 'the legal status of the correction mechanisms should be such that their provisions cannot be simply altered by the ordinary budgetary law'.[45] Principle 1 also contains the qualification that the correction mechanisms must respect the prerogatives of the national parliaments.

It has already been outlined in Section II.D how the constitutional preference stated by the Fiscal Compact has not been met by the manner in which Ireland has implemented its provisions. It is submitted here that even acting on a subconstitutional level, the requirements of Principle 1 of the Communication are not reflected by the Fiscal Responsibility Act 2012. The Act has no greater permanence than any other piece of legislation and can be amended, added to or repealed by a successive Act. There is nothing in its content that distinguishes it from other Acts. Whereas in other Member States such as France, Italy and

[43] European Commission Communication, 'Common Principles on National Fiscal Correction Mechanisms', COM(2012) 342 final.

[44] Ibid,1.

[45] Ibid, 3.

Spain, the provisions have been implemented through a version of quasi-constitutional legislation (organic law), Ireland currently has no such innovation in operation.[46]

Nevertheless, Irish law does provide one example of an attempt to give an Act a quasi-constitutional status. In an attempt to address the longstanding concern over the limited provision of abortion in Ireland, a proposal was made in 2002 to amend the Constitution by including a new Article which made reference to a specific Act of the Oireachtas. This Act, once passed by the Oireachtas, would not then be amendable by subsequent votes of the Oireachtas, in light of its reference in the Constitution. Rather, the Act could only be amended by a referendum. As this was a completely novel development at the time, it was challenged in the courts but was found to be compatible with the Constitution.[47] Kelly J stated:

> [T]here is nothing in Article 46 which expressly prohibits an amendment to the Constitution by reference to a document extraneous to it no more than there is a prohibition on the making of an amendment which is conditional upon some other event taking place. … In the absence of an express prohibition on the former I do not think that I would be justified in implying one, thereby interfering in the legislative process in its most solemn form which will involve the expression of the will of the People.[48]

The amendment to the Constitution itself was rejected in a referendum and hence the Act itself fell. However, this case demonstrates that there was nothing to stop the Irish government undertaking a more original approach to the legal provision made for the Fiscal Compact and one which would have given the balanced-budget rule much greater permanence.

B. Effectiveness of the Correction Mechanism

Undoubtedly, the correction mechanism is the most significant aspect of the Fiscal Compact, requiring as it does genuine remedial action in the event of a breach of the balanced-budget rule. The impact of such measures on fiscal and social policies in a signatory state could be profound and arguably should be decided on the basis of democratic input, and not merely on the grounds of their effectiveness.

Considering the effectiveness of the Irish mechanism, the device through which the corrections are to be achieved—the plan—merely needs to be laid before Dáil Eireann. As there is no reference to a resolution of the Dáil, there is no explicit requirement for a vote on the plan. It would appear that a speech, delivered by the Minister for Finance and covering all the required elements of sections 6(2) and (3), would suffice. It would be presumed that if the correc-

[46] See Fabbrini (n 24) 1.
[47] *Morris v Minister for the Environment* [2002] IEHC 5.
[48] Ibid, para. 36.

tion required is in any way sizeable, it will be necessary for much of it to be undertaken through changes to taxation and government spending, which would require legislation and therefore a vote of the Dáil. It is also likely that such legislation would be considered as a Money Bill, as defined under Article 22.1.1 of the Constitution.[49] A slightly different legislative process applies to Money Bills, in that they must be initiated in the Dáil, they are only laid before the Seanad (the Irish upper house) for recommendations, rather than substantive amendments and the time period given to the Seanad is significantly abridged.[50] Further, they cannot be referred to the Supreme Court under Article 26 prior to enactment to test their constitutionality.

In light of the fact that a Plan under section 6 is almost certainly going to result in a legislative process, it is submitted that it would have been better for the Fiscal Responsibility Act directly to require the drafting and passing of legislation addressing the correction. A statement outlining the package of measures set out in a Plan under section 6 lacks the cohesive momentum that voting on them as a single package would give. It is virtually impossible to see a situation where a significant deviation from the balanced-budget rule could be addressed by measures that did not require taxes to be raised or public spending to be cut—the two key components of a Money Bill. As such, having a provision in the Fiscal Responsibility Act 2012 that compelled the drafting of a Money Bill would in no way undermine the prerogatives of the national parliament as the Dáil would still have to draft and pass the Money Bill anyway.

It is significant to note that an early draft outline of the Fiscal Responsibility Bill published by the Department of Finance at the start of 2012 included a proposal for the operation of the correction mechanism.[51] Section 6 of the draft outline was considerably different from the final version. In particular, it made no reference to the government outlining a plan for dealing with the deviation. Rather, it contained a more robust direction that 'the Government shall undertake the correction measures required by regulations under [Section] 9(1) in accordance with the regulations'.[52] Section 9 of the draft was couched in mandatory terms such as 'The Minister *shall* make regulations providing for the corrective measures to be undertaken under [Section] 6.'[53] These regulations would outline the nature, size and timeframe surrounding any such corrective measures.[54] The Minister was also given the power to make other regulations

[49] 'A Money Bill means a Bill which contains only provisions dealing with all or any of the following matters, namely, the imposition, repeal, remission, alteration or regulation of taxation; the imposition for the payment of debt or other financial purposes of charges on public moneys or the variation or repeal of any such charges; supply; the appropriation, receipt, custody, issue or audit of accounts of public money; the raising or guarantee of any loan or the repayment thereof; matters subordinate and incidental to these matters or any of them.'

[50] Art 21.

[51] General Scheme of a Bill to the Called the Fiscal Responsibility Bill, 2012.

[52] A regulation is an element of secondary legislation under Irish law, which is usually made by a government minister, pursuant to powers delegated to him/her within the primary legislation.

[53] S 9(1) (emphasis added).

[54] S 9(2)(b).

incidental to the Act.[55] The position of the Dáil in relation to the corrective mechanism regulations was strengthened by the requirement that such regulations required approval by a resolution of Dáil Eireann.[56]

Section 9 of the Act as finally passed is far less detailed. No explicit reference is made to it being the device through which a correction mechanism will be implemented. Subsection 2 states that regulations adopted under section 9 'may contain such incidental, supplementary and consequential provisions as appear to the Minister to be necessary or expedient for the purposes of the regulations'. However, the section also states that the ministerial regulations can be made on the basis of common principles contained in Article 3(2) of the Fiscal Compact. Most significantly, subsection 9 repeats the stringent approach to the adoption of ministerial regulations, requiring an affirmative vote of the Dáil before they are adopted.

The Fiscal Responsibility Act 2012 and the Explanatory Memorandum are silent as to whether it was the intention of the Oireachtas that the correction mechanisms would be adopted as ministerial regulations under section 9, or whether they would be provided for in primary legislation. However, the Department for Finance has subsequently confirmed that any future correction mechanism would be undertaken through primary legislation, stating:

> Any correction plan presented to the *Dáil* would be implemented primarily through budgetary legislation, which can be supplementary if the timing of the plan warrants it. There is provision to introduce a Finance Bill, Social Welfare Bill or expenditure estimates at any time. If the correction plan sets out a multi-year correction, then;
>
> - Multi-annual revenue measures can be made through Finance or Social Welfare Bill amendments; and
> - The element related to Government expenditure (about 90% of Ireland's total general government expenditure) would be directly reflected in the Government expenditure ceiling which is being put on a statutory basis under the Minister and Secretaries (Amendment) Bill 2012.[57]

It is submitted that this approach to implementing a correction in a more open manner is preferable. Obviously, implementing a correction through secondary legislation would be attractive to a government, as it is both quicker and less complicated. Nevertheless, it would have the consequence of significantly curtailing debate. Rather than going through the stages of the legislative process that a Bill would undertake, the secondary legislation would only be subject to a single vote of approval. It is argued here that in light of the very significant consequences that would flow from a correction, involving tax increases and spending cuts, it is both appropriate and necessary that the democratically elected representatives of the people are given the fullest opportunity to debate the measures.

[55] S 9(3).

[56] S 9(5).

[57] Written response from the Minister for Finance to Deputy Catherine Murphy TD, Question 60 (13 June 2013) Ref 28510/13.

This change in approach to the implementation of the correction mechanism between the first and final draft of the legislation is significant. The draft outline Bill, which was published before the Commission Communication, already contained much of what was eventually in the final Act. As such, it would appear that the Communication was not hugely consequential regarding its content. However, the Department for Finance drew attention to the fact that the only major changes occasioned by the Communication were to the correction mechanism.[58] Referring to Principle 2 of the Communication, which required consistency of the national correction mechanisms with the wider EU fiscal framework, the Department of Finance stressed that the newer version of section 6, 'provides fully for the correction mechanism'. It is argued here that the changes made to section 6 between the original and final drafts of the legislation, which have had the effect of making the process more open, were actually motivated by the statement in Principle 1 that the correction mechanism adopted would respect the prerogatives of national Parliaments. The final version of section 6 could have continued to mandate a ministerial regulation, approved by a single vote of the Dáil, to implement the correction. Alternatively, it could have required, as suggested above, that the range of measures outlined in the plan, which the government has a leisurely two months to draw up, be drafted in a Money Bill and put to a vote of the Dáil in the context of an 'emergency budget'.

These points are not to assume that the section 6 correction mechanism will be ineffective if it is ever required. However, they demonstrate that the Irish legislature has written into the Fiscal Responsibility Act the maximum possible amount of flexibility regarding how it approaches the correction and indeed that it feels justified in doing so due to the Commission's own interpretation of the obligations placed on national governments by Article 3(2) of the Fiscal Compact.

C. Consistency with EU Framework

In relation to Principle 2, requiring consistency of Irish national rules with existing EU budgetary rules, section 1 of the Fiscal Responsibility Act makes it clear that most of the technical terms used in the Act are defined in reference to existing definitions contained in EU secondary legislation.[59] For example, 'exceptional circumstances' are defined by reference to the Stability and Growth Pact, 'general government deficit' and 'general government surplus' by reference to the 2009 Regulation, and 'medium-term budgetary objective' by reference to the 1997 surveillance and coordination Regulation.[60] Further, section 1(2)

[58] Press Release, Publication of the Fiscal Responsibility Bill, 2012 www.finance.gov.ie/viewdoc.asp?DocID=7319 (last accessed 15 April 13).

[59] S 1.

[60] Council Regulation (EC) No 1466/97 of 7 July 1997 on the strengthening of the surveillance of budgetary positions and the surveillance and coordination of economic policies [1997] OJ L 209/1.

ensures that any word or phrase used in the Act and also in the Fiscal Compact will be given the meaning it is given in the Fiscal Compact, unless the contrary is expressed.

D. The Substance of Correction Mechanisms: Activation, Nature of the Correction, Operational Instruments, Escape Clauses

In response to Principle 3 of the Communication, the Act identifies two potential routes to the activation of the correction mechanism. Section 6(1) outlines how the mechanism is activated in response to a Commission warning addressed to Ireland that there has been a breach of the balanced-budget rule. However, the government can itself determine that there is a risk of a significant deviation occurring, and thereby itself activate a correction.[61]

In the event of a Commission warning, it is clear that activation is automatic, as section 6(1) uses the mandatory phrase 'the Government shall'. It would appear that the self-activation under section 6(5) is more flexible, using as it does the phrase 'the Government may'. Obviously, it is easier for the law to provide compulsion in an ex post situation. Nevertheless, there is surely an argument that ex ante compulsion has benefits, particularly in light of the threat caused to the EU financial system as a whole from the loss of confidence resulting from the news that a Member State is at risk of breaching the balanced-budget rule. However, while the automatic nature of the correction mechanism is referred to in Article 3(1)(e) of the Fiscal Compact and the term is repeated in the Commission Communication, it is not specifically referenced in any of the seven principles set out therein.[62] As such, Ireland's approach of only providing for an automatic correction in the event of the Commission identifying an existing breach of the balanced-budget rule is compliant with the Communication.

Section 6(1) of the Act contains a widely framed direction that the plan proposed by the government must specify 'what is required to be done' in order to regain compliance. As noted above in Section III.A, this needs to contain an overall time period within which compliance will be regained, annual targets if this period is over a year, the size and type of measures on both income and expenditure side that will be undertaken, and how these will relate to different subsectors of the general government. Due to its vague nature, it could be argued that this last point does not fully meet the requirement of Principle 5 that the design of the correction mechanism will contain provisions regarding the co-ordination of the fiscal adjustment across the governmental subsectors. However, the Minister for Finance has subsequently confirmed that where the adjustment needs to include subsectors of the government, including local authorities, the relevant measure will be taken through legislation.[63]

[61] S 6(5).
[62] European Commission (n 43) 1.
[63] Above, n 57.

Section 6(3) mandates compliance of the correction process with the Stability and Growth Pact and recommendations made to the state under the Pact. Obviously, due to the specific circumstances of Ireland, there is also a requirement of compatibility with the current financial adjustment programme.

As required under Principle 6 of the Communication, the term 'exceptional circumstances' is defined in section 1 of the Act in accordance with the meaning given in the Stability and Growth Pact.[64] Within the legislation, this criterion plays a dual role. Firstly, it acts as a justification as to why either of the two measures of compliance with the balanced-budget rule, the budget condition or the adjustment part condition, are not met.[65] In both circumstances, an exceptional circumstance will only act as a reason so long as relying on it will not endanger medium-term fiscal sustainability, as per the revised Stability and Growth Pact. Secondly, it provides a justification for suspending those measures adopted under a plan drawn up by the government to restore compliance with the balanced-budget rule.[66] On this point, the Act adheres closely to the requirements of Principle 6 that the suspension must be temporary. It states that once the exceptional circumstances come to an end, a new plan must be drawn up, unless the deviation from the balanced-budget rule has ceased.

E. Role and Independence of Monitoring Institutions

The Communication deals with the monitoring institutions established to provide assessment of national compliance with the budgetary rules under Principle 7. It sees these as a key ingredient in fostering credibility and transparency.[67] The Communication sets out two broad principles regarding the design of such institutions. The Member States are given some level of flexibility regarding their structure, so that they can fit within the wider administrative infrastructure of the state. However, they must be guaranteed significant independence, both as regards their legal basis, operation, appointment of members and the provision of resources.[68]

The Fiscal Council is a completely new body within Irish law. Originally conceived as an element of the Memorandum of Understanding between Ireland, the EU and the International Monetary Fund as a condition of the economic assistance package provided in late 2010, it was enshrined in law through the Fiscal Responsibility Act 2012.[69] Section 8(1) emphasizes the independence of the Fiscal Council in performing its functions. While it is submitted that this

[64] 'Exceptional circumstances' means: (a) a period during which an unusual event outside the control of the State has a major impact on the financial position of the general government, or (b) a period of severe economic downturn.

[65] S 3(2) and (4).

[66] S 6(4).

[67] European Commission (n 43) 5. See A De Streel in this volume (Chapter 5).

[68] European Commission, ibid.

[69] Memorandum of Understanding between the European Commission and Ireland, para. 25.

is sufficient to guarantee its independence as per the requirements of Article 3(2) TSCG, by putting it on an equivalent footing to other bodies such as the Ombudsman, it is noted that the office of Comptroller and Auditor General, tasked with auditing all accounts of moneys administered by or under the authority of the Oireachtas, has always been specifically referenced within the Constitution.[70] Although the role of the Fiscal Council and the Comptroller and Auditor General are not directly comparable, it is legitimate to ask why, if ex post scrutiny of state finances is worthy of constitutional protection, ex ante scrutiny is not equally significant, particularly in light of the damage caused by failures in this area in recent years.

The Commission Communication emphasizes the importance of the monitoring institutions being able to express their analysis of economic issues in public. This criterion is key to the principle of 'comply or explain', whereby national governments are expected either to follow the advice of the monitoring institution or publically indicate the reasons for not doing so.[71] The Act implements this principle through a number of provisions.

The Fiscal Council must publish their annual assessment within ten days of submitting this to the Minister for Finance.[72] It is significant to note that the government does not have to accept a determination contained in its assessment of either a breach of the balanced-budget rule, the existence or not of exceptional circumstances, or of its own failure to implement a plan. However, section 8(6) indicates that in the event of the government refusing to accept the assessment of the Fiscal Council on one of these grounds, the government must lay a statement before the Dáil outlining the reasons for this within two months.

The Communication indicates a desire that national lawmakers would not be in a position whereby they could simply ignore high-level economic advice, but at the same time seeks to ensure that these lawmakers' responsibilities are not infringed. It is submitted that the Irish legislation has gone a long way to achieving this. It will be politically difficult for any future Irish government to be seen to disregard or contradict a determination by the Fiscal Council on any of these three crucial headings. While the limitation is political rather than legal—the only concrete restriction being the requirement of having a debate in the Dáil—nevertheless this mandates parliamentary scrutiny of economic analysis that is independent of that provided by the government, to an extent never before provided. One criticism that could be levelled at these provisions is that the two-month delay permissible before the government is required to explain why it is rejecting the assessment of the Fiscal Council is overly generous, particularly in light of the speed with which uncertainty about economic markets can rapidly create negative implications.

[70] Art 33.
[71] European Commission (n 43) 4.
[72] S 8(5).

V. IMPACT AND EFFECTIVENESS OF THE IRISH IMPLEMENTATION

Across the literature on the Fiscal Compact, certain trends emerge as to how the TCSG is being applied within the signatory states. Ireland's approach to incorporation and implementation appears to fit comfortably within these trends, though some specific features of the method of application are worthy of comment.

A. An Enhanced Role for Courts?

A number of authors have identified the Fiscal Compact as effecting a move towards a more legalized version of the financial constitution, with the courts playing an increasing role in the determination of issues.[73] Nevertheless, the evidence across the Member States does not demonstrate a dramatic shift in power to the national courts.

Like the Netherlands, the Irish approach demonstrates one that is primarily political, rather than legal, in its implementation.[74] As any future budgetary corrections will be undertaken through Money Bills, these cannot be sent to the Supreme Court for scrutiny before being signed by the President under Article 26 of the Constitution. The Fiscal Compact has not changed this situation in any way. Further, it is difficult to envisage a situation whereby a private individual would be in a position to seek to litigate under the Fiscal Responsibility Act. An applicant mounting a judicial review action claiming that the size of the correction had not gone far enough would have to face the reluctance of the Irish courts to have themselves drawn into matters of the raising and spending of state finances. In a previous case taken against the imposition of a property tax, O'Hanlon J in the High Court stated that plaintiff challenging the validity of a taxation statute passed by the Oireachtas, would face 'a very uphill battle'.[75] In the context of a case regarding the failure of the state to spend money on persons with special educational needs, Hardiman J in the Supreme Court, referring to a range of cases where the courts had refused to get involved on issues of redistribution, stated 'these are peculiarly matters within the field of national policy, to be decided by a combination of the executive and the legislature, that cannot be adjudicated upon by the Courts'.[76]

In states such as the Netherlands and Spain, the implementation of the TCSG may give the central authorities a greater scope to take judicial action against spending by regional governments.[77] However, this does not arise as an issue

[73] M Antoš in this volume (Chapter 10); G Delledonne in this volume (Chapter 9).

[74] See M Diamant and M van Emmerik in this volume (Chapter 12).

[75] *Madigan v Attorney General* [1986] ILRM 136, 152.

[76] *Sinnott v Minister for Education* [2001] 2 IR 545

[77] M Diamant and M van Emmerik in this volume (Chapter 12); G Delledone in this volume (Chapter 9) p 192.

in the Irish context, as local government is almost wholly dependent on direct central government funding.

B. Differing Models of Independent Supervision

Ireland created a completely new body to serve as the independent monitoring institution overseeing its commitment to the balanced-budget rule. This approach, similar to that in Slovakia, is in contrast to states that added the role to existing national bodies.[78] In the Netherlands, for example, the task was granted to the Council of State, an advisory body that has had a consultative role in the Dutch legislative process since the 1500s.[79] Similarly, the role in Germany has been delegated to the Council of Economic Experts, which has functioned since the 1960s. The comply-or-explain principle adopted in Ireland is similar to that used in most states, though it is relevant to note that in Hungry, the Budgetary Council formed under the new Constitution must give its approval before the state budget can be approved, thus giving it a virtual veto power.[80]

The approach adopted in the Irish legislation to the selection of the membership of the Fiscal Council demonstrates a strong bias in favour of the executive. The members of the Fiscal Council are appointed by the Minister for Finance.[81] The sole role for the Oirechtas is if the Minister wishes to terminate the appointment of one of the members, which can only be undertaken after the passing of a resolution by the Dáil. Other states already have a more active role for their national parliaments in the selection of the persons comprising their monitoring institutions, with both Slovakia and Poland having at least one member nominated by the legislative branch.[82]

C. Weakening National Parliaments?

Undoubtedly, the introduction of the Fiscal Compact and adherence to its requirements has seen a further shift in power from the national to the supranational level. However, it is submitted that the criticism of the Fiscal Compact that it erodes the prerogatives of national parliaments is less applicable in Ireland.[83] This is primarily because Ireland already experiences a major imbalance of power in favour of the executive function. As such, the decision to implement budgetary adjustments through primary legislation leaves the parliament with the same, admittedly low, level of influence that it currently enjoys, in contrast to

[78] M Antoš in this volume (Chapter 10) p 217.

[79] M Diamant and M van Emmerik in this volume (Chapter 12) p 258.

[80] M Antoš in this volume (Chapter 10) 16. Currently, Hungry is not a eurozone country and therefore is not bound in the same way by the provisions of the Fiscal Compact.

[81] Schedule to the Act, s 1(2).

[82] M Antoš in this volume (Chapter 10) pp 215–17.

[83] See L Papadopoulou in this volume (Chapter 11); S Piedrafita in this volume (Chapter 15).

the earlier proposal to undertake corrections by the even more executive dominated method of secondary legislation. Further, the creation of the Fiscal Council and the introduction of the comply-or-explain principle actually creates a new opportunity for the Dáil to question executive activity. This has the potential to, in the words of Armstrong, 'strengthen domestic accountability … of the executive to the public and parliament'.[84]

VI. CONCLUSION

While Ireland was the only EU Member State to hold a referendum to undertake ratification of the Fiscal Compact, this did not actually result in the enshrinement of the balanced-budget rule at constitutional level. Instead, the Irish government opted to give constitutional protection to legal devices undertaken on the basis of the Fiscal Compact, whether domestically or by institutions competent under the TCSG. While this method was appropriate for mediating Ireland's relationship with a body as complex as the EU, it is arguably an overly complicated approach in relation to the Fiscal Compact, the essence of which is principally the balanced-budget rule and the correction mechanism.

While the TCSG did not oblige Ireland to incorporate the balanced-budget rule into its Constitution, it has been shown that the legislative approach adopted in the Fiscal Responsibility Act in no way distinguishes this Act from any other piece of legislation. As such, this author queries whether the adoption criteria of binding force and permanent character, set out in Article 3(2) TCSG and elaborated upon in the Commission Communication, have been fully met by the legal status of the Irish measures.

The approach adopted to the correction mechanism is vague, with the Fiscal Responsibility Act failing to set out a clear path regarding how the measures to re-establish compliance with the balanced-budget rule will be achieved. While it has been subsequently clarified that the correction would be undertaken via primary legislation through an emergency budget, it has been argued here that the Act should have directly require this, rather than relying on the nebulous apparatus of a plan.

Nevertheless, the establishment of the Fiscal Council is a major development in economic planning in Ireland. Its legislative design gives it the potential to have a significant input into fiscal planning within the state. Furthermore, it creates a framework whereby the Oireachtas will have an enhanced ability to force the government to account for ill-advised economic policies. In a country which experiences executive dominance to the extent that Ireland does, and where that executive has demonstrated fiscal irresponsibility in recent years, this could prove to be the most significant legacy of the Fiscal Compact within the state.

[84] See KA Armstrong in this volume (Chapter 4).

Part 3

Towards a Genuine EMU: Democracy, Legitimacy and Integration

14

Domestic Courts, Constitutional Constraints and European Democracy: What Solution for the Crisis?

INGOLF PERNICE*

I. INTRODUCTION

THE EU IS still in the midst of a crisis, and with the ongoing financial turmoil it has become clear that the economic disturbance in many Member States is coupled with fundamental constitutional questions about, and challenges to, the democratic legitimacy of the EU altogether. With a view to retaining their sovereignty and, in particular, their budgetary autonomy, Member States take the risk of the euro breaking down and any chances to retain control over the highly speculative financial markets being lost. Important legislative packages have been adopted to strengthen the Stability and Growth Pact. With a view to enhancing co-operation among governments and to tightening up oversight over new national policies, international agreements have been concluded, all this in order to achieve short-term stability. However, with these instruments the EU is shifting towards a system of governance driven by the executive. Traditional parliamentary prerogatives regarding economic, fiscal and, consequently, redistributive policies are passed to somewhat opaque co-ordination and control mechanisms producing decisions and guidelines with a strong impact on the economic and social conditions within each of the Member States, but with little to no democratic accountability at the EU as well as at the national level. Governments seem to enjoy their new powers and appear to be reluctant to take the necessary steps towards a meaningful revision of the EU treaties that not only allocates the powers needed to lead an effective economic and fiscal policy at the EU level but also arranges for the democratic legitimacy needed to ensure that the people affected can understand themselves as the authors of these policies. National constitutional courts, in particular the German Federal Constitutional Court (GFCC), seem to be concerned with the loss of direct

* The author is grateful for the assistance of Michael Schwarz in preparing this contribution and to Linda Engelbrecht for bringing it in conformity with the style guide.

parliamentary control over their national budgets and the related redistributive policies. They establish constitutional constraints not only on the discretionary powers of their respective governments participating in the co-ordination mechanisms, but also on the terms of a possible revision of the EU treaties aiming at adapting them to the challenges ahead.

Whatever the merits and defaults of the present policies adopted to cope with the financial crisis may be,[1] the answer to the question 'what is solution to the crisis?' cannot be found, at least in a long-term perspective, in a muddling-through based upon legislative action, the legal basis of which is doubtful under the existing EU treaties (such as new sanction powers within the framework of the multilateral surveillance under Article 121 TFEU or the reversed majority rule for sanctions under Article 126 TFEU introduced by the 'six-pack', but also the new provisions on a banking union). Neither can the solution be found in paraconstitutional agreements, such as the European Stability Mechanism (ESM) Treaty and the Fiscal Compact, conferring responsibilities upon the EU institutions beyond those Article 13 TEU refers to,[2] and for the exercise of which it is open how parliamentary legitimacy can be secured. As already envisaged in the Fiscal Compact—which is merely a provisional and incomplete substitute for further reform—only a revision of the EU treaties will give an adequate answer to the question. As such revision will touch and amend profoundly the constitutional setting of the EU, it seems to be useful to undertake some theoretical reflection upon how this setting should actually be understood (Section II), as well as upon the constitutional boundaries of European integration from the point of view of the national constitutional courts (Section III), before it is possible to develop some ideas for the new provisions needed (Section IV) and, finally, to consider the path to be followed for a successful implementation of the revision of the treaties (Section V).

II. MULTILEVEL CONSTITUTIONALISM: CITIZENS' OWNERSHIP OF THE EUROPEAN UNION

It is difficult to talk about democracy in the EU as a political body without taking into account its citizens. This is specific for the EU, as opposed to traditional international organizations where states or their governments co-operate on their own account and with legal effects among themselves only. With its legislative powers applicable to the individual with direct effect, conceptualizing the EU must be based upon constitutional principles such as democracy, the respect for

[1] For a summary of the measures taken see European Commission Communication, 'A Blueprint for a Deep and Genuine Economic and Monetary Union. Launching a European Debate, COM(2012) 777 final/2, 4-9, with a general appraisal at 9 et seq.

[2] See P Craig in this volume (Chapter 2). Doubts remain insofar, though in ECJ Case C-370/12 *Pringle v Government of Ireland, Ireland and the Attorney General*, judgment of 27 November 2012, paras 155–77, the Court gives leeway to the new and additional tasks of the ECB, the Commission and the CJEU.

fundamental rights and, in particular, human dignity,[3] together with the rule of law and the principle of subsidiarity. The principle of subsidiarity plays a primary role not only for guiding the exercise of competences (Article 5(3) TEU), but also for determining the attribution of competences to one or the other level in a multilevel political system such as the EU. It deploys a special force when the constitution and further development of the EU is not regarded as a business conducted between states and governments only—like in the case of an international organization—but as a matter primarily of the citizens.

Multilevel constitutionalism[4] takes the perspective of the individual in the construction of the EU. Whatever is decided at the European or at the national level is decided in the name of, and with regard to the citizens of the Member States. It affects, as drastically shown by the austerity policies adopted to face the ongoing crisis, these citizens, who under Article 9 TEU and Article 20 TFEU, are simultaneously citizens of the EU. Whatever measure is taken, it must be based, ultimately, on their will—the Member States and the EU are founded upon and bound to, as Article 2 TEU clearly states, democracy as a fundamental value. From this perspective, the actions of the European institutions draw their legitimacy from the citizens, as national citizens indirectly through the governments which are accountable to their respective parliaments and directly through the European Parliament, which is composed of representatives of the EU's citizens (Articles 10 and 14 TEU). More importantly, however, multilevel constitutionalism envisages the establishment and further development of the EU as such to be a process originating in, and driven by, the citizens through their respective institutions. As national citizens they are represented, by their governments in negotiating the EU treaties, and by their parliaments in authorizing the ratification, if they are not acting directly through referendum. In this manner, the EU cannot be understood as an administrative agency of the Member States having delegated powers upon it,[5] but rather as a constitutional joint venture or endeavour of individuals with original powers conferred on it by the EU treaties: the citizens of the Member States first established and subsequently further developed the EU as a supranational, complementary instrument for articulating and implementing policies, which may not effectively and legitimately be implemented by the individual Member States autonomously, and so they grant themselves the common status as citizens of the EU with equal rights and obligations. The citizens, thus, are ultimately the real owners of the EU, though the awareness of this ownership is not widespread. It is, thus, at least

[3] For a comprehensive and comparative conceptual analysis of human dignity pursuant to Art 1 of the Charter of Fundamental Rights of the EU and Art 1 of the German Basic Law, see M Schwarz, 'Die Menschenwürde als Ende der Europäischen Wertegemeinschaft? Eine realistische Perspektive auf das Schutzdefizit nach Art 1 der Grundrechtecharta' (2011) 50 *Der Staat* 533–66.

[4] First developed in I Pernice, 'Constitutional Law Implications for a State Participating in a Process of Regional Integration. German Constitution and "Multilevel Constitutionalism"', in E Riedel (ed), *German Reports on Public Law Presented to the XV International Congress on Comparative Law, Bristol, 26 July to 1 August 1998* (Baden-Baden, Nomos, 1998) 40–65.

[5] This is the approach of PL Lindseth in this volume (Chapter 18) following n 8, 34.

superficial if commentators including the German Federal Constitutional Court continue to see the Member States as the 'masters of the Treaties'.[6]

Establishing institutions for exercising public authority at the supranational level, organising decision-making procedures involving national governments, providing for elections to these institutions, and conferring competences upon the institutions for issuing legislative acts and decisions with direct effect upon the individuals, enshrining individual fundamental rights of the citizens to be respected by the authorities so established, and providing for judicial review by national and European courts, all these features of the EU not only are fundamentally constitutional issues but cannot be without effect on national constitutions and the authorities they establish.

This is why most Member State national constitutions provide in their respective integration clauses for special procedures and conditions for the ratification of treaties when these are established or amended, or on their accession to the EU.[7] Under Article 23(1) of the German Basic Law, the EU must respond to the principles of democracy, federalism and subsidiarity, the rule of law, and respect of fundamental rights. The procedure for amending the German Basic Law itself also applies to the national law authorizing the ratification of the treaties (Articles 23(1), 79(2) and (3)). The constitutions at both levels are complementary parts of one constitutional system; notwithstanding their formal autonomy and original legitimacy deriving from the respective citizenry, they are interdependent and 'permeable',[8] interacting and reciprocally receptive to constitutional principles, legal provisions, patterns of regulation, and even legal and administrative cultures.

People would not confer powers on newly created common institutions at the European level and organize legislative and political action beyond the state without a real need to do so. Even less so would political leaders or governments engage in such ventures if they did not face new challenges, the solution of which required new instruments. The first of these challenges was to stop war among European states. European integration, thus, started with the European Coal and Steel Community Treaty, which brought the coal and steel production and markets under common control and so made war amongst the Member States much less likely. The next step was to ensure decent conditions of life and to promote economic prosperity and social progress within an ever-closer union of the peoples of Europe through a common market, further developed into the internal market, and European Monetary Union (EMU). Other issues followed: environmental protection, climate change, international crime and terrorism, energy security. The principle guiding the allocation of appropriate powers upon

[6] German Federal Constitutional Court (GFCC), Case BVerfGE 89, 155 Maastricht, judgment of 12 October 1993, para 190. See also GFCC, case BVerfGE 123, 267 Lisbon, judgment of 30 June 2009, paras 231, 235, 271, 289 and 334.

[7] For a comparative analysis, see M Wendel, *Permeabilität im europäischen Verfassungsrecht* (Tübingen, Mohr Siebeck, 2011) 144–370.

[8] Wendel (n 5) 7, *passim*.

the EU as well as limiting their exercise at the European level is the principle of subsidiarity, which—in a narrower sense as laid down in Article 5(3) TEU—also determines whether or not the EU may exercise those powers conferred to it, which are not exclusive. Taken at face value, it means that no power is conferred to the EU, or exercised at this level, if the objective of the proposed action can effectively be reached at the national level (Article 5(3) TEU). Consequently, powers exercised on this basis at the European level would not be considered a loss of political autonomy and power for the Member States, but in contrary, a real gain of impact, to the benefit of the citizens of the EU. This is the ultimate justification for the existence of the EU.

The establishment of the EMU can be understood as an attempt to follow this approach. EMU was felt necessary to complete the internal market with all the benefits for EU citizens that derive from economies of scale, increased competitiveness on global markets, and the price stability of a common currency. The euro, thus, was introduced and the monetary policy was centralized via the European Central Bank (ECB) and the European System of Central Banks under the Treaty of Maastricht, while Member States felt that economic, fiscal and social policies could remain in their hands as autonomous responsibilities subject only to some provision on economic policy co-ordination, fiscal discipline and general rules. As it was clear from the outset that this framework was insufficient as a corollary for the common currency, the Growth and Stability Pact was concluded in order to strengthen the rules on fiscal discipline in particular. As recent experience shows, however, the asymmetry of the EMU, the lack of fiscal and legal discipline of the Member States, and the 'malfunction' both of the surveillance mechanisms and of the markets, which did not sanction as expected the misbehaviour of some Member States, led to the quasi-breakdown of the system altogether.[9]

Is it really surprising that granting autonomy to Member States with respect to national economic and fiscal policies in a union of states with significantly diverse approaches and cultures in these policy areas under a loose system of co-ordination, instead of striving for economic convergence as envisioned, led to structural cleavages and economic imbalances of a magnitude that cannot be sustained in a monetary union? And, what is more: the internal market with free movement of capital, common competition rules including the control of state aids, together with the common currency meant that specific national measures in economic and fiscal policies had effects well beyond national borders. Does it come as a surprise in a system of interdependent markets to see that great efforts in one Member State, such as Germany, to enhance the competitiveness of its economy by moderating wages, restructuring social systems, etc, may seri-

[9] Explaining the crisis rather as a problem of democracy, see MP Maduro, 'A New Governance for the European Union and the Euro: Democracy and Justice', in *European Parliament Directorate General for Internal Policies. Policy Department C: Citizens' Rights and Constitutional Affairs*, PE 462.484 (2012) 7 et seq. For the economic reasons, see PA Hall, 'The Economics and Politics of the Euro 21 Crisis' (2012) *German Politics* 355, 357–60.

ously affect other national economies, where similar efforts have not been taken? Avoidance of such tensions was the reason why Article 121 TFEU sets out a framework for co-ordination of national economic policies. Thus far, it has not been taken seriously and the result is not what was hoped for.

On the other hand, the crisis shows that Greek economic and fiscal policies, too, had and will continue to have harsh consequences for other Member States. Is it an expression of the budgetary autonomy of the German parliament to be told that it had no alternative but to consent to the grants accorded to Greece with a view to rescuing the euro in 2010? What about the financial commitments and risks incurred by Germany following its consent to the establishment of the European Financial Stabilization Mechanism and, finally, the ESM? Not one of the members of the Bundestag can be supposed to have agreed to this voluntarily and happily. Rather, they acted under the pressure of precedents and economic disasters in other parts of the internal market with its intimately interdependent economies. They reacted as they felt necessary to regain control over the markets, but this is not what we may understand as autonomy.

Other Member States urged Germany to accept eurobonds in order to avoid excessive spreads for sovereign bonds and, eventually, to mutualize debts. But who could reasonably accept any kind of common liability without a common policy? That equates to paying the bill for policies of others without having a say.[10] The GFCC clearly excludes any kind of commitment of this nature.[11] Co-ordination of national economic and fiscal policies, based upon multilateral surveillance, has failed to bring about the necessary convergence of national economies. Why should more co-ordination with stricter surveillance do the job? Even the conditionality imposed on the countries under the rescue umbrella—measures felt by the people concerned as akin to dictatorship by the rich and the end of parliamentary autonomy or even of national sovereignty—still need to produce the results they are expected to bring about.

European integration and, in particular, the community method was invented to achieve what co-operation among sovereign states apparently could not: peace and prosperity for the people in this part of Europe, with moreover some further positive effects. Why should this approach not be applied to economic and fiscal, even for social policies? The common argument is that such sensitive and important redistribution policies lie at the core of national sovereignty and, thus, of

[10] See already: I Pernice, 'Währungsunion—Zuerst kommt die europäische Disziplin', *Handelsblatt*, 18 August 2011, also as WHI-paper 04/11, 3: 'es gibt keine Haftungsgemeinschaft ohne Handlungsgemeinschaft'. The Commission has understood this when stating in the Blueprint (n 1) 26: '[M]oving to wards more mutualisation of financial risk would require bringing the coordination of budgetary policy one step further by ensuring that there is collective control over national budgetary policy in defined situations.' More in detail, ibid, 40.

[11] GFCC, case 2 BvR 987/10 Greek rescue umbrella, judgment of 9 September 2011, headnote 3(b): 'No permanent mechanisms may be created under international treaties which are tantamount to accepting liability for decisions by free will of other states, above all if they entail consequences which are hard to calculate. Every large-scale measure of aid of the Federal Government taken in a spirit of solidarity and involving public expenditure on the international or European Union level must be specifically approved by the Bundestag.'

parliamentary autonomy.[12] But what if this autonomy, as shown, is lost? The external effects of the national policies for other countries and their people are so significant that, as Miguel Maduro rightly points out in this volume, the principle of democracy is at stake.[13] Or, as Jürgen Neyer turns the argument: 'Europe's democratic deficit originates first of all in the Member States, not in its supranational layer.'[14] Those affected cannot participate in the decision-making; those deciding do not take account of the interests of all people potentially affected by the decision.[15] What Peter Lindseth strives to maintain: '[T]he integrity of national democracies in a historically recognizable, if evolving, sense', is impossible in a world of deeply interdependent states.[16] To the extent that democratic self-determination is ineffective, as a result of the interdependence of the markets and economies, a commonly determined policy at the appropriate level is due, and this level is the EU.

Once people have taken ownership of the EU as an instrument for effectively and legitimately dealing with issues beyond the reach of the individual Member States, they will be able to appreciate it as needed to secure democratic self-government. A democratically accountable authority at the European level empowered to ensure the convergence of the economies of the Member States, thus, is required to sustain the euro and the functioning of the EMU. The institutional modalities as well as the extent of a European competence for a common economic and fiscal policy remain to be determined. This exercise has to take account of the limits of European integration in terms of national constitutional law, and it must be implemented as an open, innovative, constitutional process substantially impacting both on the national and the European constitutional levels, and essentially safegarding the balance of powers between these levels.

[12] See in particular: GFCC, case BVerfGE 123, 267 Lisbon, judgment of 30 June 2009, para 252: 'Particularly sensitive for the ability of a constitutional state to democratically shape itself are decisions on substantive and formal criminal law (1), on the disposition of the monopoly on the use of force by the police within the state and by the military towards the exterior (2), fundamental fiscal decisions on public revenue and public expenditure, the latter being particularly motivated, *inter alia*, by social policy considerations (3), decisions on the shaping of living conditions in a social state (4) and decisions of particular cultural importance, for example on family law, the school and education system and on dealing with religious communities (5).'

[13] See the Preface to this volume, and also Maduro (n 8) 9, 11, with special reference to the external effect on importing countries of the devaluation of the currency in one country (ibid, 10). For some ideas how to address this problem regarding national budgetary policies, see: I Pernice, M Wendel, L Otto, K Bettge, M Mlynarski and M Schwarz, *Die Krise demokratisch überwinden. A Democratic Solution to the Crisis* (Baden-Baden, Nomos, 2012) 115 et seq.

[14] J Neyer, *The Justification of Europe. A Political Theory of Supranational Integration* (Oxford, Oxford University Press 2012) 4, arguing that the EU helps to remedy the democratic deficits of the Member States.

[15] See already: J Habermas, *The Divided West* (Cambridge, Polity Press, 2006) 176: 'Nation states … encumber each other with the external effects of decisions that impinge on third parties that had no say in the decision-making process. Hence, states cannot escape the need for regulation and coordination in the expanding horizon of a world society that is increasingly self-programming, even at the cultural level.' See also C Joerges, 'Unity in Diversity as Europe's Vocation and Conflicts Law as Europe's Constitutional Form', LEQS Paper 28/2010 (revised April 2013) 21–22, with more references.

[16] Lindseth (n 5) following footnote 4.

III. THE GFCC AND THE CONSTITUTIONAL BOUNDARIES OF EUROPEAN INTEGRATION

Contrary to several political statements, including some by representatives of the GFCC, notably its president, this Court has not (yet) set clear and definitive boundaries to European integration and to any new steps, in particular, deemed necessary to ensure the stability of the euro. The concern of the GFCC is rather to ensure that the democratic powers exercised by the German Bundestag are not limited to an extent that renders national elections meaningless for German citizens, and so threatens the fundamental right of these citizens to participate effectively in the exercise of political power. This is why the Court has admitted constitutional complaints against the ratification of the Treaties of Maastricht and of Lisbon, as well as—more recently—against the ESM and the Fiscal Compact. It has rightly rejected, however, the argument that the new EU treaties engendered a loss of national democracy, while it has accepted to some extent that the German Bundestag too readily ceded control over further developments of the treaties through the application of the built-in *passarelles*, as well as over the national budget through its unlimited consent to take on financial risks and commitments incurred within the framework of the rescue schemes, including the ESM.

For the sake of the present chapter, it suffices to refer to some of the important statements of the GFCC in order to clarify that measures necessary to ensure the stability of the euro and the functioning of the EMU are not excluded pursuant to the German Basic Law, unless such steps would result in the creation of a European federal state, which the Court considers contrary to what it understands to be the constitutional identity of German statehood.[17] This was the message previously delivered in the Court's Maastricht judgment, and strongly confirmed by its judgment on the Treaty of Lisbon. Regarding the EMU, however, the Maastricht judgment was open not only concerning the limits on parliamentary control of the ECB as a consequence of the guarantee of its independence,[18] but also in terms of envisaging new steps towards a fully fledged EMU if needed to safeguard its functioning as a stability union. This was confirmed in the recent judgment on the ESM, where the Court holds:

> Article 79 (3) of the Basic Law does not guarantee the unchanged further existence of the law in force but those structures and procedures which keep the democratic process open and, in this context, safeguard parliament's overall budgetary responsibility. Already in its Maastricht judgment, the Federal Constitutional Court held that, in

[17] See GFCC, case BVerfGE 123, 267 Lisbon, judgment of 30 June 2009 para 228: '[I]ntegration into a free community neither requires submission removed from constitutional limitation and control nor the forgoing one's own identity. The Basic Law does not grant powers to bodies acting on behalf of Germany to abandon the right to self-determination of the German people in the form of Germany's sovereignty under international law by joining a federal state.' For a more integration-oriented interpretation of the identity, see I Pernice, 'Der Schutz nationaler Identität in der Europäischen Union' (2011) *Archiv des öffentlichen Rechts* 185-221.

[18] GFCC, case BVerfGE 89, 155 Maastricht, judgment of 12 October 1993, para 154.

> order to comply with the stability mandate, a continuous further development of the monetary union may be necessary if otherwise the conception of the monetary union, which had been designed as a stability union, would be departed from (see BVerfGE 89, 155, 205). If the monetary union cannot be achieved in its original structure through the valid integration programme, new political decisions are needed as to how to proceed further (see BVerfGE 89, 155, 207; 97, 350, 369). It is for the legislature to decide how possible weaknesses of the monetary union are to be counteracted by amending European Union law.[19]

Nothing is said about what kind of political decisions would be acceptable and which others would not. Yet, the safeguard of the 'parliament's overall budgetary responsibility' has clearly to be ensured, including 'those structures and procedures which keep the democratic process open'. This does not, however, exclude any constraint on the discretion of the parliament. The Court clarifies what the limits are:

> The principle of democracy under Article 20(1) and (2) of the Basic Law, which is oriented towards fundamental legal reversibility, may also be violated by a long-term restriction of budget autonomy by the transfer of essential budgetary decisions to bodies of a supranational or international organisation or to other states, or by the assumption of corresponding obligations under international law.[20]

It follows that a transfer of essential budgetary decisions to the EU would infringe what is meant by the 'parliament's overall budgetary responsibility'. Nevertheless, the Court admits that certain restrictions have been introduced, and it gives the example of the debt brake introduced in Germany by the constitutional amendment of 2009:

> [I]t is not anti-democratic from the outset for the budget legislature to be bound by a particular budget and fiscal policy (see BVerfGE 79, 311 <331 ff>; 119, 96 <137 ff>). By putting into specific terms and objectively tightening the rules for borrowing by Federal and *Länder* governments (in particular Article 109(3) and (5), Article 109a, Article 115 of the Basic Law new, Article 143d(1) of the Basic Law), the constitution-amending legislature made it clear that a constitutional commitment on the part of the parliaments and thus a palpable restriction of their budgetary power to act may be necessary precisely in order to preserve the democratic power to shape affairs for the body politic in the long term.[21]

Instead of excluding a substantial adaptation of the EMU based upon the lessons learned from the financial crisis, the Court adds that 'the commitment of the budget legislature to a particular budget and fiscal policy may also be made under European Union law or international law'.[22] This approach thus paves the way for a moderate European framework under which margins and limits are set up in order to constrain the budgetary autonomy of the national parliaments

[19] GFCC, case 2 BvR 1390/12 ESM, judgment of 12 September 2012, para 222.
[20] Ibid, para 223.
[21] Ibid, para 224.
[22] Ibid, para 225.

if needed to preserve the overall stability of the currency and if such measures contribute in the long run to securing the freedom of democratically elected parliaments to take political action.

The dangers that uncoordinated and incoherent national economic policies pose to the budgetary autonomy and the freedom of action of the parliament in each of the individual Member States of the eurozone has been mentioned above. Against the backdrop of these dangers it is therefore the principle of democracy itself which requires new structures and powers at the European level to ensure that legally binding decisions are taken in a democratically sufficient manner to ensure convergence of the economies, and the economic and social cohesion required for a functioning monetary system. I herewith borrow from Jürgen Habermas's explanation of the conceptual connection between popular sovereignty and state sovereignty:

> In view of a politically unregulated growth in the complexity of world society which is placing increasingly narrow systemic restrictions on the scope for action of nation states, the requirement to extend political decision-making capabilities beyond national borders follows from the normative meaning of democracy itself.[23]

IV. A FRAMEWORK FOR EUROPEAN ECONOMIC AND FISCAL POLICIES

A legal framework for a European economic and fiscal policy is therefore needed to allow for democratically legitimated and effective governance ensuring that national economies develop towards a coherent and competitive system with a stable currency and the necessary convergence of economic and social conditions throughout the EU. But how can this framework be shaped without questioning the national 'parliament's overall budgetary responsibility'? Providing for a debt brake in the national constitutions of all eurozone Member States, as required under the Fiscal Compact, is certainly an important first step. Preventive surveillance of national budget plans as part and parcel of the 'European Semester', as well as a system to provide early information about substantial reform programmes to enable timely co-ordination at the European level may be helpful tools. Co-ordination and surveillance without binding decisions, however, do not seem to be sufficient for ensuring either fiscal discipline or the convergence of national economies.

Whatever the solutions to be found may be, the first concern must be to remedy the 'democratic failure', as Maduro puts it, and to provide for meaningful democratic processes in order to guarantee that citizens not only take ownership of the EU but also sense that they have a say in its politics. Most of the official papers and proposals submitted on the subject take up democracy as

[23] J Habermas, *The Crisis of the European Union. A Response* (Cambridge, Polity Press, 2012) 15. A similar approach seems to guide also Neyer (n 14) 4.

their final point.[24] The road ahead towards substantial reforms, however, starts with democracy; citizens' trust in the EU depends not on promises but on the practical experience that their concerns are taken seriously by the competent authorities and ultimately reflected in the legislation and decisions enacted. In this respect, important steps can be taken even without amendments to the treaties (see Section IV.A below). Only on this basis, however, can a revision of the treaties remedy the asymmetry of the EMU to the extent needed to ensure the functioning and stability of the common currency (see Section IV.B below). Economic and fiscal policies at the EU level that have an impact on national budgetary and fiscal policies must, nevertheless, be rooted in and supported by an enhanced fiscal capacity of the EU, which is based upon some powers for taxation and other policies with redistributional effects (see Section IV.C below).

A. Democratic Legitimacy

Democratic legitimacy at the European level means accountability, but is in fact more than this. If citizens cast their ballots, their scrutiny must have an impact on the policies made at the European level. To this end, it is an old but still valid proposal that each family of political parties should present a candidate for Commission president together with a valid political agenda for the EU.[25] This would give people a real choice, provided that the political composition of the European Parliament has a real impact on the politics of the EU. While it is true that the political influence not only of the Commission, and in particular its President, but also of the European Parliament is limited if the majority of the national governments in the Council and in the European Council belong to different political camps, the political influence of the Commission is often underestimated. The quasi-monopoly of the Commission to propose European legislation (Article 17(2) TEU), its role in the ordinary legislative procedure, but also its composition (with staff originating from all Member States with their diverse legal and political cultures) and the particular expertise of its staff and services give it a strong stake in the framing of European policies, whatever the political colour of the majority within the Council may be. And the President of the Commission has a strong position within the Commission. Although the Member States play a role in the process of nominating the members of the Commission, the Council needs the consent of the President of the Commission in establishing a list of the other members of the Commission selected by the Member States (Article 17(7)(2) TEU). It is up to the President to decide

[24] See eg the 'Four Presidents' Report', 'Towards a Genuine Economic and Monetary Union. Report by President of the European Council, Herman Van Rompuy', EUCO 120/12 of 26 June 2012 (democracy addressed shortly as point 4). See also the Blueprint (n 1) p 30, on the 'longer-term vision for EMU', mentioning 'as a fourth element, appropriate democratic legitimacy and accountability in decision-making'. See also: the Foreign Ministers' Group on the Future of Europe, Chairman's Statement for an Interim Report, 15 June 2012, taking up democratic legitimacy at the end (p 7).

[25] See also the Blueprint (n 1) 37.

upon the responsibilities of each of the members of the college, who are carrying out the duties devolved unto them under his authority (Article 248 TFEU). A member has to resign, according to Article 17(6)(c) TEU, if the President so requests. The President, thus, has a political say on the composition as well as on the political work of all the members of the Commission. If the candidate for presidency were nominated by the European Council with due regard to the outcome of the European elections, and elected by the European Parliament (Article 17(1) TEU), and if the Commission had to be confirmed by the European Parliament after it has heard each of the candidates for the office of a Commissioner and discussed his or her political programme in informal hearings, it would be difficult to question the legitimacy of the Commission and the political powers conferred upon it. European elections, already politically meaningful, would be more meaningful were there a real choice of candidates and political agendas for the electorate to chose between. And this political impact could be further enhanced by a merger of the offices of the President of the Commission and that of the European Council. This 'double-hatted' person would not only give the EU a more personal face vis-à-vis the citizens as well as in foreign affairs, but the President of the EU would also set the political agenda of the EU and be accountable to the citizens of the EU represented in the European Parliament. For the first time, with this merger of offices, the President of the European Council would not only be controlled by the members of the European Council—each accountable to their respective national parliament—but would also be directly accountable to the European Parliament.[26]

These innovations are possible, as we know, even without any revision of the EU treaties. Other steps, namely provision for a direct control of the institutions in charge of the supervision and co-ordination of economic policies and national budgetary policies by the European Parliament, and measures in favour of a better structured interparliamentary co-operation including representation of each others' representatives in the budgetary commissions of the national parliaments,[27] may necessitate a revision of the treaties.

It seems to be a question of democracy not to exceed the powers conferred on the EU by the treaties, even in the case of apparent need, but rather to proceed to the revision necessary, in particular, with regard to the provisions of Articles 121 and 126 TFEU and the Growth and Stability Pact. Although it is regrettable that the existing provisions do not allow for an efficient European co-ordination,

[26] See already I Pernice, 'Democratic Leadership in Europe: The European Council and the President of the Union', in I Pernice and JM Beneyto Pérez (eds), *The Government of Europe—Which Institutional Design for the European Union?* (Baden-Baden, Nomos, 2004) 31, 38, 47–50; see also Pernice (n 10) 136 et seq.

[27] Such measures are envisaged in the Blueprint (n 1) 35 et seq. For more details, see Pernice et al (n 10) 45 et seq, 117 et seq; with other references I Pernice, 'What Future(s) of Democratic Governance in Europe: Learning from the Crisis', in: *European Parliament Directorate General for Internal Policies. Policy Department C: Citizens' Rights and Constitutional Affairs, Challenges of Multi-tier Governance in the European Union. Effectiveness, Efficiency and Legitimacy. Compendium of Notes*, PE 474.438 (2013) 4, 22, 24.

disciplining and sanctioning of national policies, the balance established by the TFEU cannot be modified by measures of secondary legislation such as the six-pack or the two-pack. New provisions on sanctions as outlined by Article 121 TFEU, the introduction of a macroeconomic imbalances procedure with enforcement provisions in the form of financial sanctions or the introduction of decision-making by reversed majority voting, cannot be based upon Article 136 TFEU (even if this would apply exclusively to the Member States whose currency is the euro). Any measure taken under this provision, as it emphasizes, must be 'in accordance with the relevant provisions of the Treaties'. Where new powers at the Union level seem to be necessary, and obligations of the Member States need to be more effectively enforced than the treaties so allow, the decision must be taken by the peoples of the Member States according to their respective constitutional procedures, and therefore a revision of the treaties is the way ahead.

Democracy is at stake, in particular, when a new fiscal capacity at the European level is to be established based upon own resources that substantially exceed the present EU budget and involve some measure of taxation collected at the European level. Where common policies have to be financed by resources provided directly by the taxpayers, ie the citizens of the Union, debates and—later on—decisions on European policies would include the costs of any policy. The present system to a large extent abstracts European policies from aspects of financing. The EU budget is very limited and will remain so under the political agreement resulting in the Multiannual Financial Framework for 2014–20.[28] But this budget is and will continue to be available without any need to consult citizens about what it is spent on. The euro amounts available are basically a matter of intergovernmental negotiation on the national contributions, though the Council needs the consent of the European Parliament (Article 312(2) TFEU). The iron principle 'no taxation without representation', however, holds true even if it is reversed: no representation without taxation.[29] This entails that democratic self-government presumes financial involvement or monetary contribution. Democracy in Europe, thus, would be enhanced, as would solidarity among the citizens of the EU, taking the form of a commitment to unite certain policies through common institutions.[30] It would also gain in value if it would include financial commitments by the citizens to make such policies possible. As long as finances remain a matter of a struggle over national contributions, each Member State will find ways to make sure that not only are contributions low, but also that the lion's share of its monetary contributions will be diverted at the European level to flow back into its own pocket. To be a net payer in the EU is politically difficult to defend at national level, and this would be even

[28] See ec.europa.eu/budget/mff/index_en.cfm.

[29] Similarly: Maduro (n 10) p 14. See also F Fabbrini in this volume (Chapter 19).

[30] For more details, see I Pernice, 'Solidarität in Europa. Eine Ortsbestimmung im Verhältnis zwischen Bürger, Staat und Europäischer Union', in C Calliess (ed), *Europäische Solidarität und nationale Identität—Überlegungen im Kontext der Krise im Euroraum* (Tübingen, Mohr Siebeck, 2013) 25–26, also available as WHI-Paper 01/2013, 19.

more true with regard to direct transfers to the benefit of other Member States. The answer, thus, is that democracy requires taxation at the European level to be understood as the flip-side of European policies, both to be decided through democratic procedures at the same level. This is what makes solidarity a matter not among states but among people in a democratic polity.

B. Overcoming the Asymmetry of the EMU

On the basis of more transparent and efficient procedures for democratic control and legitimization of European policies to be introduced with the European elections of 2014, new provisions in the EU treaties can be envisaged to complete the EMU and to protect its economic and social sustainability. This entails appropriate powers to adopt the legislation needed to establish a European Banking Union including the stated Commission proposals for a Single Supervisory Mechanism (SSM) of 19 March 2013,[31] for a Single Resolution Mechanism (SRM) of 10 July 2013,[32] and perhaps for a future legislative proposal on a supranational Deposit Guarantee Scheme. More importantly, however, the economic and financial policies of the Member States need more than extended and deeper co-ordination and supervision, as suggested by the Commission's Blueprint,[33] and more than a European framework for systematic surveillance of macroeconomic imbalances and competitiveness developments, as now provided for and given effect to under the 'excessive imbalance procedure' by the six-pack.

In a single market accompanied by a monetary union the lesson to be drawn from the financial crisis is that general obligations of the Member States to 'regard their economic policies as a matter of common concern' and to 'conduct them with a view to contribution to the achievement of the objectives of the Treaties', as provided for by Articles 120 and 121(1) TFEU, are not respected, at least in critical situations, and thus simply do not suffice. To the extent that it necessary to sustain the euro these policies have to become shared European policies to be implemented at both the European and national levels. The aforementioned Blueprint gives us a hint at the right direction. It envisages 'progressive further integration of the euro area towards a full banking, fiscal and economic union' in a long-term perspective, and the Commission recognizes that this will 'require

[31] See the Statement by Commissioner Michel Barnier following the trilogue agreement on the creation of the Single Supervisory Mechanism for the eurozone, MEMO/13/251 of 19 March 2013.

[32] Proposal for a Regulation establishing uniform rules and a uniform procedure for the resolution of credit institutions and certain investment firms in the framework of a Single Resolution Mechanism and a Single Bank Resolution Fund and amending Regulation (EU) No 1093/2010 of the European Parliament and of the Council, COM(2013) 0520 final.

[33] For the long-term perspective (five years and more), see Blueprint (n 1) 12 et seq: 'progressive pooling of sovereignty and thus responsibility as well as solidarity competencies to the European level, the establishment of an autonomous euro area budget providing for a fiscal capacity for the EMU to support Member States in the absoption of shocks … a deeply integrated economic and fiscal governance framework'. The latter is meant to 'allow a common issueance of public debt, which would enhance the functioning of the markets and the conduct of monetary policy'.

parallel steps towards a political union with a reinforced democratic legitimacy and accountability'.[34] New instruments proposed by the Commission in short-term perspective, such as the proposed Convergence and Competitiveness Instrument (CCI)[35] and the 'ex ante coordination of plans for major economic policy reforms',[36] would provide for financial assistance for Member States contracting internal structural reform plans and make concrete ideas already included in the Fiscal Compact, respectively. Yet, they do not affect the national responsibility for the economic policies of the Member States and are not likely to achieve what is necessary. In particular, they do not provide for binding legislation or decision-making, judicial review and enforcement under the infringement procedure of Article 258 TFEU.[37] But what processes would ensure the democratic legitimacy of such reform measures? What would happen if a Member State does not acquiesce to signing an agreement on internal reforms because of the lack of public support within the country? What would happen if such an agreed or co-ordinated action programme is not implemented? These questions remain open, as does that about the origin of the funds needed to implement the CCI.

The obligation of Member States under Article 3 of the Fiscal Compact to lay down a balanced-budget rule and to establish an automatic correction mechanism in their national constitutions, or at a similar normative level to set an internally binding limit for public expenses, is an extraordinary and unprecedented measure that is aimed at achieving budgetary discipline. It seems to be the first time ever that the introduction of such important provisions in national constitutions has been agreed upon, and has thus become mandatory under international law. To integrate it into European primary law would be a great step forward. The common commitment to financial discipline and austerity policies, however, limits the capacity of the Member States to implement growth initiatives. Whether such mandatory restrictive measures at the constitutional level are sustainable, if they are not supplemented by a common scheme ensuring that not only growth and competitiveness of the national economies, but also

[34] Blueprint (n 1) 12. For more concrete details, see ibid, 30 et seq, 35 et seq. For a critical and differentiated view, see Lindseth (n 5) following footnote 6, who asserts that increased surveillance and control of national budgetary decisions and certain aspects of a banking union (bank supervision and harmonized bank resolution rules) fall on the democratically legitimate side of 'delegated' supranational authority while the delegation of autonomous fiscal powers (taxing, borrowing and spending authority) to the EU, at least on a scale that would have a real impact on the efforts to ameliorate the crisis, fall on the far side of what he deems a possible 'reconciliation' of integration and democracy.

[35] Blueprint (n 1) p 21; Communication from the Commission to the European Parliament and the Council, 'Towards a Deep and Genuine Economic and Monetary Union. The Introduction of a Convergence and Competitiveness Instrument', COM(2013) 165 final.

[36] Blueprint (n 1) p 20; Communication from the Commission to the European Parliament and the Council, 'Towards a Deep and Genuine Economic and Monetary Union. Ex ante coordination of plans for major economic policy reforms', COM(2013) 166 final.

[37] For new judicial powers of the CJEU, see also the Blueprint (n 1) 27, on harmonization of national budgetary laws with a competence of the CJEU in the case of non-compliance, and 39 'deleting Art 126 paragraph 10 TFEU'.

in case of asymmetric shocks—at least—sufficient financial flexibility is provided for, remains a matter of debate.

What seems to be necessary is to understand that the existence and the proper functioning of a single market with a common currency cannot be reconciled with the wish to maintain and conduct autonomous economic and financial policies in the now 28 Member States. Nor can the reinforcement of budgetary and economic integration envisaged by the Commission's Blueprint in a medium-term perspective achieve what is needed. It would certainly be nice for Member States in economic distress to move 'towards more mutualization of financial risk'. But this is not the solution even if European control over national budgetary policies were to be enhanced by legally binding decisions of the Council, even if the monitoring and co-ordination of national economic policies under the two-pack was supplemented by the power of the EU institutions 'to require a revision of individual decisions of budget execution in line with European commitments', and if a 'clear competence for the EU level to harmonize national budgetary laws' was introduced, as proposed in the Blueprint.[38] The concept of command and control, even if it is based upon common principles and commonly agreed objectives, is not a solution for the EU. Even taking into account the financial incentives set within the CCI, the funding for which the Commission considers to be ensured by new powers of the scheme to 'resort to borrowing', or with the introduction of a redemption fund along the lines proposed by the German Council of Economic Experts,[39] the possible damage control is marginal as the grand design and structure of the system is bound to fail.

As long as Member States see themselves as 'owning' economic and financial policies, and as long as the principle of autonomy governs the system, new and even more violent divergences in structure and results are the inevitable outcome, whatever the governments politically agree to at the European level. Although economic policies might be considered as a 'common concern', national interests will and must prevail as long as the policies remain national and are legitimized only by the national electorates. How can competing national economies sustain a single market? Competition means that some are successful, others fail. And if one or some fail, the crisis shows, the system as such is at risk. Competition between systems, thus, cannot be the rule within the EU, unless it is serving only as a learning process based upon best practices, and acts within the limits imposed by the need to keep the system running and to make it more efficient for the benefit of all EU citizens, and therefore more competitive on the global markets.

The Blueprint, therefore, rightly envisages in a long-term perspective a move towards a fully fledged banking union and a fully fledged fiscal and economic union.[40] It is not the place here to repeat what the Commission suggests. What

[38] Ibid, 26 et seq.
[39] Ibid, 27 et seq.
[40] Ibid, 30 et seq.

seems to be relevant so far is to know whether, and if so, to what extent, the proposals would comply with the constitutional requirements set out above and what other European instruments could be considered for ensuring the necessary convergence of national economic and fiscal policies and for meeting the challenges of the EMU today and in the long run.

The Commission proposes, first, a 'central budget providing for a fiscal capacity with a stabilisation function', as a 'tool to support adjustment to asymmetric shocks, facilitating stronger economic integration and convergence and avoiding the setting up of long-term transfer flows'.[41] This would give some flexibility to the European markets as a whole as well as to the diverse parts of the European economy. It would operate like an insurance system and imply payments from and to national budgets, but it would not generally constrain the budgetary autonomy of each of the national parliaments. Nor would a new taxation power at the European level or a power to raise revenue by indebting itself on the markets involve such constraints, as long as these powers are limited in size and regarding the object. Finally, new provisions for an EMU Treasurer within the Commission as a Vice-President responsible for the organization of the 'shared policies undertaken with the common fiscal capacity', as proposed,[42] do not substantially touch upon the powers of the national parliaments.

However, where legally binding decisions on economic and fiscal policies implying specific measures directly applicable within the Member States are taken at EU level, the limits set out by the jurisprudence of the national constitutional courts become relevant. Competences for economic and fiscal policies, even social policies at the European, level do not imply that all relevant decisions in all areas are taken by European institutions. Nor does it mean that they do not leave substantial political discretion for the national authorities. The principles of subsidiarity and proportionality are the guiding principles and legally enforceable boundaries for setting up the right frame as well as for the appropriate exercise of powers conferred upon the European institutions. Only to the extent that common action is required as an expression of rational solidarity among all citizens of the EU,[43] and in particular to the extent that the stability of the euro and the functioning of the EMU so require, may European economic and fiscal policies that impinge on the Member States' fiscal and economic autonomy be implemented at this level.[44] Important decisions in the area of economic policies are already a matter of European institutions,[45] such

[41] Ibid, 31.

[42] Ibid, 34.

[43] Pernice (n 24) WHI-paper 01/13, 16, 18 et seq.

[44] For a view that 'substitutes' the normative logic of 'burden-sharing' for the notion of solidarity, see Lindseth (n 5) following footnote 57.

[45] See the analysis of I Pernice and F Hoffmeister, 'The Division of Economic Policy Powers between the European Community and its Member States—Status Quo and Proposals de lege ferenda', in A von Bogdandy, S C Mavroidis and Y Mény (eds), *European Integration and International Co-ordination, Studies in Transnational Economic Law in Honour of Claus-Dieter Ehlermann* (The Hague, Kluwer, 2002) 363–82.

as regarding competition and state aid policies, structural and cohesion policy, or social policies and foreign trade, including, since the Treaty of Lisbon, direct investments. Thus, the co-ordination of economic policies under Article 121 TFEU and of employment policies under Articles 145–50 TFEU only complete the picture. The ESM and the Fiscal Compact provide for an additional framework for participating Member States. Yet, bolder steps are necessary, but must be limited to what cannot be done effectively at the national level in order to ensure the stability of the euro.

This is what the Humboldt Group, in proposing 'a democratic solution to the crisis', ventured, referring to the road traffic model previously suggested by Guy Verhofstadt. Similarly to how we distinguish different types of roads—interstates, long-distance highways, country roads, city avenues and narrow streets—and the actual setup of a specific road—the path and direction it may take—we can distinguish the various and diverse forms of political action—eg the open method of co-ordination or the community method with its directives, regulations or decisions—and the concrete definition of the policy to be implemented.[46] It is clear that democratic legitimacy must be more directly and visibly supplied, the more a decision impacts on, figuratively speaking, the driver's choices and consequently limits the room for manoeuvring of national budgetary authorities. The application of the ordinary legislative procedure under Article 294 TFEU may have to be coupled with close interparliamentary co-operation providing awareness and understanding between the national and the European parliaments as well as among national parliaments and their budgetary committees of their specific needs and concerns. Without going too far into the details of such collaboration, the guiding principles for setting up an appropriate European framework of binding economic and fiscal policies may include the following:

1. Decisions setting up common broad guidelines for European economic and employment policies,[47] including country- or region-specific targets and provisions, and setting up a binding framework for such policies at the European and national levels that should be adopted under the ordinary legislative procedure to be supported by an intense interparliamentary dialogue at the preparatory stages.
2. Monitoring and multilateral surveillance regarding the implementation of such guidelines by the national authorities are an exercise to be led by the Commission under the special authority of its Vice-President appointed as the Treasurer. On his report, European and national parliaments' budgetary commissions should be asked for comments before the Commission proposes, if necessary, appropriate action to be taken by the Council. The European Parliament as well as the national parliament of the Member State(s) concerned may veto such action and refer with reasons the matter to the European Council for final decision.

[46] Pernice et al (n 10) 131–35.

[47] The Blueprint (n 1) 27, 37, rightly emphasizes the need for such 'integrated guidelines'.

3. A fiscal capacity of the EU should be established for providing the necessary financial flexibility and responsiveness of the EU and its Member States in the case of asymmetric shocks, based upon an insurance system with a supplement financed by the EU budget. The Treasurer is responsible for the management of this system, including the submission of proposals for decisions on contributions and payments, taking account of the cyclical developments in each part of the EU or of the Union as a whole. Such decisions shall be taken in accordance with the provisions governing the ordinary legislative procedure.
4. The overall budget of the EU shall be supplemented by additional own resources increasing the budget up to a limit of 3 per cent of EU GDP, to be financed by genuine European taxes introduced under new powers to be conferred on the EU to enact and collect taxes that are specifically related to EU activities. The revenue from such taxes shall enable the EU substantially to increase the operational amounts available to the European structural funds and, in particular, the cohesion fund, and to finance a new stabilization fund.[48] Any assistance or funding through these funds shall be supportive of structural reforms and subject to strict conditionality under agreed adjustment programmes, as appropriate, to avoid moral hazard.[49]
5. Legislative acts and decisions taken under the new provisions and their implementation shall be subject to unlimited judicial review under Articles 258–60, 263–65 and 267 TFEU.

C. Taxation and Redistributional Policies

The proposed increase in the EU budget should, as mentioned, proceed hand in hand with new powers of the EU to raise European taxes. Such taxes could include the financial transaction tax, or as Maduro suggests with a number of compelling reasons including social justice and fairness, 'even a broader tax on financial or banking activities', an additional corporate tax and a carbon emissions tax. Such European taxes would not only feed the European budget but also limit tax competition among Member States, make those who benefit most from the single market contribute most to its functioning, and could even help to avoid corporate income being exempt from austerity policies in some Member States because of the fear that these policies would drive companies and capital away.[50] The choice of the areas of European taxation, in any event, should be

[48] This is taking up some of the ideas of the Blueprint (n 1) 31–32 on the Central Budget. The operation of such a fund could be a way also to implement a scheme under which the EU only provides for collateral for debts to be issued by the Member States; see M Maduro, 'A New Governance for the European Union and the Euro: Democracy and Justice', in *European Parliament Directorate General for Internal Policies* (n 27) 27, 39 et seq.

[49] Similar to the conditions proposed by the Blueprint (n 1) 31–32, for the EMU-level stabilization-tool.

[50] Maduro (n 41) 41 et seq.

made with due regard to the benefits the EU offers for certain activities and groups of people. European taxation, thus, would not, at least in sum, burden the general public or specific national economies, but could have a positive redistributional effect and constitute an expression of solidarity among people in Europe without affecting specific national budgets.

Enhancing European solidarity through common schemes for unemployment or health insurance at the European level could also indirectly contribute not only to the stabilization and recovery of weak economies with high unemployment but also encourage and facilitate mobility. A common European social security scheme for migrant workers, even on a voluntary basis, would be greatly beneficial for the EU as a whole, since bureaucratic and financial disadvantages for people making use of the market freedoms, and in particular the freedom to move, could be avoided.

V. TOWARDS A NEW SOCIAL CONTRACT AT THE UNION LEVEL

To fix the acute problems of the EU by measures along the lines discussed in this chapter is not a matter for a simplified treaty revision procedure. It is an undertaking of great constitutional importance and impact, but it is in the common interest of all EU citizens. It is urgent because of the fragility of the present situation and it should involve the entire citizenry of the EU. Proposals on how to overcome the crisis and provide for a sustainable system should be part of the political agendas in the electoral campaigns of all families of parties participating in the European elections; details should be discussed in all political forums at all levels. The task is too serious to be left to governments, diplomats and technocrats in charge of negotiating another revision of the treaties.

What is needed is the conclusion of a new social contract at the EU level, including all citizens of the Member States determined to organize their common European future most effectively and democratically. This political process has to be initiated long before the electoral campaigns for the European elections are launched, and the Blueprint of the Commission is meant to start the debate. It has in fact already started some time ago, among others with lectures held at the Humboldt-University, Berlin since the outbreak of the crisis.[51] Eventually, the European Parliament opened the debate in 2012 with its October workshop on the challenges facing multi-tier governance in Europe.[52] The four presidents of the European Council, the European Commission, the Eurogroup and the ECB

[51] See I Pernice and R Schwarz (eds), *Europa in der Welt—Von der Finanzkrise zur Reform der Union* (Baden-Baden, Nomos, 2013), forthcoming. See also the speeches available at the website of the Walter Hallstein Institute for European Constitutional Law (Forum Constitutionis Europeae, FCE, and Humboldt-Reden zu Europa, HRE), available at www.whi-berlin.eu.

[52] See my conclusions, n 21.

have drafted reform proposals, as did a group of foreign ministers of numerous Member States.[53]

David Cameron's Bloomberg speech of 23 January 2013[54] can be taken as a positive signal too, though the UK is generally seen as one of the most sceptic Member States of all. In his speech, Cameron confirms that his country sees itself as 'a European power', he wants 'the European Union to be a success', and he wants 'a relationship between Britain and the EU that keeps us in it'. But he criticizes some aspects of the Union, stressing that 'more of the same will produce more of the same—less competitiveness, less growth, fewer jobs'. His vision to condition the EU for the twenty-first century is competitiveness of the single market, which needs to be completed in terms of services, energy and digital industries, 'the engines of a modern economy'. He does not see Britain as a member of the eurozone. He does not want 'an ever closer union among the peoples of Europe', though Britain has ratified the TFEU and subscribed to this goal. His vision is a 'flexible union', where power can also flow back to Member States. Thus, he has launched 'a balance of competence review', to give us, as he says, 'an informed and objective analysis of where the EU helps and where it hampers'. Is this unreasonable? Should we not ask this question every time when adopting new legislation? Cameron clearly gives expression to what the principle of subsidiarity is about. Contrary to the concepts agreed and laid down in Articles 10 and 11 TEU, for him 'national parliaments … are, and will remain, the true source of real democratic legitimacy and accountability in the EU'. But he is contradicting himself with his critique of the process of integration after Britain has joined the 'common market'. People, he states, 'feel that the EU is heading in a direction that they never signed up to. … They see Treaty after Treaty changing the balance between Member States and the EU. And they were never given a say.' If this is true, can the national parliaments having ratified these treaties really be the 'true source of real democratic legitimacy' as said before? A referendum is what Cameron promises to his people for any treaty revision to come. He sees the EU emerging from the eurozone crisis as 'a very different body' and proposes to work on shaping the future of the EU so to allow 'a real choice' for the British people on the 'in' or 'out' of a Union so adjusted, with certain powers flowing back to European states, as far as they prove to be misallocated at the European level. Other powers may be added to the EU, if it becomes clear that they are needed to make it function better. Hence, Cameron has also launched a debate, for a long process of negotiation and, finally, a referendum on continued UK membership of a fundamentally reshaped Union.

We could learn from this in some respects. Should a new Union not be adopted by a—parallel—referendum in all the Member States, or better by a

[53] See above, n 18.

[54] D Cameron, EU speech at Bloomberg, 23 January 2013, www.gov.uk/government/speeches/eu-speech-at-bloomberg.

European referendum?[55] Lots of provisions would have to be simplified to make them understandable for the people, before they can reasonably vote on a new treaty. This could be a new European social contract and give the EU a legitimacy that some do not believe the treaties' 'simple' ratification procedure, which rests in the hands of the national parliaments according to their respective constitutional procedures, can provide.

The present collection of contributions might be considered as one more step in the new debate and, hopefully, stimulate further European-wide discussions on the future of Europe.

[55] On this option, see I Pernice, 'Referendum sur la Constitution pour l'Europe: Conditions Risques Implications', in C Kaddous and A Auer (eds), *Les principes fondamentaux de la Constitution européenne*, (Brussels, Bruylant, 2006) 301–15, also available as WHI-paper 07/06.

15

National Parliaments' Say on the New EU Budgetary Constraints: The Case of Spain and Ireland

SONIA PIEDRAFITA

I. INTRODUCTION

THE ROLE THAT national parliaments have played in the adoption process of the new EU budgetary constraints is relevant not only because the new measures can affect the power that parliaments wield over the state budgets but also because parliaments have traditionally been considered one of the main sources of the EU's democratic legitimacy. Since the first steps towards political union in 1992, there have been more and more initiatives to enhance the role of national parliaments in the EU decision-making process, culminating in the Lisbon provisions on the role of the national parliaments in general and the control of the subsidiarity and the proportionality principles in particular. The analysis of national parliaments' say on the new EU budgetary constraints will shed some light on how these new opportunities are being used to influence EU decision-making and show whether the legitimacy of the new measures was contested by the citizens' representatives at national level.

Given their fragile financial situation, Ireland and Spain were among the group of Member States most affected by the new budgetary rules and predictably willing to raise objections. They constitute, therefore, crucial cases to analyse the degree to which these decisions were contested at national level. The selection of Ireland and Spain will also allow us to compare two Member States with different systems of parliamentary scrutiny of EU affairs. Although both were viewed as having a weak scrutiny system in the 1990s, Ireland made some progress during the 2000s, whereas changes in Spain have been much more limited. Nevertheless, this chapter will also give a general overview of the experience of other national parliaments with a stronger involvement in EU affairs.

In particular, this chapter will look into how Ireland and Spain ratified the Treaty on Stability, Coordination and Governance in the Economic and Monetary Union (TSCG) and incorporated the 'golden rule' in their legal orders, examining as well the parliamentary debates and the position of the political parties. It will also analyse the subsidiary check—and participation in political dialogue with the Commission—that the Cortes Generales and the Oireachtas made of the so-called two-pack regulations (namely, on monitoring and assessing draft budgetary plans and ensuring the correction of excessive deficits and on enhanced surveillance of eurozone members experiencing or threatened with financial difficulties). Section II reviews the concept of democratic legitimacy and the role of national parliaments in the EU. Section III examines how national parliaments, in particular the Cortes Generales and the Orteachtas, have reacted to the new provisions in the Lisbon Treaty. Section IV compares the ratification process of the TSCG in both countries, providing as well a general overview of the experience in other Member States. Section V analyses the subsidiarity checks carried out for the two-pack regulations.

II. DEMOCRATIC LEGITIMACY AND NATIONAL PARLIAMENTS IN THE EU

Political legitimacy is a contentious concept, especially when referred to non-state entities such as the EU. From a Weberian perspective, a political order can be considered legitimate when it is viewed as 'valid', ie when actions in accordance with it are considered to be normatively right. Beetham distinguished three standards of legitimacy that apply to liberal democracies:[1] *output* legitimacy, ie their capacity to deliver results and improve citizens' welfare; *procedural* legitimacy, ie respect for the democratic principles of representation and checks and balances; and *substantial* legitimacy, ie the protection and promotion of collective values and the common identity. For case of the EU, Scharpf agglutinated these three components into two: *input* and *output* legitimacy.[2] In order to be legitimate, the EU political system, institutions and decisions must be democratic and effective, ie they have to reflect the will of the people ('government by the people') and promote the common welfare ('government for the people'). National parliaments are traditionally seen as an important source of democratic legitimacy in the EU as they can aggregate and channel citizens' demands into the European decision-making and control their governments' actions in the Council. In turn, citizens can sanction their work in the national elections. National parliaments also contribute to bringing EU affairs into national debates.

Initially, the European integration process seemed to be relegating national parliaments, but the need to enhance their role soon became inescapable. The transfer of competences to the European level progressively reduced the legislative remit of national parliaments and affected the executive–legislative balance in Member States. National parliaments had no representation, or direct

[1] D Beetham, *The Legitimation of Power* (Basingstoke, Macmillam, 1991).

[2] F Scharpf, *Governing in Europe, Effective and Democratic* (Oxford, Oxford University Press, 1999).

access, to EU decision-making, and many times they lacked the information, resources and expertise properly to control their governments' actions in the EU.[3] Concerns over the democratic deficit of the EU became particularly relevant in the early 1990s in view of the stronger political and economic union that the EU was forging. In order to improve the parliamentary scrutiny of EU affairs at national level, Declaration 13 of the Maastricht Treaty (1992) foresaw in a non-binding commitment that 'the governments of the Member States will ensure that national Parliaments receive Commission proposals for legislation in good time for information or possible examination'.

The reflection group in preparation of the 1996 Intergovernmental Conference on the institutional reform reaffirmed that the main role of national parliaments in the EU was to check their governments' actions in the Council, and therefore recommended revision of the treaties to guarantee that the parliaments received the necessary information in time.[4] A protocol annexed to the Amsterdam Treaty (1997) established that legislative proposals would be included in the agenda of the Council for discussion at least six weeks after being delivered to the Member States by the European Commission, 'so that the government of each Member State *may* ensure that its own national parliament receives them as appropriate'. Therefore, the Commission had the duty to guarantee a period of time before the discussion of the proposal, but the timely reception of all legislative drafts remained the responsibility of the national governments.

The Treaty of Lisbon, which entered into force in December 2009, raised expectations about the scrutiny of EU affairs by national parliaments and their participation in EU decision-making. It was the first time that the national parliaments had been included in the body of a treaty. The Treaty of the European Union (TEU) states that national parliaments must ensure compliance of the EU with the principle of subsidiarity (Article 5) and hold their governments accountable for their actions in the Council (Article 10). Parliaments can also contribute to the good functioning of the EU (Article 12) by taking part in the evaluation mechanisms for the implementation of the EU policies in the area of freedom, security and justice in accordance with Article 70 TFEU, in the political monitoring of Europol, and in the evaluation of Eurojust's activities in accordance with Articles 85 and 88 TFEU, in the revision procedures of the treaties in accordance with Article 48 TEU and in the interparliamentary co-operation between national parliaments and with the European Parliament. They will also be notified of applications for accession to the EU, in accordance with Article 49 TEU.

The Protocol on National Parliaments (No 1 in the Lisbon Treaty) broadened the scope of the documents to be forwarded to the legislative assemblies

[3] D Judge, 'The Failure of National Parliaments?' (1995) 18 *West European Politics* 79. R Katz (ed), *The European Parliament, The National Parliaments and European Integration* (Oxford, Oxford University Press, 1999).

[4] Reflection Group, *Report by the Reflection Group: A Strategy for Europe* (Brussels, 5 December 1995).

to include all draft legislative acts, consultation documents, the annual legislative programme and any other instrument of legislative planning of the Commission, the Council's agendas and minutes, and the Annual Report of the Court of Auditors. It also increased to an eight-week period the time between a draft legislative act being made available (by the EU institutions) to national parliaments in the official languages of the EU and the date when it is placed on a provisional agenda for the Council for its adoption or for adoption of a position under a legislative procedure. A new Protocol (No 2) on the application of the principles of subsidiarity and proportionality established the conditions for the application of these principles and set out a system for monitoring possible breaches of the subsidiarity principle. Within eight weeks, any legislative chamber of the Member States may submit a reasoned opinion stating why it considers that a draft legislative act does not comply with the principle of subsidiarity. If the number of opinions that find there is a breach of the subsidiarity principle are at least one-third of the total (counting double those from unicameral parliaments), the proposal must be reviewed, although it can be maintained. For acts under the ordinary legislative procedure, if the number of negative opinions represents a simple majority of the votes and the Commission decides to maintain the proposal, the Council and the European Parliament have the possibility to reject it at the first reading.

One cannot dodge the fact that national parliaments are not given a veto power to block a proposal when they find there is a breach of the principle of subsidiarity and that the threshold for reviewing the proposal is very difficult to achieve given the close connection between the executive and the parliamentary majority in most Member States, the difficulties in coordinating 28 or more national parliaments, their lack of resources and their freedom to decide whether and when to carry out the scrutiny.[5] Moreover, most EU legislation is beyond the remit of this procedure, which does not apply to delegated and implementing acts or to decisions related to EU exclusive competencies or adopted by the open method of co-ordination. However, the implementation of the early warning mechanism and the subsidiarity checks triggered a wave of reforms in the parliamentary scrutiny of EU affairs across Member States. The *political dialogue* with national parliaments, launched in 2006 by the Barroso Commission, also encouraged national parliaments to submit their opinions on any aspects (not only questions of subsidiarity) of the legislative proposals and consultation documents; the European Commission committed to reply to these opinions and take their views into account.[6] This, together with the eight-week time frame and the broader scope of the documents to be received directly

[5] T Raunio, 'National Parliaments and European Integration: What We Know and Agenda for Future Research' (2009) 15 *Journal of Legislative Studies* 317.

[6] European Commission, Communication from the Commission to the European Council, 'Citizens' agenda. Delivering results for Europe', COM(2006) 211 final.

from EU institutions, may contribute to engaging parliaments earlier in the EU decision-making process and to reducing existing information asymmetries.[7]

Winzen's comparative study on the parliamentary control of EU affairs in Member States between 1999 and 2010 gives an account of these changes. On a scale of 0–3, he measured the level of parliamentary control in EU affairs in 1999 and 2010, taking into consideration their capacity to access information on EU affairs, their ability to process it and the enforceability of their resolutions.[8] As regards the access to information, he considered whether parliaments were receiving all legislative proposals, planning and consultation documents, as well as an attached memoranda from the government. To measure their capacity to process this information, he took into account the involvement of the European Affairs Committee (EAC) and the standing committees in the scrutiny, as well as whether the Member State had a scrutiny reserve in effect. Finally, he considered the extent to which the government was bound by parliamentary resolutions or mandates.

In line with previous studies, Winzen highlighted 'the good shape' of the scrutiny system in EU affairs that already existed in countries such as Denmark, Finland, Germany and Sweden in 1999.[9] In the case of Denmark, Austria and the Netherlands the enactment of the Lisbon Treaty brought about a further reinforcement of the parliamentary scrutiny of EU affairs. In Germany, the Act Extending and Strengthening the Rights of the Bundestag and the Bundesrat had to be amended after the Federal Constitutional Court ruled that it did not sufficiently safeguard parliament's participation rights in EU affairs. As Table 1 shows, parliamentary capacity to access information, to process it and to enforce its resolutions was also reinforced in the case of France, Italy, Portugal, Ireland and slightly in Greece. However, Belgium, Luxembourg and Spain did not seem to introduce any significant change, remaining at the bottom of the list.

The number of reasoned opinions sent by national parliaments to the Commission in the framework of the Political Dialogue also increased 55 per cent in 2010 and 60 per cent in 2011, reaching then a total of 622. Only a few of these opinions (64) stated a breach of the subsidiarity principle according to Protocol 2 (as was also the case in 2010), with the majority including comments on the substance of the Commission's proposals and initiatives. Only four chambers did not take part in the political dialogue in 2011 (compared to ten in the previous year). Moreover, in 2012 12 national parliaments issued reasoned opinions stating that the 'Proposal for a Council Regulation on the exercise of the right to take collective action within the context of the freedom of establishment and

[7] T Jans and S Piedrafita, 'The Role of National Parliaments in EU Decision-Making' (2009) *Eipascope* no 1, 25.

[8] T Winzen, 'National Parliamentary Control of European Affairs: A Cross-national and Longitudinal Comparison' (2012) 9 *West European Politics* 657.

[9] T Bergman, 'National Parliaments and EU Affairs Committees: Notes on Empirical Variation and Competing Explanation' (1997) 4 *Journal of European Public Policy* 373. A Maurer and W Wessels, 'National Parliaments after Amsterdam: From Slow Adapters to National Players?' in A Maurer and W Wessels (eds), *National Parliaments on their Ways to Europe: Losers or Latecomers?* (Baden-Baden, Nomos, 2001).

Table 1. Level of parliamentary control, Winzen (2012)

	1999	2010
Denmark	2.5	2.67
Finland	2.5	2.5
Germany	2.17	2.17
Sweden	1.83	1.83
Austria	1.67	1.83
UK	1.67	1.67
Netherlands	1.33	1.83
France	1	1.17
Italy	0.83	1.67
Spain	0.83	0.83
Belgium	0.67	0.67
Greece	0.67	0.83
Luxembourg	0.67	0.67
Portugal	0.67	1.5
Ireland	0.5	1.5

the freedom to provide services' breached the subsidiarity principle by overstepping national sovereignty. Interparliamentary co-operation and an effective lobbying campaign by the Danish parliament drew in parliament after parliament in opposition to the proposal. As a result, the threshold for the 'yellow card' was reached in the very last moment, forcing the Commission to initiate a review process. In January 2013, the Commission withdrew the proposal. Cooper has argued that the early warning mechanism could reinforce the capacity of national parliaments to influence EU legislation, provide a new channel of representation linking the citizens with the EU, and create a new forum for debating EU affairs, therefore becoming a 'virtual third chamber'.[10]

III. THE SCRUTINY SYSTEMS IN IRELAND AND SPAIN

A. The Houses of the Oireachtas

In Ireland, the reform of the system to scrutinize EU affairs began even before the European Convention had started its work. In order to allay concerns about EU democratic deficit after the failed referendum on the Nice Treaty in 2001, the European Union (Scrutiny) Bill was introduced in the Oireachtas, as a precursor

[10] I Cooper, 'A "Virtual Third Chamber" for the European Union? National Parliaments after the Treaty of Lisbon' (2010) 35 *West European Politics* 441.

to passing an Act making provision for reports and consultation by ministers with the Houses of the Oireachtas prior to consideration of proposals for directives, regulations, framework decisions, decisions or conventions to be adopted by the Council of Ministers. The European Union (Scrutiny) Act 2002 was finally adopted in October 2002. Under the new Act the government is legally obliged to lay copies of all EU legislative measures before both chambers together with a statement by the minister outlining the content, purpose and likely implications for Ireland. The scrutiny of EU legislative measures was carried out by a subcommittee of the Joint Committee on European Affairs until the creation of the Joint Committee on European Scrutiny in October 2007.

The signature of the Lisbon Treaty and the ratification process in Ireland raised concerns about the quality of the parliamentary scrutiny of EU affairs in the country. After the first failed referendum, a subcommittee of the Houses of the Oireachtas was established in October 2008, 'Ireland's Future in the European Union', which resulted in a report including a number of suggestions to enhance the role of the parliament in EU affairs. One year later, the Joint Committees on European Affairs and on European Scrutiny published the 'Joint Report on the Implementation of the Lisbon Treaty: Provisions on the Enhanced Role for National Parliaments', with recommendations on how to carry out the subsidiarity checks and improve interaction with the government and other national parliaments. However, in the end, only those amendments deemed indispensable were made to Irish statutory law in order to adapt it to the Lisbon provisions. Article 7 of The European Union Act 2009 amending the European Communities Acts 1972 to 2007 established that either House of the Oireachtas was entitled to pass a resolution to authorize the House to send a reasoned opinion regarding the breach of the subsidiarity principle of a draft legislative act not later than eight weeks after transmission. According to the 2007 Orders of Reference of the Joint Committee on European Scrutiny, this committee would carry out the subsidiarity checks and propose the reasoned opinions in consultation with the Joint Committee on European Affairs and any other select committees. Article 7 also provided that either chamber could, within a six-month period after notification, pass a resolution opposing the adoption of a *passerelle* clause by the Council (Article 48(7) TEU) or a measure concerning family law with cross-border implications (Article 81(3) TFEU).

The economic crisis and the subsequent bailout of the country revived the discussions again. In 2011, the government decided that scrutiny of EU draft legislative acts, other proposals for EU legislation and consultation documents should be mainstreamed across all Oireachtas sectoral committees. The Orders of Reference of Committees agreed by the Dáil and the Seanad in June 2011 require standing committees to consider EU matters within the remit of the relevant government department that they shadow and to engage with relevant ministers in the context of meetings of the Council of Ministers. They should report on the implications of the measures, setting their conclusions and any recommendations before the Houses of the Oireachtas (including reasoned opinions on the subsidiarity principle) or before ministers, who are legally obliged to take these into consideration. Ministries must send the relevant standing committee a report every six months on the measures, proposed measures and other developments in relation to the EU. Standing committees may also invite the relevant minister to attend in advance of relevant EU Council meetings to brief the Committee. On major policy issues and consultation papers from the EU, Committees may decide to make a contribution to the relevant EU institution.

In 2011, the Joint Committee on European Affairs became the Joint Committee on European Union Affairs, which, according to its Orders of Reference, considers EU-related bills, estimates or motions; conducts hearings in advance of the General Affairs Council; invites witnesses and guest speakers on EU policy and strategic issues; considers the European Commission's strategic planning documents; and follows up cross-sectoral policy developments at EU level. It has also to be notified on any proposal for the amendment of the treaties (pursuant of Article 48(2) TEU), any decision to move from unanimity to qualified majority or from special to ordinary legislative procedure (Article 48(7) TEU) and any application for membership (Article 49 TEU).

B. The Cortes Generales

Although Spain had previously introduced some changes on the regulation of the EAC in response to the Maastricht Treaty, in the late 1990s its system for the parliamentary scrutiny of EU affairs was still quite weak.[11] As the result of the Lisbon Treaty, the Act 8/1994 regulating the Joint Committee on the European Union (or Comisión Mixta para la Unión Europea) was modified by Act 24/2009 of 22 December, giving the Joint Committee the competence to elaborate and adopt, on behalf of the Cortes Generales, reasoned opinions on the compliance with the subsidiarity principle of draft legislative acts delivered by the EU institutions. The Act also gave the Joint Committee on the European Union the faculty to ask the government to bring action for annulment before the CJEU on grounds of infringement of the subsidiarity principle, to make a proposal for the lower and upper chamber to oppose a *passerelle* clause, to be informed of new membership applications, and to monitor Eurojust's and Europol's activities.

Although the new legislation incorporated the new powers, it did not establish specific duties for their execution, with the Joint Committee being free to exercise them extensively or only occasionally. Until July 2011, the subsidiarity check was carried out on 35 legislative proposals, ie approximately one-third of the total received (108). The members of the Bureau and the Board of Spokespersons of the Joint Committee on the European Union decide at a joint meeting, which takes place at least twice a month during legislative sessions, which proposals to scrutinize, assigning a 'rapporteur' to each of them (usually one of themselves). Rapporteurs submit to the committee either a 'reasoned

[11] Bergman (n 9). Maurer and Wessels (n 9).

opinion' (when they believe there is a breach of the principle) or a 'report' (when they believe the proposal complies with the principle). Before June 2011, only on three occasions was a reasoned opinion stating that the legislative act did not comply with the principle of subsidiarity submitted, always in line with the opinion of the government. Reports and reasoned opinions were adopted by the Committee with no debate or voting.[12]

On 23 October 2009, the main opposition party (the People's Party) also filed a motion in the EAC to amend Act 8/1994 further so as to reinforce the Joint Committee's capacity to check and shape the government's position in the Council meetings. The recitals of the proposal argued that the Joint Committee on the European Union could not exercise its new prerogatives derived from the Lisbon Treaty unless the hearings with the government members before and after the Council meetings became regulated. After some months of negotiations, the final law came into force on 20 December 2010. Act 38/2010 revising Act 8/1994 to reinforce the role of the Joint Committee on the European Union introduced a new Article 8 providing that the Bureau of the Committee shall decide—in view of the calendar of each six-month presidency—which members of the government to summon before their respective Council meetings to give account of their position. The new Article 9 lays down the duty of the Minister of Foreign Affairs or the Secretary of State for the EU to appear before the Joint Committee at the end of each presidency to explain the main achievements. This represented a considerable downgrade of the original motion, which proposed to hold a hearing with the corresponding (or related) Minister or his/her deputy before every Council meeting and one at the end of each rotating presidency. With regards to the ex ante control, the Joint Committee now has the discretion to decide on the total number of hearings with members of the government before the Council meetings (three in the IX Legislature), whereas the ex post control is confined to a hearing with the Secretary of State for the EU at the end of each presidency.[13]

In summary, although the incorporation of the Lisbon provisions implied the creation of a systematic procedure to examine EU law in Spain, this is not used to its full potential and there are indications that the scrutiny might be turning more 'legal' and mechanical in nature with a lower involvement of the standing committees. The Joint Committee for the European Union also used the momentum to improve the regulation on the parliamentary control of the executive in EU affairs, though the new rules are quite flexible and the new instruments to hold the government accountable are not used significantly. In terms of Winzen's criteria, whereas the access to information has improved, the ability of the Cortes Generales to process it and its capacity to enforce its resolutions remain weak. In Ireland, on the contrary, new measures have contributed to improving the capacity of the Houses of the Oireachtas to access information

[12] S Piedrafita, 'The Spanish Parliament and EU Affairs in the Post Lisbon Treaty Era: All Change?' (2014) 4 *Journal of Legislative Studies* (forthcoming).

[13] Ibid.

(EU documents and memoranda from the government), their ability to process it through a greater involvement of the standing committees and the enforceability of their resolutions.

IV. RATIFICATION AND IMPLEMENTATION OF THE TSCG

The TSCG was signed on 2 March 2012 by 25 Member States,[14] and entered into force on 1 January 2013 for the 16 states that had completed its ratification.[15] Ratifying Member States were required to enact laws at statutory level or higher no later than 12 months after the entry into force adopting the 'balanced-budget rule', the 'debt brake rule' and the corresponding automatic correction mechanisms in case of a breach of either rule.[16] The Treaty gave specific powers to the European Commission to monitor the implementation of these provisions at national level. In the case of non-compliant Member States, both the Commission and another Member State might bring the case before the CJEU and fines might be imposed if correction does not take place.

It has been argued that this tighter fiscal discipline, together with the stricter surveillance over the national budgets imposed by the two-pack regulations (see next section), might imply a loss of national sovereignty given that it will have direct consequences on national taxing and spending policies, as well as on the distribution of wealth between different groups in society and between Member States. In addition, the democratic legitimacy might be negatively affected given the significant powers conferred on the European Commission (an unelected body that is not accountable to the general public) and the Eurogroup (where decisions will be taken by a 'reversed qualified majority').[17] Even if Article 13 TSCG established that the European Parliament and the national parliaments will together determine the organization and promotion of a conference of representatives of the relevant committees of the European Parliament and national parliaments in order to discuss budgetary policies, this might not be enough to compensate the loss of powers and does not ensure an improvement in democratic legitimacy.

Although national parliaments did not participate in the drafting of the TSCG, each Contracting Party had to ratify the pact according to its constitutional requirements, which in all Member States except Cyprus required the approval of the parliament. With only a few exceptions (Austria, Luxembourg),

[14] All Member States signed the Treaty except the Czech Republic and the United Kingdom.

[15] For the other members of the eurozone, it will enter into force on the first day of the month following the deposit of the ratification instruments. The fiscal provisions in the Treaty (the so-called Fiscal Compact) will only apply for the non-euro Member States once they have adopted the euro unless they submit a special declaration.

[16] The 'balanced-budget rule' obliges the general state budget to be balanced or in surplus, ie that the annual structural deficit does not exceed 0.5% of GDP, or 1% when debt levels are significantly below 60%. The 'debt brake rule' establishes specific obligations and timing to reduce the government debt-to-GDP when this exceeds the 60% limit.

[17] www.publications.parliament.uk/pa/cm201012/cmselect/cmeuleg/writev/eurozone/eu01.htm.

the consent of the parliament to ratify the Treaty required a similar or higher majority than for the revision of the EU treaties, although the celebration of referendum was easier to escape. Indeed, the final draft of the pact softened the obligation to enshrine the 'golden rule' on balanced budgets into the constitutions after indications that several countries (Ireland, Finland, Denmark and Romania) would have to hold referendums in order to change their constitutions. Instead, the Treaty finally established that the budgetary rules would be implemented in the signatory Member States 'through provisions of binding force and permanent character, preferably constitutional, or otherwise guaranteed to be fully respected and adhered to throughout the national budgetary processes'. Additionally, the entry into force only required the ratification of 12 Member States. In order to facilitate and speed up the ratification process, the enactment of the European Stability Mechanism (ESM) was also made conditional on the ratification of the TSCG.

A. Ireland

Ireland was indeed the only eurozone Member State to hold a referendum after the government received legal advice that in order to ratify the TSCG and enable the Oireachtas to adopt any legislation necessary to implement the Treaty's provisions the Constitution needed to be amended. A Bill amending the constitution in Ireland requires a majority of votes from both chambers as well as a mandatory and binding referendum (Articles 46(2) and 47). Although the Irish voters had complicated the passage of both the Nice and Lisbon Treaties before, on this occasion opinion polls suggested that most people would vote to ratify the agreement. The main opposition party, Fianna Fail, joined the governing Fine Gael and Labour parties in campaigning for a 'yes' vote, with only Sinn Féin campaigning against the Treaty. Those seeking a 'yes' vote highlighted that rejection of the pact would prevent Ireland from accessing loans from the ESM in the future if necessary (the ongoing credit line was due to run out in 2013), which would destabilize the markets and increase the burden of debt repayment.[18] The government was also confident that a positive result would strengthen its hand in talks on the €30 billion promissory note for Anglo Irish Bank.[19]

On 10th May, the Sub-Committee on Referendum on the Intergovernmental Treaty on Stability, Coordination and Governance in the Economic and Monetary Union of the Joint Committee on European Union Affairs issued a report on the Treaty.[20] Meetings with 60 witnesses were held from January until April. In brief, proponents sustained that the Treaty would remedy design flaws in the euro and ensure 'good housekeeping' within the eurozone. The adoption of the new rules would improve market confidence across the eurozone and reduce the

[18] www.bbc.co.uk/news/world-europe-17528290.

[19] www.irishtimes.com/news/government-to-set-date-for-fiscal-treaty-referendum-today-1.489332.

[20] www.oireachtas.ie/parliament/media/SubCommittee-Report_10-May-2012.pdf.

difficulty of balancing Ireland's budget and reducing its public debt, which would boost exports and stimulate growth in the country. The availability of ESM funds would give significant reassurance to private lenders in the bond markets and it would even make a second bailout less likely. The rejection of the Treaty would not make a great difference as regards the fiscal rules that Ireland would have to apply but would restrict the access to the ESM and undermine Ireland's ability to negotiate economic reforms in the EU and to attract foreign investment.

For opponents, the purpose of the Treaty was rather to protect financial interests and to institutionalize austerity, and the adoption of the new rules would be detrimental to the economic recovery, the employment and the public services. Additionally, it would transfer the control of the economic policy to unaccountable officials in the European Commission. According to them, access to the ESM was made conditional to the adoption of the Treaty to frighten the public into accepting it, but there were other options for funding. And if not, the EU would never allow an Irish default and it would have to come up with a bailout mechanism even if Ireland did not ratify the TSCG.

Ireland approved the TSCG by a referendum held on 31 May by 60.29 per cent votes in favour, 39.71 against, with a participation rate of 50.6 per cent. Only 5 of the 43 constituencies rejected it.[21] Voters were asked whether to add the following in Article 29.4 of the Constitution:

> 10 The State may ratify the Treaty on Stability, Coordination and Governance in the Economic and Monetary Union done at Brussels on the 2nd day of March 2012. No provision of this Constitution invalidates laws enacted, acts done or measures adopted by the State that are necessitated by the obligations of the State under that Treaty or prevents laws enacted, acts done or measures adopted by bodies competent under that Treaty from having the force of law in the State.

The approval by referendum was subsequently enacted by the 30th Amendment Bill 2012 to the Constitution and received Presidential Assent on 27 June 2012. The government opted to wait until the Fiscal Responsibility Bill 2012, which implemented the provisions required by the Treaty into national law, was passed before formally completing the ratification. The Oireachtas passed the Fiscal Responsibility Bill on 27 November 2012 and the deposit of the ratification instrument took place on 14 December.

The Fiscal Responsibility Bill 2012 set out the legislation required to implement Articles 3 and 4 TSCG, ie the commitment for a balanced or in-surplus budget, the provision of an automatic correction mechanism and the inclusion of the 'debt rule'. If there is a significant deviation from the medium-term budgetary objective or from the agreed adjustment path towards it, the government must lay a correction plan before the Dáil within two months, specifying the deadline for the correction and the size and nature of the measures to be taken.[22]

[21] www.rte.ie/news/2012/0601/323199-fiscal-treaty-referendum-count-to-begin/.

[22] Furthermore, the plan must be consistent with recommendations made under the Stability and Growth Pact on the correction in question and the current stability programme.

The 'debt rule' establishes that where state debt to GDP ratio is in excess of 60 per cent, the difference between the actual ratio and the 60 per cent threshold must be reduced by an average of 1/20th per annum. This will start applying three years after Ireland has exited the deficit procedure. The Bill also established the Irish Fiscal Advisory Council (IFAC) on a statutory basis, which will provide public assessments of whether a significant deviation has occurred, if exceptional circumstances have begun, continue to exist or have ceased, and if a correction is proceeding in accordance with the correction plan.[23]

On the reading of the Bill in the Dáil on 10–11 October 2012, deputies from Fine Gael (government party) defended that greater budgetary discipline in all Member States was necessary to steer the European project through the current impasse, to ensure security in the eurozone and a return to growth in the economy. The enactment of the Bill would provide a statutory basis for a range of fiscal policy and expenditure management reforms which would prevent future governments from being reckless with taxpayers' money. The establishment of IFAC on a statutory basis as an independent body to monitor fiscal policy would serve to introduce greater transparency to the process. Also, enactment of the Bill would allow for ratification of the TSCG, which would play in favour of government actions to convince fellow Eurozone members to firm up details of the decisions taken at the EU summit in June in order to split Ireland's banking and sovereign debt and to find a solution for the Anglo Irish Bank promissory notes.[24]

During the reading, only a few independent deputies insisted that the Bill would damage democratic legitimacy and accountability, dismembering the welfare state with the excuse of 'balancing the books', increasing the powers of technocrats and enshrining neoliberal policies in law, which would constrain future governments wanting to implement different economic policies. They also believed the Bill would threaten the livelihoods of many people and push the economy into a downward spiral, curtailing public expenditure to deal with a problem that was essentially one of private debt and outlawing investment. The government was criticized for bending to EU demands at every turn and not getting anything in exchange, and especially for introducing property taxes, letting banks put up interest rates and cutting child benefits.

With 91 votes in favour (deputies from Fine Gael, Fianna Fáil, the Labour Party and some independents) and 27 against (deputies from Sinn Féin, People Before Profit Alliance, Workers and Unemployed Action Group South-Tipperary and a number of independents) the Bill was referred to the Select Sub-Committee on Finance.[25] On 18 October 2012, the Sub-Committee overruled a number of

[23] www.oireachtas.ie/documents/bills28/bills/2012/6612/b6612d.pdf.

[24] Debates can be followed in Dáil Éireann Debate, vol 773, nos 13 and 14 (online): http://oireachtasdebates.oireachtas.ie/debates%20authoring/debateswebpack.nsf/takes/dail2012101100007?opendocument#.

[25] http://oireachtasdebates.oireachtas.ie/debates%20authoring/debateswebpack.nsf/takes/dail2012101100021?opendocument#.

amendments proposed by Sinn Féin to include a provision making compliance with the budgetary rules dependent on social and economic development; to prioritize growth, job creation and delivery of high-quality public services; to assess the impact of any proposed measures on key social indicators, such as income equality, social inclusion and poverty reduction; and to give the government the option to derogate from the debt and deficit rules when it be in the best social and economic interests of the state. Only proposal for Amendment 9 establishing that the correction plan shall only be adopted following approval of the Oireachtas had to be put to vote, getting the support also of Fianna Fáil, but it was defeated by the votes of Fine Gael, the Labour Party and the Independent committee member. The Sub-Committee sent the Bill with no amendments back to the Dáil for adoption of the report.[26] At the Dáil, Sinn Féin tabled the same ten amendments again, obtaining the support of the deputies from the People Before Profit Alliance, the Workers and Unemployed Action Group South-Tipperary, the Socialist Party and a number of independents. Fianna Fáil also gave its support to Amendment 9. All were overturned.[27]

B. Spain

In Spain, the process went all the way around. The 'golden rule' was incorporated into the Spanish Constitution (CE) in summer 2011, some months before the TSCG had been even signed, in response to the soaring premium risk and the instability of the financial markets. The Bill implementing the new Article 135 CE (as well as Articles 3 and 4 TCSG) was submitted to Parliament on 3 March 2012, and the corresponding Act was enacted in April, after finalizing all the parliamentary proceedings. The TSCG was ratified in June 2012.

In summer 2011, the Spanish government decided to introduce the golden rule in Article 135 CE via the ordinary revision procedure (Article 167 CE), ie it needs a majority of 3/5 in both chambers and a referendum is not necessary unless it is requested by 1/10 of the members of a chamber (which was not the case). The socialist party (PSOE)—then in government—reached an agreement with the main opposition party (PP) on the constitutional reform on 26 August 2011. Two days later they tabled a motion in the Congreso de los Diputados (lower chamber) applying for an emergency debate and its adoption in a single reading.[28]

Old Article 135 CE established that the government should be authorized

[26] http://oireachtasdebates.oireachtas.ie/Debates%20Authoring/DebatesWebPack.nsf/committeetakes/FI12012101800002?opendocument#.

[27] http://oireachtasdebates.oireachtas.ie/Debates%20Authoring/DebatesWebPack.nsf/takes/dail2012110600035?opendocument#.

[28] The Rules of Procedure of each chamber (Art 150 Congreso de los Diputados, Art 129 Senado) establish that the House floor can decide to reduce the parliamentary proceedings to a single reading on the floor (with no involvement of the committee) whenever it is advisable for the nature of the legislative proposal or its simplicity).

by law to issue public debt or incur debt, and that the credit necessary to clear the payments should be always included as appropriations in the state budget. The proposal, which went through with no amendments, kept this provision in section 3 of the new Article, but included the regional governments and the obligation that the total public debt cannot exceed the limit established in the TFEU. New section 1 of the Article set out the principle of a balanced budget for all public administrations and new section 2 provided that an organic law would determine the limit of the structural deficit for the central and regional governments, which in no case should exceed that decided by the EU.[29] This organic law would also regulate the allocation of any possible deficit deviation among the public administrations, the possible exceptions, the correction mechanisms, the methodology to calculate the deficit and the sanctions (section 5).[30] An additional provision established that this Bill should be passed by 30 June 2012 and that the limits for the structural deficit would not come into force until 2020.

At the extraordinary session of the floor of the Congreso on 30 August 2012 to decide on the motion, the socialist spokesperson defended the urgent need to incorporate the budget and debt rules into the Constitution so as to reduce uncertainty in the financial markets and stop the soaring of Spain's risk premium, which could make the payment of debt unsustainable in the future. The conservative MP went further, insisting that payment of the debt limited the capacity to invest in other policies to promote growth and employment. The new article in the constitution would prevent any future government from making policies and politics. The constitutional reform would commit any future government to a balanced budget and would give Spain a leading role in the emerging economic governance in the EU. Those against the motion criticized the 'express' procedure chosen for such an important constitutional reform (even the choice for an ordinary procedure with no referendum), the exclusion of the other parliament groups from the dialogue with the government, the 'constitutionalization' of budget practices that should be regulated only by law (and that in any case are mandatory given the obligation of Spain to abide by EU treaties and secondary legislation), the limitation of the regional governments' financial autonomy and the government's capitulation to the will of the German Chancellor, the European Central Bank and the financial markets.[31]

In any case, the floor decided to consider the constitutional amendment (318 yes votes out of 336) through the emergency procedure with a single reading (317 yes votes), summoning the Congreso for its debate and adoption on 2

[29] Section 4 established the exceptions to the budget and debt rules in case of natural disasters, economic recession or extraordinary circumstances beyond the control of the state that can threaten the financial situation.

[30] www.congreso.es/consti/constitucion/indice/titulos/articulos.jsp?ini=135&tipo=2.

[31] CIU (centre-right Catalan party), ERC (left-wing Catalan party), IU (Communist party), PNV (centre-right Basque party), BNG (left-wing Gallego party), UPyD (centre-left state party) and NA-BAI (nationalist left party from Navarra) opposed the motion. UPN (regional party from Navarra) voted yes and CC (regional party from the Canary Islands) abstained.

September 2012.[32] Therefore, there was only one day to present amendments to the motion. Opposing political parties tabled 24 amendments, demanding a more extensive revision of the constitution, stronger regional powers (in this and other non-related areas), the use of the reinforced revision procedure (or the ratification by referendum) and the withdrawal of the motion.[33] All of them were declared out of order by the Bureau of the chamber or lost by the floor of the chamber.[34] In the final vote, the constitutional reform was approved by 316 votes in favour and 5 against.[35] The proposal was referred then to the Constitutional Committee of the Senate. Twenty-nine amendments were tabled on this occasion, all of them declared again out of order by the Bureau of the committee or lost by the floor of the chamber on 7 September 2011. In the final vote, the constitutional reform was approved by 233 yes to 3 no votes. Given that there was no request for a referendum by 1/10 of the members of any chamber in the 15 following days, the Bill was sanctioned by the King and published in the official diary on 27 September 2011.[36]

The Ley Orgánica 2/2012, de 27 de abril, de Estabilidad Presupuestaria y Sostenibilidad Financiera developed the principles set out in the new Article 135 CE, as well as the other open questions.[37] According to the 'balanced-budget' principle, no public administration (central, regional, local, social security) will be able to incur a structural deficit, apart from in exceptional and temporary circumstances. In the case of structural reforms with long-term budgetary effects, a structural deficit up to 0.4 per cent of GDP (or whatever lower limit is decided by the EU) will be allowed for all the public administrations together. An absolute majority of the members of the Congreso may authorize the state or a regional government to incur a structural deficit in the case of natural disasters, a deep economic recession or exceptional emergency situations beyond the control of the public administrations that can threaten the financial situation or the social and economic sustainability. According to a new 'rule on expenditure', public expenditure cannot grow more than the annual increase of the GDP. According to the 'principle of financial sustainability', the total public debt must not exceed 60 per cent of GDP, namely 44 per cent for central government, 13 per cent for all the regions, and 3 per cent for all the municipalities (or whatever other threshold is decided by the EU).

Following the recommendations by the EU, the government will define before 1 April every year the objectives (in relation to the GDP) of both the balanced budget (financial needs) and the public debt, and will refer them to the Parliament for its approval. The subsequent elaboration of the budget should comply with these targets. Before 1 October every year, the government will elaborate a

[32] www.congreso.es/public_oficiales/L9/CONG/DS/PL/PL_269.PDF#page=2.

[33] www.congreso.es/portal/page/portal/Congreso/PopUpCGI?CMD=VERLST&BASE=puw9&DOCS=1-1&DOCORDER=LIFO&QUERY=%28CDB20110905032903.CODI.%29#(Página1).

[34] Except for a grammar correction.

[35] www.congreso.es/public_oficiales/L9/CONG/DS/PL/PL_270.PDF#page=2.

[36] www.congreso.es/constitucion/ficheros/leyes_espa/rc_2011_001.pdf.

[37] www.boe.es/boe/dias/2012/04/30/pdfs/BOE-A-2012-5730.pdf.

report on the compliance of these objectives and the expenditure ceiling, taking into account the actual evolution of the GDP. Any public administration not complying with the targets must elaborate an action plan to explain the situation and the measures to steer it, and it will be sanctioned (by having to make a deposit or by the cancellation of its credit availability) in case of infringement.[38]

The Bill was tabled in the Congreso on 3 March 2012 (the day after the TSCG had been signed) by the PP (in government as from November 2011). In the first reading of the proposal (for its consideration or withdrawal), the main opposition party, the socialist PSOE, on the grounds of 'responsibility', abstained in the vote for 'amendments to the totality' presented by a few minority groups, but demanded the government 'soften' the draft. In its opinion, the rules were extremely restrictive, even beyond the obligations under the Stability and Growth Pact, and would impair economic growth and the creation of employment. The expenditure ceiling was unnecessary, enshrined neoliberal assumptions and would negatively affect the sustainability of the public services. The socialist group argued that the political agreement between both parties referred to a structural deficit of 0.4 per cent (not 0 per cent) in 2020.[39] Out of more than 200 amendments tabled by all the political groups in the Committee of Finance and Public Administration, only five minor ones were approved.[40] The floor of the lower chamber debated the committee report on 12 April 2012, and approved seven more revised amendments.[41] The Bill was passed with 192 yes, 116 no votes and 4 abstentions. In the Senate, almost 100 amendments were tabled as well, but they were all defeated.[42]

[38] Any government's action plan will need the approval of the Parliament, those by the regions will require the consent of the Consejo de Política Fiscal y Financiera, and those by the municipalities will require the approval of the local councils. Non-compliant regions and municipalities will require the authorization of the central government for further indebting and the consent of the Ministry of Finance and Public Administration to obtain state subsidies.

[39] UPyD and UPN voted with the PP against the ammendments to the totality presented by CiU, BNG, ERC, CC and GB. PNV and PSOE abstained. The debates and votes can be found online at: www.congreso.es/public_oficiales/L10/CONG/DS/PL/PL_023.PDF.

[40] Amendment no 15 referred to the Preliminary recitals, no 97 changed the title of an article, no 109 replaced the name 'delegation of experts' by 'committee of experts', no 110 added a word for the sake of clarity, and no 138 included a line in the coercive measures to assure compliance by local governments. All the amendments proposed can be found online at: www.congreso.es/public_oficiales/L10/CONG/BOCG/A/A_003-05.PDF#page=1.

The debates and votes on the amendments can be found online at: www.congreso.es/public_oficiales/L10/CONG/DS/CO/CO_063.PDF.

[41] Amendment no 9 (revisited) modified Art 18 to state that adjustments during the budgetary year would be in order to guarantee the objective of budgetary stability (rather than to avoid incurring a structural deficit); no 96 introduced two clarifications to Art 3, no 124 placed stricter limits on the rule of the expenditure (Art 12) in case of structural imbalance; no 127 specified that the report on the economic outlook to be elaborated by the Ministry of Economy to calculate the budget and debt targets should refer to both the national and all the subnational levels; no 176 modified the wording of the final provision (no 3) regarding the two regions with a special economic arrangement (Navarra and Basque Country); nos 183 and 204 modified the first transitory provision so as to include the provisions of the TSCG. The debates and votes on the amendments can be found online at: www.congreso.es/public_oficiales/L10/CONG/DS/PL/PL_027.PDF.

[42] www.congreso.es/public_oficiales/L10/SEN/DS/CO/DS_C_10_44.PDF.

The Act implementing the TSCG was more controversial than the ratification of the Treaty itself. In Spain, an absolute majority (50 per cent) in favour is required in both chambers to approve a Ley Orgánica (Organic Law) which ratifies an international treaty giving powers envisaged in the Constitution to an international organization. In the case of the TSCG, the proposal for the Ley Orgánica to authorise its ratification was submitted to the Congreso de los Diputados on 14 May 2012. Although in principle the Bill should have been referred to the Committee on Foreign Affairs, on 19 June 2012 the House floor decided to adopt the single-reading procedure, meaning the Bill would be, as in the case of the previous constitutional reform, immediately discussed and adopted on the floor (skipping the committee proceedings). Three requests for the withdrawal of the Bill in the form of 'amendments to the totality' were tabled by left-wing state and regional parties (IU, ICV/EUiA, CHA and BNG), but these were defeated. Opponents argued that the provisions in the TSCG were neoliberal and would only deteriorate even further the economic situation and increase unemployment. The PSOE retired the two amendments that they had proposed reflecting the urgent need to promote economic growth and employment, and voted in favour of the Bill. The other opposition groups (CIU, PNV, UPyD and UPyN) also gave their consent to the ratification of the Treaty. The Act was finally adopted by 311 votes in favour and 19 against and sent to the Senado for its approval. During the Senate floor proceedings on 18 July 2012, two veto proposals by left-wing parties were presented and declared lost, and the Act was finally adopted with 309 votes in favour, 19 against and 1 abstention. Official Royal Assent was given on 25 July 2012 and the ratification instrument was deposited on 27 September.

C. Findings in a Comparative Perspective

In Spain, in order to include the balanced-budget and the debt rules in both the ratification of the TSCG and the amendment to the Constitution, the ruling party moved an urgent motion in Parliament limiting discussion and restricting the opposition's capacity to table amendments. The timing of the sessions did not favour public debate either. Nevertheless, a great majority of MPs from the main political groups backed the proposals. On the contrary, the implementing law followed an ordinary legislative procedure and encountered greater opposition. Parliamentary debates were longer, more contentious and impinged on the general public. However, the comfortable parliamentary majority held by the conservative party allowed the passage of the government's proposal with only a few minor amendments. In Ireland, there was a far-reaching public debate on the TSCG, although most political parties and society as a whole backed its adoption. Most of the political parties represented in Parliament also supported the law implementing the fiscal rules.

In other countries with a stronger involvement of their parliaments in EU affairs, parliamentary ratification of the TSCG was not especially controversial either. In Denmark, where a simple majority of MPs was required, the draft was submitted to the Parliament on 11 April 2012 and adopted in May with 80 'yes' votes and 27 'no' votes. In Finland, the 50 per cent majority required for ratification was comfortably surpassed (139 yes, 38 no), with the six parties of the government coalition voting in favour—though the government had previously to secure a mandate from the Parliament in order to sign the Treaty. In Sweden, the governing centre-right Alliance for Sweden had to secure support from the Social Democratic Party to reach the necessary 50 per cent parliamentary majority against the guarantees that the Swedish labour market would be maintained and that no decision-making power would be transferred to EU institutions. Finally, 251 MPs voted in favour and only 23 against.

V: THE SUBSIDIARY CHECKS OF THE TWO-PACK REGULATIONS

The first set of rules on enhanced EU economic governance entered into force on 13 December 2011 and was known as the 'six-pack'.[43] The measures aimed to reinforce the Stability and Growth Pact, strengthening both its preventive and corrective arms. Member States were required to steer their budgetary balance towards medium-term budgetary objectives, using expenditure benchmarks alongside the structural budget balance to assess the corresponding adjustments. An interest-bearing deposit of 0.2 per cent of GDP was introduced for non-compliant eurozone countries. On the corrective side, the new rules provided that the excessive deficit procedure (EDP) should also be initiated when a Member State's debt exceeds 60 per cent of GDP and introduced the possibility to request a non-interest-bearing deposit of 0.2 per cent of GDP from a eurozone country which is placed in EDP on the basis of its deficit or its debt, as well as fines for non-compliant states. A new Macroeconomic Imbalance Procedure (MIP) was established to identify potential risks, prevent the emergence, and correct macroeconomic imbalances in Member States.[44] The new rules also

[43] They consisted of five regulations (Regulation (EU) No 1173/2011 of the European Parliament and of the Council of 16 November 2011 on the effective enforcement of budgetary surveillance in the euro area; Regulation (EU) No 1174/2011 of the European Parliament and of the Council of 16 November 2011 on enforcement measures to correct excessive macroeconomic imbalances in the euro area; Regulation (EU) No 1175/2011 of the European Parliament and of the Council of 16 November 2011 amending Council Regulation (EC) No 1466/97 on the strengthening of the surveillance of budgetary positions and the surveillance and coordination of economic policies; Regulation (EU) No 1176/2011 of the European Parliament and of the Council of 16 November 2011 on the prevention and correction of macroeconomic imbalances; Council Regulation (EU) No 1177/2011 of 8 November 2011 amending Regulation (EC) No 1467/97 on speeding up and clarifying the implementation of the excessive deficit procedure) and Council Directive 2011/85/EU of 8 November 2011 on requirements for budgetary frameworks of the Member States.

[44] The MIP is based on a gradual approach according to the gravity of the macroeconomic imbalances identified and can eventually lead to the imposition of sanctions on eurozone Member States should they repeatedly fail to meet their obligations under the corrective arm.

regulated the use of reverse qualified majority voting and set the obligation of Member States to keep their fiscal frameworks in line with minimum quality standards, cover all administrative levels and follow a multiannual perspective.[45]

The subsidiarity checks for these legislative acts were carried out by the national parliaments from October to December 2010. The Joint Committee on European Scrutiny of the Houses of the Oireachtas decided at a meeting on 4 November that given the significant nature of these proposals they should be scrutinized in detail by the committee, and it invited the Minister for Finance to make an oral presentation to the committee and take questions. The hearing with officials from the Department of Finance took place on 16 December, but no subsidiarity check or reasoned opinion was produced. In the case of Spain, the Bureau of the Joint Committee on the European Union assigned a rapporteur for each of these proposals on 10 November, and the favourable reports were approved by the Committee with no debate or voting on 9 December.

On 23 November 2011, the European Commission proposed two draft Regulations to enhance the co-ordination and surveillance of budgetary processes for all eurozone Member States, and especially for those countries that have excessive deficits, are experiencing or are at serious risk of financial instability, or are under a financial assistance programme. The 'Proposal for a Regulation on common provisions for monitoring and assessing draft budgetary plans and ensuring the correction of excessive deficit of the Member States in the euro area' (COM(2011) 821 final) provides that Member States must submit their draft annual budgetary plans before 15 October for the Commission to check whether they are in line with the Stability and Growth Pact and the recommendations of the European Semester. The Commission's opinions on Member States will be discussed in the Eurogroup. For Member States subject to a EDP the proposal also contains new obligations to inform the Commission about any fiscal policy decisions. An independent body must monitor the implementation of national fiscal rules in eurozone Member States and budgets must be built upon independent macroeconomic forecasts. The 'Proposal for a Regulation on the strengthening of economic and budgetary surveillance of Member States experiencing or threatened with serious difficulties with respect to their financial stability in the euro area' (COM(2011) 819 final) establishes an enhanced surveillance procedure for countries facing series difficulties and receiving financial assistance. The Commission may also decide to enhance surveillance for other Member States experiencing or threatened with financial difficulties.

Following negotiations with the Council, the European Parliament approved both regulations at a first reading in May 2013. The subsidiarity checks were carried out between 25 November 2011 and 26 January 2012. In Belgium, the Committee on Finance and Budget of the Lower Chamber expressed in a reasoned opinion sent to the European Commission the view of a few members

[45] Under the 'reverse qualified majority' system, a Commission recommendation or proposal to the Council is considered adopted unless a qualified majority of Member States votes against it.

of the Committee that Proposal 819 restrained the role of national parliaments in the budgetary process and therefore interfered with their democratic legitimacy, in a clear breach of both the subsidiarity and proportionality principles. Regarding Proposal 821, a few members of the Committee also stated their view that budgetary commitments should also be 'social' and 'environmental'. No other reasoned opinion was sent by any other national parliament on Proposal 819 stating a breach of the subsidiarity and proportionality principles.

As for Proposal 821, the French Senate and the Swedish Parliament also referred a reasoned opinion to the Commission. In France, the Financial Affairs Committee of the Senat downgraded the negative opinion of the European Affairs Committee to state that the current draft of Articles 3 and 4 could breach the subsidiarity principle given the broad definition of the 'independent fiscal council' and the 'independent macroeconomic forecasts', which could lead to different interpretations. In Sweden, the Riksdag adopted the resolution of the Committee on Finance stating a breach of the subsidiarity principle given that the regulation did not offer sufficient guarantees to safeguard national competence on fiscal policy.

In Ireland, both legislative proposals were considered at the meeting of the Joint Committee on Finance, Public Expenditure and Reform on 16 February 2012, which agreed that, given their major significance, they warranted further scrutiny. A subsidiarity check was not carried out but the members of the Committee had the chance to discuss the details of the proposals and the state of the negotiations with two officials from the EU and the International Division, Department of Finance, on 14 November. In Spain, the annual legislative session starts on 1 February and therefore the proposals were not referred to the Bureau of the Joint Committee on the European Union until 15 February 2012. The members of the Bureau and the spokespersons did not commission a subsidiarity check for either of these two legislative acts given that the deadline for sending a reasoned opinion had expired. The proposals were not the object of further political scrutiny in the Parliament.

VI. CONCLUSIONS

In Spain, the constitutional amendment—a prelude to the TSCG—as well as the ratification of the Treaty itself were adopted following an abbreviated single reading with little room for debate, although there was little dissent in Parliament. The adoption of the implementing law followed the ordinary legislative procedure, allowing discussions in the respective committees and giving the opposition greater scope to table amendments. However, despite strong objections from the main opposition parties, this law was finally adopted because the governing party had a comfortable parliamentary majority. The two-pack regulations were not the object of a subsidiarity check by the Cortes Generales. All this shows the weakness of the parliamentary scrutiny of EU affairs in

Spain (despite the new Lisbon provisions), as well as the strong position of the executive in the political system. In Ireland, the TSCG was ratified in a referendum, the implementing law was adopted following the standard procedure and the two-pack regulations were the object of parliamentary scrutiny. Despite the broad consensus around these measures—due perhaps to the fragile financial situation of the country—the scrutiny system in EU affairs seems to be improving and raises fewer concerns in terms of input or procedural legitimacy. In any case, contestation to EU decisions establishing budgetary constraints was also very low in Member States with a parliament traditionally more involved in EU affairs. Only the Swedish parliament questioned to some extent the TSCG and challenged the two-pack regulations.

16

Who Got to Adjudicate the EU's Financial Crisis and Why? Judicial Review of the Legal Instruments of the Eurozone

SAMO BARDUTZKY and ELAINE FAHEY*

I. INTRODUCTION

DESPITE ITS CURRENT significance for EU integration and the functioning of world banks, economies and markets, the eurozone area group of EU Member States is not an institution of EU law. Even its 'leader' is nothing more than an ordinary finance minister of one of the Member States that uses using the euro currency. The eurozone area group has been recognized as an 'informal body' since 1997 but still cannot take legally binding decisions. It is not a formation of the Council and operates technically outside of Ecofin, the formation of Finance Ministers of the Council. According to some, eurozone summit meetings could not lawfully take place within Ecofin Council formations.[1] A Protocol on the eurozone area group introduced special provisions for the meetings of the finance ministers. It thus provided for regularization of its activities through law.[2] Participation of non-eurozone states in

* This paper is a revised version of an article, 'Judicial Review of Eurozone Law: The Adjudication of Postnational Norms in the EU Courts, Plural—A Case Study of the European Stability Mechanism' (2013) 34 *Michigan Journal of International Law* 101 (available at www.mjilonline.org/wordpress/wp-content/uploads/2013/07/FaheyBardutzky.pdf), in a symposium in the *Michigan Journal of International Law*, convened by the authors. The authors are grateful to Daniel Halberstam, Chris Koedooder and Aart Loubert for comments on an earlier version of this piece and to Federico Fabbrini and participants at the conference on 'The Constitutionalization of European Budgetary Constraints', Tilburg, May 2013 for their rich comments.

[1] F Snyder, 'EMU—Integration and Differentiation: Metaphor for the European Union', in P Craig and G de Búrca (eds) *The Evolution of EU Law*, 2nd edn (Oxford, Oxford University Press, 2011) 704; see also F Snyder, 'EMU Revisited: Are We Making a Constitution? What Constitution Are We Making?' in P Craig and G de Búrca (eds) *The Evolution of EU Law* (Oxford, Oxford University Press, 1999).

[2] Protocol No 14.

eurozone meetings has led to some tensions,[3] given that their participants are not understood to be lawfully able to observe or speak at eurozone meetings. However, the International Monetary Fund (IMF) *has* been granted such privileges.[4] These practices emphasize the ambiguous contours of its configurations, decision-making and its discretionary powers despite its apparent lack of institutionalization. Such practices also indicate their possible amenability to judicial review.[5] Its spatial and textual 'grey-zone' status raises the question as to precisely whose interests the eurozone group serves. Additionally, it raises the question as to the place of law and the rule of law therein.[6]

Prima facie, the eurozone may be said to constitute a default state of EU integration. Thus the eurozone Protocol introduced an integration status for the eurozone, providing rules for what Snyder terms the 'ins'.[7] It allowed the 'ins' to develop ever-closer co-ordination and regarded Member States outside of the eurozone group as having a 'derogation' in law.[8] The precise categorization of eurozone law on this view is not so straightforward. Membership of the eurozone is a legal requirement for candidate countries who wish to accede to the EU. Thus differentiation within the eurozone law was initially viewed as temporary.[9] Yet both the UK and Denmark have permanent eurozone law derogations and eight others have had derogations.[10] Recent developments that are the subject of analysis here nevertheless suggest that the characterization of the eurozone as a *default* state of EU integration is far from accurate or convincing.

In the same way that the Eurozone operates outside of EU institutional law stricto sensu, the European Monetary Union (EMU) has remained *outside* of judicial review and arguably even non-justiciable until more recent times. In this regard, there is little case law on the EMU and in an earlier decision on

[3] For example, 'Sarkozy Tells Cameron to "Shut Up" on Eurozone' *EUObserver.com*, 24 October, 2011, http://euobserver.com/economic/114041 (accessed 30 June 2013).

[4] For example, via its representative, Christine Lagarde, on 21 June 2012. The Eurozone area leader has also attended IMF meetings: www.eurozone.europa.eu/newsroom/news/2012/06/eurogroup-overview-of-the-situation-in-the-eurozone (accessed 30 June 2013).

[5] One may note the semi-autonomous functionality of the eurozone area, evidenced not least on its website, witnessing the reliance and relationship of the area to other EU institutions, its conduct of its business in accordance with standard practices and formats of EU Institutions, and its compliance with practices of the Council of Ministers, its closest institutional allay or even home: www.eurozone.europa.eu/home (accessed 30 June 2013).

[6] I Pernice, 'What Future(s) of Democracy in Europe: Learning from Crisis' in Compendium Report, *Challenges of Multi-Tier Governance in the EU, Effectiveness, Efficiency and Legitimacy* (European Parliament, Constitutional Affairs, 2012).

[7] As referred to by Snyder (2011, n 1).

[8] As Piris states, there are many conceptions of a multispeed Europe, principally involving a two-speed Europe, acting on the assumption that all states will eventually participate or variable geometry or flexibility of differentiation, resulting in co-operation on a case-by-case basis: JC Piris, *The Future of Europe: Towards a Two-Speed EU?* (Cambridge, Cambridge University Press, 2012) 66, 70.

[9] Participation in the eurozone involves fulfilling conditions including the independence of national central banks, the convergence criteria relating to a high level of price stability, a low budgetary deficit and the durability of limited fluctuation margins within the exchange rate mechanisms: Art 140 TFEU and Protocol No 13 on the convergence criteria.

[10] Protocol No 16 on certain provisions relating to Denmark and Protocol No 15 on certain provisions relating to the UK.

the Stability and Growth Pact the CJEU is viewed as having adopted a particularly narrow construction of its role there.[11] Moreover, eurozone law *was not and could not have been* the subject of judicial review qua justifiability in the national courts until now.[12] However, the limited role for law, courts and justiciability in this domain has changed dramatically in recent times. The European Stability Mechanism (ESM) is the latest and most permanent in a series of law and governance mechanisms designed to finally resolve the eurozone qua EU's financial crisis, purporting to create an EU replica of the IMF.[13] Recently enacted law and governance mechanisms perform, cumulatively, a radical rebalancing of powers and functions, not least its temporal predecessor, the Treaty on Stability, Coordination and Governance (TSCG) which rendered the goals of previous soft law instruments justiciable and granted the CJEU judicial review powers. On the one hand, they purport to decrease dramatically Member State fiscal sovereignty through non-conventional and sometimes transitional instruments. On the other hand, they increase the capacity to protect the eurozone through funds derived from the Member States themselves, in shares apportioned relative to the size and financial capacity thereof. The ESM Treaty (ESMT) provides for institutional arrangements in situations where non-eurozone states participate on an ad hoc basis in certain financial assistance operations for eurozone states. This further operates to blur the separation between the formations acting within and outside the eurozone.[14] The ESM has been subjected to a limited number of direct judicial review challenges in the Member States and also before the CJEU. The mere fact that the ESM has survived this adjudication ostensibly reflects as much upon its character as upon the judicial machinery of the EU. Overall, the constitutional form and character of the ESM remains curious, ambivalent and strikingly postnational. And while the role of law and courts in EMU law may have changed dramatically in recent times, the result of this process is not neces-

[11] Case C-27/04 *Commission v Council* [2004] ECR I-6649. There, the Commission initiated an EDP against France and the Council, acting on a Commission recommendation, decided that France had an excessive deficit, following a similar situation in respect of Germany in the previous year. In 2003 at a meeting of Ecofin all Member States except France and Germany voted on the recommendation of the Commission to make the Council's recommendation public; France and Germany garnered support from other states to block the vote. The Council agreed not to act and the Commission brought an application to annul measures concerning Germany and France. The Court held that the Council had to respect treaty rules on its role in decision-making procedures and institutional balance. The Court held that the Commission was not entitled to require the Council to make recommendations public or to oblige a Member State to take specific measures. The Council could act pursuant to an alternative principle outside of the treaties. The decision has been described as one where the Court adopted an alliance between the Court and Commission to act as defenders of EC law (as it then was).

[12] That is, in the absence of a mechanism capable of generating judicial review in the Member States.

[13] These include the so-called 'six-pack' (five regulations and a directive on reinforced economic governance), the Treaty on Stability, Coordination and Governance, a so-called 'two-pack', Single Supervisory Mechanisms, and the predecessors to the ESM, the ESF and ESFM. See the overview provided by C Joerges, 'A Crisis of Executive Managerialism in the EU: No Alternative?', Maastricht Faculty of Law Working Paper 2012/7, 20-22.

[14] See recital 9 of the Preamble to the ESMT and Art 6/III ESMT.

sarily much different. Judicial review here has had a limited impact, or to quote the oft-cited comment of Tushnet, it has only delivered 'limited noise' at 'zero'.[15]

The account here argues that the adjudication of the ESM is a rich case study of the character of law in contemporary EU integration and the state of postnationalism. Moreover, the account here contends that it constitutes an example of suboptimal adjudication in the EU courts, plural.[16] This argument is rooted in both the character of eurozone law and a rather flawed procedural matrix for judicial review, in the form of the preliminary reference mechanism, pursuant to Article 267 TFEU. We seek to argue that retrospectively courts possibly offered a *unique forum for participation and contestation* for these esoteric mechanisms. This is because these mechanisms sought to render fiscal affairs *justiciable*.[17] Accordingly, in our analysis, first and foremost, we consider the characterization of the ESM, in light of how it was conceived by its framers (Section II). Secondly, we consider what happened when it was assessed by several European courts, national and supranational (Section III). Thirdly, we examine the preliminary reference mechanism as the tool that could have facilitated a more participatory and orchestrated judicial response, but did so to a very limited extent (Section IV), followed by our conclusions (Section V).

II. THE CHARACTER OF THE ESM AS AN INSTRUMENT OF POSTNATIONALISM

The demise of the nation state as a solitary actor and its increasing operation within transnational constructs or in the shadow of supranational institutions is a fact of contemporary life, albeit that it still remains the 'ultimate actor'.[18] Certain scholars have deployed terms such as postnational law or postnational democracy to depict 'the state of the State', the postmodern decline of the boundaries of orthodoxy in society.[19] At its core, postnationalism implies that the performance

[15] M Tushnet, *Taking the Constitution Away from the Court* (Princeton, Princeton University Press, 1999) 153.

[16] As our account analyses the totality of the courts in the EU—both the supranational courts of the EU as well as the national courts (of the Member States) that belong to the judiciary of the EU *lato sensu*, we chose the nomenclature of 'EU courts, plural' to describe the totality.

[17] See R Cichowski, *The European Court and Civil Society: Litigation, Mobilization and Governance* (Cambridge, Cambridge University Press, 2007). The argument that we make is at variance with that made by others in this volume, seeking a more deferential stance to the legislature. We make this argumentation on the basis of our interpretation of the character of the eurozone instrument studied here, and make this argumentation retrospectively, ie looking back at the path of the adjudication.

[18] See, most famously, S Sassen, *Losing Control? Sovereignty in the Age of Globalization* (New York, Columbia University Press, 1996); S Sassen, *Territory, Authority, Rights: From Medieval to Global Assemblages*, 2nd edn (Princeton, Princeton University Press, 2008).

[19] D Chalmers, 'Post-nationalism and the Quest for Constitutional Substitutes' (2000) 27 *Journal of Law and Society* 178; N Krisch, *Beyond Constituitonalism: The Pluralist Structure of Postnational Law* (Oxford, Oxford University Press, 2011); N Walker, 'Postnational Constitutionalism and Postnational Public Law: A Tale of Two Neologisms' (2012) 3 *Transnational Legal Theory* 61; G Shaffer, 'A Transnational Take on Krisch's Pluralist Postnational Law' (2012) 23 *European Journal of International Law* 565; KH Ladeur, 'The Theory of Autopoiesis as an Approach to a Better Understanding

of constitutionalism and politics is no longer configured around or constructed *within* the territorial strictures of the nation state.[20] While, as Chalmers states, postnationalism often understates the importance of the nation state, it signifies the importance of the proliferation of new forms of law and politics, interactions between legal orders and political disordering. Postnationalism is arguably less a study of single or specific instruments or policies. Instead, it is probably more accurately a broader methodology to study shifts in norms, actors and processes. Nonetheless, the instruments of postnational organizations generate many questions. Postnationalism has not resulted in any accepted normative idea of postnational law as a phenomenon, especially not in legal scholarship. At its height, the deployment of postnationalism in legal scholarship has even been critiqued as EU-centric and court-centric. It has been argued to lack relevance to any legal order or field outside of the context of the EU.[21] Nonetheless, we suggest that it provides a rich depiction of the breakdown in the boundaries in rule-making in the EU currently. We say that the manipulation of the character of Member States in the legal instruments in eurozone law altered the role for courts as a phenomenon of postnationalism. It may merit further attention beyond the simple descriptor of 'hat-switching',[22] given that it indicates evolving, living practices of a postnational democracy, albeit that their health or evolving status may be less than organic.[23]

We thus turn to the characterization of the ESM as the latest eurozone instrument. As to its conception, the ESM had numerous distinctive features as a matter of EU law that suggested it was intentionally and explicitly an esoteric instrument which had shortcomings and deficiencies. The ESM was enacted by way of a parallel agreement by the Member States inter se *outside* of the EU treaties, using a vehicle of public international law: the ESMT.[24] The ESM was anchored in Article 136 TFEU, through the device of a European Council decision to amend the treaties. It was thus entered into by a broader configuration than merely the eurozone. This decision purported to use the simplified revision procedure to achieve the end result: the ESMT.[25] The explicit reference in the ESMT to Article 273 TFEU jurisdiction of the CJEU self-characterized

of Postmodern Law From the Hierarchy of Norms to the Heterarchy of Changing Patterns of Legal Inter-relationships', EUI Working Paper Law 1999/3; E Eriksen, C Joerges and F Rödl (eds), *Law and Democracy in the Post-national Union* (2006/1 ARENA Report).

[20] Chalmers, ibid, 178.

[21] Whether lawmaking takes place in this forum or rulemaking or a combination of both is a decidedly unexplored point: postnational law is nonetheless a limited and descriptive working term of art, perhaps at odds with the rich matrix that it evokes. EU-centrism within its ideology is perhaps forgivable and self-evident given that the EU is an evolving organization.

[22] B De Witte and T Beukers, 'The Court of Justice Approves the creation of the European Stability Mechanism outside the EU Legal Order: *Pringle*' (2013) 50 *Common Market Law Review* 805, 825–27.

[23] See D Curtin, *The EU as a Postnational Democracy in Search of a Political Philosophy* (The Hague, Kluwer, 1997). See also D Curtin, *Executive Power of the European Union: Law, Practices and the Living Constitution* (Oxford, Oxford University Press, 1999).

[24] It was signed by the 17 Member States of the eurozone on 2 February 2012 and entered into force on 27 September 2012.

[25] European Council Decision of 25 March 2011 amending Article 136 of the Treaty on the

the ESMT as a 'special agreement', further emphasizing its exceptional character.[26] The legal form of the ESMT as a 'special agreement' deploying public international law was not beyond the letter of the treaties or past practices. Rather, it has become a phenomenon of recent reforms.[27] Nevertheless, it was as exceptional as it was problematic in a number of ways. First and foremost, it created its own parallel institutional structure outside the EU treaties and borrowed the EU institutions such as the Commission for certain tasks.[28] This enhanced the complexity of the institutional design of the EU and at the same time avoided input or control from the European Parliament. This is arguably the antithesis of the EU project post-Lisbon.[29] Secondly, the heads of state or government used a variant of simplified treaty revision procedure to insert the new third paragraph of Article 136 TFEU. This was arguably motivated by a desire to avoid referendums in the Member States[30] and a desire to legitimize the new organization through the veneer of law. Thirdly, it has been shaped as a tool for international co-operation, yet constructed deliberately beyond the EU treaties *for the moment*, until the ESM is integrated into the EU treaties.[31] Last but not least, the ESMT removed the veto power of the smaller eurozone states by providing that it would enter into force if ratified by states that together would contribute 90 per cent of the funds for the mechanism.[32] This has de facto and de jure generated the phenomenon of legally insignificant states in EMU

Functioning of the European Union with regard to a stability mechanism for Member States whose currency is the euro (2011/199/EU), [2011] OJ L91/1.

[26] ESMT, Recital 16 of the Preamble.

[27] See inter alia the analysis of the use of the term 'special agreement' in the Fiscal Compact Treaty in A Kocherov et al, 'Another Legal Monster? An EUI Debate on the Fiscal Compact Treaty Law', EUI Law Working Paper 2012/09. On past practices deploying such techniques and mechanisms, see B De Witte, 'The European Treaty Amendment for the Creation of a Financial Stability Mechanism' (2011) 6 *European Policy Analysis* 1. See also GM de Alberto, 'Legal Developments in the Economic and Monetary Union During the Debt Crisis: The Mechanisms of Financial Assistance' (2012) 49 *Common Market Law Review* 1613.

[28] The ESMT envisages, inter alia, that the Commission will 'negotiate, in liaison with the European Central Bank ("ECB"), the economic policy conditionality attached to each financial assistance' under the mandate given by the ESM Board of Governors (Art 5(6)(g)). The Commission shall be entrusted with assessment tasks in the process of granting stability support (Art 13(1)) as well as with negotiating and signing the memoranda of understanding with the ESM member requesting stability support (Art 13(2) and (3)) and then take part in the monitoring of the compliance with the memorandum (Art 13(7)). See also C-370/12 *Thomas Pringle v Government of Ireland, Ireland and The Attorney General* [2012] I-000, nyr, para 56 with regard to the tasks allocated to the Commission and para 157 with regard to tasks allocated to the ECB.

[29] M Ruffert, 'The European Debt Crisis and EU Law' (2011) 48 *Common Market Law Review* 1777; K Tuori 'The European Financial Crisis—Constitutional Aspects and Implications', EUI Law Working Paper 2012/28, 36.

[30] B De Witte, 'Treaty Revision Procedures after Lisbon' in A Biondi, P Eeckhout and S. Ripley (eds) *EU Law After Lisbon* (Oxford, Oxford University Press, 2012) 107. P Craig, *The Lisbon Treaty: Law, Politics and Treaty Reform* (Oxford, Oxford University Press, 2010) 443.

[31] See eg the Opinion of the European Central Bank of 17 March 2011 on a draft European Council Decision amending Article 136 of the Treaty on the Functioning of the European Union with regard to a stability mechanism for Member States whose currency is the euro (CON/2011/24), [2011] OJ C140/8, para 8; referred to in the *Riigikohus* judgment, recital 220: see n 40 below.

[32] Art 48 ESMT.

law.[33] Given that the largest contributor is Germany, contributing 27 per cent of the funds, the reality of the power dynamic of the ESM and its functional operation is apparent.[34] This is perhaps best revealed through the position of the courts, tribunals and committees regarding the compatibility of the ESMT with national sovereignty. In a number of the challenges to the ESM, sovereignty was considered through the 'legitimacy link'[35] mediated between national parliaments and the ESM by Member States' representatives on the ESM Board of Governors. However, this link varied substantially between the Member States. It depended upon the architecture of the legislative and executive branches and political control thereof, as well as the difference between debtor and creditor states of the ESM.[36] More importantly, unanimity in decision-making in the ESM Board of Governors is subject to exceptions and Member States may find themselves de facto and de jure excluded from decision-making in certain circumstances, such as if they are outvoted.[37] Overall, one can say that every possible step and device to construct 'postnational' arrangements has been availed of in this process. The esoteric character of these arrangements is thus further reinforced by its operational impact *upon* the Member States.

The decision of the creators of the ESM to avail themselves of a plethora of postnational devices resulted in the ESM being immune both to challenges of direct democracy that present a risk to integration processes as well as to oversight within the framework of supranational representative democracy—the European Parliament. The ESM, we might say, was hence envisaged to sail comfortably and safely between Scylla of national *demoi* and Charybdis of the European *demos* through its constitutive phase. This image would be persuasively intergovernmental were it not for the fact that the ESM also introduced, as we have mentioned, legally irrelevant states. It thus protected itself from the risks posed by consensual decision-making. The ESM, prior to its adjudication in the EU courts, plural, was a project with far-reaching consequences and little or no possibility for it to be controlled by the usual guardians. We claim that, postadjudication, the ESM remains standing after having been effectively vali-

[33] See on this specific point Advocate General J Kokott (2013) 34 *Michigan Journal of International Law*, www.mjilonline.org/wordpress/wp-content/uploads/2013/07/Kokott1.pdf.

[34] See Annex I to the ESMT for the Contribution Key. Spain (ESM Key: 11.9%), France (20.4%) and Italy (17.9%) are the only other countries with shares large enough to be able to prevent the entry into force pursuant to Article 48.

[35] See n 41 below: BVerfG judgment, recital 270.

[36] See eg the *Eduskunta* Grand Committee Statement SuVL 3/2011vp of 2 September 2011 ('Revision of the EFSF and ESM Agreements') 4. The Riigikohus referred to the size of Estonia's share and the relevance thereof for parliamentary control over ESM in recital 184. Similarly, see the Finnish Constitutional Law Committee, Report of the Constitutional Law Committee PeVL 5 and 12/2011; see Tuori (n 29) 40. The Irish Supreme Court found the combination of unanimous decision-making in the ESM Board of Governors and the controls of Parliament to suffice as a matter of sovereignty: *Pringle v The Government of Ireland* [2012] IESC 47, para 17. See MP Maduro, '*A New Governance for the European Union and the Euro: Democracy and Justice*' report for European Parliament, Committee for Constitutional Affairs (2012) http://cadmus.eui.eu/handle/1814/24295 (accessed 30 June 2013) 18, on the uncertainty of parliamentary control upon the ESM.

[37] See Art 4(4) and (8). See the BVerfG judgment recital 266.

dated by a number of courts. As we argue later on, it was also brought within the confines of EU law on the one hand and domestic constitutional law on the other hand by those same courts. By strengthening the link between the ESM and the national parliaments, the former has been brought within the sphere of oversight of the latter. The parliaments, in turn, have been activated to legitimize the ESM. The criteria established for the review of the ESM in the CJEU *Pringle* case can be expected to judicialize further the sphere of eurozone law. This is not to dismiss the comparative argument of judicial deference to representative democracy in the area of fiscal and monetary governance.[38] What we claim is that the present situation of eurozone law offers a specific situation in which the intervention of the EU courts, plural, was desired from the perspective of institutional balance.

Judicial review of these arrangements thus raises many questions and challenges for the rule of law. We examine next where and why the ESM was adjudicated.

III. THE ADJUDICATION OF THE ESM IN THE EU COURTS

The ESM was subject to judicial review in the highest courts of four Member States: the Supreme Court of Ireland,[39] the Estonian Supreme Court (Riigikohus),[40] the German Constitutional Court (Bundesverfassungsgericht)[41] and the Austrian Constitutional Court (Verfassungsgerichtshof).[42] At the time of writing, judicial review of the ESM was pending in the Constitutional Tribunal of Poland (Trybunal Konstytucyjni).[43] Only the Supreme Court of Ireland decided to engage in a formal judicial 'dialogue' with the CJEU pursuant to the preliminary reference mechanism. This followed the refusal of the Irish High Court below it to do so, as was within its discretion.[44] The other courts, it seems, did not even consider the possibility of referring questions to the CJEU.[45] In retrospect, the fact that the ESM was subject to several different judicial proceedings in a

[38] F Fabbrini, 'The Fiscal Compact, the 'Golden Rule' and the Paradox of European Federalism' (2013) 36 *Boston College International and Comparative Law Review* 1, and also in this volume.

[39] *Pringle v Government of Ireland* [2012] IESC 47.

[40] Supreme Court of Estonia, judgment of the Supreme court *en banc* of 12 July 2012, Case No 3-4-1-6-12, www.riigikohus.ee/?id=1347? (accessed 30 June 2013).

[41] Federal Constitutional Court, judgment of the Second Senate of 12 September 2012, Case No 2 BvR 1390/12, www.bundesverfassungsgericht.de/entscheidungen/rs20120912_2bvr139012.html (accessed 30 June 2013).

[42] Austrian Constitutional Court, judgment of March 16, 2013, Case No SV 2/12-18.

[43] With regard to the case before the Polish Constitutional Tribunal, www.trybunal.gov.pl/OTK/ezd/sprawa_lista_plikow.asp?syg=K%2033/12. Additionally, the ESM was the subject of review before the Constitutional Committee of the Finnish Parliament (Eduskunta) and the European Union Committee of the House of Lords of the United Kingdom. While these two bodies cannot strictly be considered a part of 'EU courts, plural', we list them here to highlight the amount of (quasi-) judicial attention that the ESM attracted—as well as the consequences of this attention. Also, we occasionally refer to the argumentation used by the Eduskunta.

[44] *Pringle v The Government of Ireland* [2012] IEHC 296.

[45] The Verfassungsgerichtshof was the only high court of a Member State that did not refer a

number of courts and review bodies across the EU implied that its creators, the EU Member States, ran the risk of facing diverging outcomes. Given that aspects of domestic procedural rules and litigation strategies varied across the Member States, the judicial review of the ESM would not generate similar outcomes. For example, the Riigikohus ruled on the ESMT itself,[46] the Bundesverfassungsgericht reviewed the ratification statutes introducing the ESM into the German legal order adopted by the German legislature, whilst the procedure in the Irish courts was initiated against both the European Council decision as well as the ratification statute of the ESMT itself, the European Communities (Amendment) Act 2012, along with a sovereignty challenge based upon Irish Constitutional law. The CJEU in turn, ruled on the validity of the European Council decision as an EU Act and on the question of whether a eurozone Member State was entitled to enter into and ratify an international agreement such as the ESMT, having regard to primary EU law (and general principles). This generated a tricky question as to the powers of the Court itself and its jurisdiction.[47]

Nevertheless, as the courts' rulings were in formal terms about differing legal norms, numerous 'suboptimal' outcomes for judicial review were possible. Firstly, the contested provisions of the legal instruments involved (European Council Decision, the amendments to the treaties, the ESMT, the ratifying statutes) are interconnected. However, the *fundamental basis* of the entire ESM structure was the European Council Decision which provided for a revision of the TFEU through a 'simplified' procedure. A finding of invalidity thereof would not have necessarily sent the creators of the ESM back to the drawing board since, in theory, the Decision qua Treaty amendment merely 'confirmed' the powers of the Member States to do this. However, it could have called into question the legitimacy of the procedures and instruments used. At the same time, whereas negative outcomes in the Riigikohus and in the Bundesverfassungsgericht would have prevented the respective state parties from ratifying the Treaty, in the case of Germany, as its largest shareholder, a negative outcome could possibly have killed off the ESM project.[48] Secondly, while a court might have technically ruled on the validity of one legal norm and pronounced on its validity in the operative part of its judgment, it was almost impossible not to transgress or indirectly review connected norms in its reasoning. A striking example of this is found in the judgment of the Bundesverfassungsgericht. Its decision was formally a ruling on the constitutionality of the German ratification statutes and in substance an appraisal of the legal instruments that the German legislature ratified—the

question to the CJEU and pronounced a ruling after the CJEU judgment in *Pringle* had already been delivered. The Verfassungsgerichtshof, however, referred to the CJEU judgment in its judgment.

[46] That is, Art 4(4) ESMT.

[47] C-370/12 *Thomas Pringle v Government of Ireland, Ireland and The Attorney General* [2012] I-000, nyr, para 28.

[48] S Schmidt, 'A Sense of Déja Vu? The FCC's Preliminary European Stability Mechanism Verdict' (2013) 14 *German Law Journal* 1, 2; B Ackerman and M Maduro, *Broken Bond*, Foreign Policy (17 September 2012), www.foreignpolicy.com/articles/2012/09/17/germany_euro_broken_bond (accessed 30 June 2013).

European Council Decision and the ESMT. Thus the complexity of the legal structure of the mechanism meant that there were several instruments exposed to contestation.

The interconnection between the legal instruments that form the 'multilevel fabric of the ESM is further revealed by the fact that the Bundesverfassungsgericht engaged in a review of compatibility of the ESM with EU primary law. In reviewing the German statute ratifying the ESMT,[49] the Court discussed a number of features of the ESM against the yardstick of the 'haushaltspolitische Gesamtverantwortung' ('overall budgetary responsibility') of the Bundestag. One of the features reviewed was the 'possible interplay'[50] between the ESM and the European Central Bank (ECB). The parties to the proceedings claimed that the ESM might become a vehicle of unconstitutional financing of the Member States through the ECB. In addressing this concern, the Bundesverfassungsgericht cited Article 123 TFEU as the provision prohibiting such financing and then mentioned the possibility that such financing is already precluded by the provision of Article 21/I ESMT. The Court saw no other option but to exclude all possible interpretations of the ESMT that would not be compatible with EU law. The explanation for this demand for the ESMT to be interpreted in conformity with the EU law—as provided by the German court—ties back into our observations on the esoteric character of the ESM. It is at this point that the Bundesverfassungsgericht unveiled its characterization of the ESMT: it is an 'internes Abkommen' ('internal agreement') between EU Member States and as such, it has to be interpreted in conformity with primary EU law.[51] As this point, we submit, the desired action of the Bundesverfassungsgericht would be to refer the issue of interpretation of primary law for a preliminary ruling to the CJEU. Less than three months later, the CJEU presented its own view of interpretation of Article 123 TFEU in relation to the ESM in *Pringle*.[52] Was the review of ESMT against Article 123 TFEU really necessary in the procedure before the Bundesverfassungsgericht? We can observe that in considering other features of the ESM, the Court usually quite meticulously lays down the connection between the provision of the ESMT and the 'overall budgetary responsibility' of the Bundestag. This is because the latter concept enabled it to link the review back to the invoked provisions of the Grundgesetz. In contrast, the Court does not expound on how the 'possible interplay' between ESM and ECB would have an impact on the overall budgetary responsibility. It seems plausible to believe there would be another possibility, couched in German constitutional language, to dismiss this contestation.

Among the three national high courts that form a part of *EU courts, plural*

[49] *Gesetz zu dem Vertrag vom 2 Februar 2012 zur Einrichtung des Europaeischen Stabilitaetsmechanismus*. See the Bundesverfassungsgericht judgment, paras 239 and 240.

[50] This is the Court translation of the phrase 'etwaiges Zusammenwirken', para 272.

[51] The Bundesverfassungsgericht relied on the CJEU judgment C-235/87 *Matteucci v Communauté française de Belgique* [1988] ECR 5589.

[52] C-370/12 *Pringle v Government of Ireland*, paras 123 et seq. See also the speech of Advocate General J Kokott delivered to the 'Justizpressekonferenz', Karlsruhe, 6 March 2013 (n 33).

in this account and have attracted our attention, the Riigikohus perhaps stood out with regard to how prevalently its ruling was worded in the language of national constitutional law. This is in comparison to—on the one hand—the Irish Supreme Court, which phrased the proceedings in *Pringle* clearly in terms of EU law and subsequently engaged in judicial dialogue with the CJEU and—on the other hand—with the Bundesverfassungsgericht which engaged in review of the ESMT against the yardstick of EU primary law but abstained from judicial dialogue. At the same time, the Riigikohus embraced to a large extent a version of, to borrow Halberstam's formulation, the 'embedded openness'[53] of the Estonian Constitution. Significantly, it even read some of its pro-EU stance into the constitutional text when it declared the economic and financial sustainability of the eurozone to belong to the constitutional values of Estonia as of the time Estonia became a member of the eurozone.[54] The abstention of the Riigikohus from the engagement in the judicial dialogue, coupled with a reading of the domestic constitutional text in a way that is open to claims of judicial authority from parallel legal systems, begs further the question: what was the reason that the Riigikohus majority's readiness to accommodate EU law in Estonian constitutional law did not result in an inclination towards further judicial dialogue? The possible reason for this dissonance could be in the unorthodox character of the ESMT. It can be concluded that the Riigikohus invested its energy into trying to classify the treaty it was reviewing. What was apparently embraced in the end was the Estonian government's theory of the ESMT as a 'dualist' treaty, although this was far from unanimously accepted when we take into account the stances of the dissenting judges.[55]

The specific reasons why the decisions of the different courts overlapped or varied because of jurisdictional limitations and the like is not, in our opinion, a convincing explanation for the incoherence in the judicial review of the ESM across the Member States. On the contrary, the adjudication of the ESM can be presented as an argument for a better co-ordinated system of judicial review in Europe. We submit that the ESM represents a context in which courts provide a unique participatory forum for contestation. The procedures before the three national courts that we look at show, on the one hand, a readiness to acknowledge the standing of the 'concerned citizen' (in Germany, the review of the ESM was triggered by a massive influx of individual constitutional complaints resembling a popular petition) and on the other hand, the interest of ombudsman-like organs in the exercise of control of the political and legal responses to the financial crisis (the procedure in Riigikohus was at the request of Estonia's Legal

[53] Discussing mutual embedded openness as part of the claim of pluralists: D Halberstam, 'Systems Pluralism and Institutional Pluralism in Constitutional Law: National, Supranational, and Global Governance' in M Avbelj and J Komárek (eds), *Constitutional Pluralism in the European Union and Beyond* (Oxford, Hart Publishing, 2012).

[54] Recitals 162–63 of the Riigikohus judgment. This was apparently not uncontroversial within the Court, taking into account the dissenting opinion of Justice Luik, para 15.

[55] See the dissenting opinion of Justice Jõks and five other Justices to the Riigikohus judgment, para 2.

Chancellor). The fact remains that the European judicial apparatus has been availed of. The Irish Supreme Court referred questions concerning the ESMT to the CJEU, and the CJEU engaged in substantive analysis thereof. We submit that this is proof that the preliminary ruling was an available and, to some extent, also a useful tool in the adjudication of the ESM. Accordingly, we look next at the character of the ESM through the 'lens' of the mechanism of a reference for a preliminary ruling to the CJEU. We consider the structural problem as to why the ESMT was not referred to the CJEU more widely. Looking for the answer to the question why the ESM is a case of suboptimal judicial dialogue, we can identify three possible approaches—which are not mutually exclusive. In fact, these approaches are intertwined. First, it could be that the framework for judicial dialogue among EU courts, plural, is to a certain extent flawed. Second, it is possible that the actions (or inaction) of the individual courts are problematic—within a system that is objectively well designed. Third, it is possible that it is the unorthodox legal solutions woven into the fabric of ESM that are responsible for the 'clogging' of the European judicial looms.

IV. THE EU COURTS, PLURAL AS A UNIQUE HOLISTIC FORUM FOR PARTICIPATION AND CONTESTATION: DEVICES, TIMES, LINKS AND INTERESTS

The fundamental link between national courts and the CJEU in the EU treaties is the preliminary reference mechanism (Article 267 TFEU), and the CJEU has carefully fostered a balance of roles therein.[56] The interaction between the CJEU and national courts within this device is widely depicted as a very successful dialogue mechanism. This does not reflect the fact that when we speak in terms of *Realpolitik*, it establishes a hierarchy.[57] Article 267 TFEU provides that last-instance courts must refer questions to the CJEU in a broad formulation of circumstances, albeit subject to vast exceptions.[58] However, there are many last-instance courts in the EU which, controversially, have never made a preliminary reference to the CJEU, such as the German Bundesverfassungsgericht.[59] Moreover, specialized constitutional courts may implicitly or explicitly reduce

[56] F Mayer, 'The European Constitution and the Courts' in A von Bogdandy (ed), *Principles of European Constitutional Law*, 2nd edn (Oxford, Hart Publishing and CH Beck, 2010) 287–88; T De La Mare and C Donnelly, 'Preliminary Rulings and EU Legal Integration: Evolution and *Stasis*' in P Craig and G de Búrca (eds), *The Evolution of EU law*, 2nd edn (Oxford, Oxford University Press, 2011) ch 13. G de Búrca and J Weiler (eds) *The European Court of Justice* (Oxford, Oxford University Press, 2011); A Dashwood and A Johnston *The Future of the Judicial System of the European Union* (Oxford, Hart Publishing, 2001); P Allott, 'Preliminary Rulings—Another Infant Disease' (2000) 25(2) *European Law Review* 538.

[57] See the account of JHH Weiler, 'Deciphering the Political and Legal DNA of European Integration' in J Dickson and P Eleftheriadis (eds), *Philosophical Foundations of European Union Law* (Oxford, Oxford University Press, 2012) 138.

[58] Most notably, through the doctrine of *acte claire*: see Case 283/81 *Srl CILFIT v Ministero della sanita*' [1982] ECR 4315.

[59] Or have only just begun (Spanish Constitutional Court): Case C-399/11 *Stefano Melloni v Minis-*

the extent to which they become part of the decentralized system of adjudication of EU law. This creates a structural problem for Article 267 TFEU.[60] It is thus a highly imperfect device and, arguably, a seriously flawed mechanism, although we pursue this theme less in the present context for reasons of space.

A more practical problem was posed by the expediency of resolving judicial review challenges to the ESM, assuaging markets and crucially 'funding' the eurozone, however indirect. The delay between sending a reference to the CJEU and receiving a decision from the Court became substantial over decades of expansion of the EU, sometimes rising to over 20 months. This delay was perceived to be so great as possibly to discourage national courts and litigants from seeking references. It resulted in new procedural rules.[61] In *Pringle v The Government of Ireland*, the Irish Supreme Court availed itself of these procedural provisions. It sought a ruling by way of the accelerated procedure pursuant to Article 104a of the Rules of Procedure of the CJEU on account of 'exceptional urgency' and possible damage to the eurozone from delayed ratification.[62] The decision of the CJEU on the reference from Ireland was hastily delivered after 34 days and a 'view' of the Advocate General published thereafter.[63] The Court thus accepted the urgency characterization. This urgency characterization, unmatched in any other jurisdiction, is highly significant. Urgency was referred to in passing in Estonia and the German Bundesverfassungsgericht delivered judgment on a temporary injunction. For Ireland, a small eurozone country, access to the ESM was essential.[64] Yet this characterization was also transferrable across all of the other Member States in various ways, including to its largest creditor, Germany. Its acceptance by the CJEU is perhaps a subtle point but nonetheless a critical

terio Fiscal [2013] ECR I–000. Also, the French Conseil Constitutionnel's first referral is pending before the CJEU at the time of writing.

[60] Mayer (n 57) 287–88.

[61] Memorandum by D Chalmers to the UK House of Lords, European Union Committee; Justice and Institutions Sub-Committee, 'Inquiry into the Workload of the Court of Justice of the European Union' (24 September 2010), written evidence, 17–18, www.parliament.uk/documents/lords-committees/eu-sub-com-e/courtofjustice/euewrittenevidence.pdf (accessed 30 June 2013).

[62] Supreme Court of Ireland: *Pringle v The Government of Ireland* [2012] IESC 47.

[63] Case C-370/12 *Thomas Pringle v Government of Ireland, Ireland and the Attorney General*, View of Advocate General Kokott delivered on 26 October 2012 [2013] ECR I-000.

[64] Not only that, the Irish courts found that other Member States had a similar interest:

> The High Court accepted evidence from the State to the effect that the ESM Treaty Members, including Ireland, and the Member States of the European Union all have pressing interest in Ireland's timely ratification of the ESM Treaty and that the stability of the euro area would be seriously damaged by delayed ratification. … The State says that a range of adverse consequences may ensue if Ireland does not ratify the ESM Treaty in the short term, for example, detrimental impact on Ireland's phased re-entry into the financial markets and a serious set-back to the substantial progress made to date by Ireland towards completing and exiting the EU-IMF programme by 2013. … In evidence placed before the Supreme Court on the injunction issue, it was suggested that a failure to ratify and implement the measures contained within the ESM Treaty at the earliest possible stage would lead to irreparable harm both to the interests of Ireland and those of the euro zone generally.'

Supreme Court of Ireland, *Pringle v The Government of Ireland* [2012] IESC 47, para 17. Although the subsequent adequacy of the ESM for Ireland has been under review since *Pringle*.

one. The related practical issues of caseload and the time required to deliver a judgment can be connected to the first possible reason for the suboptimal use of judicial dialogue. We have observed that the procedural order itself features mechanisms available when expediency is of essence. However, at the same time, we have highlighted the indications that courts in Member States were pressured to deliver judgments without any delay. We cannot do away with the possibility that the courts, feeling the time pressure, took this as a justification for abstaining from judicial dialogue. In that sense, the uncertainty of the duration of the procedure before the CJEU can represent a flaw of the judicial architecture that could have led to the suboptimal course of the ESM saga.

To return to the larger question of the function of the preliminary reference mechanism, the metaphor of the preliminary reference mechanism as a dialogue arguably wears thin where courts simply do not deploy it. This prevails irrespective of whether they are preciously guarding their autonomy or generously interpreting exceptions to the preliminary reference obligation, especially where an urgent request *was* possible. We suggest that the German, Estonian and Finnish courts, tribunal and Committee. respectively could have through their own motion referred questions similar to the Irish Supreme Court. To put it another way, one can say that the protection of their own autonomy or the procedural limitations of the proceedings before them countenanced referrals, but this was not insurmountable. In the end, there is a distinct lack of dialogue with the CJEU, which could and should have been the case, on account of the esoteric form and character of the ESMT. The specific manner in which EU institutions and national participation and contestation has been limited in the construction of the ESM, even curtailed and manipulated, entails that judicial review thereof may operate as a powerful check on its character. The legalization of governance through courts is a palpable feature of contemporary EU law[65] and courts can provide more legitimate fora for contestation of norms in certain circumstances.[66] Given the awkward relationship of postnational rules such as the ESM with both the nation state and supranational EU treaty law, the EU courts, plural, may provide a unique and appropriate forum for contestation. The courts of the Member States uniquely operate as the forum for checks and balances of the ESM, with limited further review possible before the CJEU, also on account of the nature of the ESM as an entity conceived outside of the EU treaties. It manipulated the character of its instruments and the place of the Member States. In this regard, the preliminary reference mechanism is thus not only an important device in the EU treaties linking legal orders: it also provides a unique forum for the participation of interests.

Our claim of EU courts, plural, being a unique participatory forum may face relevant contestation in light of the fact that all the courts that have ruled on the

[65] RD Kelemen, 'Eurolegalism and Democracy' (2012) 50 *Journal of Common Market Studies* 55; *Eurolegalism: The Transformation of Law and Regulation in the EU* (Cambridge MA, Harvard University Press, 2012).

[66] See Cichowski (n 18).

ESM so far have *validated* it and thus delivered limited noise at zero through judicial review, displaying what we might term 'soft' or less than hard-edged reviewability.[67] What fuels this contestation are indications that the courts, to varying extents, have acted in a result-oriented manner and entered into adjudicative processes with strong reluctance toward slowing down or even effectively terminating the ESM project.[68] To borrow Borger's words (regarding the CJEU), the courts allegedly did 'what [they] were expected', the outcome of their work was 'unsurprising'.[69] An examination of how the analysed courts reached certain conclusions that enabled them to reject the claims against the ESM provides support for the criticism of result-oriented adjudication. We take the Bundesverfassungsgericht's ruling on the provision of Article 4(8) ESMT as an example. If one was to summarize the fundamental message of the German ESM case on the back of a business card, it would be the concern for the safeguarding of the budgetary powers and responsibilities of the Bundestag as the timeless embodiment of representative democracy in German against ephemeral decisions taken by the composition of the Bundestag at any given moment.[70] A failure to comply with Germany's financial obligations would lead to suspension of voting rights (pursuant to Article 4(8) ESMT) and temporarily shut down the 'overall budgetary responsibility' of the Bundestag, the central constitutional value in the Bundesverfassungsgericht's judgment. Nevertheless, the Bundesverfassungsgericht found Article 4(8) ESMT 4(8) constitutionally unproblematic, apparently satisfied with the argument that it is the obligation of Germany *anyway* to pay its dues. In the eyes of the Court, Germany's respect for its obligation 'practically excludes' the possibility that Germany's voting rights would be suspended.[71] The preparedness of the Court to rely on the willingness and capability of the other two branches of government to pay the ESM contributions is surprising when observed against the principal constitutional canon followed by the Bundesverfassungsgericht in the ESM case. It thus hints at the result-oriented readiness of the Court to loosen up some of its constitutional apparatus to accommodate for some of the solutions in the ESM. There is also an example in the CJEU *Pringle* judgment where the interpretative path taken by the Court hints towards result-oriented adjudication: it is how the CJEU reconciled the ESM with the 'no-bailout' provision in Article 125 TFEU.[72] In Borger's words, this was the most difficult task for the CJEU in *Pringle*.[73] The Court's relativization of the prohibition of financial assistance in Article 125 ('shall not assume …'), which

[67] In addition to the courts we put most focus on in this piece, we should at this point recall that the ESM was also upheld in the High Court of Ireland before the Supreme Court engaged in judicial dialogue.

[68] We are grateful to Paul Craig for his comments on this issue.

[69] V Borger, 'The ESM and the European Court's Predicament in Pringle' (2013) 14 *German Law Journal*, 113.

[70] See para 228 of the BVerfG judgment (n 41).

[71] Ibid, BVerfG judgment, para 268.

[72] C-370/12 *Thomas Pringle v Government of Ireland* (n 12) paras 130 et seq.

[73] Borger (n 69) 124.

in turn enables the Court to lay down the conditions under which the ESM can be validated, is founded in part on the finding that the text of the prohibition that stems from the text of Article 123 ('shall be prohibited …') is stricter. In our opinion, to use the nuanced difference between the texts of the provisions of Articles 123 and 125 as grounds for such a weighty interpretation hints at the possibility that the Court was acting in a result-oriented manner.

Taking these doubts into consideration, we find convincing arguments for the counterclaim that while the courts might have bent the established canon of interpretation to a certain degree in order not to block the process of construction of the ESM, they have nevertheless played a role within the system of checks and balances and exercised judicial control of the other branches of government on the basis of judicial review generated by EU law. While they have validated the ESM project, they have nevertheless drawn various boundaries. We find support for this counterclaim in the following examples. First, the jurisdiction of CJEU to answer the first question (the validity of the European Council Decision amending the text of the TFEU) referred by the Irish Supreme Court was far from unequivocally recognized. No less than ten Member States, the majority of eurozone countries, as well as the European Council and the European Commission contested the jurisdiction of the Court with the argument that the Court cannot assess the validity of the EU treaties.[74] The CJEU, however, asserted jurisdiction and thereby also established a precedent in judicial review of the new simplified treaty revision procedure.[75] The link to the provision of Article 19 charging the CJEU with 'ensuring that the law is observed' is in a way a 'mini *Marbury v Madison*', basing judicial power of review on a textually open, near-programmatic provision. In the context of our discussion focusing on the way the EU courts, plural, cope with new forms of governance in the area of eurozone law, we find that the Court took an important step towards maintaining a check on future lawmaking. Similarly, while the Bundesverfassungsgericht with its judgment of 12 September 2012 effectively validated the ESM and gave a green light to Germany to enter the Mechanism, its affirmation has already been dubbed as a 'yes, but …'.[76] The most assertive conditions of the Bundesverfassungsgericht in order for the ESM to be validated are the demands for the Federal Republic to ensure—in the process of the ratification—that the members of the ESM will interpret the provisions of the ESMT in conformity with the German constitution.[77] A 'yes, but …' answer is not the only pattern developed

[74] C-370/12 *Thomas Pringle v Government of Ireland* (n 12) para 30.

[75] For a more extensive discussion of this development, see De Witte and Beukers (n 22) 825–27.

[76] K Schneider, 'Yes, But … One More Thing: Karlsruhe's Ruling on the European Stability Mechanism' (2013) 14 *German Law Journal* 53, 54. Schneider connects this conditional approach in the 2012 ESM judgment with the pattern of previous 'European case law' of the Bundesverfassungsgericht.

[77] Federal Constitutional Court, judgment of the Second Senate of 12 September 2012, Case No 2 BvR 1390/12, paras, 25–253. For a press release with details on the interpretative statement issued by the signatories upon the initiative of Germany, see: www.bundesfinanzministerium.de/Content/EN/Pressemitteilungen/2012/2012-09-26-federal-government-paves-the-way-for-permanent-esm.html?view=renderPrint (accessed 27 June 2013).

by the Bundesverfassungsgericht in its 'European case law' and followed in the ESM judgment. Wendel notes 'numerous and profound critique' of the Court's approach to standing to file a constitutional complaint in these cases, construing 'the right to vote as the key to the admissibility of the constitutional complaints, and thus enables virtually every German citizen with the right to vote to initiate a de facto objective review of constitutionality regarding domestic acts approving the ratification of EU reform measures'.[78] In the case of the ESM, this understanding of access to judicial review is confirmed in the rapidly changing area of eurozone law.[79] In that sense, we see it as a signal of the Court's willingness to exercise judicial control over new and innovative legal solutions in this area that might emerge in the future. While there is no general possibility of individual interests in the form of *amicus curiae* representations before the CJEU yet, Member States have a broad discretion to intervene and participate in preliminary references from other Member States, availed of in *Pringle* but not necessarily uniformly or consistently with their own judicial or parliamentary bodies.[80] Thus, participation must be more broadly and successfully fostered amongst the EU courts, plural, within this specific judicial architecture.

V. CONCLUSIONS

The ESM 'saga', if we may term it that, retells a familiar tale of the dialogue between Member State courts and the CJEU. It also tells the tale of the subtle contest between postnationalism and the Member States, procedurally and substantively. Procedurally, the adjudication of the ESM emphasizes how the discretionary exceptions and limitations of the preliminary ruling mechanism fundamentally impinge upon its intent. In the absence of any indication by the Member State courts that did not refer the case the CJEU on whether this option was at all considered, we do not know with certainty the reasons for non-referral. As we have outlined here, time pressures as well as the safeguarding of constitutional autonomy may constitute possible explanations for the reluctance to engage in interjudicial dialogue. The desire on the part of the domestic courts to retain the competence for review rooted in the concern for constitutional autonomy connects to the second possible reason for the suboptimal course of the multilevel adjudication in the case of ESM that we have identified above: within the objectively efficient matrix of the procedure of preliminary ruling,

[78] M Wendel, 'Judicial Restraint and the Return to Openness: The Decision of the German Federal Constitutional Court on the ESM and the Fiscal Treaty of 12 September 2012' (2013) 14 *German Law Journal* 21, 24.

[79] With the words of the Bundesverfassungsgericht, in the area of 'Ersatzunionsrecht'. Federal Constitutional Court, judgment of the Second Senate of 12 September 2012, Case No 2 BvR 1390/12, para 259,

[80] On the historically uneven use of this procedure, see MP Granger, 'When Governments Go to Luxembourg …: The Influence of Governments on the European Court of Justice' (2004) 29 *European Law Review* 1.

the national courts choose actions that reduce the strength of this mechanism. However, the third possible reason for the suboptimal course should be considered: that the ESM with its esoteric character was too elusive for the national courts to act in a more orchestrated manner. In other words, the ambiguity of the ESM lead courts to different conclusions on what was the proper forum for its review.

These issues need to be reflected upon in future discourse on the role of courts not only in the sphere of eurozone law, but also more broadly. While the former, to a large extent, remains intrinsically connected to the caseload issue that the CJEU continues to face, the latter invites a discussion on the role of Member States' courts in the architecture of the EU judiciary. Accordingly, and more substantively, the complex balance between the Member States and the EU that we can observe in the ESM instruments in terms of tasks, functions and obligations entails that the future development of eurozone law may see further 'innovation' between the supranational and national levels. The ESM saga indicates that if the Member States continue to avail themselves of creative instruments of esoteric postnational character curbing or purporting to curb judicial review or national plebiscites on their character, this will require a rethink of the architecture of the EU judiciary, at supranational and national level, as much as the instruments themselves.

17

The Impact of Stronger Economic Policy Co-ordination on the European Social Dimension: Issues of Legitimacy

FRANCESCO COSTAMAGNA*

I. INTRODUCTION

MOST OF THE measures taken by the EU[1] in response to the crisis have the primary aim of remedying the structural weaknesses of the European Economic and Monetary Union (EMU), in order to contribute to its consolidation. Strengthening economic policy co-ordination represents a building block of this strategy, since, as duly emphasized by the so-called Four Presidents' Report, it 'is essential for the smooth functioning of the EMU and is an essential counterpart to the financial and fiscal frameworks'.[2]

An important step in that direction has been taken with the creation of the European Semester, an umbrella framework that brings together different co-ordination processes, connecting them with existing or new surveillance mechanisms. The interplay between the different components of the Semester gives EU institutions an unprecedented capacity for policy formulation, guidance and monitoring of virtually the entire spectrum of Member States' economic and social policies. This feature aims at avoiding the possibility that national authorities may keep adopting unsustainable policy choices, which could jeopardise the stability of the EMU and, thus, endanger the future of the common currency. On the other side, such an evolution touches upon a key prerequisite for the legitimacy of the European integration process, as it affects the socioeconomic

* The author wishes to thank the participants at the conference 'The Constitutionalization of European Budgetary Constraints: Comparative and Interdisciplinary Perspectives', Tilburg Law School, 30–31 May 2013 for their useful comments on an earlier version of this paper. Furthermore, he is grateful to Ornella Porchia, Annamaria Viterbo and Andrea Spagnolo for their help in the finalization of the chapter. All errors remain my own.

[1] See generally R Cisotta and A Viterbo, 'La crisi del debito sovrano e gli interventi dell'UE: dai primi strumenti finanziari al "Fiscal Compact"' (2012) *Il Diritto dell'Unione europea* 323, 323–66.

[2] 'Towards a Genuine Economic and Monetary Union', report prepared by the President of the European Council in collaboration with the Presidents of the Commission, the Eurogroup and the European Central Bank, EUCO 120/12, 26 June 2012, 6.

model that is at the basis of the European integration process, by prioritizing a narrow set of economic objectives over other competing ones. Furthermore, the new mechanism impinges on the relationship between the supranational level and the national one in key policy areas, putting severe constraints on Member States' autonomy in the exercise of some of their core social functions.

This chapter aims at assessing the impact of the measures taken to strengthen economy policy co-ordination on the European social dimension and, in particular, on the relationship between economic and social objectives in the context of the European integration process. The chapter is structured as follows. First, it looks at the evolution of the European social dimension and at the relationship between the 'economic' and the 'social', arguing that the need to find a balance between these two dimensions does represent an essential prerequisite for the legitimacy of the European integration process. Secondly, the analysis focuses on the European Semester, examining its architecture and its main components. Thirdly, it takes into consideration the impact of the new co-ordination mechanism on the relationship between the supranational level and the national one in the social domain, by focusing on the extensive powers granted to EU institutions to intervene in this field. Fourthly, it examines the way in which the European Semester, at least in its early cycles, has tended to prioritize a narrow set of economic objectives, such as budgetary discipline and economic growth, over social ones.

II. THE EUROPEAN SOCIAL DIMENSION AND THE LEGITIMACY OF THE EUROPEAN INTEGRATION PROCESS

The European social dimension has been traditionally conceived as a rebalancing factor against the disruptive effects caused on the functioning of national social security systems by the deepening of the supranational economic integration process. In other words, its creation and progressive strengthening has primarily aimed at safeguarding the so-called 'European Social Model',[3] by restoring the balance between the 'economic' and the 'social' within the EU.

The need to find a point of equilibrium between these two dimensions has been considered an essential prerequisite for the legitimacy of the European integration process since its inception. This concern was a key determinant of the choice made by the Treaty of Rome of 1957 to decouple the economic sphere from the social one—leaving the latter firmly in Member States' hands, while opening the former to supranational intervention. Indeed, rather than a sign

[3] F Scharpf, 'The European Social Model: Coping with the Challenges of Diversity' (2002) 40 *Journal of Common Market Studies* 645, 645–70. This chapter uses the admittedly controversial concept of a 'European social model' to identify a socioeconomic order in which economic growth and social cohesion are seen as objectives having an equal status and that thus have to be jointly pursued by striking a workable balance between competing interests and values.

of the founding fathers' 'social frigidity',[4] the creation of a double-track model was meant to enhance the legitimacy of the common market's legal order, by allowing the process of economic integration to proceed without affecting the capacity of national social security systems to absorb any negative social effect deriving from it.[5] Furthermore, this choice rested on the assumption that the benefits accruing from an integrated market at supranational level would have even contributed to reinforcing national social security systems, by increasing Member States' capacity to engage in redistributive functions. This vision was translated into the European legal order, by excluding almost any possibility for the then European Economic Community to intervene into the social sphere. The only partial exception was the conferral of the power to adopt those social measures that were functional to the realization of the integrated market, such as the co-ordination of social security systems to facilitate the free movement of workers.[6]

The deterioration of the economic situation in the mid-1970s contributed to the demise of the embedded liberalism compromise,[7] progressively altering the relationship between the 'economic' and the 'social' within the European integration process. In particular, as aptly observed by Giubboni, '[t]he order of political values and priorities was reversed [as] the market ... (re)assumed a position at the top of the list of objectives'.[8] The original division of labour between the national and the supranational levels came under severe pressure, due to the progressive deepening and widening of economic integration following the adoption of the internal market programme and the Single European Act, as well as the infiltration of internal market rules into the social spheres of the Member States.[9] The latter evolution can be mainly ascribed to the Court of Justice of the European Union (CJEU), which, especially from the 1990s onwards, started to assess the compatibility of key components of national welfare states with internal market rules. This was the case, for instance, with the application of competition and state aid rules to social insurance monopolies or norms on the freedom to provide services to cross-border medical treatments.[10]

The infiltration of internal market law has been perceived as a threat to the

[4] GF Mancini, 'Principi fondamentali del diritto del lavoro nell'ordinamento delle Comunità europee' in *Il lavoro nel diritto comunitario e l'ordinamento italiano* (Padova, Cedam, 1988) 33.

[5] See especially S Giubboni, 'European Citizenship and Social Rights in Times of Crisis', LPF Working Paper No 2 (2013) 7–8.

[6] Art 51 of the Treaty Establishing the European Economic Community.

[7] See especially K Polanyi, *The Great Transformation. The Political and Economic Origins of Our Times* (Boston, Beacon Press, 2001)—although there are tensions between its use by Polanyi and its use today. See especially G Dale, 'Lineages of Embeddedness: On the Antecedents and Successors of a Polanyian Concept' (2011) 70 *American Journal of Economics and Sociology* 306, 306-39.

[8] S Giubboni, *Social Rights and Market Freedom in the European Constitution. A Labour Law Perspective* (Cambridge, Cambridge University Press, 2006) 20.

[9] G Lyon-Caen, 'L'infiltration du droit du travail par le droit de la concurrence' (1992) *Droit Ouvrier* 313, 313–59.

[10] See generally F Costamagna, 'The Internal Market and the Welfare State: Anything New After Lisbon?', in M Trybus and L Rubini (eds), *The Treaty of Lisbon and the Future of European Law and Policy* (Cheltenham and Northampton, MA, Edward Elgar, 2011) 382–84.

viability of national social solidarity arrangements[11] and, consequently, as potentially affecting the legitimacy of the economic integration process. Indeed, this evolution upset the balance between the economic and the social dimensions, as the progressive infiltration of supranational economic law into the social sphere, and the ensuing erosion of Member States' social sovereignty, has not been matched by the strengthening of supranational social governance mechanisms.[12] Lack of political consensus blocked any attempt to fill the constitutional gap between market-creating and market-correcting functions, leaving the EU without legal powers, or financial capabilities, to engage in proper redistributive activities, so to compensate for the reduced capacity of Member States to intervene.

The Treaty of Lisbon sought to remedy to this situation, by trying to enhance the safeguard of social interests vis-à-vis economic ones and by explicitly making the balance between the pursuit of economic objectives and the safeguard of social ones a fundamental principle of the EU legal order. This feature is very much evident with regard to the modification of the catalogue of aims to be pursued by the EU. The new Article 3 TEU gives unprecedented visibility to a host of social objectives, establishing, for instance, that the EU 'shall work for the sustainable development of Europe based on … a highly competitive social market economy, aiming at full employment and social progress', and it 'shall combat social exclusion and discrimination, and shall promote social justice and protection, equality between women and men, solidarity between generations and protection of the rights of the child'. The proclamation of these objectives may sound hollow,[13] especially if read in the light of the choice not to confer on the EU any new legal powers to pursue them. However, the added value of this provision lies in the choice to put these aims on a par with more traditional economic ones, such as the establishment of an internal market. A corollary of this choice is the duty for EU and national institutions to strike a balance between competing objectives that enjoy the same constitutional status.

This duty is expressly imposed by the so-called 'horizontal social clause' contained in Article 9 TFEU. The provision establishes that 'in defining and implementing its policies, the Union shall take into account requirements linked to the promotion of a high level of employment, the guarantee of adequate social protection, the fight against social exclusion and a high level of education, training and protection of human health'. The clause has been defined as 'the most important innovation of the Lisbon Treaty', marking the 'appearance within the constitutional arena of [a] potentially strong [anchor] that can induce

[11] Compare C Joerges, 'A Reinassance of the European Economic Constitution?', in U Neergard, R Nielsen and LM Roseberry (eds), *Integrating Welfare Functions into EU Law* (Copenhagen, Djøf Publishing, 2009) 37–51. See also M Ferrera, 'Friends not Foes: European Integration and National Welfare States' (2010) URGE Working Paper No 10/2006, 3.

[12] Giubboni (n 8) 26 speaks about a 'joint sovereignty trap' to describe such a situation.

[13] For a critical assessment of the reference to the concept of 'social market economy', see C Joerges and F Rödl, '"Social Market Economy" as Europe's Social Model?', EUI Working Paper No 2004/8(2004), 19–21.

and support all EU institutions … in the task of finding an adequate (and more stable) balance between economic and social objectives'.[14] This assessment may sound overoptimistic, if measured against the uncertain language used in the provision to define the obligations of EU institutions. However, it can be hardly denied that the clause has an important value from a constitutional perspective, as it clarifies that the need to find a balance between economic and social objectives lies at the core of the European legal order, representing a requirement for the legitimacy of EU action.

A similar function can be also performed by the EU Charter of Fundamental Rights (Charter) and, in particular, by the social rights contained therein, which now enjoy the 'same legal value as the Treaties'.[15] This recognition is admittedly accompanied by many doubts as to the scope of the legal obligations descending from the Charter's provisions on social rights, due, inter alia, to the reference to the unclear distinction between rights and principles.[16] However, the new status acquired by the Charter strengthens the role of social rights as a shield,[17] ie as a balancing factor vis-à-vis the disruptive effects that the application of EU law may have on the functioning of social security systems. Their capacity to perform such a defensive role was already recognized even when the legal value of the Charter was still uncertain[18] and, therefore, it cannot but be reinforced once it has become a primary source of EU law.

Although certainly welcome, all these reforms have an eminently defensive character, mainly seeking to reassert the original division of powers in the social sphere in the face of the activism of the CJEU with regard to the application of internal market law. Conversely, there is little going forward, as the Treaty of Lisbon left substantially untouched the allocation of competences in this domain,[19] ruling out any possibility of introducing stronger social anchors at supranational level. Therefore, respect for the capacity of Member States to carry out their redistributive functions still represents a building block of the EU social dimension and, hence, a prerequisite for the legitimacy of actions undertaken by EU institutions.

[14] M Ferrera, 'Modest Beginnings, Timid Progresses: What's Next for Social Europe?', in B Cantillon, H Verschueren and P Ploscar (eds), *Social Inclusion and Social Protection in the EU: Interactions between Law and Policy* (Cambridge, Antwerp and Portland, Intersentia, 2012) 29.

[15] Art 6 TEU.

[16] C Hilson, 'Rights and Principles in EU Law: A Distinction Without Foundation?' (2008) 15 *Maastricht Journal of European and Comparative Law* 193, 193–215.

[17] D Damjanovic and B De Witte, 'Welfare Integration through EU Law: The Overall Picture in the Light of the Lisbon Treaty', in Neergaard, Nielsen and Roseberry (n 11) 80

[18] M Poiares Maduro, 'The Double Constitutional Life of the Charter of Fundamental Rights of the European Union', in T Hervey and J Kenner (eds), *Economic and Social Rights under the EU Charter of Fundamental Rights: A Legal Perspective* (Oxford, Hart Publishing, 2003) 284–86.

[19] Arts 153 and 168 TFEU—concerning, respectively, social protection and healthcare—confirm that the EU can only intervene to complement and support the activities of Member States, while fully respecting their competences in organizing, funding and managing national social security systems.

III. THE EUROPEAN SEMESTER AND ITS COMPLEX LEGAL ARCHITECTURE

A stronger economic co-ordination represents a cornerstone of the new European economic governance,[20] tentatively filling the original EMU constitutional gap that derives from the choice of creating a common currency without having an economic union in place.[21] One of its main objectives is to foster economic convergence in a number of key policy areas, so as to remedy to structural imbalances and, thus, ensure the smooth functioning of the EMU. On the other side, it helps to strengthen supranational control over economic and fiscal decisions taken at national level. This was perceived as a necessary countermeasure to the profligacy of certain Member States, mostly southern ones, that, according to the dominant narrative of the crisis,[22] was one of the main causes for the dire situation that is endangering the future of the European integration process.[23]

The fulcrum of the new system is the European Semester,[24] a framework that, after being launched as a code of conduct for the implementation of the Stability and Growth Pact (SGP),[25] has been fully codified by the so-called 'six-pack'[26] and, in particular, by Regulation (EU) No 1175/2011 that amended Regulation (EC) No 1466/97 on the preventive arm of the SGP. The Semester brings under the same umbrella different strains of EU policy co-ordination and surveillance that touch upon both economic and social policy aspects, with the specific objec-

[20] Four Presidents' Report (n 2) 3.

[21] F Snyder, 'EMU Revisited. Are We Making a Constitution? What Constitution Are We Making?', EUI Working Paper No 98/6 (1998) 13–17.

[22] P Tsoukala, 'Narratives of the European Crisis and the Future of (Social) Europe', Georgetown Public Law and Legal Theory Research Paper No 13-012 (2013).

[23] See generally D Adamski, 'National Power Games and Structural Failures in the European Macroeconomic Governance' (2012) 49 *Common Market Law Review* 1319, 1325–29.

[24] On the mechanism see M Hallerberg, B Marzinotto and GB Wolff, 'An Assessment of the European Semester', Study for the European Parliament's Committee on Economic and Monetary Affairs, IP/A/ECON/ST/2010-24 (Brussels, 2012).

[25] Commission Communication, 'Reinforcing Economic Policy Coordination' ,COM(2010) 250.

[26] It consists of six normative measures that entered into force on 13 December 2011 and that aim to strengthen fiscal and macroeconomic surveillance at the EU level. As for the fiscal side, the six-pack strengthened the SGP, through the adoption of the following acts: Regulation (EU) No 1175/2011 of the European Parliament and of the Council of 16 November 2011 amending Council Regulation (EC) No 1466/97 of 7 July 1997 on the strengthening of the surveillance of budgetary positions and the surveillance and coordination of economic policies [2011] OJ L306/12; Regulation (EU) No 1177/2011 of the European Parliament and of the Council of 8 November 2011 amending Council Regulation (EC) No 1467/97 of 7 July 1997 on speeding up and clarifying the implementation of the excessive deficit procedure [2011] OJ L306/33; Regulation (EU) No 1173/2011 of the European Parliament and of the Council of 16 November 2011 on the effective enforcement of budgetary surveillance in the euro area [2011] OJ L306/1; Council Directive No 2011/85/EU of 8 November 2011 on requirements for budgetary frameworks of the Member States [2011] OJ L304/41. Furthermore, the six-pack also introduced the so-called Macroeconomic Imbalance Procedure, with the adoption of Regulation (EU) No 1176/2011 of the European Parliament and of the Council of 16 November 2011 on the prevention and correction of macroeconomic imbalances [2011] OJ L306/25 and Regulation (EU) No 1174/2011 of the European Parliament and of the Council of 16 November 2011 on enforcement measures to correct excessive macroeconomic imbalances in the euro area [2011] OJ L306/8.

tive of increasing consistency among instruments that have different legal bases and rely upon distinct enforcement mechanisms. For this reason, the Semester's function has been aptly described as 'the coordination of coordination'.[27]

The Semester rests upon three main pillars, namely the Europe 2020 Integrated Guidelines, the SGP and the Macroeconomic Imbalances Procedure. In more detail, as provided for by Article 2a of Regulation (EC) No. 1466/97, its constituent parts are: definition, and surveillance over the implementation, of the Broad Economic Policy Guidelines and of the Employment Guidelines; submission and assessment of Members States' Stability or Convergence Programmes (SCPs), as well as of National Reform Programmes (NRPs); and, lastly, surveillance to prevent and correct macroeconomic imbalances.

The whole process starts in November with the adoption of the Annual Growth Survey (AGS) by the Commission. The AGS is a policy document detailing a list of priorities and objectives for the EU and Member States aimed at ensuring that their policies align with the SGP and Europe 2020 Strategy. After its endorsement by the European Council in the spring meeting, the content of the AGS should feed into Member States' NRPs and SCPs. NRPs are policy documents adopted under the Europe 2020 Strategy that set out Member States' strategy in areas such as economic growth, employment and social inclusion for the following 12 months. They have to be drafted and implemented by following the guidance offered by the Europe 2020 Integrated Guidelines,[28] which have been adopted by the Council in 2010 in order to contribute to Europe 2020 priorities[29] and to achieve its headline targets.[30] Furthermore, NRPs should also make reference to the measures adopted under the Euro Plus Pact,[31] at least for

[27] K Armstrong, 'The Lisbon Agenda and Europe 2020: From the Governance of Coordination to the Coordination of Governance', in P Copeland and D Papadimitriou (eds), *The EU's Lisbon Strategy: Evaluating Success, Understanding Failure* (Basingstoke, Palgrave Macmillan, 2012) 208–28.

[28] The Integrated Guidelines merge the Employment Guidelines (Council Decision 2010/707/EU of 21 October 2010 on guidelines for the employment policies of the Member States [2010] OJ L308/46) and the Broad Economic Policy Guidelines (Council Recommendation of 13 July 2010 on broad guidelines for economic policies of the Member States and of the Union, [2010] OJ L191/28). The document contains 10 guidelines: ensuring the quality and sustainability of public finances, addressing macroeconomic imbalances, reducing imbalances in the eurozone, optimizing support for R&D and innovation, strengthening the knowledge triangle and unleashing the potential of the digital economy, improving resource efficiency and reducing greenhouse gases emissions, improving the business and consumer environment and modernizing the industrial base, increasing labour market participation and reducing structural unemployment, developing a skilled workforce responding to labour market needs, promoting job quality and lifelong learning, improving the performance of education and training systems at all levels and increasing participation in tertiary education, promoting social inclusion and combating poverty.

[29] The Europe 2020 strategy aims to enable the EU to achieve growth that is smart, sustainable and inclusive (Commission Communication, 'Europe 2020: A Strategy for Smart, Sustainable and Inclusive Growth, COM(2010) 2020).

[30] Increasing the employment rate of the population aged 20–64 to 75%; investing 3% of GDP in R&D; reducing carbon emissions by 20%, increasing the share of renewable energies by 20% and increasing energy efficiency by 20%; reducing the school dropout rate to less than 10% and increasing the proportion of tertiary degrees to 40%; reducing the number of people threatened by poverty by 20 million.

[31] The Pact has been agreed in 2011 by 23 Member States that committed to adopt a series

those states that signed this political commitment to enhance policy co-ordination. On the other hand, Stability Programmes—which take the name of Convergence Programmes for non-eurozone states—are to provide the Commission with all the necessary information for the purpose of multilateral surveillance to be conducted under Article 121 TFEU. According to Articles 3 and 7 of Regulation No 1466/97, SCPs represent 'an essential basis for the sustainability of public finances which is conducive to price stability, strong sustainable growth and employment creation'. To this end, they must contain a long list of detailed information on, inter alia, the medium-term budgetary objective (MTBO) together with the adjustment path toward it,[32] implicit or contingent government liabilities, the consistency of the SCP with the national reforms plan, and the main assumptions about economic developments covering the preceding, the current and the following three years.

Both these documents have to be submitted by 30 April every year, a point at which national budgetary processes are still at an early phase or are yet to begin. The two-pack[33] invites eurozone states to submit their documents and, in particular, their fiscal plans even earlier, by 15 April, although this is no longer mandatory as it was in the original proposal presented by the Commission in November 2011.[34] In May, the Commission evaluates national reform and fiscal plans and issues country-specific recommendations that set out the actions to be taken by the state concerned. These recommendations are, first, endorsed by the European Council and, then, discussed by the employment, economic and finance, and competitiveness formations of the Council. In July, country-specific recommendations are finally approved by the ECOFIN Council.

The approval of the two-pack[35] and, in particular, the adoption of Regulation

of actions in order to achieve five broad objectives contained therein: fostering competitiveness, fostering employment, contributing to the sustainability of public finances, reinforcing financial stability and strengthening tax policy co-ordination (see European Council Conclusions of 24/25 March 2011, EUCO10/1/11 of 20 April 2011, Annex 1).

[32] The definition of the MTBO, which should provide a realistic budgetary target for the state has been defined as 'the central duty' of states in the context of balanced budget regimes: D Chalmers, 'The European Redistributive State and a European Law of Struggle' (2012) 18 *European Law Journal* 667, 677–78. However the MTBO methodology has been criticized for 'focus[ing] on a handful of fiscal and growth variables and thus leav[ing] aside other important determinants of the sustainability of public finances': P Biraschi, M Cacciotti, D Iacovoni and J Pradelli, 'The New Medium-Term Budgetary Objective and the Problem of Fiscal Sustainability After the Crisis', Department of the Treasury, Ministry of the Economy and Finance Working Paper No 8 (2010), 6.

[33] Below, n 35.

[34] Proposal for a Regulation of the European Parliament and the Council on common provisions for monitoring and assessing draft budgetary plans and ensuring the correction of excessive deficit of the Members States in the euro area, COM(2011) 821 final.

[35] Composed by two different legislative measures, both addressing eurozone states only: Regulation (EU) No 472/2013 of the European Parliament and the Council of 21 May 2013 on the strengthening of economic and budgetary surveillance of Member States in the euro area experiencing or threatened with serious difficulties with respect to their financial stability [2013] OJ L140/1 and Regulation (EU) No. 473/2013 of the European Parliament and of the Council of 21 May 2013 on common provisions for monitoring and assessing draft budgetary plans and ensuring the correction of excessive deficit of the Member States in the euro area [2013] OJ L140/11.

(EU) No. 473/2013 adds a further step to the Semester, at least with regard to eurozone states. Indeed, the latter are now required to submit to the Commission, by 15 October, a draft budgetary plan for the following year, including a series of information regarding, for instance, general government expenditure by function—including on education, healthcare and employment—as well as the description and the quantification of expenditure and revenue measures included in the national draft budget. This allows the Commission to look into the measures proposed by national governments at the point at which these measures, and their modes of implementation, are discussed by national parliaments. The Commission has the power to step into the debate and, should it identify serious non-compliance with SGP obligations, even request the state concerned to submit a revised plan within three weeks.[36]

IV. THE EUROPEAN SEMESTER AS A FORM OF CO-GOVERNMENT: THE IMPACT ON MEMBER STATES' SOCIAL POWERS

A feature of the European Semester that must be considered in assessing its impact on the EU social dimension is its capacity to reach across the entire spectrum of Member States' economic and social policies. This enables EU institutions to exercise policy formulation, supervision and guidance on issues, such as the provision of social services or the regulation of the labour market, that fall within the competence of Member States. This does not represent an absolute novelty in the EU legal order, as EU institutions were capable of exercising these functions in the context of already existing policy co-ordination processes having a soft character. However, the creation of the Semester brings about some relevant innovations in this regard, considerably enhancing the capacity of EU institutions to intervene. The new framework is not a mere sum of past soft law processes, as co-ordination activities are now carried out under the shadow of hard law measures, or even financial sanctions for eurozon states, that can be adopted against those Member States that fail to comply with the recommendations. These measures can be adopted under the SPG, which has been revised and reinforced by the six-pack, or the macroeconomic imbalance procedure, which has been introduced ex novo by the same legislative package.

The interplay between the different components of the Semester brings EU institutions and Member States into a process of co-government that 'goes to the structure and rationale of a State fiscal and welfare system'.[37] Admittedly, the use of this notion may seem an overstatement of the role that EU institutions

[36] Art 6 of Regulation (EU) No 473/2013.

[37] Chalmers (n 32) 679–81. The author uses this concept only with regard to the three regimes aiming at securing balanced budgets, avoiding excessive deficits and avoiding and correcting macroeconomic imbalances. However, as this paragraph will seek to demonstrate, the notion can be used to describe the functioning of the Semester as a whole.

can play in this context. However, the term is worth using as it captures the essence of a process that goes beyond merely setting quantitative constraints on the spending capacities of Members States. Indeed, the whole process gives EU institutions unprecedented capacity to shape and control national social policies.

This feature emerges since the early phases of the Semester. On the one side, Article 2a of Regulation (EU) No 1466/97 empowers the Council to assess the programmes submitted by the Member States and to 'address guidance' to them making full use of the instruments provided for by the treaties, the SGP and the macroeconomic imbalances procedure. On the other, this provision requires Member States to take due account of the guidance 'in the development of their economic, employment and budgetary policies before taking *key decisions* on their national budgets' (emphasis added).

The element is also present in other stages of the process. As has been rightly observed,[38] in all these cases, the focus is not simply on whether the state is meeting the quantitative targets aimed at securing balanced budgets, avoiding excessive deficits or preventing macroeconomic imbalances, but on whether it is doing all it takes to move in that direction, by following the advice issued by EU institutions. This gives them wide discretion in the exercise of powers that, albeit often described as having a mere technical character, are eminently political in nature.

As for the excessive imbalance procedure, Article 8 of Regulation (EU) No 1176/2011 requires any 'Member State for which an excessive imbalance procedure is opened [to] submit a corrective action plan', detailing the remedial strategy. The plan is to be endorsed by the Council that, acting on a Commission's reports, may list the specific actions required and set a timetable for surveillance. Furthermore, Article 9 gives the Commission the power to carry out IMF-style missions in the concerned country, with the possibility to involve social partners and other national stakeholders in a dialogue.

A similar procedure is also envisaged in the context of the SGP. As for its preventive arm, Article 5 of Regulation (EU) No 1466/97 asks Member States to indicate, in their SCPs, their MTBO and an adjustment path toward it. In the event of a significant deviation from the path, the Commission may issue a warning and the Council, acting on a Commission's recommendation, may indicate which policy measures should be taken. The same feature is also very much present in the SGP's corrective arm, which may be launched should the Council decide on the existence of an excessive deficit or debt. In this case, the Council, acting on a recommendation from the Commission, may first recommend and, then, impose on the State the adoption of specific measures, as respectively provided for by paragraphs 7 and 9 of Article 126 TFEU. The so-called 'two-pack' further strengthens this process of co-government in the context of the excessive deficit procedure, at least with regard to eurozone states. Indeed, Article 9 of Regulation (EU) No 473/2013, transposing into the EU

[38] Ibid, 677.

legal order a duty imposed by Article 5 TSCG,[39] compels eurozone states under an EDP to present to the Commission and the Council an economic partnership programme. This programme has to describe the policy measures and the structural reforms needed to ensure a durable correction of the deficit. It is worth highlighting that this programme should also identify a number of specific priorities aimed at enhancing competitiveness and long-term sustainable growth, by taking fully into account 'Council recommendations on the implementation of the integrated guidelines for the economic and employment policies of the Member State concerned.' The implementation of the programme is to be monitored by the Commission and the Council.

Lastly, the Commission is planning to further enhance the steering capacity of EU institutions in this context, by introducing within the European Semester a binding framework for ex ante co-ordination concerning major national economic reform plans.[40] If adopted, this framework would require Member States to submit, before adopting them, their major reform proposals[41] to the Commission. These plans should, then, be assessed and discussed by the Commission and the Council, which, in turn, may even suggest modifications if necessary to ensure the smooth functioning of the EMU.[42]

This feature of the European Semester raises some doubts as to its compatibility with the allocation of competences provided for by the Treaties in fields such as the social one. Indeed, as seen above, the mechanism de facto puts Member States' social autonomy under EU discipline, in way that seems to go beyond the limits envisaged by the treaties. Contrary to what happens with the infiltration of internal market law into the social sphere, in this case it is not just a matter of constraining national authorities' room for manoeuvre by requesting them to exercise their social powers in a way that does not unduly restrict the free circulation of goods, services and persons or violate competition rules. The co-ordination mechanism allows EU institutions to exercise quasi-normative functions in this field, enabling them to impose on national authorities the adoption of specific measures and to intervene in the national decision-making process. The fact that these functions are exercised through the adoption of instruments not having a normative character cannot alter this conclusion.

[39] The Treaty on Stability, Coordination and Governance in the Economic and Monetary Union was signed in March 2012 by representatives of all EU Member States, apart from the UK and Czech Republic. It entered into force on 1 January 2013. For an analysis of its legal form and content, as well as its contradictory relationship with EU law, see P Craig, 'The Stability, Coordination and Governance Treaty: Principle, Politics and Pragmatism' (2012) 37 *European Law Review* 231, 231–48 and LS Rossi, '"Fiscal Compact" e Trattato sul Meccanismo di Stabilità: aspetti istituzionali e conseguenze dell'integrazione differenziata nell'UE' (2012) *Il Diritto dell'Unione europea* 293, 293–307.

[40] Commission Communication, 'Towards a Deep and Genuine Economic and Monetary Union. Ex Ante Coordination of Plans for Major Economic Policy Reforms', COM(2013) 166 def.

[41] The Commission proposes to identify them by referring to their possible spillover effects 'on other Member States and/or on wider euro area and wider EU' (ibid, 3). In the light of the high level of interdependence between Member States' economies, this criterion, if taken seriously, would broaden the scope of the framework so to encompass almost any reform plan elaborated at national level.

[42] Ibid, 4–6.

As seen above, despite retaining the formal status of recommendations, these acts have binding effects, as failure to obey might trigger the adoption of hard law measures. Instead, their lack of 'rule-like qualities and check and balances'[43] raises further concerns as to their legitimacy and it may end up unduly broadening EU institutions' discretion in exercising their steering functions.

V. THE EUROPEAN SEMESTER IN ACTION: THE PRIORITIZATION OF ECONOMIC OBJECTIVES OVER SOCIAL ONES

A. A Second-Tier Status for Social Objectives?

To evaluate the impact of the co-ordination efforts on the European social dimension it must be borne in mind that the exercise of these steering functions takes place in the context of a mechanism that has been created with the primary aim of remedying the structural defects of the EMU. Therefore, it is hardly surprising that it has tended to focus on a narrow set of policy objectives, such as budgetary discipline and, more recently, economic growth, which are directly connected to this goal, prioritizing them over potentially conflicting objectives, such as social ones.

This is not to say that social considerations have been completely absent: for instance, both the 2012[44] and 2013[45] AGSs put 'tackling the social consequences of the crisis' among the priorities for EU action. Moreover, especially in the 2013 cycle of the Semester, a number of recommendations have focused on core social objectives, such as reducing poverty and social exclusion. Some Member States, eg Latvia and Lithuania, have been requested to adopt specific measures to extend the coverage of their social assistance systems in order to provide a better answer to these challenges.

However, this cannot hide the fact that social objectives still enjoy a second-tier status in this context. Indeed, as will be seen in the following paragraphs, most of the recommendations touching upon the functioning of social protection systems or labour market regulation have been strongly concerned with ensuring their financial sustainability and efficiency, with little attention paid to the effects on their capacity to perform core social functions. The need for a more balanced approach has been recognized even by the Commission. In a speech delivered in front of the European Parliament on 22 May 2013, Commissioner Olli Rehn called for a strengthening of 'the social pillar of the EMU', by enhancing the monitoring system and, in particular, the macroeconomic imbalance procedure. Although several key aspects of the initiative remain fairly obscure at the time of writing, this represents an important recognition of the need to find a

[43] Chalmers (n 32) 682–84.
[44] Commission Communication, 'Annual Growth Survey 2012', COM(2011) 815 final, 3.
[45] Commission Communication, 'Annual Growth Survey 2013', COM(2012) 750 final, 3.

better balance between achieving key economic objectives and safeguarding the European social dimension.

B. Budgetary Discipline and the European Social Dimension

Budgetary discipline has constantly represented the main objective of the co-ordination system. This is hardly surprising for a system the stated aim of which is ensuring the smooth functioning of the EMU. Indeed, budgetary discipline has been long recognized as a key component of the economic and monetary regime established by the Maastricht Treaty,[46] and, more recently, it has been enshrined in Protocol No 12 attached to the treaties. Some of the measures adopted in the aftermath of the crisis have further enhanced its status, as is the case of Article 3 TSCG which required Contracting Parties to give effect to the so-called 'golden rule'[47] through binding provisions, 'preferably constitutional'.

The 2011 AGS duly confirmed that its 'first priority' was 'to set budgetary policies on a sound footing through rigorous fiscal consolidation'.[48] In this context, it takes the precedence over any other objective, included social ones. Indeed, as observed in the 2012 AGS, fiscal consolidation is 'a basis … to securing the future of the European social model' and, hence, it comes inevitably first.

In this context, social security systems have been primarily, if not exclusively, taken into consideration because of their impact on public finances. Accordingly, reduction of social expenditure has been one of the main items of the reform agenda invariably proposed by EU institution, especially during the 2011 and 2012 cycles of the Semester. In particular, several Member States have been required to proceed with the reform of their pension systems, in order to align the retirement age with increased life expectancy, and of their healthcare systems, in order to ensure their long-term sustainability.

As for pensions, this has been the case with regard to Austria, Belgium, Bulgaria, Cyprus, Czech Republic, Lithuania, Luxembourg, Malta, the Netherlands, Poland, Slovakia, Slovenia and Spain. In the case of Slovenia, for instance, the 2012 Council Recommendation required national authorities to adopt a detailed list of measures aimed at ensuring long-term sustainability of the system, such as equalizing the statutory retirement age for men and women, increasing the effective retirement age, reducing early retirement possibilities and reviewing

[46] J Herdegen, 'Price Stability and Budgetary Restraints in the Economic and Monetary Union: The Law as Guardian of Economic Wisdom' (1998) 35 *Common Market Law Review* 9, 10.

[47] L Azoulai et al, 'Another Legal Monster? An EUI Debate on the Fiscal Compact Treaty', EUI Working Paper No 2012/9 (2012) 4–5. See also F Fabbrini, 'The Fiscal Compact, the "Golden Rule", and the Paradox of European Federalism' (2013) 36 *Boston College International and Comparative Law Review* 1, 1–38.

[48] Commission Communication, 'Annual Growth Survey: Advancing the EU's Comprehensive Response to the Crisis', COM(2011) 11 final, 9.

the indexation system for pensions.[49] Similar recommendations have also been adopted with regard to healthcare and other welfare-related sectors. Belgium, for instance, has been required, in 2012, to '[curb] health-related expenditure, including health expenditure', while, in 2013, to improve cost-effectiveness of public spending with regard to long-term care.[50]

The focus on the reduction of social expenditure as one of the main routes toward fiscal sustainability can be justified by the economic relevance of this item in the state budget. Public spending for social policies, covering both pensions and healthcare, accounts for around 30 per cent of GDP on average in EU Member States. However, the recommendations issued in the early cycles of the European Semester seems to have gone too far, paying little attention to the need to find a balance between budgetary discipline and other competing objectives and values, such as social ones. In this regard, the European Semester codifies and makes permanent the approach that characterized, even more intensely, the financial assistance packages devised to rescue EU Member States that have been hard hit by the financial crisis. In all these cases, recipient states have been required to adopt a set of fiscal consolidation measures aimed at halting and reverting the deterioration of their public finance position. Adjustment programmes invariably rested upon draconian measures, all entailing severe cuts to public spending, in particular, on social expenditure.[51] In keeping with this evolution, which goes to the core of the European social model, it can be argued that the new co-ordination mechanism contributes to what Joerges has defined as the transformation of the European economic constitution into 'a general mandatory commitment to budgetary discipline'.[52]

However, it is worth observing that the Commission has recently been forced to partially soften its stance on this issue. Although budgetary discipline still represents the main priority for any effort aimed at ensuring stronger economic policy co-ordination, it has been progressively accepted that this objective cannot be pursued without paying any consideration to other equally important aims. This change of attitude concerned first and foremost the relationship between budgetary discipline and economic growth. However, some of the 2013 country-specific recommendations would suggest that a similar development is also taking place with regard to its relationship with social objectives, in order to make the mechanism operate in a way that is more consistent with the model enshrined in the treaties. For instance, both Spain and Lithuania have been

[49] This request was reiterated, although in a less detailed manner, in the 2013 Council Recommendation on Slovenia.

[50] The same request, with regard to the whole healthcare sector, is contained in the 2013 Council Recommendation on Spain.

[51] See generally F Costamagna, 'Saving Europe Under Strict Conditionality: A Threat for EU Social Dimension?', LPF Working Paper No 7 (2012). For a recent criticism of the austerity-driven approach used in the case of Greece, see IMF, 'Greece: Ex Post Evaluation of Exceptional Access under the 2010 Stand-By Arrangement', IMF Country Report 13/156 (2013) 20–28.

[52] C Joerges, 'The European Constitution and its Transformation Through the Financial Crisis' in D Patterson and A Södersen (eds), *Blackwell Companion to EU Law and International Law* (Oxford, Blackwell, forthcoming).

expressly recommended to adopt targeted measures to reduce poverty and social exclusion, while the UK has been urged to stop the increase in child poverty. Nevertheless, this evolution is still limited and it cannot be taken as proof of a definitive reversal of the one-sided approach that characterized the EU early response to the crisis.

C. Economic Growth and the European Social Dimension

The promotion of economic growth and employment represents another key aim of the co-ordination mechanism. This objective has progressively achieved a status that stands on a par with that of budgetary discipline as a priority of EU strategy, as also exemplified by the emphasis put on the need to pursue a 'growth-friendly fiscal consolidation'. Albeit certainly welcome, this evolution, which rests on the belated recognition that '[f]iscal consolidation and financial repair are not sufficient in themselves',[53] may end up worsening the prospects of the European social dimension.

As observed with regard to budgetary discipline, this set of recommendations tends to make the functioning of social protection systems and the regulation of the labour market subject to the achievement of overarching economic objectives, such as economic growth, competitiveness and job creation. In this context, social policy is primarily, if not exclusively, seen as a productive factor and, thus, it must be shaped accordingly. Recommendations are mostly about enhancing efficiency, cost containment and private participation, while they tend to disregard principles, such as solidarity, equity, inclusion and cohesion, which represent the bedrock of the traditional paradigm of the welfare state.

By these means, the European Semester allows EU institutions to elaborate and enforce a positive vision on how the welfare state and labour relations should be organized. The paradigm[54] places much emphasis on the principles of equality of opportunities, individual responsibility and reduced welfare dependency. Increased access to employment, to be achieved through the introduction of higher levels of flexibility in the labour market and the reduction of wages, is considered as the main instrument for fostering social inclusion. Accordingly, activation policies play a pivotal role, as access to social assistance is made conditional upon the need for the beneficiary to take specific steps toward his integration or reintegration into the labour market. All in all, this paradigm is characterized by a low level of decommodification,[55] as individuals have to rely first on the market to satisfy their needs, while social safety nets should

[53] 2012 AGS (n 44) 7.

[54] J Vignon and B Cantillon, 'Is There a Time for "Social Europe"? Looking Beyond the Lisbon Strategy Paradigm', OSE Opinion Paper No 9 (2012), 5.

[55] See especially G Esping Andersen, *The Three Worlds of Welfare Capitalism* (Princeton, Princeton University Press, 1990). For a more recent and empirical assessment of the concept, see L Scruggs and J Allan, 'Welfare State Decommodification in 18 OECD Countries: A Replication and Revision' (2006) 16 *Journal of European Social Policy* 55, 55–72.

be targeted and highly selective in their functioning. This conveys the idea of a residual welfare state, to be managed and financed through a greater involvement of private actors.

Several of the recommendations issued in the context of the European Semester are very much consistent with this model, which has a strong neoliberal flavour. For instance, the 2011, 2012 and 2013 AGSs stress the importance of creating job opportunities by removing labour market rigidities through, inter alia, reforming employment protection legislation so to reduce 'over-protection of workers with permanent contracts'.[56] The 2012 AGS, after a reference to the need to implement 'balanced flexisecurity policies', requires Members States to move forward in 'revising wage setting mechanisms … to better reflect productivity developments'.[57] The 2013 AGS goes even further, by praising the 'ambitious reforms' that have been implemented across Europe in order to 'facilitate flexible working arrangements within firms, reduce severance pay for standard contracts and simplify individual or collective dismissal procedures'.[58] Furthermore, all these documents reiterate the need to make social benefits conditional upon activation measures.[59] The 2013 AGS expressly points to the need to strengthen 'the link between social assistance and activation measures', as it considers the latter one of the main strategies to promote social inclusion and tackle poverty.[60]

These advices are a constant feature of the country-specific recommendations issued during the 2011, 2012 and 2013 cycles of the Semester. Belgium, Cyprus, France, Italy, Lithuania, Luxembourg, Malta, Poland, Slovenia and Spain have all been recommended to amend their labour market legislation in order to enhance their competitiveness. In particular, they have been required to revise, in consultation with the social partners and in accordance with national practices, the wage bargaining and indexation systems, to modify the law on dismissal, and to introduce greater flexibility with regard to permanent contracts and working time arrangements. A similar emphasis is put on activation policies, which, in the case of the 2012 Council Recommendation on Lithuania, are considered as the only way to tackle poverty and social exclusion.

Lastly, it is worth observing that these recipes can also be found in the so-called Social Investment Pact,[61] a policy instrument that had been originally proposed as a counterbalance to the process of social retrenchment caused by the austerity-driven response to the crisis.[62] Conversely, this document, in the version adopted by the Commission, seems to keep going in that direction, by putting sustainability and efficiency above adequacy of social provisioning.

[56] 2011 AGS (n 48) 7.

[57] 2012 AGS (n 44) 10.

[58] 2013 AGS (n 45) 10.

[59] 2011 AGS (n 48) 6; 2012 AGS (n 44) 10.

[60] 2013 AGS (n 45) 12.

[61] Commission Communication, 'Toward Social Investment for Growth and Cohesion—Including Implementation of the European Social Fund 2014–2020', COM(2013) 83 final.

[62] F Vandenbroucke, A Hemerijck and B Palier, 'The EU Needs a Social Investment Package', OSE Opinion Paper No 5 (2011).

For instance, the Pact reiterates the need to move toward more targeted social policies, in order to reduce the financial burden over public finances, as well as to make social support conditional upon the adoption of activation measures.[63] Furthermore, this document puts much emphasis on the need to attract private actors, including for-profit ones, to complement public sector efforts, and innovative approaches to financing, including 'participation of the public sector and financial engineering',[64] so as to compensate for the reduced financial capabilities of Member States.

The model proposed through the European Semester is by no mean new. Indeed, these recommendations are fully in line with the 'welfare state modernization'[65] discourse and programmatic agenda that had been elaborated by the Commission since the early 2000s and that was further articulated through the Open Method of Coordination.[66] In particular, the 2005 Mid-Term Review of the Lisbon Strategy stressed the need for the whole process to focus on the promotion of growth and employment, by enhancing competitiveness and productivity.[67] This contributed to a toning-down of core welfare objectives, such as social inclusion, by making them an ancillary aspect of the jobs and growth agenda. The assumption, which has been criticized for not being supported by empirical evidence,[68] was that more employment and a more competitive economy would have seamlessly led to greater social inclusion and less poverty. The process of 'colonization of the welfare state by economic policy-making process'[69] continued with the launch of the Europe 2020 Strategy,[70] although the latter, for the first time, has given a specific and quantitative target to anti-poverty efforts.[71] Indeed, Europe 2020 confirms the tendency to subordinate social policy to economic policy goals, such as economic growth and job creation. This is very much evident in line with the Commission's definition of the inclusive growth priority, conceived as 'fostering a high-employment economy delivering economic, social and territorial cohesion'. Furthermore, it is worth observing that most of the structural reforms envisaged to achieve an inclusive growth concern

[63] Social Investment Pact (n 61) 9–12.

[64] Ibid, 6.

[65] The 2013 AGS (n 45) 5 considers the 'modernization of social protection systems' as a critical step 'to ensure their effectiveness, adequacy and sustainability'.

[66] The OMC is a soft mode of governance that started in 1997 with regard to employment policy co-ordination and that, with the adoption of the Lisbon Strategy in 2000, was extended to social protection. Moreover, in 2001 an OMC-like process was launched on pensions and, in 2004, on healthcare. Lastly, in 2005 all these separate processes were consolidated in a single OMC for social protection and social inclusion.

[67] Commission Communication, 'Working Together for Growth and Jobs. A New Start for the Lisbon Strategy', COM(2005)24 final, 12–14.

[68] C Saraceno, 'The Undercutting of the European Social Dimension', LIEPP Working Paper No 7 (2013) 2

[69] D Chalmers and M Lodge, 'The Open Method of Co-ordination and the European Welfare State', CARR Discussion Paper No 11 (2003) 10 use this expression with regard to the OMC.

[70] Commission Communication (n 29).

[71] The reduction in the number of Europeans living below the national poverty lines by 25%, lifting over 20 million people out of poverty (Europe 2020, 11).

the 'modernization' of the labour market and the social protection systems with the aim of achieving higher employment rates.

However, although not new in their content, these recipes take a new meaning, especially with regard to their impact on the European social dimension, once they are included in recommendations issued in the context of the European Semester. Indeed, as seen above, this framework gives EU institutions and, in particular, the Commission, stronger legal capabilities to pursue their agenda by going beyond the well-known limits of soft modes of governance, such as the OMC. Therefore, in this case Member States may be forced to reform their social protection system, by adopting, at least in part, the model 'proposed' by the Commission.

This evolution can have far-reaching effects on the legitimacy of the whole integration process, by, inter alia, upsetting the precarious balance between internal market law and the national welfare state.[72] Indeed, one of the key features of this model is the push toward the introduction of greater competition in the national welfare schemes, in order to enhance the efficiency of the provision of the services, by opening up new spaces to the participation of private actors. This may contribute to bringing these schemes within the scope of EU competition law, thus posing further constraints on Member States' autonomy in the exercise of their social functions.

VI. CONCLUSION

The measures taken to strengthen economic policy co-ordination in the EU may be seen as a necessary attempt to fill what has been rightly identified 'as a major institutional gap at the heart of European integration', by creating, at least *in nuce*, an institutional space for taking decisions 'about political priorities and choices among competing social values'.[73]

The strengthening of economic policy co-ordination has taken place through the creation of a framework—the European Semester—that reaches across the entire spectrum of Member States' economic and social policies, by putting them under supranational control. This is amplified by the fact that the failure of Member States to comply with the recommendations issued under the Semester may lead to the adoption of hard law measures, and even financial penalties, under the reinforced SPG and the newly created macroeconomic imbalance procedure. The whole system works in a way that goes beyond merely setting quantitative constraints on Members States' spending capacities, as it gives EU institutions unprecedented capacity to take part and influence the decisions

[72] See especially J van de Gronden, 'The Transformation of EU Competition and Internal Market Law by the Stability and Growth Pact: Competence Creeps into the National Welfare States', Nijmegen State and Law Research Papers Series No 2012/01 (2013).

[73] Snyder (n 21) 55.

adopted by national authorities even in domains that fall under Members States' exclusive competence.

At least in its early cycles, the new co-ordination framework has focused on strengthening budgetary discipline and promoting growth and competitiveness. In this context, structural reforms, touching upon key aspects of Member States' welfare and labour systems, have primarily aimed at reducing the burden of social provisioning on public finances or at enhancing their efficiency, by forcing states to introduce greater competition in the management of their welfare schemes. These recipes have paid little attention to the effects that these reforms may have on fundamental social objectives that lie at the core of the EU social dimension. Such a one-sided approach touches upon one of the essential prerequisite for the legitimacy of the whole integration process, as it fails to strike a proper balance between the pursuit of economic objectives and the safeguard of the European social dimension.

In this regard, it is worth observing that there are signs of a progressive reorientation of the strategy adopted at supranational level. The recommendations adopted in the 2013 cycle of the European Semester pay greater attention to social objectives, as a number of states have been specifically required to adopt targeted measures to reduce poverty and social exclusion. The Commission itself has recently recognized the need for a more balanced approach, calling for a sort of re-embedding of the European social dimension in the EMU.

These signs are certainly promising, showing that the mechanism is flexible enough to accommodate interests and objectives that go beyond those considered so far. At the same time, they are still far too limited and rather occasional. The strengthening of the European economic governance, through the creation of steering mechanisms that go to the core of states' social systems, postulates a deep reconfiguration of the role and status of the European social dimension, so to re-establish the balance between the 'economic' and the 'social' at supranational level. Simply reasserting the old division of labour, even in an updated version, would be fictitious and useless, as EU institutions are now fully entitled to exercise policy formulation, supervision and guidance on key social aspects. Therefore, there is the need to ensure that, as a minimum, their action fully contributes to the pursuit of fundamental social objectives that lies at the core of national welfare states and that are now enshrined in the list of EU aims. This step, which might eventually lead to a strengthening of EU legal competences and financial capabilities[74] to develop a proper social policy at supranational level, is necessary to preserve the legitimacy of the integration process and, ultimately, its very raison d'être.

[74] M Poiares Maduro, 'A New Governance for the EU and the Euro: Democracy and Justice', RSCAS Policy Paper No 2012/11 (2012) 11–21.

18

Power and Legitimacy in the Eurozone: Can Integration and Democracy Be Reconciled?

PETER L LINDSETH

THE TITLE OF this chapter—and more importantly the question in the subtitle—were suggestions of the editors of this timely and important collective volume. I am happy to try to address the question here because it touches on one of the most fundamental issues raised by the eurozone crisis. Among this volume's contributors, I see my role as primarily conceptual rather than technical; I do not pretend to duplicate the many outstanding contributions in terms of legal detail, both national and supranational, all of which is directly pertinent to the question of integration and democracy in the context of the eurozone crisis. My aim, rather, is to provide some broader reflections on the potentially far-reaching changes that the eurozone crisis has effected in European public law, understood capaciously to encompass both the national and supranational levels.

My answer to the question posed by the editors is a deeply qualified 'yes'—there are indeed ways to reconcile integration and democracy even in the context of this crisis, although not in the manner suggested by several of my fellow contributors.[1] My response, moreover, is subject to several important provisos and reservations, building on the 'administrative, not constitutional' interpretation of integration that I set out in my most recent book, *Power and Legitimacy: Reconciling Europe and the Nation-State* (Oxford University Press, 2010).

The operative concept in both that book and this contribution is the difficult process of 'reconciliation'. The focus is on those aspects of European public law that strive to balance the evident functional demands for supranational regulatory solutions, on the one hand, with the continued political-cultural attachment to the nation-state as the primary locus of democratic and constitutional legiti-

[1] See eg the contributions of Federico Fabbrini and Ingolf Pernice in this volume. For more details, see below nn 29–42 and accompanying text.

macy in Europe, on the other.[2] This approach thus takes as its premise the idea that, at this point in Europe's history, supranational governance lacks its own autonomous democratic and constitutional legitimacy in a historically recognizable sense, something that cannot be easily engineered at, or transferred to, the supranational level in the short or intermediate term. Despite the diffusion and fragmentation of regulatory power in the European system—a consequence of the evident functional demands of economic interdependence—the national level remains the locus of democratic *identity* (government 'of the people'),[3] which in turn confers on national level institutions much greater resources of democratic and constitutional legitimacy, if not necessarily of power.

The reconciliation of integration and democracy is thus intimately bound up with the historic effort to bridge the disconnect between (supranational) regulatory *power* and (national) democratic and constitutional *legitimacy* in the integration process. There are other kinds of legitimacy, of course—legal, technocratic, indeed even 'messianic'[4]—and I discuss them below in relation to the EU and the eurozone crisis. But my essential point is that, in the effort to achieve a specifically democratic reconciliation, one must focus on those aspects of European public law that seek to

> establish a legitimating framework within which the otherwise undoubted complexity of Europe's policymaking processes—characterized by significant amounts of functionally autonomous regulatory power, distributed across multiple levels of governance—can operate *without evident democratic and constitutional legitimacy of their own*, at least as classically understood.[5]

In the present context, interpreting integration as an 'administrative' rather than autonomously 'democratic' and 'constitutional' process suggests that any durable solution to eurozone crisis—even one that pursues functionally necessary transfers of fiscal-disciplinary or bank-supervisory powers to the supranational level—must be vigilant in maintaining the integrity of national democracies in Europe and not allow them to be eclipsed by, or subsumed into, a set of supranational institutions whose autonomous democratic and constitutional legitimacy is still tenuous. In more concrete terms, this reconciliation implies three elements in European public law in the context of the eurozone crisis. Firstly, it points to the need, at least in extremis, for substantive constitutional limitations on the scope of authority delegable to the supranational level, consistent with the demand of preserving democracy on the national level (this likely precludes, most importantly, proposals to shift expanded fiscal capaci-

[2] PL Lindseth, *Power and Legitimacy: Reconciling Europe and the Nation-State* (Oxford, Oxford University Press 2010) 14.

[3] PL Lindseth, 'Of the People: Democracy, the Eurozone, and Lincoln's Threshold Criterion' [2012] *Berlin Journal* 4–7.

[4] JHH Weiler, 'The Political and Legal Culture of European Integration: An Exploratory Essay' (2011) 9 *International Journal of Constitutional Law* 678–94.

[5] Lindseth (n 2) 14 (emphasis in original).

ties—taxing, spending, and borrowing authority—to the European Parliament).[6] Secondly, even concerning more limited and otherwise constitutionally delegable powers (eg in the area of fiscal discipline/surveillance), there must still be some form of ongoing nationally mediated legitimation ('oversight', if not 'control'), of supranational action.[7] Finally, each participating state in the EMU, as a responsible 'democratic' actor in an otherwise 'demoi-cratic' enterprise,[8] bears some liability for the design flaws that led to this crisis, as well as the considerable 'legacy costs', both political and economic, which those flaws have engendered.[9]

With these elements in mind, I conclude that supranational surveillance of national budgets, as well as certain aspects of banking union (supranationalized bank supervision, harmonized bank resolution rules), are consistent with the demands of democracy-preservation on the national level, based on a so-called 'pre-commitment' theory of European integration that I describe below.[10] By contrast, moves toward an autonomous fiscal capacity in the EU—ie taxing, spending and borrowing authority, accompanied by a transformation in the role of the European Parliament (in short, some form of 'political union')—would likely be a step too far.[11] Taking such a step would not only necessitate a profound constitutional transformation in a number of Member States, not least Germany, but more profoundly there would need to be a fundamental political-cultural transformation in prevailing understandings of what constitutes 'democracy' in Europe and where it is located (national vs. supranational). I do not envision such a transformation in the near term, nor do I think one could be easily engineered in the manner advocated by the most strongly pro-European elements of EU legal-elite opinion.[12]

[6] See nn 39–42 and accompanying text.

[7] See nn 21–24 and accompanying text.

[8] K Nicolaïdis, 'The Idea of European Demoicracy' in J Dickson and P Eleftheriadis (eds), *Philosophical Foundations of European Union Law* (Oxford, Oxford University Press 2012).

[9] See nn 75–84 and accompanying text. See, more generally, PL Lindseth, 'Fault, Not Solidarity: A Normative Argument to Save the Eurozone?', *EUtopialaw*, 20 July 2012, http://eutopialaw.com/2012/07/30/fault-not-solidarity-a-normative-argument-to-save-the-eurozone/ (accessed 1 May 2013).

[10] See nn 50–53 and accompanying text.

[11] See nn 38–42, 46–48 and accompanying text.

[12] See eg M Maduro, 'A New Governance for the European Union and the Euro: Democracy and Justice', report commissioned by the European Parliament Constitutional Affairs Committee, PE 462.484 (2012), reprinted as Robert Schuman Centre for Advanced Studies, Global Governance Programme, RSCAS Policy Paper 2012/11, network.globalgovernanceprogramme.eu/wp-content/uploads/2012/10/report.pdf (accessed 17 August 2013); for a commentary, see PL Lindseth, 'Thoughts on the Maduro Report: Saving the Euro Through European Democratization?', *EUtopialaw.com*, 13 November 2012, www.eutopialaw.com/2012/11/13/1608/ (accessed 17 August 2013). See also European Commission, 'A Blueprint for a Deep and Genuine Economic and Monetary Union: Launching a European Debate', COM(2012) 0777 final, 2013, www.eur-lex.europa.eu/LexUriServ/LexUriServ.do?uri=COM:2012:0777:FIN:EN:PDF (accessed 17 August 2013); H Van Rompuy, 'Towards a genuine Economic and Monetary Union: Report by President of the European Council', EUCO 120/12 of 26 June 2012 (the 'Four Presidents' Report'), http://europa.eu/rapid/press-release_PRES-12-296_en.htm?locale=FR (accessed 9 September 2013); and J Habermas, 'Democracy, Solidarity and the European Crisis', lecture at KU Leuven, Belgium, 26 April 2013, www.kuleuven.be/

Nevertheless, consistent with the democratic responsibility of each EMU state severally in the eurozone crisis, there must be some form of burden-sharing in the 'legacy costs' of the EMU's flawed design, which to date have been borne almost entirely by the 'debtor' countries. Greater burden-sharing of legacy costs by 'creditor' countries (probably in the form of debt restructuring rather than outright transfers) is entirely consistent with the democratic responsibility of each participating state in the EMU and, indeed, is arguably essential to the ongoing effort to reconcile integration and democracy in the eurozone.

However, unless the crisis greatly aggravates to the point that it poses once again an existential threat to the common currency, a significant amount of burden-sharing may not occur—certainly not at the level commensurate with the legacy costs themselves. Because of the Member States' failure to recognize shared democratic responsibility for the crisis, one could expect the ECB to continue playing something of a 'heroic' role in combating threats to the survival of the euro through an array of non-standard measures[13] that carry with them significant challenges in terms of democratic legitimation of the supranational central-banking technocracy. Consequently, without the Member States stepping up to their shared democratic obligation to address the mutually inflicted legacy costs of a deeply flawed EMU, the only other option is a technocratic solution centered around the European Central Bank (ECB), which would have the ironic virtue of being both suboptimal to addressing the crisis while also being democratically questionable.

* * *

I begin with my 'administrative' interpretation of European governance,[14] which is certainly in tension with a good deal of legal scholarship over many decades that has sought to understand the integration phenomenon in terms of 'constitutionalization'—terminology that is in fact reflected in the title of this volume. I have long argued, by contrast, that European integration is best understood as an extension of modern administrative governance as it developed over the course of the twentieth century.[15] By this I mean that integration is an extension of the functional diffusion and fragmentation of regulatory power *away* from the historically 'constituted' bodies of self-government on the national level, whether legislative, executive or judicial. Because this framework has often been misunderstood, however, let me begin by setting out some standard clarifications regarding what the administrative rubric does *not* mean, whether applied

communicatie/evenementen/evenementen/jurgen-habermas/en/democracy-solidarity-and-the-european-crisis (accessed 17 August 2013).

[13] See the contribution of S Baroncelli in this volume (Chapter 7); see also nn 86–90 below and accompanying text.

[14] See generally Lindseth (n 2).

[15] See eg PL Lindseth, 'Democratic Legitimacy and the Administrative Character of Supranationalism: The Example of the European Community' (1999) 99 *Columbia Law Review* 628–738.

to the EU or otherwise, in order to avoid confusion from the very beginning of the discussion.

First and foremost, the 'administrative' label does *not* mean that such a regime is merely 'limited' or 'specialized',[16] indeed even entirely 'non-political'.[17] Administrative governance is 'deeply political', even if the opposite view has been (mis) attributed to me in the past.[18] Anyone with knowledge of modern administrative governance understands that the authority delegated to the administrative sphere is often functionally autonomous and yet deals with questions of values and the allocation of scarce resources—in short, distributive justice—the very essence of politics.[19]

What defines 'administrative' is not, in fact, the *nature* of the power exercised (political or not) but rather its *separation* from bodies understood to embody or express the capacity of a historical political community to rule itself in a strongly legitimated, ie *constitutional* sense, whether legislative, executive or judicial. By the latter, I mean elected assemblies, plebiscitarian political leadership at the summit of the executive (prime ministers, presidents, and their cabinets), and the court system—the classic *trias politica*. The challenge in administrative governance, as a kind of 'fourth branch'[20] vis-à-vis this *trias*, has been 'maintaining the connection between each of the [three constitutional] institutions and the paradigmatic function which it alone is empowered to serve, while also retaining a grasp on [diffused administrative governance] as a whole that respects our commitments to the control of law'.[21] What administrative bodies lack, despite their autonomous *power*, is autonomous democratic and constitutional *legitimacy* to exercise that power without some mechanisms of oversight by strongly legitimated bodies residing elsewhere (what I call 'mediated legitimacy').[22] This

[16] See G de Búrca, 'Reflections on the EU's Path from the Constitutional Treaty to the Lisbon Treaty', Fordham Law Legal Studies Research Paper No 1124586 (2008) 8, http://papers.ssrn.com/sol3/papers.cfm?abstract_id=1124586 (accessed 31 March 2012) (arguing that '[t]he depiction of the EU as an expert agency writ large, with specialized limited "administrative" functions delegated to it by internally democratic states which remain the primary source of its legitimacy is increasingly strained and difficult to defend'), citing, inter alia, Lindseth (n 15).

[17] D Curtin, *Executive Power of the European Union: Law, Practices, and the Living Constitution* (Oxford, Oxford University Press 2009) 37, citing Lindseth (n 15).

[18] HHC Hofmann and AH Türk, 'The Development of Integrated Administration in the EU and its Consequences' (2007) 13 *European Law Journal* 253, 267, though earlier (ibid, 264), these authors suggest that I maintain the opposite, again citing Lindseth (n 15), conflating me with HP Ipsen, *Europäisches Gemeinschaftsrecht* (Mohr 1972).

[19] In the first article in which I advanced the 'administrative' rubric for integration, I in fact stressed how the jurisdiction of administrative bodies had often been depicted as 'technical' in order to justify the delegation of power but that this depiction has never altered the essentially 'political' character of the power itself, in the sense of dealing with questions of values or the allocation of scarce resources. See Lindseth (n 15) 687–88; see also PL Lindseth, '"Weak" Constitutionalism? Reflections on Comitology and Transnational Governance in the European Union' (2001) 21 *Oxford Journal of Legal Studies* 145, 157, n 51.

[20] See G Majone, 'The European Community: An "Independent Fourth Branch of Government?"', in G Brüggemeier (ed), *Verfassungen für ein ziviles Europa* (Baden-Baden, Nomos, 1994) 23.

[21] PL Strauss, 'Formal and Functional Approaches to Separation-of-Powers Questions—A Foolish Inconsistency?' (1987) 72 *Cornell Law Review* 488, 488.

[22] See Lindseth (n 2); for the national origins of mediated legitimacy in the twentieth-century

is as true in the administrative state as it is in the process of European integration, as the evolution of European public law over the last six decades in fact suggests.[23] This means that, in the case of integration, supranational institutions lack democratic and constitutional legitimacy of their own, despite the fact that they have been partly constructed to mimic strongly legitimated legislative, executive and judicial bodies on the national level. Rather, supranational institutions ultimately depend for democratic and constitutional legitimacy on the legislative, executive and judicial bodies of the Member States, despite the fact that supranational institutions are also intended to exercise power autonomously from the control of those same national bodies.

This interpretation of the separation of power and legitimacy in the integration process thus challenges the idea, widespread among legal scholars, that European governance is built on a set of 'institutions constitutionally separated from national legitimation processes'.[24] Mediated legitimacy via national constitutional bodies—something *Power and Legitimacy* traces in detail in integration legal history—has been essential to the reconciliation of supranationalized administrative 'governance' with conceptions of democratic and constitutional 'government' inherited from the past. It is only through such a reconciliation that forms of administrative governance, whether *within* or *beyond* the state, are still experienced as 'democratic' and 'constitutional' in some historically and culturally recognizable way, despite the diffusion and fragmentation of normative power to an administrative (ie delegated) sphere now stretching beyond the confines of the state.

To my mind, the idea of an autonomous, supranational process of 'constitutionalization' is based on a partly valid[25] but nevertheless incomplete legal-historical perspective, rooted in the comparison of European institutions to the emergence of international organizations (IOs) over the course of the twentieth century. This perspective operates, we might say, along a dimension from public international law (IOs) to supranational constitutionalism (the EU)—which, when applied to Europe, becomes what we might call the 'constitutional, not international' framework. I would maintain, however, that the EU and IOs are better seen as denationalized expressions of the diffusion and fragmentation of

administrative state, see PL Lindseth, 'The Paradox of Parliamentary Supremacy: Delegation, Democracy, and Dictatorship in Germany and France, 1920s–1950s' (2004) 113 *Yale Law Journal* 1341–1415.

[23] See generally Lindseth (n 2).

[24] A Menon and S Weatherill, 'Legitimacy, Accountability, and Delegation in the European Union' in A Arnull and D Wincott (eds), *Accountability and legitimacy in the European Union* (Oxford, Oxford University Press 2002) 118.

[25] Especially so with regard to international or supranational adjudicative authority in the protection of human rights against the excesses of state power. See JHH Weiler, 'The Geology of International Law—Governance, Democracy and Legitimacy' (2004) 64 *Zeitschrift für ausländisches öffentliches Recht und Völkerrecht* 547, 551 (referring to 'a third stratum of [international] dispute settlement which may be called constitutional, and consists in the increasing willingness, within certain areas of domestic courts to apply and uphold rights and duties emanating from international obligations. The appellation constitutional may be justified because of the "higher law" status conferred on the international legal obligation').

regulatory power *away* from the constitutional bodies of self-government on the national level, which is the essential characteristic of modern administrative governance. This process of diffusion and fragmentation in fact began in the mid-nineteenth century (at least) and continued apace in the twentieth, in the face of the demands of regulating modern industrial and later post-industrial society. It is a reflection of what two global historians have called the 'leaky' container of the modern nation-state.[26]

From this perspective, neither the EU nor IOs are 'constitutional' in themselves, in the sense of representing a historically grounded political community conscious of itself as 'entitled to effective organs of political self-government'.[27] Rather, despite efforts to democratize and constitutionalize supranational institutions, these bodies remain fundamentally technocratic and juristocratic, possessing ultimately delegated normative power, grounded in mediated legitimacy. The key difference between the EU and IOs is in their relative *degree of autonomous discretion* in the exercise of delegated power (the EU enjoys much more autonomy, as is well known), which in turn intensifies the challenge of legitimation in the case of the EU. To arrive at this conclusion is not to ignore the real difficulties that arise when the locus of governance shifts beyond the confines of the state, thus greatly complicating mediated legitimation in an administrative sense. But the difference between the EU and IOs is one of degree and not of kind—both are manifestations of modern administrative governance, functionally diffused and fragmented beyond the confines of the state in order to address certain pressing regulatory and political problems.

The problem with a primarily constitutionalist terminology to describe integration, however subtly or critically deployed,[28] is that it risks giving license to those prepared to assume what is fundamentally contested in the integration process: the capacity of European supranationalism to legitimize its normative power in fully autonomous democratic and constitutional terms, as if integration were a site of such authority in its own right, apart from the Member States that created it.[29] If 'there is no convincing account of democracy without demos', as Weiler has rightly put it,[30] I would assert that there is also not a convincing account of a European constitutionalism in the most robust sense of the term, and ultimately for similar demos-based reasons. Following the lead of

[26] *Cf* C Bright and M Geyer, 'Where in the World Is America? The History of the United States in the Global Age' in T Bender (ed), *Rethinking American History in a Global Age* (Berkeley, University of California Press, 2002).

[27] N MacCormick, *Questioning Sovereignty : Law, State, and Nation in the European Commonwealth* (Oxford, Oxford University Press 1999) 173. This democratic and constitutional self-consciousness need not be grounded in exclusionary ethnic, religious or linguistic affinities; indeed, as MacCormick has also shown, this demos-consciousness can also be 'civic', although it still must be grounded in a 'historical' and indeed 'cultural' experience for that particular community (ibid, 169–74).

[28] See eg JHH Weiler and JP Trachtman, 'European Constitutionalism and its Discontents' (1996) 17 *Northwestern Journal of International Law and* Business 354–97.

[29] See eg the contributions of Federico Fabbrini and Ingolf Pernice in this volume.

[30] Weiler (n 25) 560.

Jed Rubenfeld[31] and Bruce Ackerman,[32] we should recognize that democratic and constitutional legitimacy are inextricably connected in the modern era. They are tied to the construction of a polity's identity over time, and thus they emerge historically together. It is thus profoundly difficult to claim that the EU has an autonomously 'constitutional' character (except in only the most formal sense) if Europeans refuse to grant it autonomous 'democratic' legitimacy, unmediated through the Member States.

Even for the most sophisticated constitutional theorists of the EU, the evolution of European public law and supranational authority ultimately is a question of the functional demands of interdependence as they perceive them.[33] This ignores the complex interplay between the functional, political and cultural dimensions of institutional change[34] and leads to the temptation to view European legitimacy as primarily a matter of institutional engineering, most often revolving around expanded powers for the European Parliament.[35] The European Parliament no doubt participates in the exercise of real legislative power in the process of European integration. Moreover, it is isomorphically modelled along the lines of a national legislative assembly. And nevertheless, despite these elements, it does not represent, as yet, a historically coherent political community ('demos') capable of legitimizing the European Parliament in an autonomously 'constitutional' sense. Thus, as Kalypso Nicolaïdis has nicely put it, 'there is no EU-wide polity in which most citizens would be willing to accept to be subjected to the rule of a pan-European majority'.[36]

What this means is that the European Parliament may often serve a critically important *functional* purpose in integration, providing a forum for forging policy compromises and providing an avenue for electoral participation and legislative-style transparency and oversight of supranational actors. But from a *political-cultural* perspective the European Parliament cannot serve an autonomously democratic and constitutional role in the integration process—with the full panoply of taxing, spending and borrowing powers that this implies—precisely because the citizens of Europe do not experience it as an embodiment or expression of the capacity of a new European demos to rule itself in autonomously democratic and constitutional terms. Rather, the European Parliament, like its counterparts in the European Commission or the CJEU, has only a delegated ('administrative, not constitutional') legitimacy, which in turn ultimately defines the scope of the power it may reasonably be expected to exercise.

No doubt, European integration enjoys many kinds of legitimacy. It enjoys, for example, a *legal* legitimacy as a consequence of the commitments made by

[31] J Rubenfeld, *Freedom and Time: A Theory of Constitutional Self-Government* (New Haven, CT, University Press, 2001).

[32] BA Ackerman, *We the People: Foundations* (Boston, MA, Harvard University Press, 1991).

[33] See eg Maduro (n 12); see also the contributions of Fabbrini and Pernice in this volume.

[34] Lindseth (n 2) 13–14.

[35] See eg the 'Blueprint' as well as the 'Four Presidents Report' (n 12); for a critique of this view, see Lindseth (n 12).

[36] Nicolaïdis (n 8) 256.

the Member States under European law, both primary and secondary, as well as the substantive rights and judicial apparatus that have been established to enforce them. It also enjoys (one hopes) a *technocratic* legitimacy as a consequence of the putative expertise that is brought to bear on the policy choices that emerge out of its rulemaking, enforcement and adjudicative processes, which leads (again one hopes) to some measure of *output* legitimacy for the integration process (admittedly under strain in the crisis, to put it mildly). It enjoys, moreover, some measure of *input* legitimacy as a consequence of growing electoral and regulatory participation and transparency rights that are embedded in EU law. Finally, it enjoys a kind of *idealistic* legitimacy derived from the 'messianic' ambition[37] to overcome the past (war) and to seize the future ('ever closer union', continued geopolitical significance, human rights, etc).

This is all a significant amount of legitimacy. But despite the fervent hopes of many advocates of intensified integration, the resulting legitimacy is only to do certain things and not others. Some kinds of power remain beyond the reach of the European Parliament because they require strongly legitimated institutions of outright self-'government' in a historically recognizable sense.[38] This strong legitimation continues to reside at the national level, despite the functional diffusion of regulatory power to the EU. In short, democratic and constitutional legitimacy is not simply a question of what is functionally demanded, conceptually possible or normatively appealing, particularly with regard to the powers of the EP.[39] Rather, it is even more fundamentally a question of where the average European perceives the proper locus of ultimate self-government to be. This political-cultural foundation, not institutional engineering or elite conceptual theorizing, is the true source of democratic and constitutional legitimacy in European integration.

As Stefano Bartolini presciently warned before the onset of the crisis, 'the risk of miscalculating the extent to which true legitimacy surrounds the European institutions and their decisions … may lead to the overestimating of the capacity of the EU to overcome major economic and security crises'.[40] When it comes to the sort of transnational taxing, borrowing and spending authority that the eurozone crisis seems to demand for the EU, the lack of robust democratic and constitutional legitimacy has been a barrier to formulating policies of real macroeconomic significance at the supranational level (not the 1 per cent of European GDP that is the current EU budget).[41] Without these supranational fiscal capaci-

[37] Weiler (n 4).

[38] *Cf* J Pisani-Ferry, 'Whose Economic Reform?', *Project Syndicate*, 30 July 2013, www.project-syndicate.org/commentary/the-purpose-and-strategy-of-structural-reofrm-by-jean-pisani-ferry (accessed 22 August 2013) (referring to 'a line in the sand beyond which only governments can set priorities and act').

[39] See eg Maduro (n 12); see also the contributions of Fabbrini and Pernice in this volume.

[40] S Bartolini, *Restructuring Europe: Centre Formation, System Building, and Political Structuring between the Nation State and the European Union* (Oxford, Oxford University Press 2005) 175.

[41] *Cf* Paul Krugman, 'What a Real External Bank Bailout Looks Like', *Conscience of a Liberal*, 17 July 2012, krugman.blogs.nytimes.com/2012/06/17/what-a-real-external-bank-bailout-looks-like/ (accessed 17 August 2013).

ties—and more importantly without the autonomous democratic and constitutional legitimacy to support them—the central instrument used to pay for the eurozone crisis has understandably been national austerity, combined with national precommitments to fiscal discipline enforced by supranational institutions—a very different animal from the autonomous fiscal capacities at the EU level that many in the European legal elite seek to engineer in the European Parliament.[42]

In the integration process, it is always crucially important to ask the question: 'legitimate for what?'[43] The 'administrative, not constitutional' (ie delegated) character of integration suggests that European public law instead requires an integration analogue to the German *Vorbehalt des Gesetzes* or the Italian *riserva di legge*, with the ultimately fundamental legislative power (at least with regard to taxation, spending and borrowing) remaining national.[44] In other words, there are necessarily domains of normative authority that must remain with the Member States in order to preserve their historically recognizable democratic and constitutional character, even as they otherwise allow integration to proceed. Moreover, as to those domains that *can* be delegated, the exercise of power on the supranational level must be sufficiently transparent and accountable in order to permit some minimal level of oversight by *national* democratic and constitutional bodies—executives, parliaments and high courts—just as in the process of administrative governance nationally.[45]

* * *

So what does the 'administrative, not constitutional' character of the EU mean more specifically for the reconciliation of integration and democracy in the context of the Eurozone crisis?

First and foremost, as I have already suggested, it means that certain constitutional 'fault lines' need to be respected, in order to preserve the historically recognizable character of democracy on the national level.[46] At this juncture, the delegation of autonomous taxing, spending and borrowing power to the

[42] See eg the contributions of Fabbrini and Pernice in this volume; see also Maduro (n 12).

[43] PL Lindseth, 'Author's Reply: "Outstripping", or the Question of "Legitimate for What?" in EU Governance' (2012) 8 *European Constitutional Law Review* 153–64.

[44] Arguably, the German Federal Constitutional Court suggested as much in its Lisbon Decision, 2 BvE 2/08, 30 June 2009, translated into English at www.bundesverfassungsgericht.de/entscheidungen/es20090630_2bve000208en.html (accessed 6 July 2013) specifically para.247 (signaling that there are 'content-related limits to the transfer of sovereign powers' analogous to the *Vorbehalt des Gesetzes* that applies nationally) and para 351 (suggesting that, in those '[e]ssential areas of democratic formative action', there is a need for both interpretive constraint and heightened oversight, both by national representative institutions and the Court, consistent with the demands of 'living democracy' on the national level). For a discussion, see Lindseth (n 2) 184–85.

[45] See generally Lindseth (n 2).

[46] PL Lindseth, 'Understanding the German Constitutional Fault Lines in the Eurozone Crisis: Der Spiegel's interview with Udo Di Fabio', *EUtopialaw*, 12 January 2012, http://eutopialaw.com/2012/01/12/understanding-the-german-constitutional-fault-lines-in-the-eurozone-crisis-der-spiegels-interview-with-udo-di-fabio/ (accessed 1 May 2013).

supranational level—ie 'political union'—is out of the question, at least on scale that would matter in this crisis.[47] In a polity lacking such autonomous legitimacy (both the EU as well as the eurozone), such actions are perceived as giving money away to 'others'.[48] In Europe's current environment, you cannot surmount this essential obstacle without a fundamental political-cultural transformation that cannot be simply engineered through increased European Parliament powers.

Once we appreciate this limit on integration, we can begin to appreciate better why the response to the eurozone crisis to date has relied almost exclusively upon national austerity, as well as national precommitments to fiscal discipline enforced by supranational institutions. Conveniently, this combination of policy tools makes (as yet) no direct redistributive demands on 'Europe' as a collectivity; all essential costs—political and economic—are borne internally, by the individual states. In this way, the current approach ultimately relies on—and in fact validates—the democratic and constitutional legitimacy of national institutions as a central foundation of the European project.

In addition, on a conceptual level at least, the creation of mechanisms of supranational surveillance to ensure that the Member States meet their commitments to fiscal discipline—however misguided this may be from an economic and political perspective (because procyclical)[49]—is constitutionally acceptable from a democracy standpoint.[50] Modern governance is built on a set of policy or institutional 'precommitments', through delegation of authority to institutions such as constitutional courts, central banks or administrative agencies. The very purpose of these bodies is, in some sense, to constrain the sovereign rights of democratic institutions in service of broader policy goals. European integration generally, and the eurozone specifically, builds on this foundation of modern governance, albeit with the twist that the delegations now occur to institutions operating *beyond* the nation-state.[51] Indeed, the new mechanisms of fiscal surveillance in European public law—the 'six-pack' and 'two-pack', etc—are arguably different *only in degree*, but *not in kind*, from the sort of commit-

[47] See PL Lindseth, 'The Eurozone Crisis, Institutional Change, and "Political Union"', in F Allen et al (eds.), *Political, Fiscal, and Banking Union in the Eurozone?* (Philadelphia, Wharton Financial Institutions Center Press, 2013) 149.

[48] PL Lindseth, 'Cyprus … or Why the "No-Demos Problem" Defines the Policy Response to the Eurozone Crisis', *EUtopialaw*, 27 March 2013, http://eutopialaw.com/2013/03/27/cyprus-or-why-the-no-demos-problem-defines-the-policy-response-to-the-eurozone-crisis/ (accessed 1 May 2013).

[49] As the old adage puts it, 'What is constitutional is not necessarily wise.'

[50] Indeed, given the extensive transparency and data-exchange obligations in this regime, one could fairly argue that such supranational surveillance can also be, in important respects, democracy-enhancing on the national level. This is a point that Kenneth Armstrong advanced in the paper presented at the conference leading to this volume, although the point did not make it into his final published version.

[51] PL Lindseth, 'Greek "Sovereignty" and European "Democracy"', *EUtopialaw*, 9 November 2011, http://eutopialaw.com/2011/11/09/greek-%e2%80%98sovereignty%e2%80%99-and-european-%e2%80%98democracy%e2%80%99/ (accessed 19 May 2013).

ment mechanisms that have been the foundation of European integration and governance in the past.[52]

In such a regime, whether the delegation of power is to an institution operating inside or outside the nation-state, the key moment of democratic and sovereign decision necessarily comes at the moment of delegation itself, subject to forms of ongoing national participation in subsequent decision making pursuant to that delegation (ie mediated legitimacy). Even as delegation shifts legal constraints to the supranational level, the democratic legitimation of those constraints remains fundamentally national. These constraints would have *no validity* without that national affirmation, through ratification of supranational policy goals defined in the various European treaties. Moreover, the democratic and constitutional foundations of these constraints have remained national even if the enforcement mechanisms of these 'precommitments' are clearly supranational. This arguably accounts for the deeply 'hybrid' character of the system of governance that is emerging from this crisis.[53]

The difficulty, however, is that by so constraining the fiscal policy of Member States (and thus deeply interfering in the democratic life of the various European 'demoi', particularly in the 'programme' countries of the periphery), the peoples of the eurozone are finding it increasingly difficult to experience this 'precommitment' system as democratic and constitutional in a historically recognizable sense. This is a genuine concern: no delegation of authority, on a 'precommitment' basis or otherwise, can be of such an indeterminate scope as to constitute an abdication of the democratic character of national institutions.[54] This is a point echoed by numerous national high courts in their European jurisprudence of the last two decades.[55] As the Danish Supreme Court (the Højesteret) put it in 1998, the really difficult challenge is in determining whether and how supranational delegation might imperil 'the constitutional assumption of a democratic system of government' on the national level.[56]

The German Federal Constitutional Court, through the articulation of the so-called *Demokratieprinzip* in the context of the eurozone crisis, has struggled to realize the same legal concept.[57] In my reading of the German Court's various decisions arising out of the crisis (as of this writing, July 2013),[58] the *Demokra-*

[52] Lindseth (n 2) 110–11. See in particular the contributions in Part 2 of this volume.

[53] See contribution of KA Armstrong in this volume (Chapter 4).

[54] PL Lindseth, 'Greek "Sovereignty" and European "Democracy"—A Bit of a Walk-back, Due to Some "Colossal" Concerns', *EUtopialaw*, 15 February 2012, http://eutopialaw.com/2012/02/15/greek-sovereignty-and-european-democracy-a-bit-of-a-walk-back-due-to-some-colossal-concerns/ (accessed 18 May 2013).

[55] See generally Lindseth (n 2), ch 4.

[56] *Carlsen and Others v Rasmussen*, Case No I-361/1997 of 6 April 1998, 1998 UfR 800, reprinted in A Oppenheimer, *The Relationship between European Community Law and National Law: The Cases*, 2 vols (Cambridge, Cambridge University Press, 1994/2003) vol 2, 191.

[57] PL Lindseth, '"Dual Legitimation", Banking Union, and the Demokratieprinzip in Germany: Initial Thoughts after the Recent European Summit', *EUtopialaw*, 9 July 2012, http://eutopialaw.com/2012/07/09/dual-legitimation-banking-union-and-the-demokratieprinzip-in-germany-initial-thoughts-after-the-recent-european-summit/ (accessed 6 July 2013).

[58] BVerfG, Greek Bailout Decision, 2 BvR 987/10, 2 BvR 1485/10, 2 BvR 1099/10, 7 September

tieprinzip has both a substantive and procedural dimension. The former seeks to define the outer bounds of constitutionally permissible delegation, generally defined in terms of maintaining the Bundestag's budgetary autonomy.[59] The latter focuses on the nature of national—particularly parliamentary—oversight which is constitutionally mandated in order to legitimize otherwise delegable powers.[60] In my view, as I have stressed elsewhere, this German jurisprudence in fact expresses more general principles as to the relationship between democracy and delegation that should be available to any national high court in a demoicratic (ie delegated/administrative) Europe, not just in the 'core' but also in the 'periphery'.[61] Jurisprudentially, what is good for the German 'goose' should also be good for the Greek, Irish, Portuguese or Spanish 'gander'.[62]

With regard to the German jurisprudence specifically, there are several interesting open questions going forward. The first relates to how the Constitutional Court might treat the various 'non-standard measures' undertaken by the ECB to address the crisis.[63] The most important has been the promise to undertake so-called Outright Market Transactions (OMTs), which the ECB announced in September 2012 to the great relief of the bond markets. In the Court's hearing on the constitutionality of the ESM Treaty on 11–12 June 2013, the OMT programme was a major focus of the judges' attention. Readers will almost certainly know the Court's ruling before the publication of this volume, so there is little point

2011, www.bundesverfassungsgericht.de/entscheidungen/rs20110907_2bvr098710.html (accessed 6 July 2013); Bundestag Right of Participation/EFSF, 2 BvE 8/11, 28 February 2012 www.bundesverfassungsgericht.de/entscheidungen/es20120228_2bve000811.html (accessed 6 July 2013); Bundestag Right of Information ESM/Euro Plus Pact, 2 BvE 4/11, 19 June 2012, www.bundesverfassungsgericht.de/entscheidungen/es20120619_2bve000411.html (accessed 6 July 2013); and Rejection of Temporary Injunctions ESM/Fiscal Compact, 2 BvR 1390/12, 2 BvR 1421/12, 2 BvR 1438/12, 2 BvR 1439/12, 2 BvR 1440/12, 2 BvE 6/12, 12 September 2012, www.bundesverfassungsgericht.de/en/press/bvg12-067en.html (accessed 6 July 2013).

[59] See, in particular, the *Greek Bailout Decision* (n 58) para124 ('if supranational legal obligations were created without a corresponding decision by the free will of the Bundestag, then the parliament would find itself in the roll of a mere rubber-stamp [a *Nachvollzug*—literally a "re-enacting"] and could no-longer exercise overall responsibility for spending policy within the framework of its budgetary rights'), as well as para 125 ('in particular [the Bundestag] is not permitted, even by statute, to subject itself [*sich ausliefern*— literally to "deliver itself up"] to any mechanism of financial effect, which—whether on the basis of its overall conception or an overall assessment of its individual measures—could lead to unclear burdens of budgetary significance, be they expenditures or revenue losses, without prior constitutive consent' of the Bundestag).

[60] See especially Bundestag Right of Participation/EFSF (n 58) and Bundestag Right of Information ESM/Euro Plus Pact (n 58).

[61] Lindseth (n 54).

[62] Although not precisely in defence of an analogue to the *Demokratieprinzip*, the recent case law of the Portuguese Constitutional Court in the context of the Eurozone crisis is arguably in the same spirit, vindicating what the Court perceives to be essential national constitutional norms in the face of supranationally imposed measures. See 'Portugal Court Finds Provisions of 2013 Budget Unconstitutional', 6 April 2013, http://jurist.org/paperchase/2013/04/portugal-court-finds-provisions-of-2013-budget-unconstitutional.php (accessed 14 September 2013); and 'Portugal High Court Strikes Down Government Employee Austerity Measure', 30 August 2013, http://jurist.org/paperchase/2013/08/portugal-high-court-strikes-down-austerity-measure.php# (accessed 14 September 2013).

[63] Again, see the contribution of S Baroncelli in this volume (Chapter 7).

in detailed speculation on the actual outcome (particularly should the Court dismiss the case rather than reaching the merits). But the overarching substantive questions in the case are reasonably clear: by undertaking OMTs and other non-standard measures, the question is whether the ECB is acting within its monetary-policy mandate to promote 'price stability' or conversely is engaged in quasi-fiscal activities that come dangerously close to, or even encroach upon, the sort of monetary financing that is banned under the treaties. And even if OMTs and other non-standard measures are found not to violate the ECB's mandate, the question remains whether and to what extent such actions have budgetary implications for Germany, thus necessitating some manner of parliamentary oversight or control at the national level.

My guess is that, consistent with the urgings of the German government at the June 2013 hearing (via the finance minister, Wolfgang Schäuble),[64] the Court will bend over backwards to give broad deference to the ECB to determine whether OMTs fit within its monetary-policy mandate. Nevertheless, even if the Court defers on that question, the Court might still be persuaded that the OMTs carry some financial or budgetary risk for Germany (perhaps via the Bundesbank's share in the equity of the ECB, whose balance sheet could deteriorate as a consequence of these actions). This could then lead the Court to invoke the procedural dimension of the *Demokratieprinzip* and mandate some form of national parliamentary involvement.[65] Such a step would be fraught with difficulties, however, both because of the practical impact on the OMT programme itself, as well as because of the legal impact on the independence of the ECB. As I wrote in another context but in terms pertinent here as well: 'A decision along these lines … would require the Court to revisit its notoriously complacent handling of the independence of the ECB in its *Maastricht Decision* of 1993 (see paras 95–96).'[66]

The second open question raised by the German jurisprudence is whether and to what extent the Constitutional Court will respond to the decision by the Member States to extend the powers of the ECB to banking supervision—the so-called 'single supervisory mechanism' (SSM)—or perhaps also to some role in the resolution of failed banks. Again, allow me to refer to something I wrote previously, soon after that SSM decision was taken during the June 2012 European summit:

> Given the realities of the current crisis, which have given vastly greater importance to the ECB's financial stability role, this area would seem ripe for heightened political (and particularly parliamentary) oversight. Indeed, one could imagine, based on the

[64] A Wiedemann, 'Overview of the Karlsruhe Hearing on OMT—Summary', *Bruegel Blog*, 13 June 2013, www.bruegel.org/nc/blog/detail/article/1109-overview-of-the-karlsruhe-hearing-on-omt-summary/ (accessed 7 July 2013).

[65] See eg Bundestag Right of Participation/EFSF (n 58) and Bundestag Right of Information ESM/Euro Plus Pact (n 58).

[66] Lindseth (n 57), citing *Brunner v European Union Treaty* (the '*German Maastricht Decision*'), Cases 2 BvR 2134/92 and 2159/92 of 12 October 1993, BVerfGE 89, 155, [1994] 1 CMLR 57, reprinted in Oppenheimer (n 56) vol 1, 527–75.

> [Court]'s decisions on Bundestag involvement in the Greek bailout in September 2011 and the EFSF in February 2012 [and now one should add the first decision on the ESM in June 2012], that the Court might see this heightened oversight as a *constitutional imperative*, should the question ever come before the Court.
>
> ... [But] given the role of the European Parliament (EP) in this area as well, it would also force the Court to revisit the adequacy of the system of 'dual legitimation' in the EU, via both the national parliaments and the EP. Given the Court's apparent skepticism of the EP as an instrument of genuine democratic legitimation, at least as evidenced in the *Lisbon Decision* of 2009 (see paras 274–95)[67]—not to mention the financial stakes for the German taxpayer and German democracy in this crisis—it would hardly be surprising if the Court were to privilege Bundestag over EP supervision in this domain, again should the question ever come before the Court.[68]

As of this writing (July 2013), the question has not in fact come before the Court. But the German government is apparently not taking any chances. In the negotiations over the SSM, the German government insisted that the final legislation include provisions for national parliamentary oversight of ECB actions in bank supervision.[69] The compromise proposal on SSM apparently included some provision for national parliamentary scrutiny, but it gave the bulk of the scrutiny rights to the European Parliament. Moreover, the language relating to national parliamentary scrutiny was permissive while the corresponding language for the European Parliament is mandatory and much more detailed.[70] Whether such a compromise will prove satisfactory to the German Federal Constitutional Court remains to be seen.[71]

[67] BVerfG, German Lisbon Decision (n 44).

[68] Lindseth (n 57).

[69] G Steinhauser and L Norman, 'Single Supervisor? Not So Fast', *Real Time Brussels*, 27 March 2013, http://blogs.wsj.com/brussels/2013/03/27/single-supervisor-not-so-fast/?mod=wsj_streaming_stream (accessed 18 May 2013).

[70] Compare Arts 17 and 17aa, Council of the European Union, 'Proposal for a COUNCIL REGULATION conferring specific tasks on the European Central Bank concerning policies relating to the prudential supervision of credit institutions', 16 April 2013, http://register.consilium.europa.eu/pdf/en/13/st07/st07776-re01.en13.pdf (accessed 18 May 2013).

[71] On 12 September 2013, just prior to the final submission of this contribution to the volume's editors, the European Parliament, in first reading, adopted a 'Position ... with a view to the adoption of Council Regulation (EU) No .../2013 conferring specific tasks on the European Central Bank concerning policies relating to the prudential supervision of credit institutions', www.europarl.europa.eu/sides/getDoc.do?pubRef=-//EP//TEXT+TA+20130912+ITEMS+DOC+XML+V0//EN&language=EN#sdocta4 (accessed 14 September 2013). This position shifts the relevant provisions on European Parliament and national parliamentary oversight to Arts 20 and 21 but does not alter the substance of the April compromise cited in n 70. However, as a condition for approving this position, the presidents of the European Parliament and ECB, Martin Schulz and Mario Draghi, agreed that an Interinstitutional Agreement between the European Parliament and ECB would provide 'for strong [European Parliament] oversight of the ECB's supervisory tasks through regular exchanges of views with Parliament's responsible committee, confidential oral discussions with the Bureau of that committee, and further access to information including to a record of proceedings of the Supervisory Board'. See 'Declaration of the President of the European Parliament and of the President of the European Central Bank', 12 September 2013, www.europarl.europa.eu/news/en/news-room/content/20130912IPR19704/html/Declarationof-the-President-of-the-EP-and-of-the-President-of-the-ECB (accessed 14 September 2013). No similar access, particularly with regard to the proceedings of the supervisory board, is expressly contemplated for national parliaments.

* * *

The SSM is not the only issue in which the German negotiating position reflects concerns over a high court reaction. German demands for treaty changes in support of both the ESM[72] as well as, more recently, a full-blown bank-resolution scheme,[73] arguably reflect similar concerns. But perhaps the best example is Germany's refusal to acknowledge any responsibility for the 'legacy costs' of the crisis.[74] As one commentator has put it, 'Germany and the creditors resist any suggestion that they should be made to pay for the problems of others.'[75]

One convenient justification for this resistance is that the assumption of responsibility for legacy costs could entail precisely the sort of open-ended, indeterminate liability that the German Federal Constitutional Court has previously declared incompatible with the *Demokratieprinzip*.[76] I think this view is both misguided as a political matter and unjustifiable in terms of the *Demokratieprinzip*. As a committee of economic experts assembled by the Institute for New Economic Thinking (INET) put it in a report in July 2012, burden-sharing among both debtor and creditor states is not merely 'necessary' but also 'just':

> It is *just* [emphasis in original] because the problems that the deficit countries are struggling with were not caused by these countries in isolation, but were the result of a flawed euro zone design that encouraged both reckless borrowing (in the deficit countries) and reckless lending (in the surplus countries). Hence, all countries that signed up to this design, and took part in the lending and borrowing boom, bear responsibility for the crisis.[77]

In my view, this argument should be developed further, specifically in legal terms. Properly developed, it might help ward off a legal challenge on the basis of the *Demokratieprinzip* against any eventual assumption of liability for 'legacy costs' by a creditor country like Germany.[78] It would *not* be a violation of the *Demokratieprinzip*, I would maintain, to hold the German people at least partly accountable for the consequences of the democratic choice their elected representatives made in favour of adhering to what has proven to be a deeply flawed

[72] L Phillips, 'Battle Over Treaty Change Divides Europe Ahead of Summit', *EUObserver*, 28 October 2010, http://euobserver.com/institutional/31148 (accessed 18 May 2013).

[73] W Schäuble, 'Banking Union Must Be Built on Firm Foundations', *Financial Times*, 12 May 2013, www.ft.com/intl/cms/s/0/8bdaf6e8-b89f-11e2-869f-00144feabdc0.html#axzz2ThdfLclW (accessed 18 May 2013).

[74] See eg 'Joint Statement of the Ministers of Finance of Germany, the Netherlands and Finland', 25 September 2012, www.vm.fi/vm/en/03_press_releases_and_speeches/01_press_releases/20120925JointS/name.jsp> (accessed 19 May 2013); Lindseth (n 9).

[75] Charlemagne, 'Step by Step, with a Ripped Map', *The Economist*, 14 December 2012, www.economist.com/blogs/charlemagne/2012/12/eu-summit-and-euro-crisis (accessed 18 May 2013).

[76] See n 59 above; see also n 81 below and accompanying text.

[77] INET Council on the Euro Zone Crisis, 'Breaking the Deadlock: A Path Out of the Crisis', Institute For New Economic Thinking (23 July 2012) para 8, http://ineteconomics.org/sites/inet.civicactions.net/files/INET%20Council%20on%20the%20Euro%20Zone%20Crisis%20-%2023-7-12.pdf (accessed 6 July 2013).

[78] Lindseth (n 9).

EMU, with all its perverse incentives, resulting imbalances, and illusory and contradictory 'protections' (eg the 'no-bailout' clause). Moreover, it would be unacceptable, on the basis of protecting democracy on the national level, to allow a Member State to walk away from those consequences, particular given that the German Court had itself previously held that adherence to the EMU was constitutional.[79] Burden-sharing thus may be justified both in terms of the *Demokratieprinzip* as well as Germany's constitutional 'openness to European law' (*Europarechtsfreundlichkeit*).

Germany would not be alone, of course, in sharing the burdens for the costs of this crisis. Rather, responsibility would take the form of both suffering through austerity and fiscal discipline (say, Greece, Ireland, Spain or Portugal) as well as taking the necessary haircuts in the immediate term to help fix the problem of legacy costs (say, Germany). However, to survive constitutional scrutiny, the burden-sharing must also be strictly *proportionate* to the inherent risks associated with the initial decision to adhere and the incentives, imbalances, and contradictions that the flawed EMU created. The INET report, to its credit, seems cognizant of this limitation. The reforms it contemplates would no doubt 'take euro zone institutions significantly beyond the status quo (particularly the banking union and the debt restructuring regime)' (para 14)—and hence significant changes to the existing treaties would be required. Nevertheless:

> [I]t is important to note what is not in the proposal: a permanent mechanism for common euro zone debt issuance and a mechanism for countercyclical fiscal transfers. Indeed, there is no common liability in any of our long-term proposals beyond those necessary to establish and backstop the banking union and the ESM, and both are subject to strict safeguards.[80]

Clearly the economist-authors of the INET report are sensitive to the concerns raised by the German high court in its prior case law on the crisis, particular the prohibition against 'indeterminate budgetary authorizations' [*unbestimmte haushaltspolitische Ermächtigungen*], as the Court put it in the *Greek Bailout Decision* (specifically para 124).[81] But the report's limitation on open-ended financial commitments also turns on a critical distinction that the authors themselves draw—between steps needed to address the legacy costs caused by the original flawed design/perverse incentives of the EMU and those needed to fix the EMU over the long term. As the report argues:

> [T]he critical requirement for tackling the crisis is to separate the solution of the 'legacy problem'—stopping the on-going recessions, reducing debt levels, and lowering current account surpluses and deficits within the currency union—from the problem of fixing the structural flaws of the euro zone for the long term. The former requires

[79] See European Monetary Union Constitutionality Case, Cases 2 BvR 1877/97 and 50/98 of 31 March 1998, BVerfGE 97, 350, as translated in Oppenheimer (n 56) vol 2, 258–69.

[80] INET Council on the Euro Zone Crisis (n 77) para 14.

[81] BVerfG, Greek Bailout Decision (n 58).

significant burden sharing. But it does not follow that the latter requires permanent transfers or jointly and severally issued debt.[82]

For those observers concerned that, by confronting the question of shared responsibility directly, one capitulates to the German 'moral' reading of the crisis (reckless debtors, upright creditors), I would respond that it is in fact essential to join issue with Germany *precisely on the terrain* of morality, responsibility, and indeed democracy.[83] The key point is that the (highly imperfect) 'economic interdependence' that allowed banks in the core to lend to the periphery so extensively were *the consequence of policy choices in the construction of the EMU* that the core's own elected governments knowingly undertook. This is precisely the terrain of moral (and, frankly, legal) responsibility on which advocates for the eurozone periphery must now engage Germany.

I have no doubt, however, that the process of burden-sharing would be both a politically delicate and complex undertaking, involving very difficult allocations of responsibility among the various Member States.[84] Nevertheless, although quite difficult, the allocation of responsibility would also be calculable through a political process of negotiation and hence adequately determinate; a commitment to open-ended transfers in the future, by contrast, would not. The latter almost certainly falls on the wrong side of the constitutional 'fault-line' needed to preserve some semblance of democracy on the national level.[85] But that does not mean that all members of the eurozone cannot share the burden for 'legacy costs'—either in the form of fiscal discipline/austerity or defined (if substantial) fiscal transfers or debt-restructuring—because all are, in a very real sense, 'democratically' at fault by virtue of their participation in the flawed EMU itself and the perverse incentives, imbalances, and contradictions it has enabled.

* * *

Do I think that such a 'democratic' apportionment of responsibility among the Member States is likely any time soon? Certainly not in the very short term: Moralistic, 'us vs them'-type narratives are proving very tenacious, particularly where they help avoid recognizing costly obligations to share fiscal burdens to address the crisis. The only way such obstacles might be overcome is if the crisis aggravates once again, thus confronting the Member States with urgent functional demands of co-operation and co-ordination.

Alas, given the incomplete policy responses to date (notably the failure to address the gross undercapitalization of banks throughout the eurozone), a reaggravation of the crisis is hardly out of the question. The Council agree-

[82] INET Council on the Euro Zone Crisis (n 77) para 7.

[83] Lindseth (n 57).

[84] See eg J Fernández-Villaverde, L Garicano and T Santos, 'Did the Euro Kill Governance in the Periphery?', *VoxEU*, 30 April 2013, www.voxeu.org/article/did-euro-kill-governance-periphery (accessed 19 May 2013).

[85] Lindseth (n 46).

ment of June 2013 on bank resolution, with its primary reliance on unsecured creditor bail-ins combined with extremely limited ESM contributions,[86] shows that 'Europe's national governments are clearly incapable and unwilling to fill the gap' in the banking sector's capital needs,[87] which is perhaps the principal legacy-cost category. Talk now is simply of 'diluting' the sovereign-bank link,[88] rather than, as the Eurogroup promised in June 2012, of 'breaking' it entirely.[89] The result is 'a policy version of pretend and extend', in which national governments 'pretend not to see the losses, and extend the crisis'.[90]

In these circumstances, the ECB may again find itself compelled to engage in more heroic measures to keep liquidity flowing to banks or to hold down sovereign interest-rate spreads—the democratic legitimation of which might be increasingly hard to establish. Moreover, as Mario Draghi stressed recently, 'there are limits to what monetary policy can achieve. … Now governments and parliaments need to do all they can to raise growth potential, strengthen competitiveness and build a stronger, more stable EMU'.[91] The failure to take a credible step toward providing the necessary funding for bank recapitalization may simply suggest that, for a creditor country such as Spain, 'the only way … to solve its zombie bank problem would be by leaving the eurozone', as one commentator recently put it.[92] Certainly the prospect of such a step would concentrate the minds of eurozone governments. Perhaps only then would they begin to see how they must share responsibility for the legacy costs of such a poorly designed monetary union, if not via outright transfers, then via debt restructuring on a broader scale.[93]

But to survive constitutional review in Germany or elsewhere, a plausible 'democracy'-based normative theory will be needed to legitimize such policies. I would argue that the EMU, in its original flawed design, was in effect a legal 'tort' that the Member States, through their democratically elected leaders, mutually inflicted on each other and for which all participating states are, in a democratic sense, jointly and severally liable. This theory is persuasive precisely because it

[86] Council of the European Union, 'Council Agrees on Bank Resolution', Brussels, 27 June 2013, www.consilium.europa.eu/uedocs/cms_data/docs/pressdata/en/ecofin/137627.pdf (accessed 7 July 2013).

[87] W Münchau, 'Europe Is Ignoring the Scale of Bank Losses', *Financial Times*, 23 June 2013, www.ft.com/intl/cms/s/0/f4577204-d9ca-11e2-98fa-00144feab7de.html#axzz2YOzqMG82 (accessed 7 July 2013).

[88] O Rehn, 'The Future of EMU: Deepening the Debate' (7 May 2013) http://europa.eu/rapid/press-release_SPEECH-13-389_en.htm (accessed 7 July 2013).

[89] Euro Area Summit Statement, Brussels, 29 June 2012, www.consilium.europa.eu/uedocs/cms_data/docs/pressdata/en/ec/131359.pdf (accessed 7 July 2013) ('We affirm that it is imperative to break the vicious circle between banks and sovereigns').

[90] Münchau (n 87).

[91] M Draghi, President of the ECB, 'Introductory Remarks at the French Assemblée Nationale', Paris, 26 June 2013, www.ecb.int/press/key/date/2013/html/sp130626.en.html (accessed 7 July 2013).

[92] W Münchau, 'Schieritz on Banking Union', *Eurointelligence*, 28 June 2013, www.eurointelligence.com/news-details/article/schieritz-on-banking-union.html?no_cache=1 (accessed 7 July 2013)

[93] W Buiter, 'Markets Insight: Eurozone Crisis Demands Swift Debt Restructuring', *Financial Times*, 8 May 2013, http://www.ft.com/intl/cms/s/0/1590c0b6-b701-11e2-841e-00144feabdc0.html#axzz2YP3hz0EZ (accessed 8 July 2013).

can be recast in terms of fault, causation, responsibility and proportionality that are deeply familiar to the legal mind of national high court judges who might be asked to rule on the constitutionality of such burden-sharing. The challenge is to avoid idealist appeals to intra-European solidarity (no matter how attractive they be in certain quarters)[94] and instead ground the normative principle of burden-sharing in the idea of democratic and constitutional responsibility of each participating state in the EMU.[95]

[94] See eg Habermas (n 12).
[95] For the original articulation of this theory, see Lindseth (n 9).

19

From Fiscal Constraints to Fiscal Capacity: The Future of EMU and its Challenges

FEDERICO FABBRINI

I. INTRODUCTION

SINCE THE BEGINNING of the euro crisis, the main strategy pursued by the member states and the institutions of the EU to address the fiscal emergency threatening the foundations of Economic and Monetary Union (EMU) has been to strengthen the constraints governing budgetary policies. As the chapters of Part 1 of this book have made clear, during the last three years the *Leitmotif* in the reforms of the constitutional architecture of EMU has been the introduction of greater fiscal discipline, combined with new mechanisms of financial stabilization and a revised framework for economic co-ordination and adjustment. To this end, tighter budgetary rules, new independent institutions charged with reviewing fiscal policy and automatic mechanisms of fiscal corrections have been established at the EU level. At the same time, EU member states have been requested to change their legal systems and constitutionalize European budgetary constraints with the aim of increasing the ownership and effectiveness of EU fiscal rules. As the chapters of Part 2 of this book have reported, by and large, member states across the EU have incorporated supranational budgetary constraints in their domestic systems, harmonizing their laws to the principles of sound fiscal policy and balanced budgets. Whereas the early rules of the Stability and Growth Pact had proved to be largely ineffectual, the recent reforms of EMU have significantly strengthened budgetary constraints and fiscal discipline at the EU and state level.

However, as the EU institutions and member states continued in their efforts to reform the EU architecture of fiscal governance in the direction of a deeper and more genuine EMU, a proposal which has attracted increasing attention has been the establishment of a fiscal capacity for the EMU—that is, a central budget, possibly funded through new own resources, by which to assuage asymmetric shocks and carry out countercyclical policies no longer possible at the national level due to budgetary constraints. As Miguel Maduro has argued in a report commissioned by the European Parliament,

> Whatever our view on the benefits and costs of constitutionalizing fiscal discipline, there are two things that are clear in the current EU context: such discipline is a necessity, if not to reestablish market trust, surely to reestablish trust between the member states; but such discipline is also insufficient to address the current crisis.[1]

As an alternative, therefore, Maduro proposed an increased EU budget supported by real EU revenue sources, finalized to address the economic emergency of the eurozone, ensure its future stability and foster its democratic legitimacy.[2] With different emphases, similar proposals have also made their way in the report of the President of the European Council 'Towards a Genuine EMU',[3] as well as in the blueprint of the European Commission 'For a Deep and Genuine EMU'[4] which are currently shaping action by policymakers in the debate about the future of EMU.

The purpose of this chapter is to examine the recent legal proposals in favour of a fiscal capacity for the EMU and to discuss the constitutional challenges that the establishment of this power raise. As I will explain, a number of different options have been so far advanced by policymakers as to how to endow the EMU with a fiscal capacity. However, I argue that the establishment of a viable fiscal capacity would have to face at least three constitutional challenges, which I term: the challenge of asymmetry, the challenge of unanimity and the challenge of representation. In a nutshell, the challenge of asymmetry is generated by the differences in size, wealth, and economic performances among member states. The challenge of unanimity is triggered by EU Treaty requirements that decisions in the area of taxation be taken by unanimous vote in the Council. And the challenge of representation is born out of the current lack of powers by the European Parliament—the only EU institution representing directly the EU citizens—in tax policy.

As this chapter points out, the proposals to introduce a fiscal capacity aspire to complement the new tight budgetary rules and improve the architecture of EMU, by providing a long-lasting solution to the euro crisis and yet offering also a new justification for the process of EU integration. In order to achieve these ambitious results, however, the establishment of a fiscal capacity needs necessarily to address the three above-mentioned constitutional challenges. As I will claim, indeed, each of these challenges may be potentially fatal to the achievement of the purposes that animates this new project of EMU reform. No fiscal capacity can endure if it falls prey of the trap of asymmetry in which wealthier

[1] M Maduro, 'A New Governance for the European Union and the Euro: Democracy and Justice', Report commissioned by the European Parliament Constitutional Affairs Committee, PE 462.484 (2012) 16.

[2] Ibid, 19

[3] President of the European Council, Final Report 'Towards a Genuine EMU', 5 December 2012.

[4] Commission Communication, 'A Blueprint for a Deep and Genuine EMU: Launching a European Debate', COM(2012)777 final.

states transfer money to poorer member states. Equally, no fiscal capacity can be effectively set up if own resources for the EMU—ie EU taxes replacing inter-state transfers—are subject to unanimity rule for their approval. And finally, no fiscal capacity can be legitimated unless the European Parliament—as the only body directly representing the citizens of the EU—is finally endowed with a status at least a co-equal to that of the Council—the body representing the member states and responsive to their interests—in the field of taxation.

As the chapter suggests, a number of legal options are available—in the framework of the current EU Treaties—if not to solve, at least to minimize, the burden that the above-mentioned challenges place on the creation of a successful fiscal capacity for EMU. The challenge of asymmetry can be addressed by replacing state contributions to the EU budget with new, real EU own resources, levied autonomously by the EU and directly connected to the wealth it generates. The challenge of unanimity in the adoption of tax measures at the EU level can be sidestepped by greater resort to enhanced cooperation. And the challenge of representation may be bypassed through the '*passerelle* clauses' that allow the European Parliament to be involved on a par with the Council even in fields which would be subject to special lawmaking procedures at the exclusive discretion of the Council. None of this solution may be optimal. In the end, more substantive amendments to the constitutional foundations of the EU may be needed to ensure the success of a fiscal capacity. However, beginning a discussion of what the potentials of EU law are in this context is a due diligence before engaging in the grand project of Treaty revision.

Many of the chapters of Part 3 of this book have emphasized how further political integration in the EMU should be a deliberate democratic response to increased interdependence and not the inevitable consequence of economic integration. In my view, the proposal in favour of a fiscal capacity should be seen as a welcome step toward more effective and legitimate self-government in the EMU. Yet, this is no easy proposal. While the establishment of a fiscal capacity for the EMU ultimately lies in the political will of the European citizens and member states, exploring the constitutional challenges facing fiscal capacity will shed light on the risks and opportunities that surround the future of EMU. The chapter is structured as follows. Section II maps the proposals in favour of creating a fiscal capacity and summarizes the state of the debate in the field. Sections III, IV and V analyse separately the challenges of asymmetry, unanimity and representation and discuss how each of these could—and ought to—be addressed in designing an EMU fiscal capacity. Section VI concludes with some final remarks.

II. TOWARDS A FISCAL CAPACITY

The proposals to endow the EMU with a fiscal capacity are extremely recent. The October 2010 report of the task force chaired by the President of the European Council, 'Strengthening Economic Governance in Europe', which served as the basis for most of the reforms in the architecture of the EMU adopted to respond to the euro crisis, did not contain any hint about this idea.[5] In fact, the first time the term 'fiscal capacity' was used in an EU official document was in the October 2012 interim report of the President of the European Council, 'Towards a Genuine EMU'.[6] Although even in its June 2012 inaugural report[7] the President of the European Council had suggested that '[a] fully fledged fiscal union would imply the development of a stronger capacity at the European level, capable to manage economic interdependences, and ultimately the development at the euro area level of a fiscal body, such as a treasury office',[8] it is in the October 2012 report that one finds a first articulate presentation of the idea of fiscal capacity and its form. In its discussion about the next pillars of EMU reform—a Banking Union, a Fiscal Union, an Economic Union and a new framework for democracy, legitimacy and accountability—the President of the European Council stated that 'strengthening [fiscal] discipline is … not sufficient' and suggested that '[i]n the longer term, there is a need to … go beyond the current steps to strengthen economic governance to develop a fiscal capacity for the EMU'.[9]

According to the President's interim report, a fiscal capacity would pursue functions which are not covered by the EU budget, the so-called multi-annual financial framework (MFF). In particular, 'one of the functions of such a new fiscal capacity could be to facilitate adjustments to country-specific shocks by providing for some degree of absorption at the central level'.[10] At the same time, '[a]nother important function of such a fiscal capacity would be to facilitate structural reforms that improve competitiveness and growth'.[11] These ideas were later developed by the President of the European Council in the December 2012 final report,[12] where the establishment of a fiscal capacity was clearly linked to the creation of a 'shock-absorption function' to improve the resilience of EMU.[13] As the President's final report underlined, in fact, 'while the degree of centralization of budgetary instruments and the arrangements for fiscal solidarity against adverse shocks differ, all other currency unions are endowed with a central fiscal capacity'.[14] The economic rationale of this instrument lay in the reduction of the impact of country-specific shock and in the prevention of contagious effects across the currency union.[15] Because of its 'insurance-type' nature, at the same

[5] See Report of the Task Force of the European Council, 'Strengthening Economic Governance in the EU', 21 October 2010 (identifying five pillars for reform, namely: (1) greater fiscal discipline, (2) broader economic surveillance, (3) deeper economic coordination via the European Semester, (4) more robust framework for crisis management, (5) stronger institutions for more effective economic governance).

[6] President of the European Council, Interim Report 'Towards a Genuine EMU', 12 October 2012.

[7] President of the European Council, Report 'Towards a Genuine EMU', 25 June 2012.

[8] Ibid, 5.

[9] President Interim Report (n 6), 4.

[10] Ibid, 5.

[11] Ibid.

[12] President Final Report (n 3).

[13] Ibid, 5.

[14] Ibid, 9.

[15] Ibid, 10.

time, the President's report suggested alternative macro- or micro-economic approaches to set-up a fiscal capacity,[16] and emphasized that its design would still have to avoid 'the risk of moral hazard inherent in any insurance system'.[17]

In the vision outlined in the President's final report, therefore, the fiscal capacity of the EMU would largely operate as a sort of 'rainy day fund'—that is, like a savings fund to which member states contribute in times of economic upswing and from which they would be able to draw in times of economic downswing, to cushion the effects of a recession.[18] In fact, although the final report leaves open the possibility that the fiscal capacity may be funded by own financial resources, including a capacity to borrow via the establishment of an EU Treasury,[19] the acknowledgement that 'the financial implications for national budget would depend on the [fiscal capacity's] precise design and parameters'[20] suggests that state contributions would be, at least in the short term, the main sources of its funding. In terms of timing, moreover, the President's final report suggested the possibility to achieve a fiscal capacity in stages. In a first phase, 'limited, temporary, flexible and targeted financial incentives'[21] would be developed to support structural reforms in those member states in fiscal difficulties that are willing to enter into contractual arrangements with the EU institutions, while in the long run a more stable instrument to provide 'fiscal solidarity … over economic cycles' would have to be put in place.[22]

Analogous ideas for the establishment of a fiscal capacity were also advanced by the European Commission. The November 2012 blueprint 'For a Deep and Genuine EMU',[23] in fact, endorsed the idea of a fiscal capacity to underpin structural reforms at the national level and provide a stabilization tool at EMU level to support adjustment to asymmetric shocks. Moreover, the Commission suggested a distinction be made between a short term, in which 'the economic governance framework should be strengthened further by creating a "convergence and competitiveness instrument" [CCI] within the EU budget—but separate from the MFF—to support the timely implementation of structural reforms, on the condition that "contractual arrangements" are concluded between member states and the Commission',[24] and a medium–long term in which a real fiscal capacity for the eurozone would be fully established. In this light, in March 2013 the

[16] Ibid, 11 (distinguishing between a macro-economic approach, which looks at contribution to, and disbursement from, the fiscal capacity in light of fluctuations in the economic cycle; and a micro-economic approach, focused instead on specific public functions such as unemployment insurance).

[17] Ibid, 10

[18] On the 'rainy day' fund mechanism in the US system of fiscal federalism, see R Inman and D Rubinfeld, 'Fiscal Federalism in Europe: Lessons from the United States Experience' (1992) 36 *European Economic Review* 654, 655

[19] President Final Report (n 3), 12.

[20] Ibid, 11.

[21] Ibid, 9.

[22] Ibid.

[23] Commission Communication (n 3).

[24] Commission Memo, 'A Blueprint for a Deep and Genuine EMU', 28 November 2012, MEMO/12/909, 2,

Commission presented as a first step a Communication for the introduction of the CCI, emphasizing the link between structural reform and financial support to be provided by member states.[25]

These proposals for the creation of a fiscal capacity have found a mild endorsement by the EU heads of states and governments in the European Council. Tellingly, while the Conclusions of the December 2012 European Council largely endorsed the President's report and followed in its footsteps to outline the process of future reforms of the EMU, no reference is made to the term 'fiscal capacity'.[26] More modestly, the Conclusions refer to 'solidarity mechanisms'[27] aimed at supporting member states who agree through contractual arrangements to undertake structural reforms, as suggested both by the President's report and the Commission's blueprint. However, the idea of endowing the eurozone with an autonomous budget has received the individual support of prominent institutional players within the European Council. While the German Chancellor had already embraced the idea in a speech before the European Parliament in November 2012,[28] recently the French President and the Italian Prime Minister also spoke in its favour.[29]

Moreover, the idea of a fiscal capacity has found increasing backing in the European Parliament. In its November 2012 resolution 'Towards a Genuine EMU',[30] the Parliament had underlined how 'the innovative idea of a central budget for the euro area funded by members of the euro area is now being proposed as the ultimate guarantee for … financial solidarity'[31] and expressed its view

> that a 'genuine EMU' cannot be limited to a system of rules but requires an increased budgetary capacity based on specific own-resources … which should in the framework of the Union budget, support growth and social cohesion addressing imbalances, structural divergences and financial emergencies which are directly connected to the monetary union.[32]

In its recent May 2013 resolution 'On Future Legislative Proposals on EMU',[33] then, the Parliament clarified that it considered the CCI proposed by the

[25] Commission Communication, 'The Introduction of CCI', 20 March 2013, COM(2013)165 final.

[26] European Council Conclusions, 13–14 December 2012, EUCO 205/12.

[27] Ibid, 5.

[28] See European Parliament, Communique de Presse, 'Angela Merkel donne sa vision d'une UE renouvelée', 7 November 2012.

[29] See F Hollande, Président de la Republique Francaise, 'Intervention liminaire de lors de la conférence de presse', 16 May 2013, 7 (speaking in favour of 'une nouvelle étape d'intégration avec une capacité budgétaire qui serait attribuée à la zone euro.') and E Letta, Prime Minister of Italy, 'Keynote Speech at Annual Dinner Brugel', 9 September 2013, 5 (arguing that 'there is room to reflect on a fiscal capacity for the euro area').

[30] European Parliament Resolution 'Towards a Genuine EMU', 20 November 2012, P7_TA(2012)0430.

[31] Ibid, para CR.

[32] Ibid, para 11.

[33] European Parliament Resolution 'On Future Legislative Proposals on EMU', 23 May 2013, P7_TA(2013)0222.

Commission as 'building blocks towards a genuine fiscal capacity.'[34] And it expressed its clear wish that 'this mechanism should be funded by means of a new facility triggered and governed under the Community method as an integral part of the EU budget, but outside the MFF ceiling, so as to ensure that the European Parliament is fully involved as a legislative and budgetary authority.'[35]

Overall, therefore, there seems to be a slow but growing institutional consensus toward the idea of complementing the constitutional architecture of EMU with a form of fiscal capacity. As the fiscal discipline side of EMU is made ever more secure by being entrenched in constitutional norms at EU and state level, greater awareness on the necessity to create new supranational instruments to support fiscal adjustments in the EMU is gaining ground among EU policy-makers. Yet, important divergences still exist among the various models of fiscal capacity so far advanced, due to different ideas about its appropriate size, sources of revenue and functions. Leaving to others the task of discussing how best to design a fiscal capacity from an economic point of view,[36] the next sections discusses three major constitutional challenges that a successful fiscal capacity would have to meet. Because the purpose of creating a fiscal capacity is to contribute to resolve the euro crisis and complete the EMU, it is crucial that these challenges be taken into account in framing the format of this new power for the EMU, or else this project will be made vain.

III. THE CHALLENGE OF ASYMMETRY

A first constitutional challenge that any model of fiscal capacity would have to withstand is what I call the challenge of asymmetry. In the EU, member states differ in size, wealth and economic performance. While in itself this is nothing special in a currency union, in the EU asymmetry has over time become a particularly relevant factor because of the way in which the EU manages its fiscal policy. Asymmetry, in particular, shapes the decision-making process underlying the EU budget—the MFF. As is well know, the EU budget is for the most part made up of contributions by the member states: as a result, the decision-making process about the EU budget has been caught up in endless negotiation among the member states about the precise costs and benefits that each member state would incur. Because no member state its willing to transfer *its* money to the EU budget for the benefit of *other* member states, discussions about the MFF have become increasingly costly and decreasingly effective—every member state having a veto power on how much resources the EU should raise and how it should spend. The latest evidence of this are the recent events relating to the MFF for 2014–20, where the European Council was first unable to reach a compro-

[34] Ibid, para 22.

[35] Ibid, para 26.

[36] See eg J Pisani-Ferry et al, 'Options for a Euro-Area Fiscal Capacity', Bruegel Policy Contribution 1/2013.

mise on the EU budget, and then found a minimum level convergence which, by reducing the size of the overall budget, was voted down by the European Parliament.[37]

The asymmetry between the member states in size, wealth and economic performance, and the implication of this state of affairs on EU fiscal policy, however, has been magnified by the euro crisis. The intergovernmental method by which the euro crisis has been handled, and the wide recourse that member states have made to international agreements outside the EU legal order, have deepened the differences between the member states, exacerbating the cleavage between creditor countries—states that have been net contributors to the newly created mechanisms of stabilization of the EMU—and debtor countries—states that have largely benefited from financial transfer to address their fiscal troubles. As has been argued, the euro crisis and the responses to it have weakened the balance between member states and favoured their polarization.[38] member states that were net contributors to the rescue of the EMU have become increasingly impatient towards debtor states and as a result have demanded harsh programs of economic adjustments to assisted countries as a condition for further help. At the same time, member states that were net benefiters of rescue measures have become increasingly impatient toward creditor states and have perceived the austerity measures conditioning rescue packages as forms of hegemonic rule.

The European Stability Mechanism (ESM)—as the main institutional mechanism devised by the member states to manage financial emergencies in the eurozone and address its long-term stability—reflects the challenge that asymmetry generates in the EMU.[39] The ESM, which is an international treaty ratified by all eurozone states, is endowed with an authorized capital stock of €700 billion.[40] Eurozone member states contribute to the capital of the ESM pro-quota, on the basis of the subscription by their national central banks to the capital of the European Central Bank (ECB).[41] Decisions by the ESM are then taken by a Board of Governors—composed by the Ministries of Finance of the eurozone member states—on the basis of unanimity rule.[42] Pursuant to Article 4(4) ESM Treaty, nevertheless, 'an emergency voting procedure shall be used where the Commission and the ECB both conclude that a failure to urgently adopt a decision to grant or implement financial assistance … would threaten the economic and financial sustainability of the euro area'. In this case a decision requires only a qualified majority of 85 per cent of the votes cast, calculated on the basis of the contributing shares to the ESM capital.[43]

[37] European Parliament Resolution, 'On the MFF', 13 March 2013, P7_TA(2013)0078, para 1.

[38] See E Chiti and PG Teixeira, 'The Constitutional Implications of the European Responses to the Financial and Public Debt Crisis' (2013) 50 *Common Market Law Review* 683.

[39] See G Napolitano, 'La nuova *governance* economica europea' [2012] *Giornale di diritto amministrativo* 461.

[40] ESM Treaty, Art 9

[41] ESM Treaty, Art 11 & Annex 1.

[42] ESM Treaty, Art 4(1).

[43] ESM Treaty, Art 4(4).

Because of the ways in which the ESM is designed—with state contributions being the source of ESM funding—bigger and richer member states transfer *more money* to the ESM capital. As a result, states such as Germany, France and Italy, contribute a larger share of the ESM capital. Conversely, however, the governance system of the ESM grants to the bigger and richer contributors *more power* of decision-making. In fact, no decision by the ESM can effectively be taken against the wish of Germany, France or Italy. As such, the ESM does not address the challenge of asymmetry of the EMU: on the contrary, it institutionalizes it.[44] Yet a system of fiscal governance which is unable to neutralize the challenge of asymmetry presents shortcomings that threaten its capacity to endure in the long run. As Miguel Maduro has argued, in terms of effectiveness, such a system leaves the governance of the euro 'dependent on a permanent "negotiation" with national democracies [boosting] the uncertainty as to the extent of financial and political support underlying the common currency'.[45] At the same time, in terms of legitimacy, this system fosters mistrusts between states: 'States paying will think they are carrying other states on their shoulders and rewarding moral hazard. [States] being "disciplined" will take as being governed by those loaning the money.'[46]

The unsustainability of a fiscal union based on financial transfers between member states has been acknowledged by multiple quarters. Expressing the concerns of creditor states, the German Chancellor in February 2012 made clear that further steps toward closer economic ties in the EMU should not open the door toward a 'Transfer Union', with permanent payments from richer to poorer states.[47] At the same time, among debtor states, discomfort has grown about the harsh conditionality that has accompanied financial aid.[48] It is with the aim to address this problem that proposals have been made to disentangle the EU budget and the EMU fiscal capacity from the contributions of the member states and to connect it, instead, with the wealth that the EU generates, for instance through the functioning of the internal market.[49] According to Miguel Maduro, in particular, '[i]t is essential that the Union is seen as redistributing the Union wealth and not the wealth of some states. It is equally important for such solidarity to be related to the different degree to which different social groups benefit from European integration.'[50] If conceived in this way, moreover, an EMU fiscal capacity would not only neutralize the challenge of asymmetries and what this

[44] See also C Ginter and R Narits, 'The Perspective of a Small member state to the Democratic Deficiency of the ESM' (2013) 38 *Review of Central & Eastern European Law* 54.

[45] Maduro Report (n 1) 18.

[46] Ibid.

[47] See T Czuczka, 'Merkely Says Euro-Area Fiscal Union Won't Be "Transfer Union"', *Bloomberg. News*, 7 February 2012.

[48] See A Higgins, 'Europe Pressed to Reconsider Cuts as Cure', *New York Times*, 27 April 2013.

[49] See eg I Pernice et al, 'Challenges of Multi-Tier Governance in the European Union', Report commissioned by the European Parliament Constitutional Affairs Committee, PE 474.438 (2013).

[50] Maduro Report (n 1), 21.

comports, but also contribute to a clearer justification of the project of European integration by pointing out to the European citizens what the EU does.[51]

In designing a fiscal capacity for the EMU, policymakers should therefore break the false equation between fiscal capacity and inter-state transfers. The challenge of asymmetry in a currency union such as the EMU can only be addressed if resources for a fiscal capacity are not drawn from state contributions but rather from own resources that the EMU levies *as a Union*. It is in this light that one should address with some skepticism the proposal—lately advanced especially by the Commission in its Communication on the CCI—to develop a bulk fiscal capacity, at least in the short term, through the grant of financial support to member states that contractually agree to undertake structural reforms. According to the Commission's proposal, in fact, the CCI would be financed by direct contributions by the member states,[52] and therefore would not escape the perverse dynamic that has traditionally characterized the management of the EU budget (with states asking how much do they pay and how much do they get) and more recently shaped the responses to the euro crisis (with creditor states asking why they should pay for the financial follies of the debtor states, and debtor states asking whether they are in fact being ruled by foreign lenders).

From this point of view, the European Parliament has perfectly grasped with the source of the problem when, in its November 2012 resolution 'Towards a Genuine EMU', it recommended the Commission 'to return to the spirit and letter of the [Treaties]'[53] and develop a budgetary capacity *funded by own resources*. In its resolution the Parliament emphasized especially the economic advantages of this move: at a time of budget consolidation at the national level, the existence of EU own resources would free the member states from the duty to increase their contributions to finance the EU budget (or a fiscal capacity of the EMU). Nevertheless, the Parliament's proposal would also have a clear political advantage, as it would free the EU heads of states and governments from incurring very high political costs for every new negotiation on the financial resources of the EU. And for the reasons mentioned above, it would break the vicious dynamics produced by state transfers, by making clear that the EU budget is the result of the wealth that the EU generates. Addressing the challenge of asymmetry therefore requires engaging 'in a progressive return to a situation in which the Union budget is financed by genuine own resources'.[54] This implies, however, the capacity for the EU (or the EMU) to levy taxes, which raises a new challenge of its own.

[51] Ibid.
[52] Commission Communication (n 25), 8.
[53] European Parliament Resolution (n 30), Recommendation 2.4.
[54] Ibid.

IV. THE CHALLENGE OF UNANIMITY

If the EU, or the EMU, were to develop a system of own resources independent from the financial contributions of the member states, the question arises as to what powers of taxation are entrusted to the EU institutions under the current EU Treaties to achieve this goal. In this regard, it appears that the founding Treaties provide the legal bases for a taxing power, but raise a clear challenge to the ability of the EU to exercise this power effectively. The only explicit acknowledgement of the competences of the EU in tax affairs is made in Article 113 TFEU which empowers the Council, acting unanimously and after consulting the European Parliament, to 'adopt provisions for the harmonisation of legislation concerning turnover taxes, excise duties and other forms of indirect taxation to the extent that such harmonisation is necessary to ensure the establishment and the functioning of the internal market and to avoid distortion of competition'. Yet, this clause, which is located in the TFEU's Title on Common rules on competition, taxation and the approximation of laws, is not directly focused on the introduction of a new European tax, but rather on the harmonization of tax rates across the member states.

However, Article 311 TFEU states that '[t]he Union shall provide itself with the means necessary to attain its objectives and carry through its policies'. And although this clause, which is located in the TFEU's Title on Financial Provisions, does not explicitly mention EU taxation, it affirms that '[w]ithout prejudice to other revenue, the budget shall be financed wholly from own resources'. Moreover, whereas the old text of Article 269 TCE only allowed the Council to lay down provisions relating to the system of own resources of the Community, which it was to recommend to the member states for adoption in accordance with their respective constitutional requirements, the Lisbon Treaty has now modified Article 311 TFEU, enlarging the power of the Council to shape the EU's own resources. Pursuant to Article 311(3) TFEU, in fact, the Council, acting unanimously and after consulting the European Parliament shall

> adopt a decision laying down the provisions relating to the system of own resources of the Union. In this context it may establish new categories of own resources or abolish an existing category. That decision shall not enter into force until it is approved by the member states in accordance with their respective constitutional requirements.

The exact interpretation of the provisions of the TFEU related to taxes is a matter of debate among tax lawyers.[55] In principle, the EU Treaties could be construed restrictively, arguing that the own-resources clause is intended simply to prohibit the member states from refusing to contribute to the EU budget. The Commission, however, has construed Article 311 TFEU in a more constructive manner and argued that, if combined with Article 133 TFEU, it could be read as granting

[55] See E Traversa and A Maitrot de la Motte, 'Le fédéralisme économique et la fiscalité dans l'Union européenne', paper presented at the Conference 'L'Union européenne et le fédéralisme économique', Paris, 21 June 2013.

to the EU the power to adopt new taxes for the benefit of the EU budget. In its June 2011 proposal for a Council decision 'On the system of own resources of the EU',[56] in fact, the Commission proposed to the Council to introduce as a new category of own resources under Article 311 TFEU a financial transaction tax (FTT), to be collected by the member states and transferred to the EU budget in lieu of other contributions currently in place. And in its subsequent proposal for a Council directive on a FTT,[57] the Commission indicated that its draft legislative text would be based on Article 133 TFEU, and thus on the harmonization clause in the TFEU, but that the revenues of the tax would be appropriated by the EU with the aim to feed the EU budget and free the member states from parts of their current contributions.

Nevertheless, whatever the precise interpretation of Articles 113 and 311 TFEU, and even assuming that their combined effect may empower the EU to levy new taxes, it is clear that these two provisions raise a new constitutional challenge on the road toward the establishment of a fiscal capacity—what I call the challenge of unanimity. Pursuant to Article 113 TFEU, in fact, the adoption of any legal measure for the harmonization of tax laws must be taken by the Council *unanimously*. At the same time, under Article 311 TFEU the establishment of new own resources for the EU requires a *unanimous* decision by the Council—to be approved moreover by every member state in accordance with its constitutional requirement. The existence of a unanimity rule in the field of taxation places a formidable burden on the ability of the EU to make steps ahead in the process of European integration. Joseph Weiler famously emphasized how the 'shadow of the veto' shaped policy-making in the EU before the introduction of qualified majority voting (QMV).[58] As has been stated, '[u]nder the prevailing unanimity rule in fiscal matters, an individual member state can adamantly oppose to any surrender of tax sovereignty to the EU level'.[59] States' opposition to EU taxation may be due to political reasons—such as the 'often visceral rejection of anything that suggests a federal state of affairs'[60]—but also on economic reasons, namely the preservation of state's interest in protecting the fiscal status quo.

The fate of the Commission proposal for a Council directive introducing a FTT reflects in a tangible manner this state of affairs. In November 2011 the Commission brought forward draft legislation to introduce a common system of FTT, with the aim inter alia of ensuring that the financial sector would make a fair contribution to cover the costs of the recent crisis. The proposal, however, was the object of fierce opposition by several member states wary of intro-

[56] Commission Proposal for a Council Decision 'On the System of Own Resources of the EU', 29 June 2011, COM(2011)510 final.

[57] Commission Proposal for a Council Directive 'On a Common System of FTT', 28 November 2011, COM(2011)594 final.

[58] See JHH Weiler, 'The Transformations of Europe', (1991) 100 *Yale Law Journal* 2423.

[59] S Plasschaert, 'Towards an Own Resource for the European Union? Why? How? And When?' [2004] *European Taxation* 470, 476

[60] Ibid.

ducing legislation which would affect their thriving financial markets.[61] Eventually, in June 2012 the European Council had to acknowledge that the differences between the member states were unbridgeable and that 'the proposal for a FTT will not be adopted by the Council within a reasonable time'.[62] Because a FTT was often indicated, together with a carbon tax or corporate tax, as the most feasible way to endow the EU (or the EMU) with a fiscal capacity,[63] the difficulties with which the Commission proposal was met cast a pale light on the challenge that the rule of unanimity poses on the road toward the establishment of a fiscal capacity. The existing EU decision-making process in tax matters, in fact, entrenches the rule of unanimity, placing a heavy burden on the ability of the EU institutions and member states to overcome idiosyncratic state vetoes.

It is in this context that a number of proposals have been made to resort to enhanced cooperation as a way to bypass the deadlock of unanimity. As has been stated,

> The political difficulties in the way of a genuine EU tax … could, in principle, be overcome if a substantial number of member states were to muster the political will to move ahead, conceivably within the 'enhanced cooperation' framework, thus sidestepping the unanimity rule which remains staunchly defended by a few member states.[64]

This was precisely the strategy followed in the case of the FTT. After the failure to reach unanimity on the Commission proposal, eleven member states asked authorization to adopt a FTT through enhanced cooperation. The European Parliament consented to this in December 2012,[65] and the Council authorized the cooperation in January 2013.[66] Because—as I have argued elsewhere—enhanced cooperation is constitutionally permitted when states disagree *whether* to act at the EU level,[67] in the case at hand the decision to resort to enhanced cooperation was legitimate and in February 2013 the Commission advanced a Council directive, readapting its original proposal to introduce a FTT among the states participating to enhanced cooperation.[68] Yet, leaving aside the legal challenge that has been raised against the FTT,[69] it appears that the use of enhanced coop-

[61] See 'Europe's Financial Transaction Tax: Oops', *The Economist*, 27 April 2013.

[62] European Council Conclusions, 28 June 2012, EUCO 76/12, 13.

[63] See Maduro Report (n 1) 21; Commission Proposal (n 56) 4.

[64] Plasschaert (n 59) 479.

[65] European Parliament Legislative Resolution, 'On the proposal for a Council decision authorizing enhanced cooperation in the area of the creation of a FTT', 12 December 2012, P7_TA(2012)0498.

[66] Council Decision 2013/52/EU, [2013] OJ L22/11.

[67] See F Fabbrini, 'Enhanced Cooperation Under Scrutiny: Revisiting the Law and Practice of Multi-Speed Integrtation in Light of the First Involvement of the EU Judiciary' (2013) 40 *Legal Issues Economic Integration* 197.

[68] Commission Proposal for a Council Directive 'Implementing enhanced cooperation in the area of a FTT', 14 February 2013, COM(2013)71 final.

[69] See Case C-209/13, *United Kingdom v Council*, application lodged on 18 April 2013 (challenging the legality of the Council decision authorizing enhanced cooperation for the introduction of a financial transaction tax for its compatibility with the internal market).

eration in taxing matters complicates the possibility to use the revenues of this tax for the purpose of creating a fiscal capacity.

In fact, while the original November 2011 Commission proposal clearly linked the introduction of the FTT to the creation of 'a new own resource to be entered into the budget of the EU',[70] the new February 2013 proposal, taking stock of the fact that only a few member states will introduce the FTT via enhanced cooperation, suggests less ambitiously that 'part of the receipts generated by the FTT shall constitute an own resource' reducing the direct contribution by these member states.[71] Otherwise, the differentiated participation of the member states in levying the tax creates equal complications on the spending side. If at least all the member states of the eurozone were involved in the enhanced cooperation, the revenues of the FTT could reasonably be used to create a EMU fiscal capacity: but as long as only a group of EMU countries are subject to the FTT, it seems inevitable—as the European Parliament acknowledged—that 'such a budgetary capacity could naturally only benefit the member states contributing to it'.[72] In conclusion, therefore, while enhanced cooperation may be a pragmatic mechanism to minimize in the short term the challenge of unanimity, it seems difficult to disagree with the recommendations of the European Convention Working Group VI on Economic Governance 'that some changes should be made to the existing decision-making procedures in order to facilitate progress in the area of fiscal policy' through the use of QMV.[73] Yet, this proposal, besides requiring an amendment to the EU treaties, carries with itself another challenge that the EU can no longer postpone.

V. THE CHALLENGE OF REPRESENTATION

If—as explained above—a sustainable fiscal capacity demands own resources to be levied through EU taxes, and assuming the challenges of unanimity in fiscal affairs can be addressed via resort to enhanced cooperation (or, in the long term, through the introduction of QMV via a reform of the EU Treaties), a third challenge still would arise. Drawing on the celebrated motto 'no taxation without representation' which served as a rallying cry for American revolutionaries, I shall call this the challenge of representation. It is indeed an everlasting principle of constitutionalism, from the Magna Carta of 1215, through the revolutionary experiences of seventeenth- and eighteenth-century England, America and France, up to contemporary models of constitutional government, that the power of taxation must be legitimized and controlled by adequate democratic representation.[74] Pursuant to this constitutionalist tradition, no governmental

[70] Commission Proposal (n 57) 3.

[71] Commission Proposal (n 68) 4.

[72] European Parliament Resolution (n 33) para 23.

[73] European Convention, Working Group VI on Economic Governance, Final Report, 21 October 2002, CONV 357/02, WG VI 17, 6.

[74] See eg B Ackerman, 'Taxation and the Constitution', (1999) 99 *Columbia Law Review* 1.

authority in fiscal affairs can be justified unless it is at the origin authorized by the people through their representatives.[75] In other words, representation—as the way to endow governmental decisions with democratic legitimacy and accountability—is the foundation of governmental authority in the fiscal domain (and beyond).

Now, in the current institutional system of the EU, the principle of representation is only partially accomplished. The European Parliament, which pursuant to Article 10(2) TEU 'directly represent[s European citizens] at the Union level', and has been elected since 1979 by direct universal suffrage throughout the territory of the EU, exercises decision-making power on a par with the Council in the budgetary field. However, the European Parliament has only a consultative role in the field of taxation, because decisions on tax harmonization under Article 113 TFEU or on the creation of new tax-based EU own resources under Article 133 TFEU are taken exclusively (and unanimously) by the Council. Surely, as Wojciech Sadurski suggested, the Council (and the European Council) still lives up to the principle of democratic representation, since each of its members represents a state and the citizens thereof—and is often directly elected by them, or at least responsible towards those directly elected by them (ie national parliamentarians).[76] According to Article 10(2) TFEU, in fact, 'member states are represented in the European Council by their Heads of State or Government and in the Council by their governments, themselves democratically accountable either to their national Parliaments, or to their citizens.'

However, precisely because the Council represents member states and reflects their interests, it can hardly offer adequate justification to decisions which are supranational in scope, operating beyond state lines and affecting directly the interests of European citizens. As the euro crisis has made plain, an intergovernmental method of governance centered on the Council (and European Council) meets 'difficult hurdles in dealing with the legitimacy dilemma'.[77] The Council, as a quasi-diplomatic body, operates in a secretive manner and, although it formally abides by the principle of equality of its members, it has become evident that several bigger member states enjoy greater leeway and influence on its decisions. Individuals affected by these decisions have only limited capacity to influence them, control them or revert them when needed. The exclusive role of the Council in decisions about taxes implies that European citizens in their collective capacity may somehow be subject to taxation without representation, since the institution that directly represents them—the European Parliament—has no voice in the field. While a balance between representation of the citizens and

[75] Of course, representative democracy is not the only form of constitutional government—direct democracy being another possible form of legitimation of political power. For the purpose of this work, however, I will take it for granted that the EU, not least for its sheer size, cannot meaningfully be governed by a principle of direct democracy.

[76] W Sadurski, 'Democratic Legitimacy of the European Union: A Diagnosis and Some Modest Proposals' (2013) *Polish Yearbook of International Law* 22.

[77] S Fabbrini, 'Intergovernmentalism and its Outcomes: The Implications of the Euro-Crisis on the European Union' [2013] *Comparative Political Studies* 23.

representation of the member states is inevitable in a Union of states such as the EU, the establishment of a fiscal capacity demands therefore that steps be taken in order to ensure that the current imbalance—with the attribution of powers in taxation exclusively to the Council (representing directly the states) at the expenses of the Parliament (representing directly the European citizens)—be redressed.

Tellingly, even top EU decision-makers seem to have taken notice of this need, as questions of legitimacy and accountability feature in both the reports of the President of the European Council and the blueprint of the Commission 'For a Deep and Genuine EMU'. In particular, as the President's June 2012 inaugural report acknowledged 'moving towards more integrated fiscal and economic decision-making between countries will … require strong mechanisms for legitimate and accountable decision-making'.[78] The President later reformulated this position in the October 2012 interim report as the principle that 'democratic control and accountability should occur at the level at which decisions are taken'[79]—a sentence repeated literally also in the December 2012 conclusive report,[80] where the President additionally remarked how 'the creation of a new fiscal capacity should also lead to adequate arrangements ensuring its full democratic legitimacy and accountability', to be detailed on the basis of its specific features, founding sources, decision-making processes and scope of activities.[81]

Yet, whereas the European Council has repeated as a refrain its support for the principle of democratic legitimacy and accountability at the level at which decisions are taken and implemented,[82] it has fallen short of devising any effective means by which to make this promise real. In fact, the main idea voiced by the European Council to enhance the EU decision-making process has been to encourage inter-parliamentary cooperation between national parliaments and the European Parliament.[83] However, for the very same reasons why national governments in the Council and European Council cannot legitimately deliver EU public goods—because they *represent their states* and are responsive to national constituencies—it is unclear how a committee of national parliamentarians—elected, once again, to *represent the constituents of their states*—would do the trick. In fact, as the President of the European Council rightly emphasized:

> [T]he provisions for democratic legitimacy and accountability should ensure that the common interest of the [U]nion is duly taken into account; yet national parliaments are not in the best position to take it into account fully. This implies that further integration of policy making and a greater pooling of competences at the European

[78] President Report (n 7) 6.
[79] President Interim Report (n 6) 8.
[80] President Final Report (n 3) 16.
[81] Ibid, 17.
[82] See European Council Conclusions, 18 October 2012, EUCO 156/12, 10; European Council Conclusions, 14 December 2012, EUCO 205/12, 5; European Council Conclusions, 28 June 2013, EUCO 104/2/13, 9.
[83] See also Fiscal Compact Treaty, Art 13.

> level should first and foremost be accompanied with a commensurate involvement of the European Parliament in the integrated frameworks for a genuine EMU.'[84]

Ensuring a commensurate involvement of the European Parliament in the new architecture of EMU may require a number of political changes aimed at politicizing parliamentary elections—for instance the establishment of transnational party lists of candidates for the election of the European Parliament (as suggested by the rapporteur of the European Parliament Constitutional Affairs Committee)[85] or the nomination of a party candidate for the post of Commission President (as proposed recently by the Commission)[86]. However, it also requires legal changes. Under the framework of the current EU Treaties, in particular, it is possible to resort to a '*passerelle* clause' shifting to the co-decision procedure the competences which would otherwise be reserved to the exclusive purview of the Council.[87] This is precisely what the European Parliament asked in its resolution authorizing the use of enhanced cooperation for the introduction of the FTT, to enhance the role of the Parliament in decision-making related to taxation. As the European Parliament emphasized, on the basis of Article 333(2) TFEU,

> [w]here a provision of the Treaties which may be applied in the context of enhanced cooperation stipulates that the Council shall adopt acts under a special legislative procedure, the Council, acting unanimously … may adopt a decision stipulating that it will act under the ordinary legislative procedure.

Hence, the European Parliament 'call[ed] on the Council to adopt a decision pursuant to Article 333(2) TFEU, stipulating that when it comes to the proposal for a Council Directive implementing enhanced cooperation in the area of FTT pursuant to Article 113 TFEU, it will act under the ordinary legislative procedure'.[88]

In conclusion, addressing the challenge of representation demands that the power of taxation—as the source of financing for an EMU fiscal capacity—be made legitimate and accountable through the involvement of the European Parliament. Whether this is feasible is a question to which opposing answers are given in other chapters of this book. While Peter Lindseth, approaching the theme from an administrative perspective, regards this step as going too far, by breaking the agency that links EU institutions to democracy at the national level, Ingolf Pernice suggests that, despite these difficulties, the increase of the powers of the European Parliament in the fiscal domain is a possible—and neces-

[84] President Final Report (n 3) 16.

[85] See European Parliament Committee on Constitutional Affairs, Draft Report by Rapporteur A Duff 'On a Proposal for the Modification of the Act Concerning the Election of Members of the European Parliament by Direct Universal Suffrage', 5 November 2010, 2009/2134(INI).

[86] Commission Communication, 'Preparing for the 2013 European Election: Further Enhancing their Democratic and Efficient Conduct', 12 March 2013, COM(2013) 126 final, 6.

[87] On the potential of the '*passerelle* clauses' to induce reforms within the framework of the existing Treaties, see G Amato, 'Future Prospects for a European Constitution', in G Amato et al (eds), *Genesis and Destiny of the European Constitution* (Brussels, Bruylant, 2007), 1271, 1272.

[88] European Parliament Legislative Resolution (n 65) para 2.

sary—step to ensure that the people affected by decisions de facto taken at the supranational level can understand themselves as the authors of these policies. Whether one endorses a more or less optimistic vision of the future of democratic representation in the EU, there is no doubt that there is still a long way to go. In its recent July 2013 resolution 'On the Political Agreement on the MFF', the European Parliament insisted on its full authority in the fiscal domain and 'regret[ted] the fact that the member states continue to underestimate the role of the EU budget, and its contribution to, strengthening economic governance and fiscal coordination across the EU'.[89] Nevertheless, it seems to be equally clear that, from a constitutional-democratic point of view, the new powers that the establishment of a fiscal capacity would entail (in terms of taxing authority for the EMU) should be tamed by adequate principles of representation.

VI. CONCLUSION

Recently, the focus of EU policy-making talks has increasingly shifted from fiscal constraints to fiscal capacity. Fiscal discipline being by now mostly entrenched in the constitutional law of the EU and the member states, EU institutions, state governments and scholars have with growing emphasis begun debating about further integration in the EMU. Fiscal capacity—that is, a central budget for the EMU, possibly funded through new resources, by which to assuage asymmetric shocks and carry out countercyclical policies no longer possible at the national level due to the budgetary constraints—has increasingly gained ground as the frontier of reform in EMU. Yet, as this chapter has explained, the proposal to establish a fiscal capacity faces several hurdles. From a constitutional point of view, I have argued that three main challenges would need to be address for a fiscal capacity to succeed. The challenges of asymmetry, unanimity and representation raise critical tests to the establishment of a fiscal capacity that wants to avoid falling prey of endless negotiations on inter-states money transfers, insurmountable deadlock in decisions about the adoption of EU own resources and lack of representation by those individuals who would be directly subject to new EU taxation.

As this chapter has claimed, these challenges are not impossible to face. The introduction of EU own resources can address the challenge of asymmetry and break the vicious equation between financial solidarity and inter-state transfers. The resort to enhanced cooperation can address the challenge of unanimity and sidestep the deadlock that virtually automatically arises in the field of tax policy whenever proposals are made for new, real EU taxes. The possibility of the '*passerelle* clauses', finally, can address the challenge of representation and ensure that the only institution directly representing the European citizens—the European Parliament—has a say on decisions which involve EU taxation, on a

[89] European Parliament Resolution, 'On the Political Agreement on the MFF', 3 July 2013, P7_TA(2013)0304, para 6.

par with the Council. Yet, even if each of the proposals suggested above were impossible, one cannot but agree with the crude assessment made by Miguel Maduro: '[T]he question soon to be faced by European politicians is which, among several impossible proposals, may be the easiest to present to [the] citizens.'[90] Endowing the EMU with a fiscal capacity is a desirable development to solve the euro crisis and strengthen democracy in the EU. Only the political will, however, can remove the constitutional challenges that obstruct the future path toward a deeper and more genuine EMU.

[90] Maduro Report (n 1) 6.

Index

www.ingramcontent.com/pod-product-compliance
Ingram Content Group UK Ltd.
Pitfield, Milton Keynes, MK11 3LW, UK
UKHW020131290926
15471UKWH00003B/408

9 781509 907052